황토빛이야기

The Color of EARTH

KIM DONG HWA

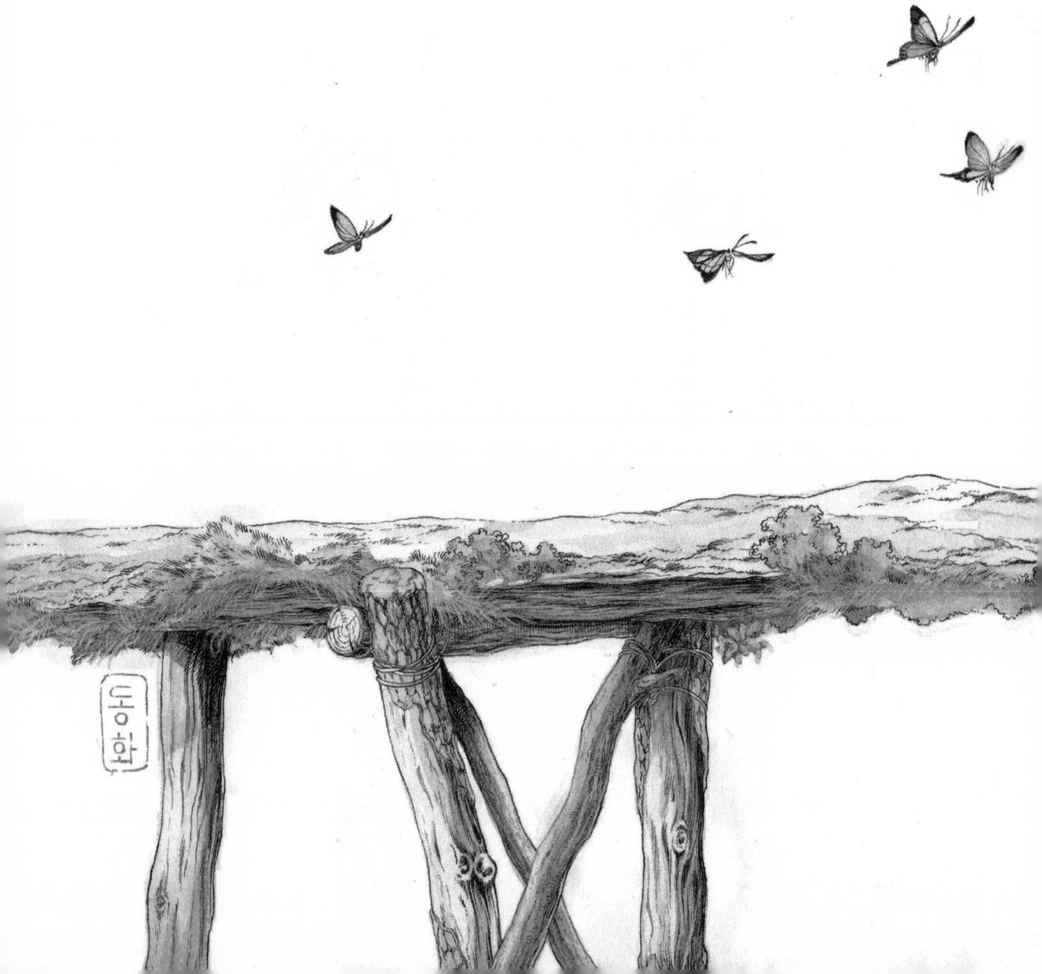
동화

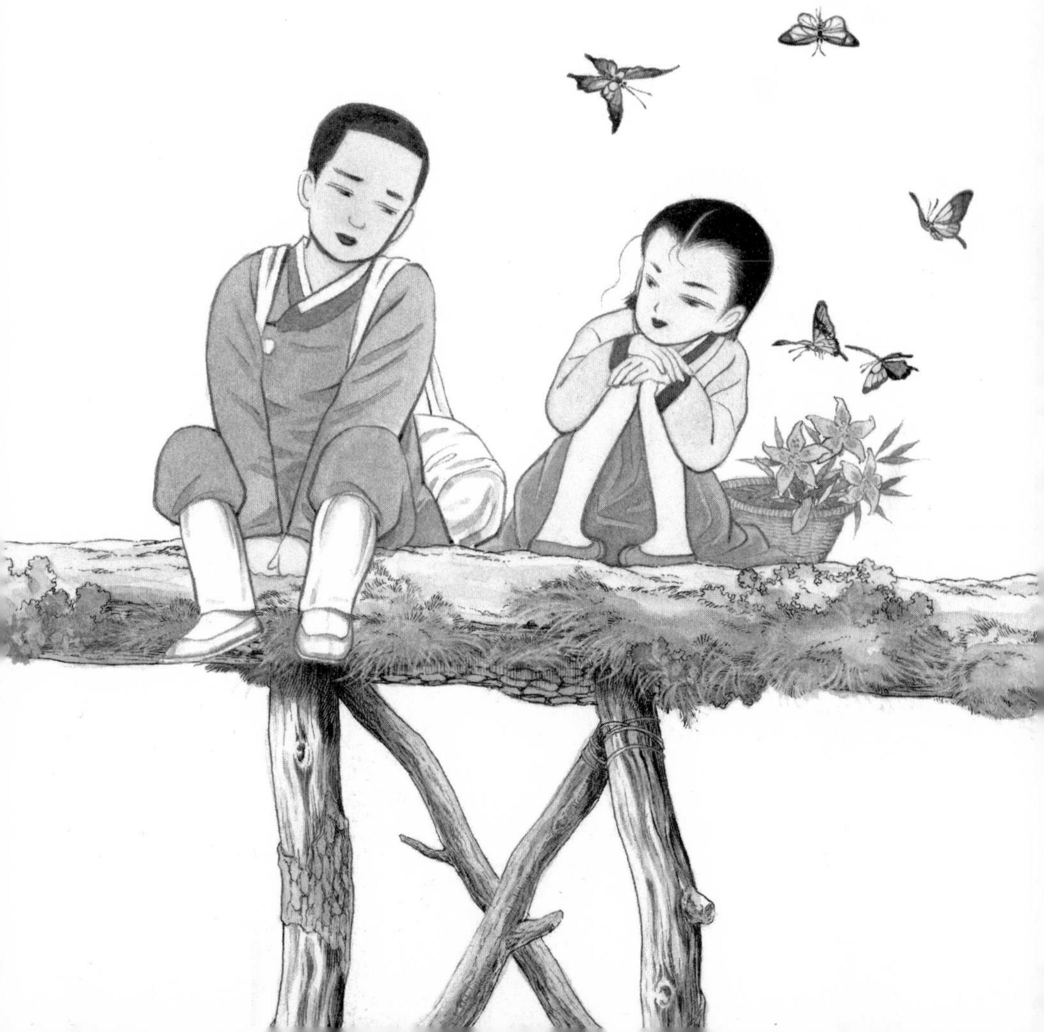

First Second

New York & London

The Story of Life on the Golden Fields Vol. 1 © 2003 by Kim Dong Hwa
All Rights Reserved
English translation copyright © 2009 by First Second

Published by First Second
First Second is an imprint of Roaring Brook Press,
a division of Holtzbrinck Publishing Holdings Limited Partnership
175 Fifth Avenue, New York, NY 10010

Distributed in Canada by H. B. Fenn and Company Ltd.
Distributed in the United Kingdom by Macmillan Children's Books,
a division of Pan Macmillan.

First published in Korea in 2003 by Kim Dong Hwa
English translation rights arranged with Kim Dong Hwa through Orange Agency
English-language edition © 2009 by First Second
Afterword by Hwang Min-Ho
Afterword translated by Alexis Siegel

Cataloging-in-Publication Data is on file at the Library of Congress.

ISBN-13: 978-1-59643-458-5
ISBN-10: 1-59643-458-9

First Second books are available for special promotions and premiums.
For details, contact: Director of Special Markets, Holtzbrinck Publishers.

First American Edition April 2009
Printed in the United States of America
1 3 5 7 9 10 8 6 4 2

황토빛이야기

The Color of EARTH

KIM DONG HWA

Translated from the Korean by Lauren Na

First Second

New York & London

My beloved has arrived, but rather than greeting him,
All I can do is bite the corner of my apron with a blank expression–
What an awkward woman am I.

My heart has longed for him as hugely and openly as a full moon
But instead I narrow my eyes, and my glance to him
Is sharp and narrow as the crescent moon.

But then, I'm not the only one who behaves this way.
My mother and my mother's mother were as silly and stumbling as I am
when they were girls...

Still, the love from my heart is overflowing,
As bright and crimson as the heated metal in a blacksmith's forge.

Deeply etched on my mother's face are wrinkles as fine as the strands on a spider's web. As I remove these threads, one at a time, I see her transform into a blushing sixteen-year-old girl.

Now, open for you to read, is the tale of this clumsy sixteen-year-old girl. From an era where time stood still, her story is revealed in bits and pieces, a tale that slowly escapes from the past.

Little gems from my mother's life at sixteen...

Ochre-colored earth stories...

From the West Bridge–
Kim Dong Hwa

CONTENTS

Little gems from my mother's life at sixteen...

Chapter One

SPRING RAIN

PART 1: THE BEETLES

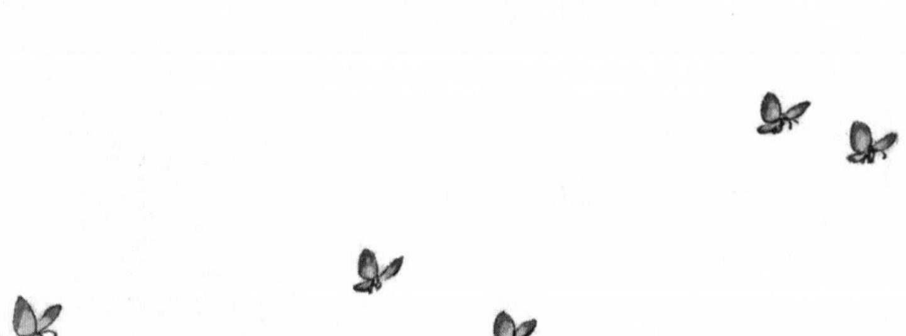

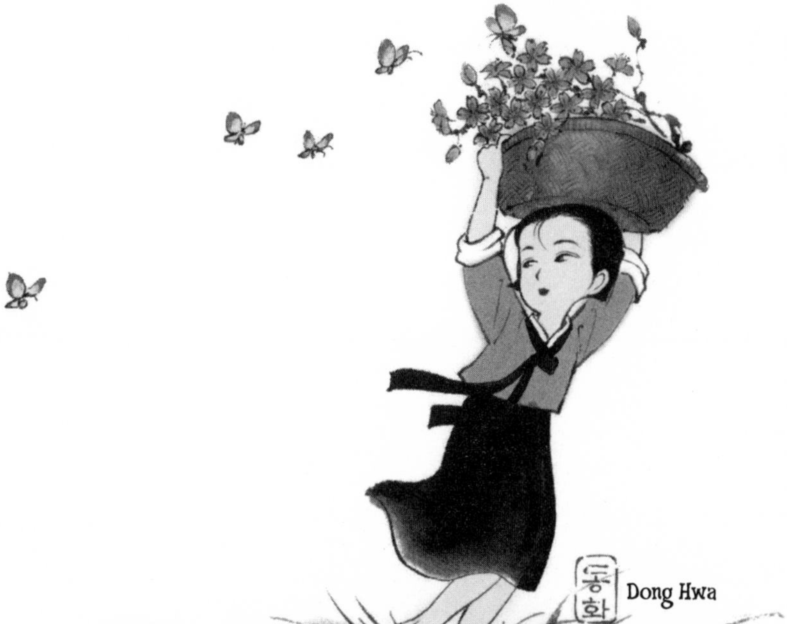
동화
Dong Hwa

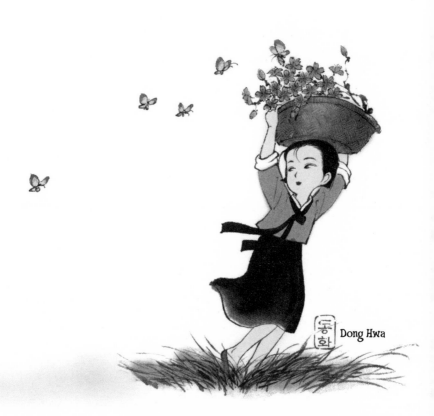

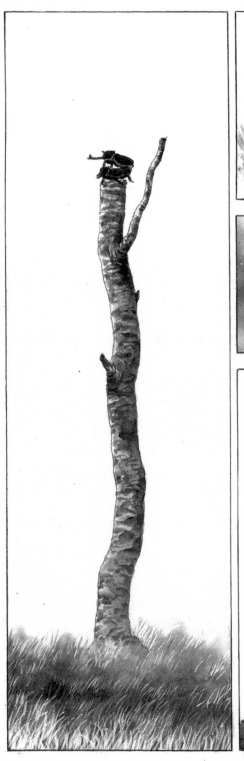

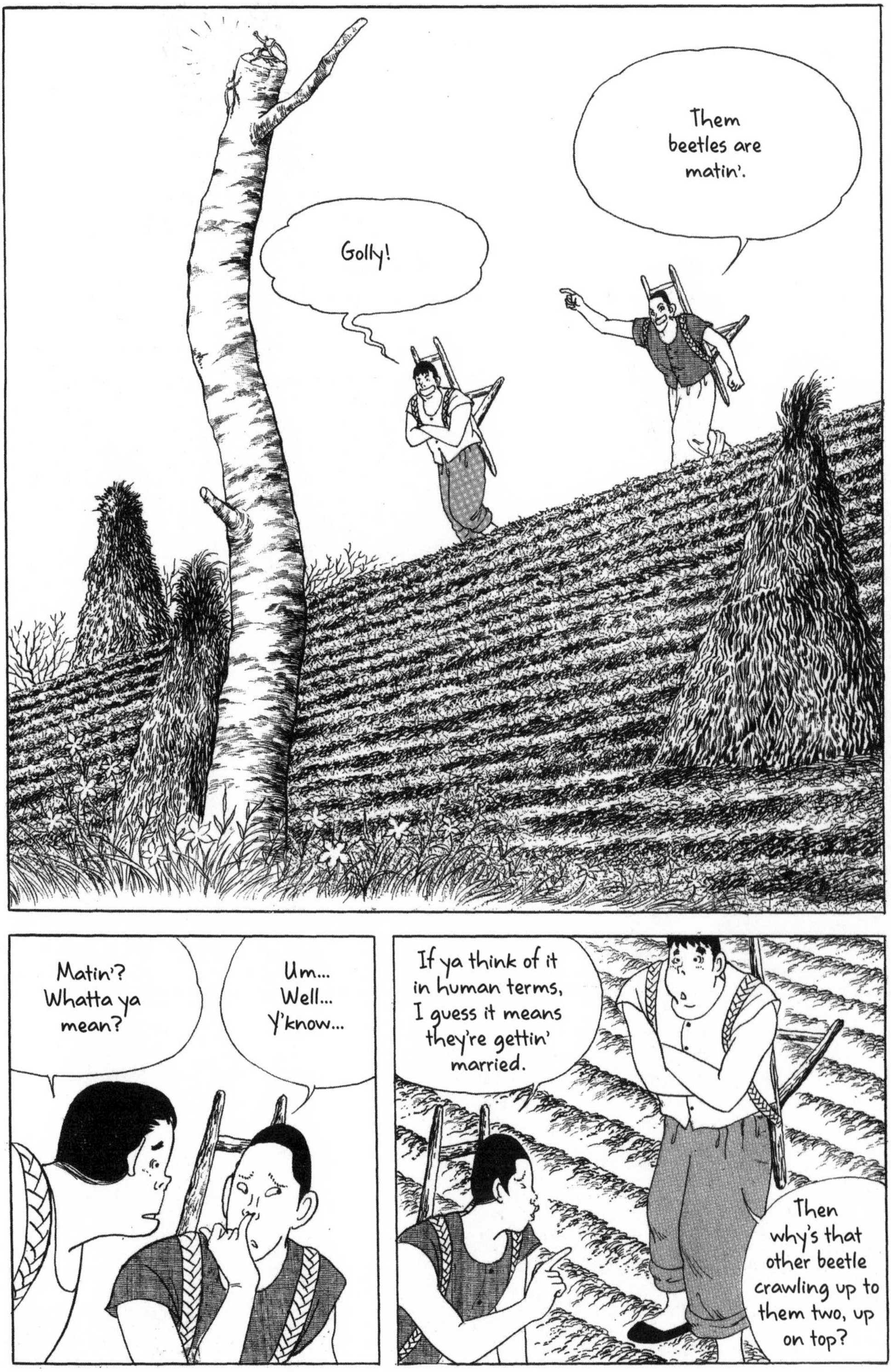
Them beetles are matin'.
Golly!
Matin'? Whatta ya mean?
Um... Well... Y'know...
If ya think of it in human terms, I guess it means they're gettin' married.
Then why's that other beetle crawling up to them two, up on top?

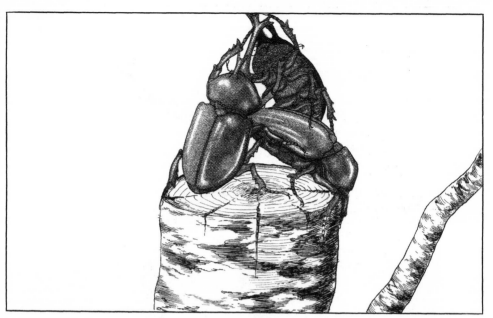

That one's plannin' on stealin' the girl beetle from the other boy beetle.

Gee. Yeah. He stopped matin' and now he's fightin' the beetle what's bothering 'em.

Looks like the girl beetle's gonna watch the two boys till the fight's all over.

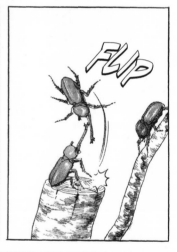

FLIP

Aw man! The beetle that interrupted 'em won.

Now look carefully.

14

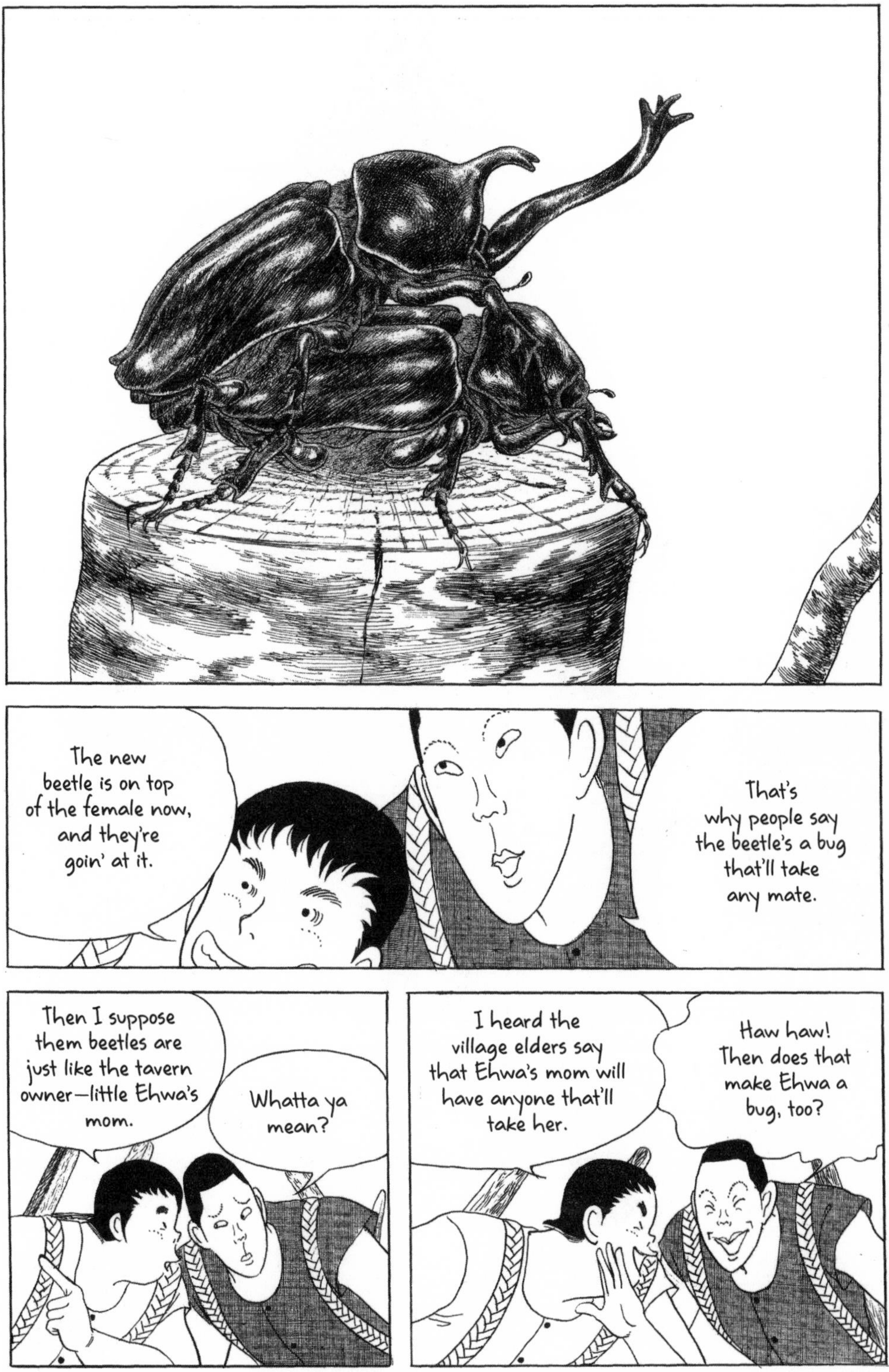
The new beetle is on top of the female now, and they're goin' at it.
That's why people say the beetle's a bug that'll take any mate.
Then I suppose them beetles are just like the tavern owner—little Ehwa's mom.
Whatta ya mean?
I heard the village elders say that Ehwa's mom will have anyone that'll take her.
Haw haw! Then does that make Ehwa a bug, too?

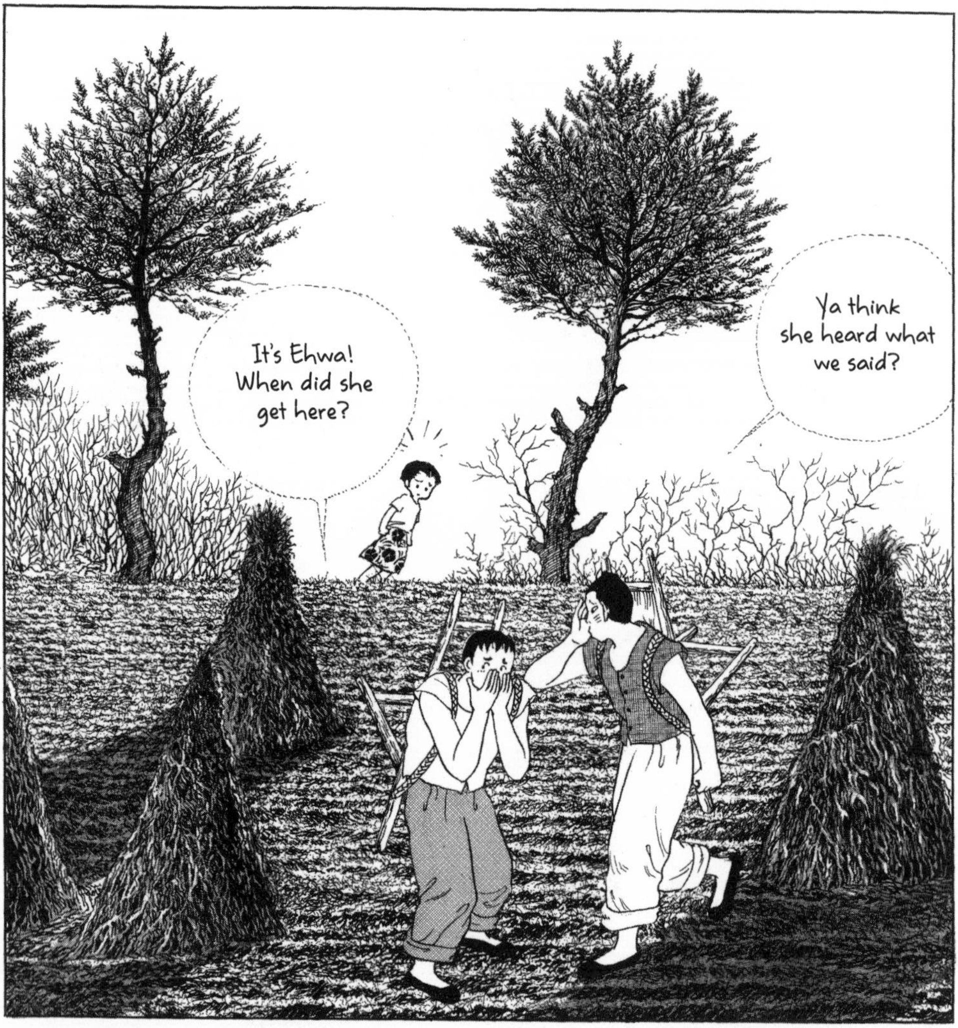
It's Ehwa! When did she get here?
Ya think she heard what we said?

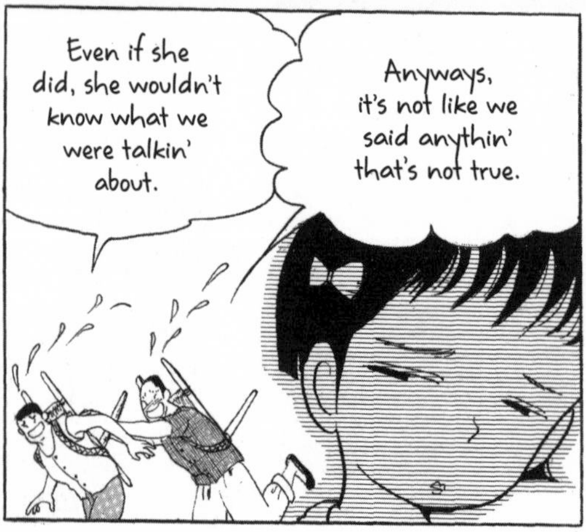
Even if she did, she wouldn't know what we were talkin' about.
Anyways, it's not like we said anythin' that's not true.

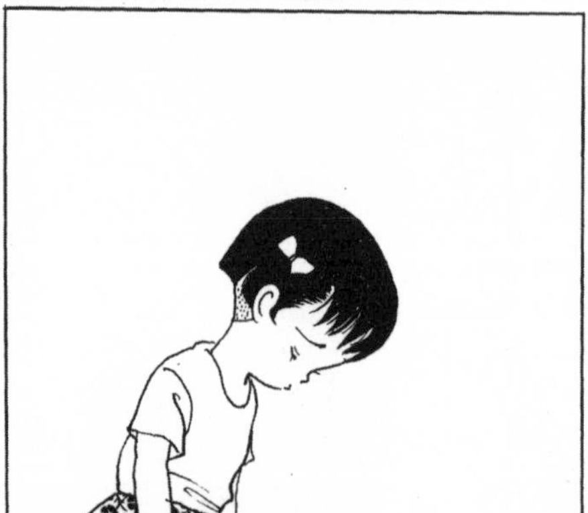

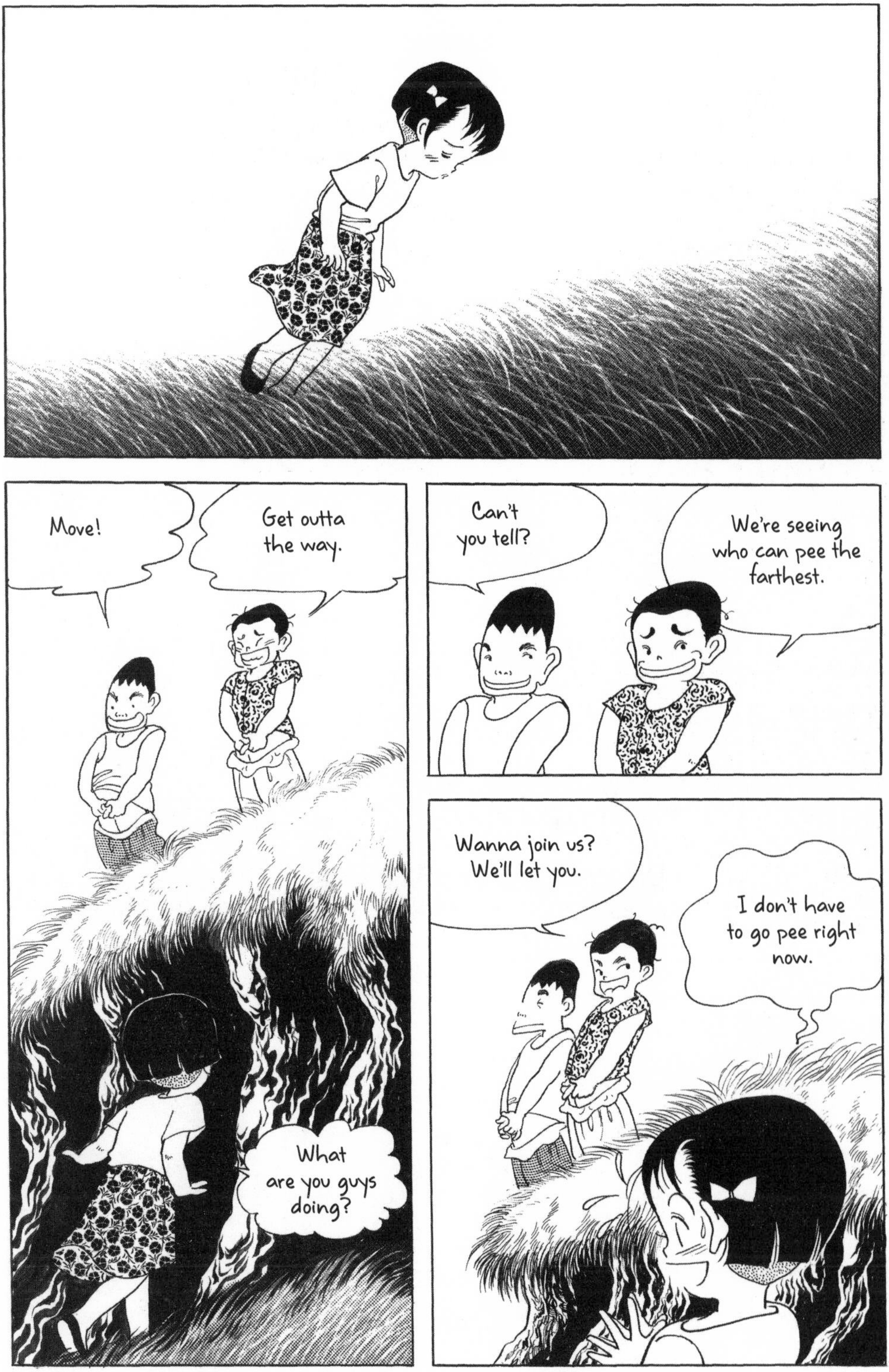
Move!
Get outta the way.
Can't you tell?
We're seeing who can pee the farthest.
What are you guys doing?
Wanna join us? We'll let you.
I don't have to go pee right now.

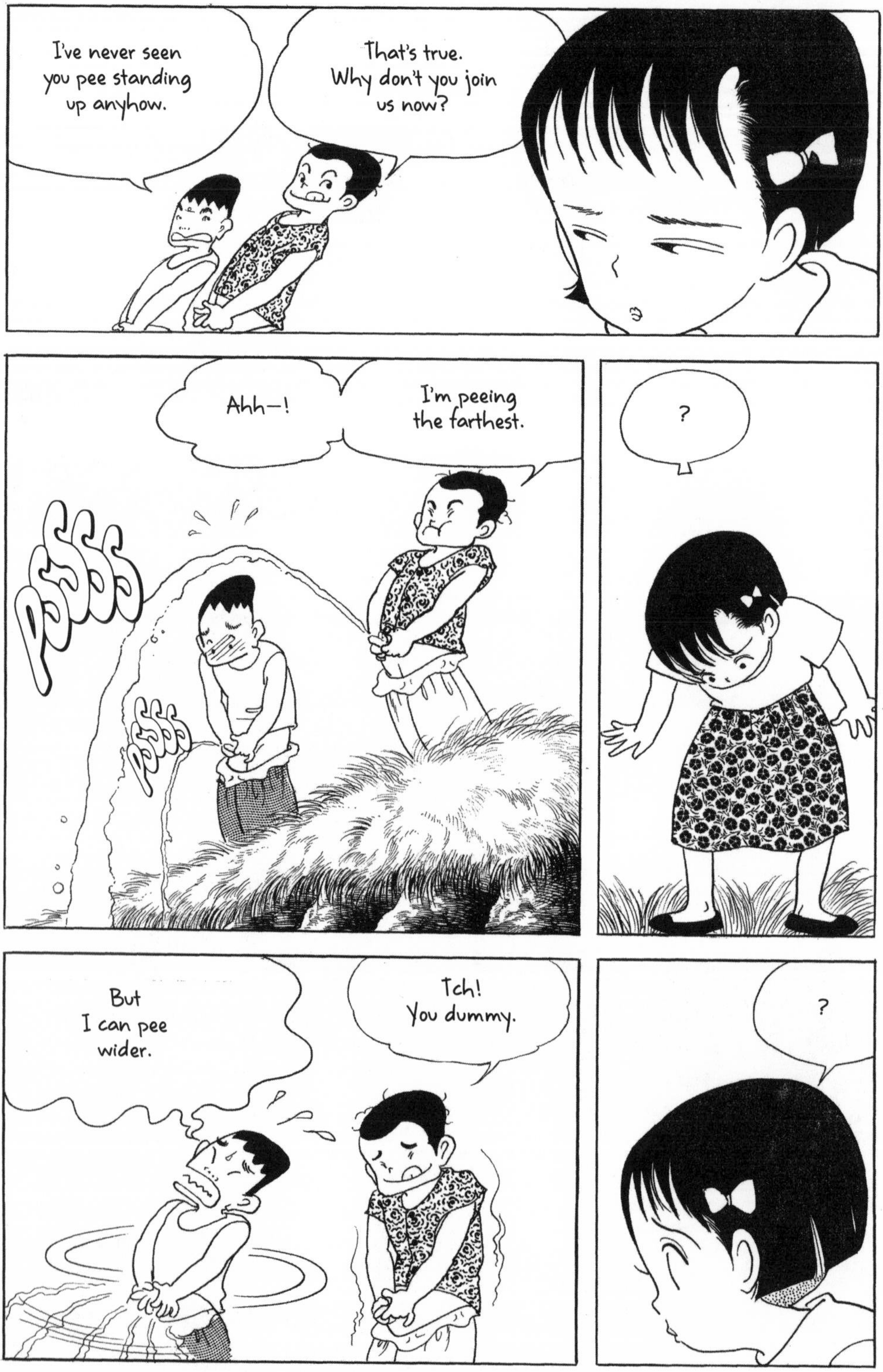
I've never seen you pee standing up anyhow.
That's true. Why don't you join us now?
Ahh—!
I'm peeing the farthest.
PSSSS
PSSSS
?
But I can pee wider.
Tch! You dummy.
?

What's that thing you guys have in between your legs?

You saw it?

It's a gochoo.*

Why is a gochoo in your pants instead of out on the field?

Are you saying you don't have one?

Everyone has one! Ehwa must be deformed.

Um... I do have one! Mine is as big as a kim-jang gochoo.**

Really?

Wow! Let me see it.

No way. I knew people would want to see it, so I hid it.

Is it hidden underneath your skirt?

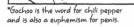

*Gochoo is the word for chili pepper and is also a euphemism for penis.

**Kimjang refers to the season of pickling various green produce. In this context Ehwa is saying that her gochoo is as big as the kimjang chili pepper (about six inches long).

19

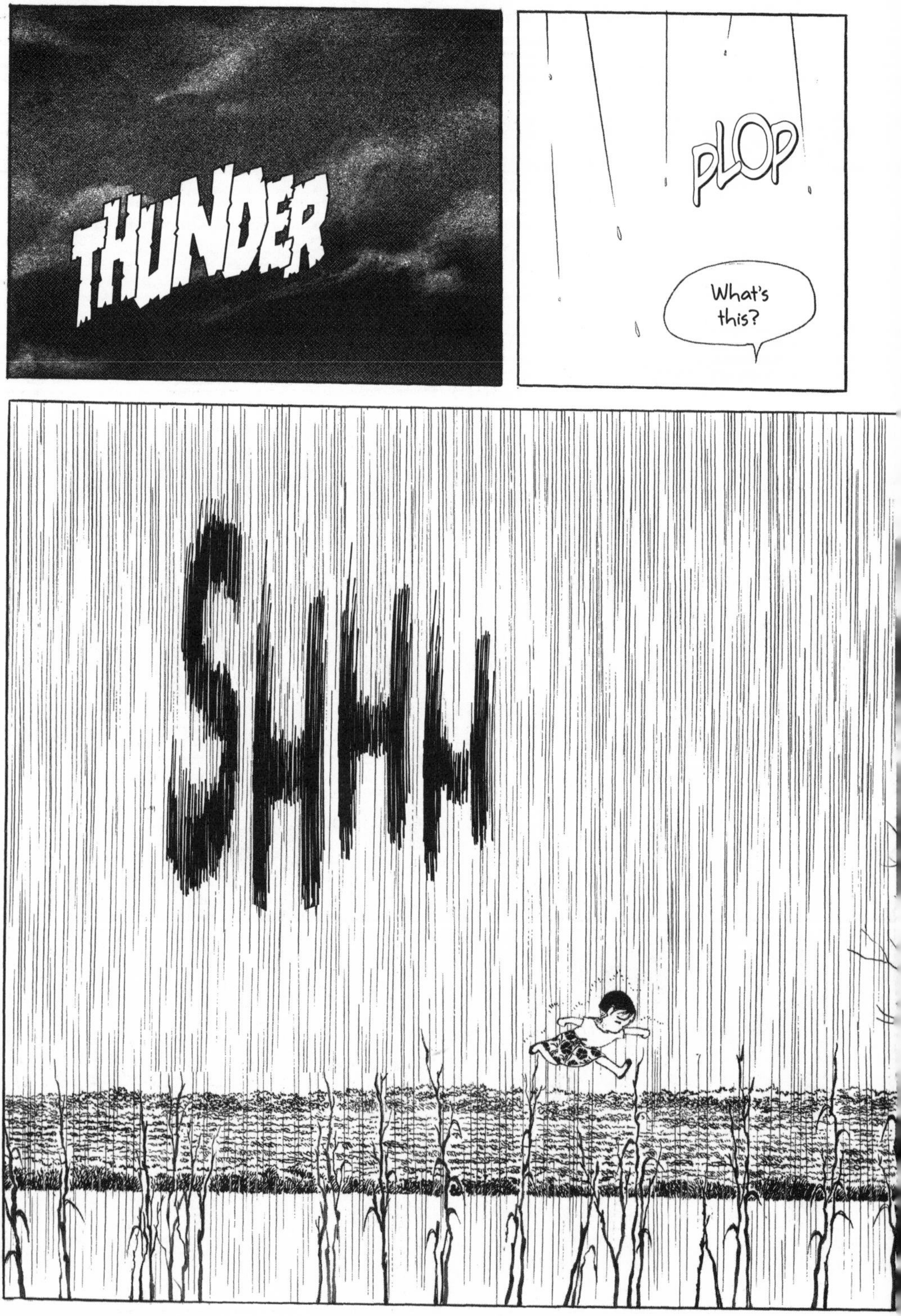
THUNDER
PLOP
What's this?
SHH

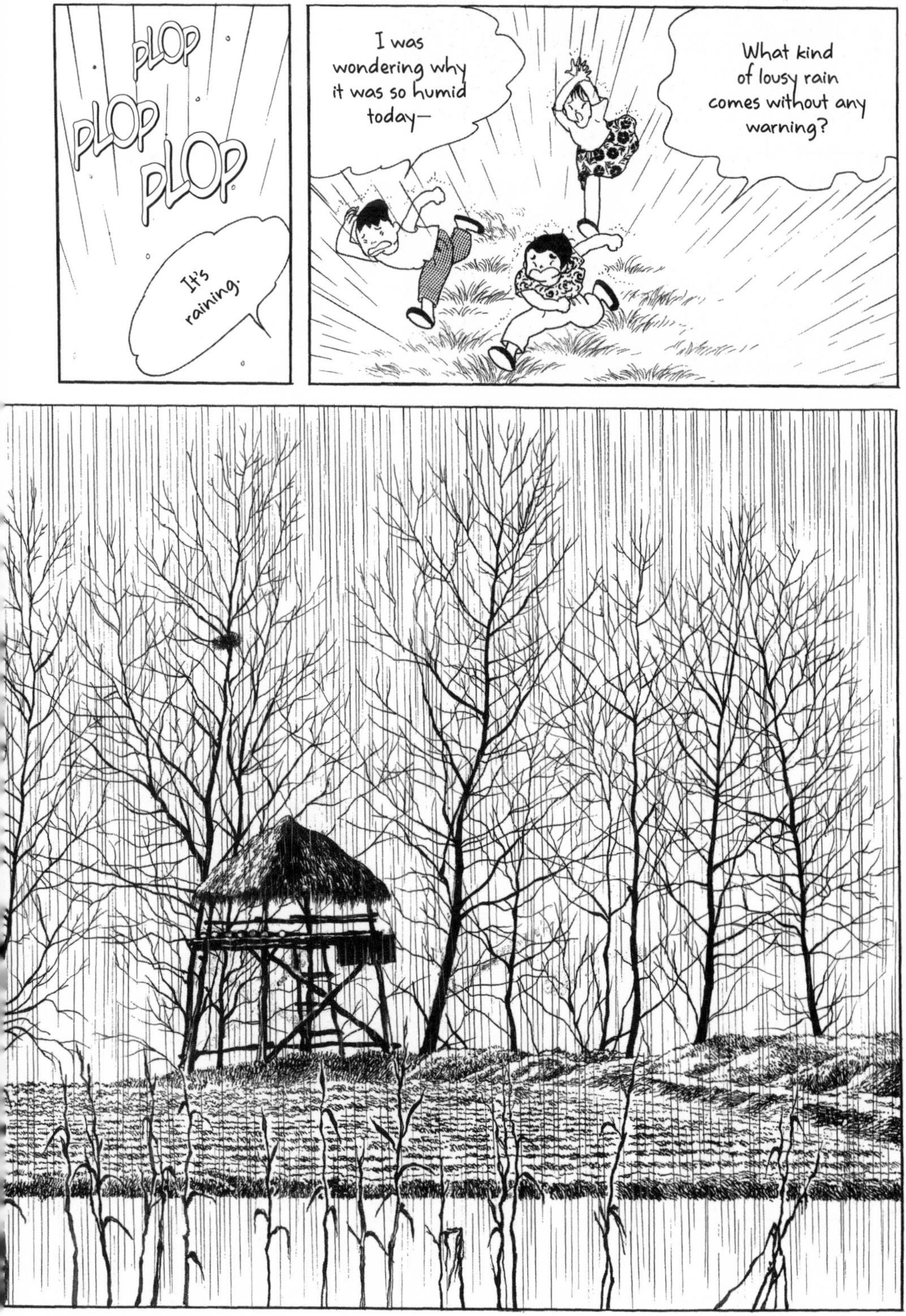
PLOP
PLOP
PLOP
It's raining.
I was wondering why it was so humid today—
What kind of lousy rain comes without any warning?

Maybe Dongchul is right that I am deformed. Why don't I have one too?

But when we were bathing in the creek, Bongeh's mom didn't have one either.

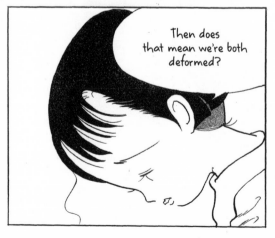

Then does that mean we're both deformed?

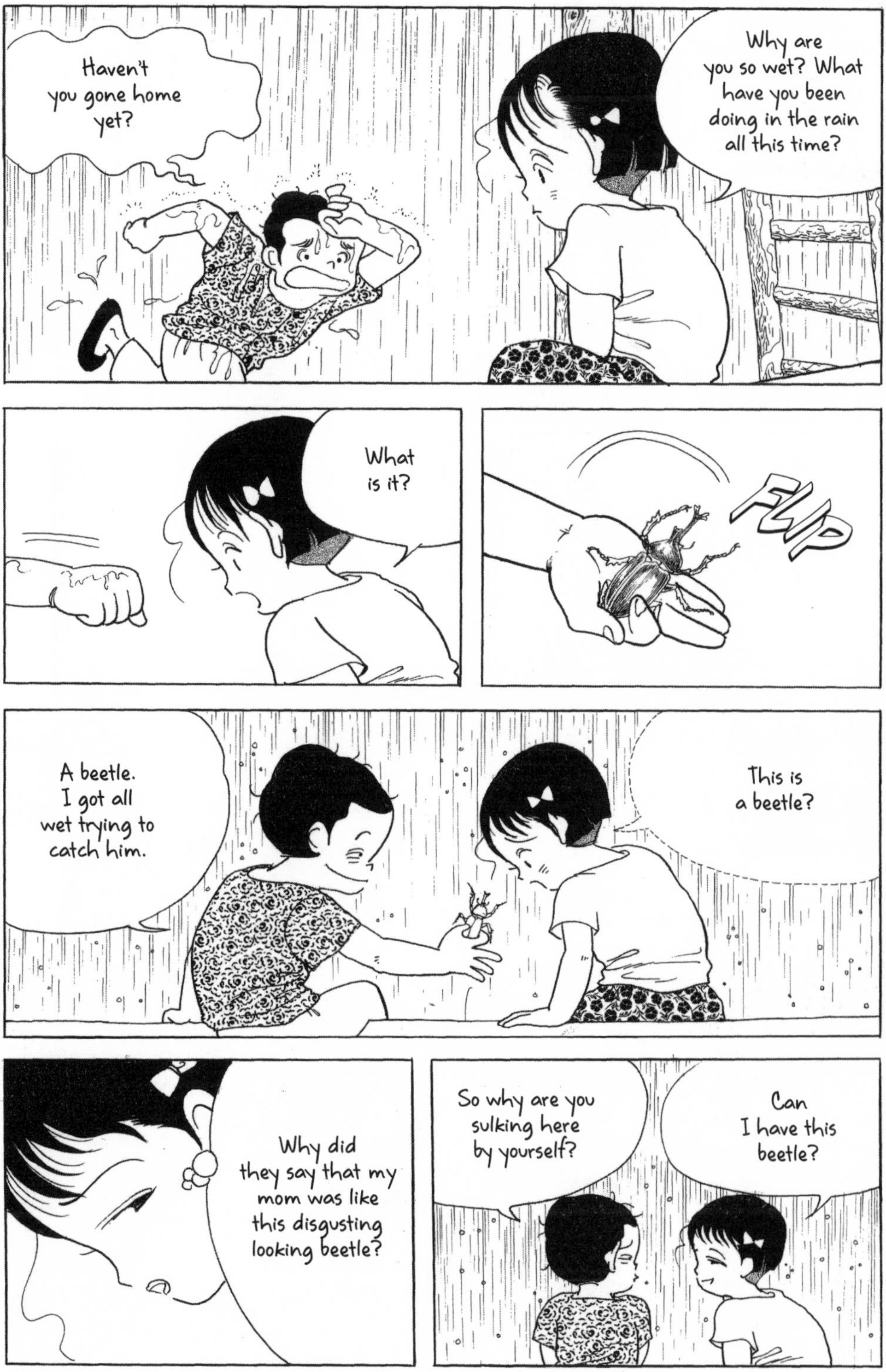
Haven't you gone home yet?
Why are you so wet? What have you been doing in the rain all this time?
What is it?
FLIP
A beetle. I got all wet trying to catch him.
This is a beetle?
Why did they say that my mom was like this disgusting looking beetle?
So why are you sulking here by yourself?
Can I have this beetle?

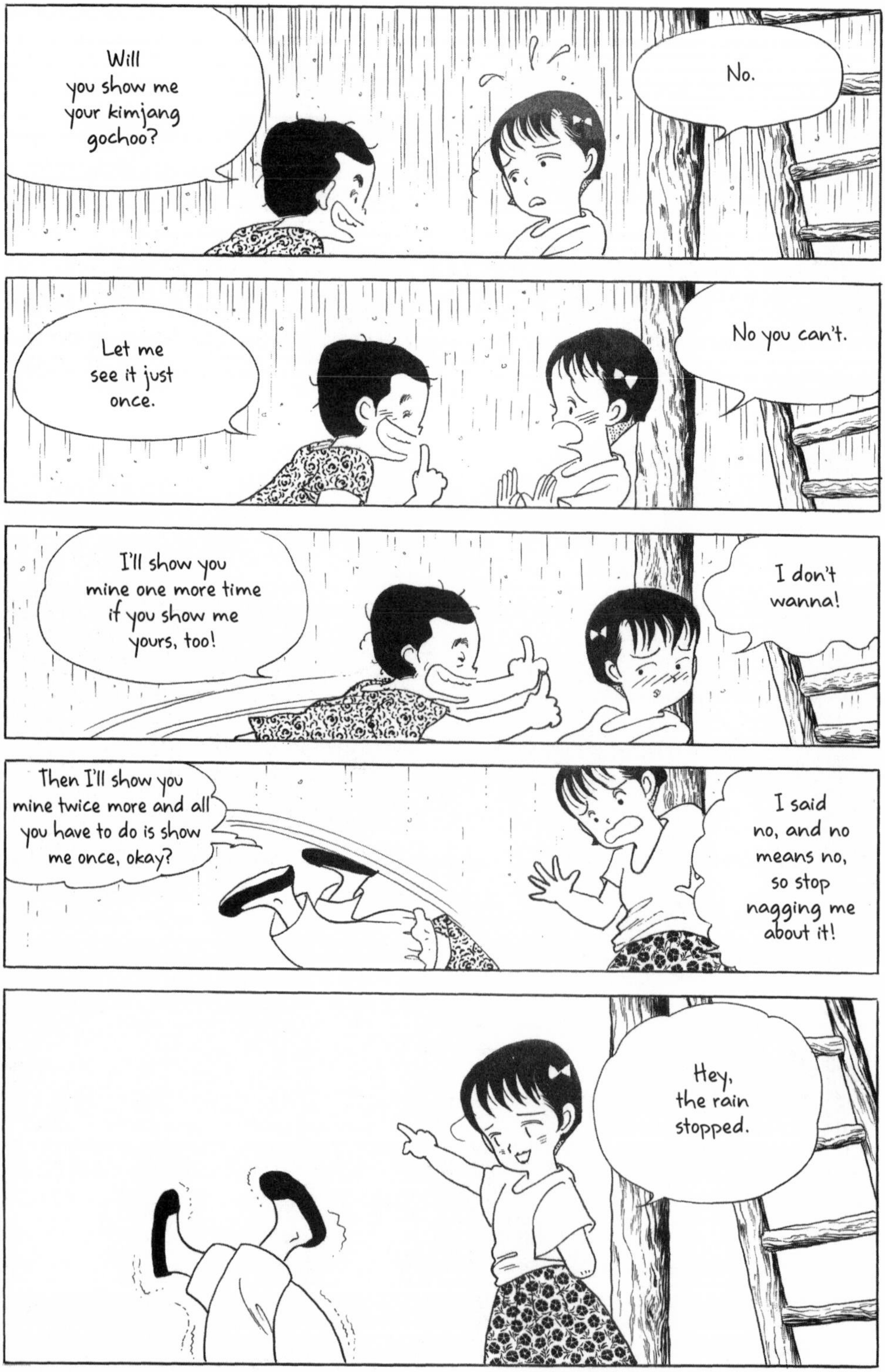
Will you show me your kimjang gochoo?
No.
Let me see it just once.
No you can't.
I'll show you mine one more time if you show me yours, too!
I don't wanna!
Then I'll show you mine twice more and all you have to do is show me once, okay?
I said no, and no means no, so stop nagging me about it!
Hey, the rain stopped.

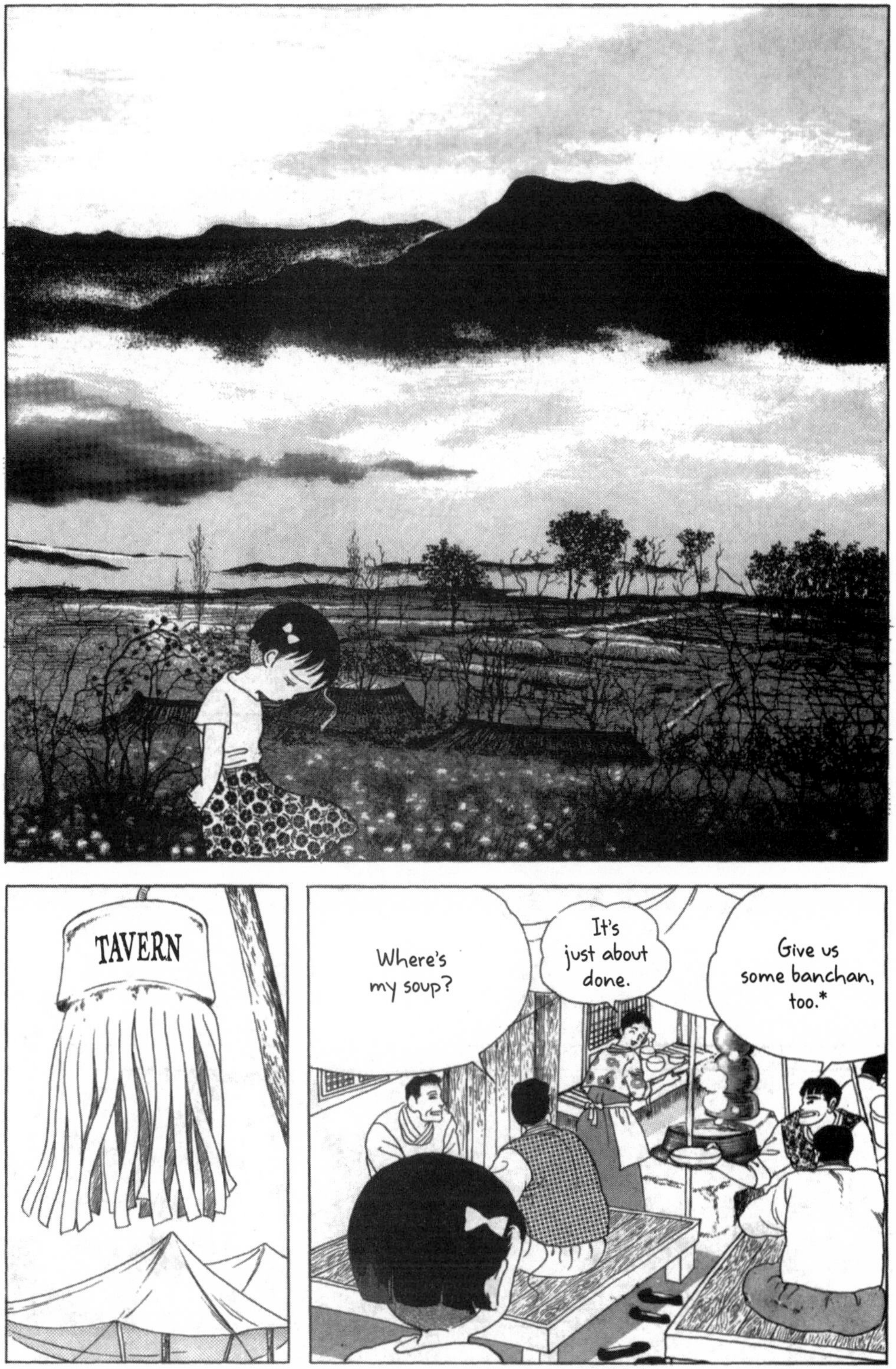
TAVERN
Where's my soup?
It's just about done.
Give us some banchan, too.*

*Banchan is a side dish that accompanies rice and soup. It can be anything from kimchee to sautéed vegetables, tofu, cuttlefish; etc.

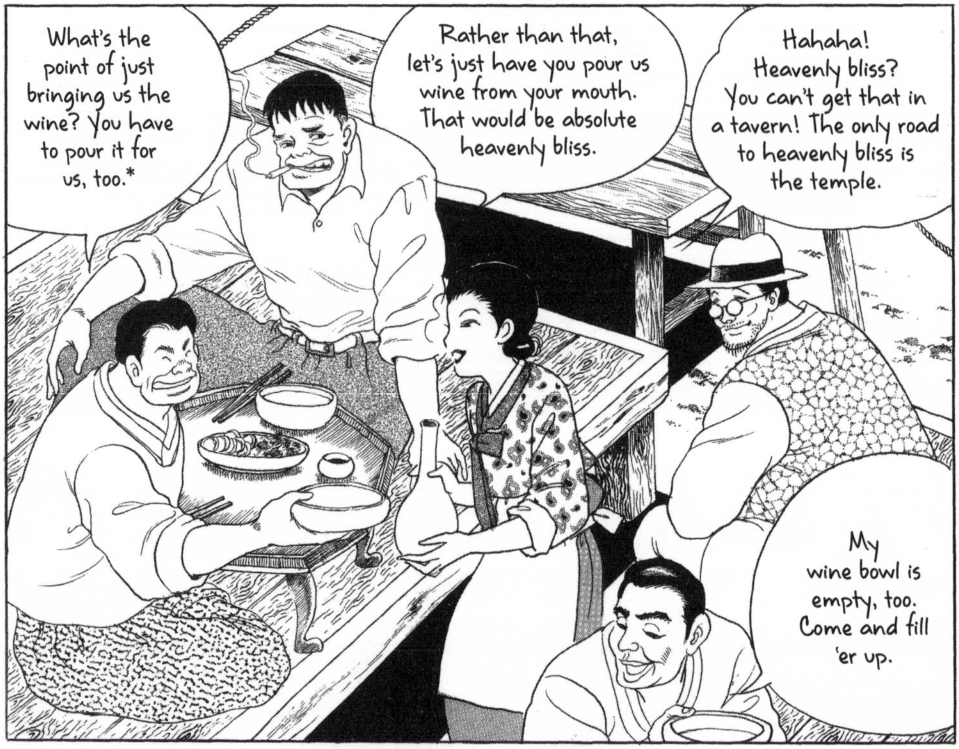
What's the point of just bringing us the wine? You have to pour it for us, too.*
Rather than that, let's just have you pour us wine from your mouth. That would be absolute heavenly bliss.
Hahaha! Heavenly bliss? You can't get that in a tavern! The only road to heavenly bliss is the temple.
My wine bowl is empty, too. Come and fill 'er up.

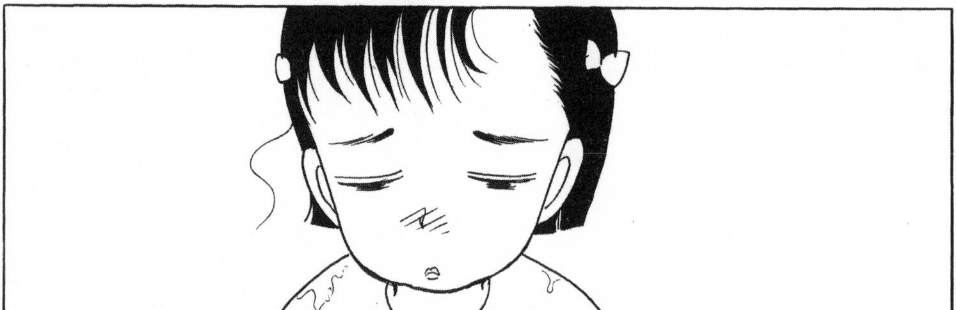

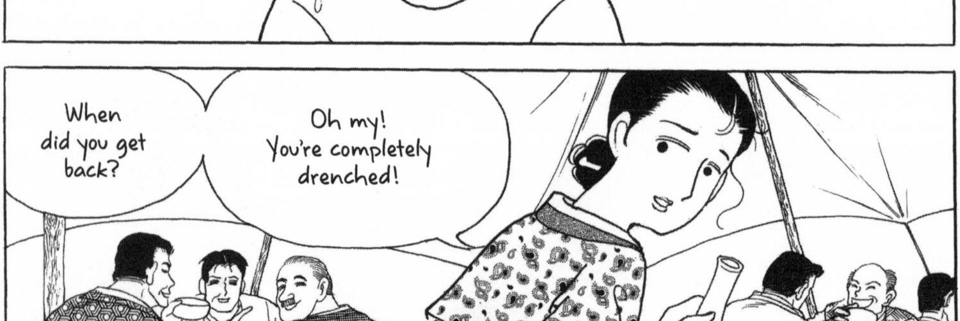
When did you get back?
Oh my! You're completely drenched!

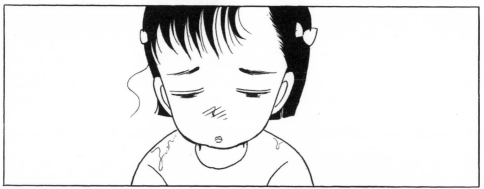

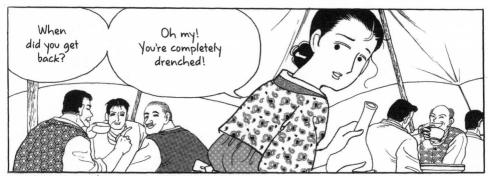

* A woman pouring alcohol for a man has two connotations: she's catering to his whims and she's being subservient to the dominant male.

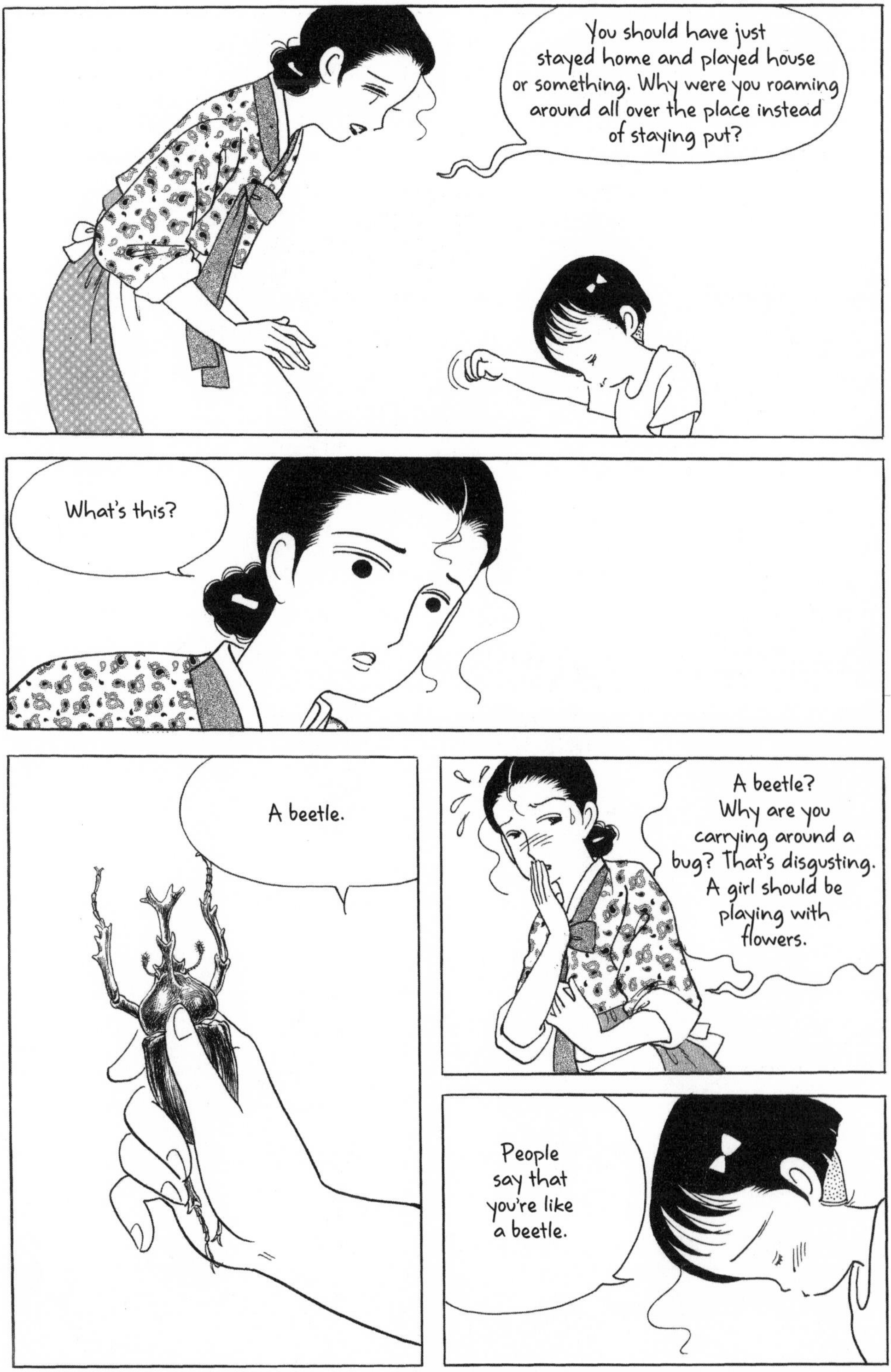
You should have just stayed home and played house or something. Why were you roaming around all over the place instead of staying put?
What's this?
A beetle.
A beetle? Why are you carrying around a bug? That's disgusting. A girl should be playing with flowers.
People say that you're like a beetle.

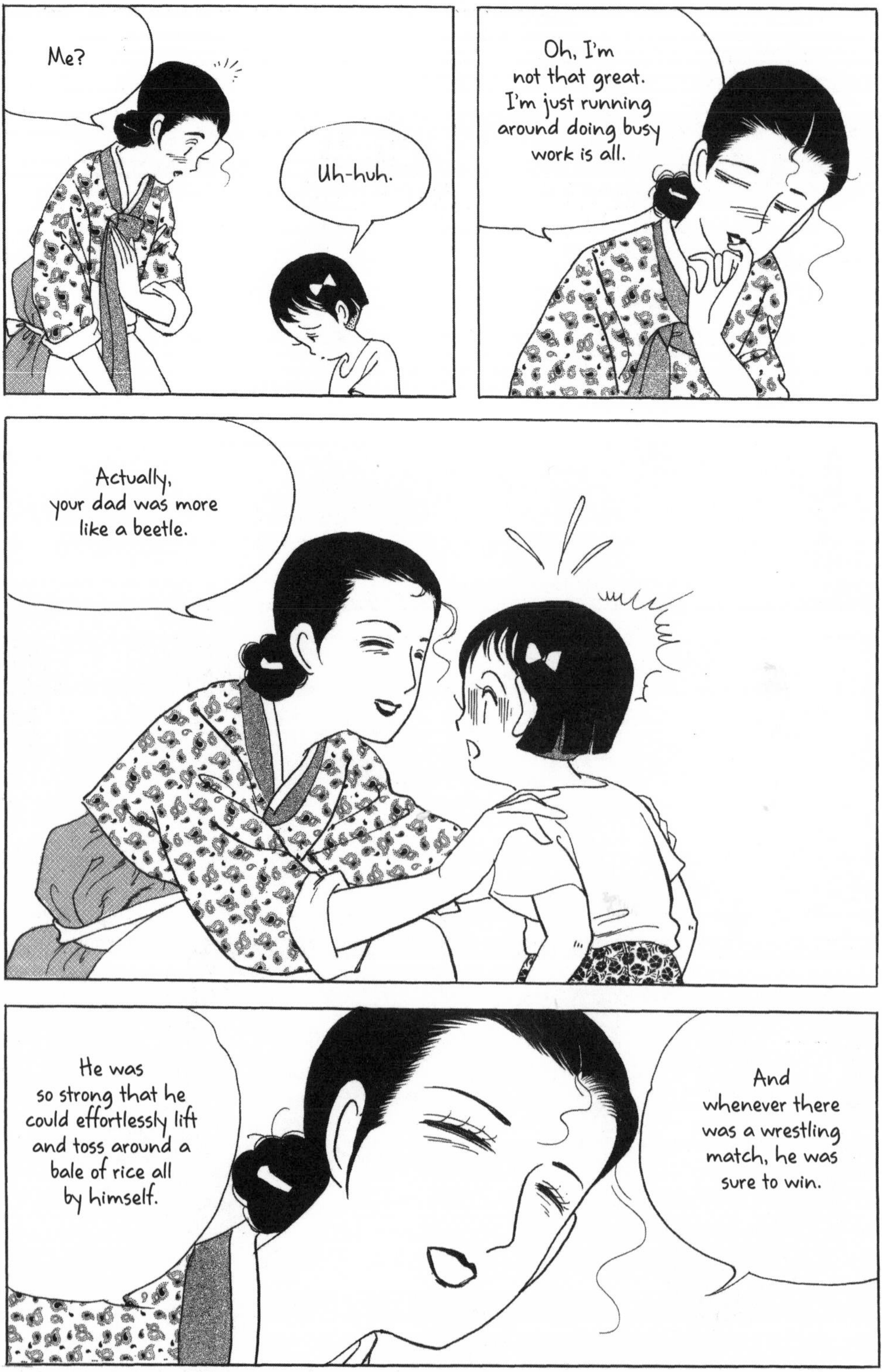
Me?
Uh-huh.
Oh, I'm not that great. I'm just running around doing busy work is all.
Actually, your dad was more like a beetle.
He was so strong that he could effortlessly lift and toss around a bale of rice all by himself.
And whenever there was a wrestling match, he was sure to win.

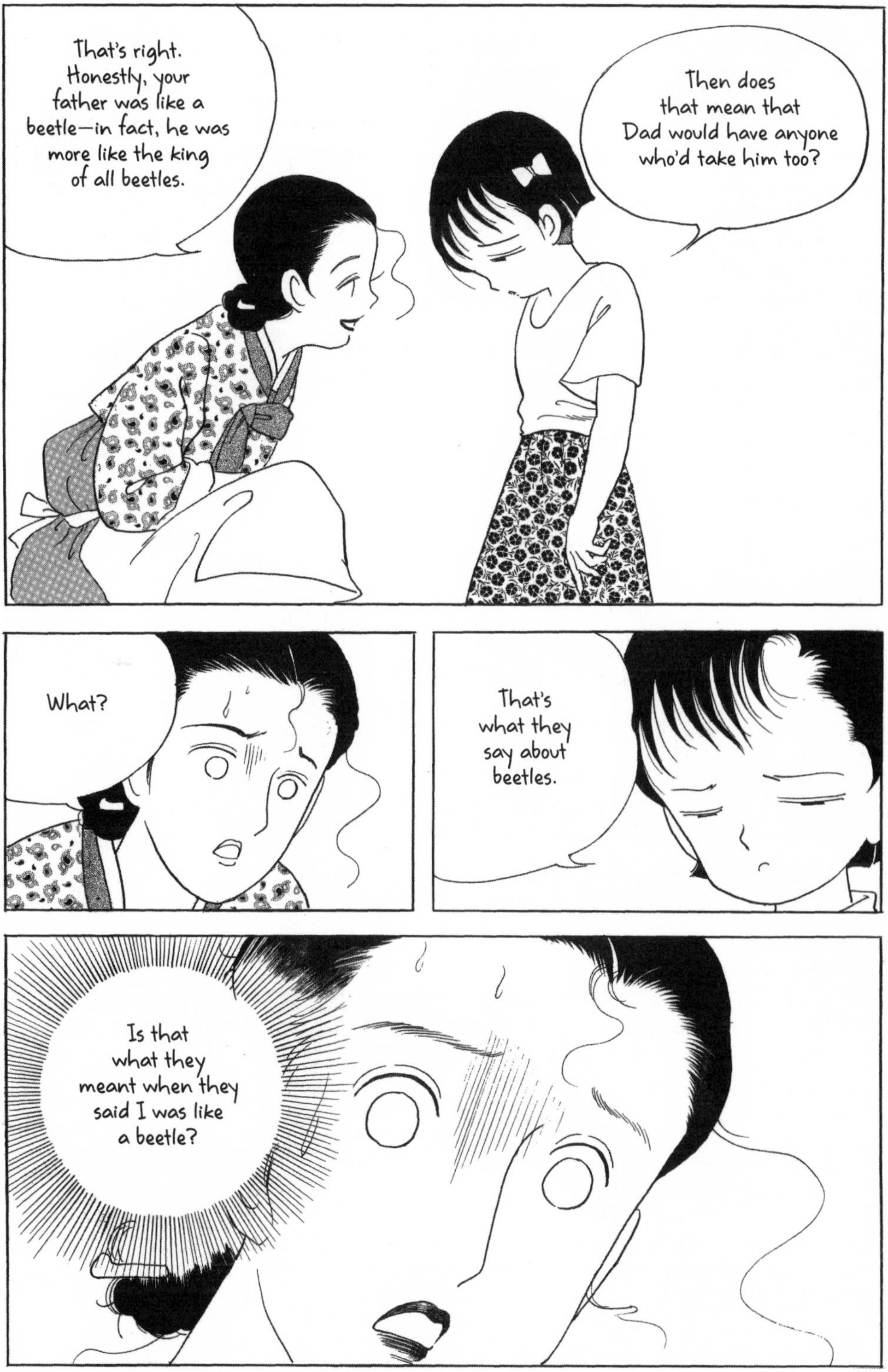
That's right. Honestly, your father was like a beetle—in fact, he was more like the king of all beetles.
Then does that mean that Dad would have anyone who'd take him too?
What?
That's what they say about beetles.
Is that what they meant when they said I was like a beetle?

Here I am doing my best to make a living while raising a child by myself, and they go around spreading false gossip. Those bastards, the least they could do is be kind.

As a tavern owner, I can't be choosy about who I serve. If they come to my place I have to welcome them with a smile whether I like them or not.

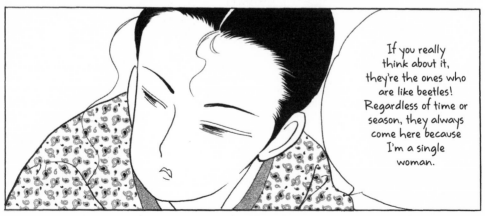

If you really think about it, they're the ones who are like beetles! Regardless of time or season, they always come here because I'm a single woman.

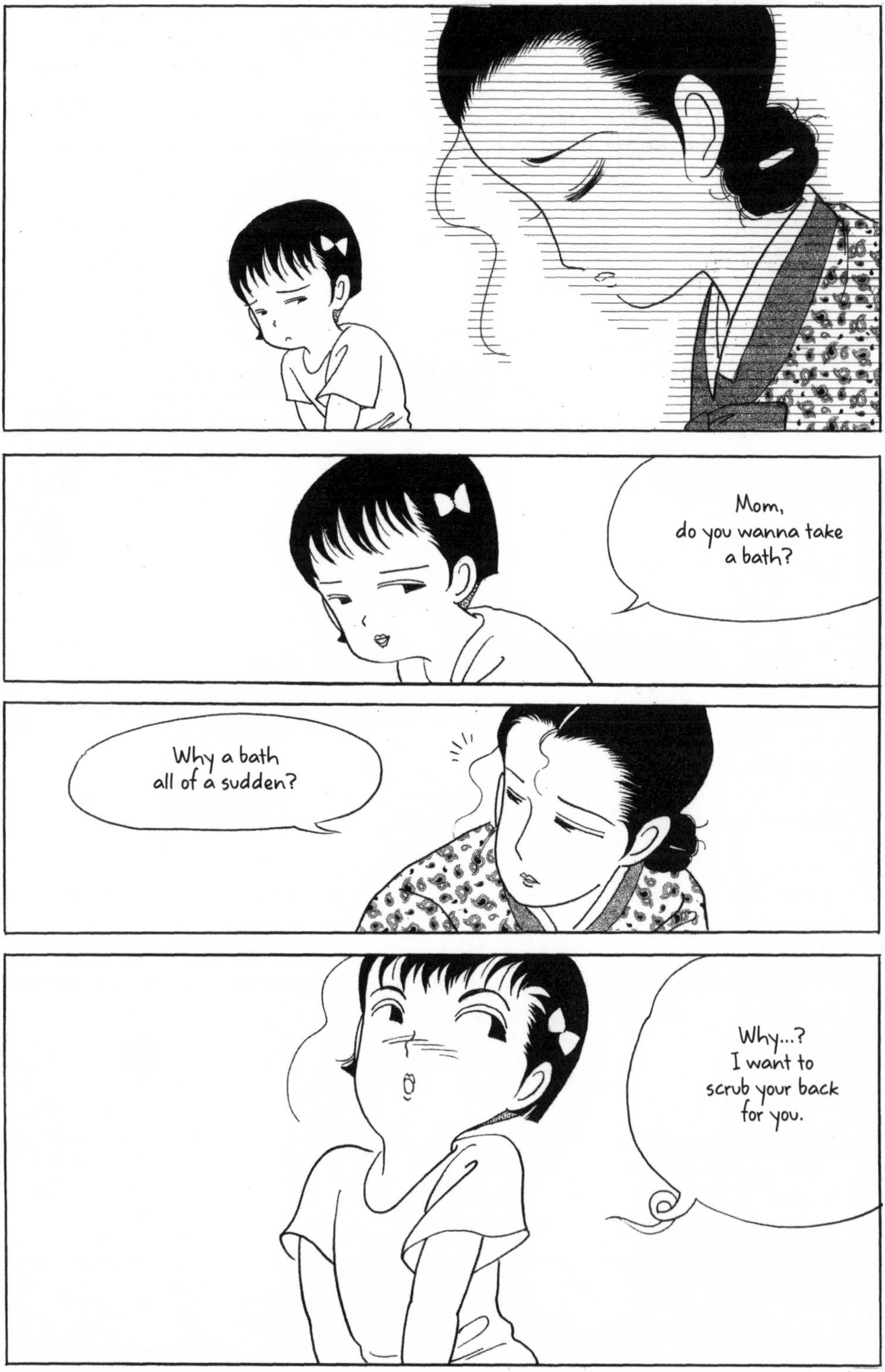

Mom, do you wanna take a bath?
Why a bath all of a sudden?
Why...? I want to scrub your back for you.

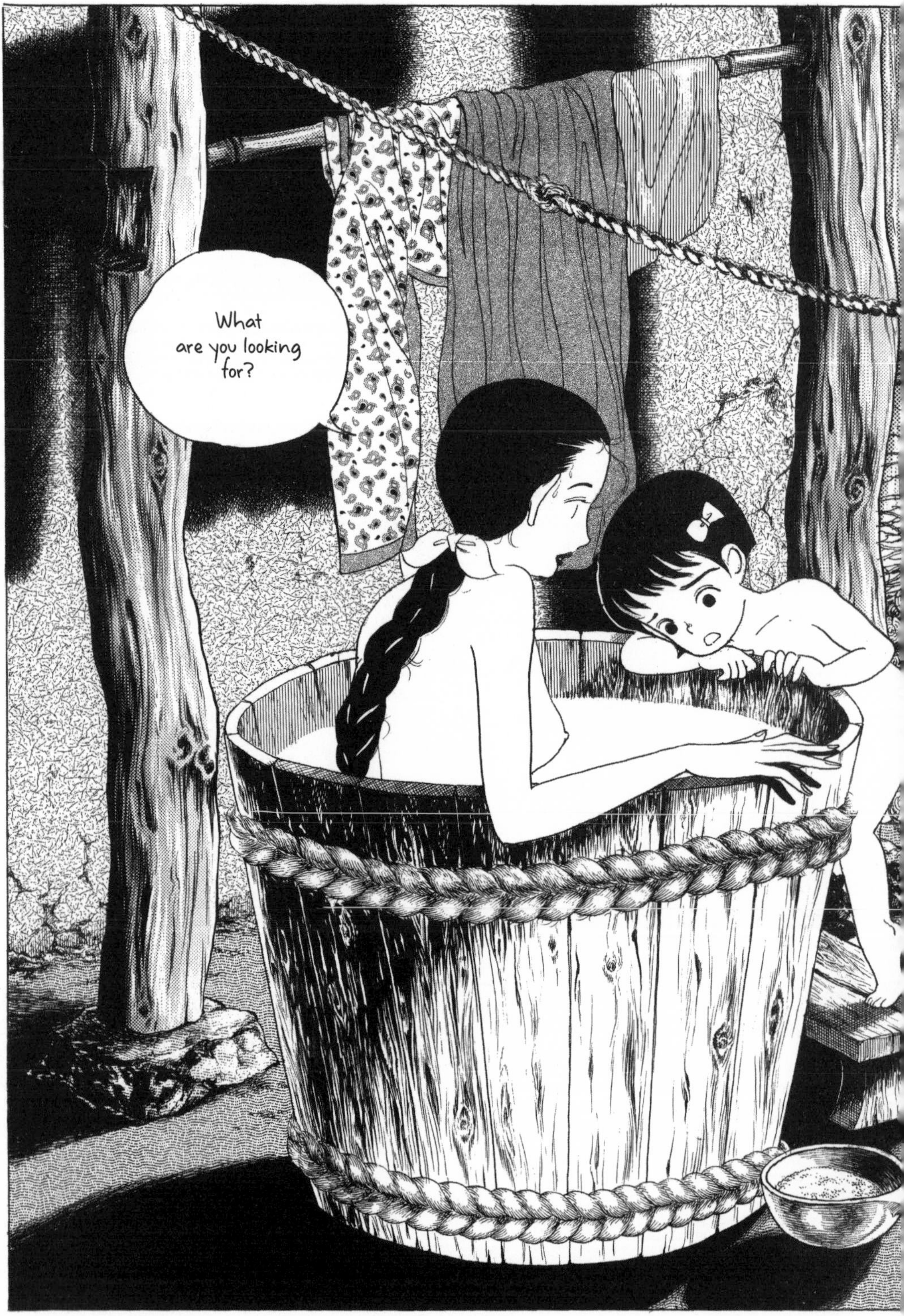
What are you looking for?

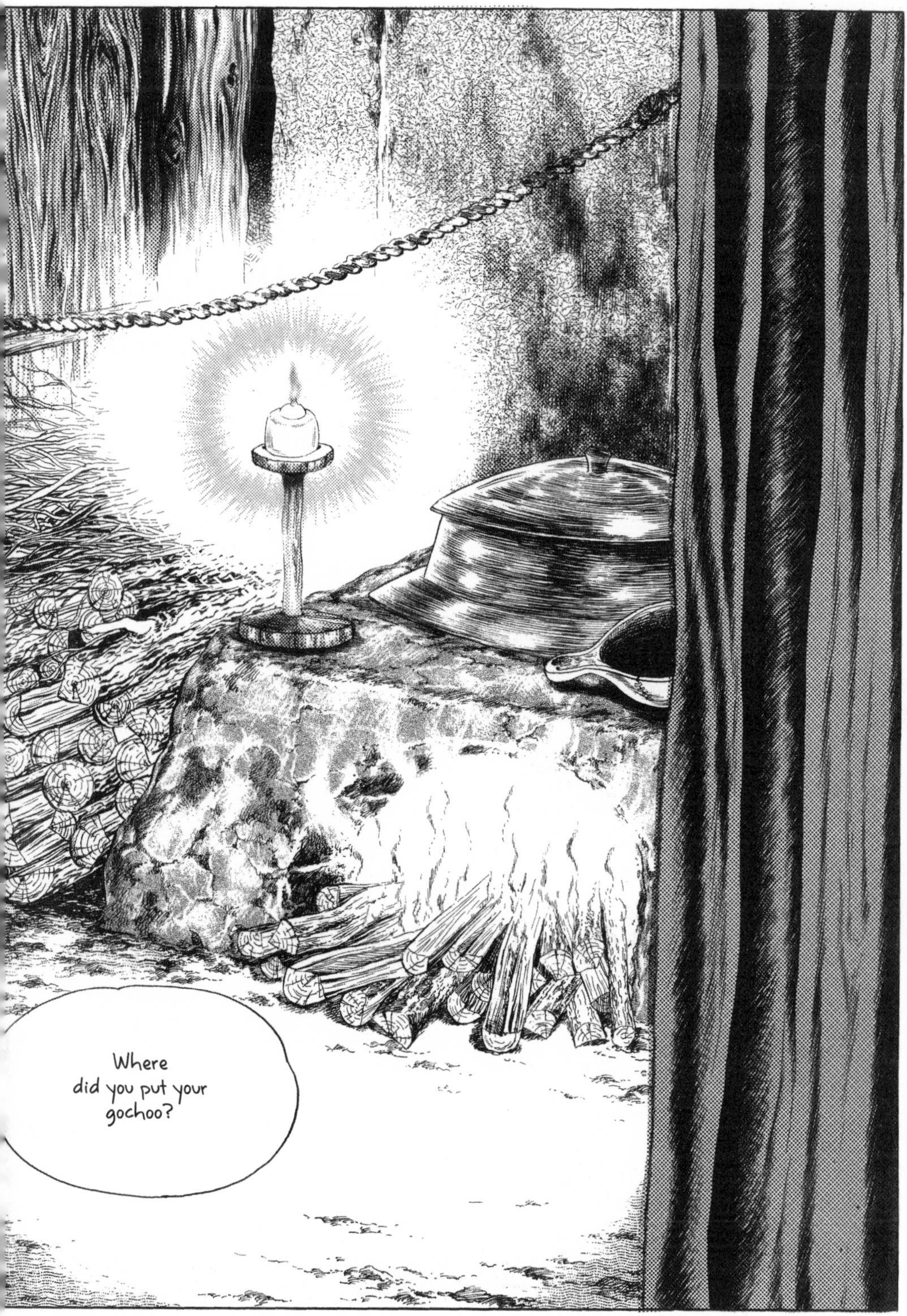
Where did you put your gochoo?

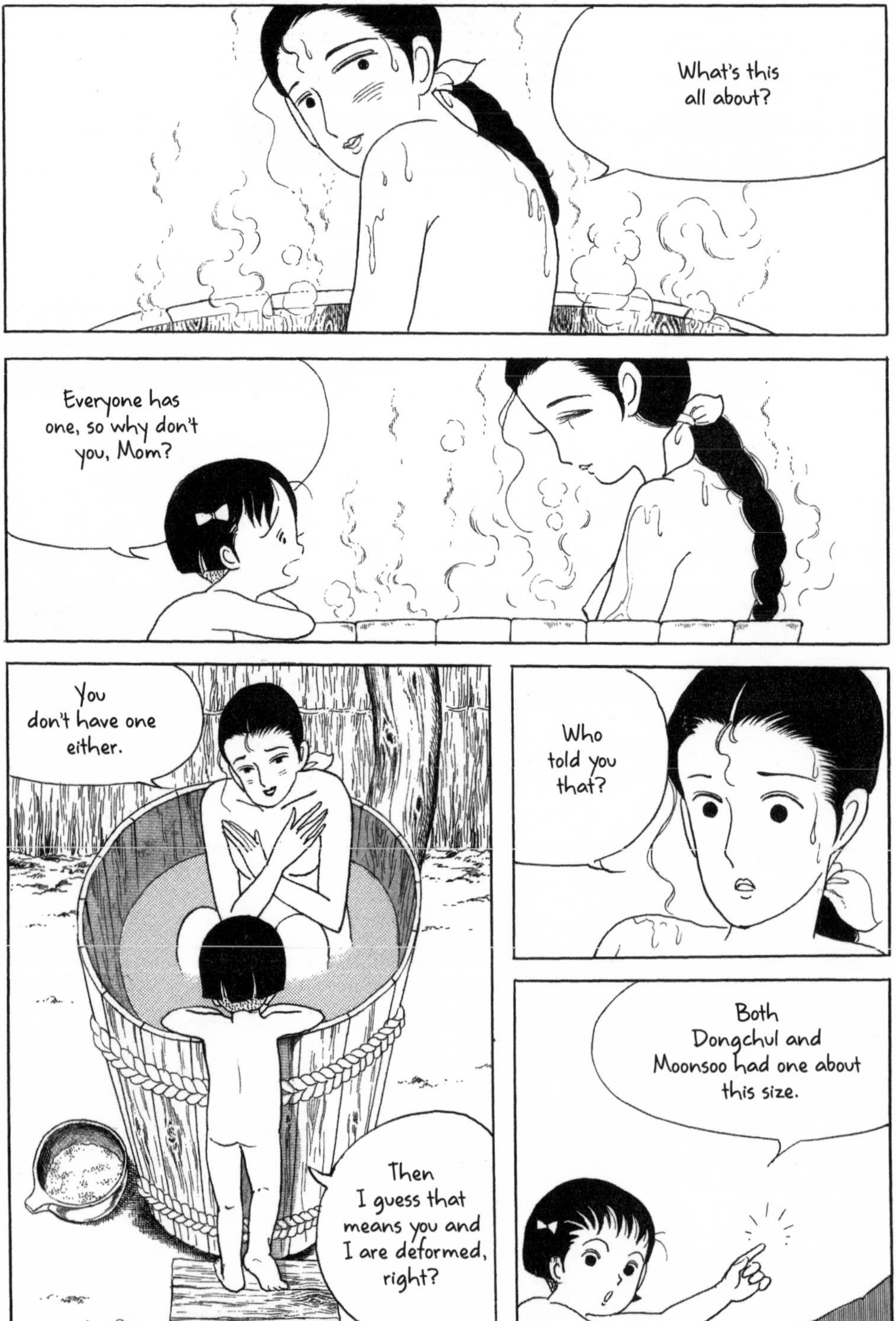
What's this all about?
Everyone has one, so why don't you, Mom?
You don't have one either.
Then I guess that means you and I are deformed, right?
Who told you that?
Both Dongchul and Moonsoo had one about this size.

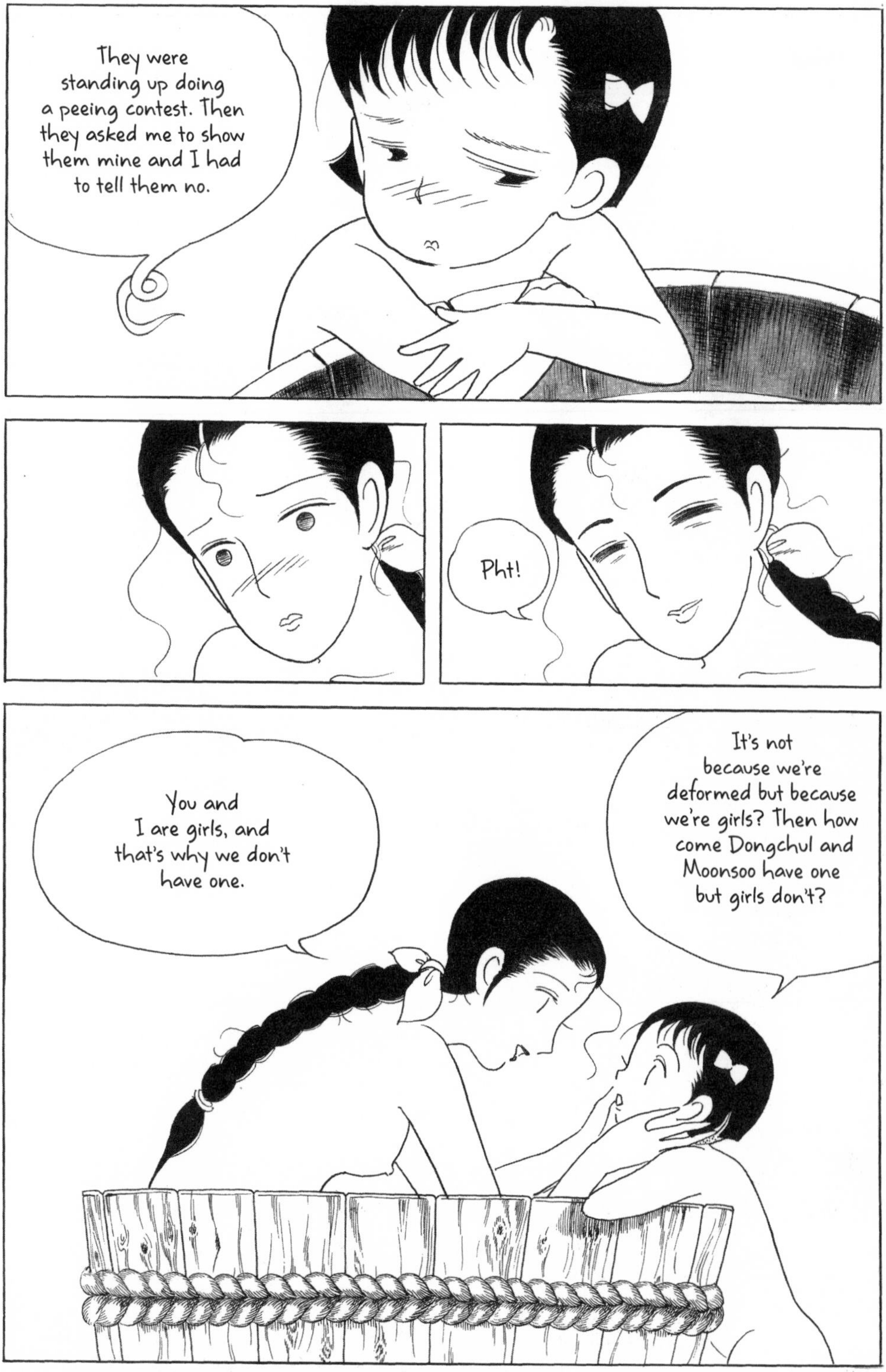
They were standing up doing a peeing contest. Then they asked me to show them mine and I had to tell them no.
Pht!
You and I are girls, and that's why we don't have one.
It's not because we're deformed but because we're girls? Then how come Dongchul and Moonsoo have one but girls don't?

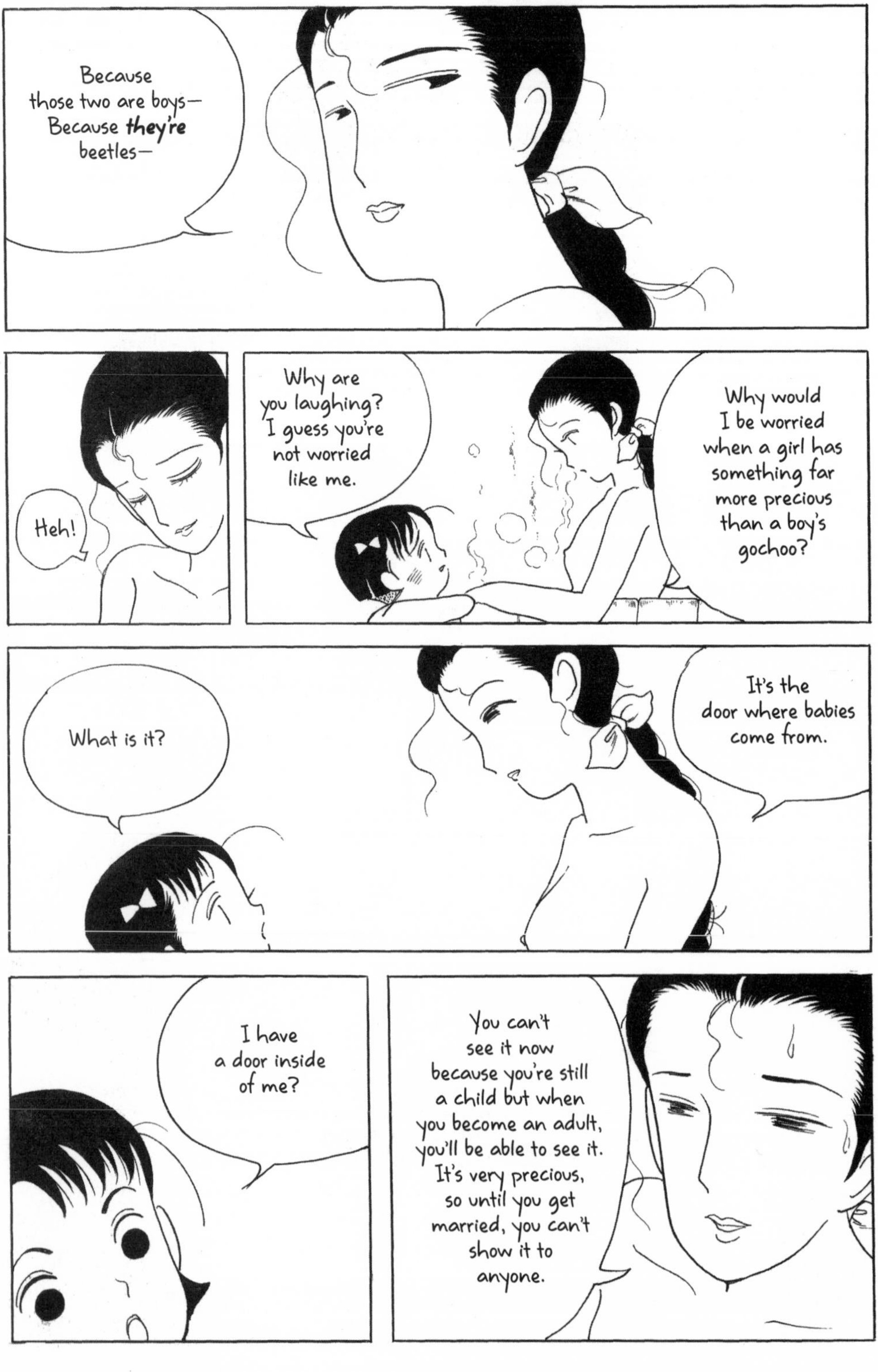
Because those two are boys— Because **they're** beetles—
Heh!
Why are you laughing? I guess you're not worried like me.
Why would I be worried when a girl has something far more precious than a boy's gochoo?
What is it?
It's the door where babies come from.
I have a door inside of me?
You can't see it now because you're still a child but when you become an adult, you'll be able to see it. It's very precious, so until you get married, you can't show it to anyone.

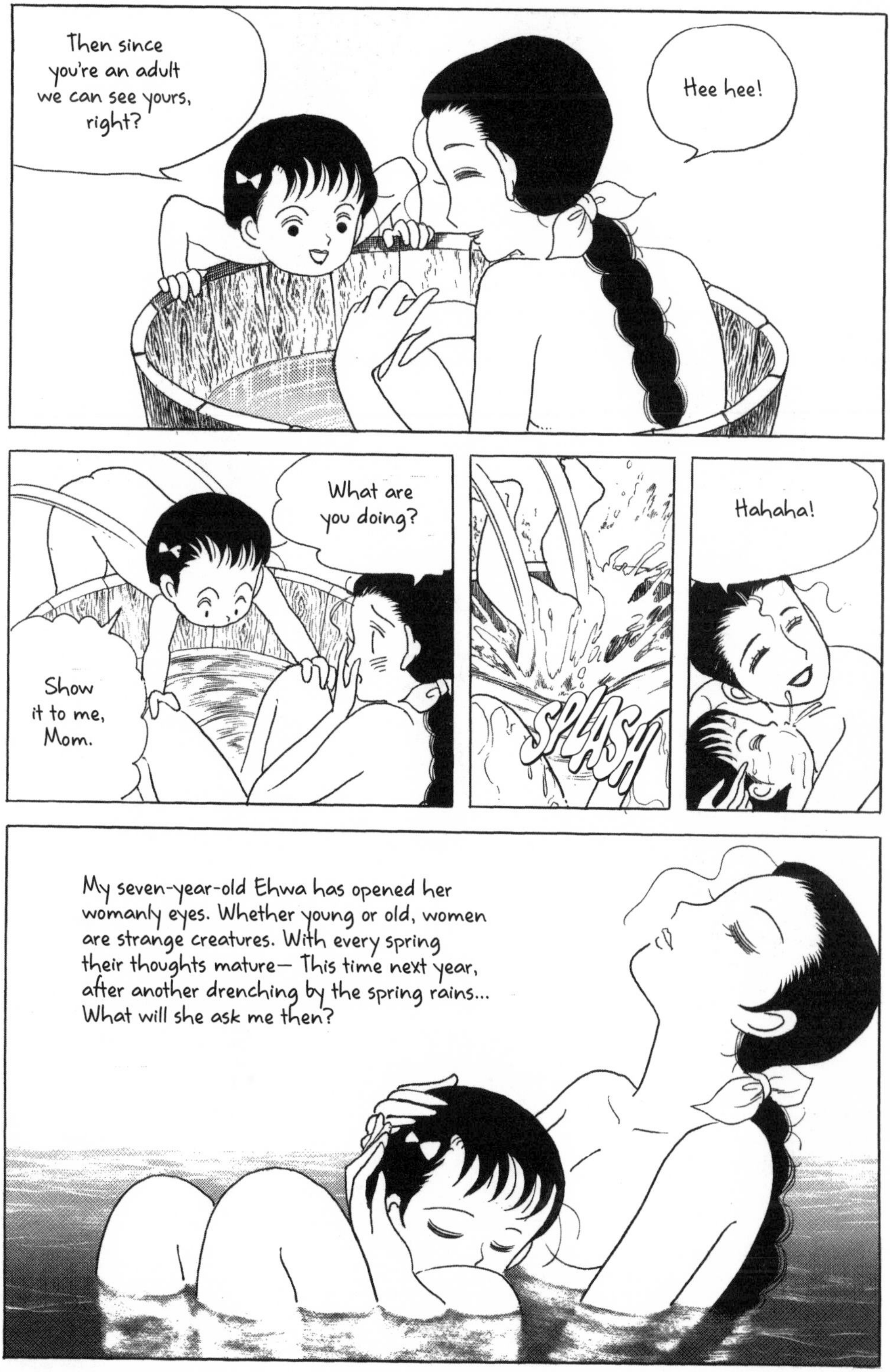
Then since you're an adult we can see yours, right?
Hee hee!
What are you doing?
Show it to me, Mom.
SPLASH
Hahaha!
My seven-year-old Ehwa has opened her womanly eyes. Whether young or old, women are strange creatures. With every spring their thoughts mature— This time next year, after another drenching by the spring rains... What will she ask me then?

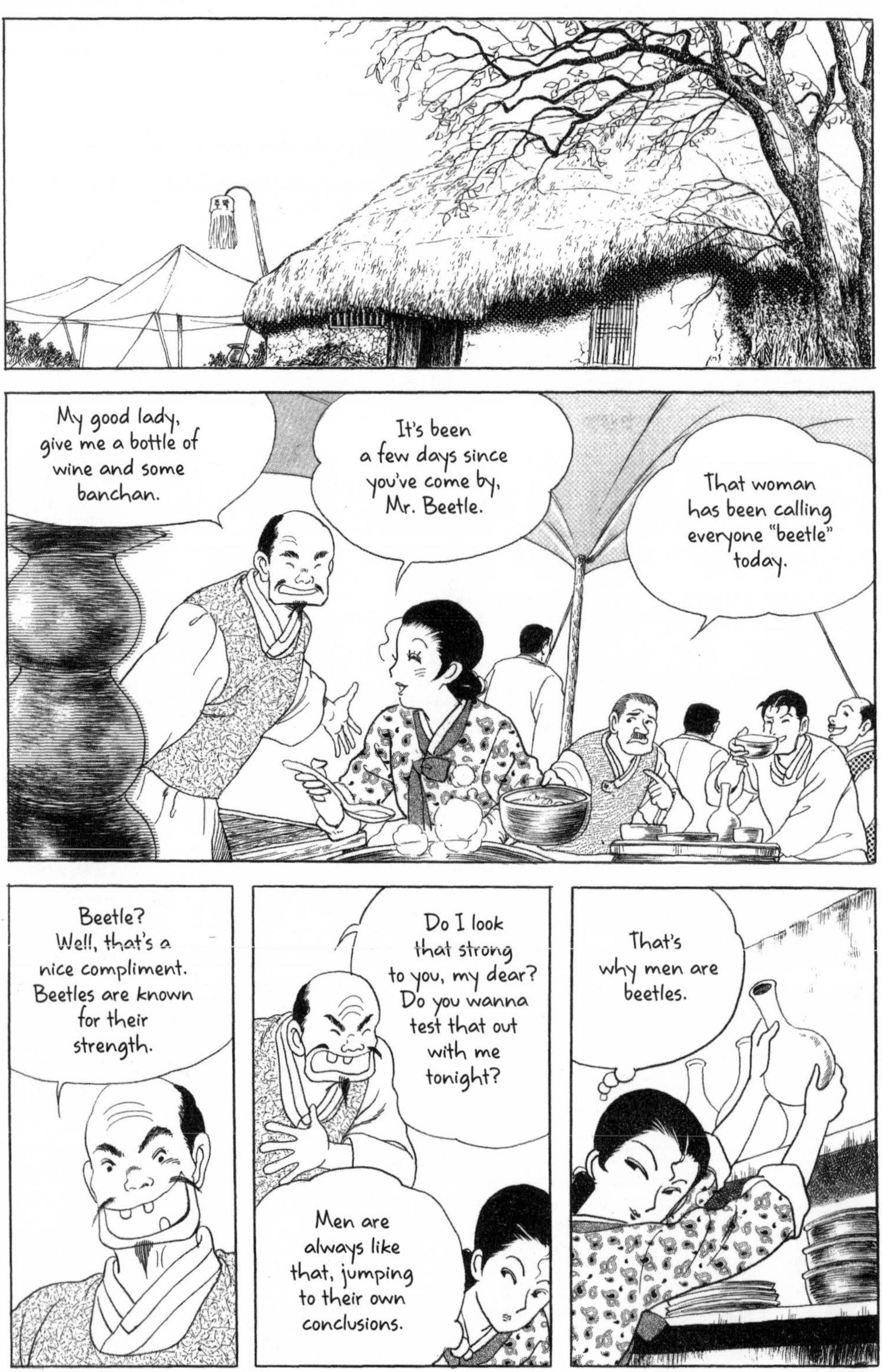
My good lady, give me a bottle of wine and some banchan.
It's been a few days since you've come by, Mr. Beetle.
That woman has been calling everyone "beetle" today.
Beetle? Well, that's a nice compliment. Beetles are known for their strength.
Do I look that strong to you, my dear? Do you wanna test that out with me tonight?
Men are always like that, jumping to their own conclusions.
That's why men are beetles.

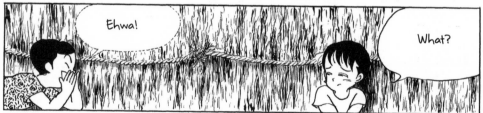

Ehwa!

What?

If I catch you a frog will you show me your kimjang gochoo?

Nope.

You just have to show me one time.

It's precious. I hid it away really well so you can't see it.

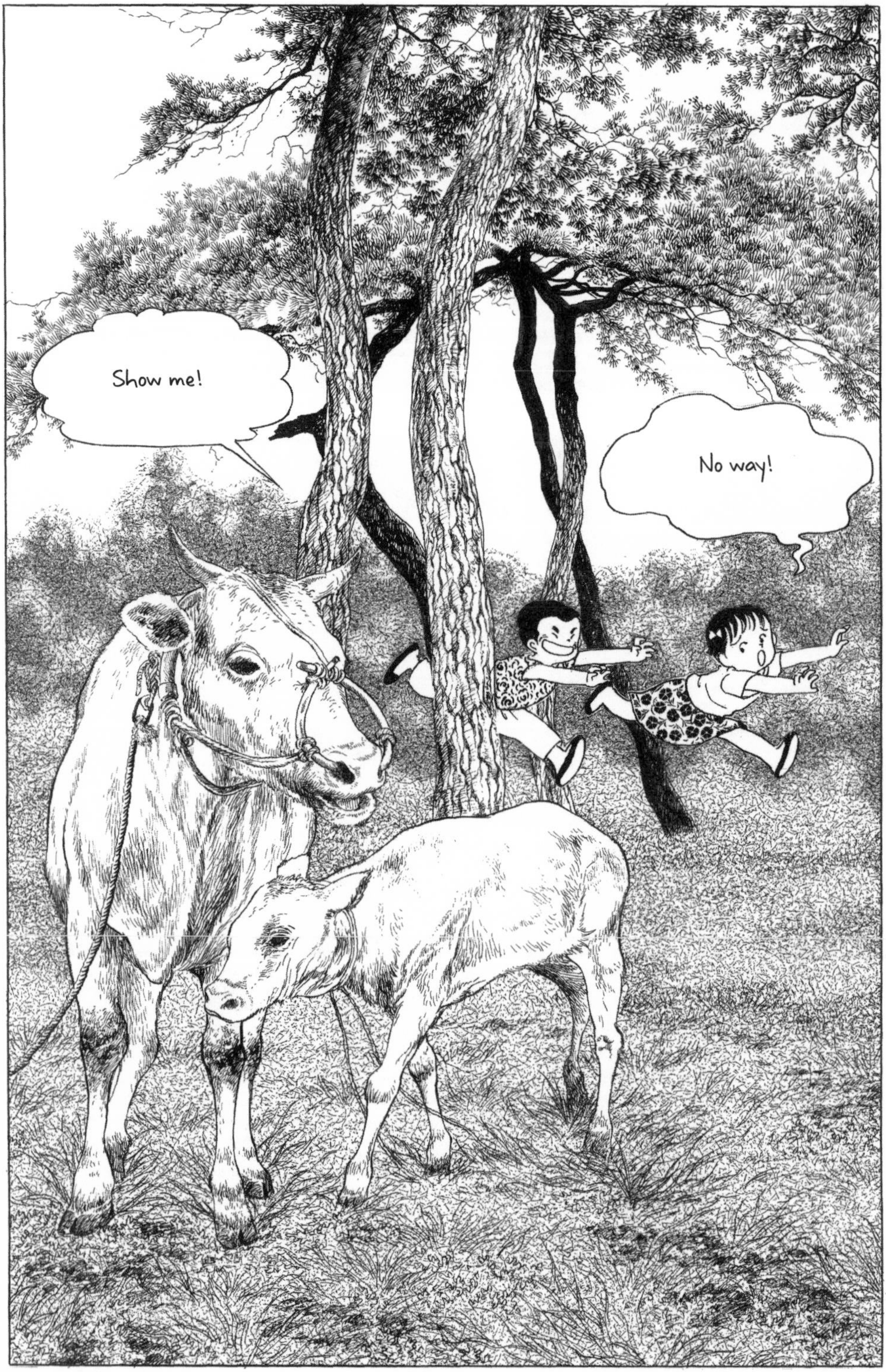
Show me!
No way!

Chapter Two
SPRING RAIN
PART 2: THE STINKY POO TREE

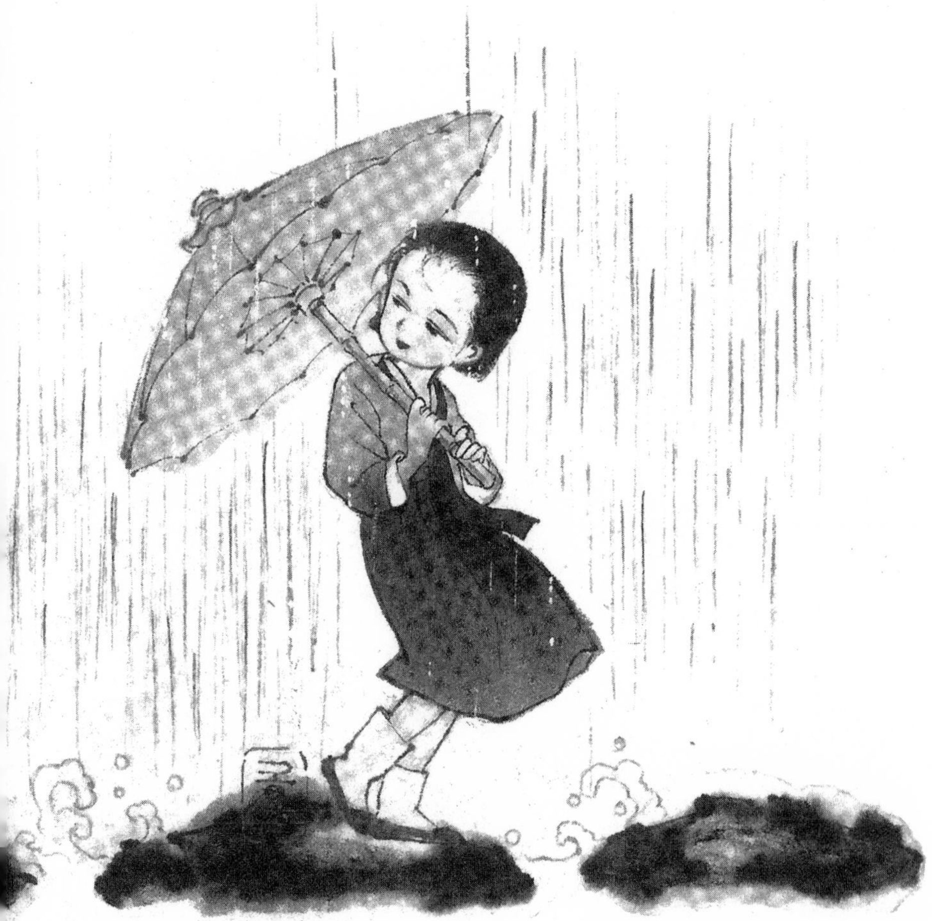

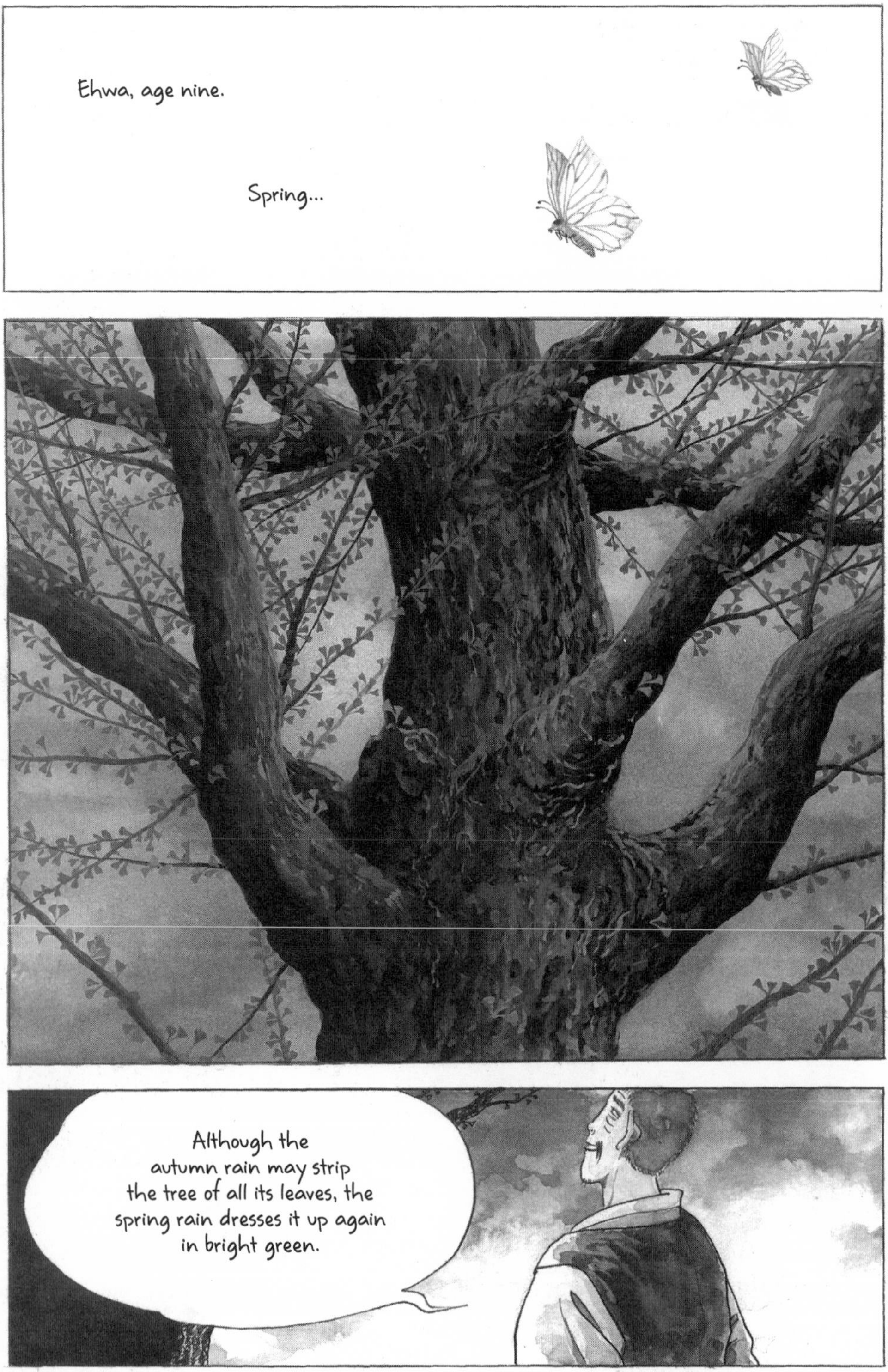
Ehwa, age nine.
Spring...
Although the autumn rain may strip the tree of all its leaves, the spring rain dresses it up again in bright green.

I don't like that stinky poo tree, but it looks like **you** like it, Grandpa Dorbang.*

Why do you call it a stinky poo tree, you little rascal? This is a ginkgo tree.

Last autumn when I opened one of the fruits, it smelled really bad.

The smell was worse than a baby's dirty diaper.

I see, so it was you who picked the unripe fruit off this tree last autumn?

No, it wasn't me. I only picked five and they smelled so bad that I thought they were rotten, and I threw them all away. It was Bongsoon who took most of the fruit. She plucked an entire skirt-full of those stinky things.

Well, even though she did, I was still able to harvest over two large bags of nuts. Doesn't that tell you how amazing this tree is?

* This man isn't Ehwa's biological grandfather. It's a polite way of addressing an older man, since in Korea people don't address people older than themselves by their first names.

45

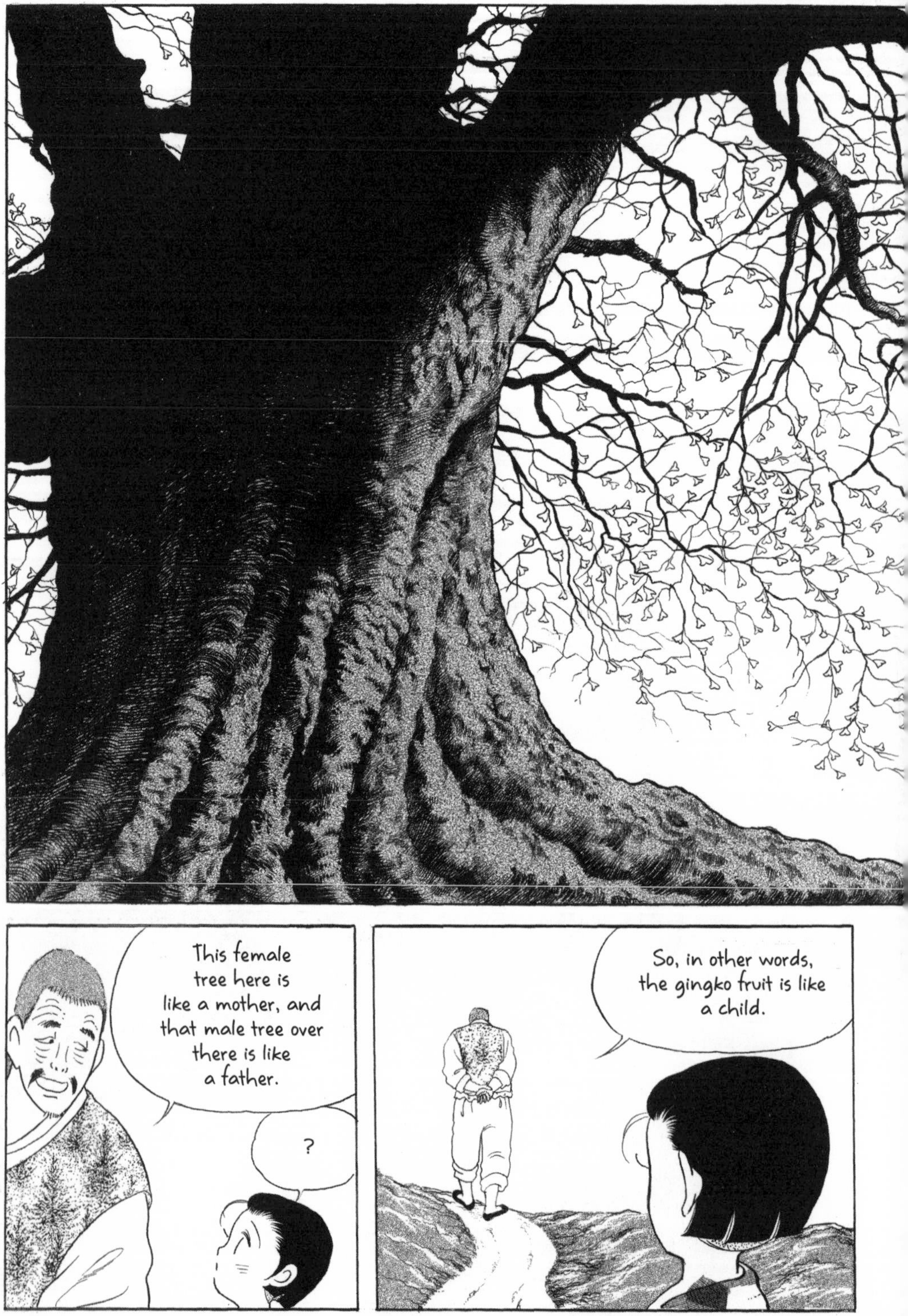
This female tree here is like a mother, and that male tree over there is like a father.
?
So, in other words, the gingko fruit is like a child.

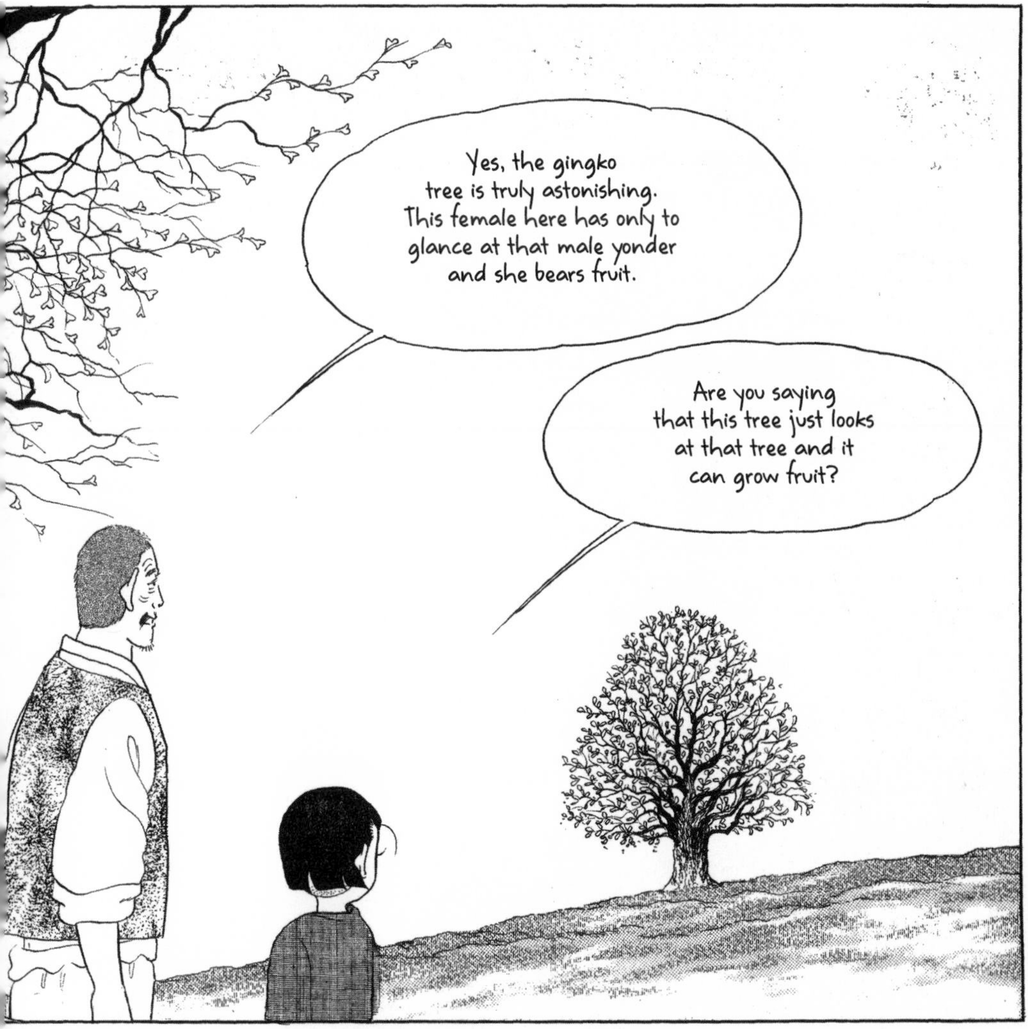
Yes, the gingko tree is truly astonishing. This female here has only to glance at that male yonder and she bears fruit.
Are you saying that this tree just looks at that tree and it can grow fruit?

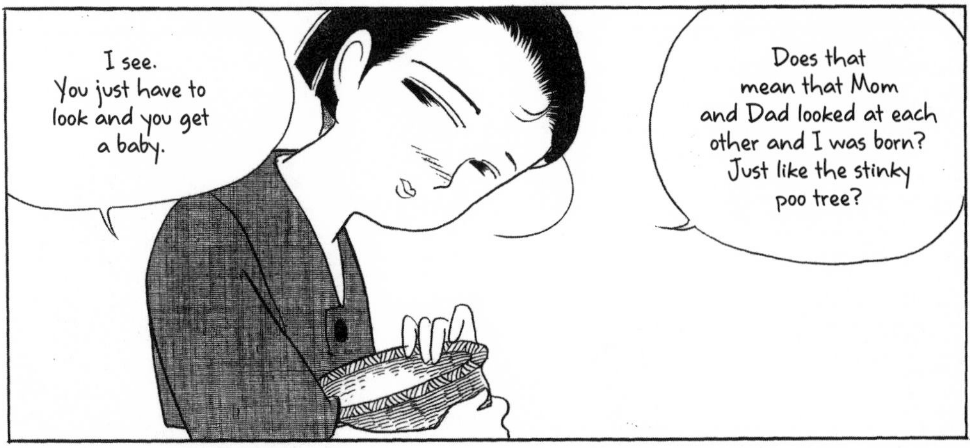
Does that mean that Mom and Dad looked at each other and I was born? Just like the stinky poo tree?
I see. You just have to look and you get a baby.

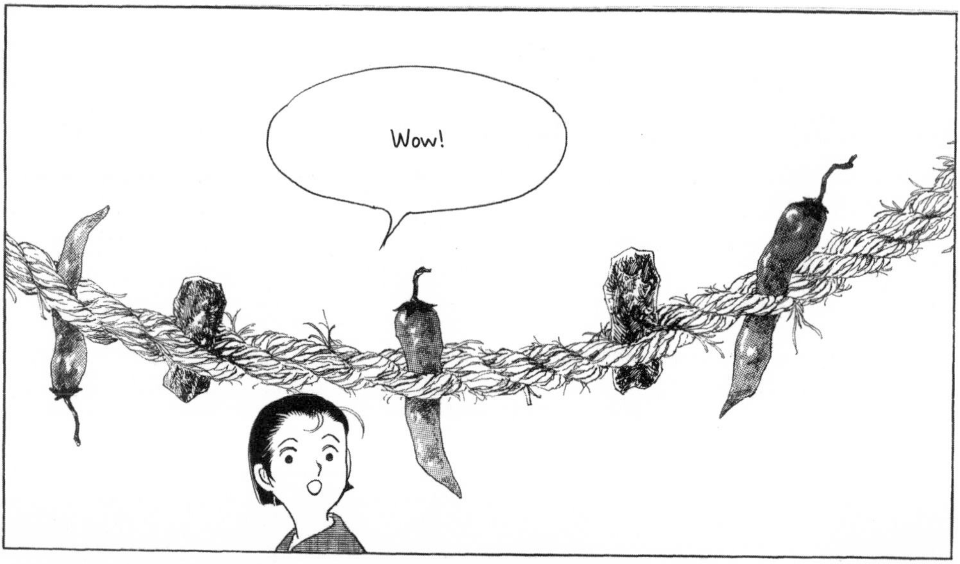
Wow!

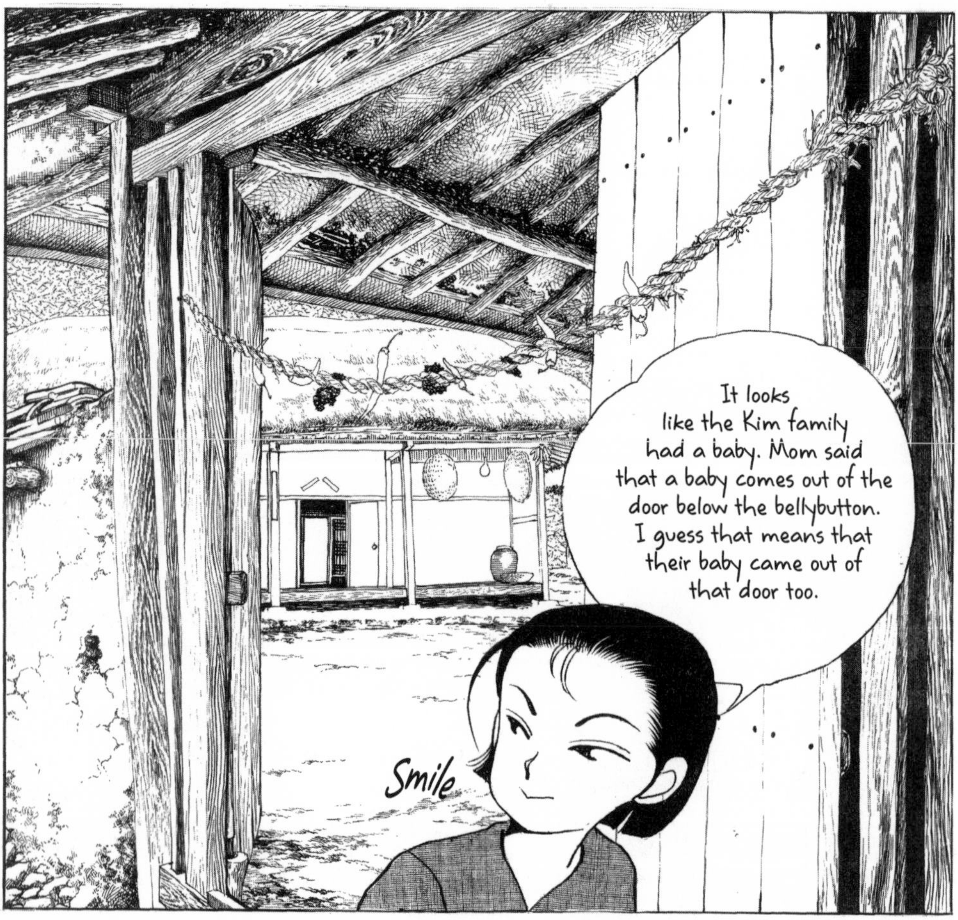
It looks like the Kim family had a baby. Mom said that a baby comes out of the door below the bellybutton. I guess that means that their baby came out of that door too.
Smile

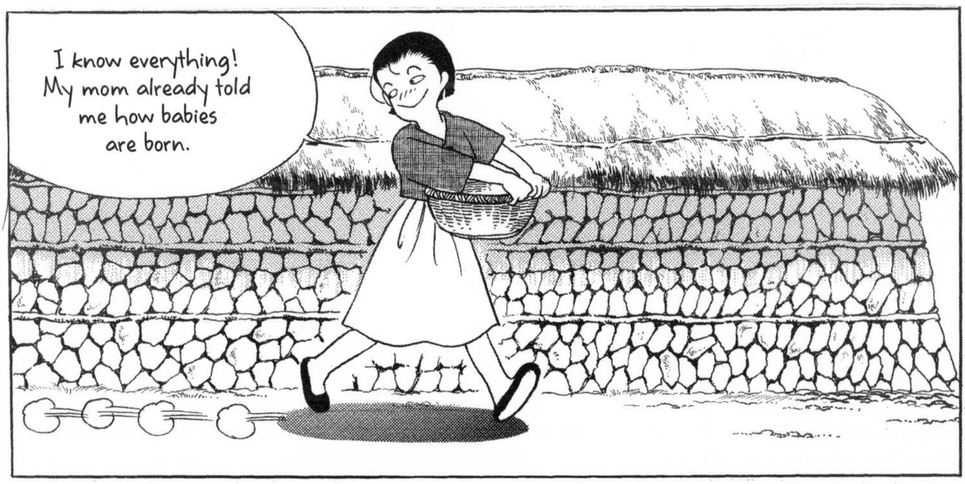
I know everything! My mom already told me how babies are born.

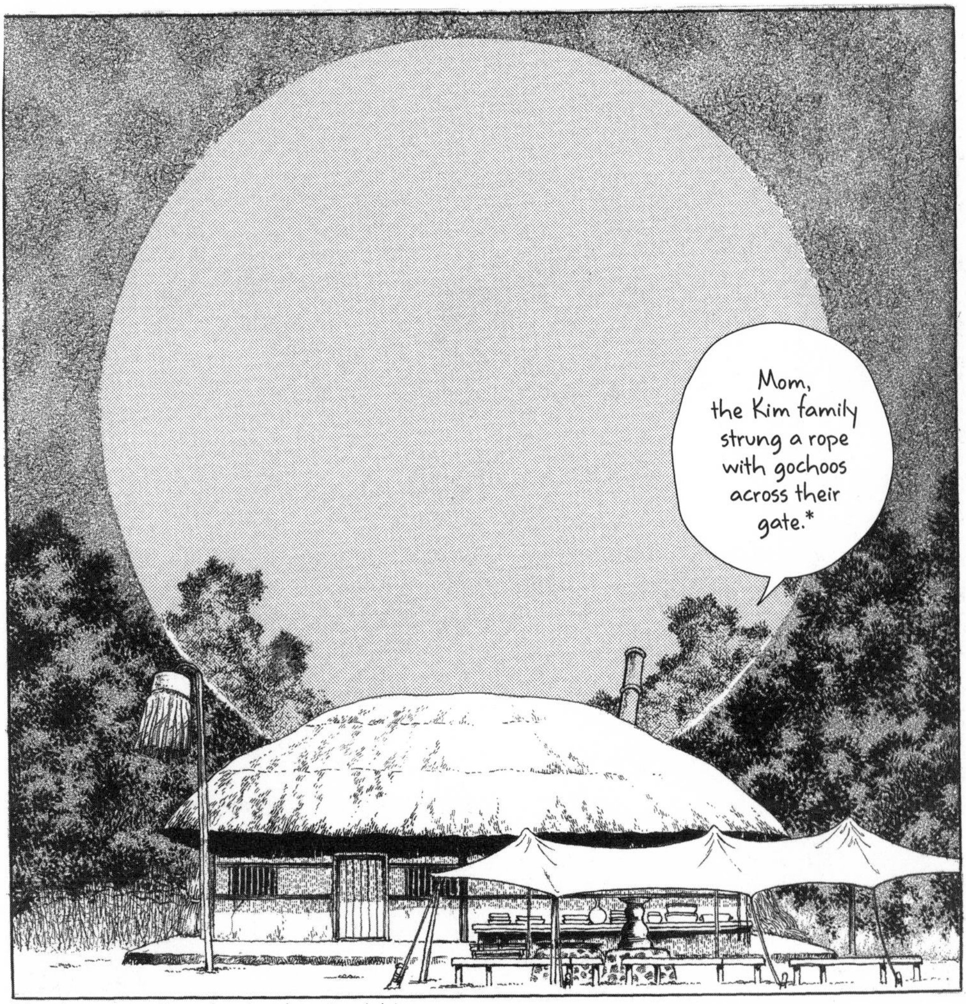
Mom, the Kim family strung a rope with gochoos across their gate.*

* A reed rope woven with pine branches, charcoal, and chili peppers is draped across the outer gate to signify the birth of a boy.

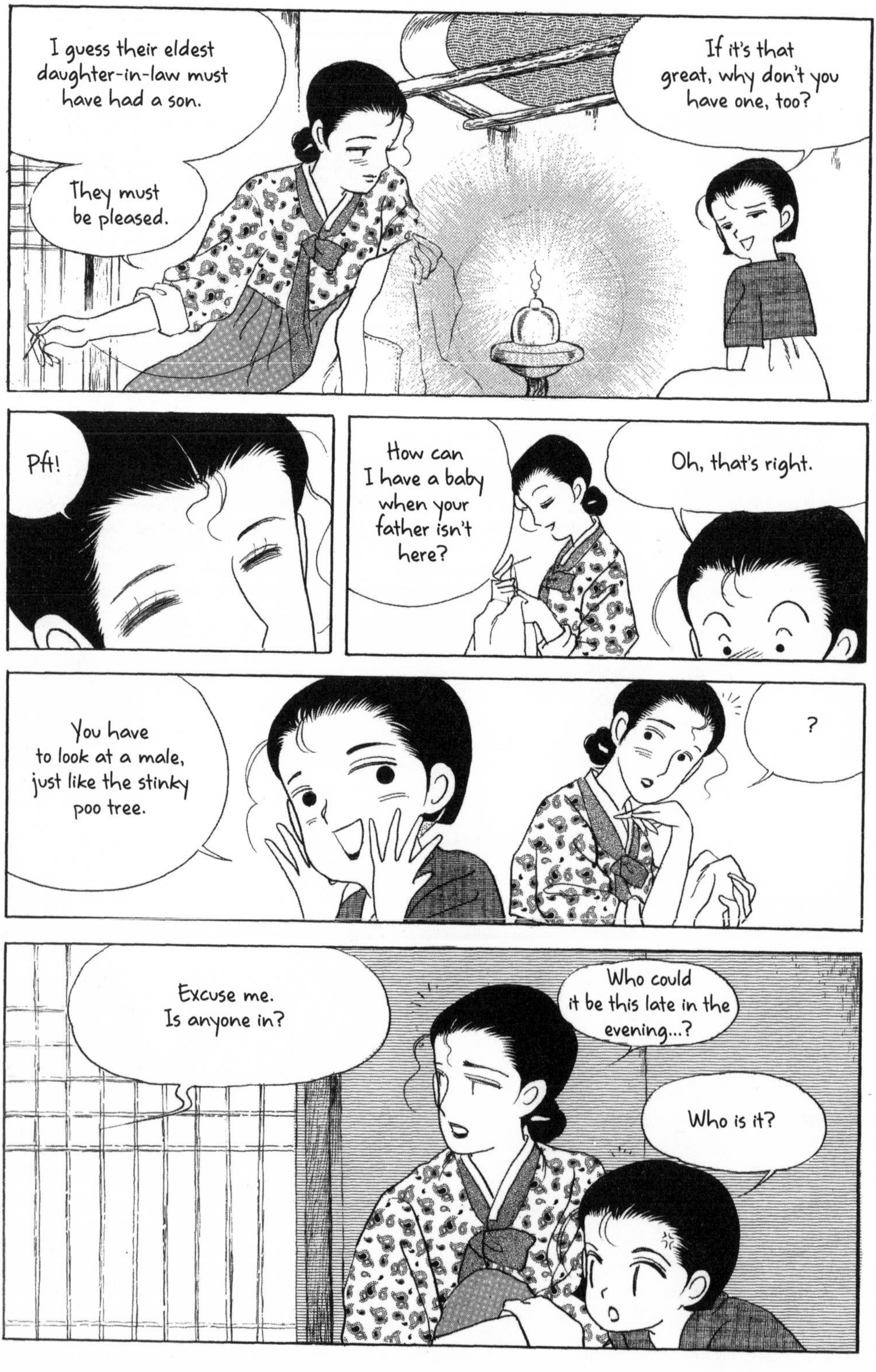

I guess their eldest daughter-in-law must have had a son.
They must be pleased.
If it's that great, why don't you have one, too?
Pft!
How can I have a baby when your father isn't here?
Oh, that's right.
You have to look at a male, just like the stinky poo tree.
?
Excuse me. Is anyone in?
Who could it be this late in the evening...?
Who is it?

I was heading for Goonsan and lost my way. I'm hungry and tired. I was hoping you could rent me a room for the night and give me some food?

Oh! There's no problem about the food. I just need to light a fire and I can get it to you shortly. But I really don't have a place I can rent to you.

We rarely have travelers pass through our town, so we have no spare room for guests.

I see. Then can you direct me to the nearest temple?

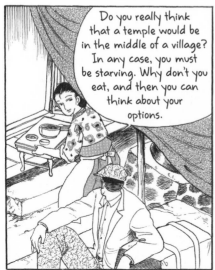

Do you really think that a temple would be in the middle of a village? In any case, you must be starving. Why don't you eat, and then you can think about your options.

SLURP

MUNCH MUNCH

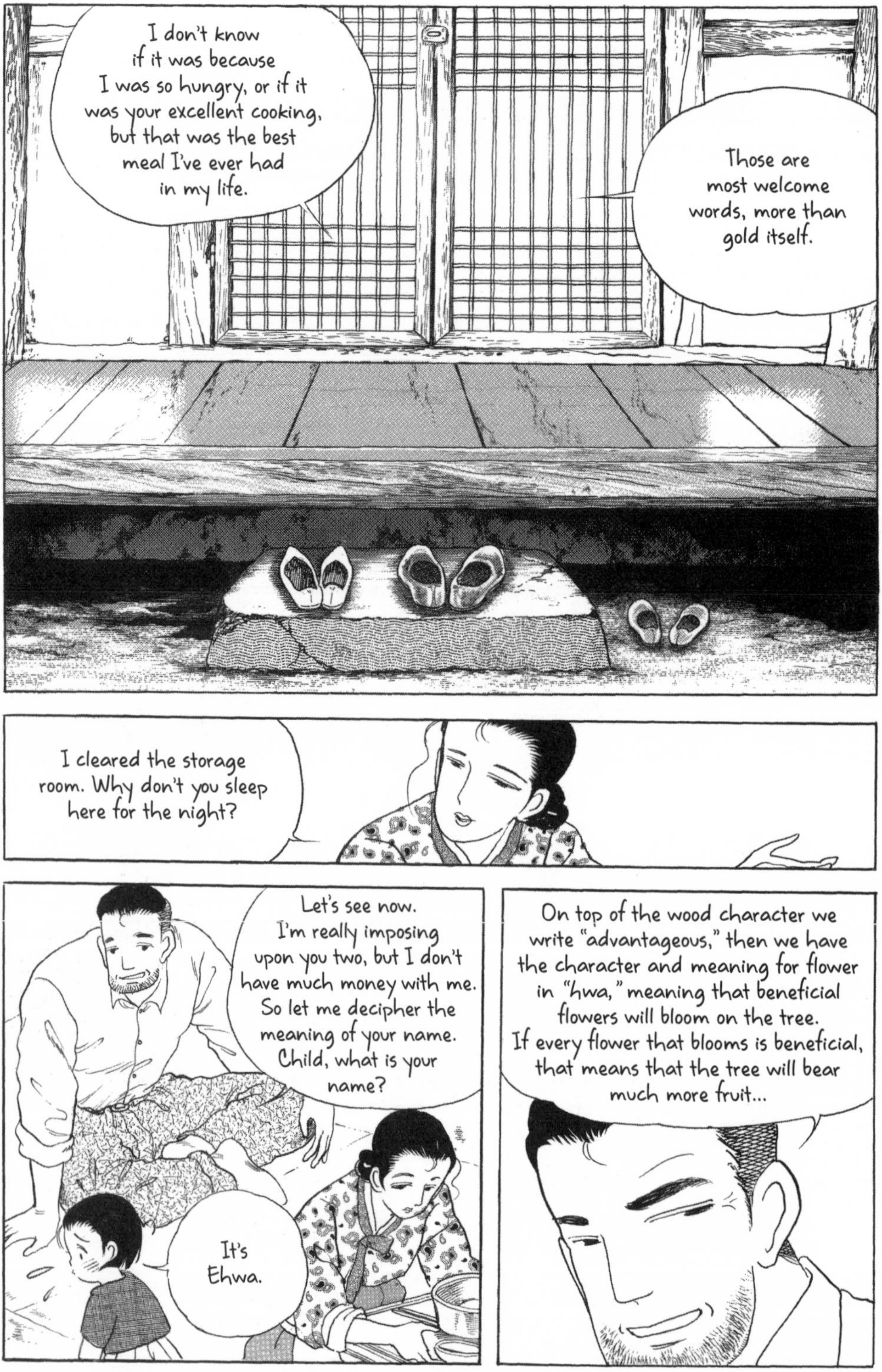
I don't know if it was because I was so hungry, or if it was your excellent cooking, but that was the best meal I've ever had in my life.
Those are most welcome words, more than gold itself.
I cleared the storage room. Why don't you sleep here for the night?
Let's see now. I'm really imposing upon you two, but I don't have much money with me. So let me decipher the meaning of your name. Child, what is your name?
It's Ehwa.
On top of the wood character we write "advantageous," then we have the character and meaning for flower in "hwa," meaning that beneficial flowers will bloom on the tree. If every flower that blooms is beneficial, that means that the tree will bear much more fruit...

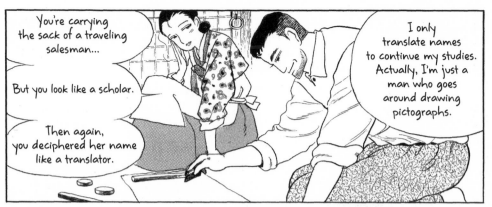

You're carrying the sack of a traveling salesman...

But you look like a scholar.

Then again, you deciphered her name like a translator.

I only translate names to continue my studies. Actually, I'm just a man who goes around drawing pictographs.

Amazing— it's pictures and words representing Ehwa's name. You did it so quickly!

Is this my name?

The pear blossom in Ehwa's name is a flower that blooms in the spring. For a girl to have a flower that blooms in the spring means she will mature early for her age. You will need to instruct and guide her very well.

I never knew that a single name had so much depth behind it.

Yes, it's true. Just as one single glance can convey the depths of one's love to another...

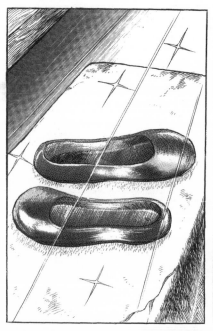

?

I feel so refreshed. It's wonderful to sleep in such a warm room.

There's nothing better than sleeping on a hot floor. That's why I used some firewood to heat up your room.

The room was well heated even until the morning. You must have tended to the fire long into the night.

It was fine. Sitting in front of the fire gave me an opportunity to think.

I placed a log in, then another log, but it just didn't seem like enough. So I placed another log in, and I still wasn't satisfied. So I placed another one in, but the fire was so small that I placed another log in...

Hmm. Isn't that something a woman does nearly every day?

This is different. On certain nights, the fire is special.

On such a night, even if you were not here, I'd probably spend the entire night warming up an empty room.

54

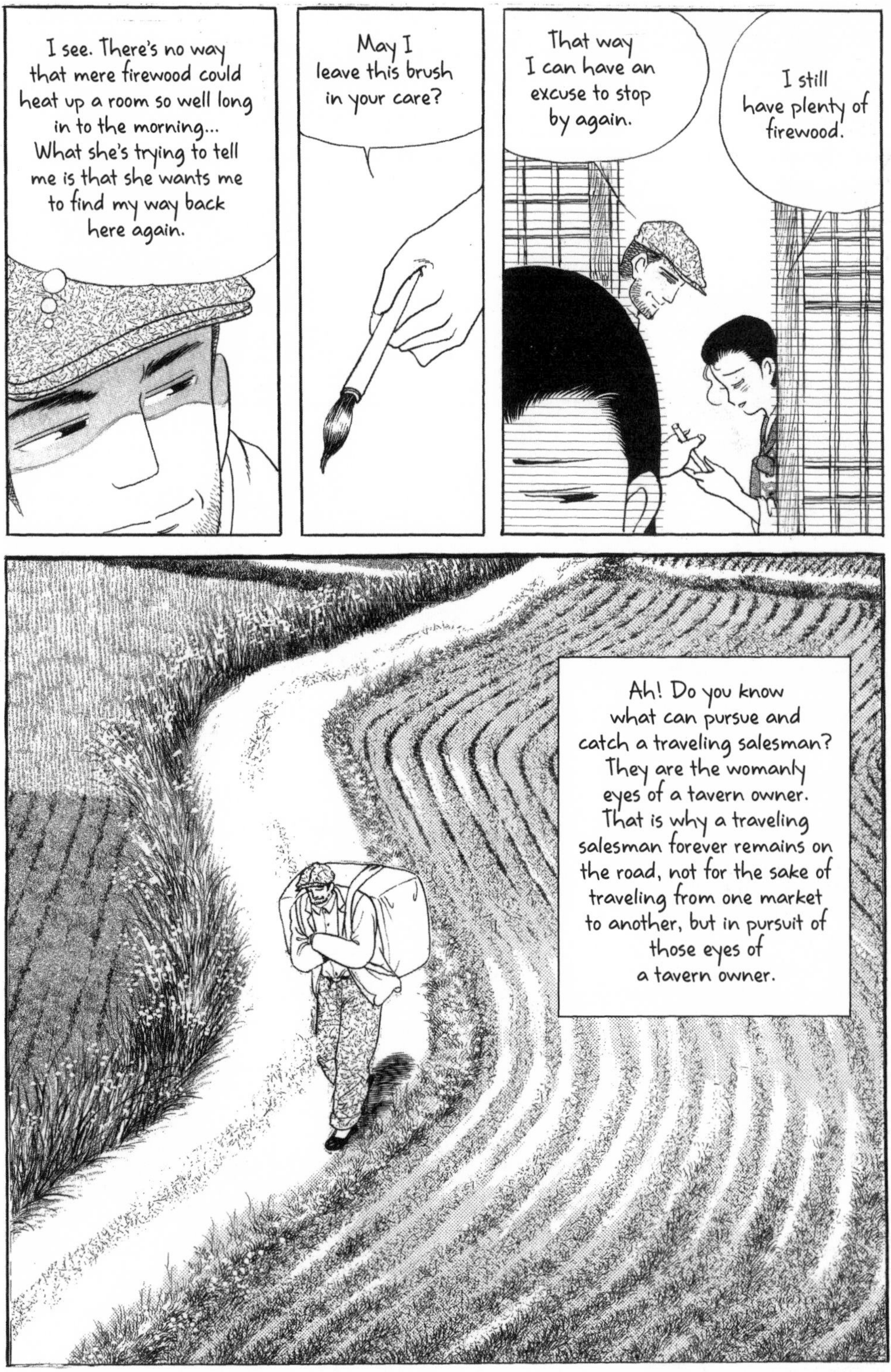
I see. There's no way that mere firewood could heat up a room so well long in to the morning... What she's trying to tell me is that she wants me to find my way back here again.
May I leave this brush in your care?
That way I can have an excuse to stop by again.
I still have plenty of firewood.
Ah! Do you know what can pursue and catch a traveling salesman? They are the womanly eyes of a tavern owner. That is why a traveling salesman forever remains on the road, not for the sake of traveling from one market to another, but in pursuit of those eyes of a tavern owner.

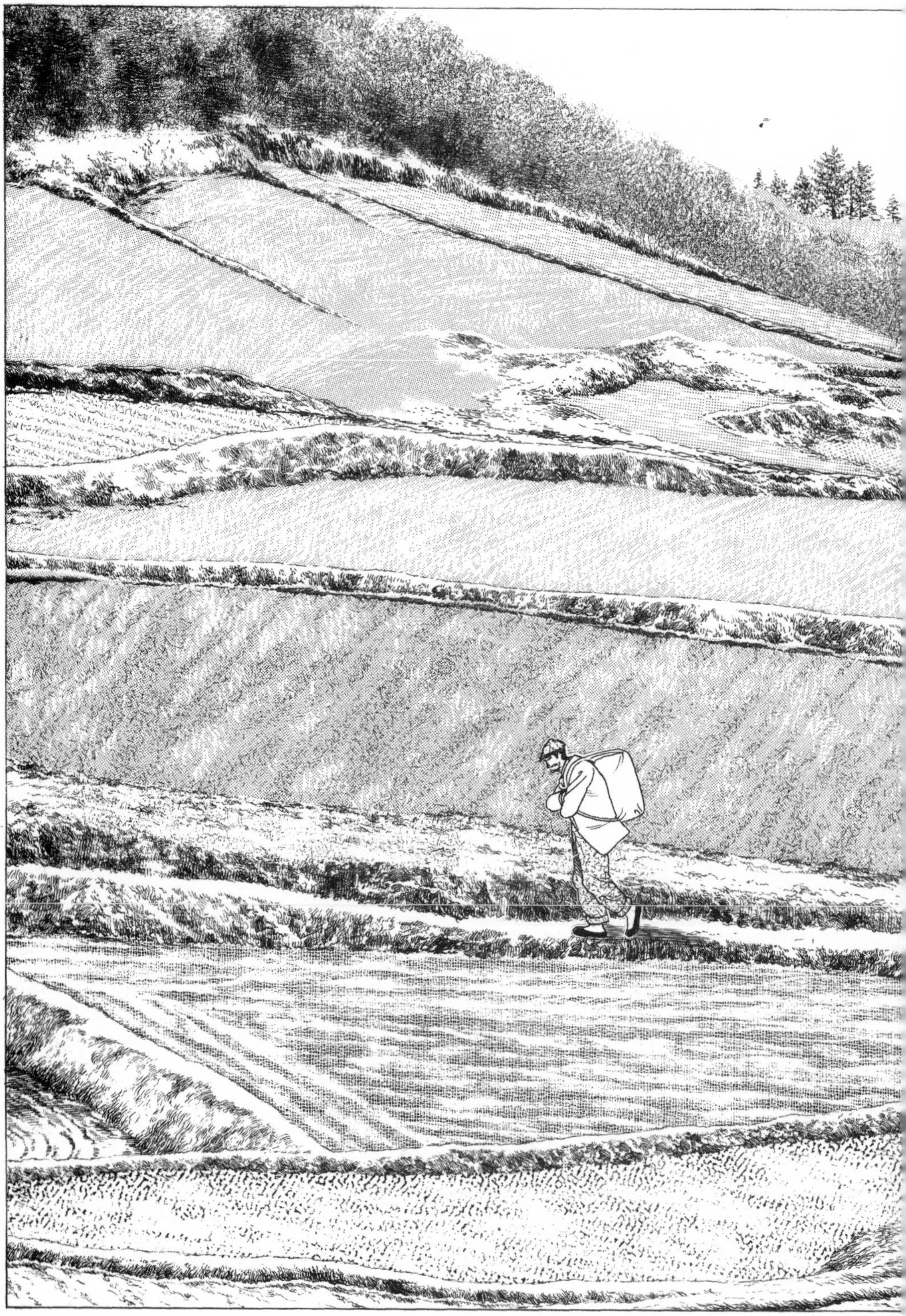

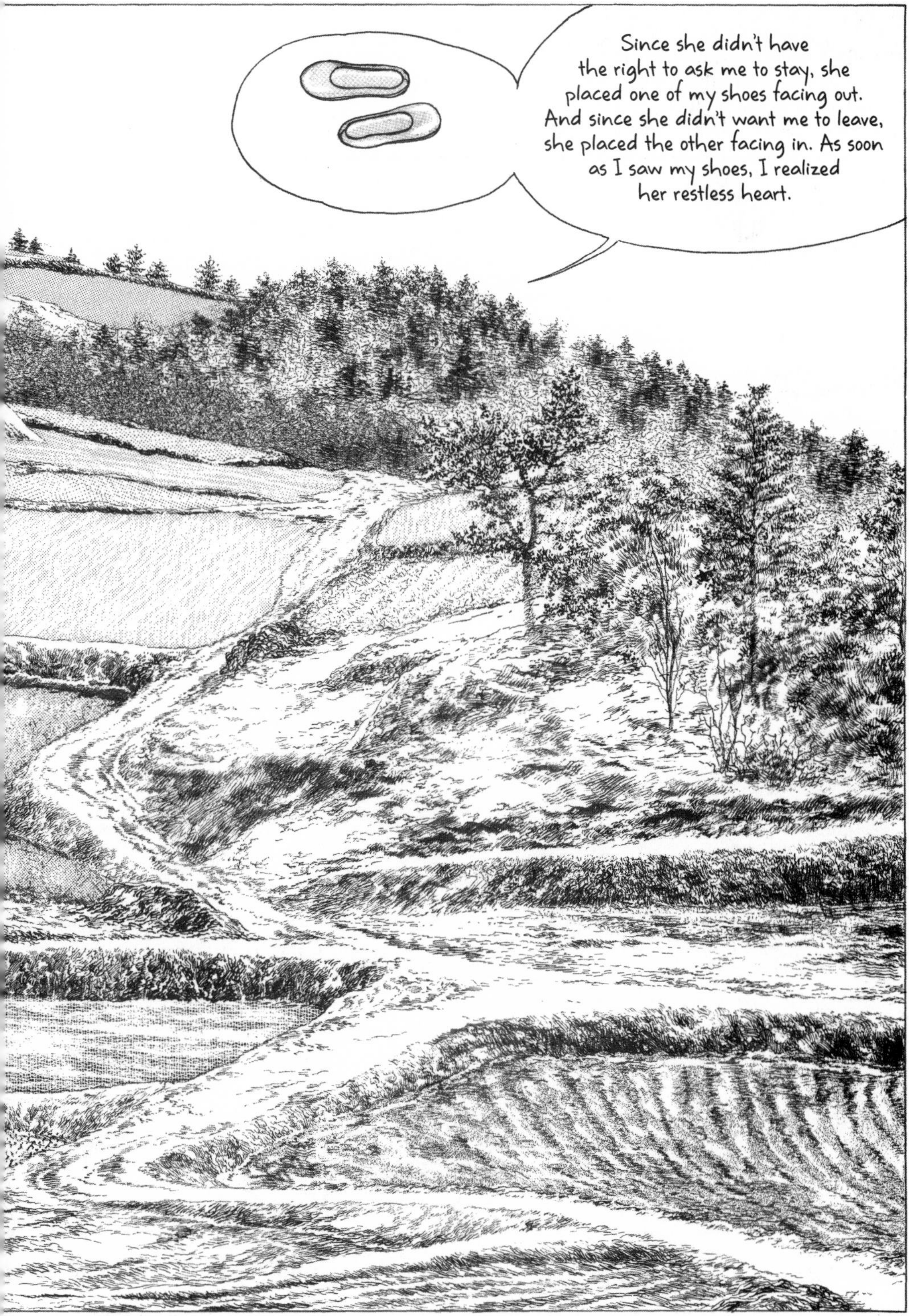
Since she didn't have the right to ask me to stay, she placed one of my shoes facing out. And since she didn't want me to leave, she placed the other facing in. As soon as I saw my shoes, I realized her restless heart.

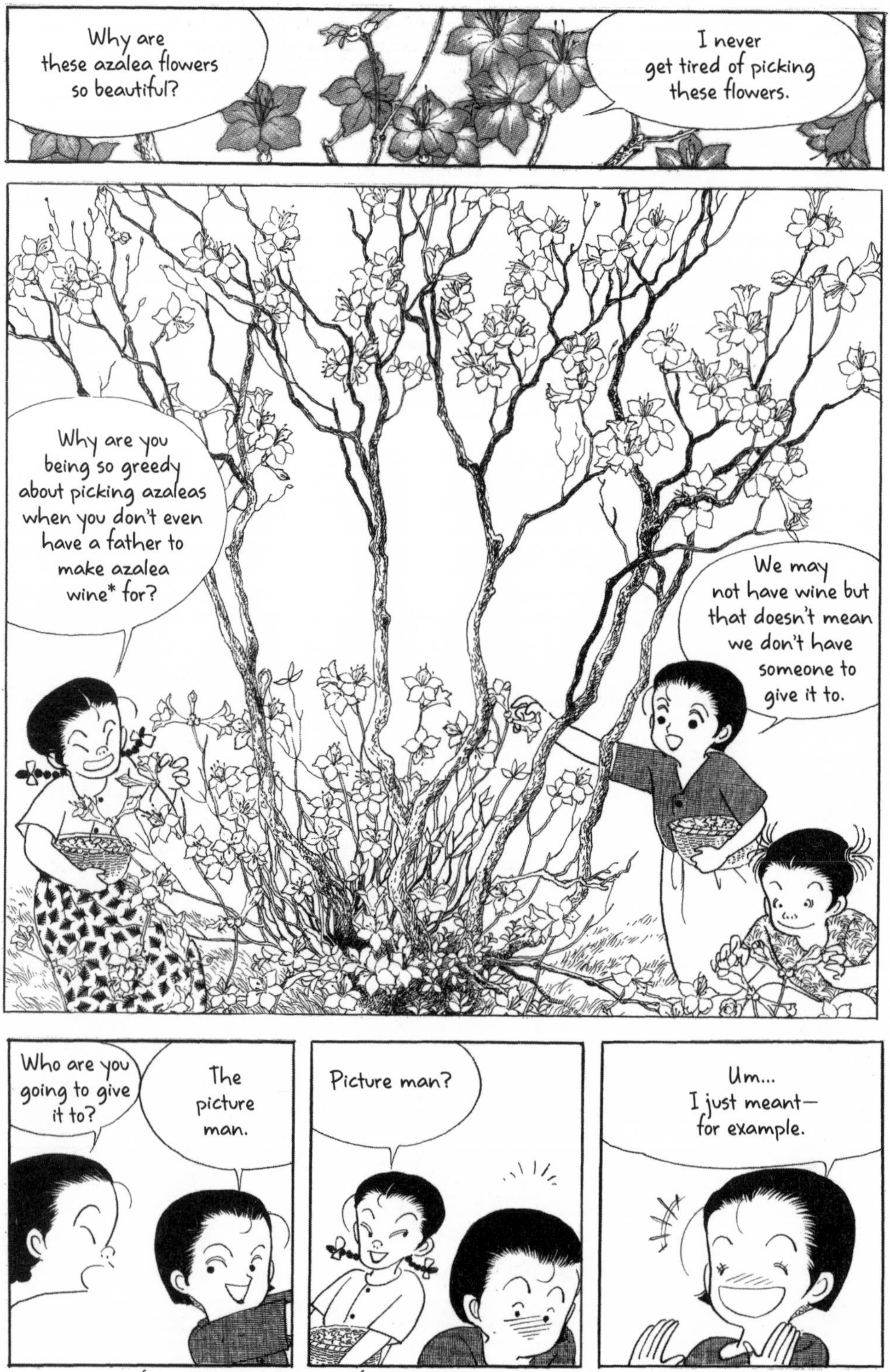
Why are these azalea flowers so beautiful?
I never get tired of picking these flowers.
Why are you being so greedy about picking azaleas when you don't even have a father to make azalea wine* for?
We may not have wine but that doesn't mean we don't have someone to give it to.
Who are you going to give it to?
The picture man.
Picture man?
Um... I just meant— for example.

* A sweet wine made from azalea petals which is reserved for special people or occasions.

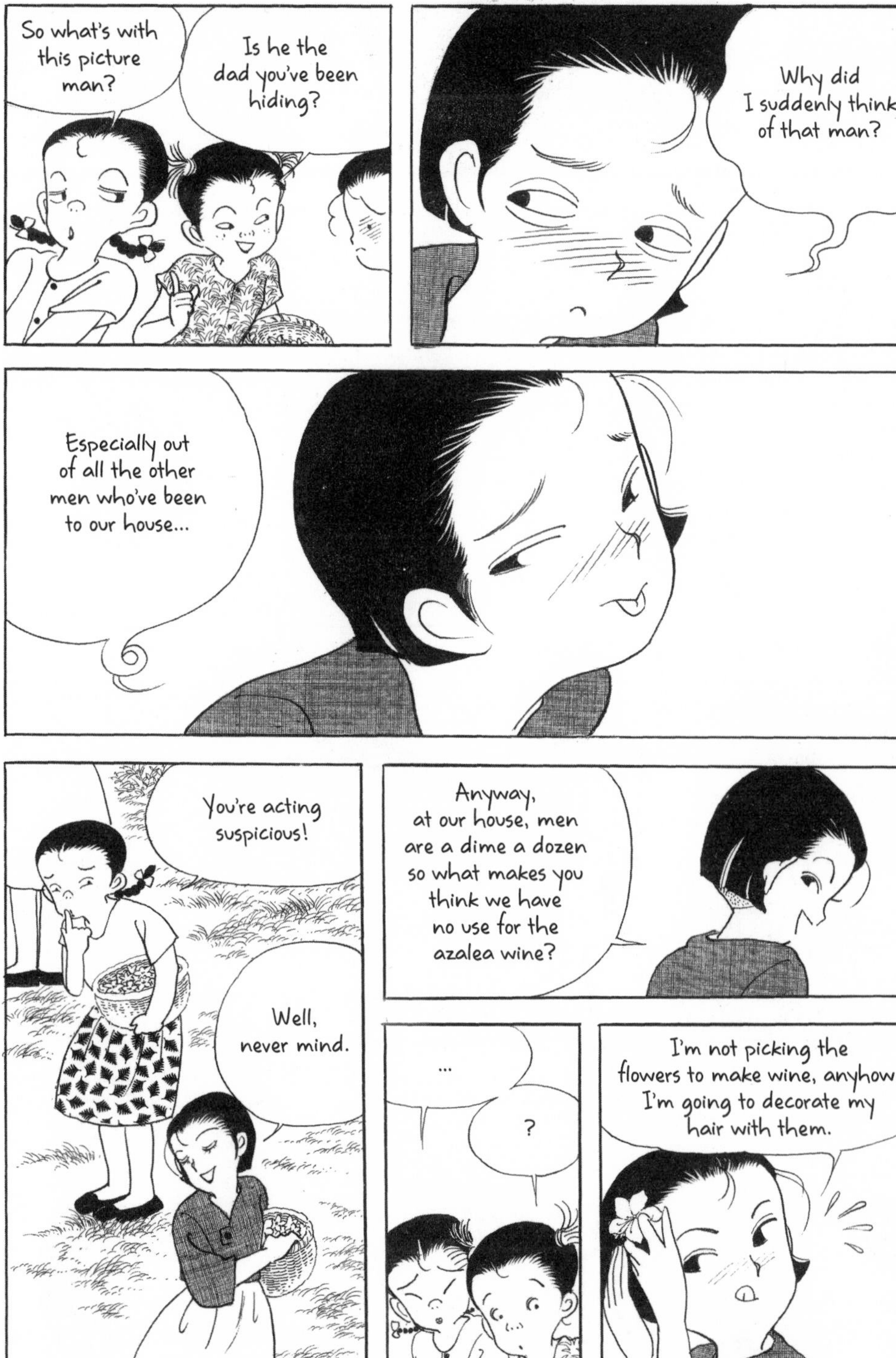
So what's with this picture man?
Is he the dad you've been hiding?
Why did I suddenly think of that man?
Especially out of all the other men who've been to our house...
You're acting suspicious!
Well, never mind.
Anyway, at our house, men are a dime a dozen so what makes you think we have no use for the azalea wine?
...
?
I'm not picking the flowers to make wine, anyhow. I'm going to decorate my hair with them.

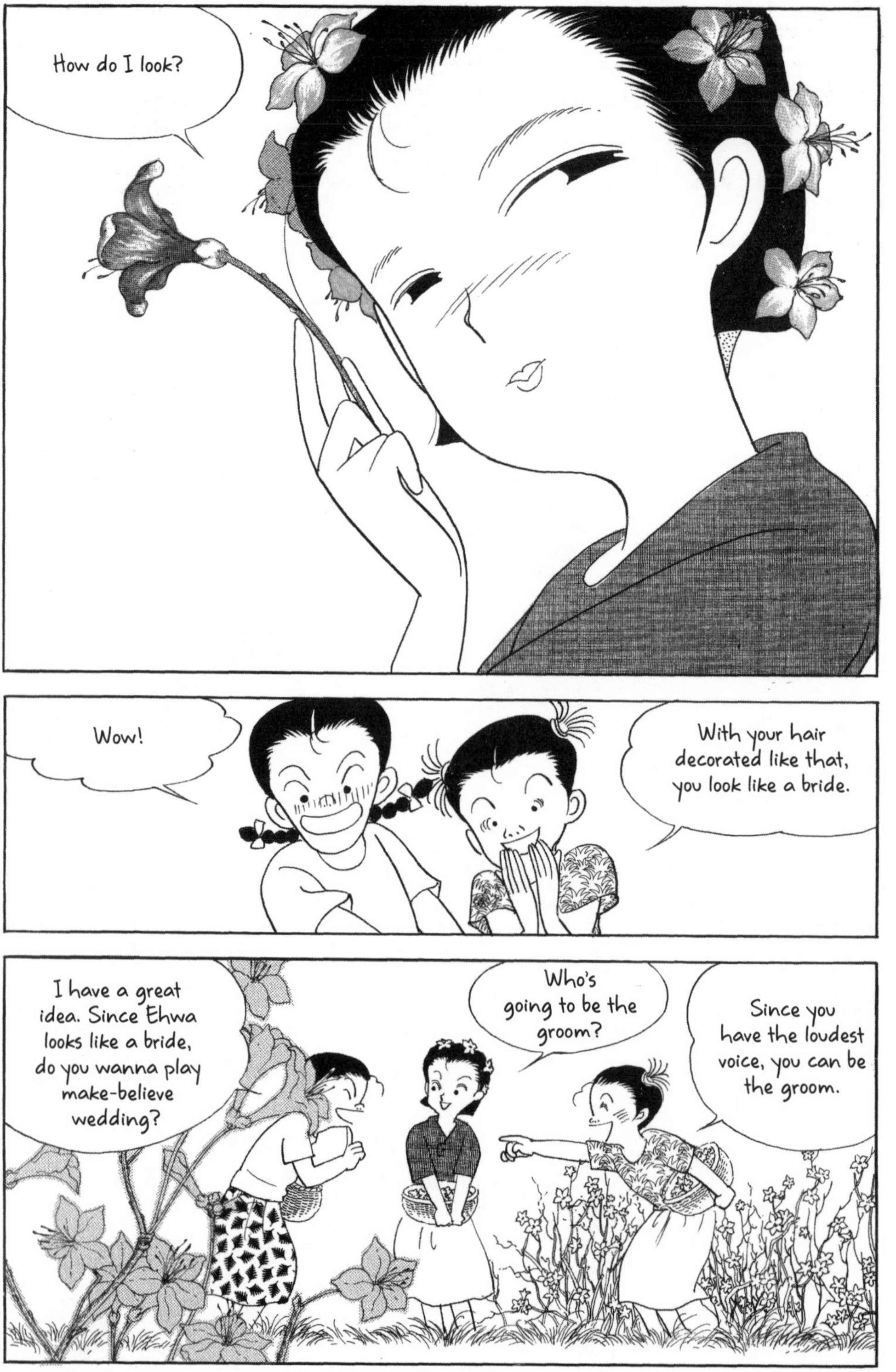
How do I look?
Wow!
With your hair decorated like that, you look like a bride.
I have a great idea. Since Ehwa looks like a bride, do you wanna play make-believe wedding?
Who's going to be the groom?
Since you have the loudest voice, you can be the groom.

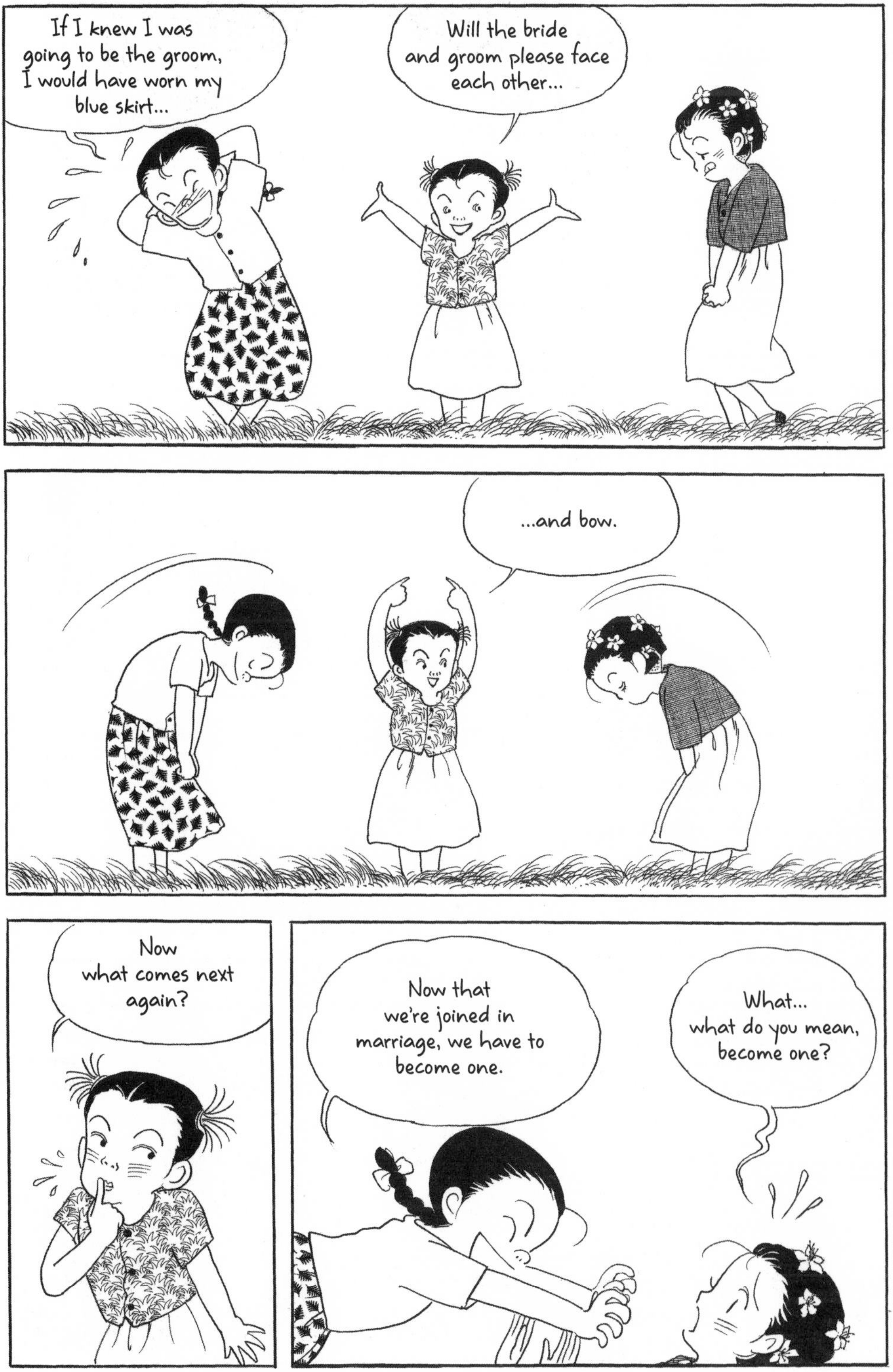
If I knew I was going to be the groom, I would have worn my blue skirt...
Will the bride and groom please face each other...
...and bow.
Now what comes next again?
Now that we're joined in marriage, we have to become one.
What... what do you mean, become one?

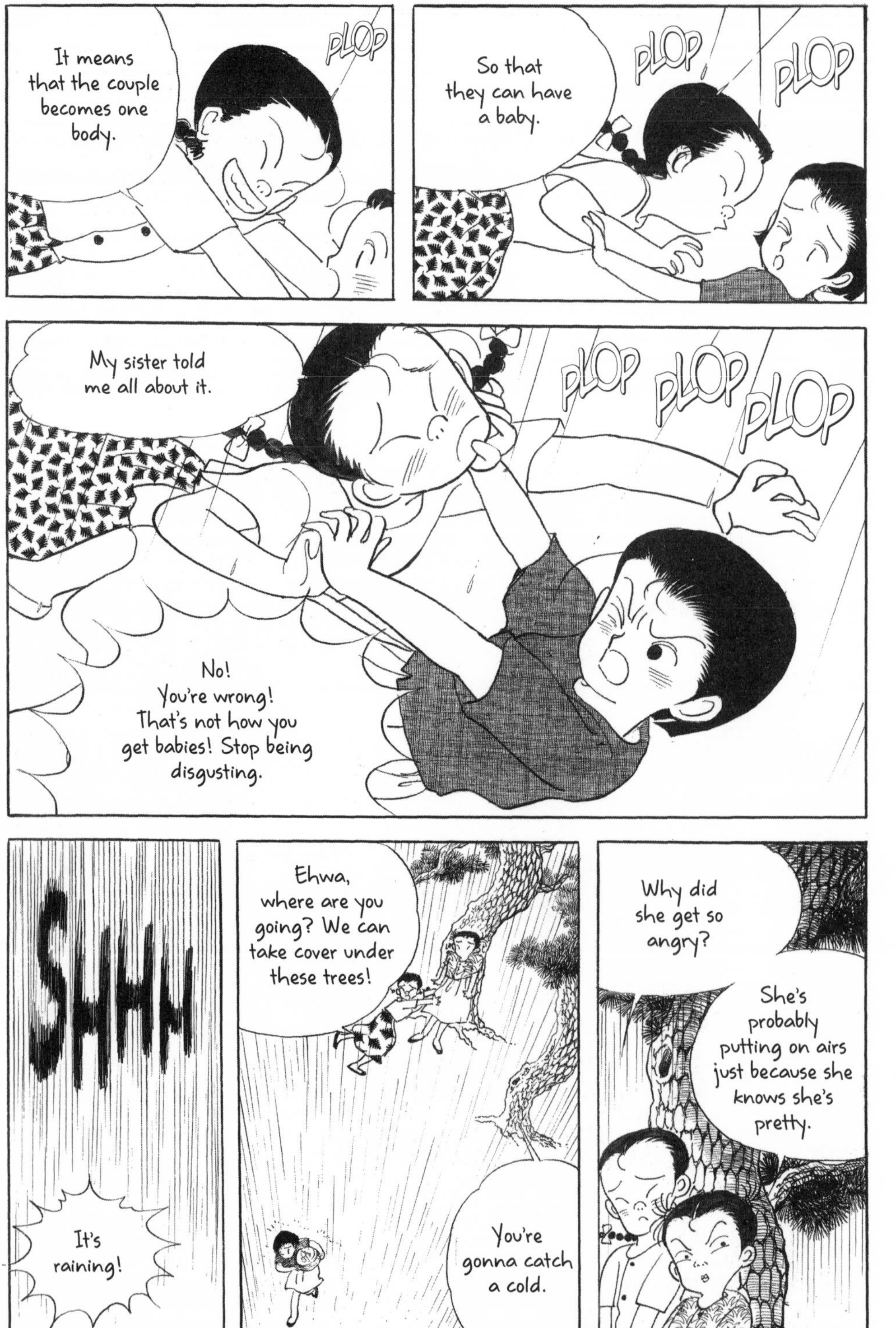
PLOP
It means that the couple becomes one body.
PLOP
PLOP
So that they can have a baby.
My sister told me all about it.
PLOP
PLOP
PLOP
No! You're wrong! That's not how you get babies! Stop being disgusting.
SHHH
It's raining!
Ehwa, where are you going? We can take cover under these trees!
You're gonna catch a cold.
Why did she get so angry?
She's probably putting on airs just because she knows she's pretty.

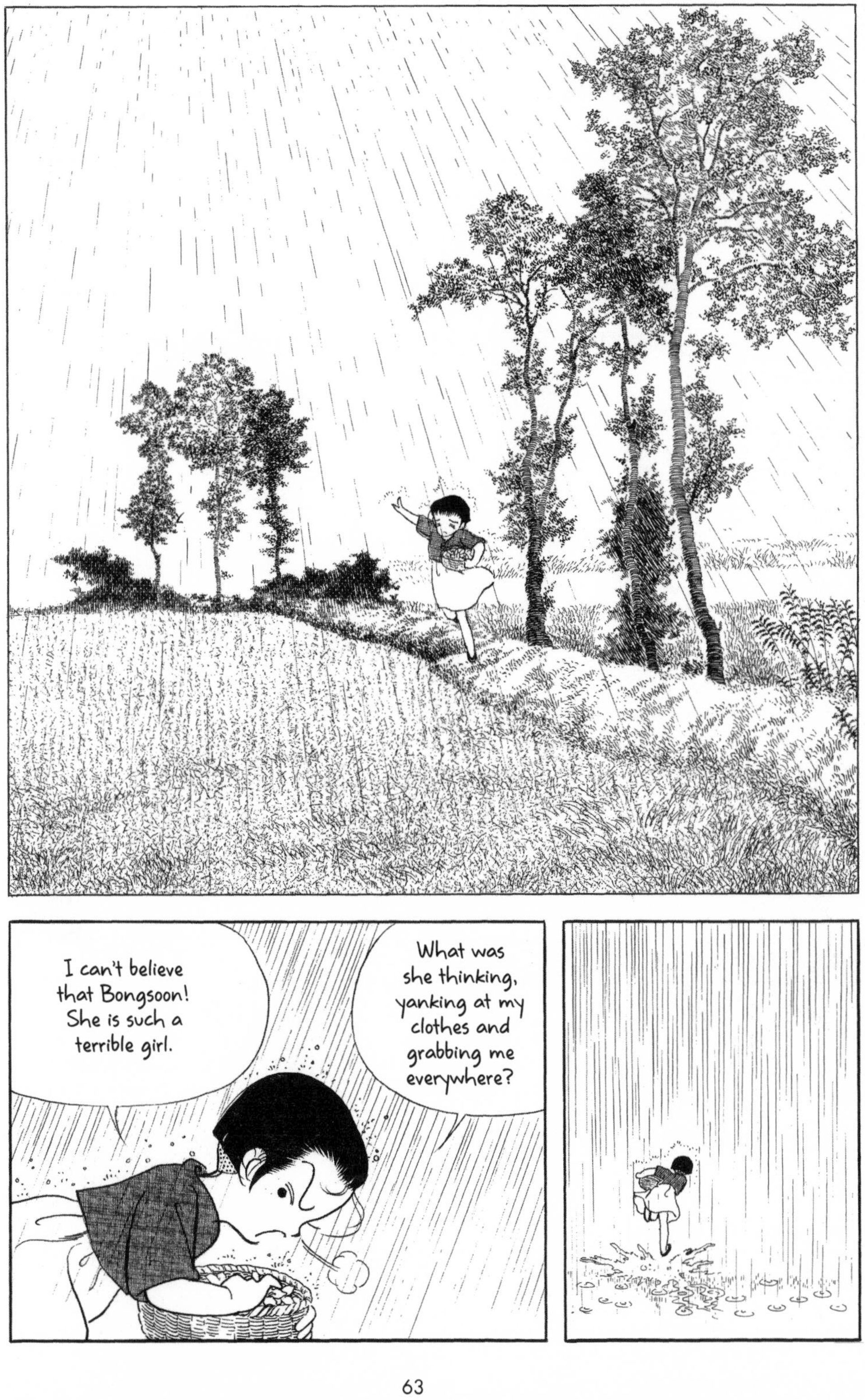
I can't believe that Bongsoon! She is such a terrible girl.
What was she thinking, yanking at my clothes and grabbing me everywhere?

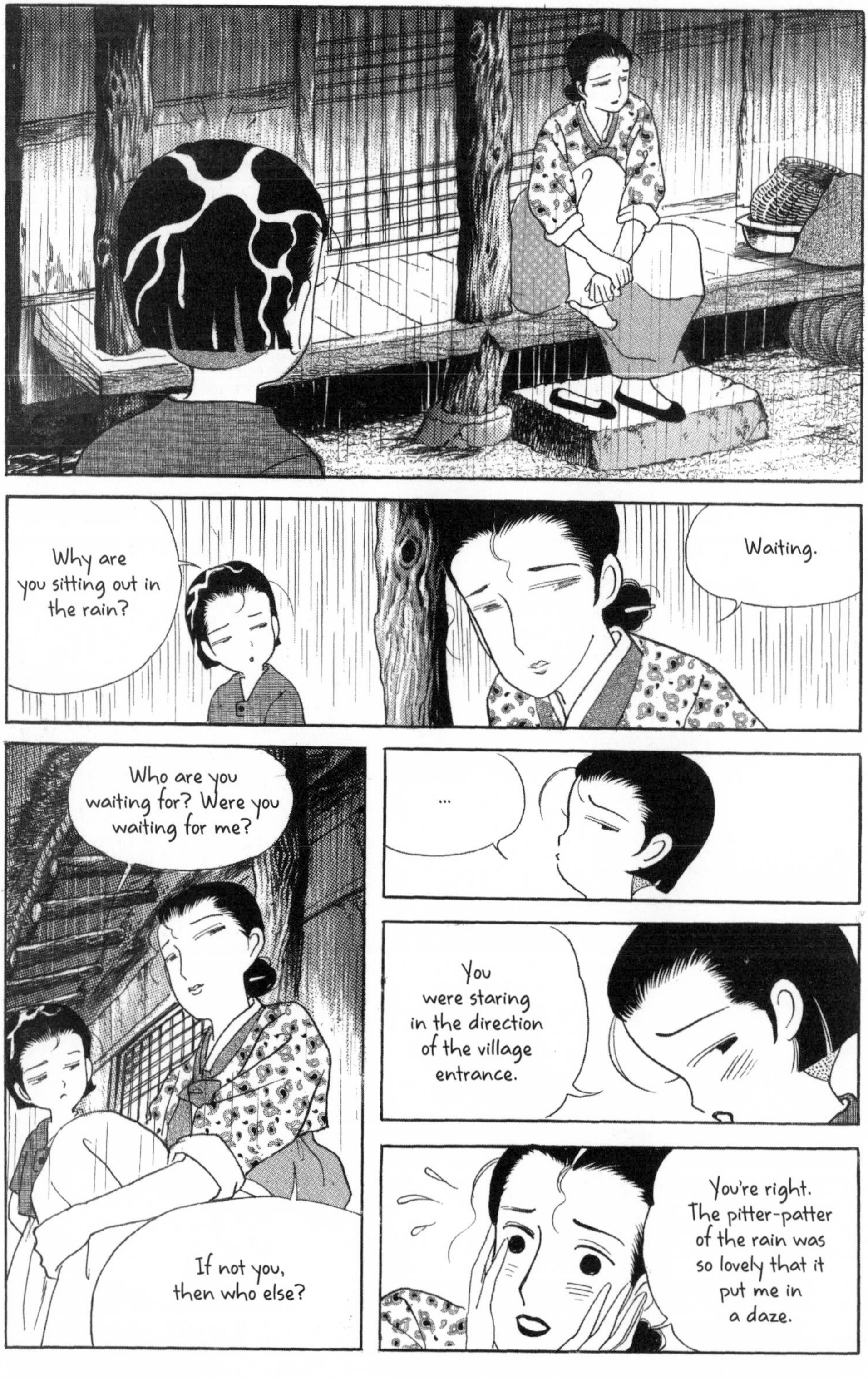
Why are you sitting out in the rain?
Waiting.
Who are you waiting for? Were you waiting for me?
If not you, then who else?
...
You were staring in the direction of the village entrance.
You're right. The pitter-patter of the rain was so lovely that it put me in a daze.

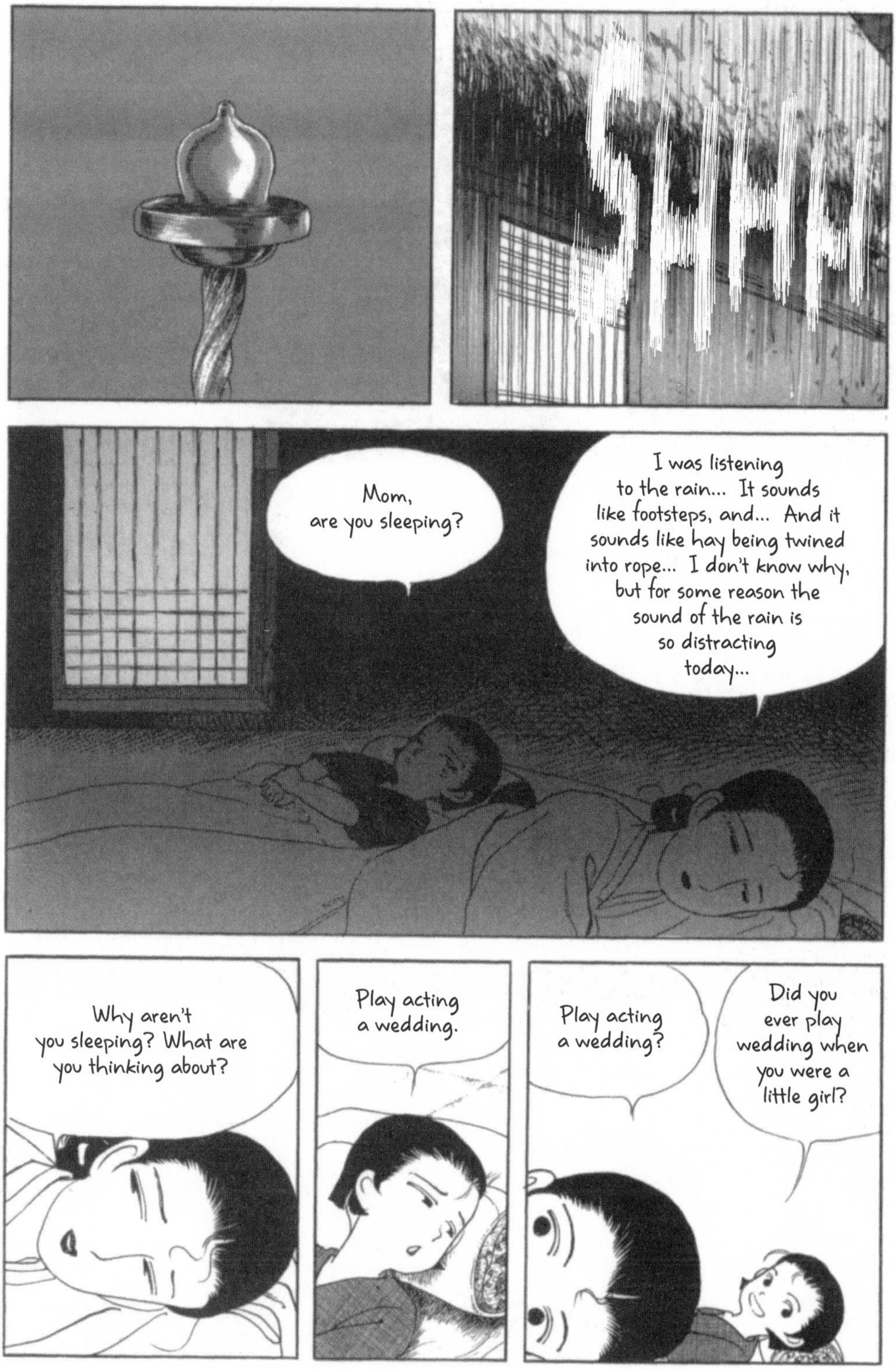
SHHH
Mom, are you sleeping?
I was listening to the rain... It sounds like footsteps, and... And it sounds like hay being twined into rope... I don't know why, but for some reason the sound of the rain is so distracting today...
Why aren't you sleeping? What are you thinking about?
Play acting a wedding.
Play acting a wedding?
Did you ever play wedding when you were a little girl?

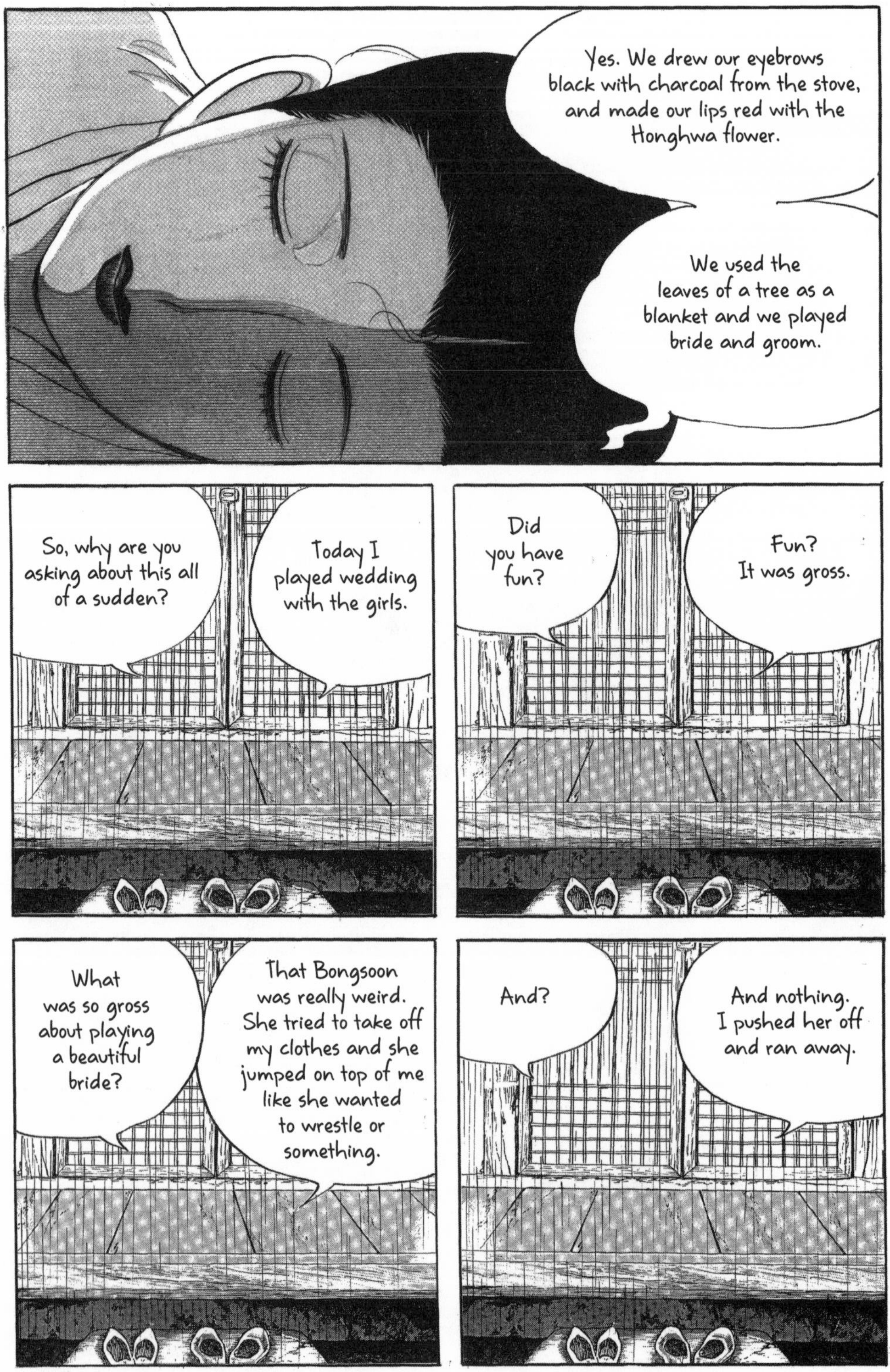
Yes. We drew our eyebrows black with charcoal from the stove, and made our lips red with the Honghwa flower.
We used the leaves of a tree as a blanket and we played bride and groom.
So, why are you asking about this all of a sudden?
Today I played wedding with the girls.
Did you have fun?
Fun? It was gross.
What was so gross about playing a beautiful bride?
That Bongsoon was really weird. She tried to take off my clothes and she jumped on top of me like she wanted to wrestle or something.
And?
And nothing. I pushed her off and ran away.

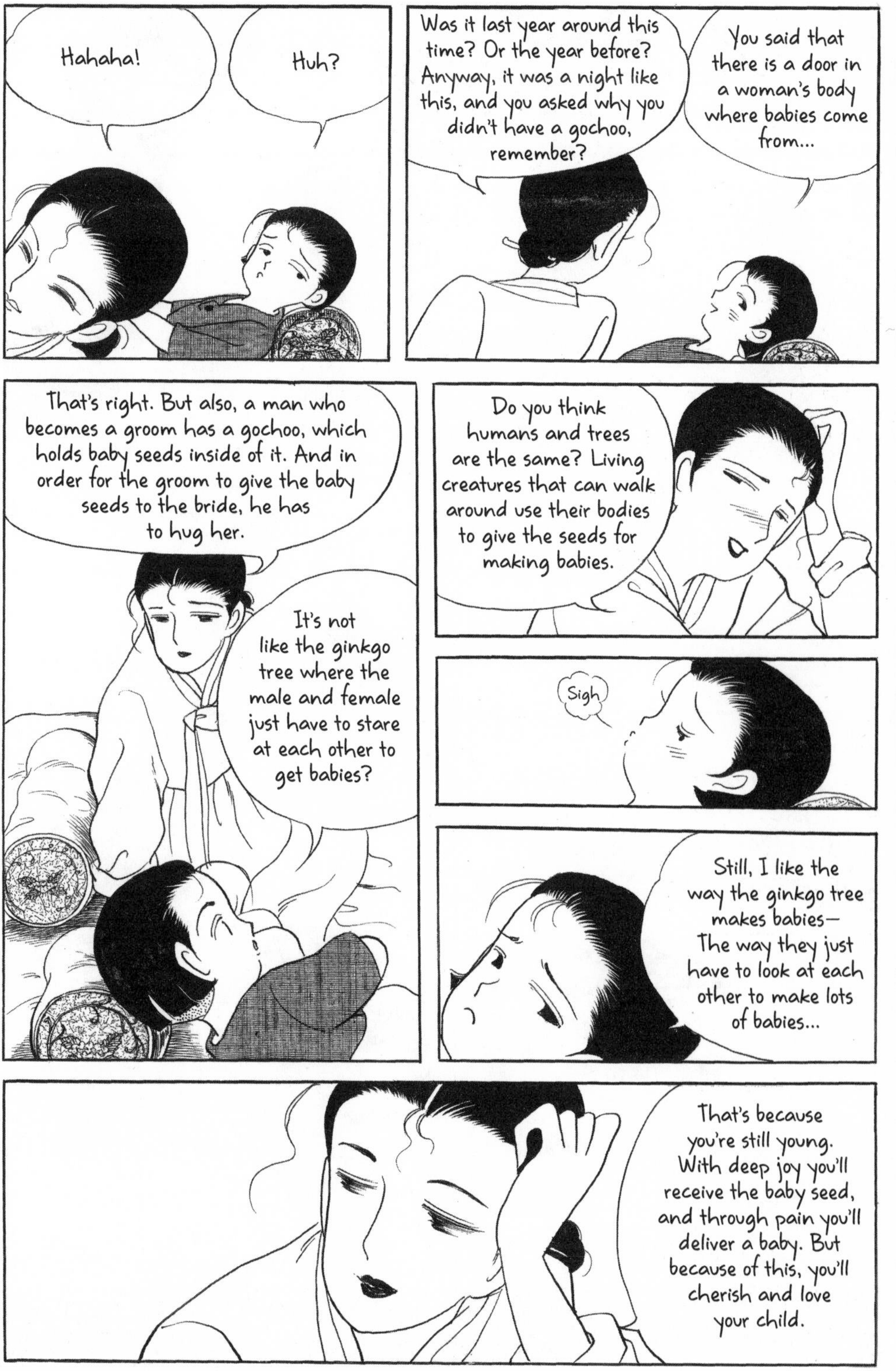
Hahaha!
Huh?
Was it last year around this time? Or the year before? Anyway, it was a night like this, and you asked why you didn't have a gochoo, remember?
You said that there is a door in a woman's body where babies come from...
That's right. But also, a man who becomes a groom has a gochoo, which holds baby seeds inside of it. And in order for the groom to give the baby seeds to the bride, he has to hug her.
It's not like the ginkgo tree where the male and female just have to stare at each other to get babies?
Do you think humans and trees are the same? Living creatures that can walk around use their bodies to give the seeds for making babies.
Sigh
Still, I like the way the ginkgo tree makes babies— The way they just have to look at each other to make lots of babies...
That's because you're still young. With deep joy you'll receive the baby seed, and through pain you'll deliver a baby. But because of this, you'll cherish and love your child.

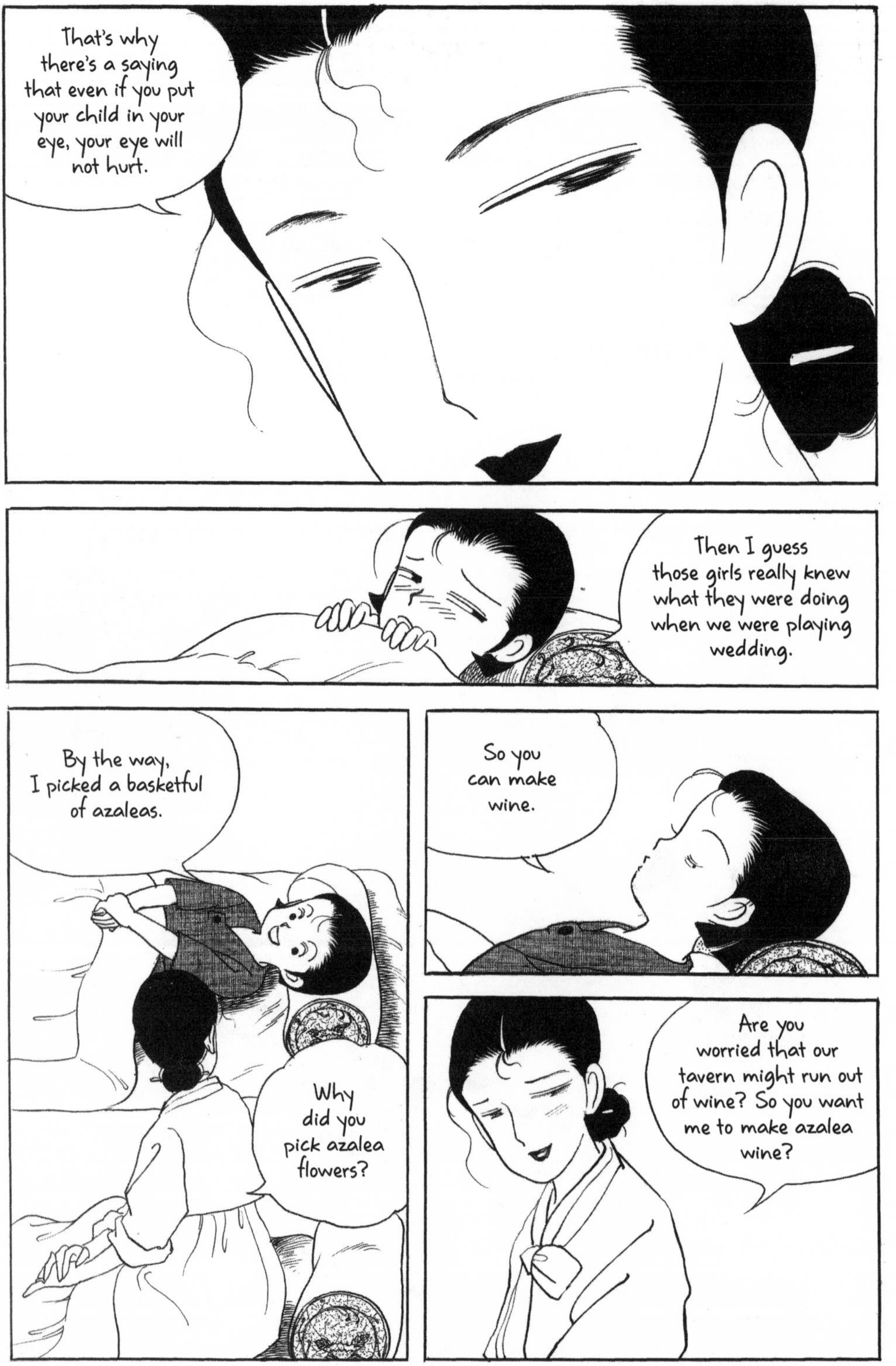
That's why there's a saying that even if you put your child in your eye, your eye will not hurt.
Then I guess those girls really knew what they were doing when we were playing wedding.
By the way, I picked a basketful of azaleas.
Why did you pick azalea flowers?
So you can make wine.
Are you worried that our tavern might run out of wine? So you want me to make azalea wine?

That's not it. Since the azalea wine is special, the person you serve it to will see the dedication you put into making it. I thought there might be someone to serve it to...

And who would that "someone" be?

How would I know? You would know better than me.

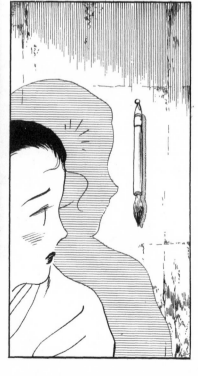

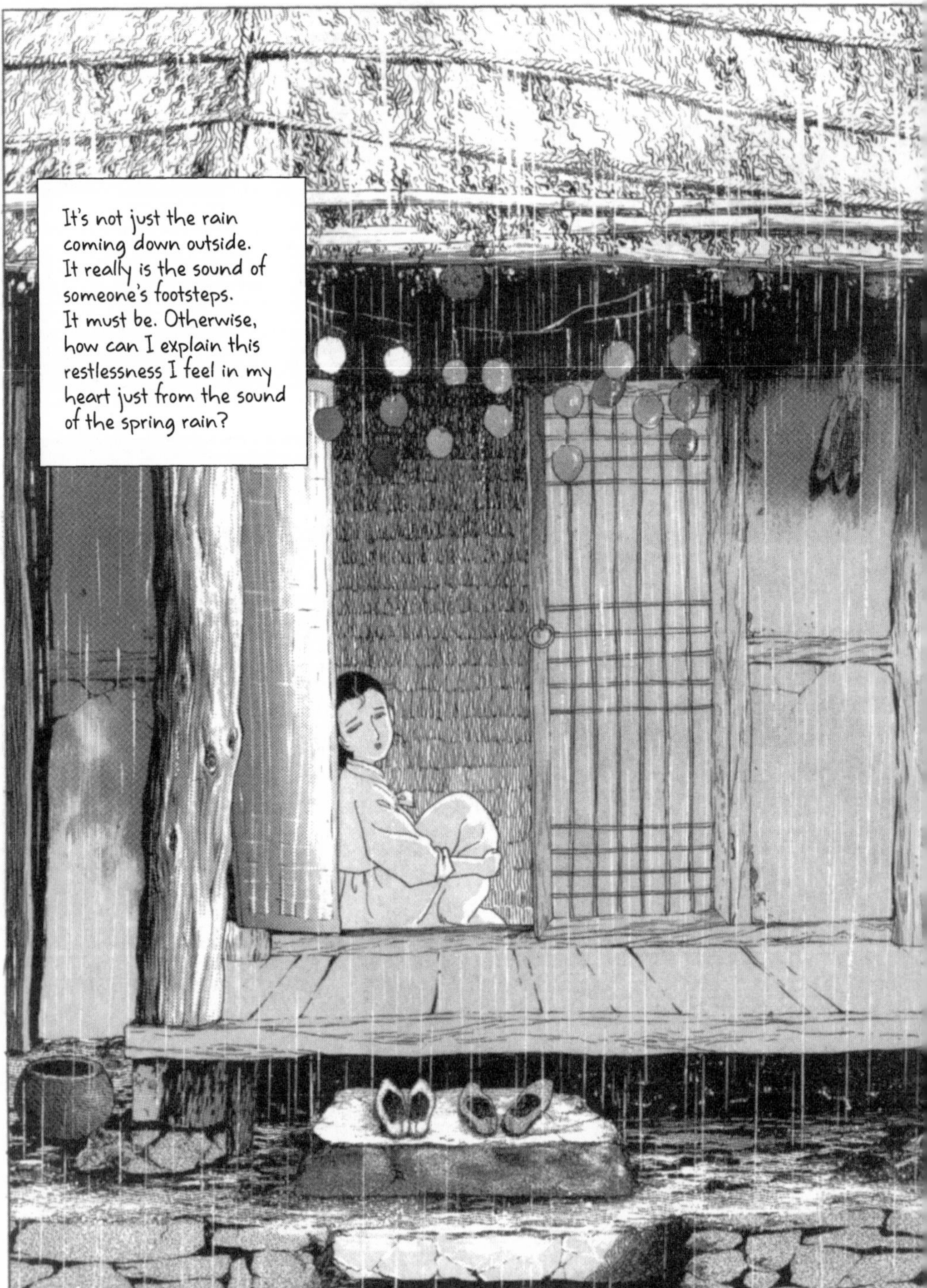
It's not just the rain coming down outside. It really is the sound of someone's footsteps. It must be. Otherwise, how can I explain this restlessness I feel in my heart just from the sound of the spring rain?

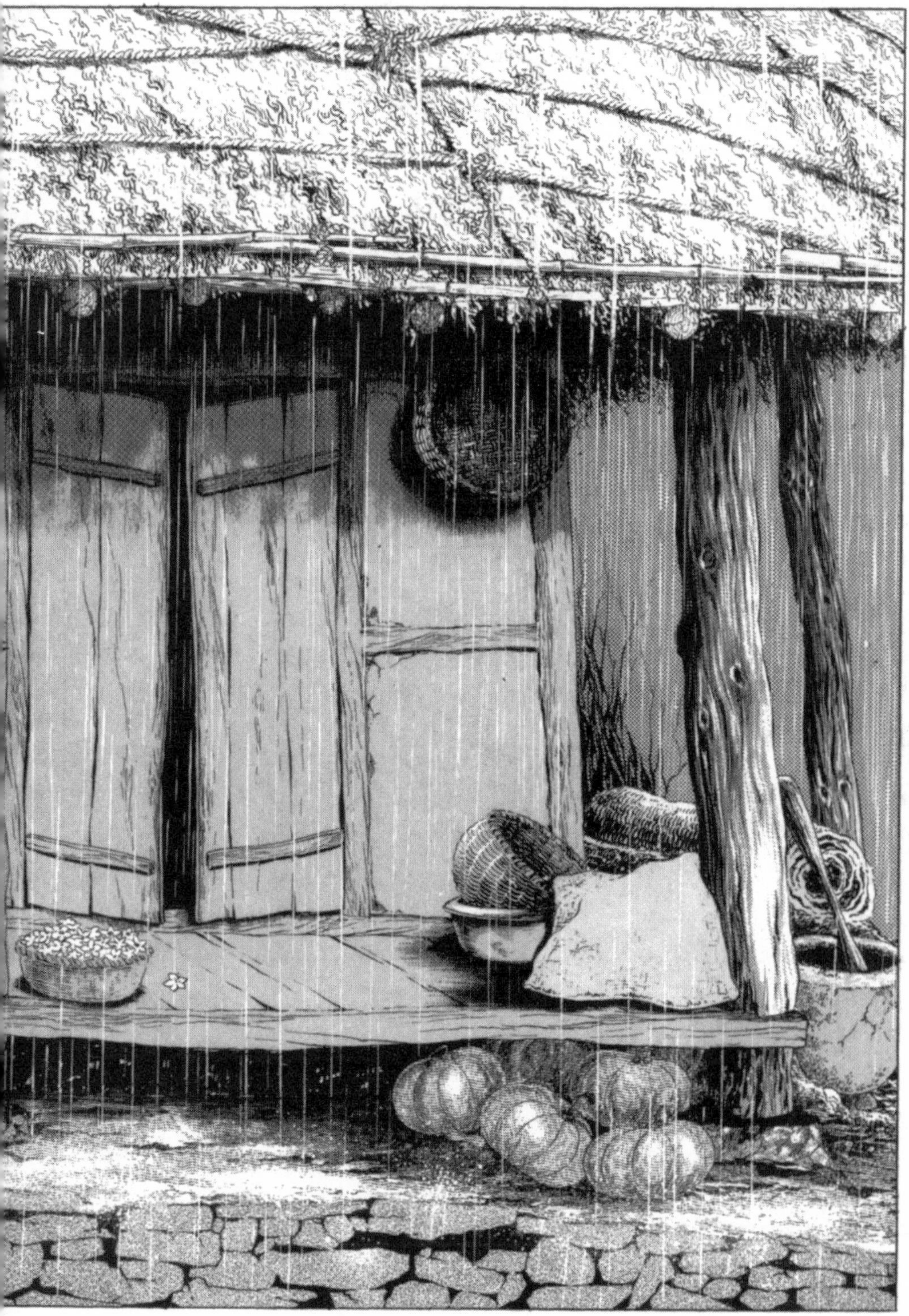

Chapter Three

THE GOURD FLOWER

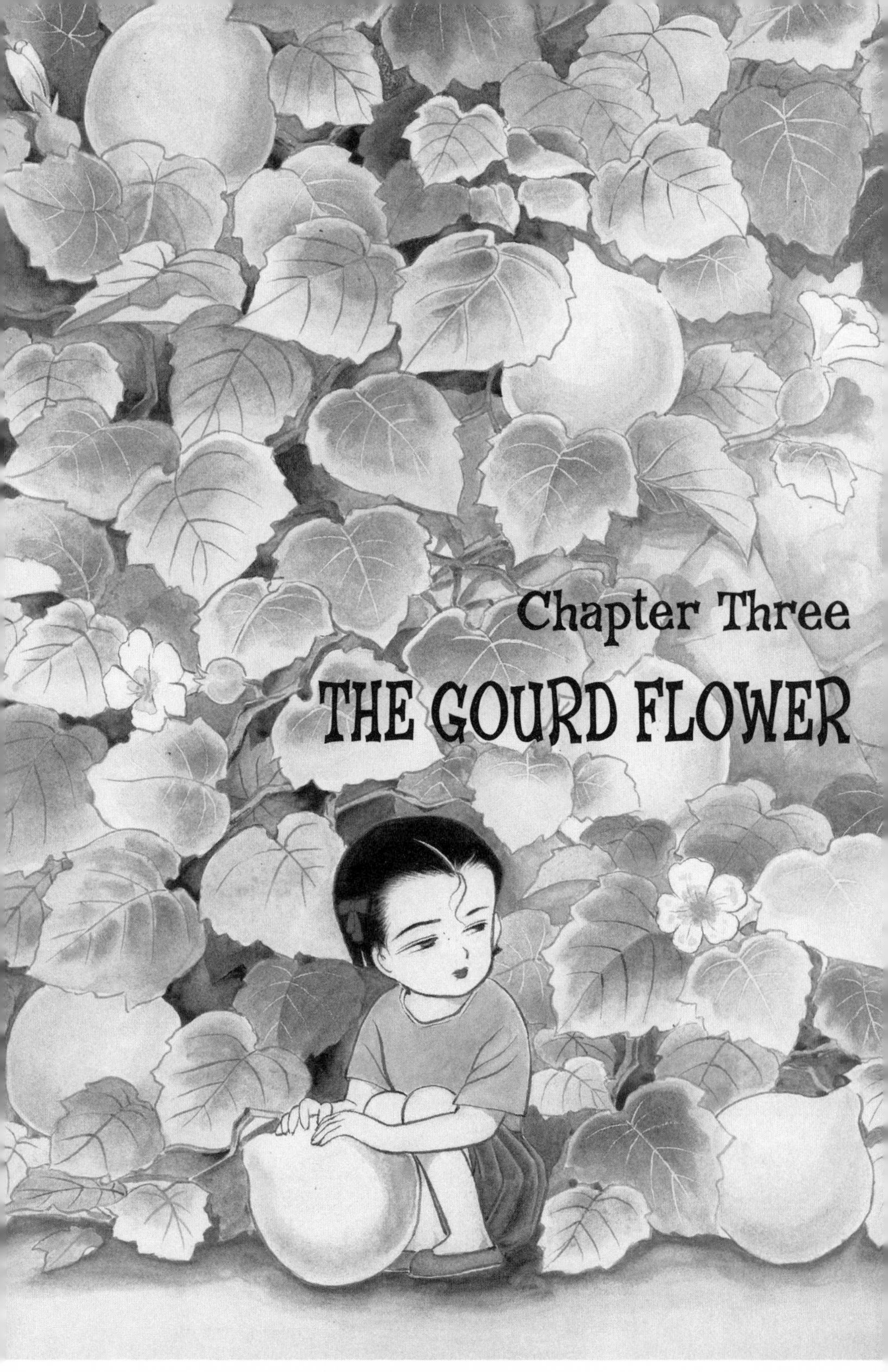

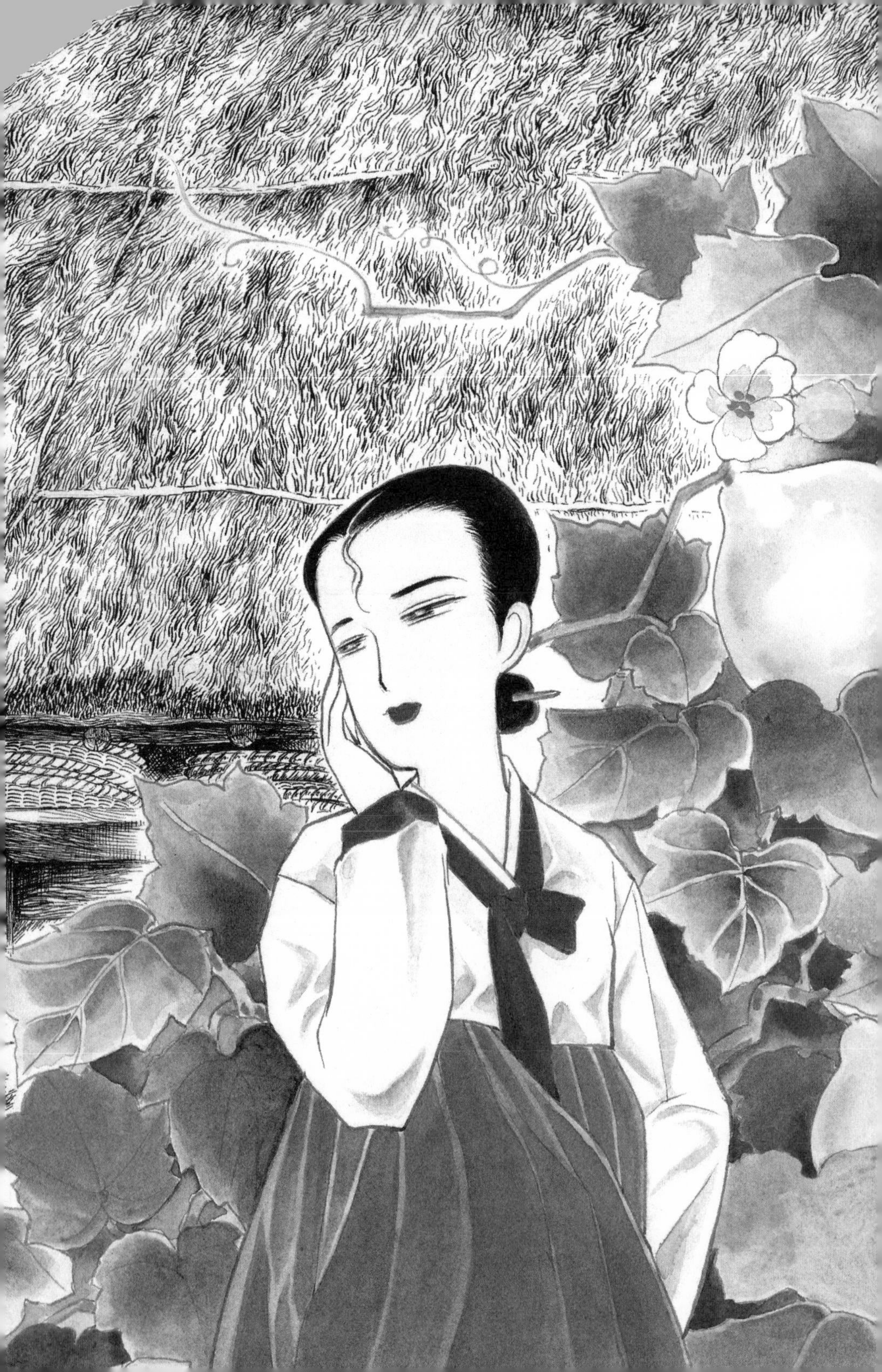

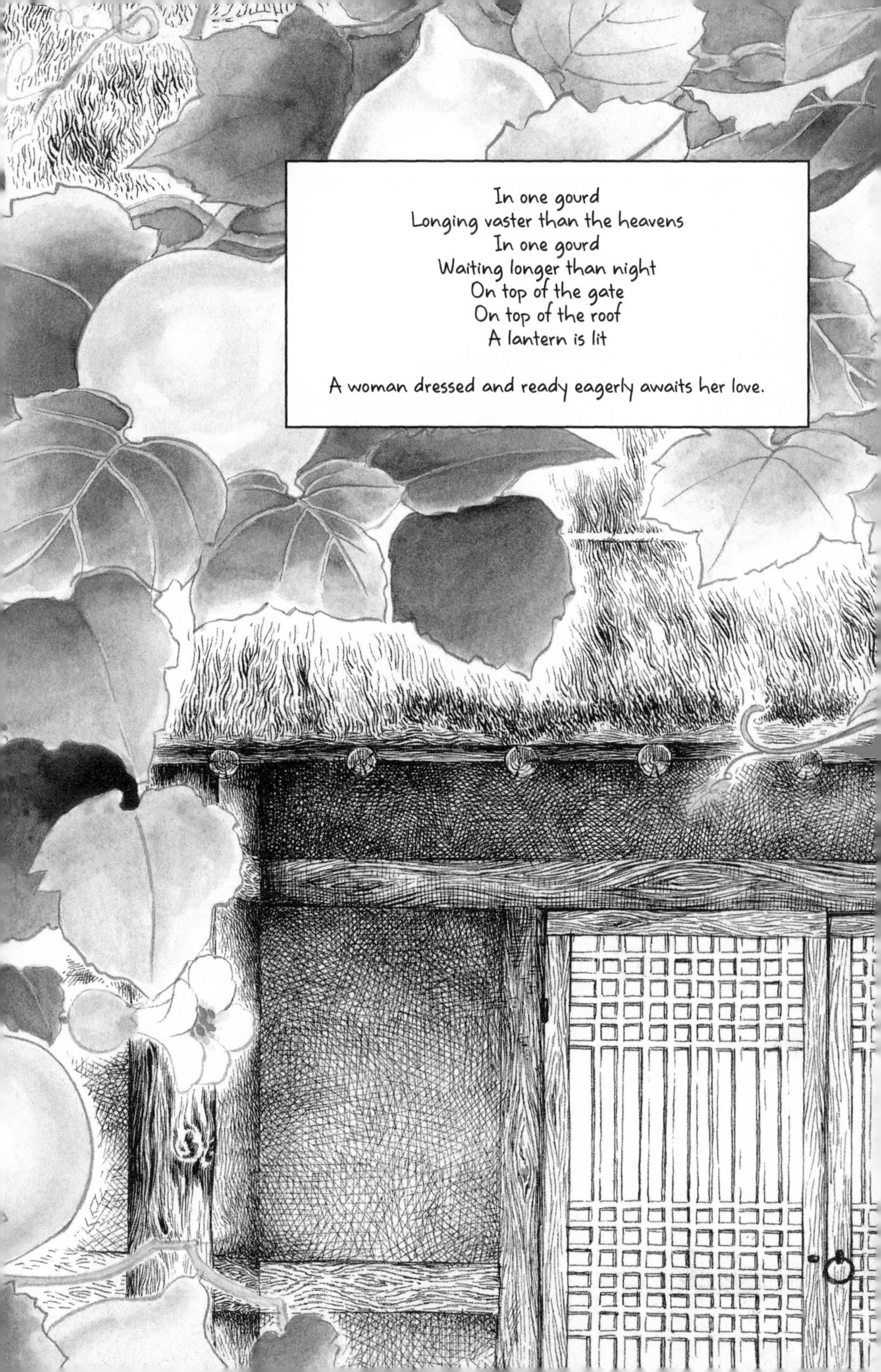
In one gourd
Longing vaster than the heavens
In one gourd
Waiting longer than night
On top of the gate
On top of the roof
A lantern is lit
A woman dressed and ready eagerly awaits her love.

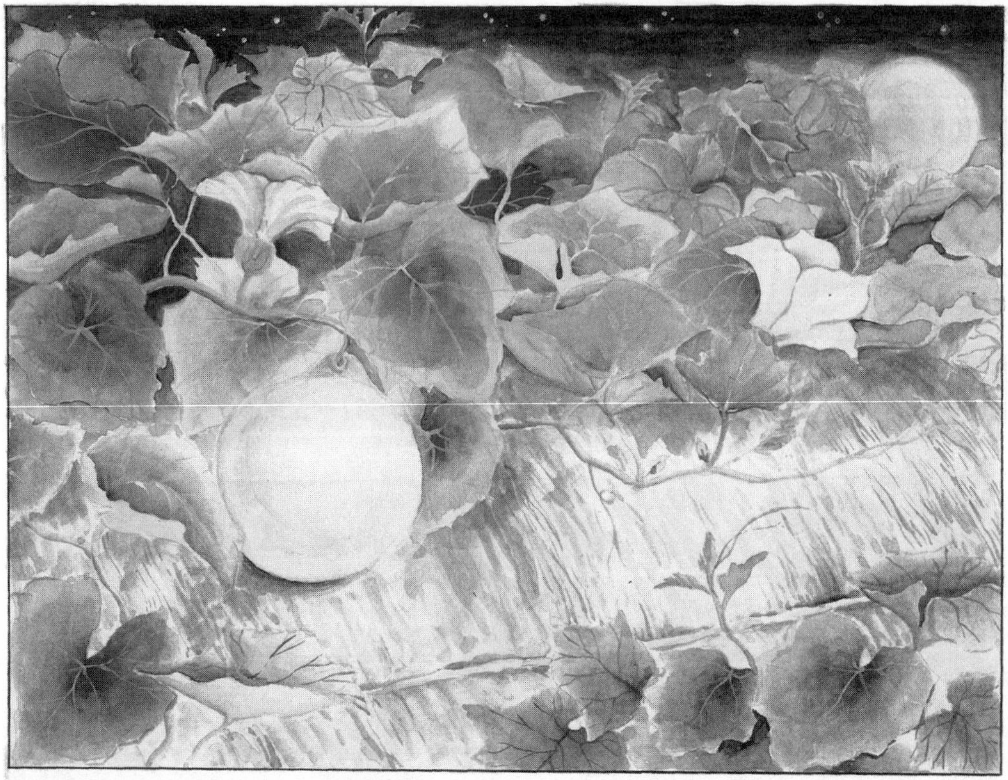

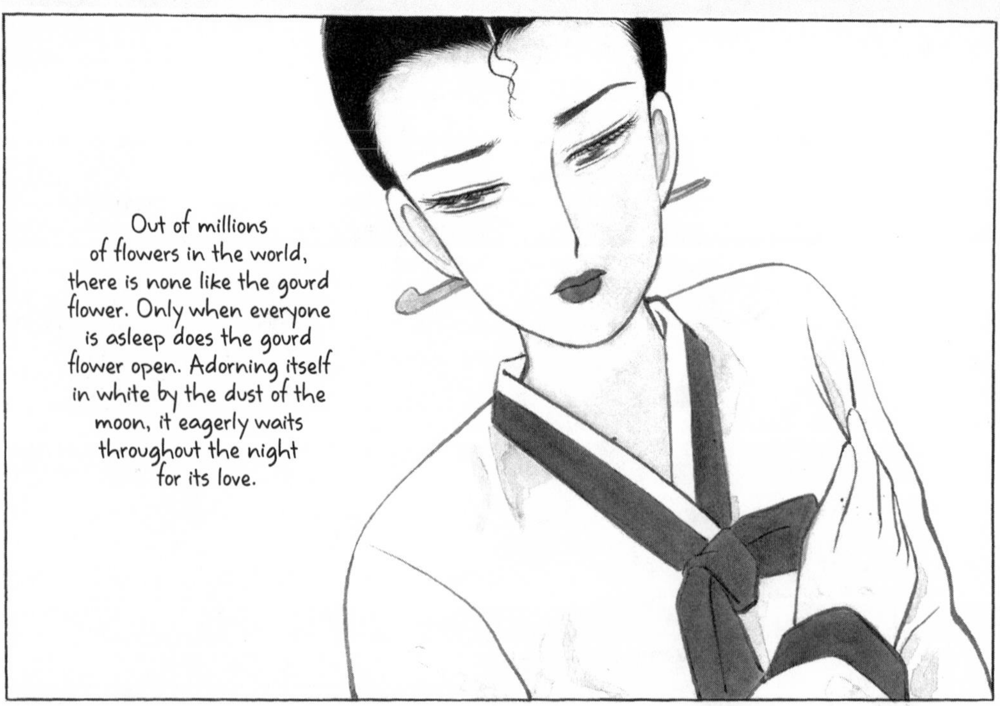
Out of millions of flowers in the world, there is none like the gourd flower. Only when everyone is asleep does the gourd flower open. Adorning itself in white by the dust of the moon, it eagerly waits throughout the night for its love.

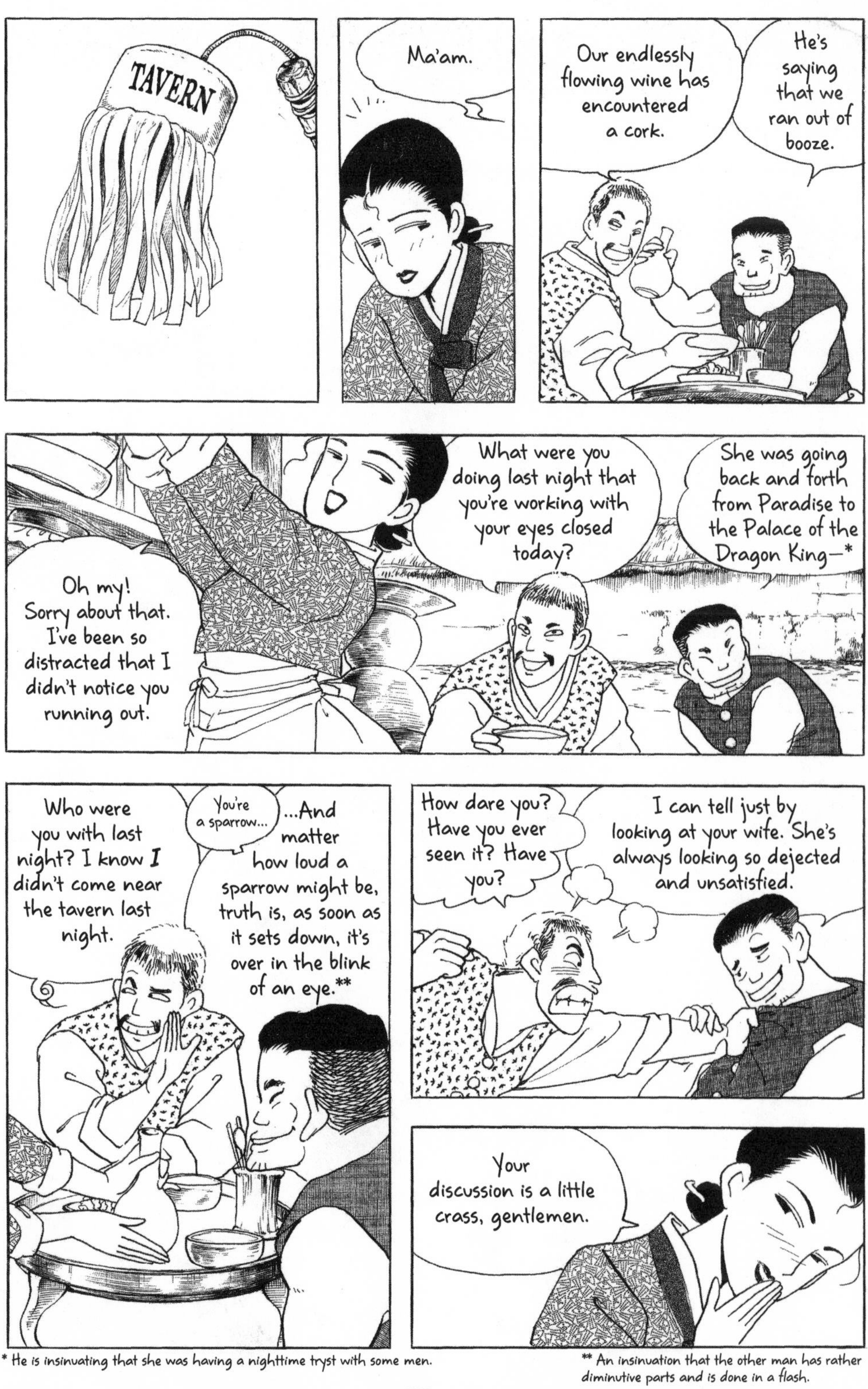
TAVERN
Ma'am.
Our endlessly flowing wine has encountered a cork.
He's saying that we ran out of booze.
Oh my! Sorry about that. I've been so distracted that I didn't notice you running out.
What were you doing last night that you're working with your eyes closed today?
She was going back and forth from Paradise to the Palace of the Dragon King—*
Who were you with last night? I know I didn't come near the tavern last night.
You're a sparrow...
...And matter how loud a sparrow might be, truth is, as soon as it sets down, it's over in the blink of an eye.**
How dare you? Have you ever seen it? Have you?
I can tell just by looking at your wife. She's always looking so dejected and unsatisfied.
Your discussion is a little crass, gentlemen.

* He is insinuating that she was having a nighttime tryst with some men.

** An insinuation that the other man has rather diminutive parts and is done in a flash.

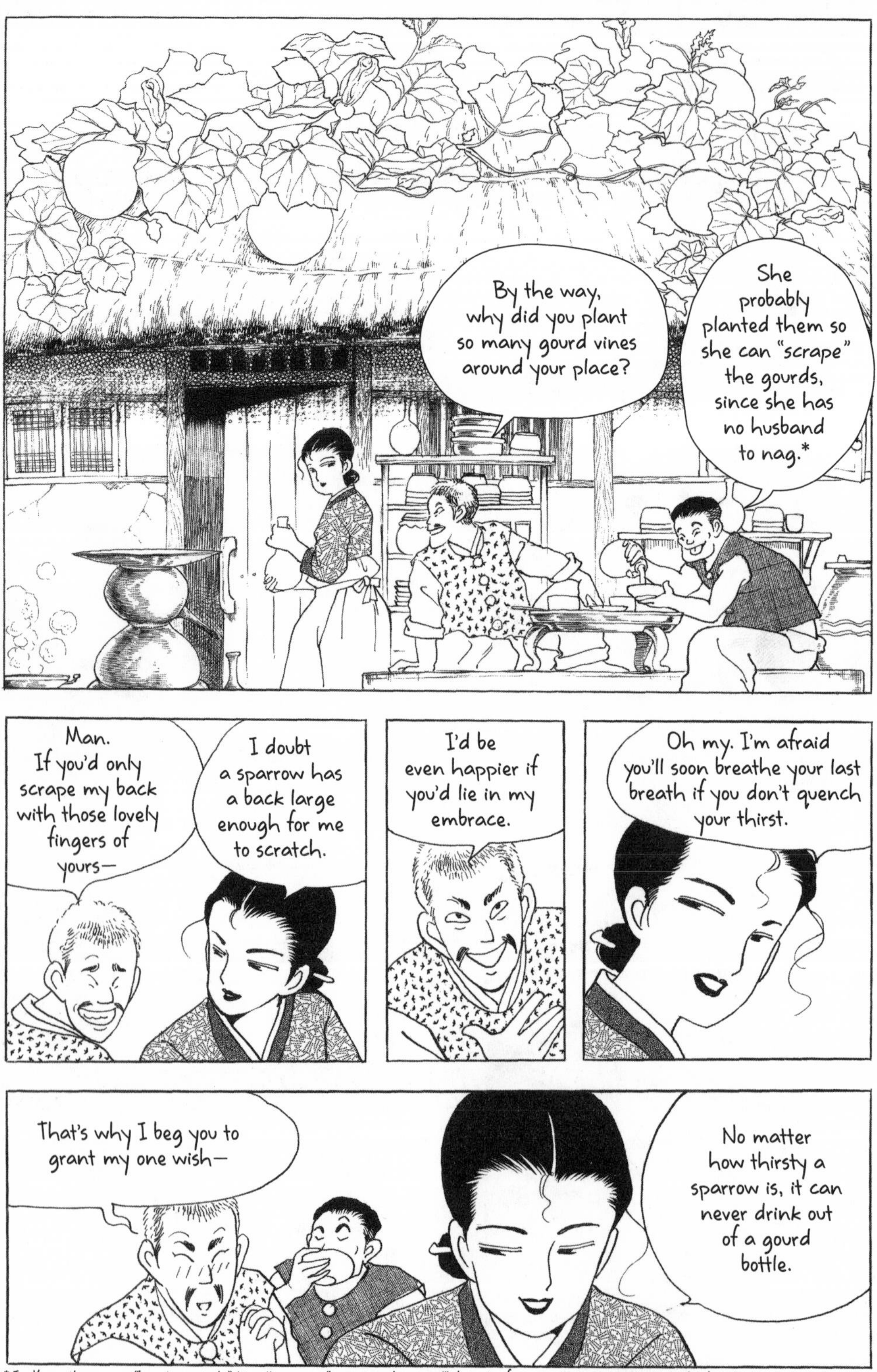
By the way, why did you plant so many gourd vines around your place?
She probably planted them so she can "scrape" the gourds, since she has no husband to nag.*
Man. If you'd only scrape my back with those lovely fingers of yours—
I doubt a sparrow has a back large enough for me to scratch.
I'd be even happier if you'd lie in my embrace.
Oh my. I'm afraid you'll soon breathe your last breath if you don't quench your thirst.
That's why I beg you to grant my one wish—
No matter how thirsty a sparrow is, it can never drink out of a gourd bottle.

* In Korea the saying "bagajee guk da" literally means "to scrape the gourd", but also figuratively means to nag at a husband.

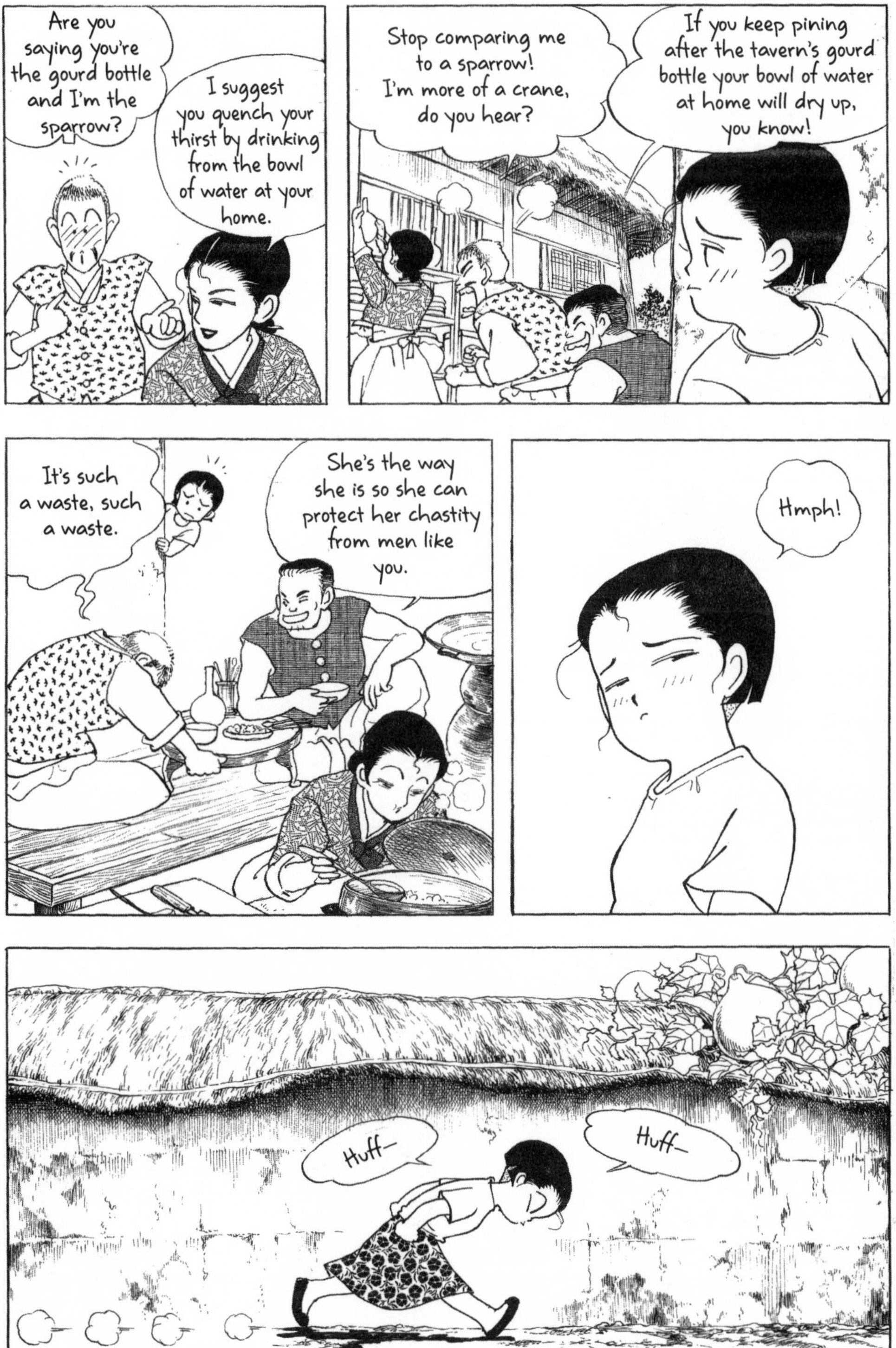
Are you saying you're the gourd bottle and I'm the sparrow?
I suggest you quench your thirst by drinking from the bowl of water at your home.
Stop comparing me to a sparrow! I'm more of a crane, do you hear?
If you keep pining after the tavern's gourd bottle your bowl of water at home will dry up, you know!
It's such a waste, such a waste.
She's the way she is so she can protect her chastity from men like you.
Hmph!
Huff–
Huff–

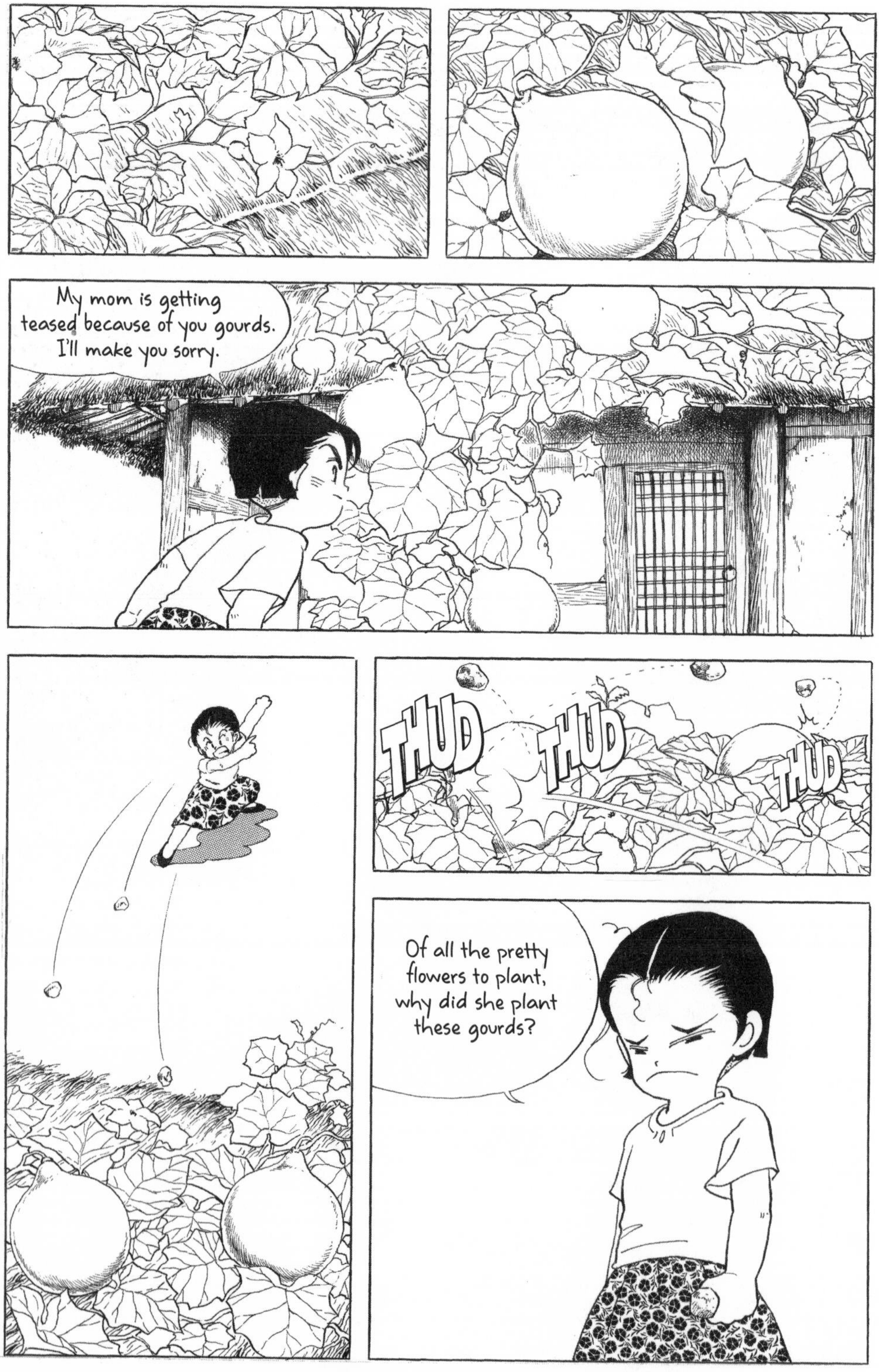
My mom is getting teased because of you gourds. I'll make you sorry.
THUD
THUD
THUD
Of all the pretty flowers to plant, why did she plant these gourds?

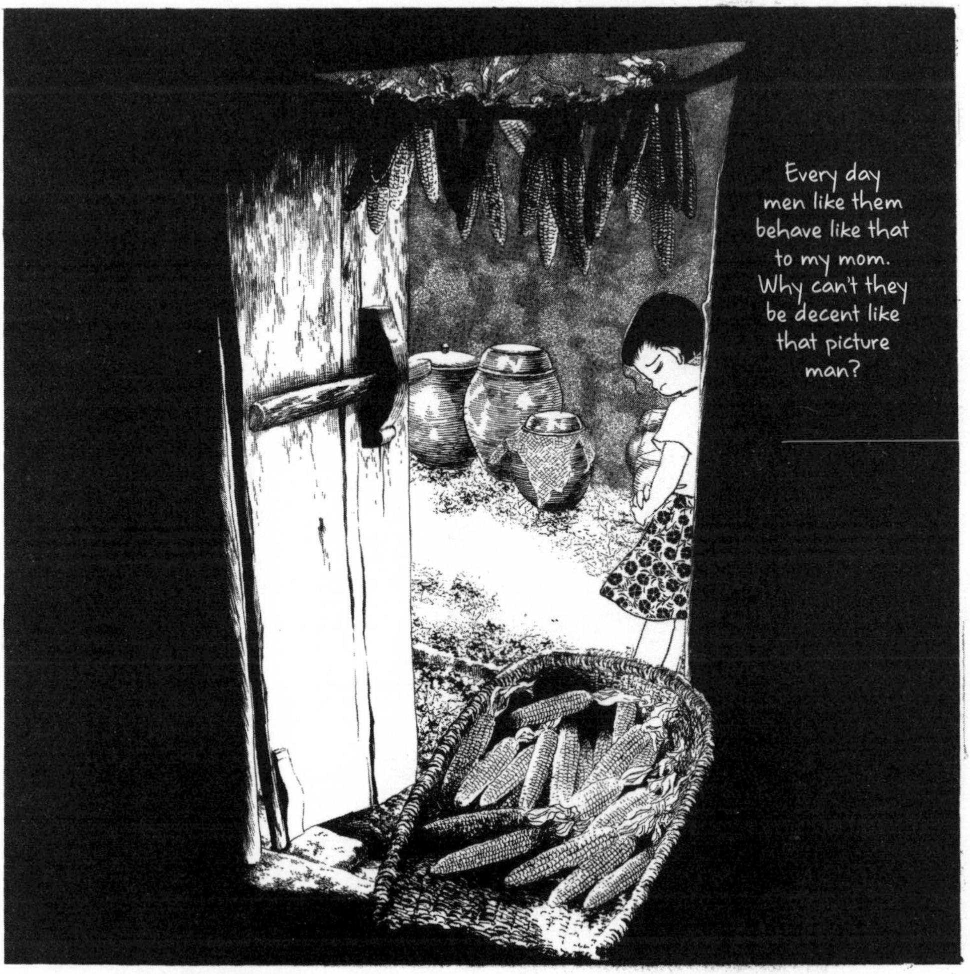
Every day men like them behave like that to my mom. Why can't they be decent like that picture man?

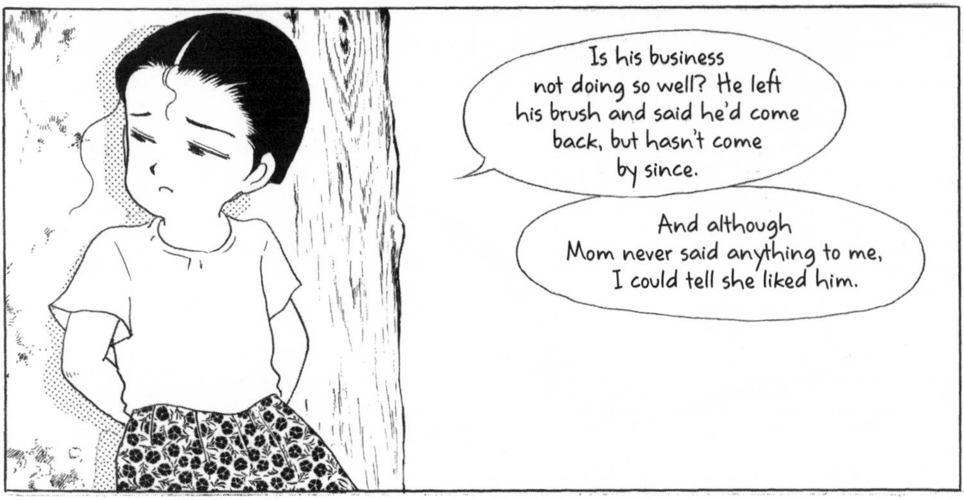
Is his business not doing so well? He left his brush and said he'd come back, but hasn't come by since.
And although Mom never said anything to me, I could tell she liked him.

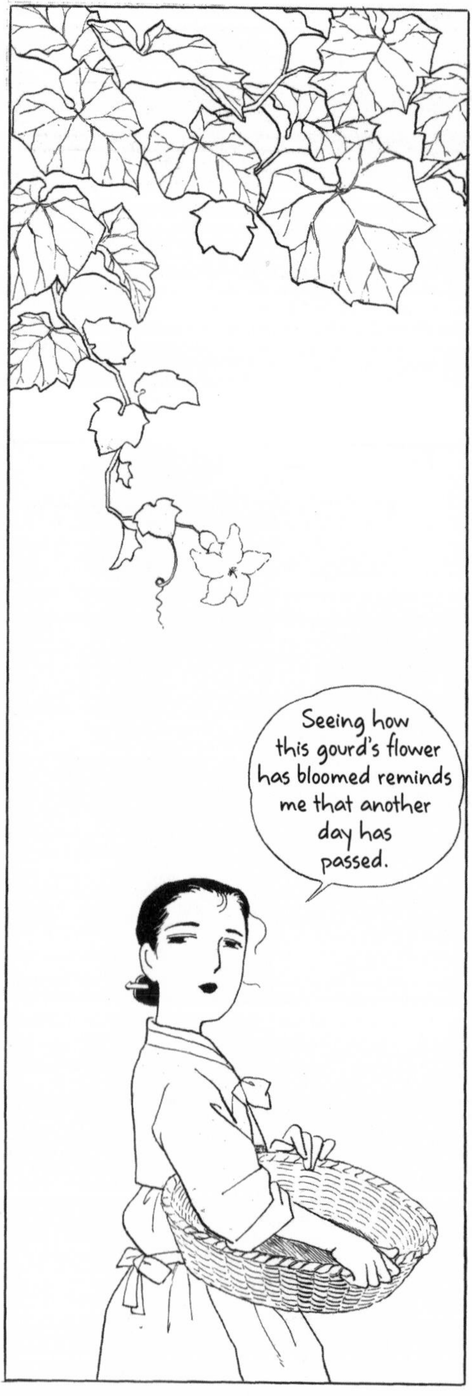
Seeing how this gourd's flower has bloomed reminds me that another day has passed.

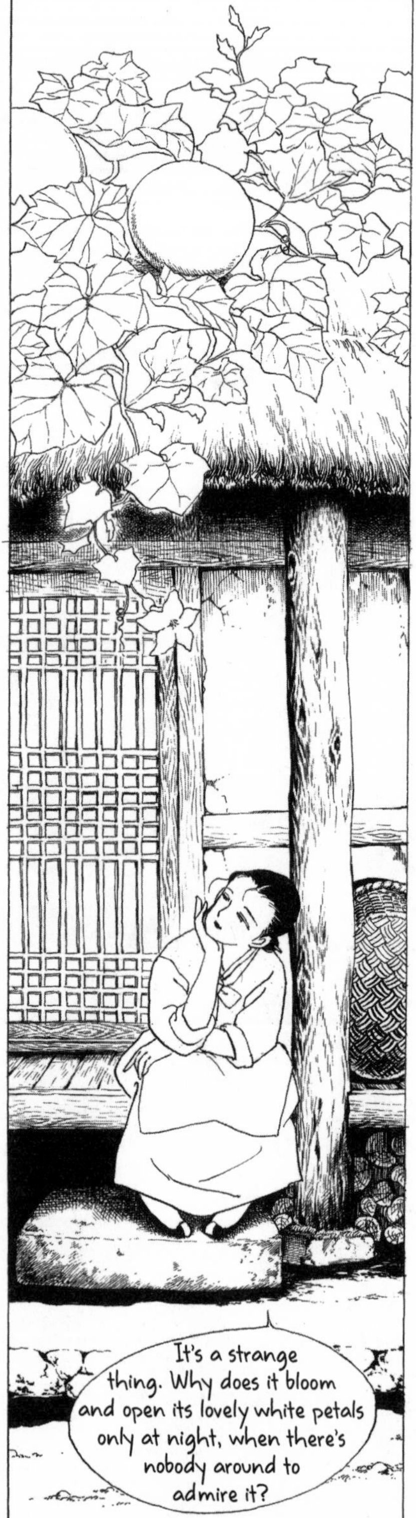
It's a strange thing. Why does it bloom and open its lovely white petals only at night, when there's nobody around to admire it?

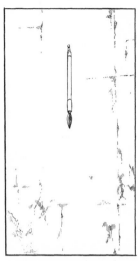

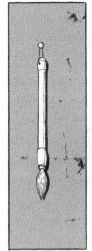

RUSTLE

Mom—

TURN

The lights
have been off for
a while now. Why aren't
you sleeping?

Can we get rid
of the gourd vine and
replace it with pretty
flowers like peonies
and hollyhocks?

Why do you want to
get rid of the gourd vine?
If you want to plant
some other flowers,
just plant them
next to it.

Because people
make fun of us.

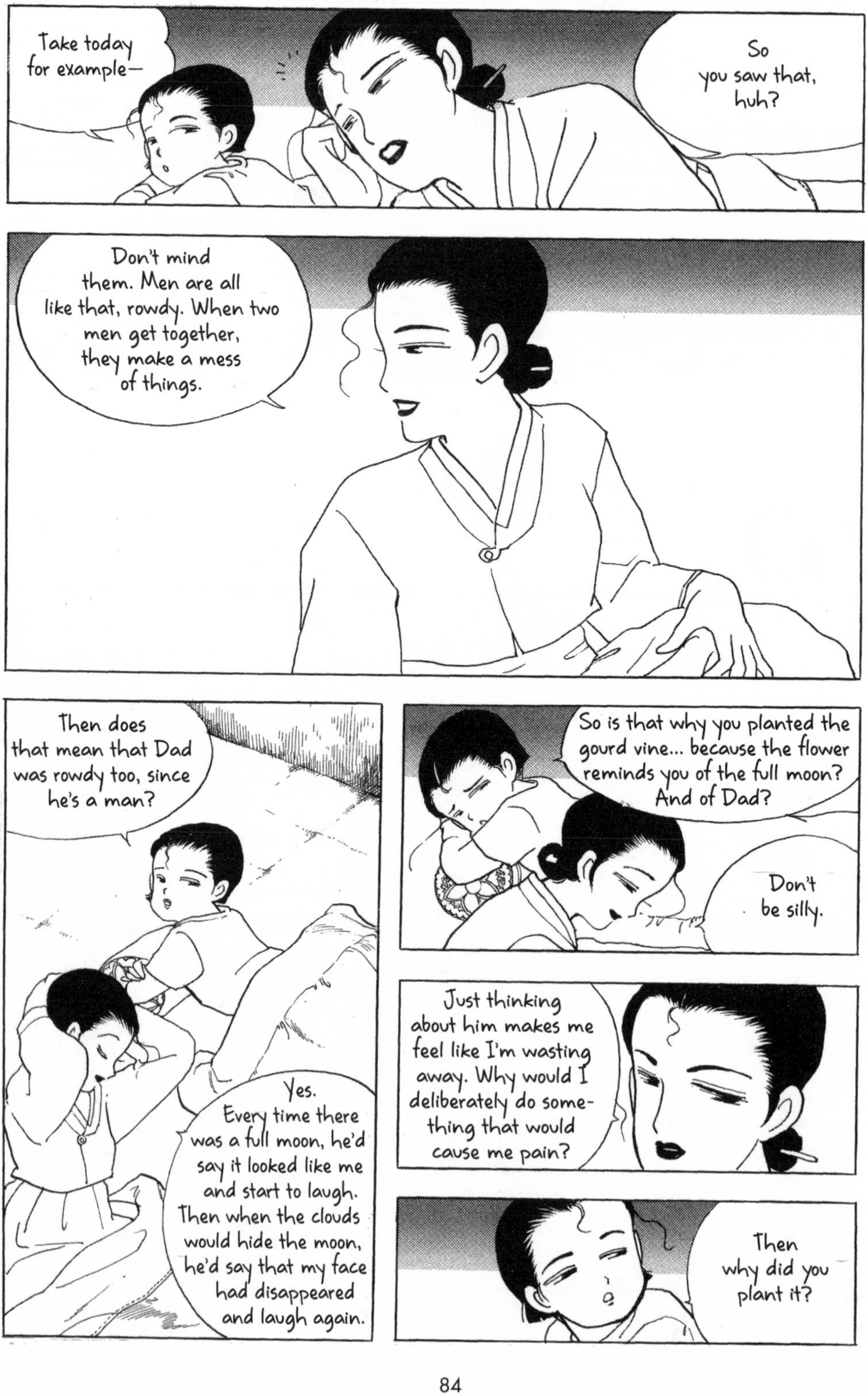
Take today for example—
So you saw that, huh?
Don't mind them. Men are all like that, rowdy. When two men get together, they make a mess of things.
Then does that mean that Dad was rowdy too, since he's a man?
Yes. Every time there was a full moon, he'd say it looked like me and start to laugh. Then when the clouds would hide the moon, he'd say that my face had disappeared and laugh again.
So is that why you planted the gourd vine... because the flower reminds you of the full moon? And of Dad?
Don't be silly.
Just thinking about him makes me feel like I'm wasting away. Why would I deliberately do something that would cause me pain?
Then why did you plant it?

I don't know. Maybe it's because the flower does look like me— Or maybe because the flower is like my heart—

Just, why did it have to be the gourd flower of all things? When I grow up, I'm going to look like a pink hollyhock instead—

Oh, I forgot! Tomorrow when you wake up, you'll need to go to your aunt's house for a few days.

Why this all of a sudden?

There's been a death in the family and she needs someone to watch the children.

Where are you going, right now?

I'm a bit thirsty—

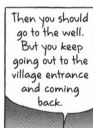

Then you should go to the well. But you keep going out to the village entrance and coming back.

That's because, sometimes there are some thirsts that a well can't quench...!

So once again I stare at the gourd flower...

85

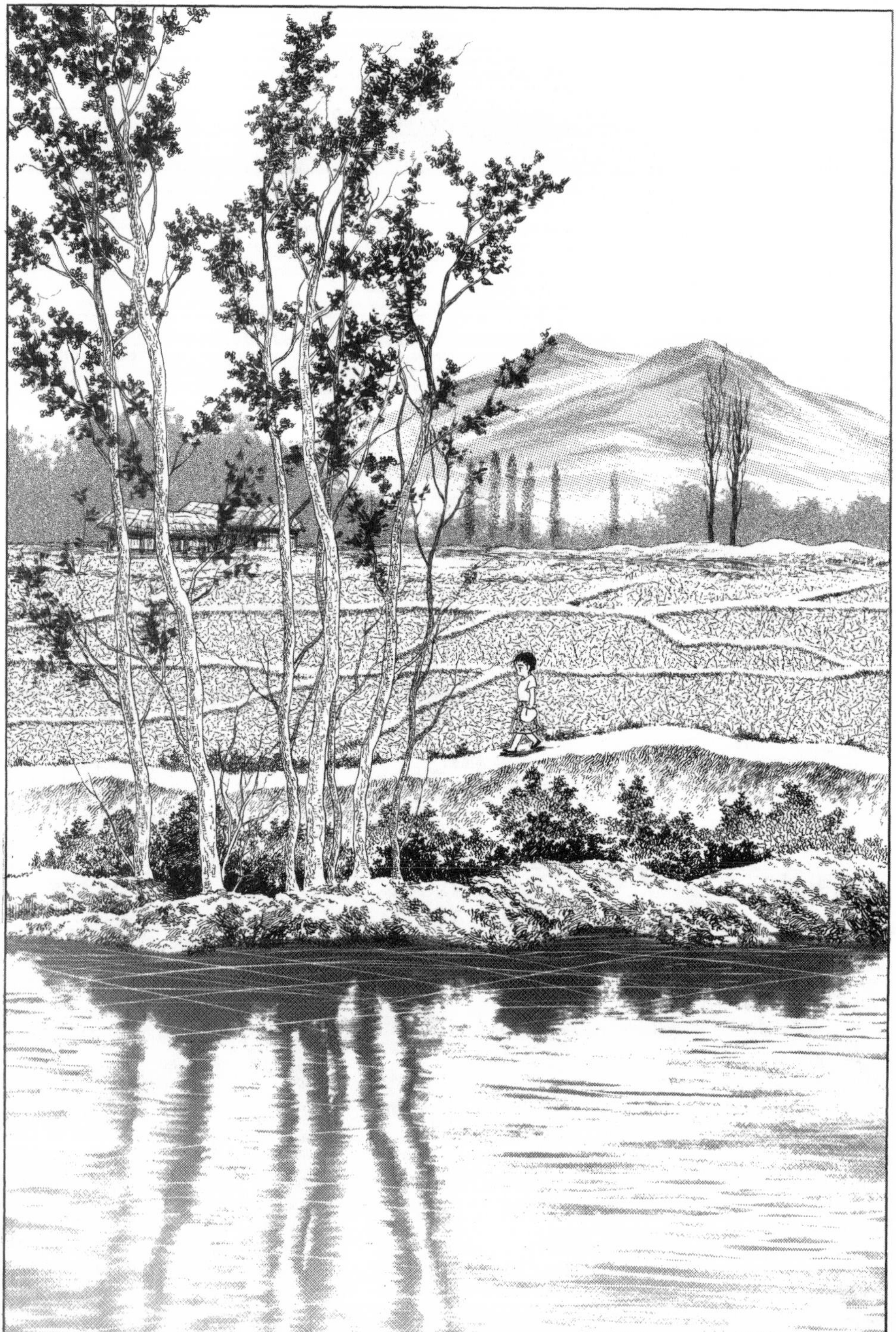

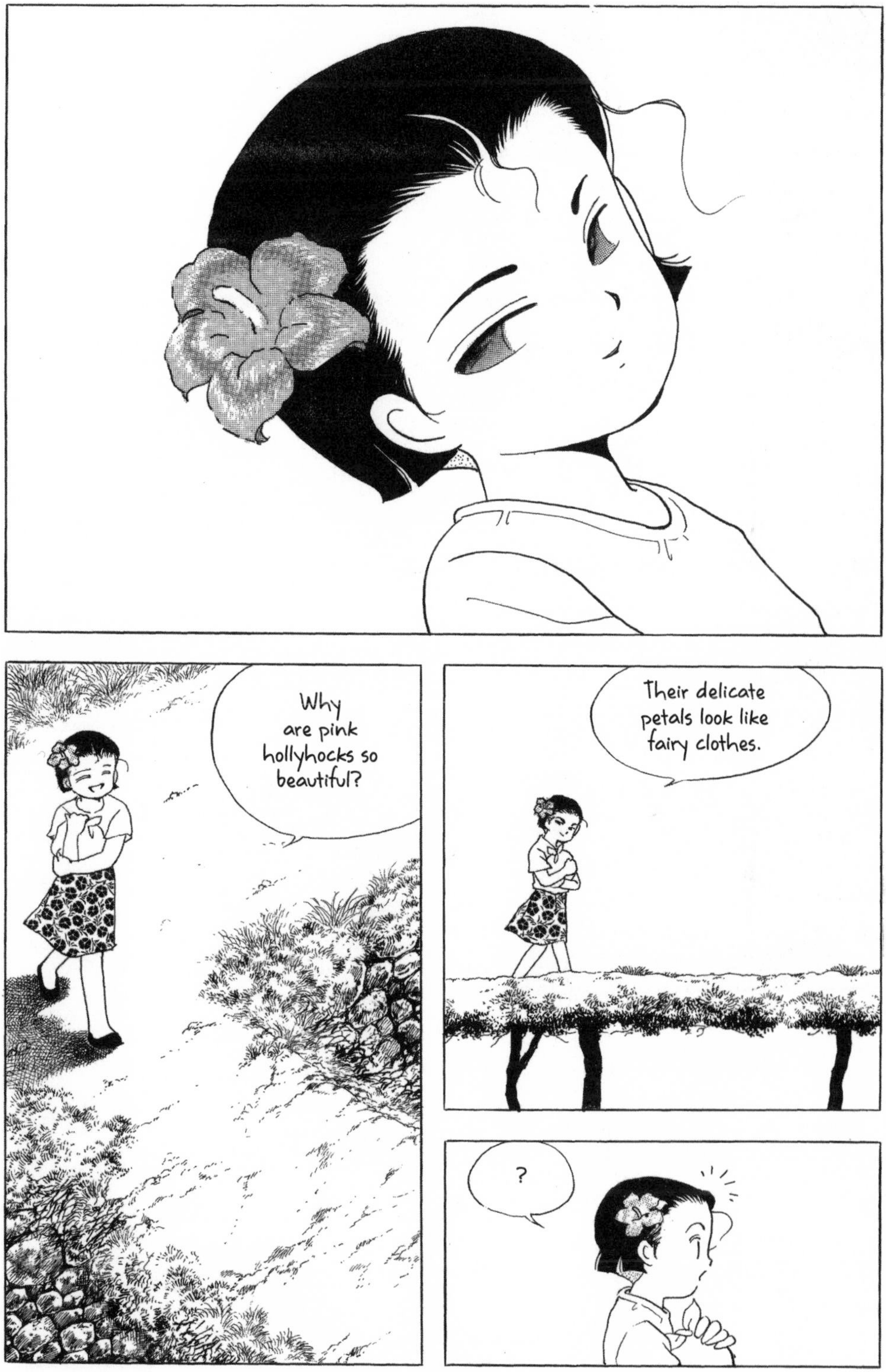
Why are pink hollyhocks so beautiful?
Their delicate petals look like fairy clothes.
?

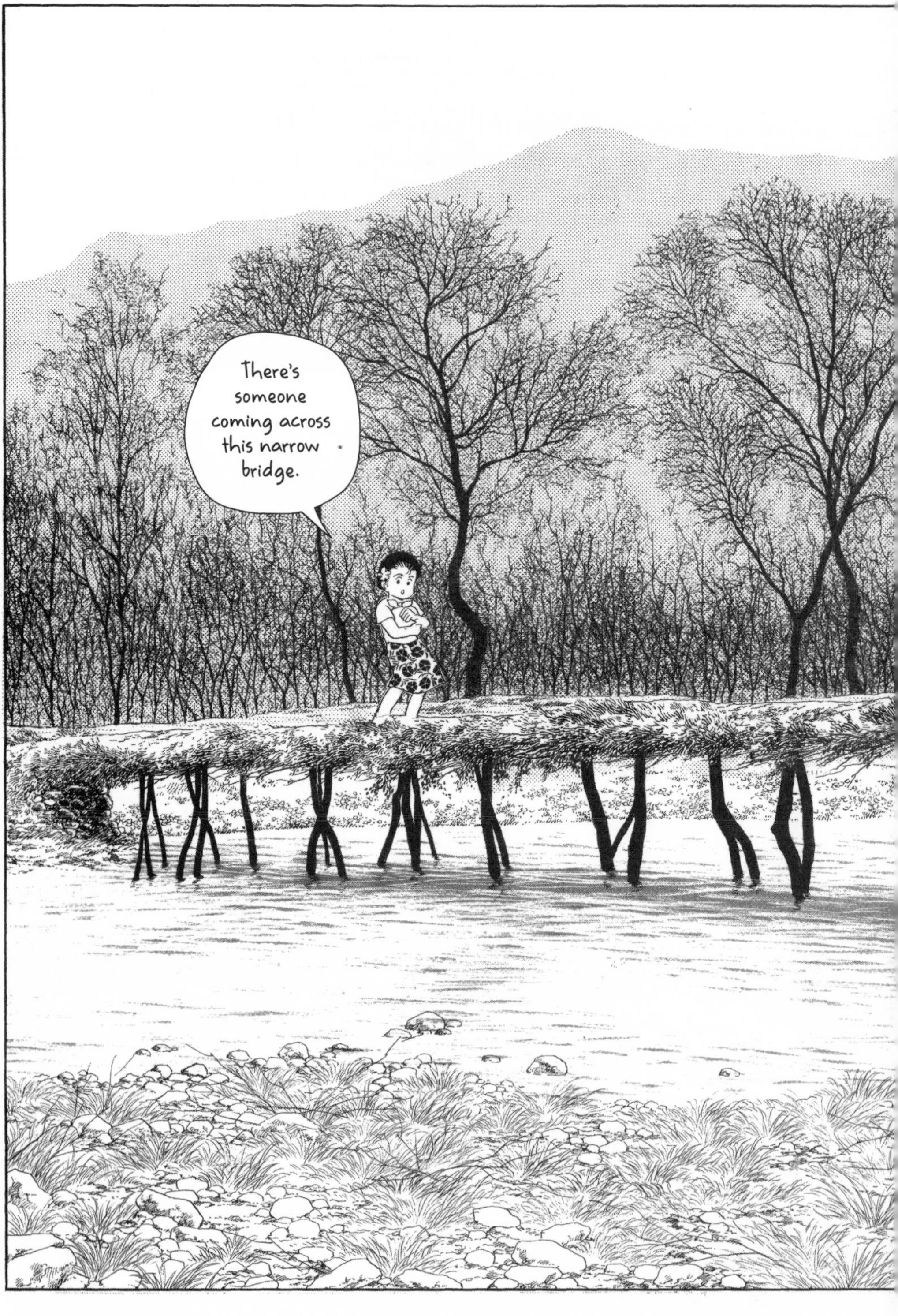
There's someone coming across this narrow bridge.

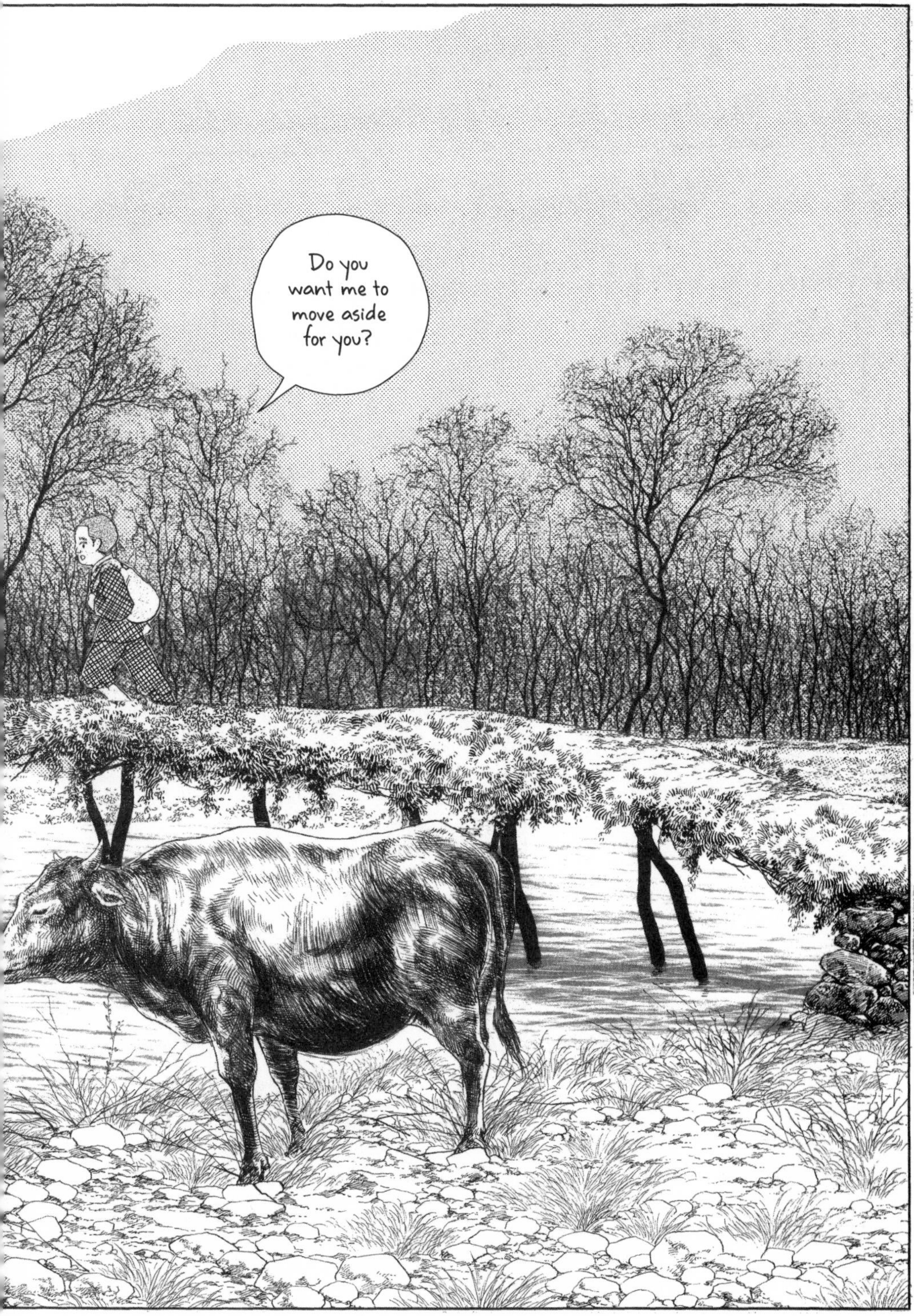
Do you want me to move aside for you?

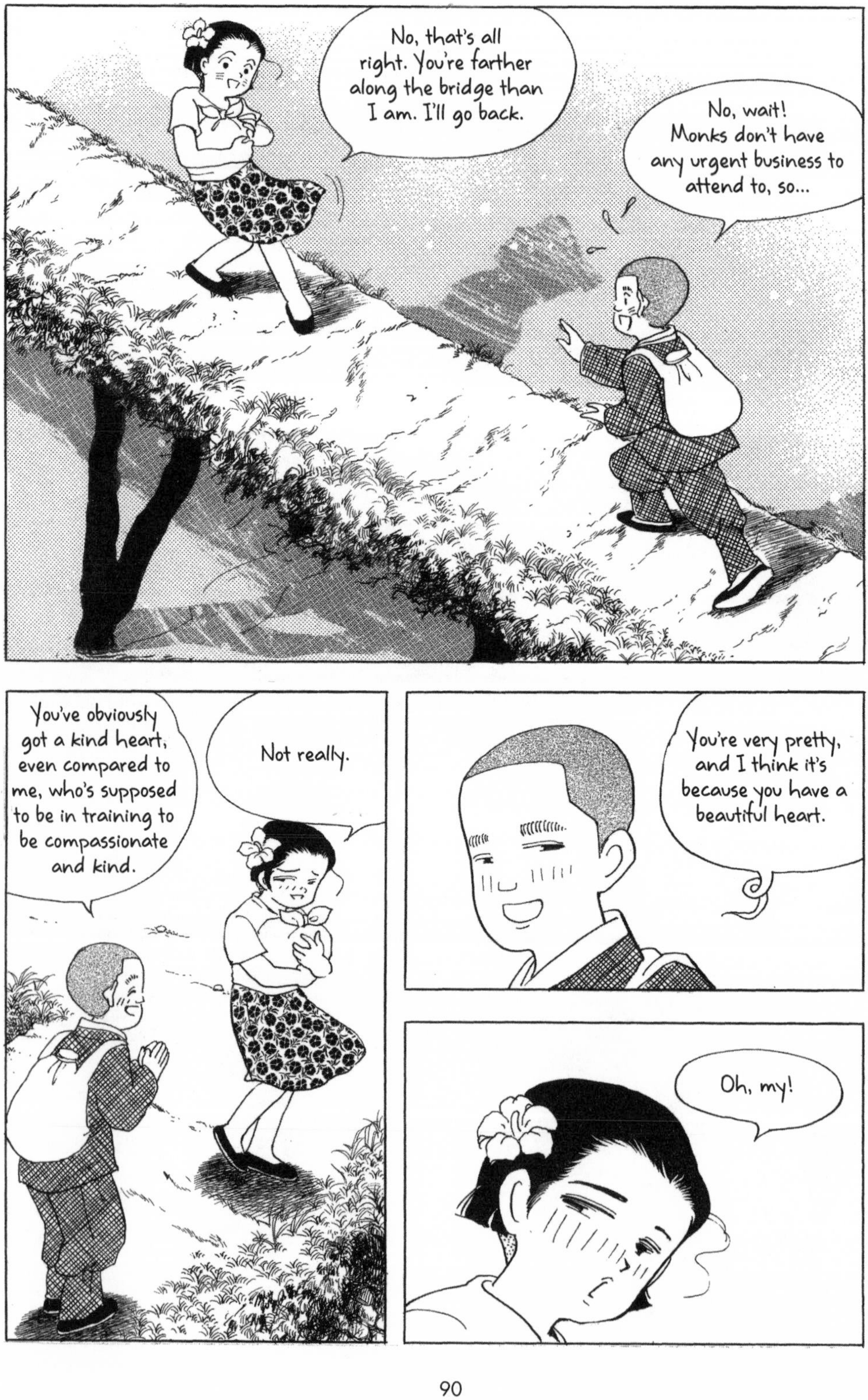
No, that's all right. You're farther along the bridge than I am. I'll go back.
No, wait! Monks don't have any urgent business to attend to, so...
You've obviously got a kind heart, even compared to me, who's supposed to be in training to be compassionate and kind.
Not really.
You're very pretty, and I think it's because you have a beautiful heart.
Oh, my!

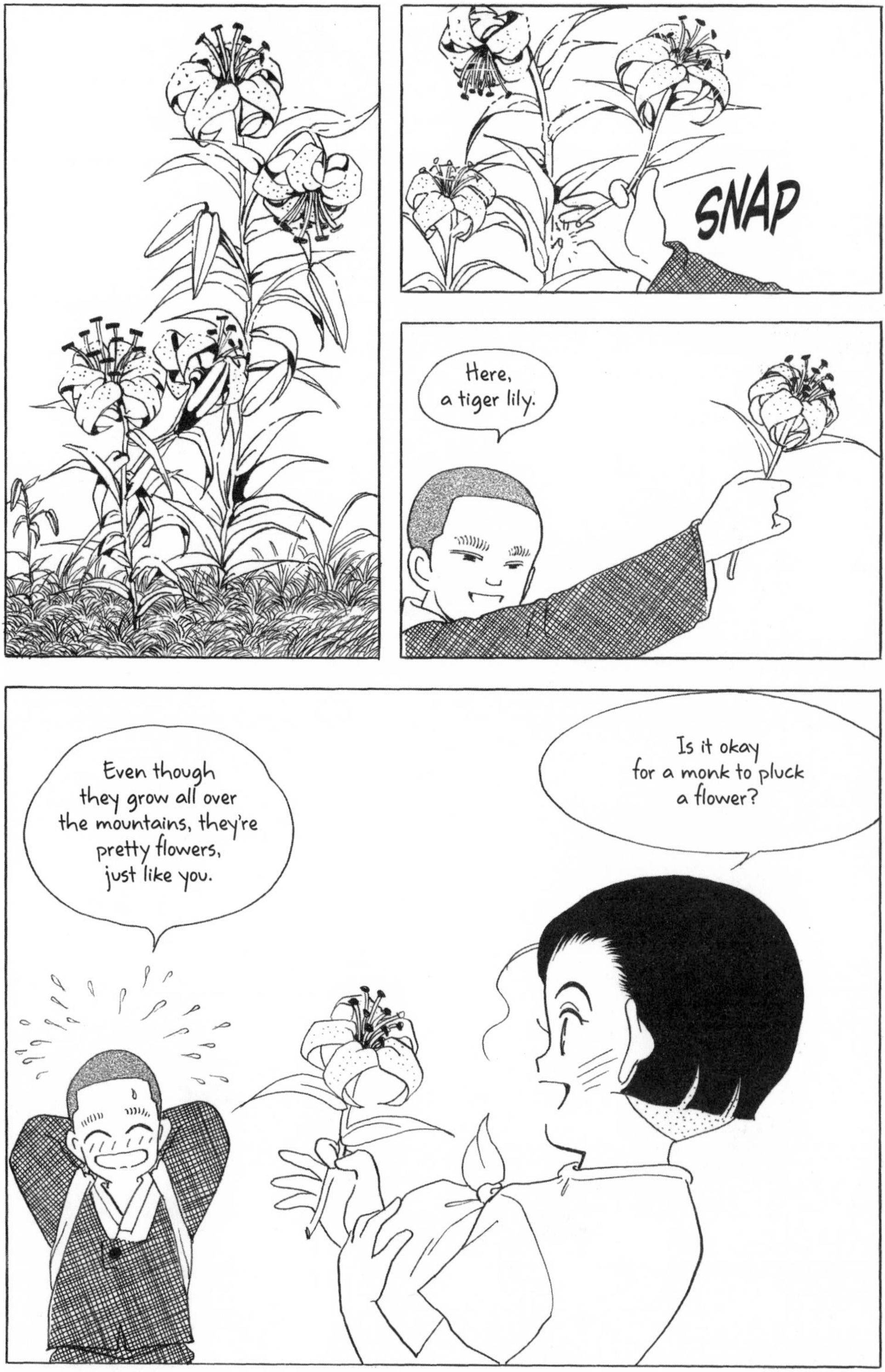
SNAP
Here, a tiger lily.
Is it okay for a monk to pluck a flower?
Even though they grow all over the mountains, they're pretty flowers, just like you.

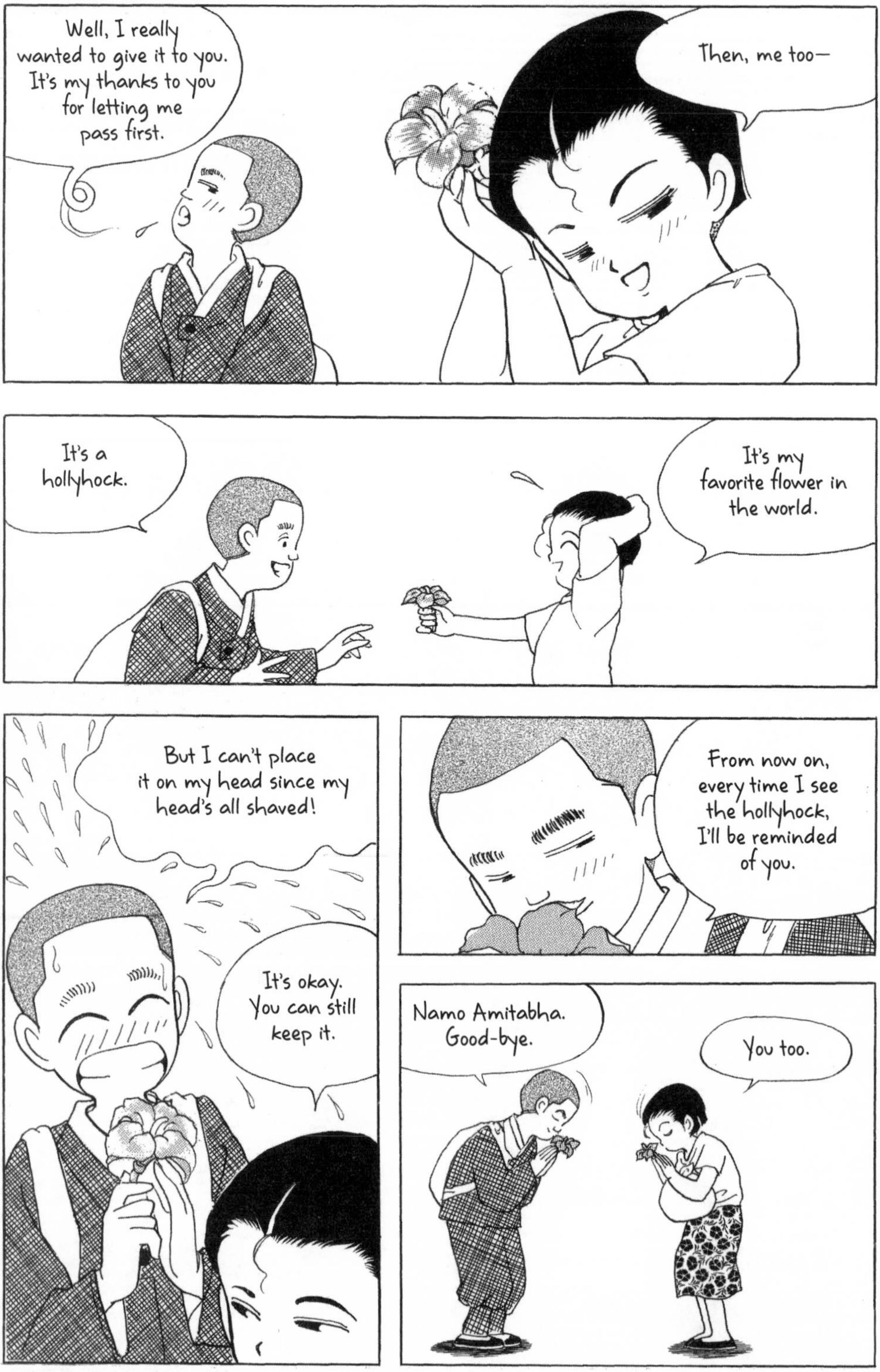
Well, I really wanted to give it to you. It's my thanks to you for letting me pass first.
Then, me too—
It's a hollyhock.
It's my favorite flower in the world.
But I can't place it on my head since my head's all shaved!
It's okay. You can still keep it.
From now on, every time I see the hollyhock, I'll be reminded of you.
Namo Amitabha. Good-bye.
You too.

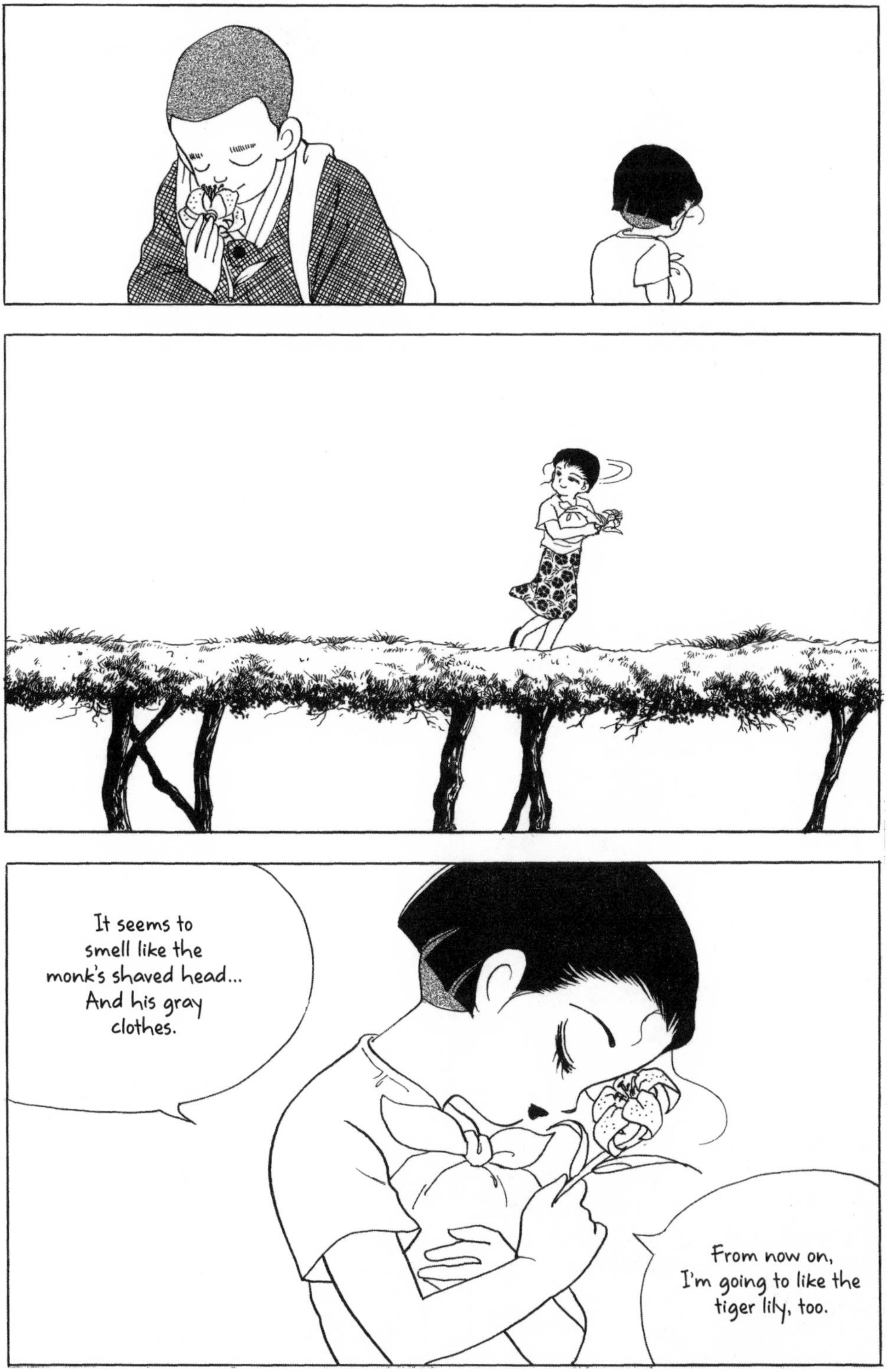
It seems to smell like the monk's shaved head... And his gray clothes.
From now on, I'm going to like the tiger lily, too.

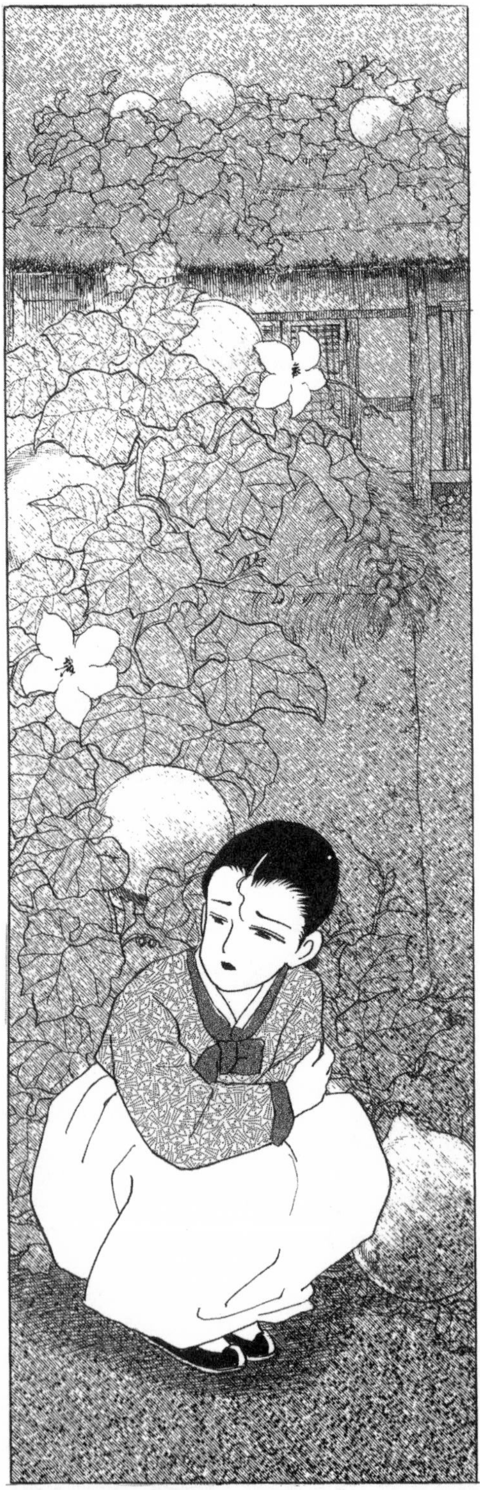

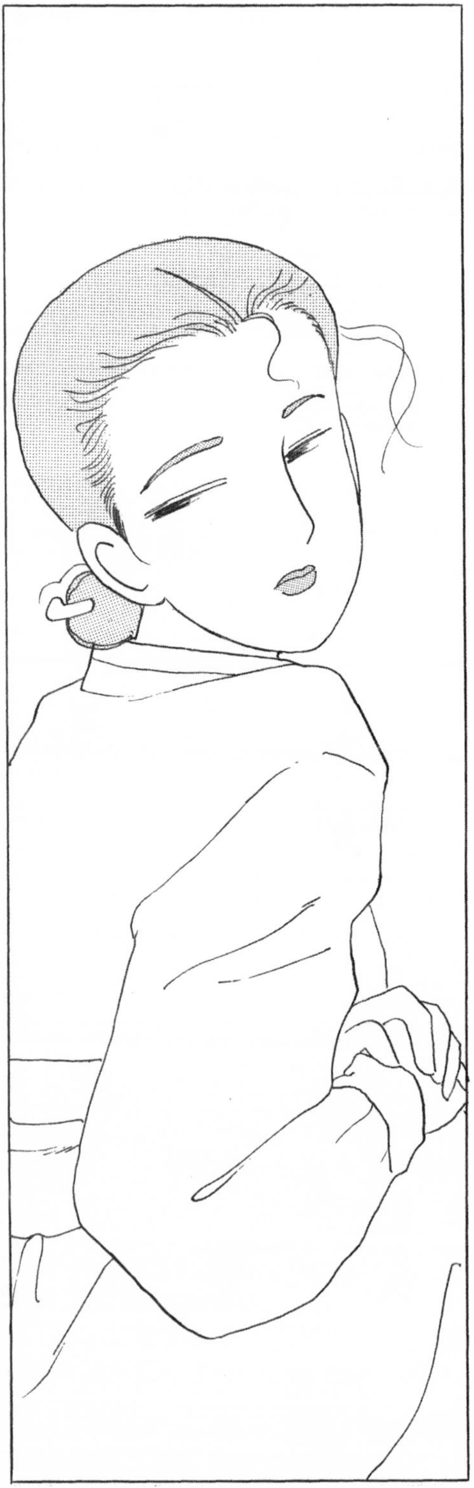

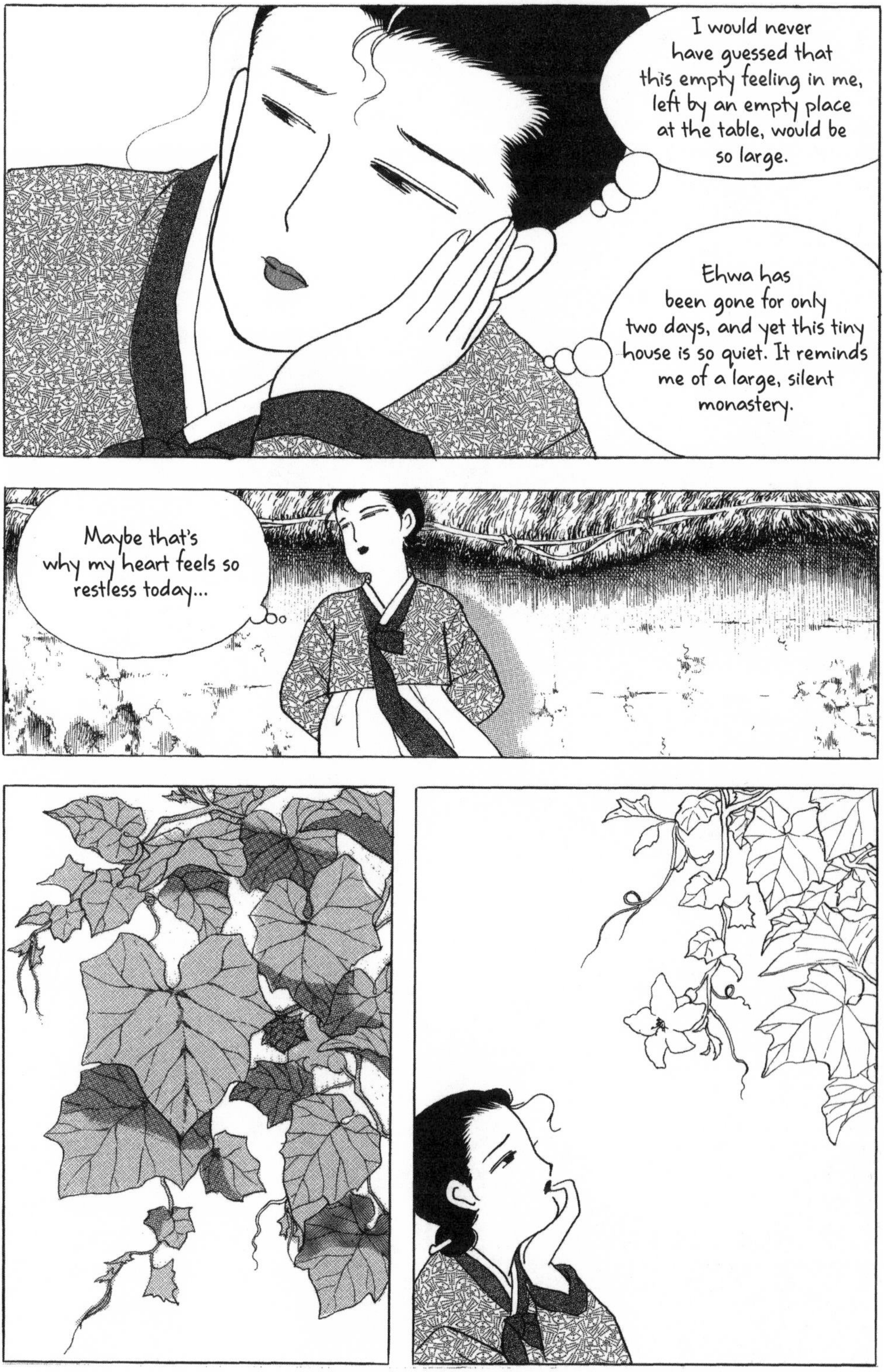
I would never have guessed that this empty feeling in me, left by an empty place at the table, would be so large.
Ehwa has been gone for only two days, and yet this tiny house is so quiet. It reminds me of a large, silent monastery.
Maybe that's why my heart feels so restless today...

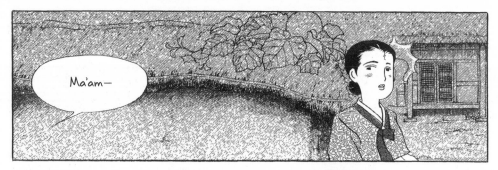

Ma'am—

I know it's a bit late, but I wonder if I can trouble you for some food?

There's no problem about the food. I just need to light a fire...

While you're at it, perhaps you can give me lodging as well.

We rarely have travelers pass through our town so we have no spare room for guests.

Then I guess I'll just have to share a room with you.

?!

And while I'm at it, I can pick up that brush I left with you when I was last here.

Ah...

It's you!

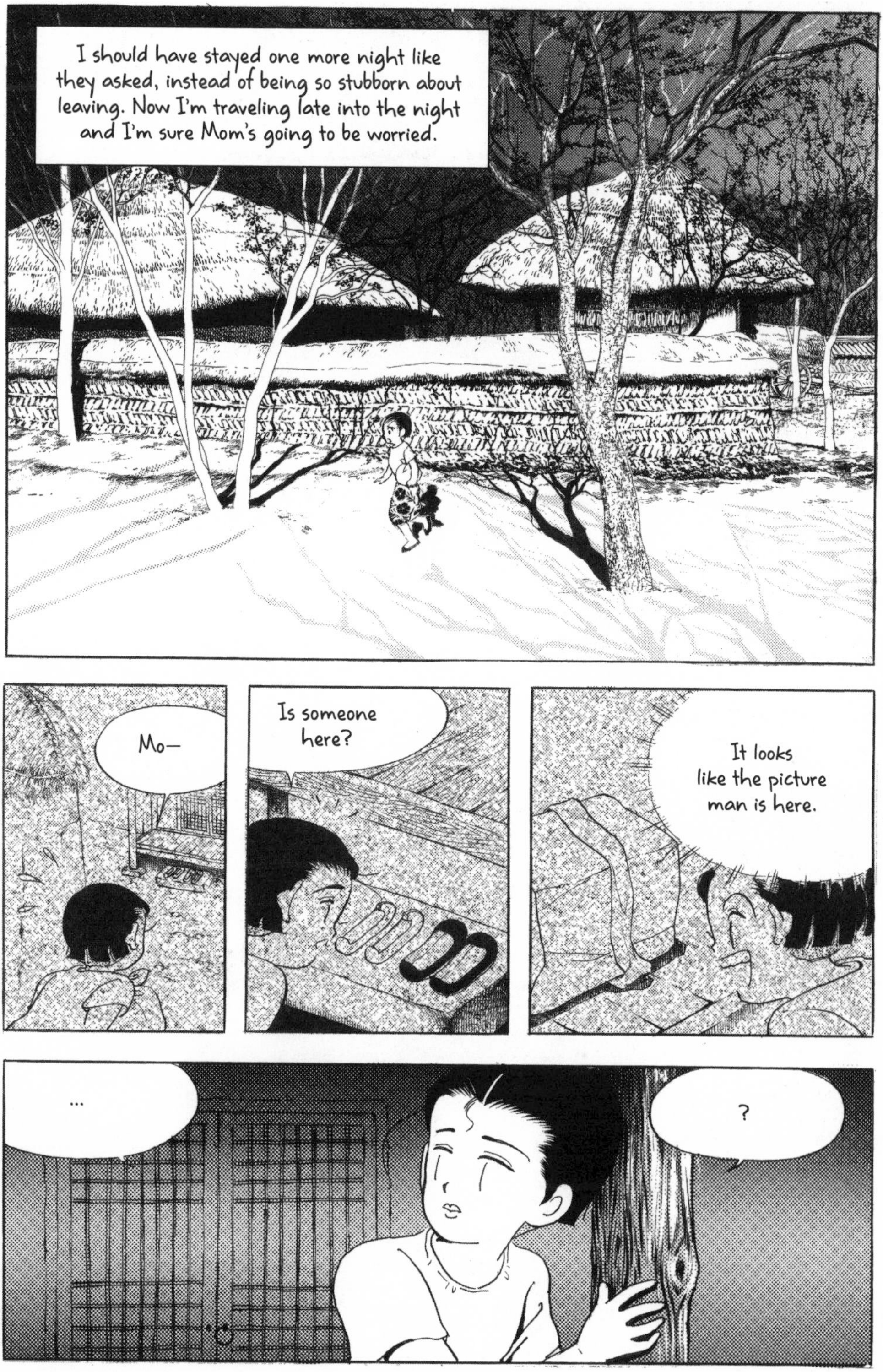
I should have stayed one more night like they asked, instead of being so stubborn about leaving. Now I'm traveling late into the night and I'm sure Mom's going to be worried.
Mo—
Is someone here?
It looks like the picture man is here.
...
?

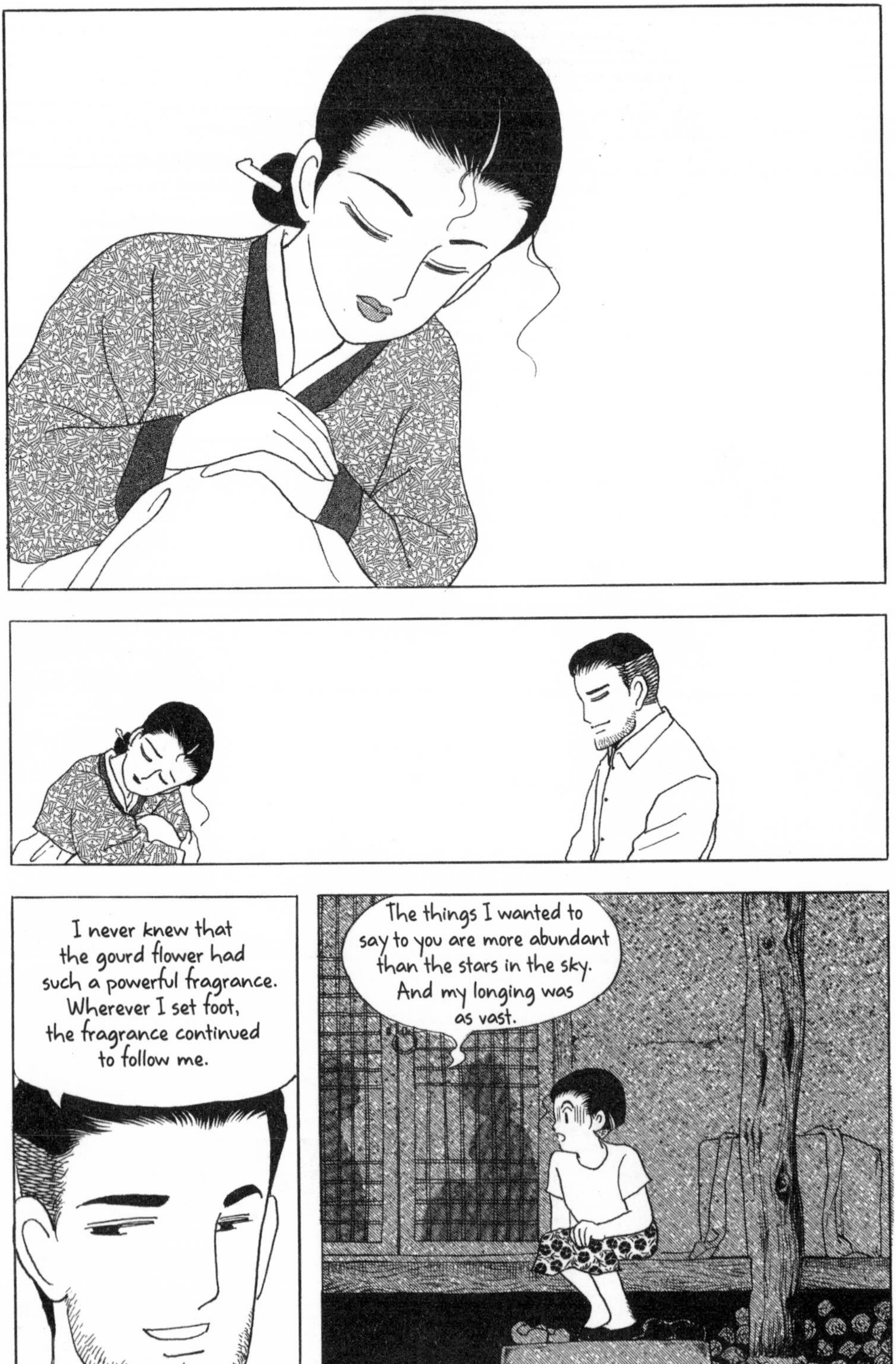
I never knew that the gourd flower had such a powerful fragrance. Wherever I set foot, the fragrance continued to follow me.
The things I wanted to say to you are more abundant than the stars in the sky. And my longing was as vast.

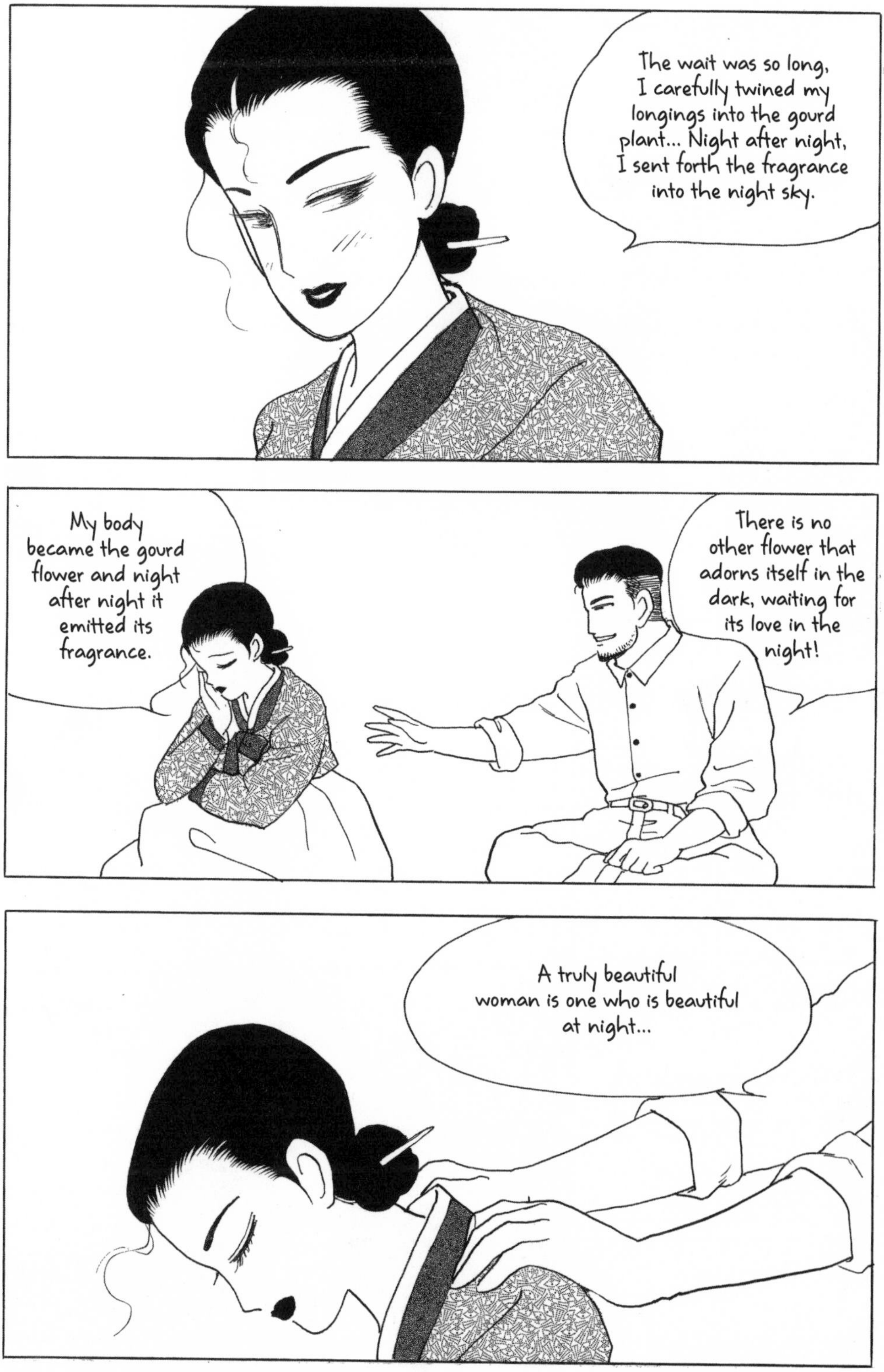
The wait was so long, I carefully twined my longings into the gourd plant... Night after night, I sent forth the fragrance into the night sky.
My body became the gourd flower and night after night it emitted its fragrance.
There is no other flower that adorns itself in the dark, waiting for its love in the night!
A truly beautiful woman is one who is beautiful at night...

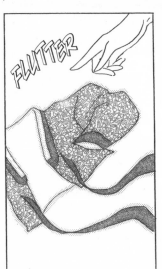

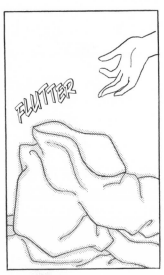

FLUTTER
FLUTTER
FLUTTER
?
Ah...
I thought it was the gourd flower that called me here, but it was you.
Thump...
Thump...

Since the picture man is a man, he's being rowdy with Mom.

Is that what all men are like?

Are they all really like that?

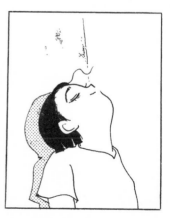

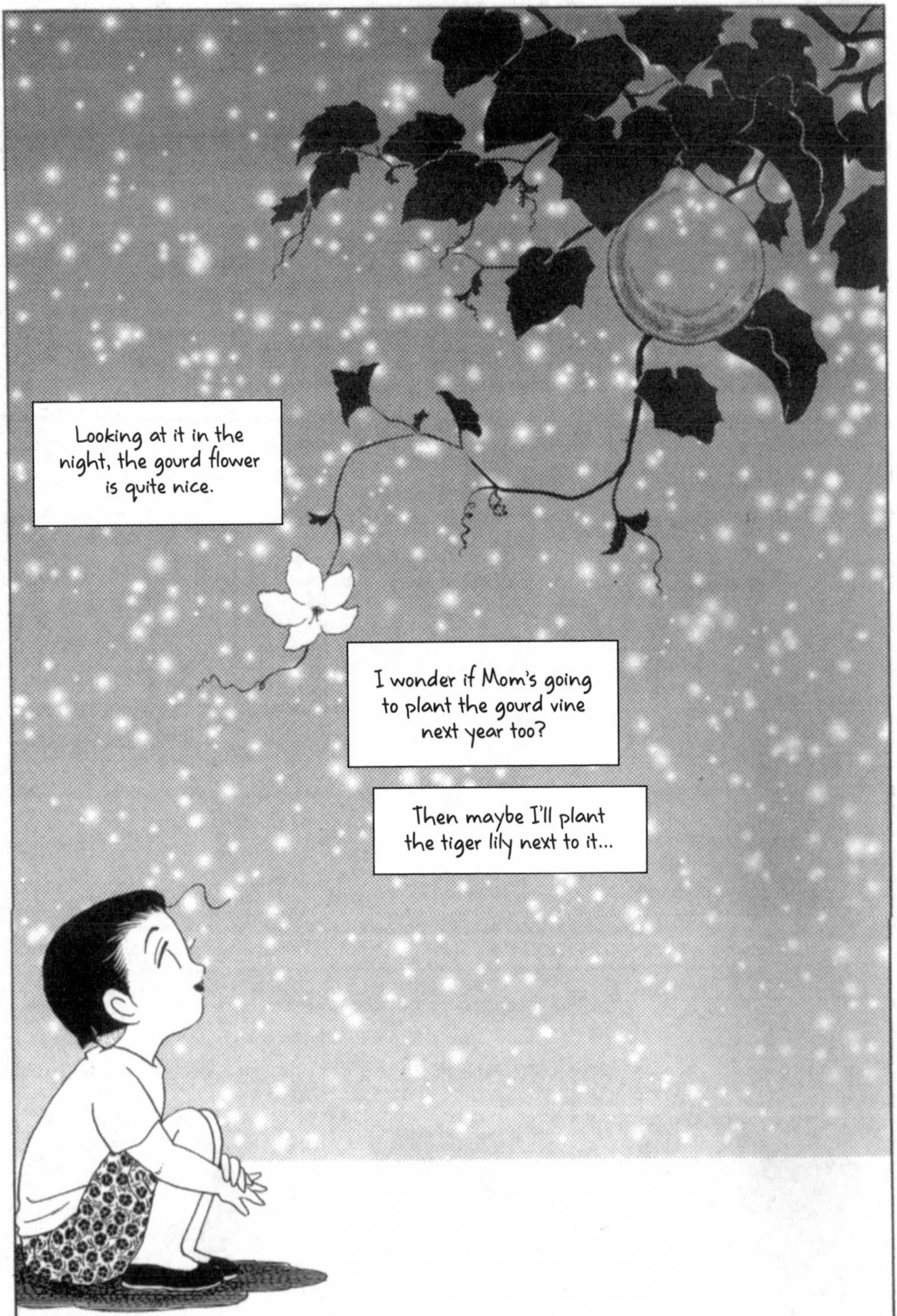
Looking at it in the night, the gourd flower is quite nice.
I wonder if Mom's going to plant the gourd vine next year too?
Then maybe I'll plant the tiger lily next to it...

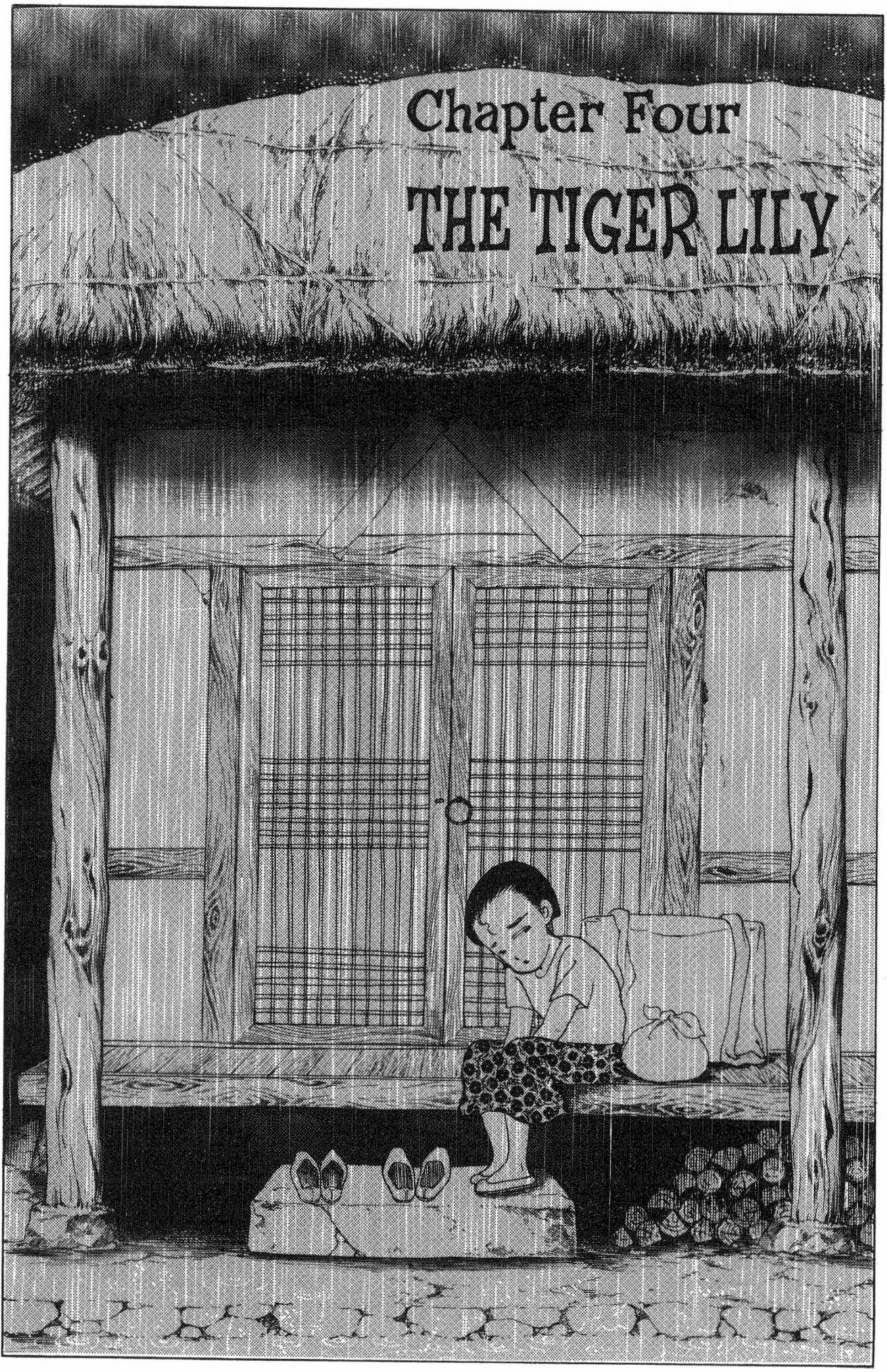
Chapter Four
THE TIGER LILY

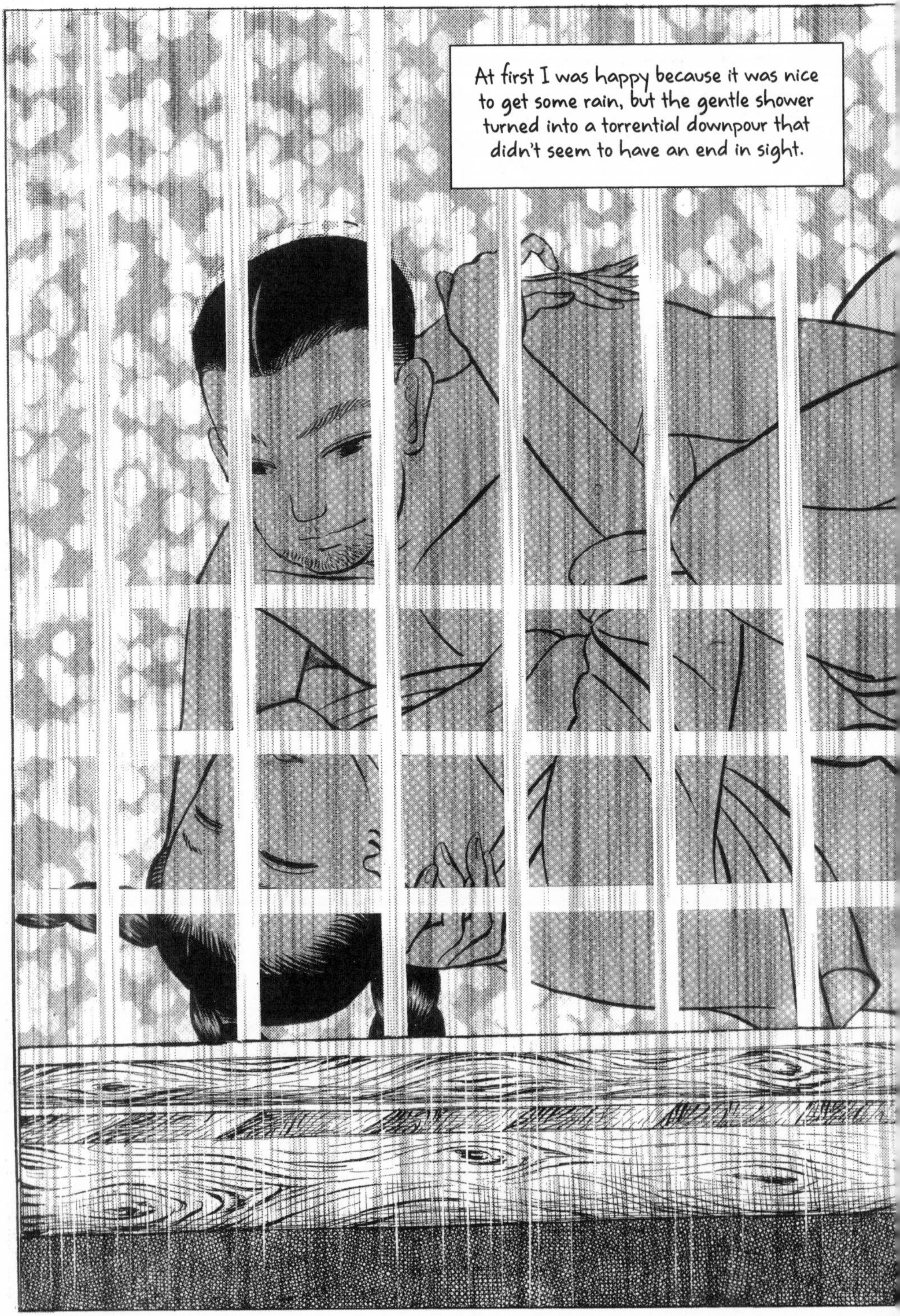
At first I was happy because it was nice to get some rain, but the gentle shower turned into a torrential downpour that didn't seem to have an end in sight.

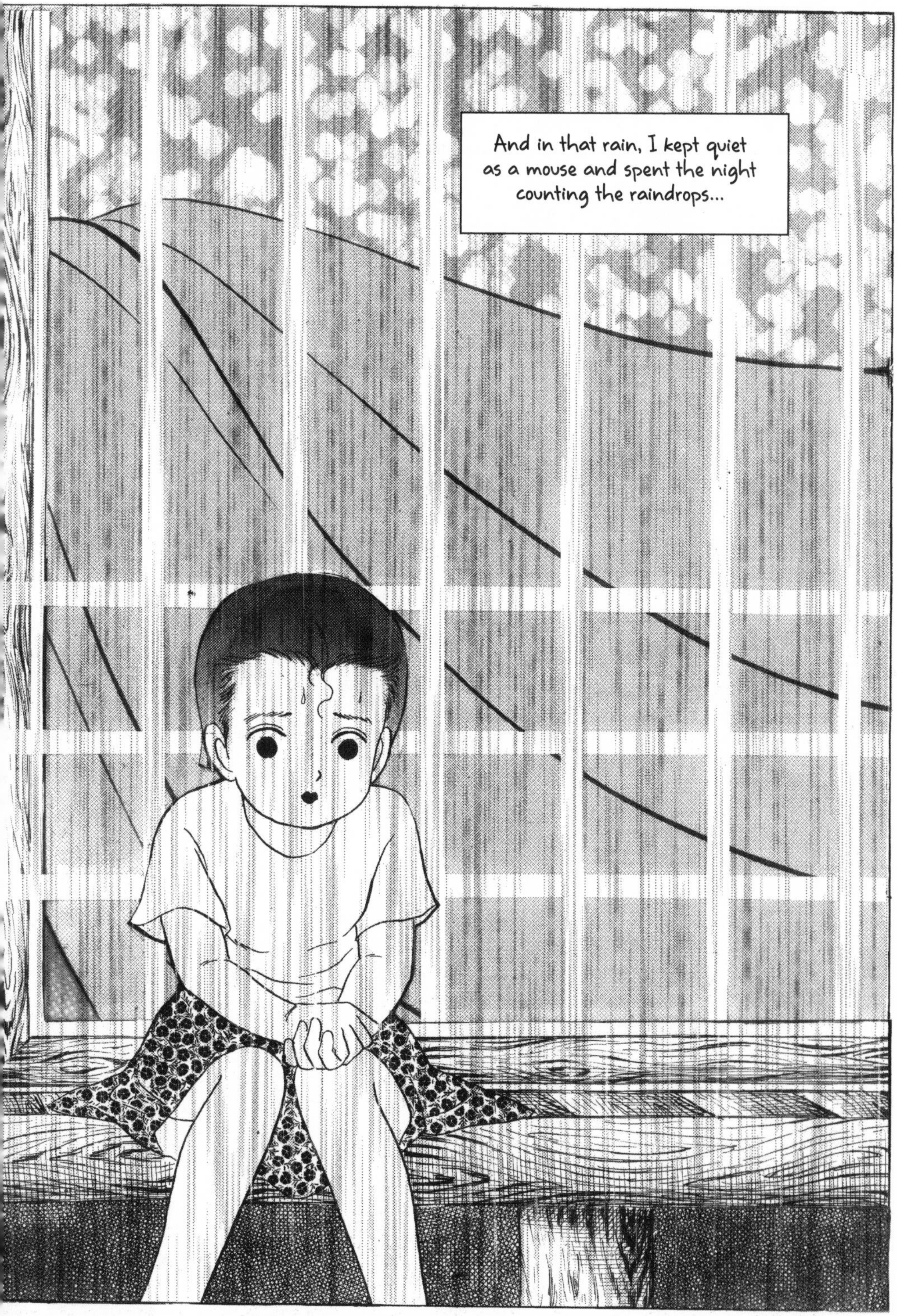
And in that rain, I kept quiet as a mouse and spent the night counting the raindrops...

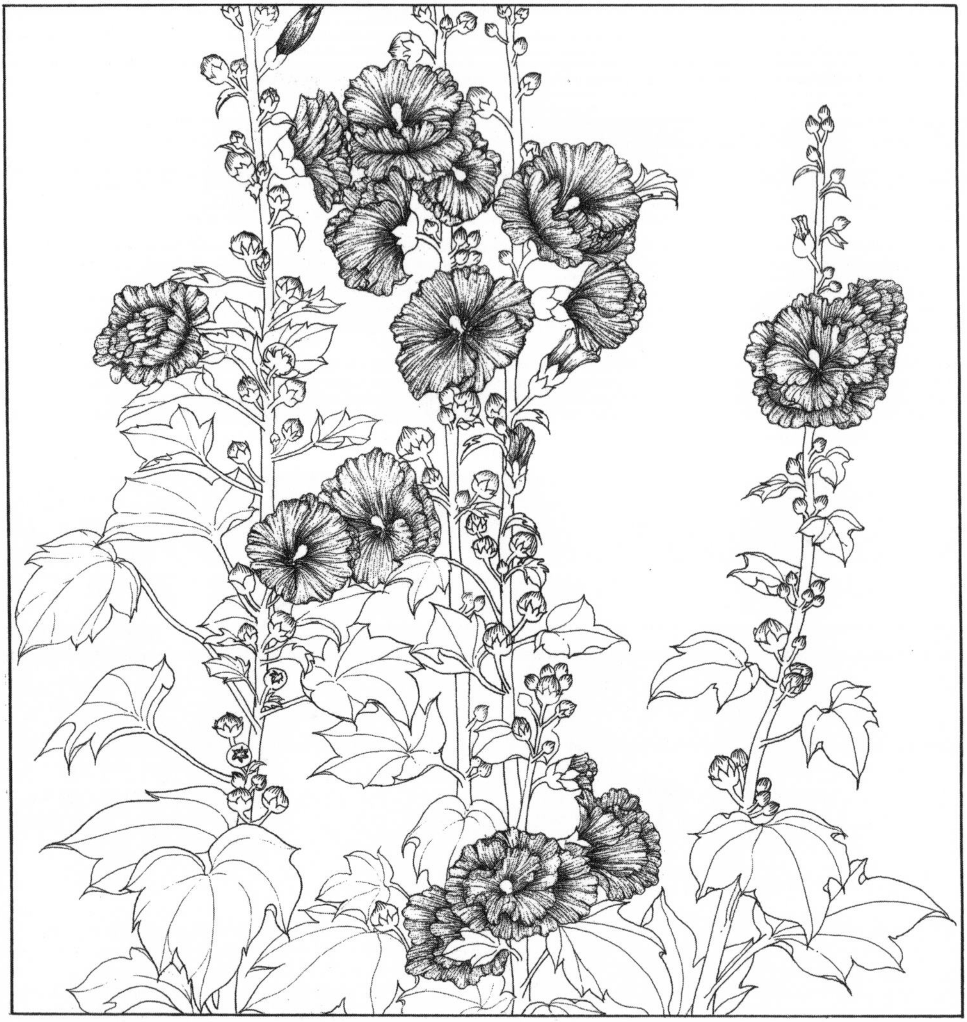

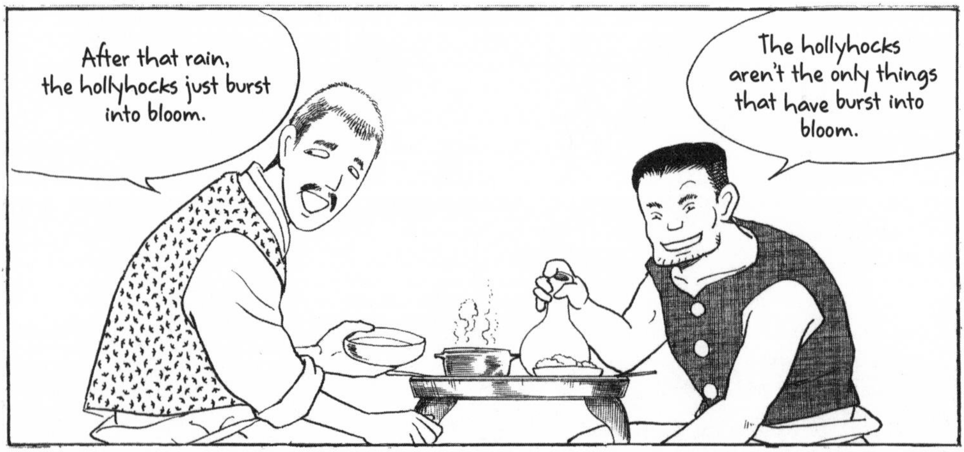
After that rain, the hollyhocks just burst into bloom.
The hollyhocks aren't the only things that have burst into bloom.

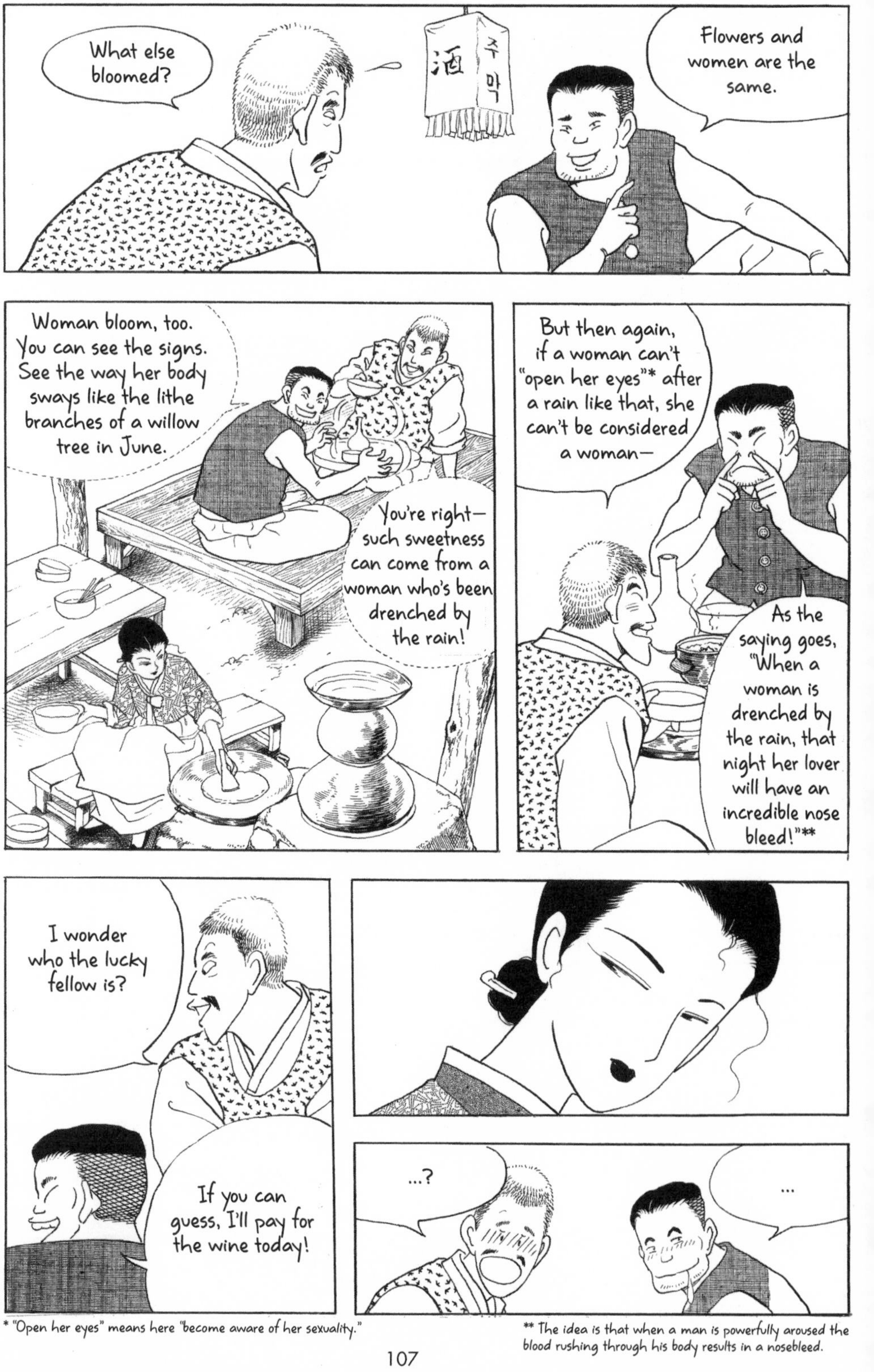
What else bloomed?
酒
주막
Flowers and women are the same.
Woman bloom, too. You can see the signs. See the way her body sways like the lithe branches of a willow tree in June.
You're right— such sweetness can come from a woman who's been drenched by the rain!
But then again, if a woman can't "open her eyes"* after a rain like that, she can't be considered a woman—
As the saying goes, "When a woman is drenched by the rain, that night her lover will have an incredible nose bleed!"**
I wonder who the lucky fellow is?
If you can guess, I'll pay for the wine today!
...?
...

* "Open her eyes" means here "become aware of her sexuality."

** The idea is that when a man is powerfully aroused the blood rushing through his body results in a nosebleed.

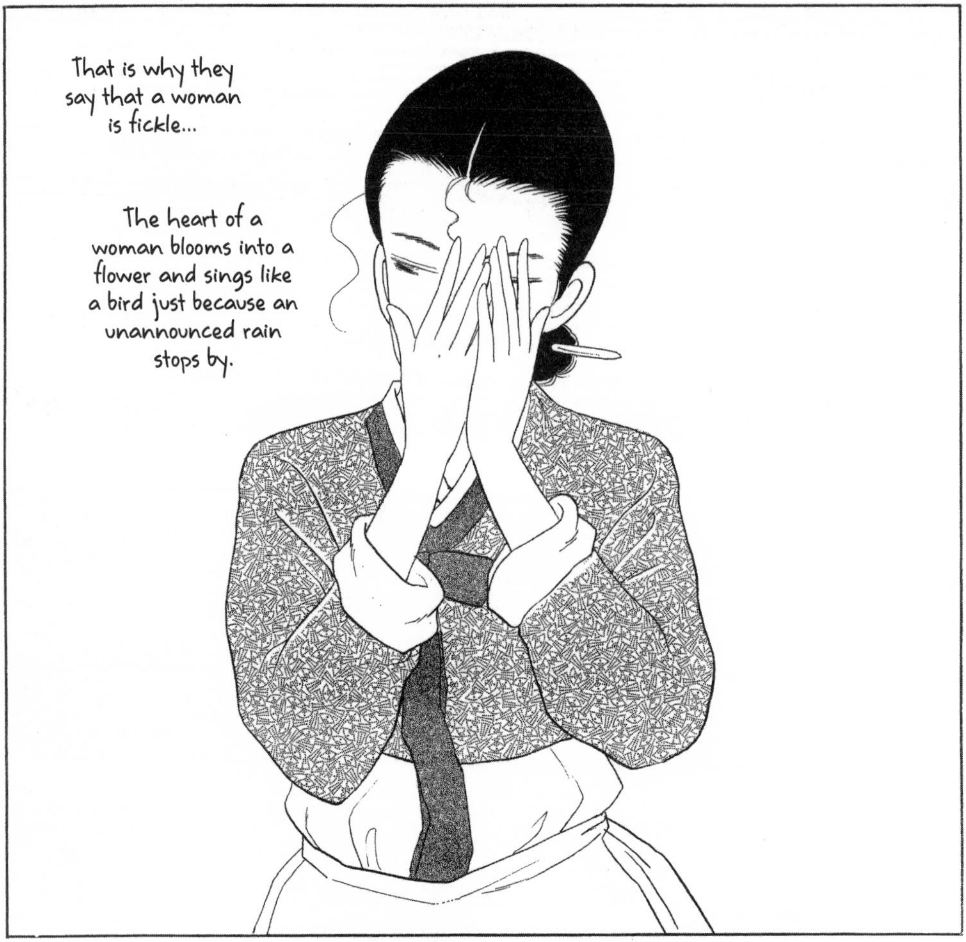
That is why they say that a woman is fickle...
The heart of a woman blooms into a flower and sings like a bird just because an unannounced rain stops by.

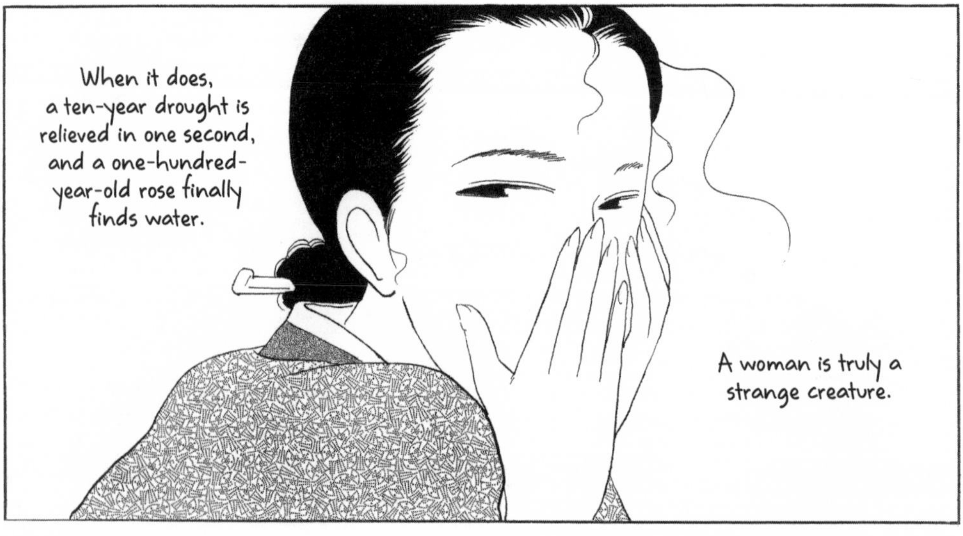
When it does, a ten-year drought is relieved in one second, and a one-hundred-year-old rose finally finds water.
A woman is truly a strange creature.

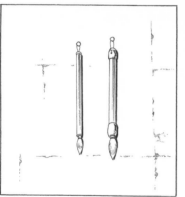

Mom, why did the picture man spend the night here?

He travels from place to place, and since he has no home, he spends his nights in taverns. Why else would a traveling salesman spend the night?

Well, he came to get his brush back, but instead he left another one, so...

Maybe this time he plans to be back twice as soon.

Then does that mean that you're going to plant twice as many gourd vines this time?

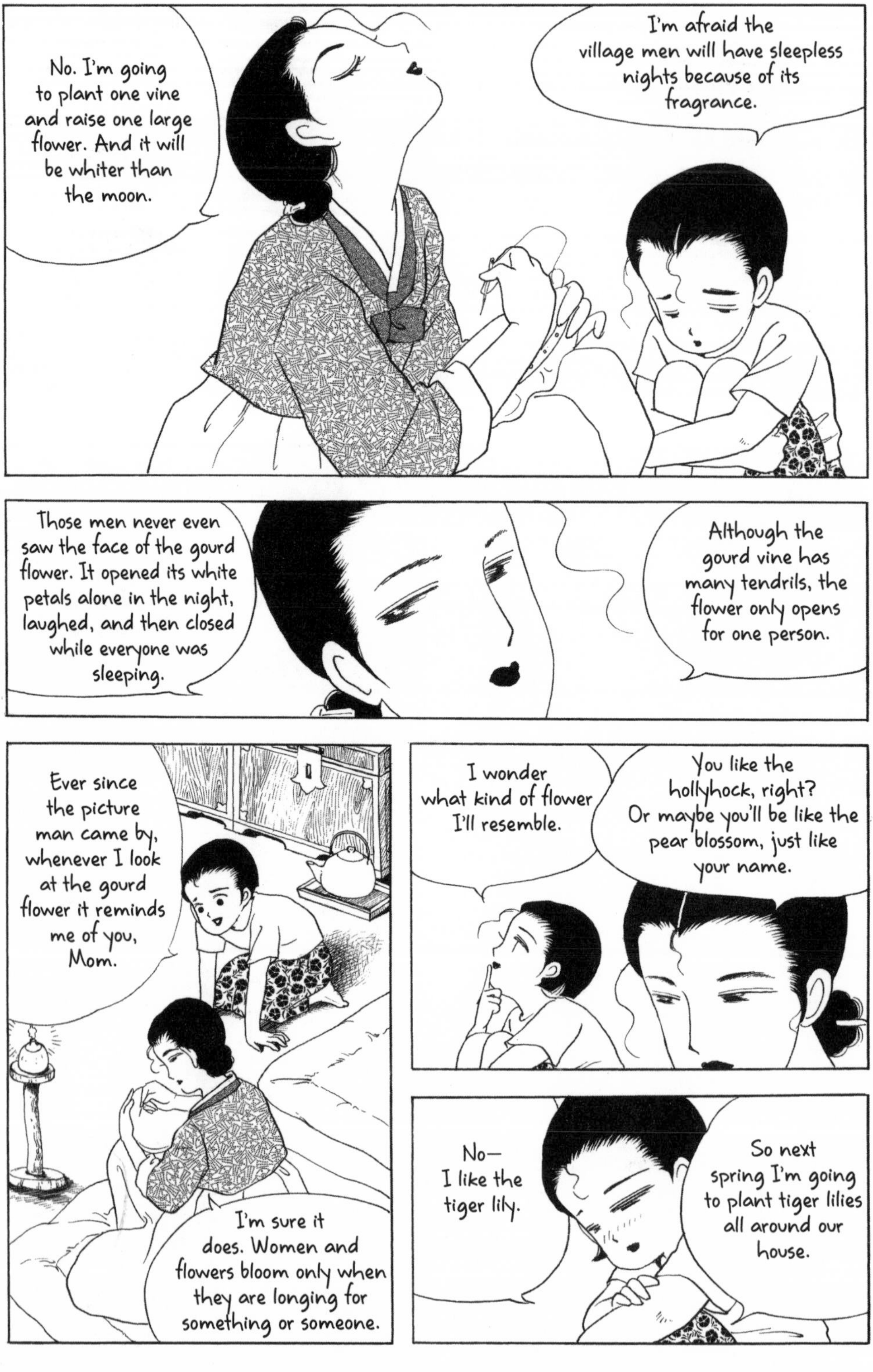
No. I'm going to plant one vine and raise one large flower. And it will be whiter than the moon.
I'm afraid the village men will have sleepless nights because of its fragrance.
Those men never even saw the face of the gourd flower. It opened its white petals alone in the night, laughed, and then closed while everyone was sleeping.
Although the gourd vine has many tendrils, the flower only opens for one person.
Ever since the picture man came by, whenever I look at the gourd flower it reminds me of you, Mom.
I'm sure it does. Women and flowers bloom only when they are longing for something or someone.
I wonder what kind of flower I'll resemble.
You like the hollyhock, right? Or maybe you'll be like the pear blossom, just like your name.
No— I like the tiger lily.
So next spring I'm going to plant tiger lilies all around our house.

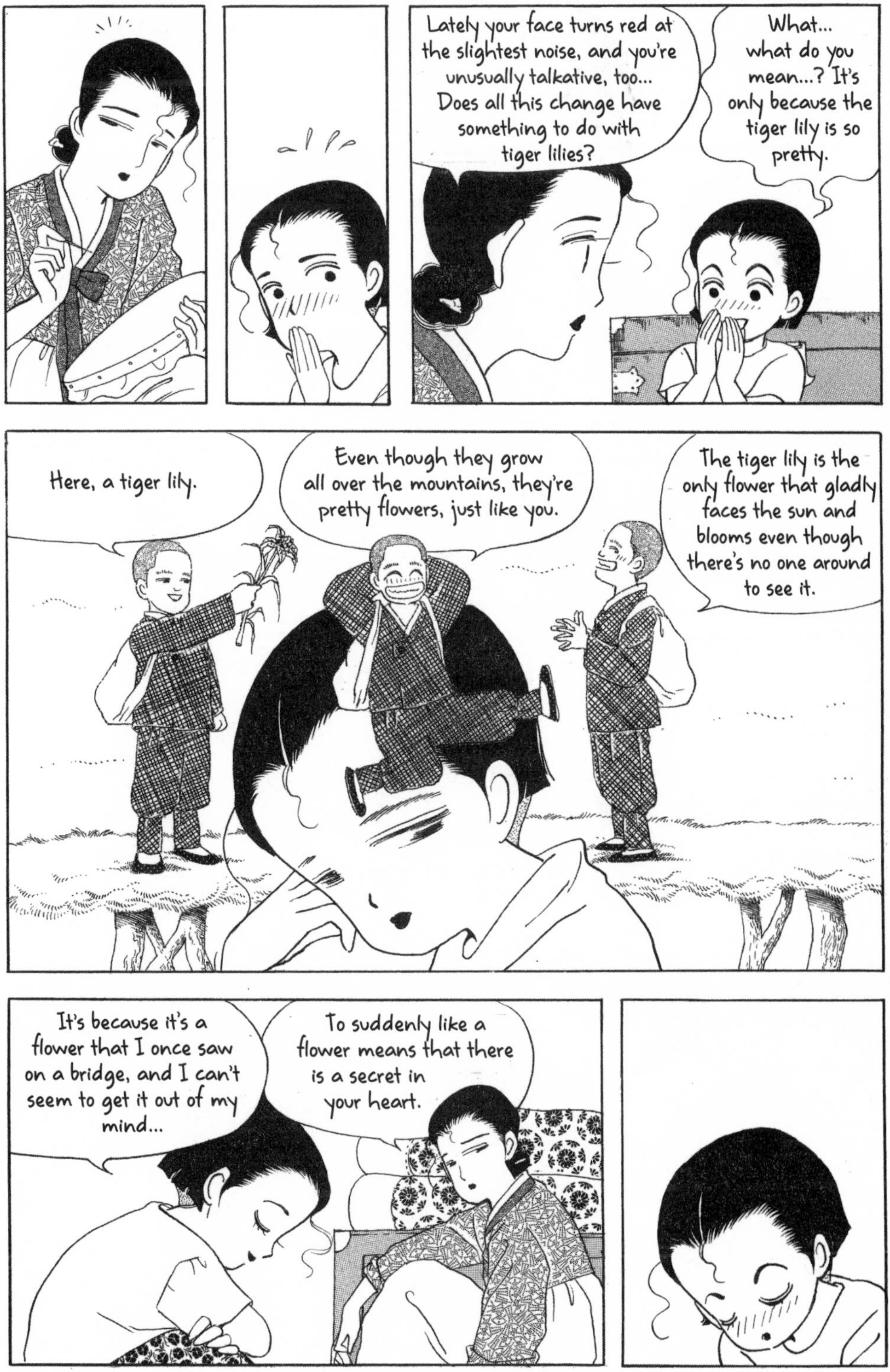
Lately your face turns red at the slightest noise, and you're unusually talkative, too... Does all this change have something to do with tiger lilies?
What... what do you mean...? It's only because the tiger lily is so pretty.
Here, a tiger lily.
Even though they grow all over the mountains, they're pretty flowers, just like you.
The tiger lily is the only flower that gladly faces the sun and blooms even though there's no one around to see it.
It's because it's a flower that I once saw on a bridge, and I can't seem to get it out of my mind...
To suddenly like a flower means that there is a secret in your heart.

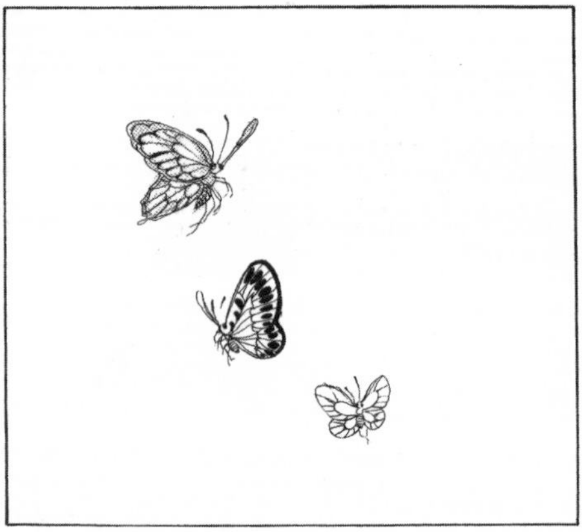

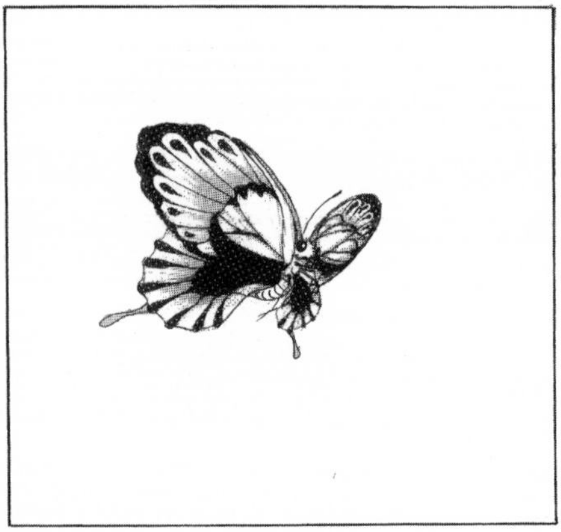

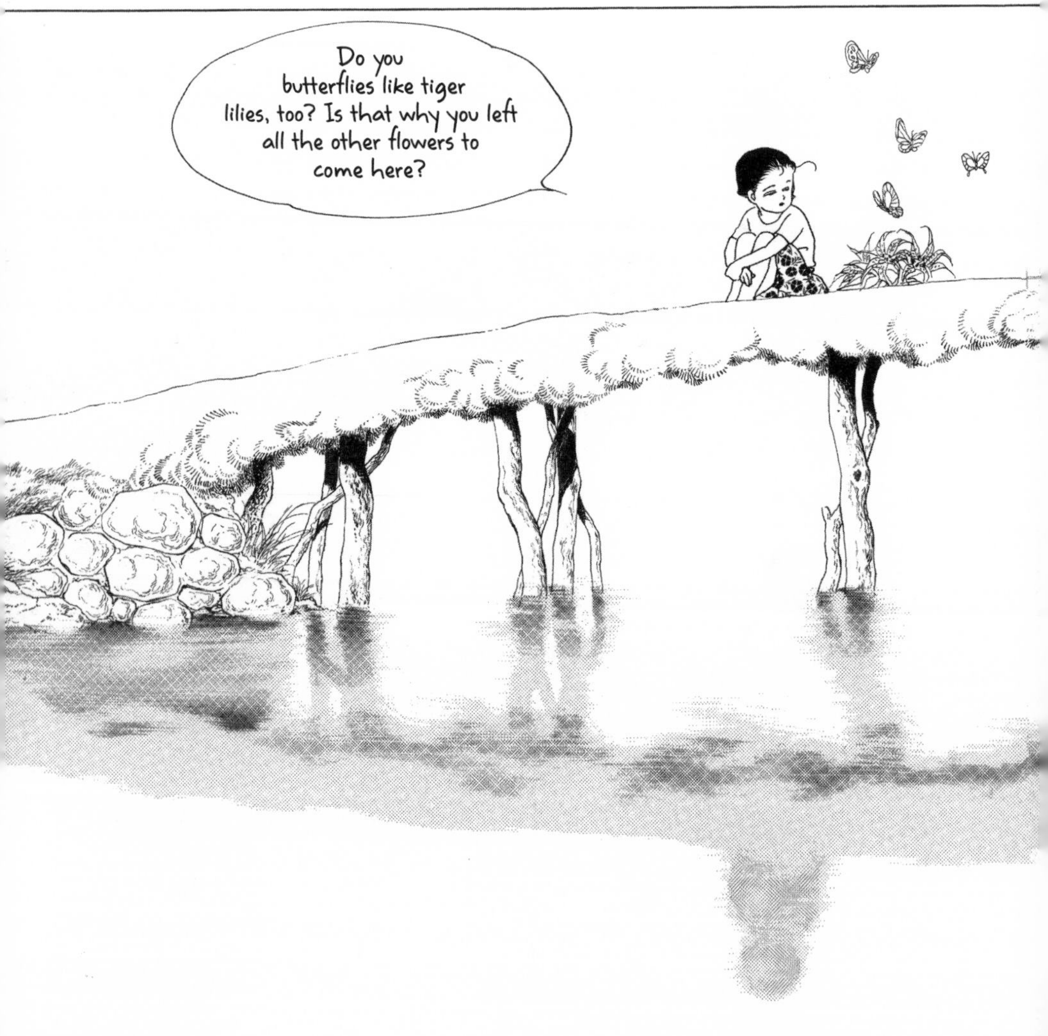
Do you butterflies like tiger lilies, too? Is that why you left all the other flowers to come here?

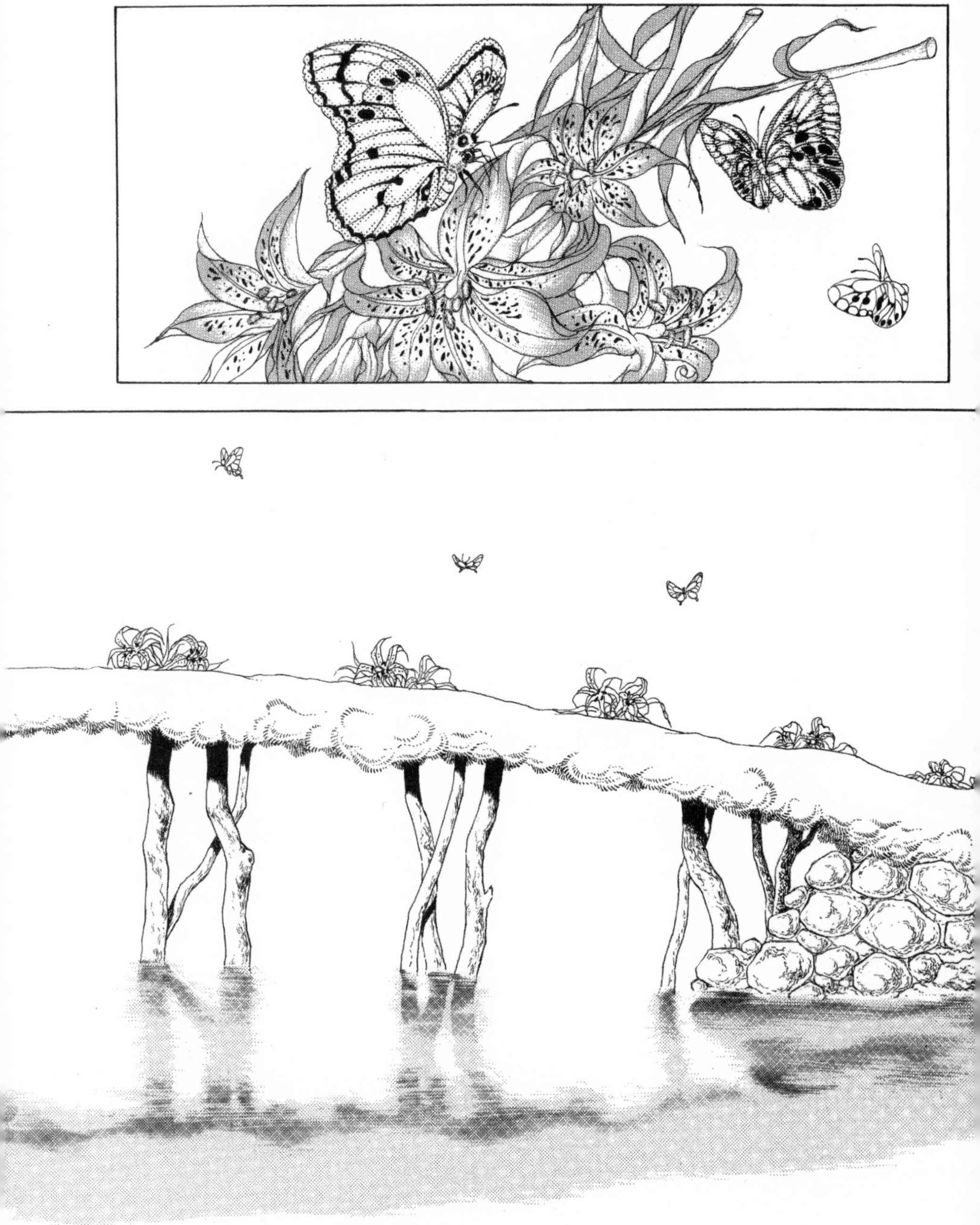

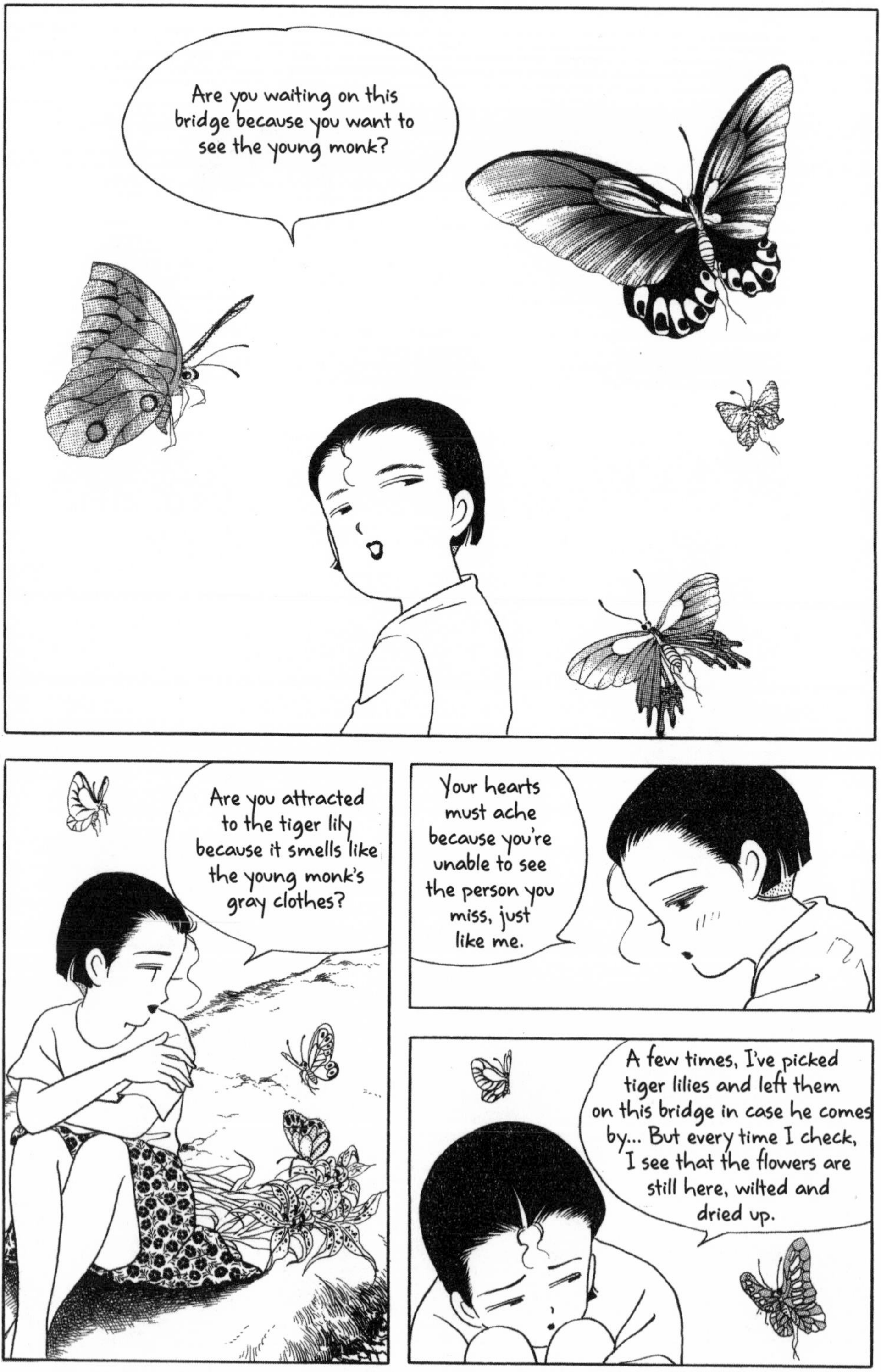
Are you waiting on this bridge because you want to see the young monk?
Are you attracted to the tiger lily because it smells like the young monk's gray clothes?
Your hearts must ache because you're unable to see the person you miss, just like me.
A few times, I've picked tiger lilies and left them on this bridge in case he comes by... But every time I check, I see that the flowers are still here, wilted and dried up.

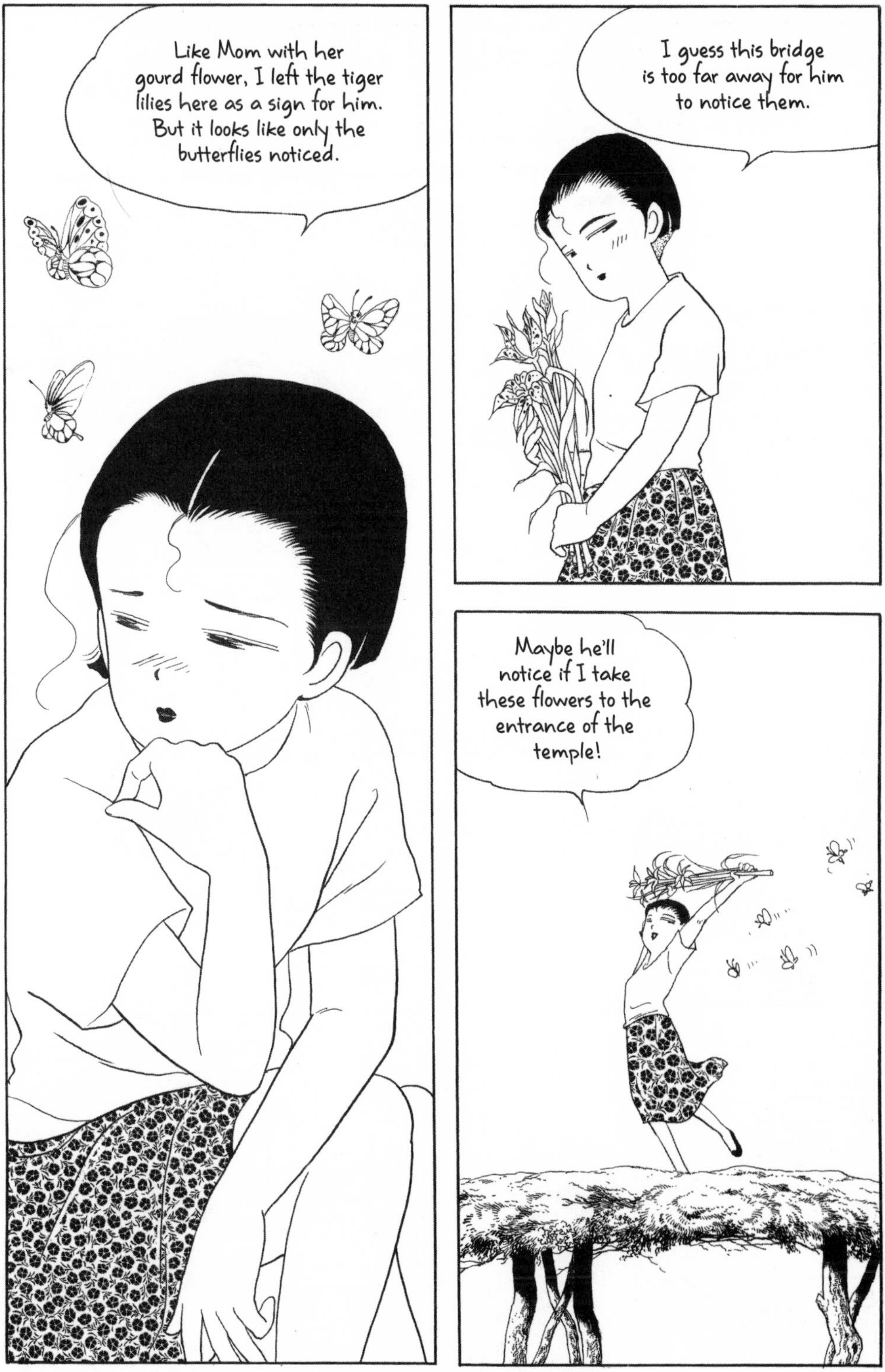
Like Mom with her gourd flower, I left the tiger lilies here as a sign for him. But it looks like only the butterflies noticed.
I guess this bridge is too far away for him to notice them.
Maybe he'll notice if I take these flowers to the entrance of the temple!

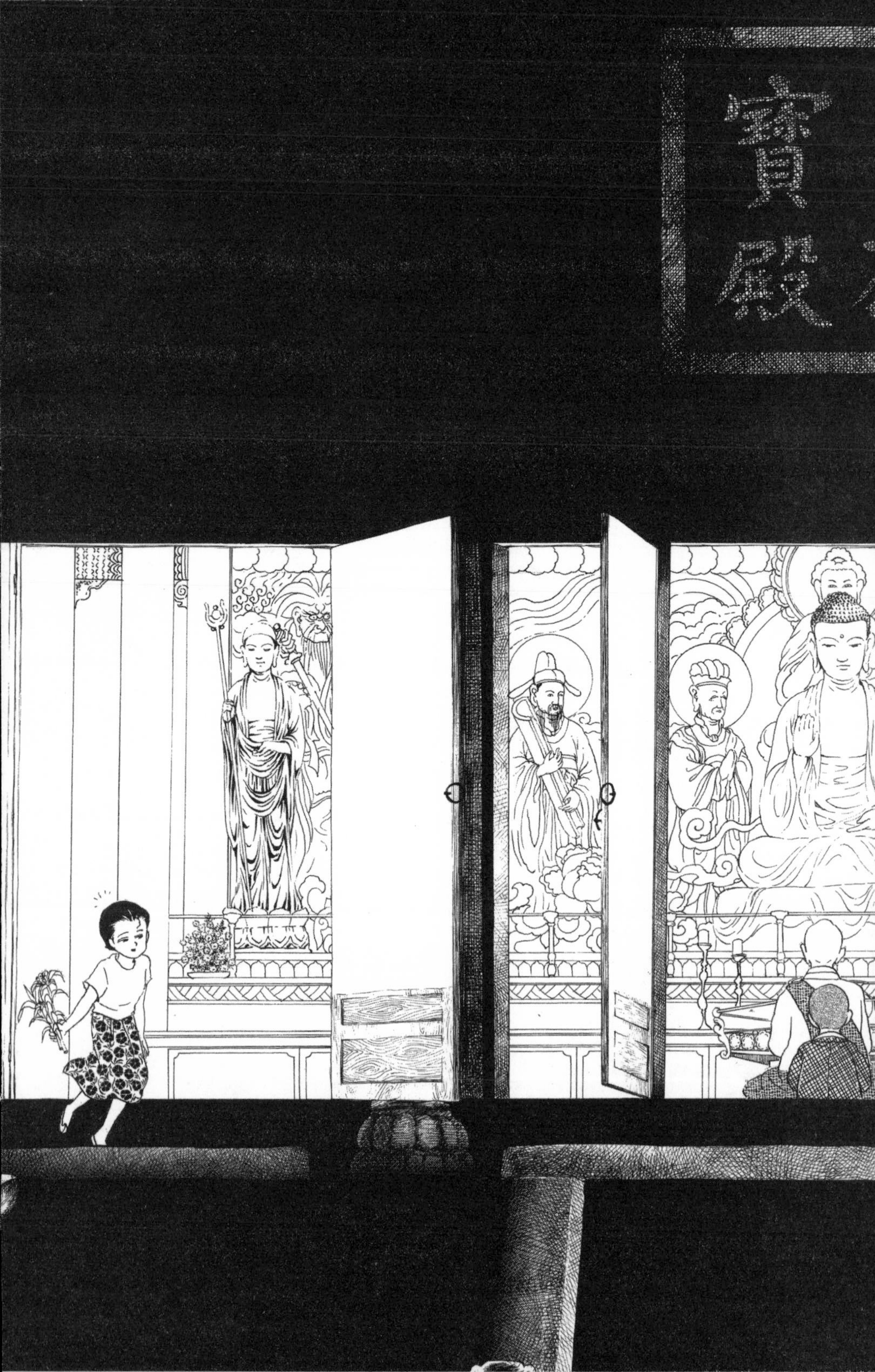
寶殿

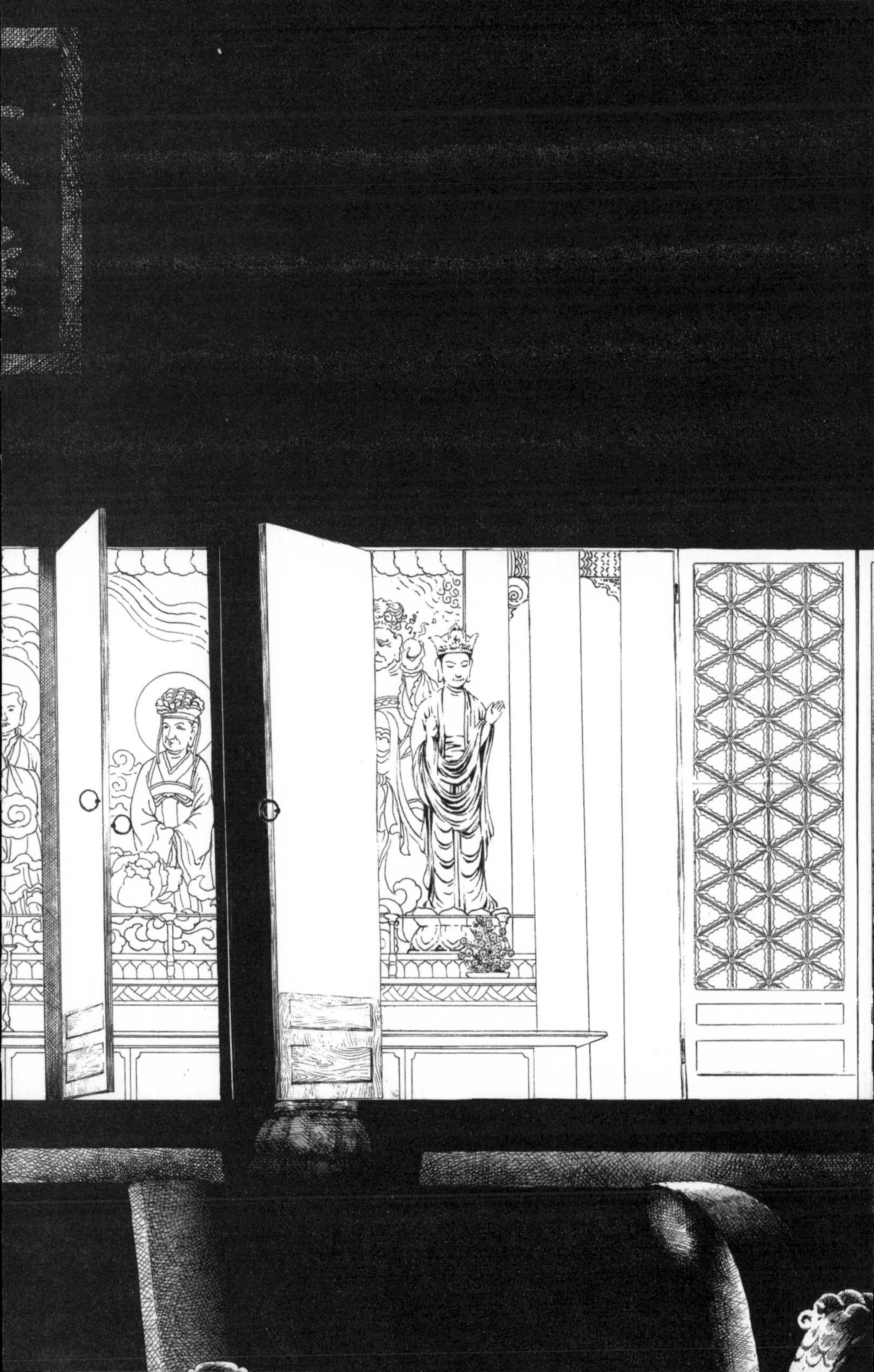

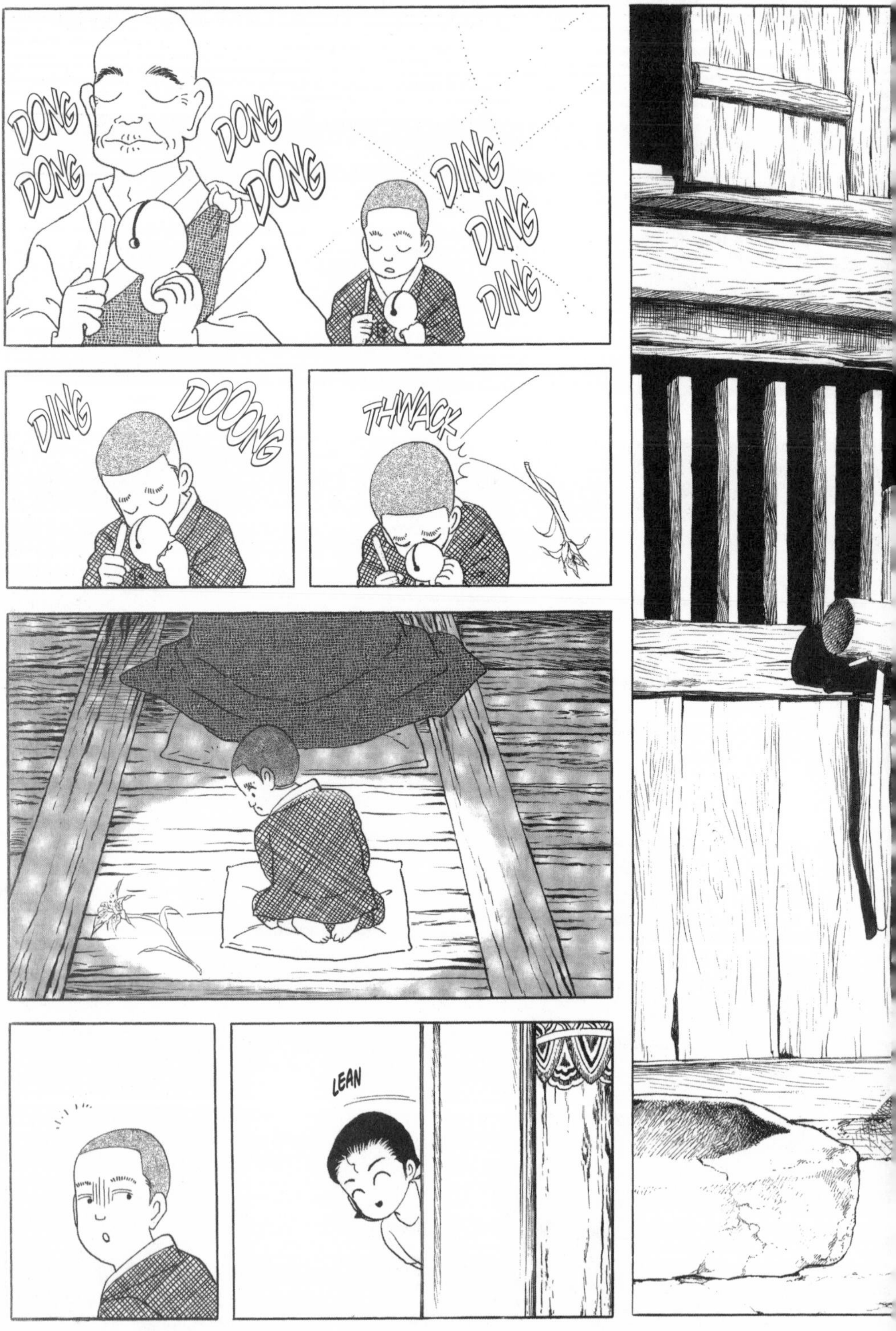
DONG
DONG
DONG
DONG
DING
DING
DING
DING
DOOONG
THWACK
LEAN

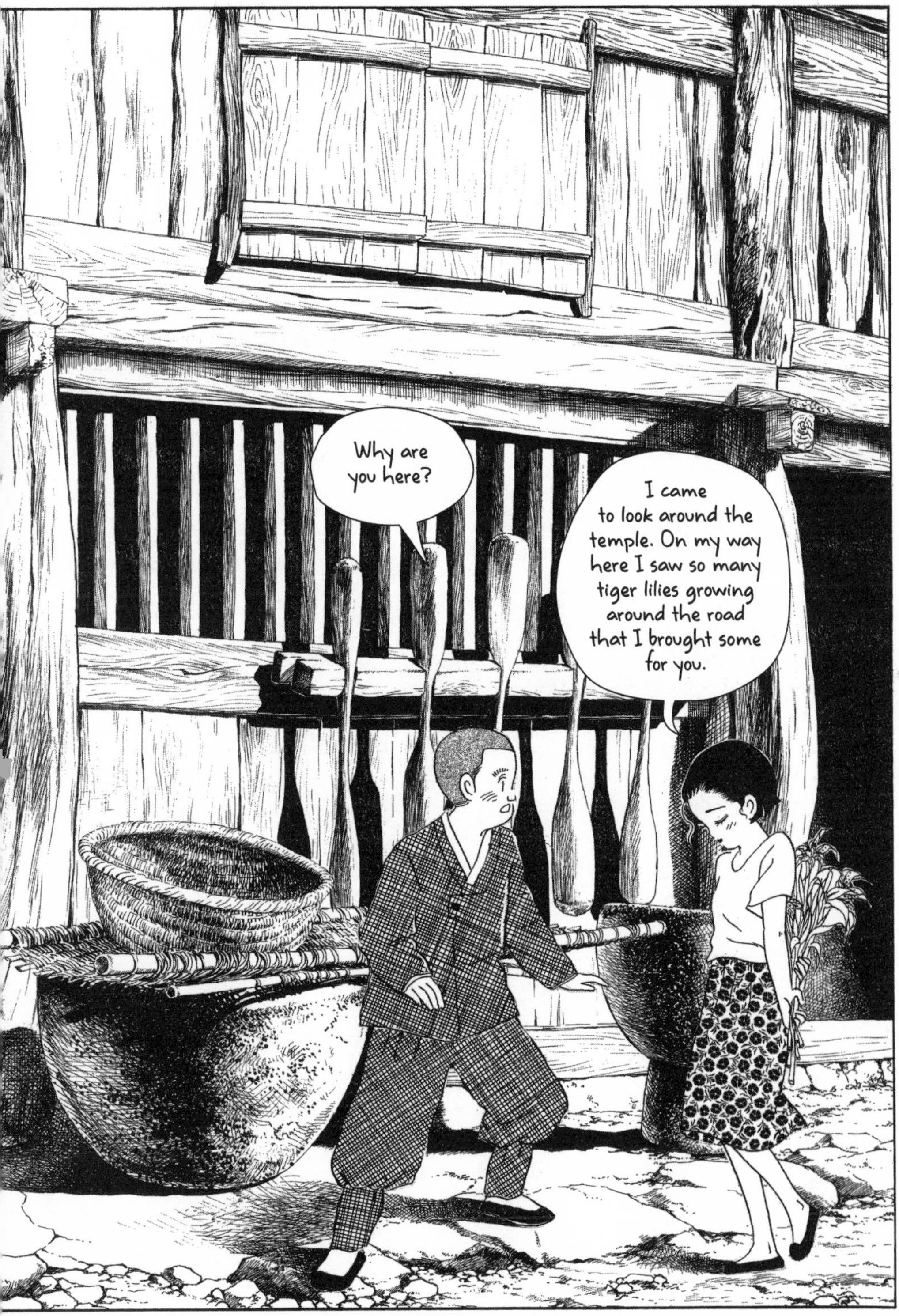
Why are you here?
I came to look around the temple. On my way here I saw so many tiger lilies growing around the road that I brought some for you.

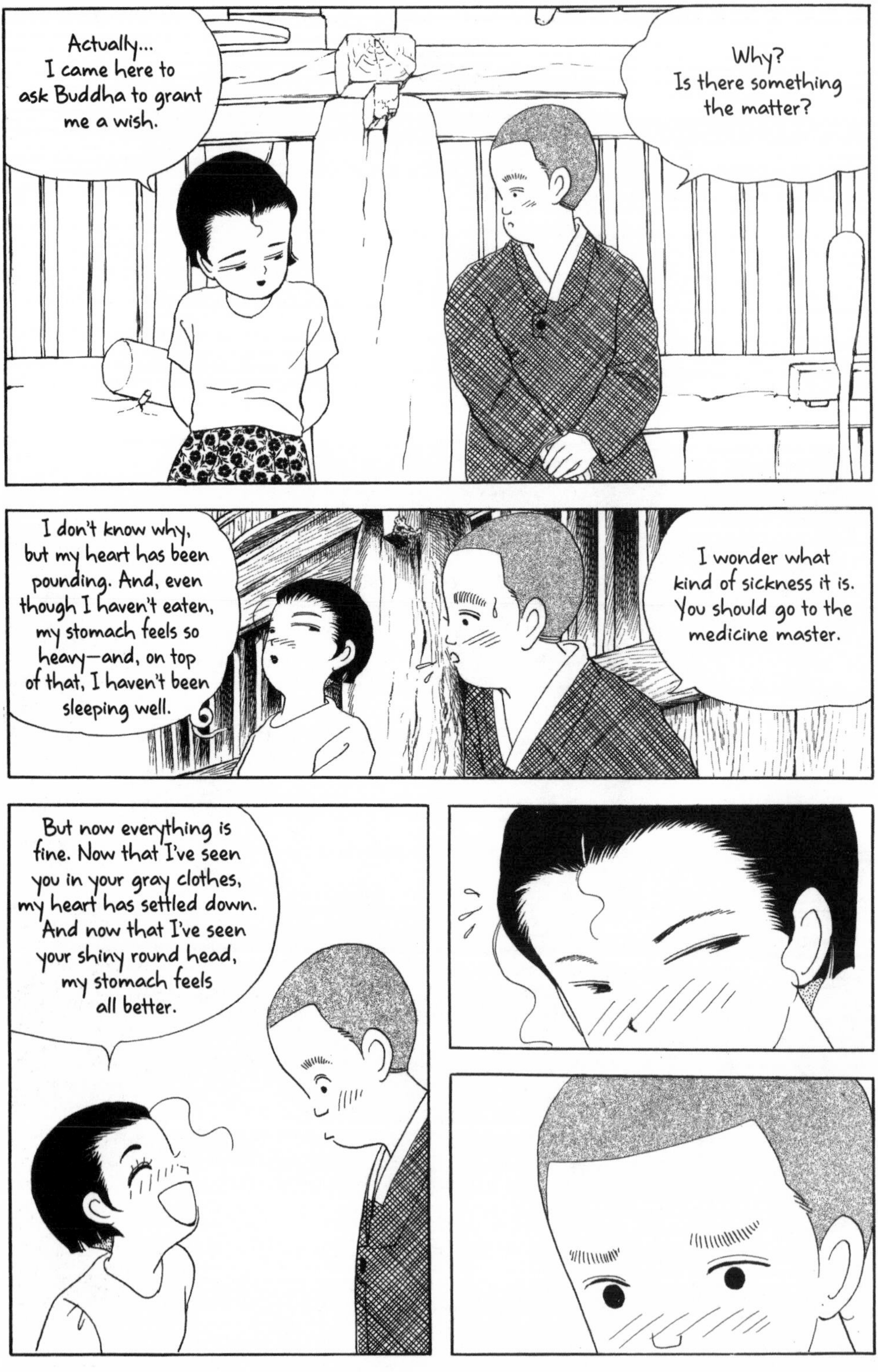
Actually...
I came here to ask Buddha to grant me a wish.
Why?
Is there something the matter?
I don't know why, but my heart has been pounding. And, even though I haven't eaten, my stomach feels so heavy—and, on top of that, I haven't been sleeping well.
I wonder what kind of sickness it is. You should go to the medicine master.
But now everything is fine. Now that I've seen you in your gray clothes, my heart has settled down. And now that I've seen your shiny round head, my stomach feels all better.

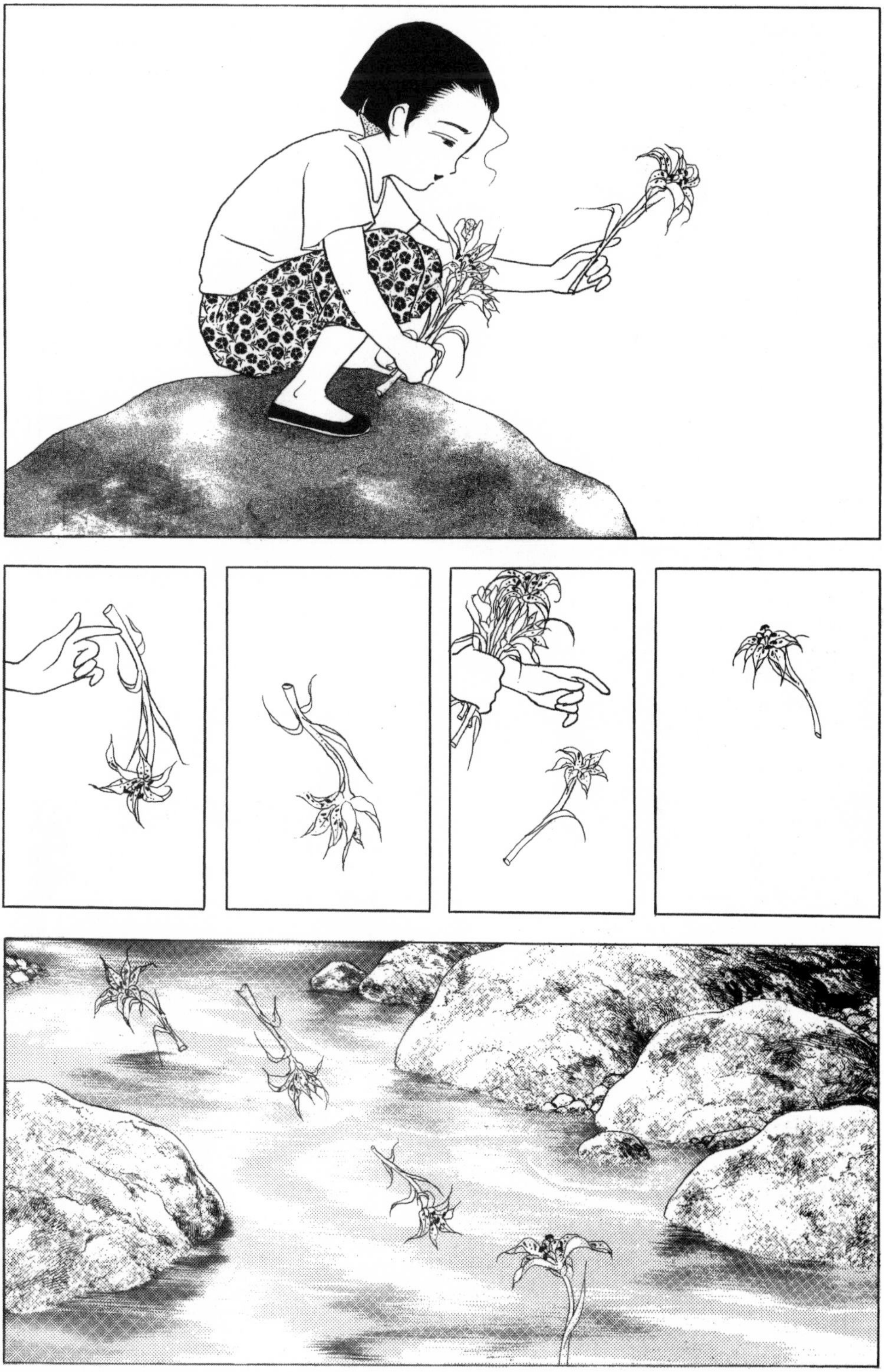

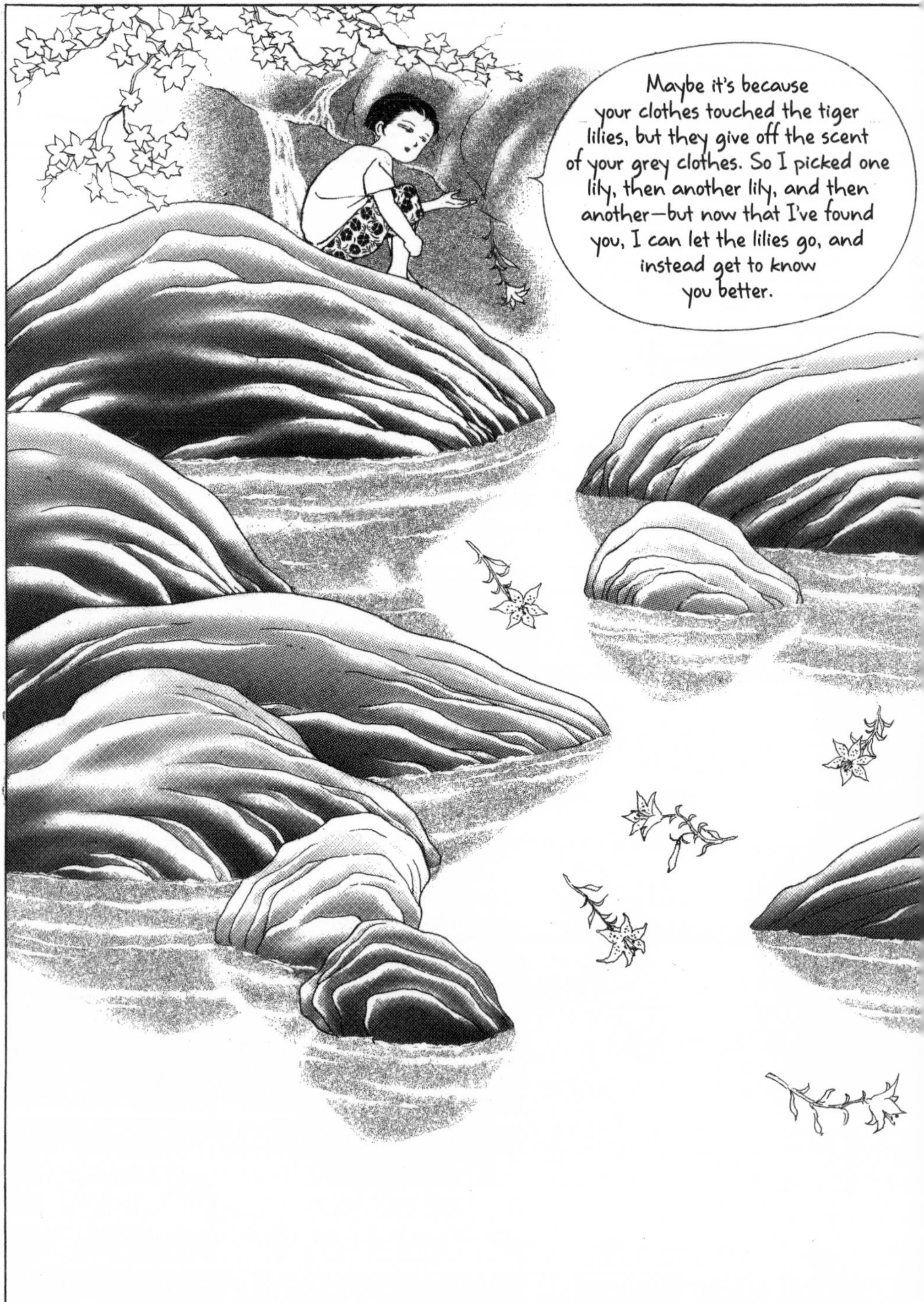
Maybe it's because your clothes touched the tiger lilies, but they give off the scent of your grey clothes. So I picked one lily, then another lily, and then another—but now that I've found you, I can let the lilies go, and instead get to know you better.

...Ehwa.

My name is Chung-Myung. What's yours?

Your name is prettier than a flower and you're prettier than your name.

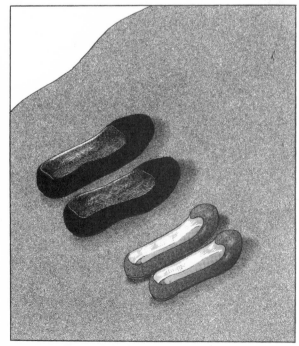

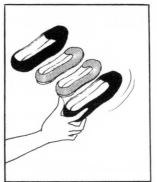

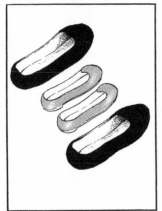

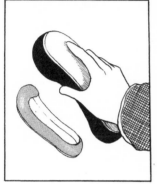

Do you want to see what this is?
What is it?
Aren't these hollyhock seeds?
Recently, I went to collect alms and I got these seeds from the Ubnae school.*
Next spring, I plan to sow these seeds all over the temple courtyard.

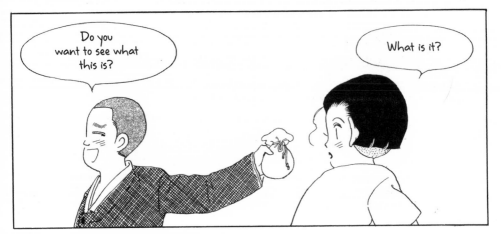

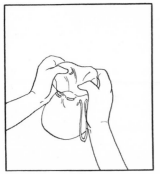

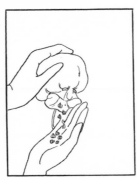

*Monks travel throughout the countryside asking for alms, which pay for their food and clothing. In return, the monks offer prayers and blessings to those who give.

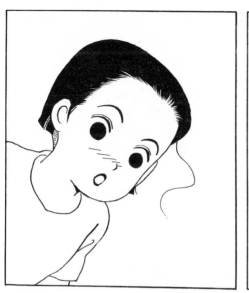

Just like you,
I've come to like the
hollyhock.

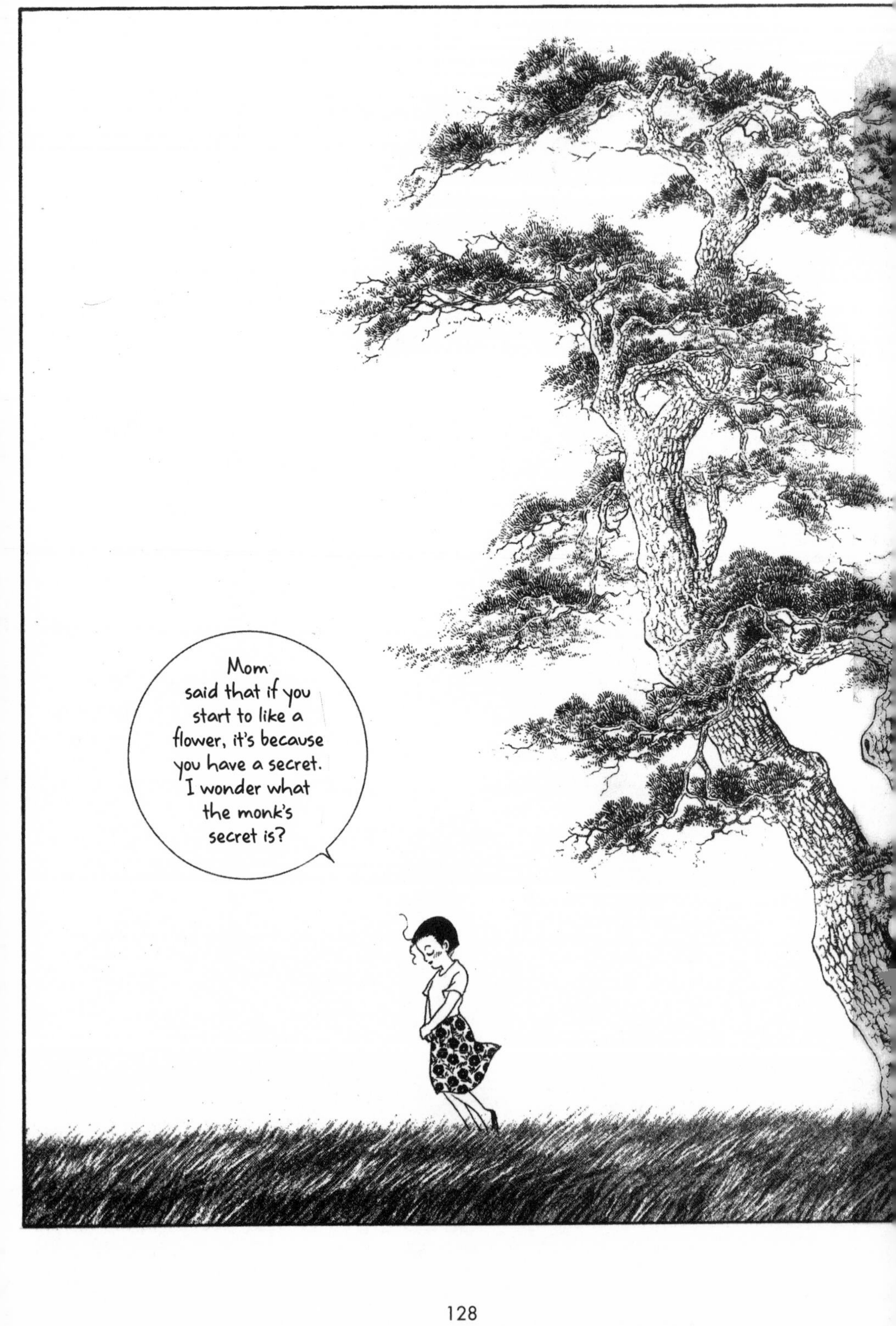
Mom said that if you start to like a flower, it's because you have a secret. I wonder what the monk's secret is?

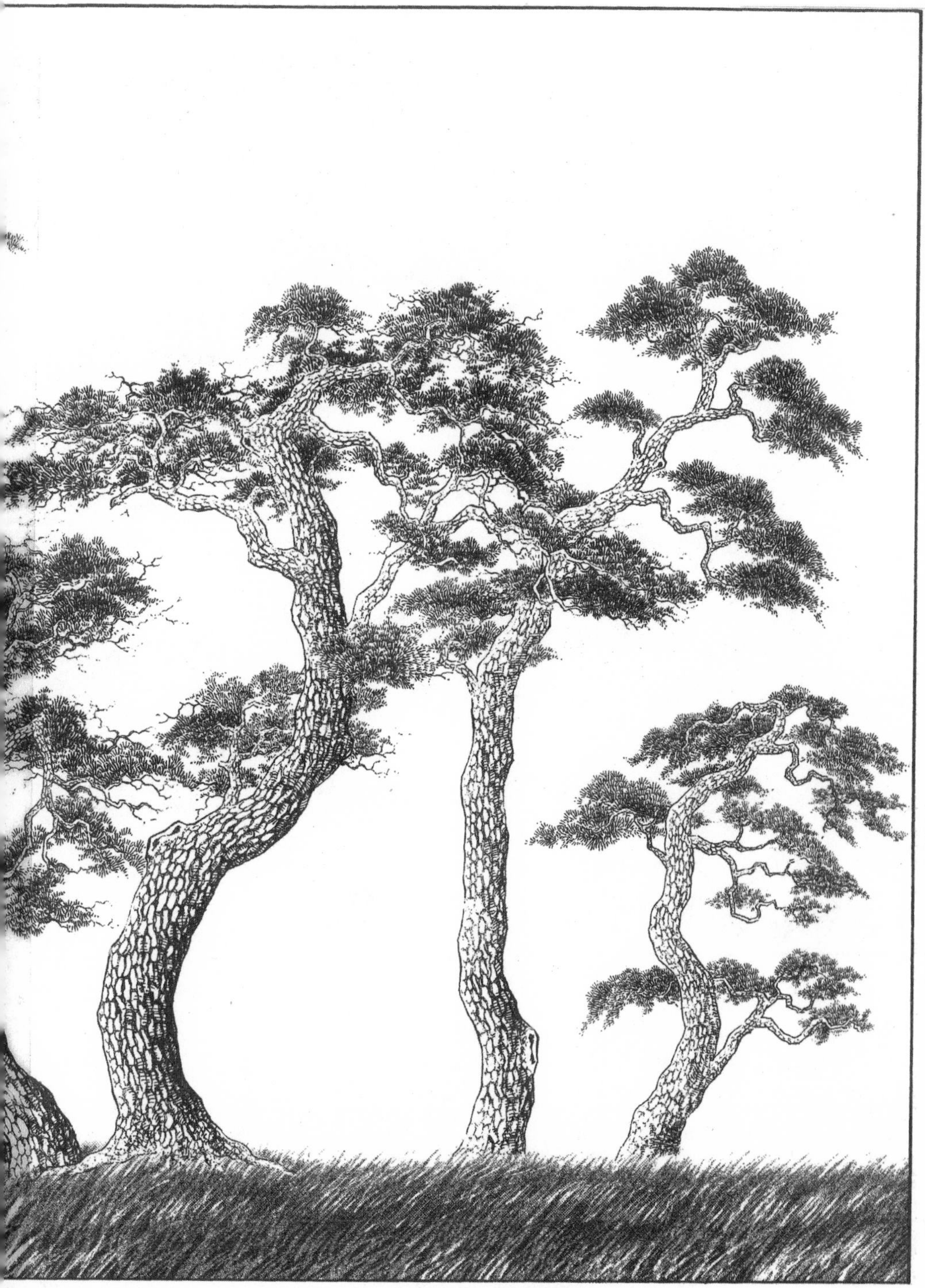

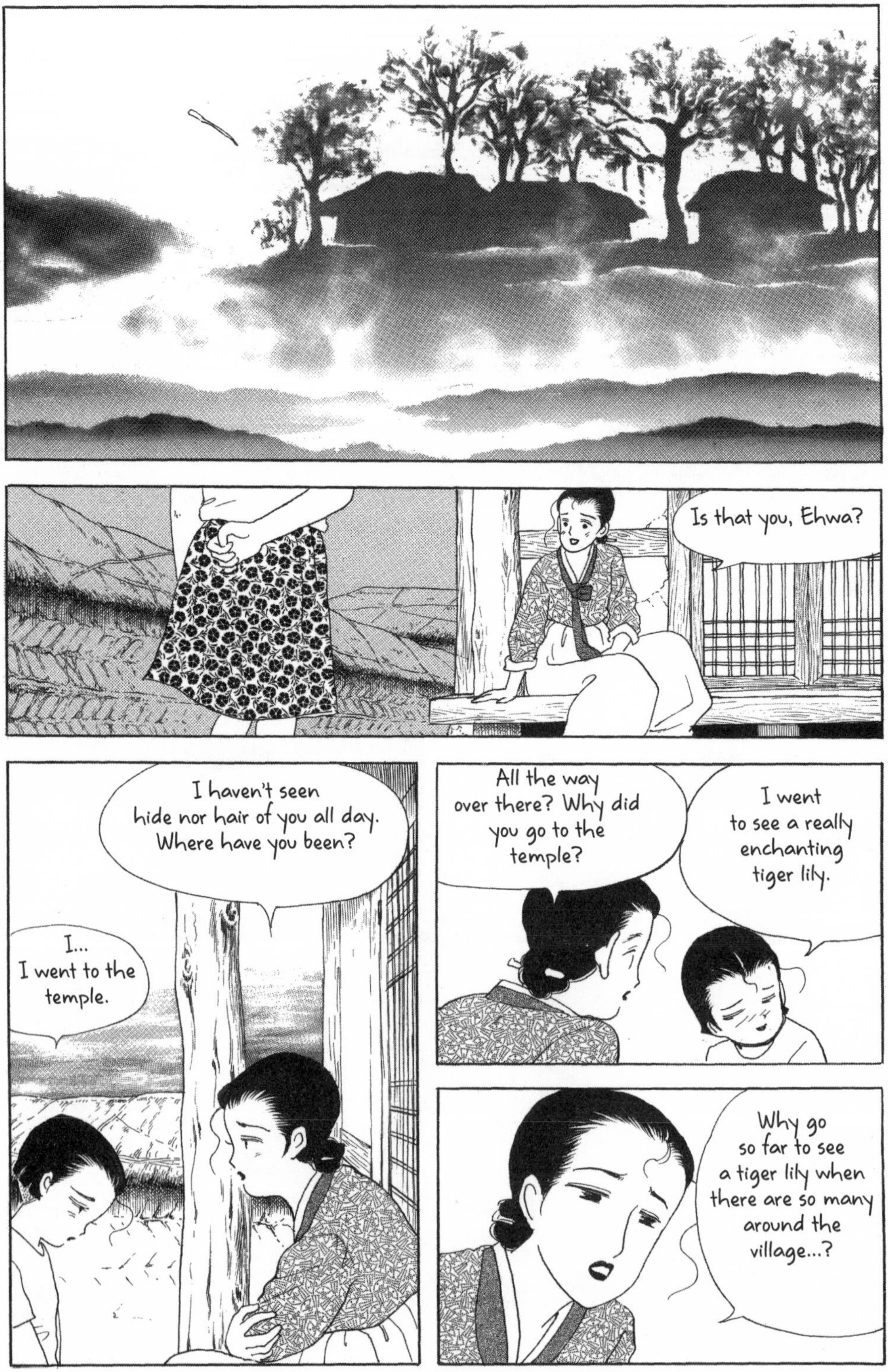
Is that you, Ehwa?
I haven't seen hide nor hair of you all day. Where have you been?
I... I went to the temple.
All the way over there? Why did you go to the temple?
I went to see a really enchanting tiger lily.
Why go so far to see a tiger lily when there are so many around the village...?

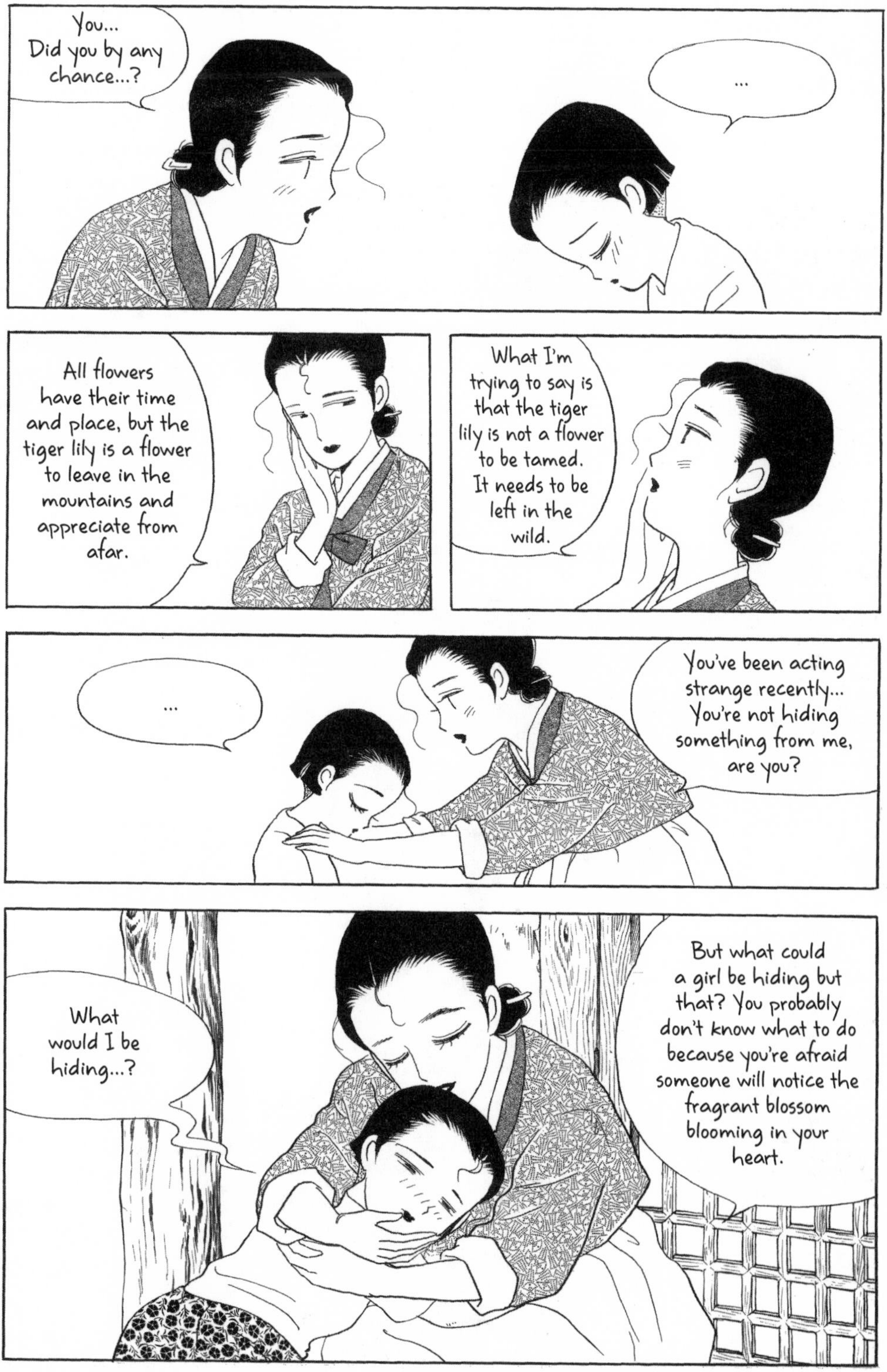
You... Did you by any chance...?
...
All flowers have their time and place, but the tiger lily is a flower to leave in the mountains and appreciate from afar.
What I'm trying to say is that the tiger lily is not a flower to be tamed. It needs to be left in the wild.
...
You've been acting strange recently... You're not hiding something from me, are you?
What would I be hiding...?
But what could a girl be hiding but that? You probably don't know what to do because you're afraid someone will notice the fragrant blossom blooming in your heart.

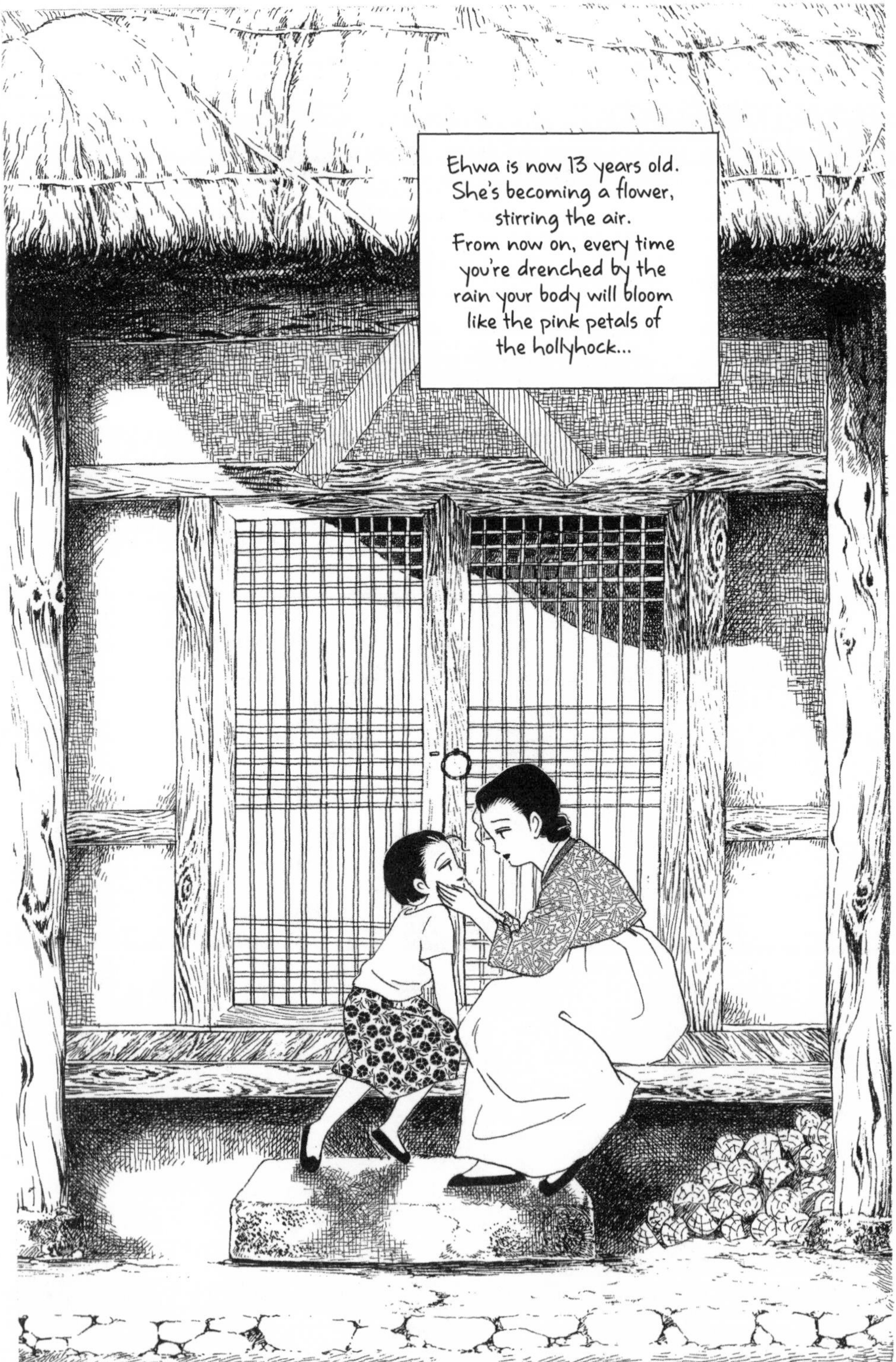
Ehwa is now 13 years old.
She's becoming a flower,
stirring the air.
From now on, every time
you're drenched by the
rain your body will bloom
like the pink petals of
the hollyhock...

Chapter Five

THE CAMELLIA SEEDS

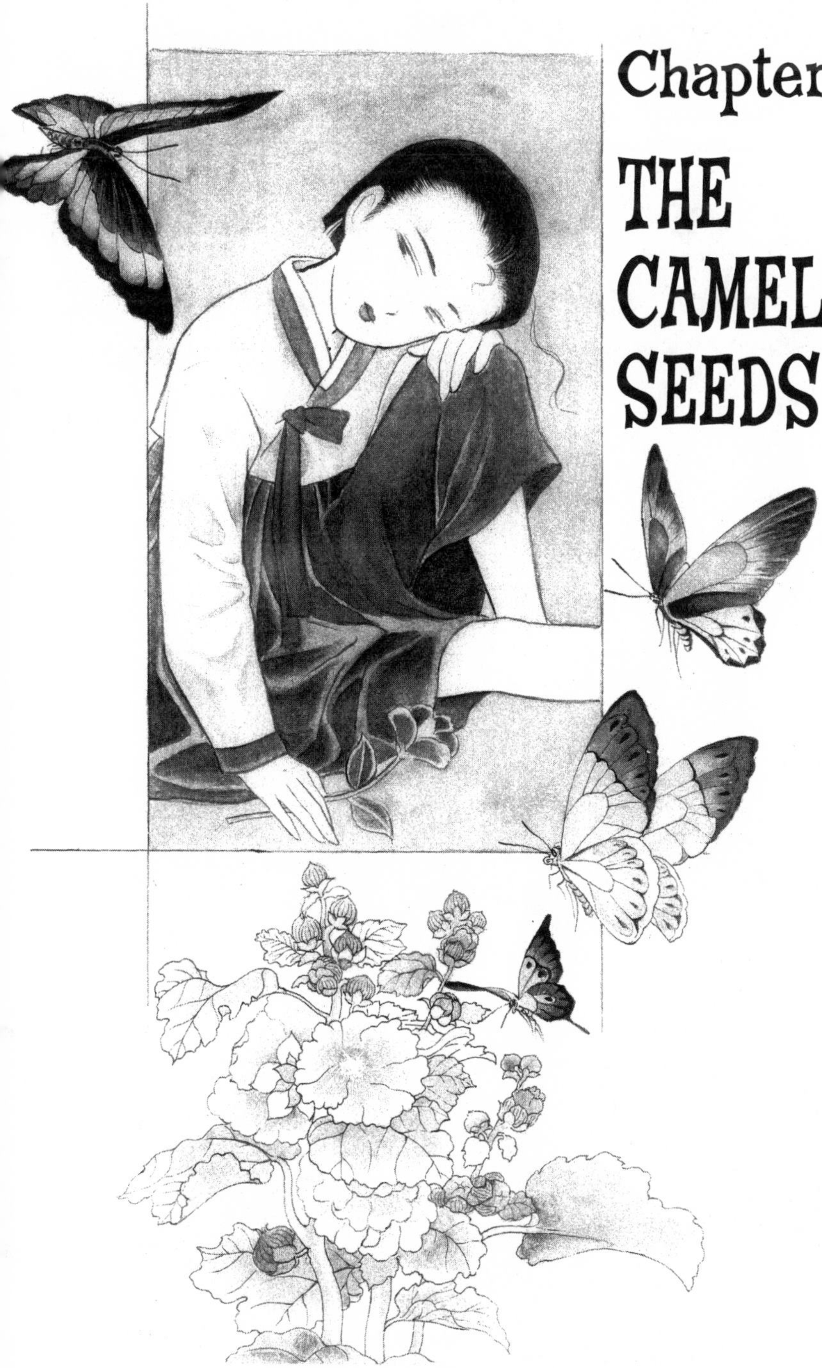

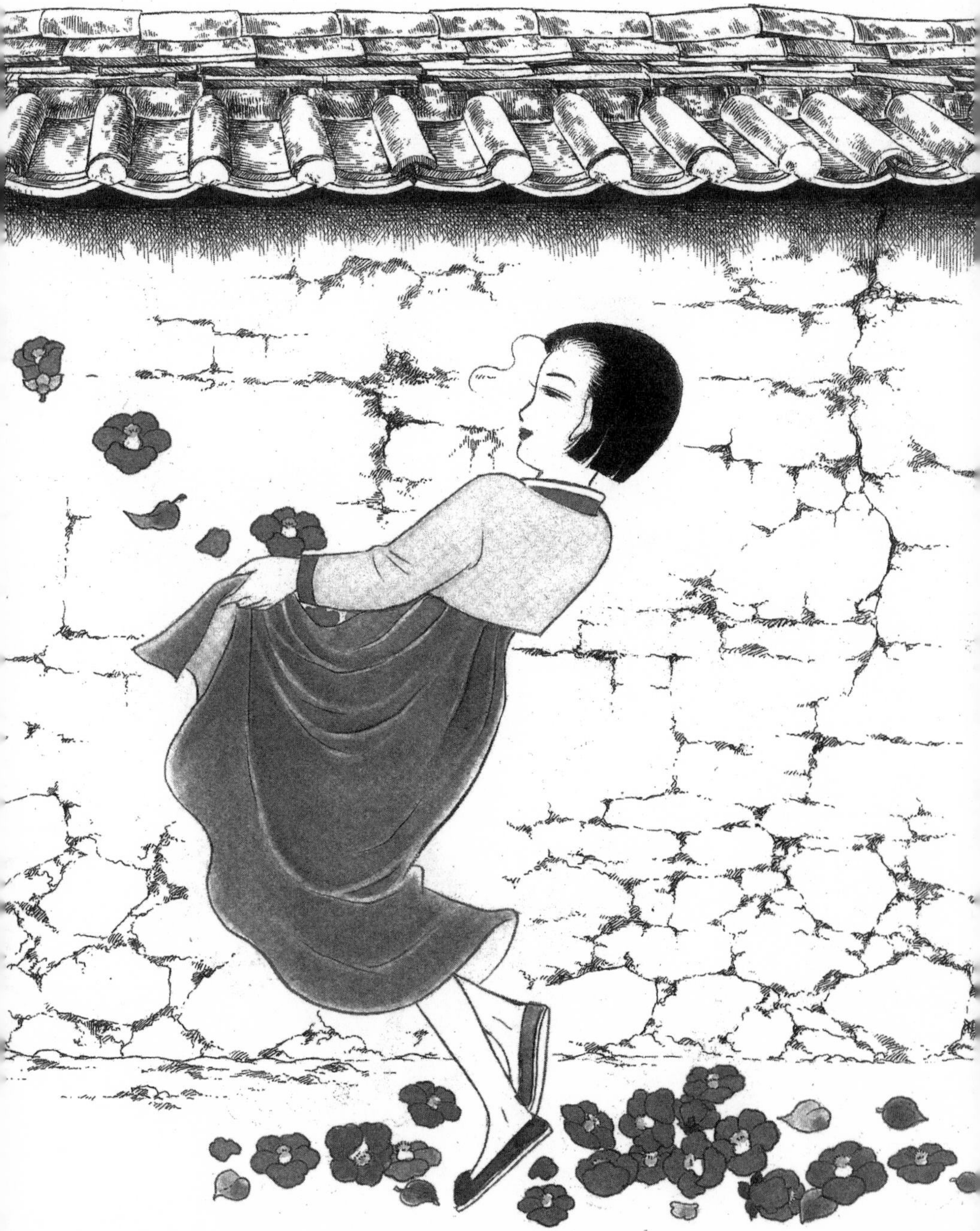

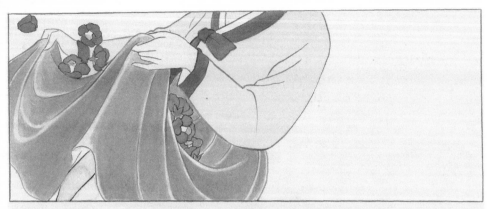

Mmmmm
Mmmmm
SPURT
?
SHUFFLE

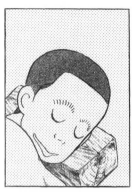

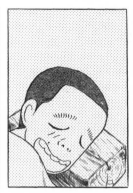

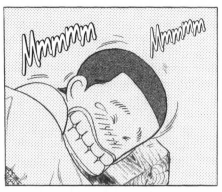

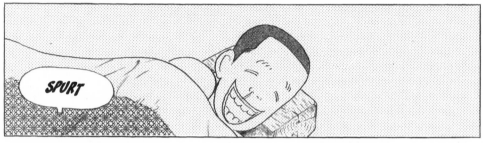

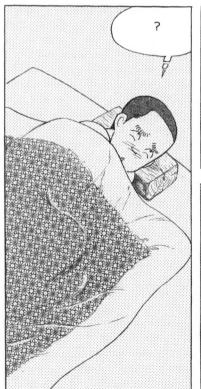

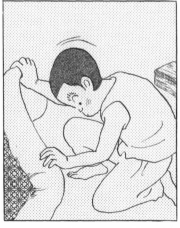

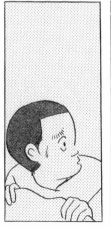

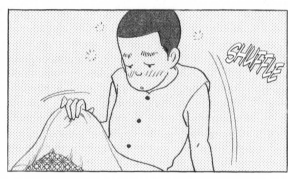

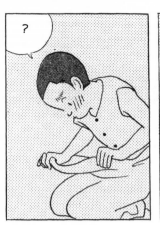
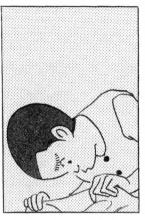

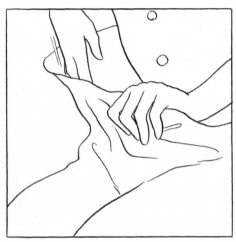
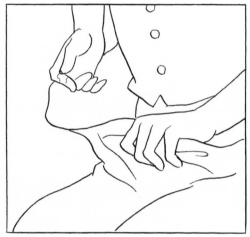
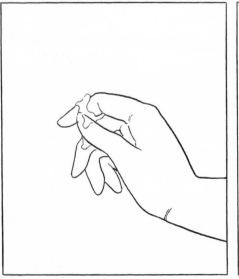
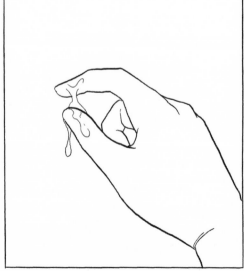

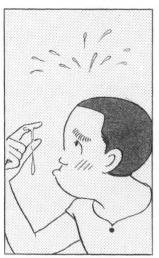
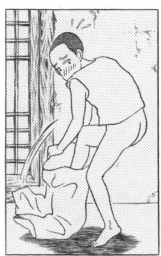
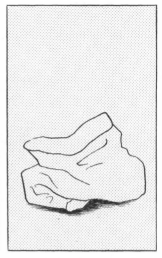

SPLASH

SPLASH

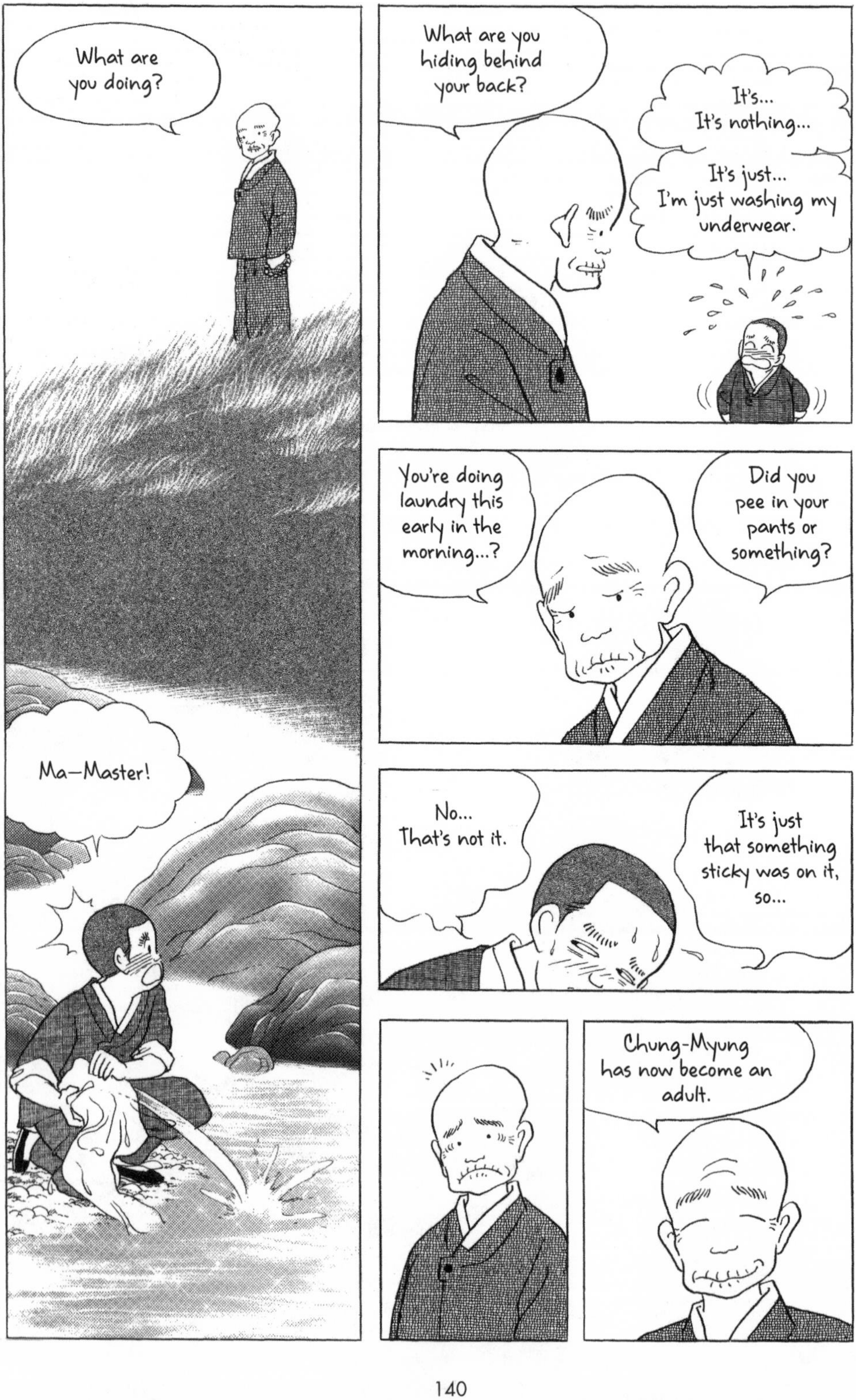
What are you doing?
Ma—Master!
What are you hiding behind your back?
It's... It's nothing...
It's just... I'm just washing my underwear.
You're doing laundry this early in the morning...?
Did you pee in your pants or something?
No... That's not it.
It's just that something sticky was on it, so...
Chung-Myung has now become an adult.

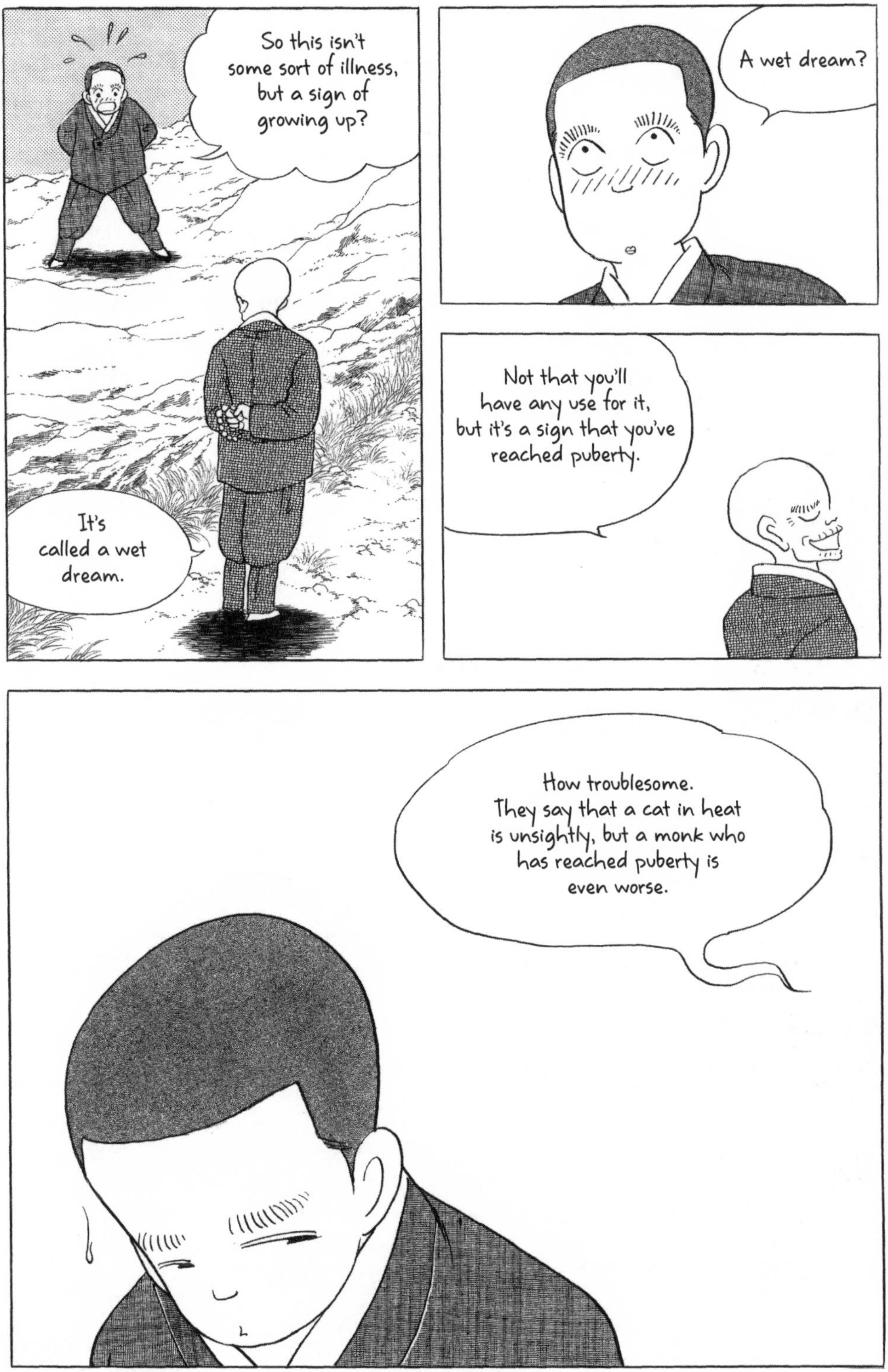
So this isn't some sort of illness, but a sign of growing up?
It's called a wet dream.
A wet dream?
Not that you'll have any use for it, but it's a sign that you've reached puberty.
How troublesome. They say that a cat in heat is unsightly, but a monk who has reached puberty is even worse.

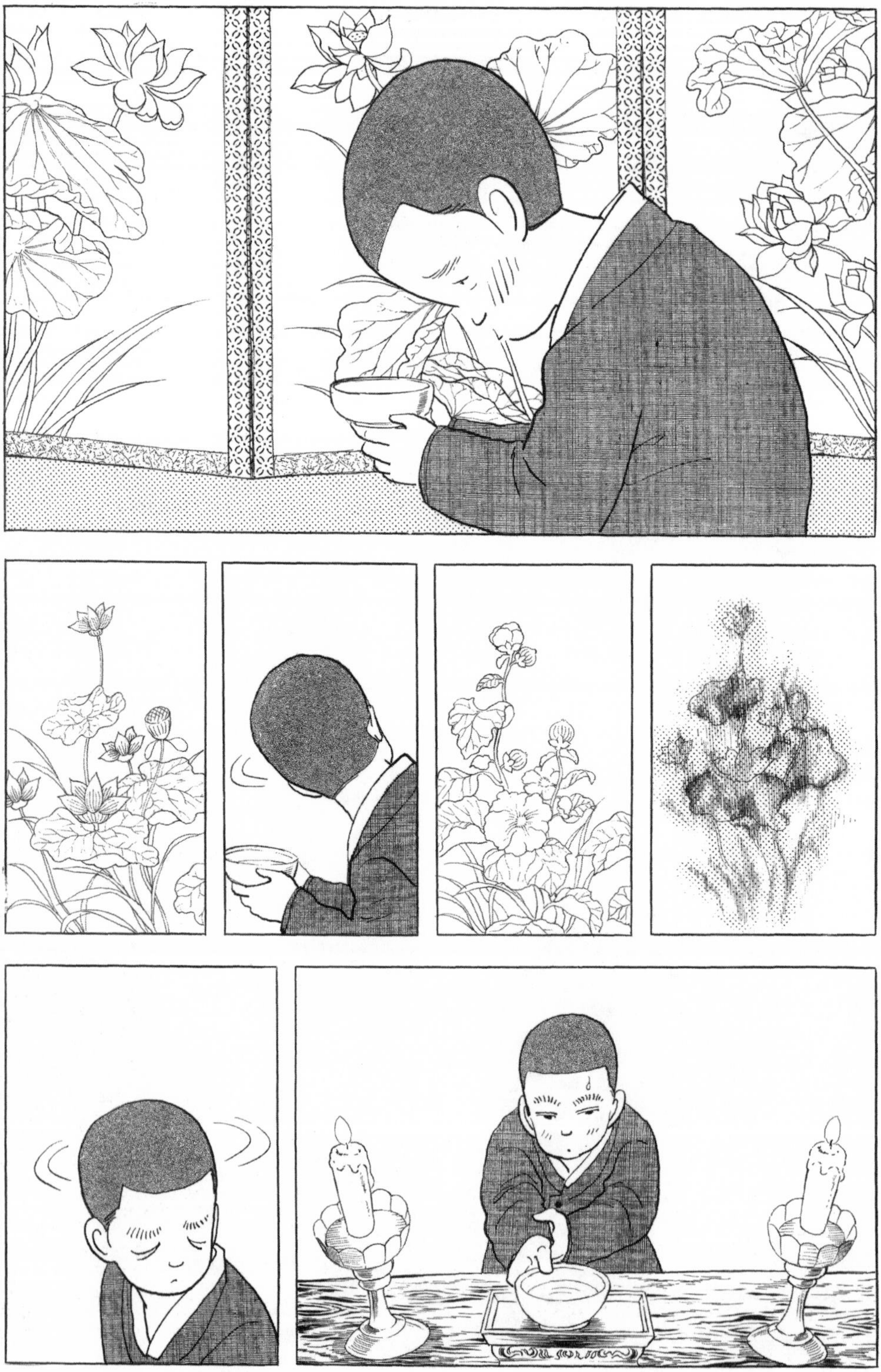

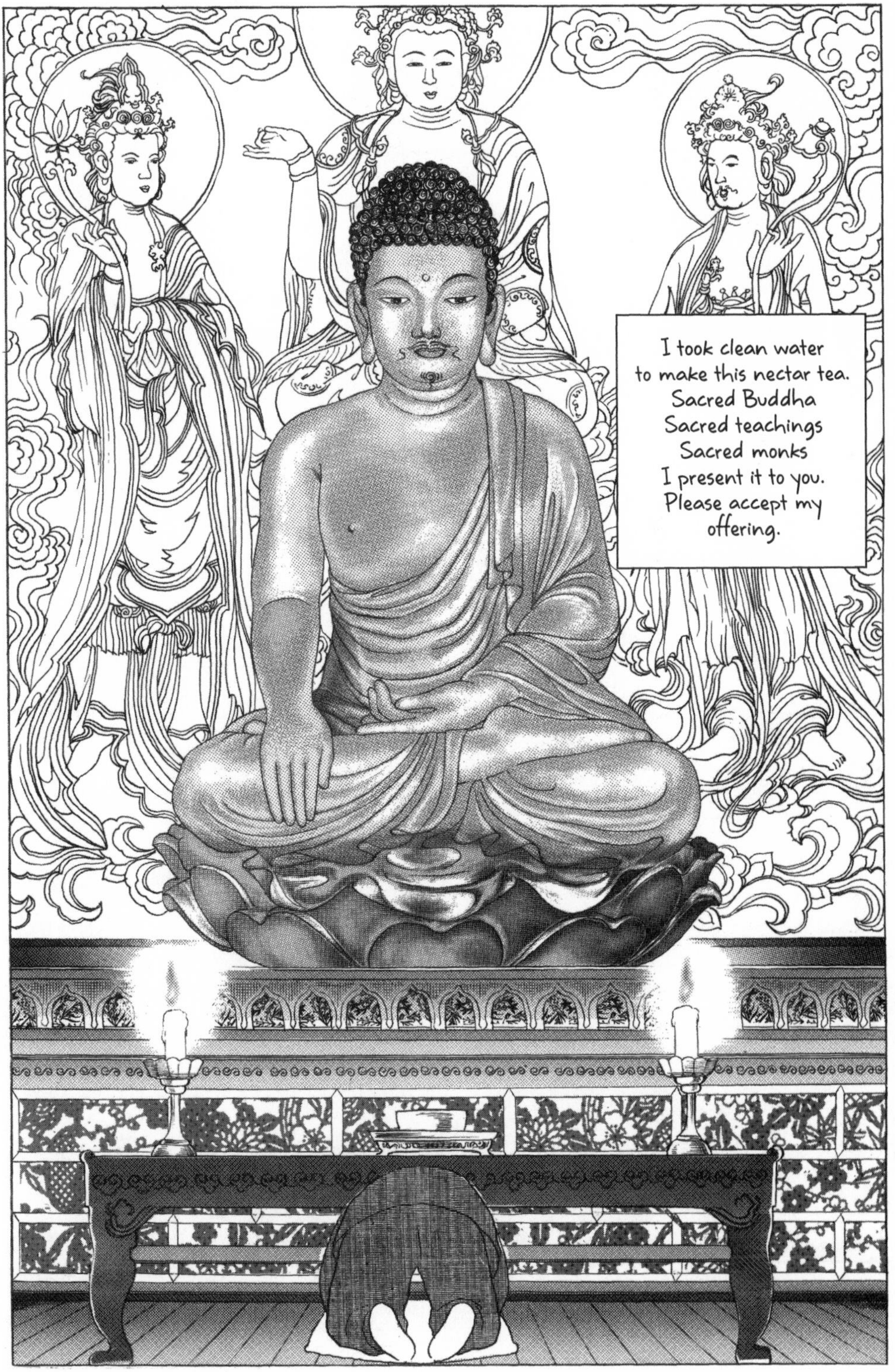
I took clean water to make this nectar tea. Sacred Buddha Sacred teachings Sacred monks I present it to you. Please accept my offering.

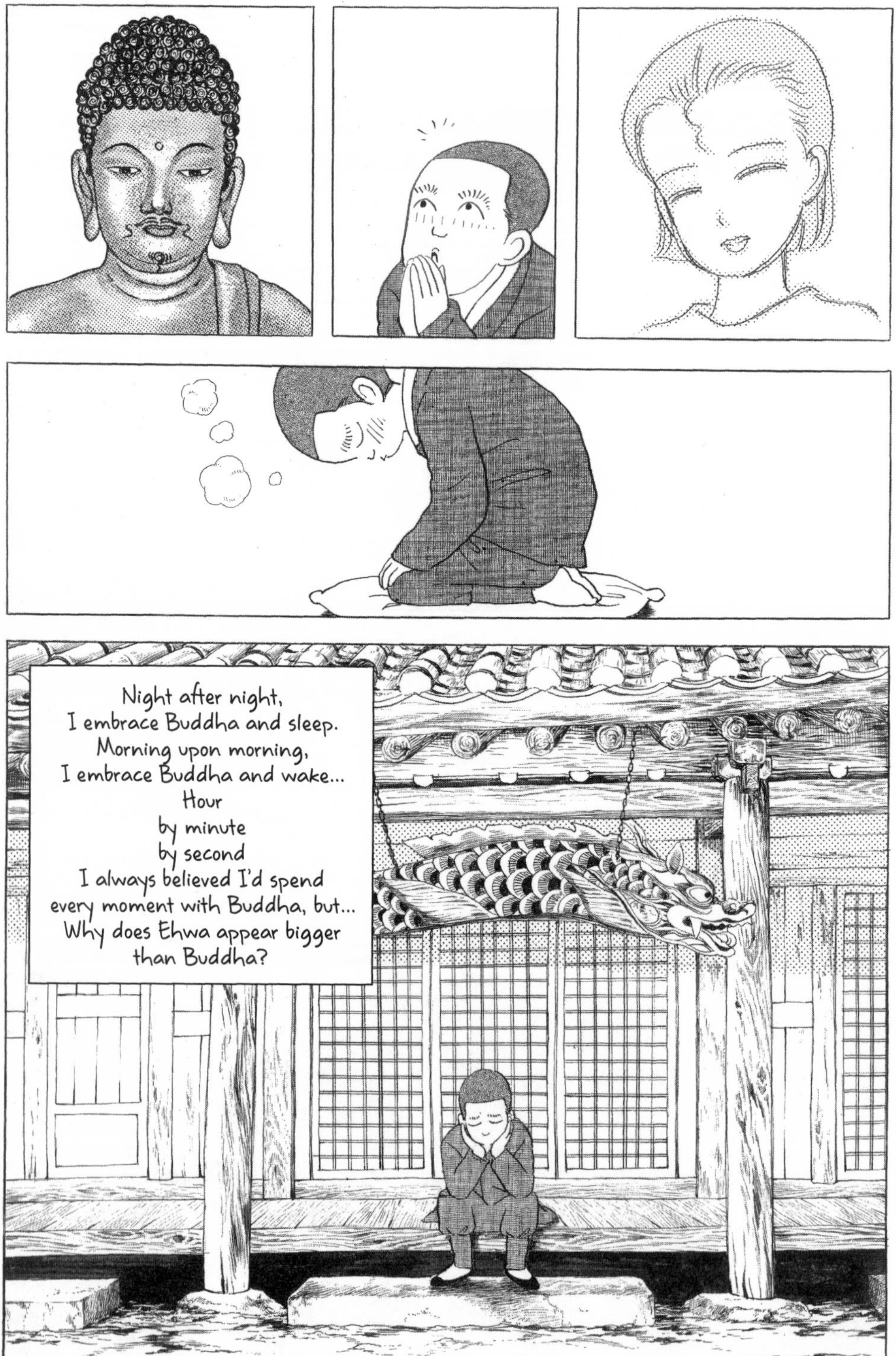
Night after night,
I embrace Buddha and sleep.
Morning upon morning,
I embrace Buddha and wake...
Hour
by minute
by second
I always believed I'd spend
every moment with Buddha, but...
Why does Ehwa appear bigger
than Buddha?

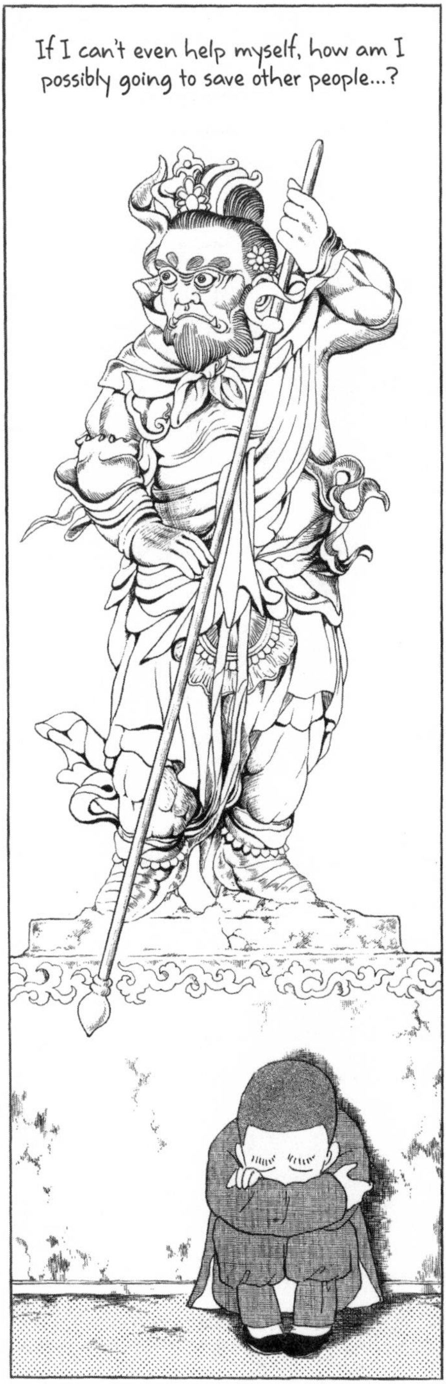
If I can't even help myself, how am I possibly going to save other people...?

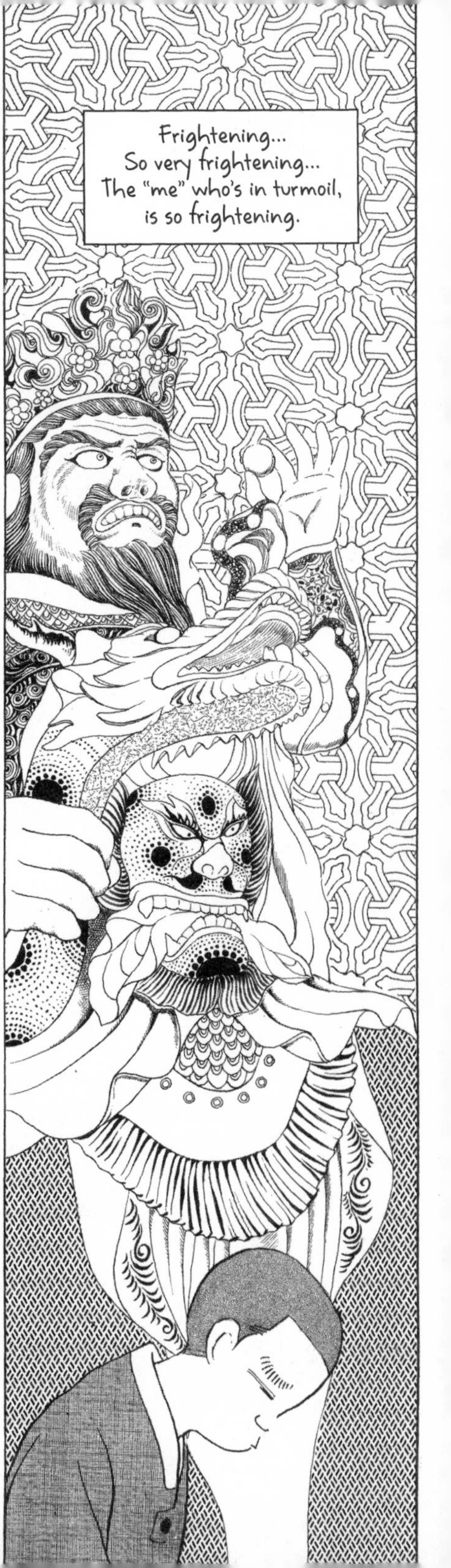
Frightening...
So very frightening...
The "me" who's in turmoil,
is so frightening.

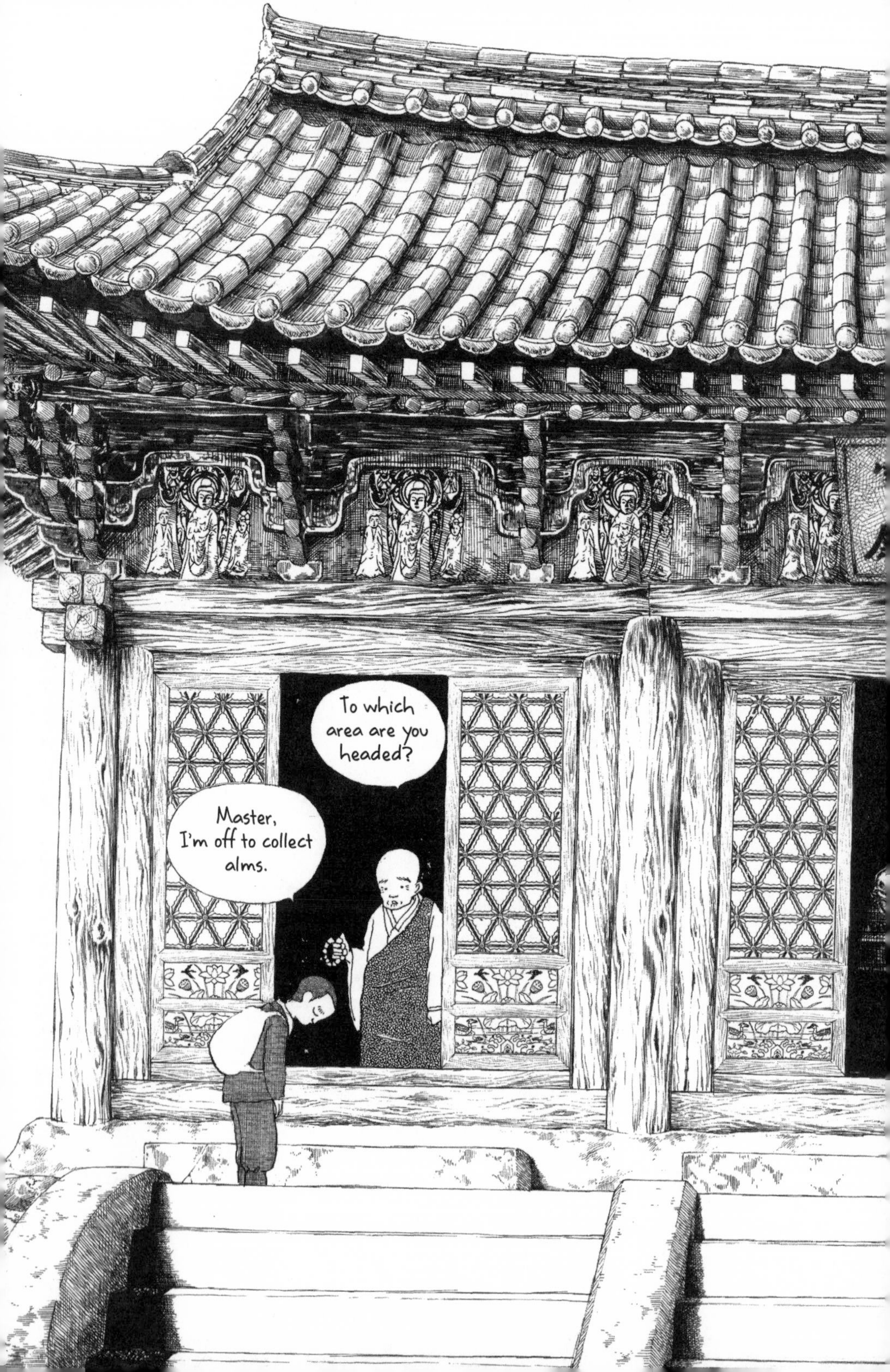
To which area are you headed?
Master, I'm off to collect alms.

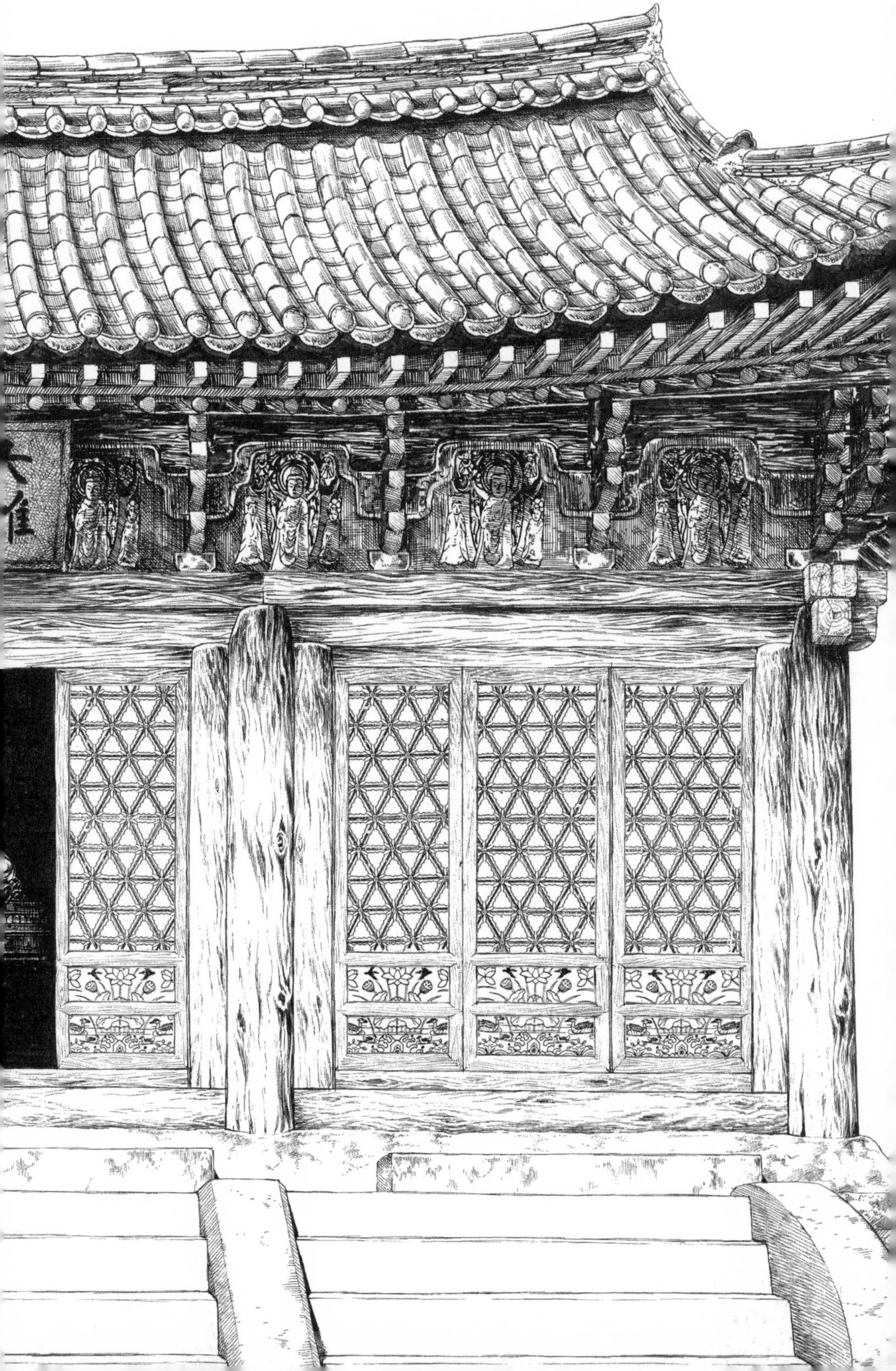

I'm thinking of heading toward Namwon.

Is there a river on the way there?

There's a small stream.

Make sure to toss your gloom into the stream. To gain hundreds of blessings, you must be willing to throw out one.

Tsk tsk tsk... How will you be able to help the masses looking like that? Your face is littered with a million worldly desires.

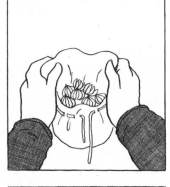

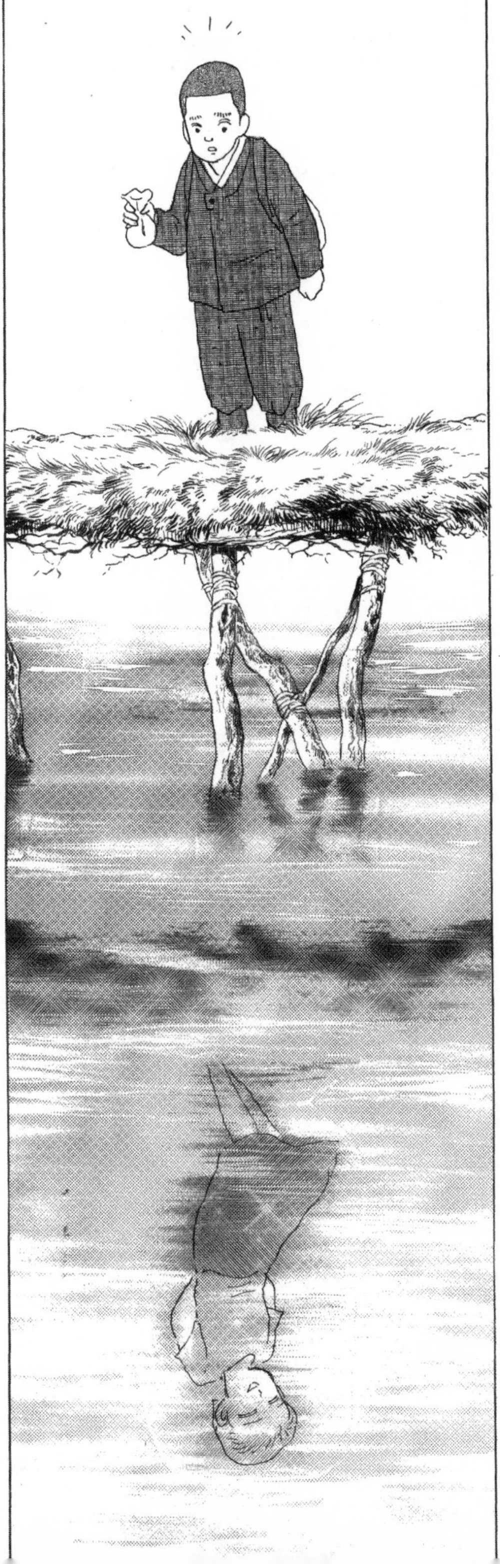

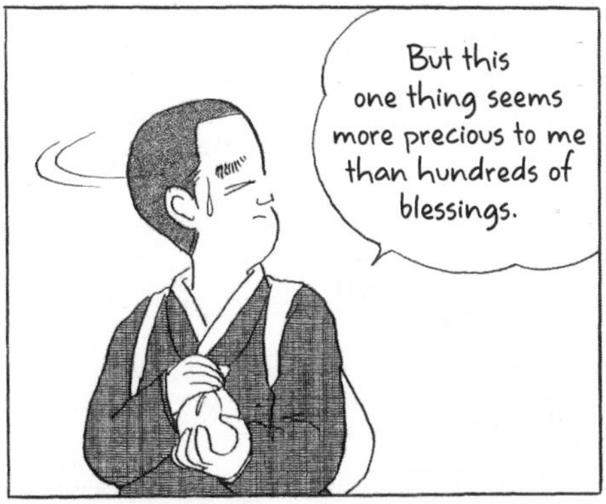
But this one thing seems more precious to me than hundreds of blessings.

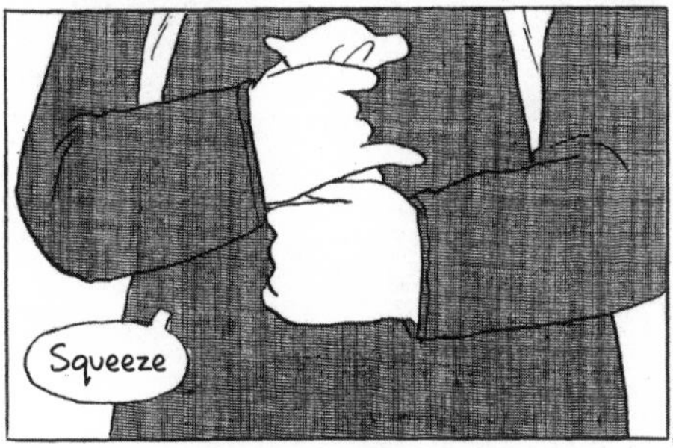
Squeeze

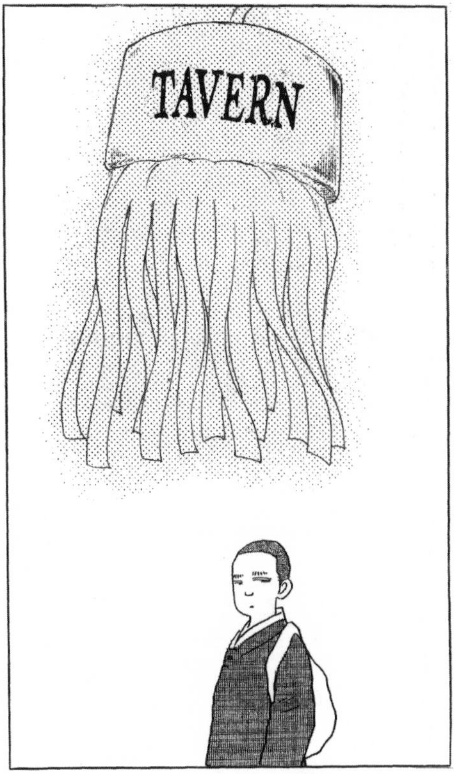
TAVERN

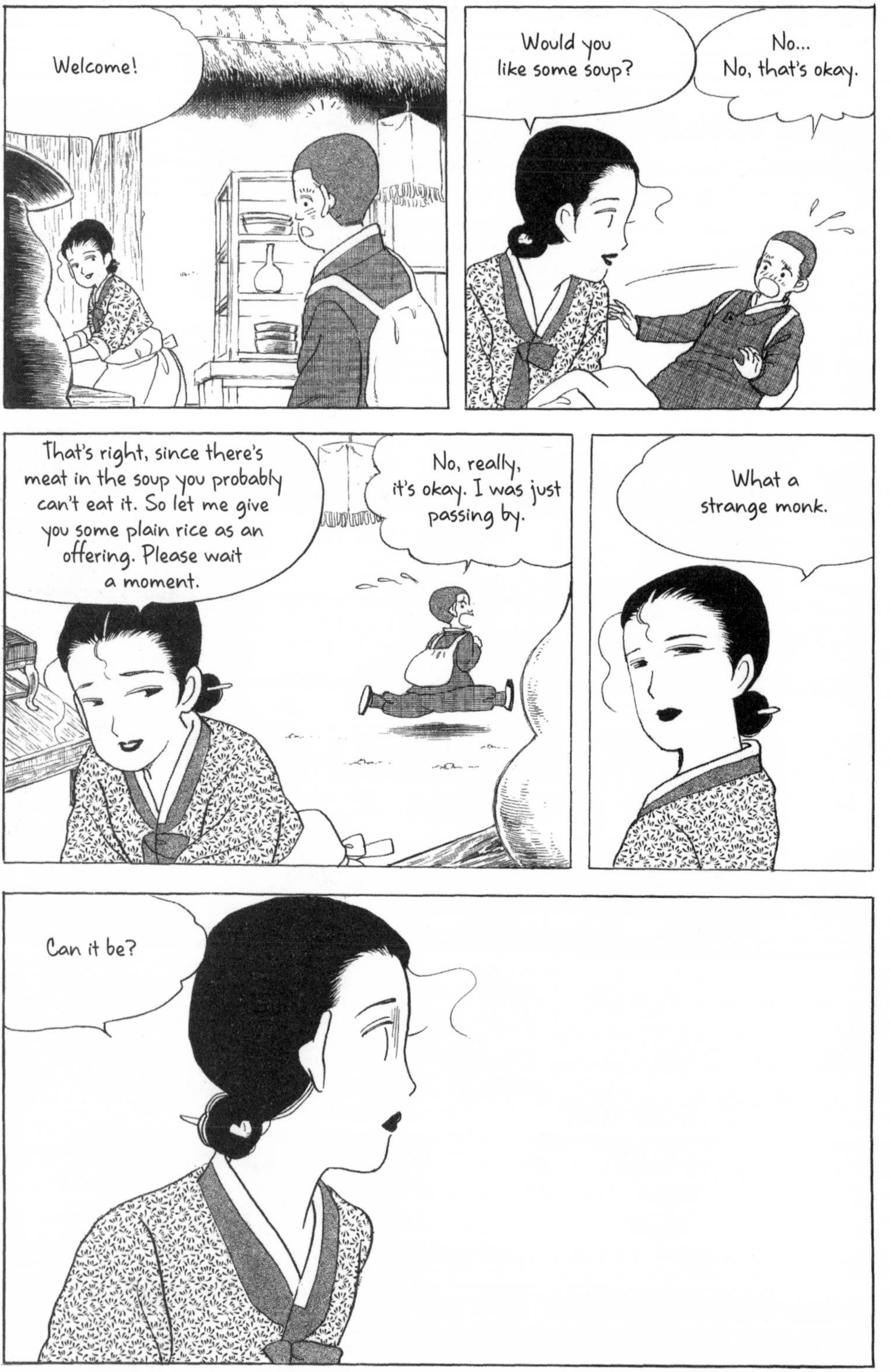
Welcome!
Would you like some soup?
No... No, that's okay.
That's right, since there's meat in the soup you probably can't eat it. So let me give you some plain rice as an offering. Please wait a moment.
No, really, it's okay. I was just passing by.
What a strange monk.
Can it be?

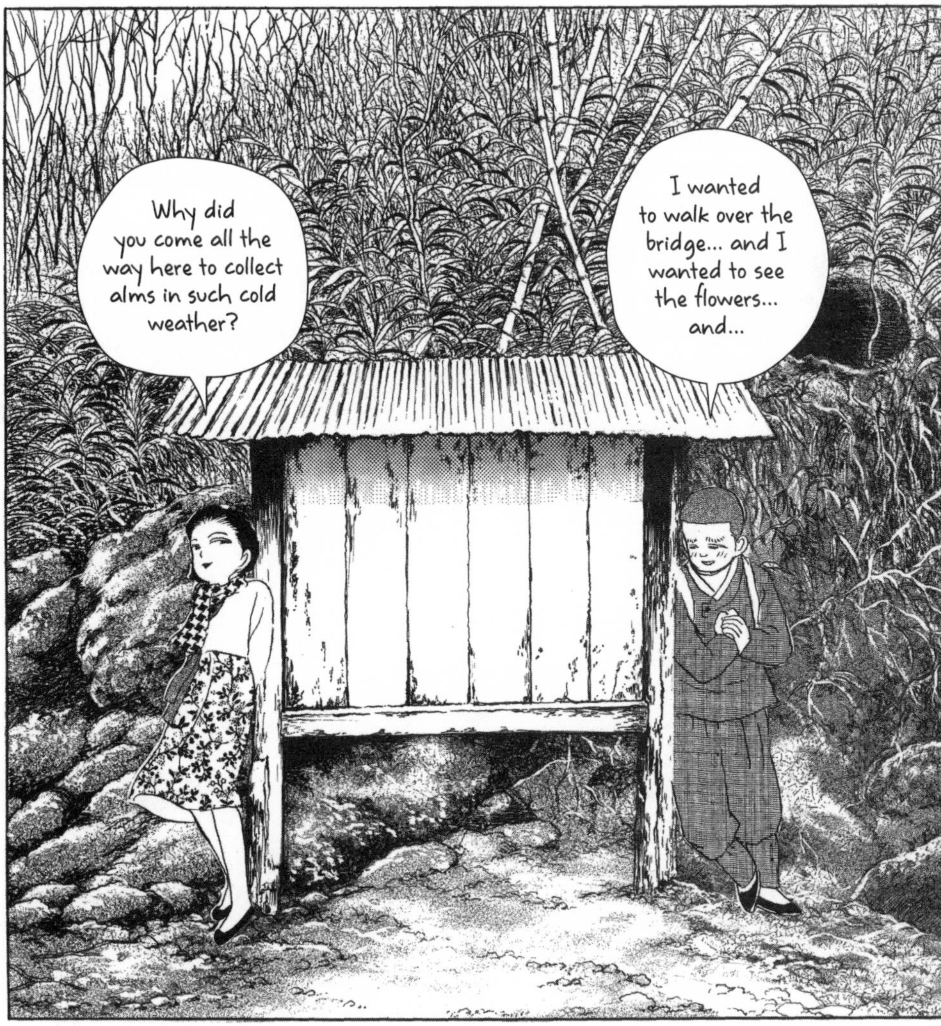
Why did you come all the way here to collect alms in such cold weather?
I wanted to walk over the bridge... and I wanted to see the flowers... and...

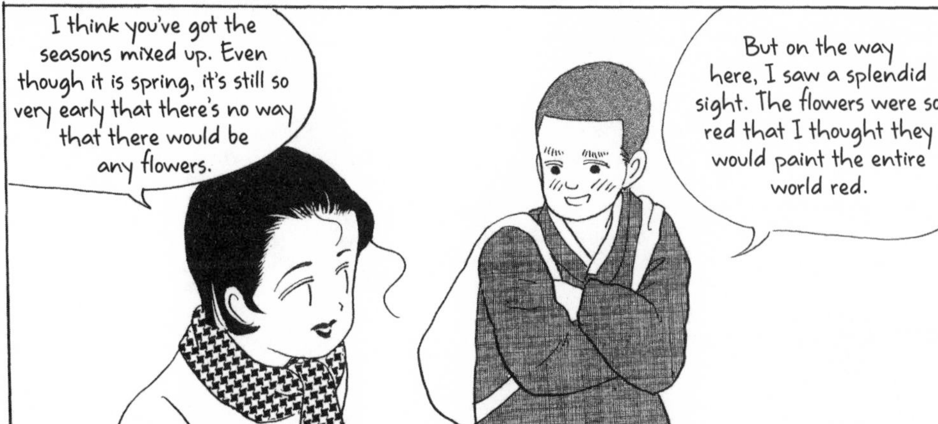
I think you've got the seasons mixed up. Even though it is spring, it's still so very early that there's no way that there would be any flowers.
But on the way here, I saw a splendid sight. The flowers were so red that I thought they would paint the entire world red.

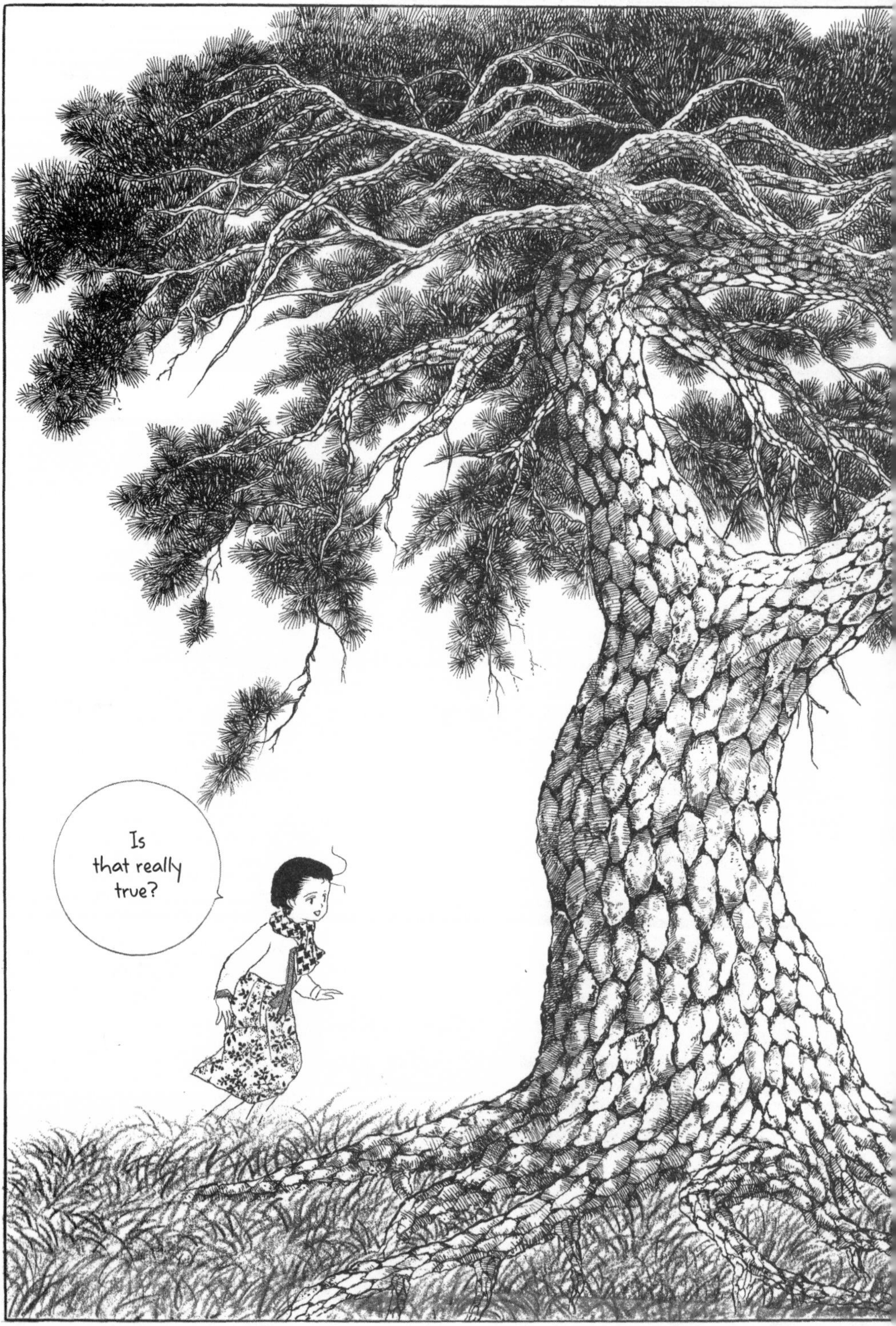
Is that really true?

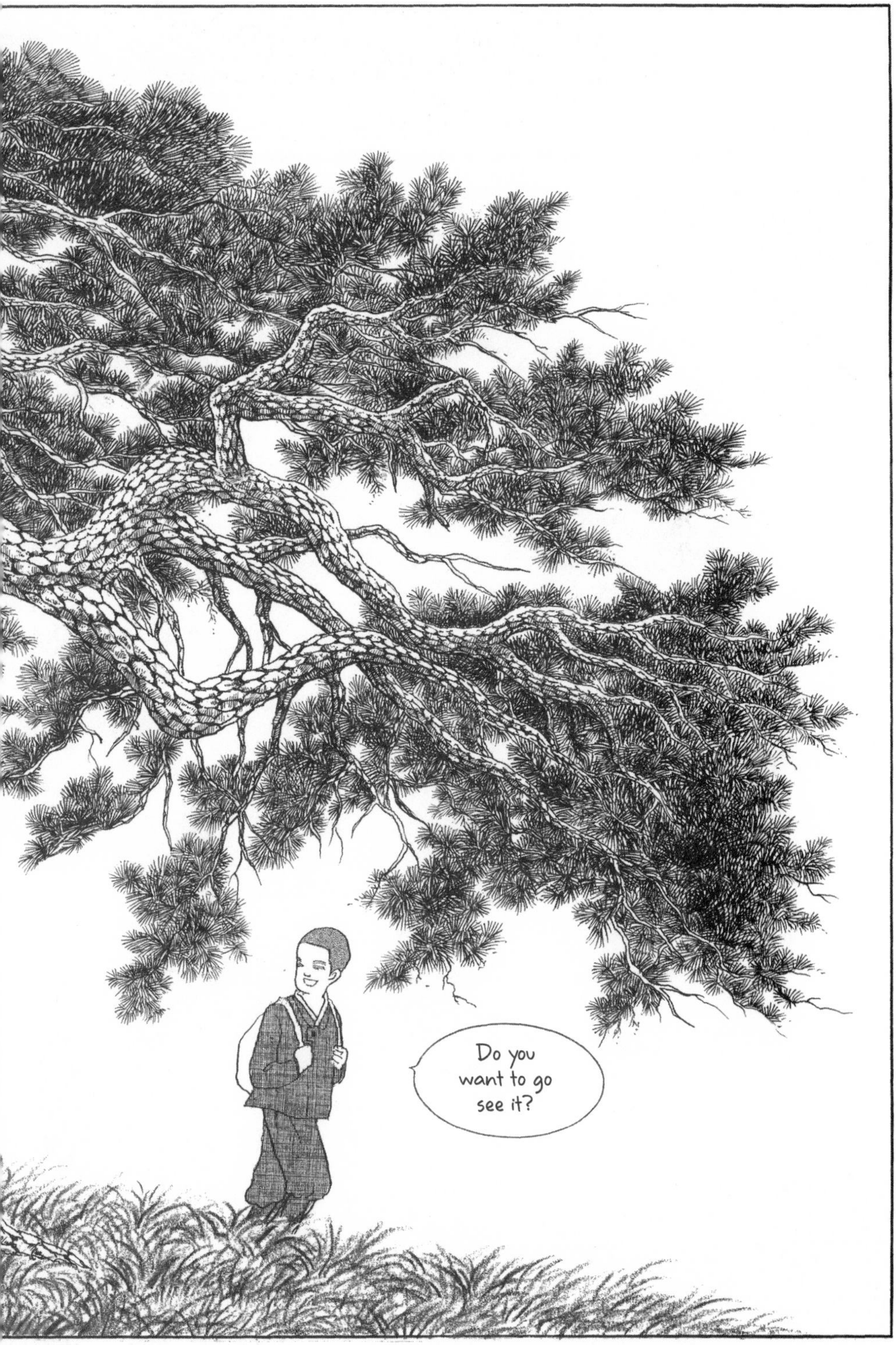
Do you want to go see it?

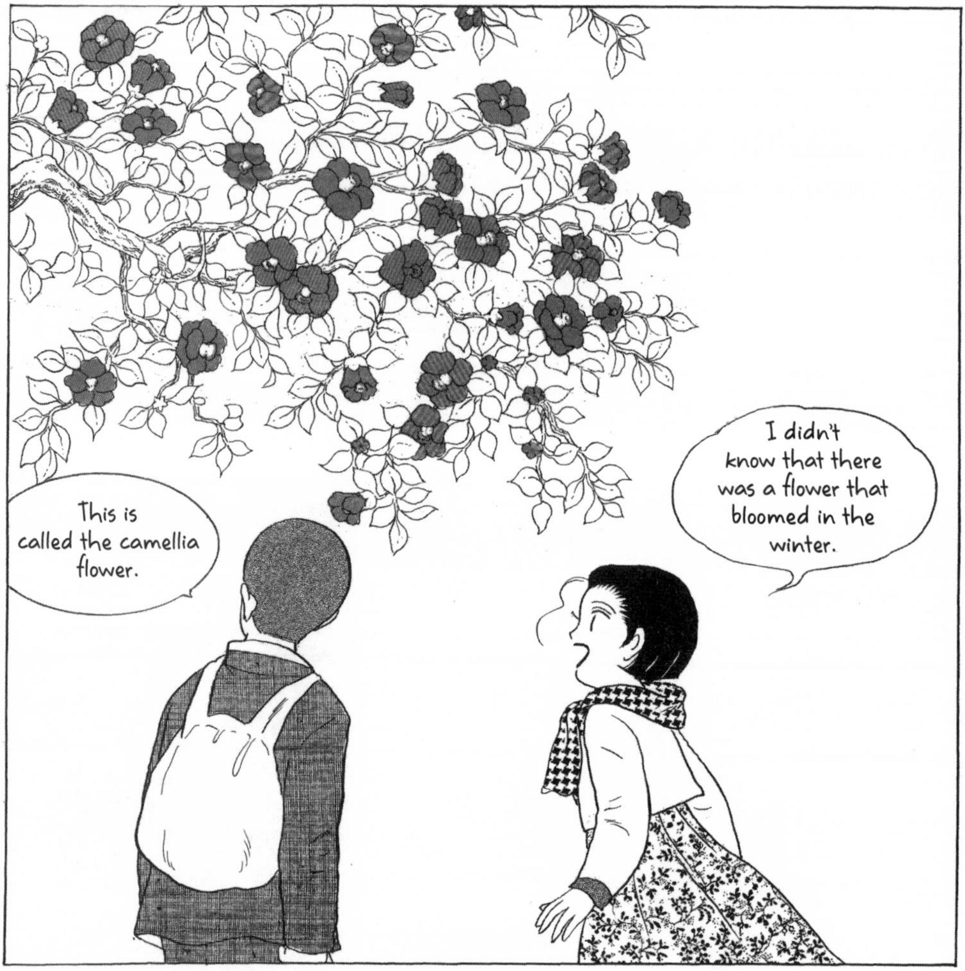
This is called the camellia flower.
I didn't know that there was a flower that bloomed in the winter.

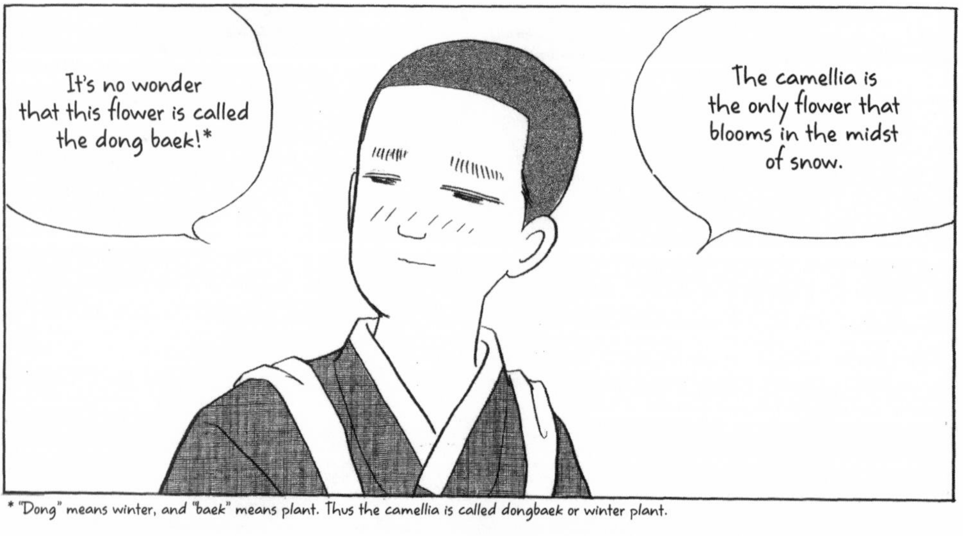
The camellia is the only flower that blooms in the midst of snow.
It's no wonder that this flower is called the dong baek!*

* "Dong" means winter, and "baek" means plant. Thus the camellia is called dongbaek or winter plant.

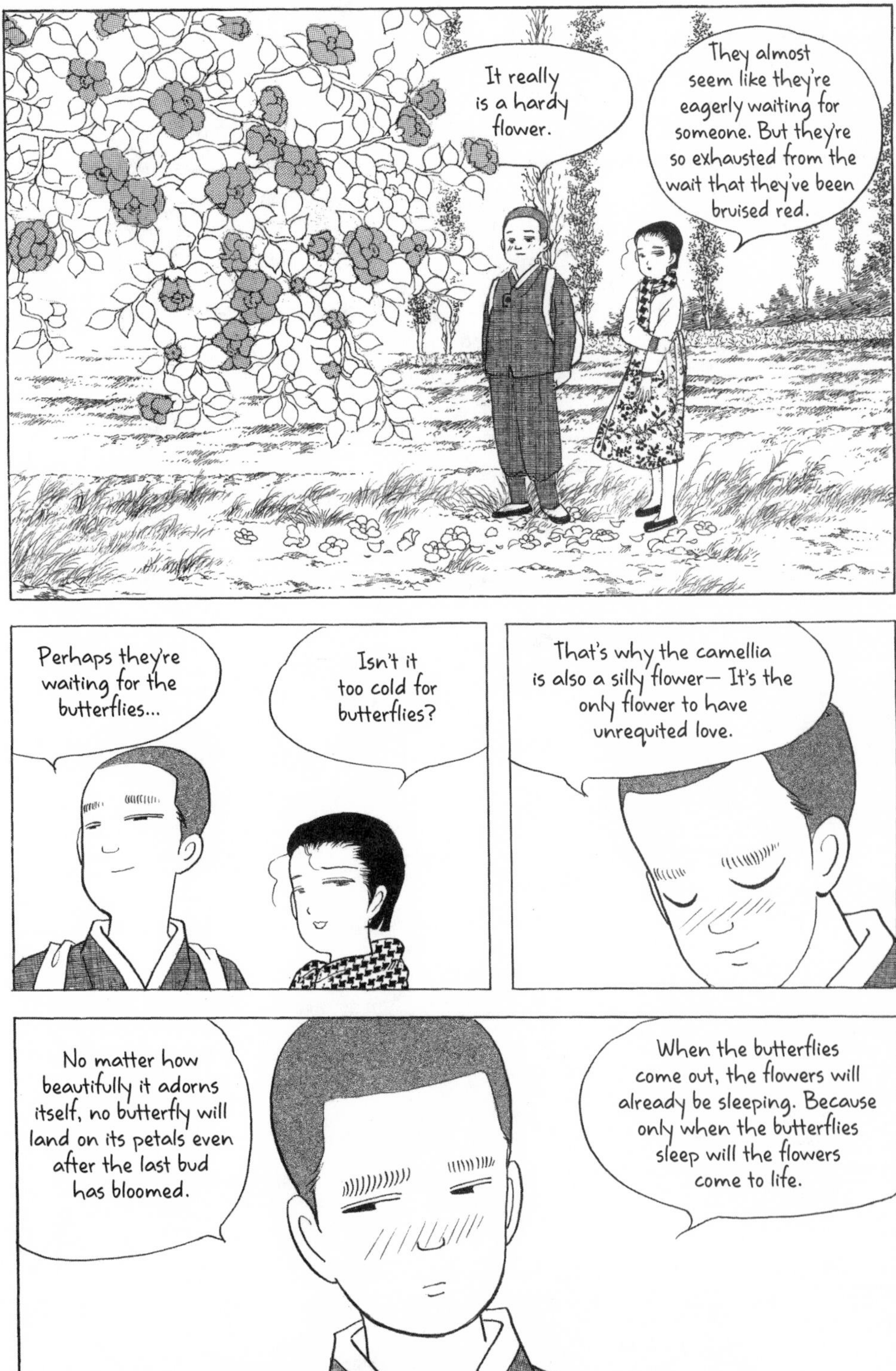
It really is a hardy flower.
They almost seem like they're eagerly waiting for someone. But they're so exhausted from the wait that they've been bruised red.
Perhaps they're waiting for the butterflies...
Isn't it too cold for butterflies?
That's why the camellia is also a silly flower— It's the only flower to have unrequited love.
No matter how beautifully it adorns itself, no butterfly will land on its petals even after the last bud has bloomed.
When the butterflies come out, the flowers will already be sleeping. Because only when the butterflies sleep will the flowers come to life.

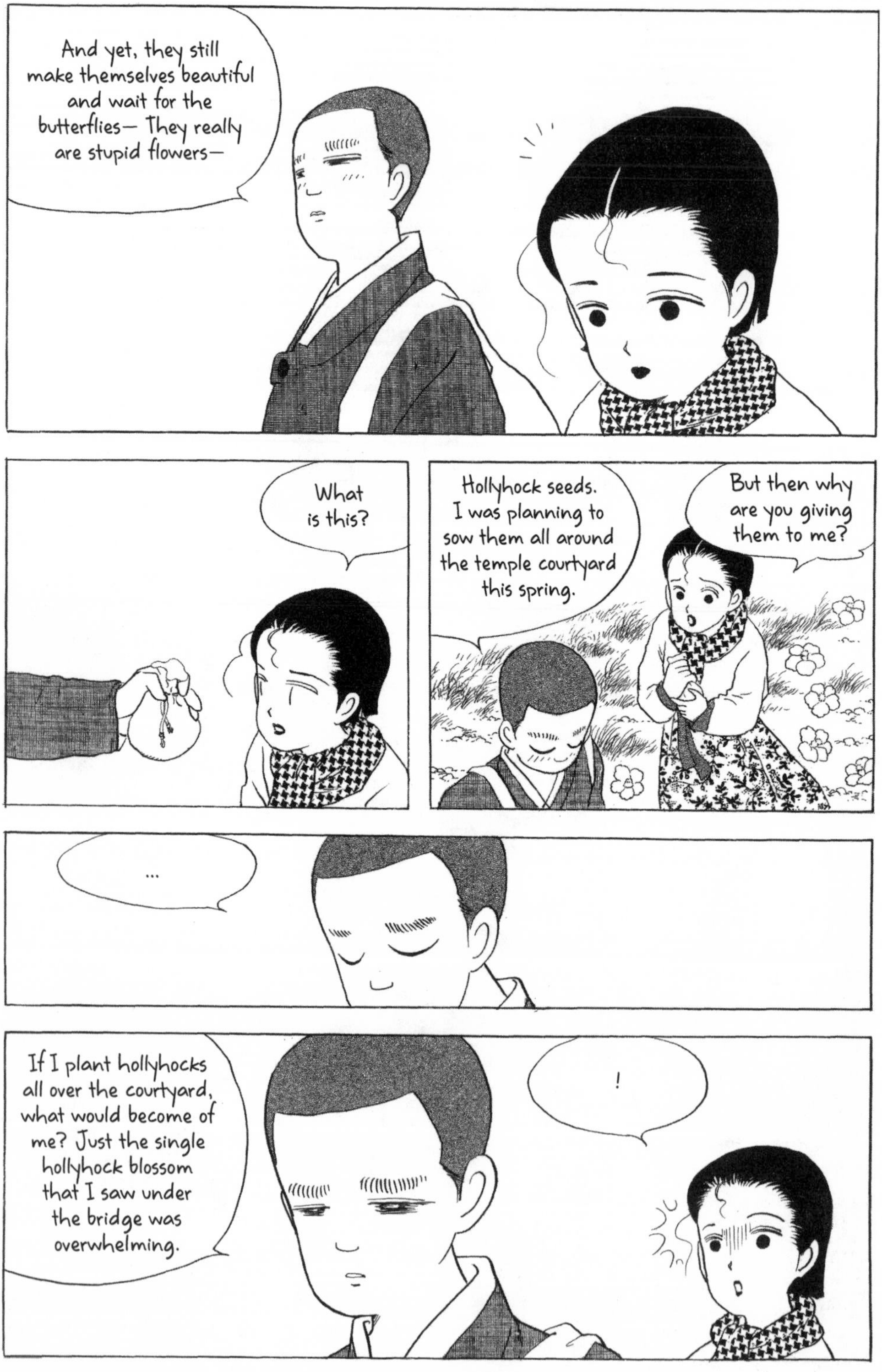

And yet, they still make themselves beautiful and wait for the butterflies— They really are stupid flowers—
What is this?
Hollyhock seeds. I was planning to sow them all around the temple courtyard this spring.
But then why are you giving them to me?
...
If I plant hollyhocks all over the courtyard, what would become of me? Just the single hollyhock blossom that I saw under the bridge was overwhelming.
!

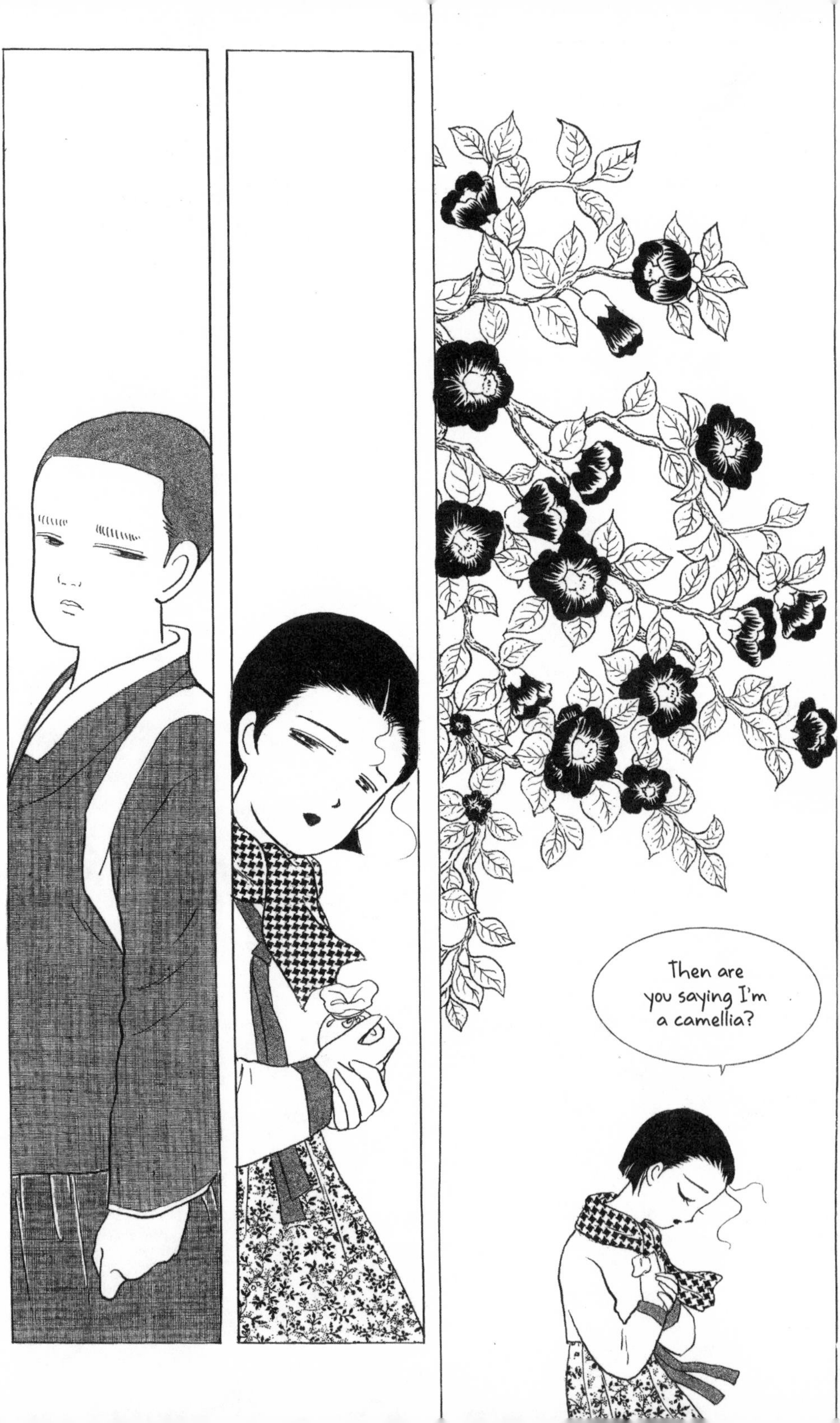
Then are you saying I'm a camellia?

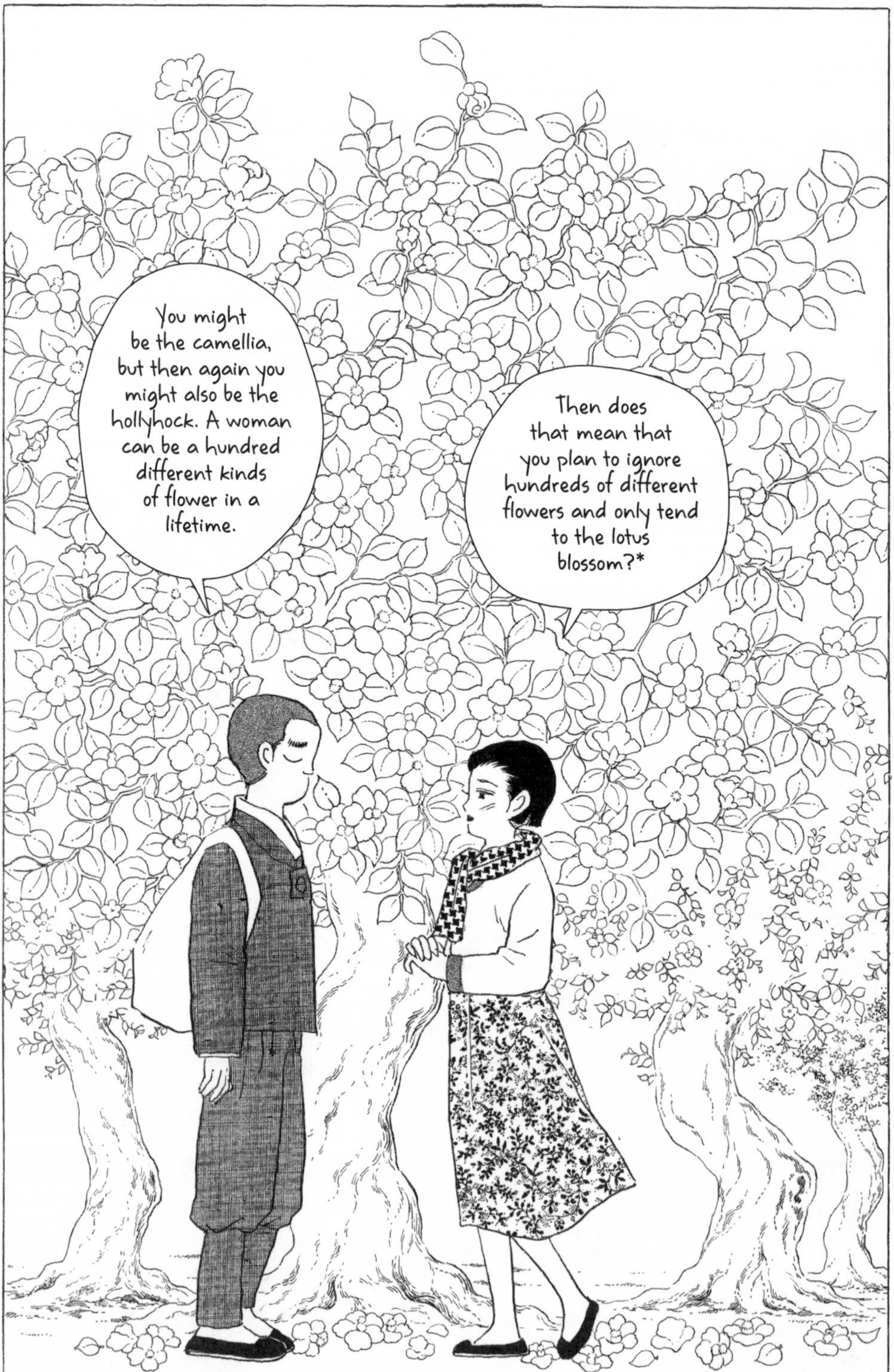
You might be the camellia, but then again you might also be the hollyhock. A woman can be a hundred different kinds of flower in a lifetime.
Then does that mean that you plan to ignore hundreds of different flowers and only tend to the lotus blossom?*

* The Lotus blossom is synonymous with Buddhism. The implication is that he will continue in his devotion to being a monk and forgo all other pleasures.

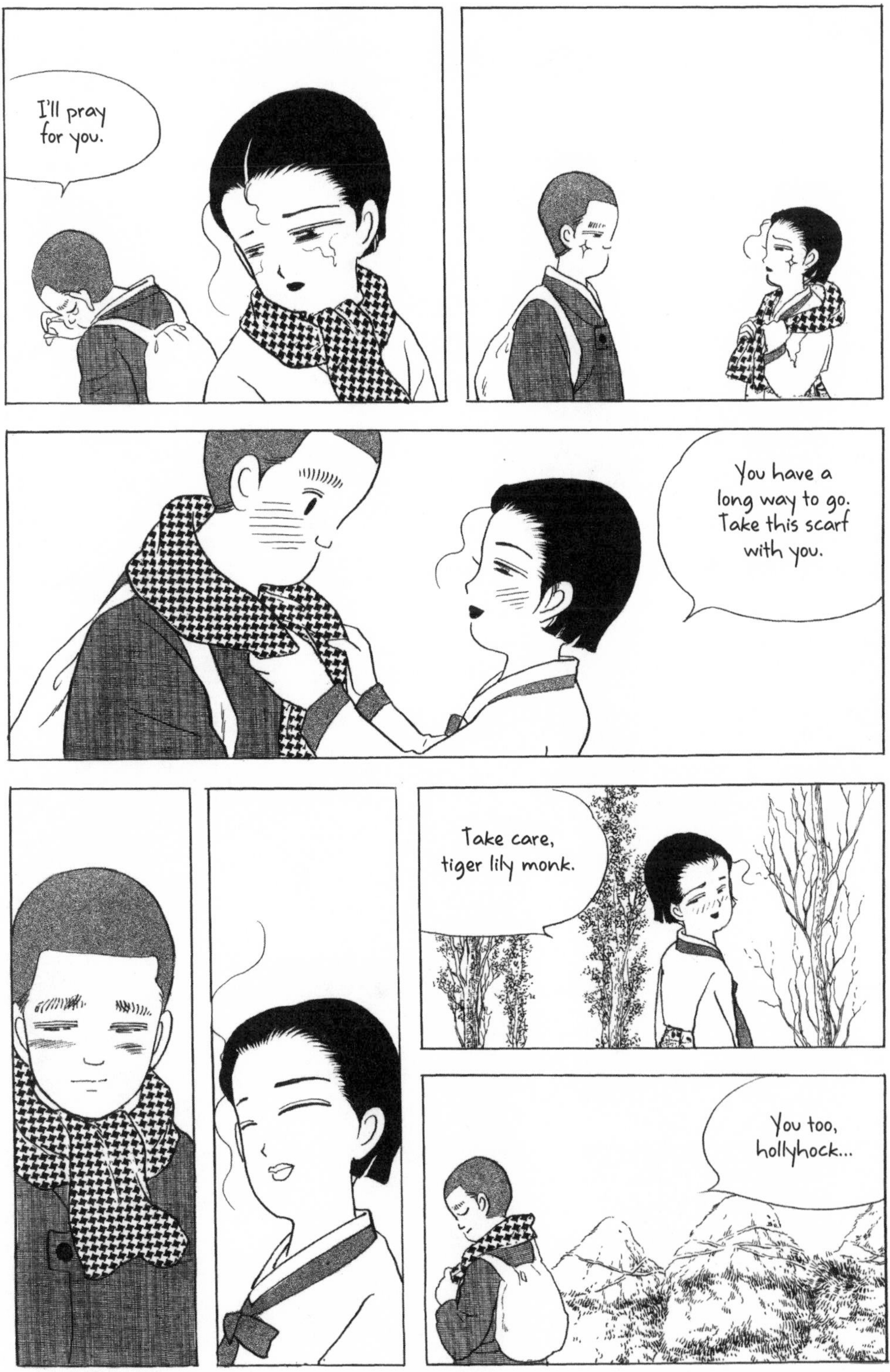
I'll pray for you.
You have a long way to go. Take this scarf with you.
Take care, tiger lily monk.
You too, hollyhock...

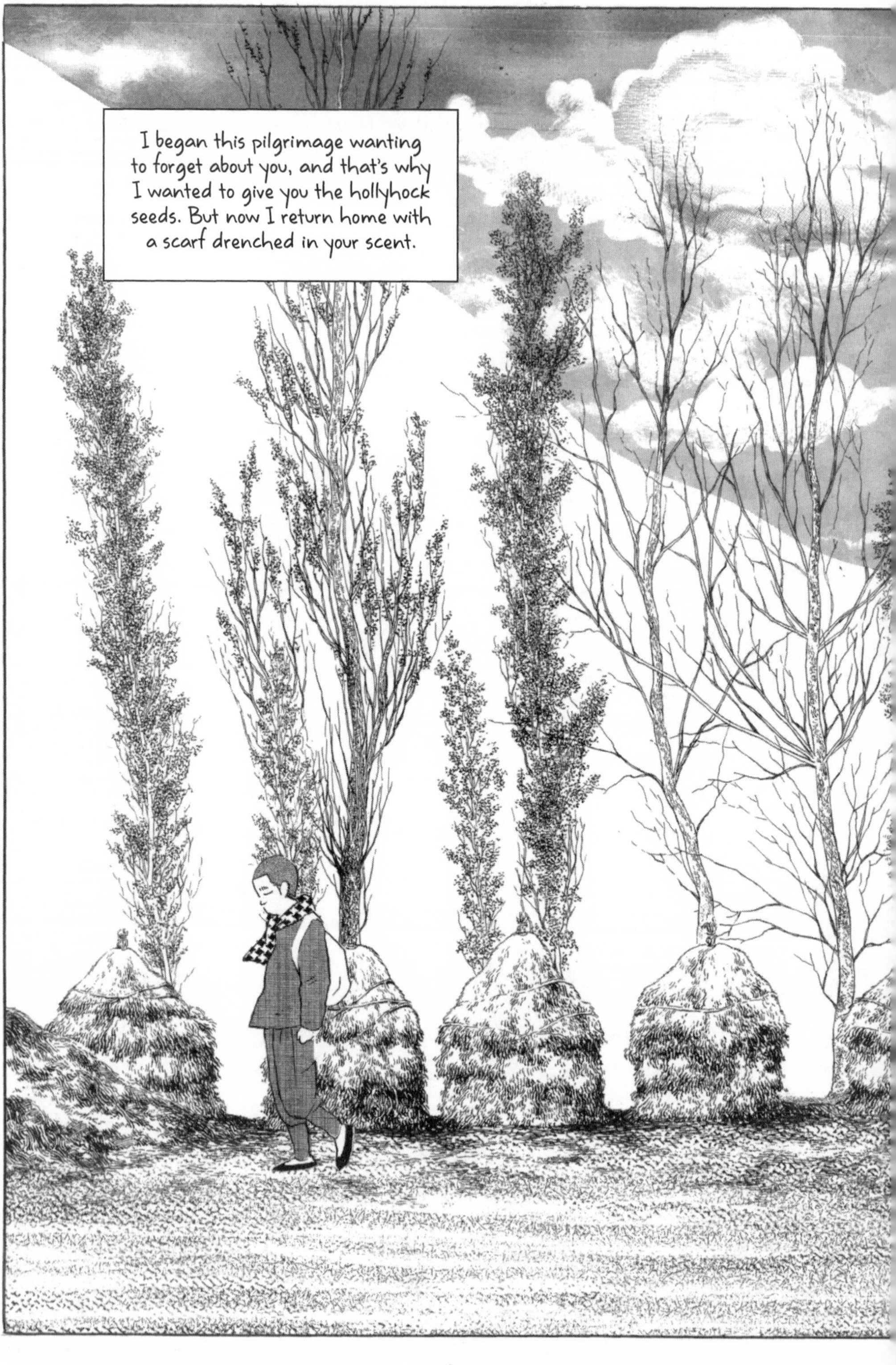
I began this pilgrimage wanting to forget about you, and that's why I wanted to give you the hollyhock seeds. But now I return home with a scarf drenched in your scent.

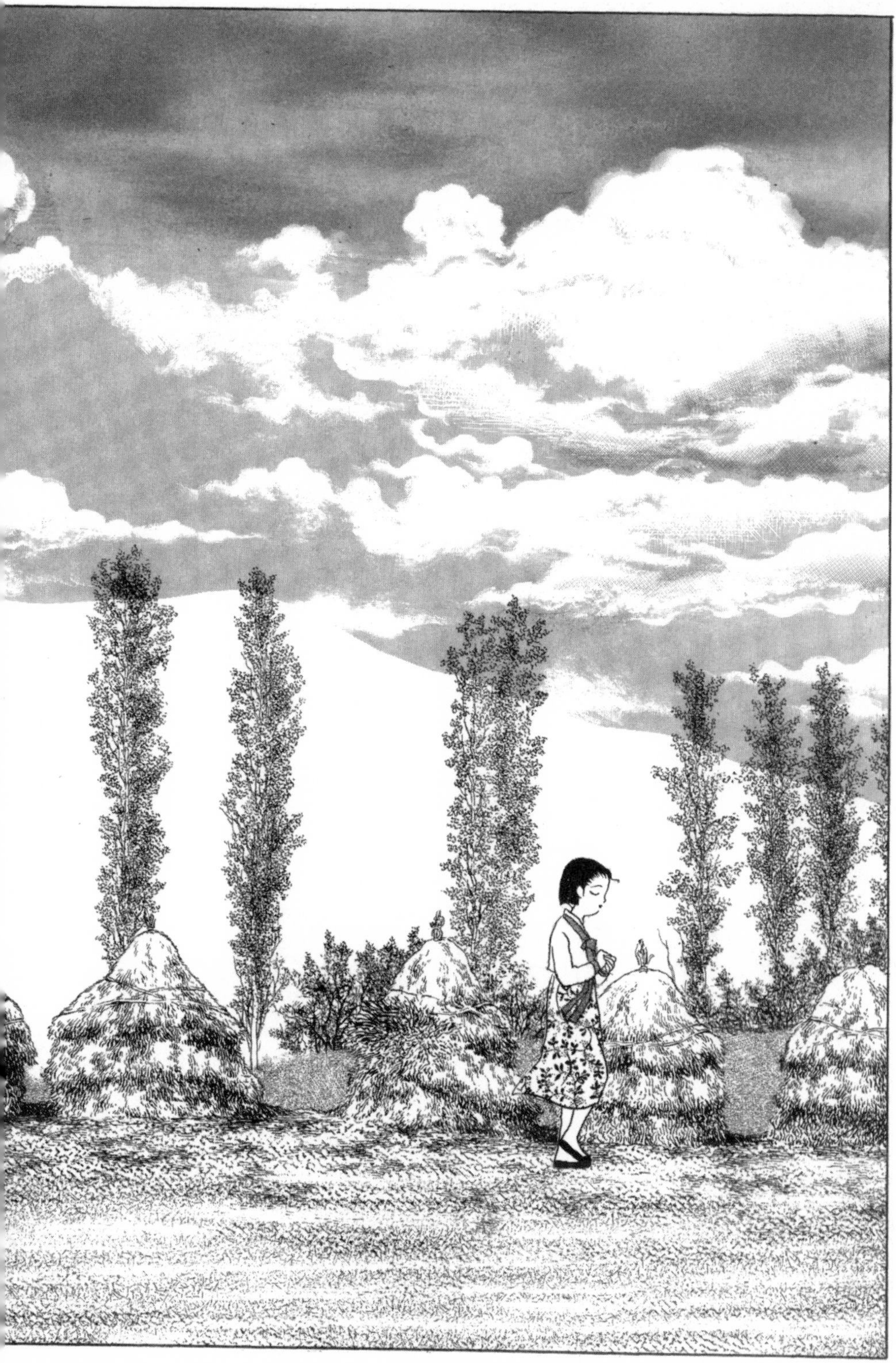

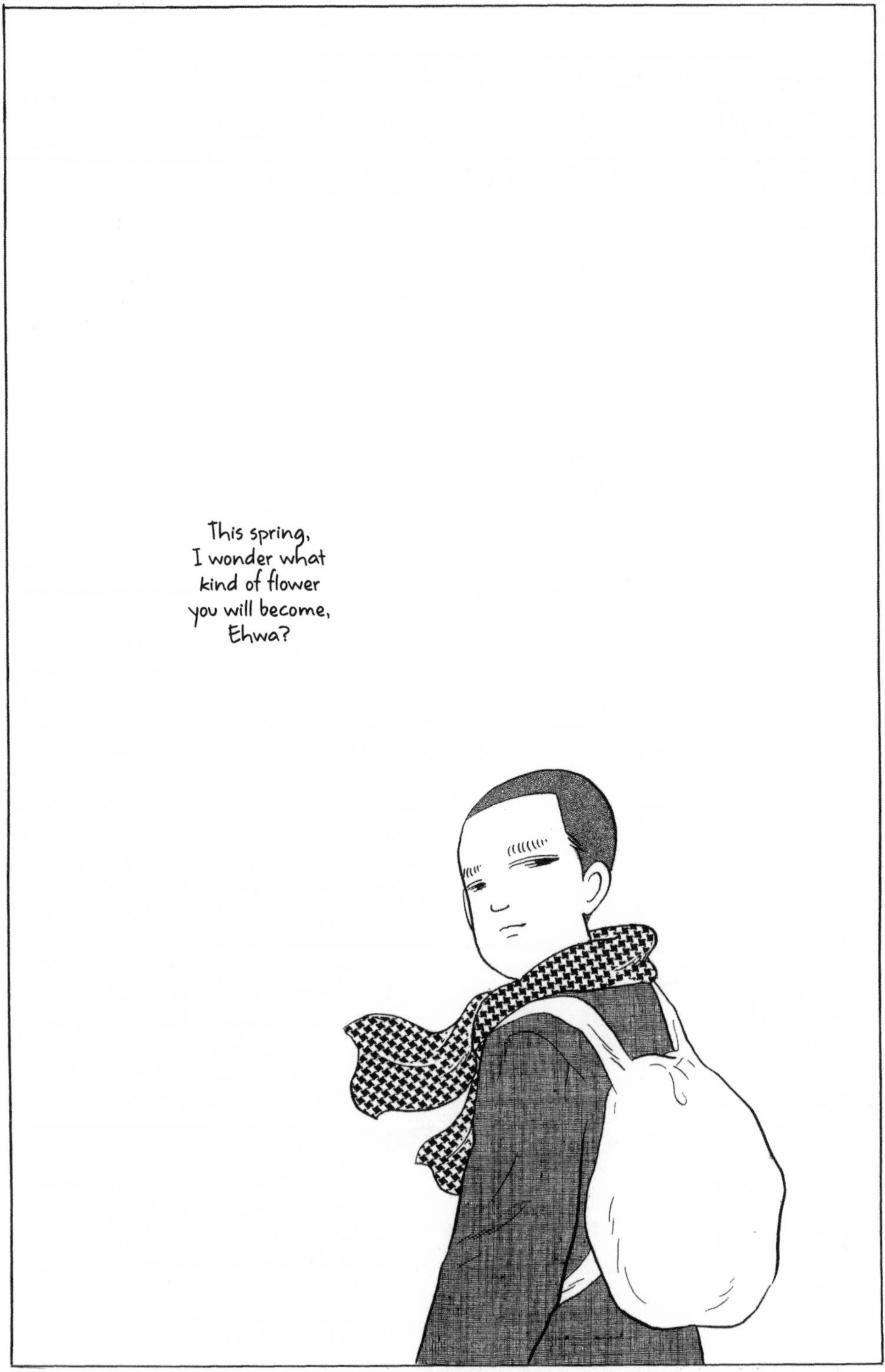
This spring,
I wonder what
kind of flower
you will become,
Ehwa?

Chapter Six

THE SPRING RAIN TELLS ME TO BLOSSOM LIKE A FLOWER

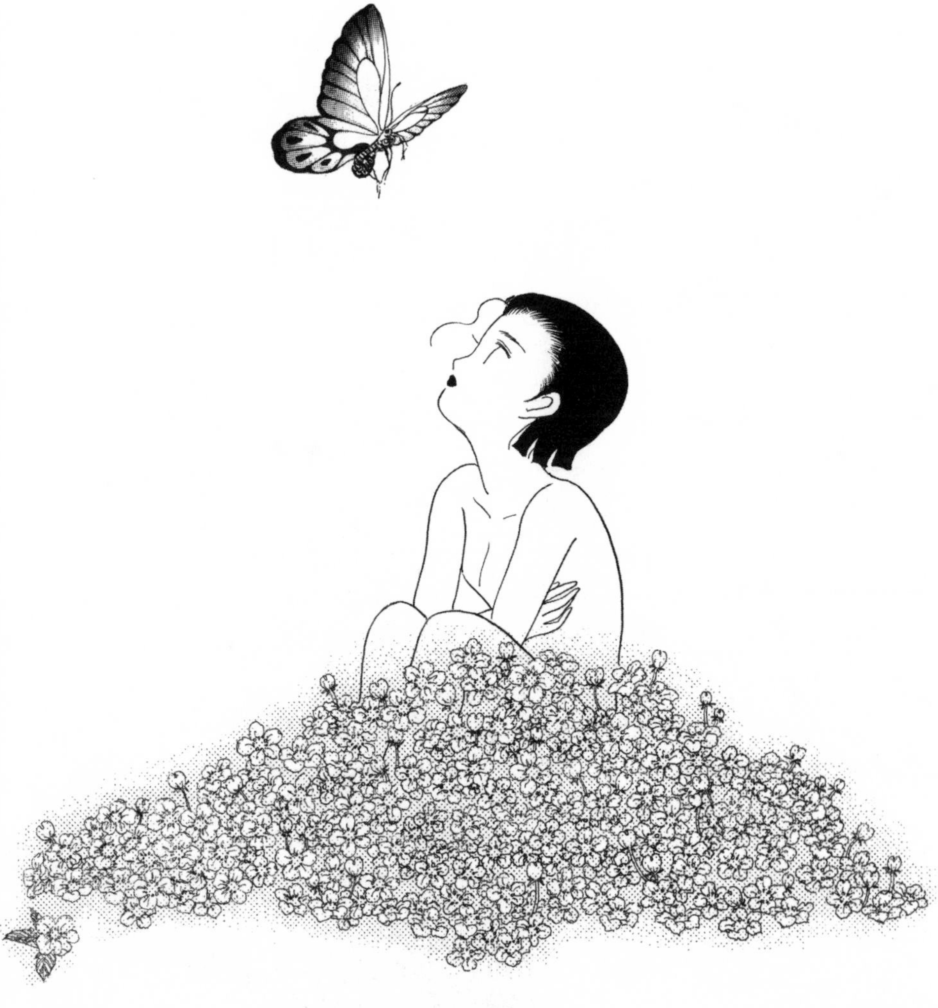

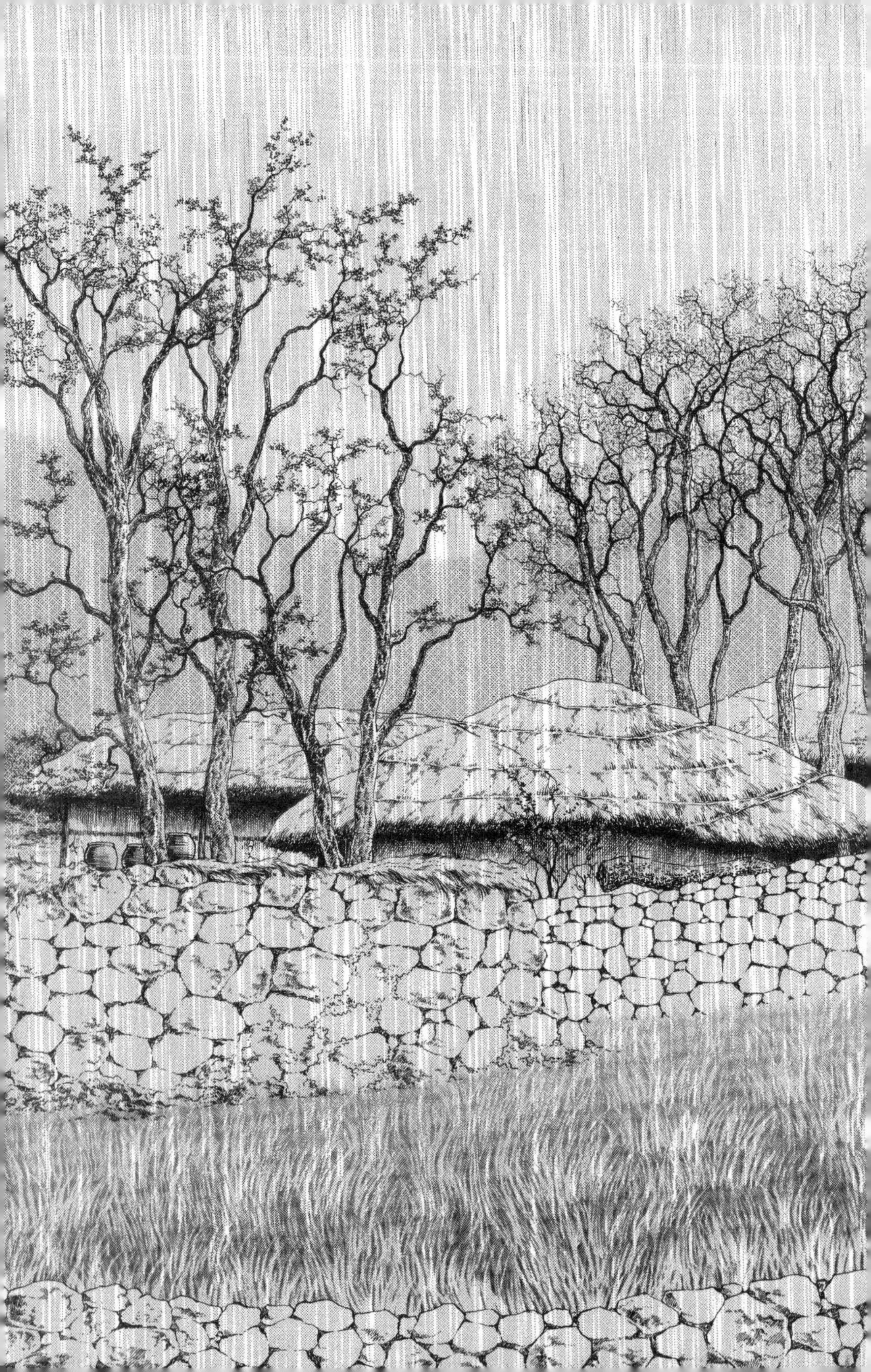

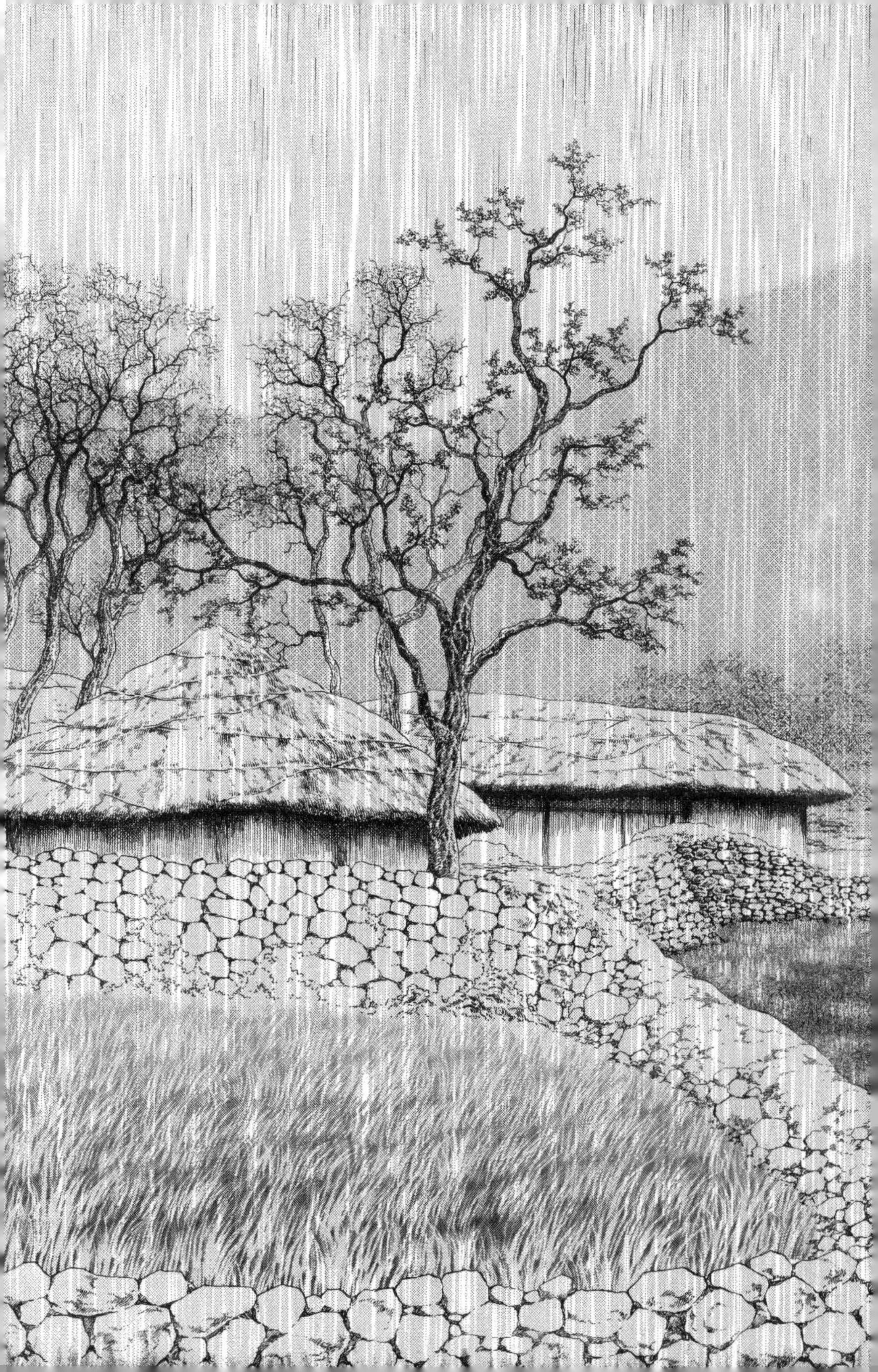

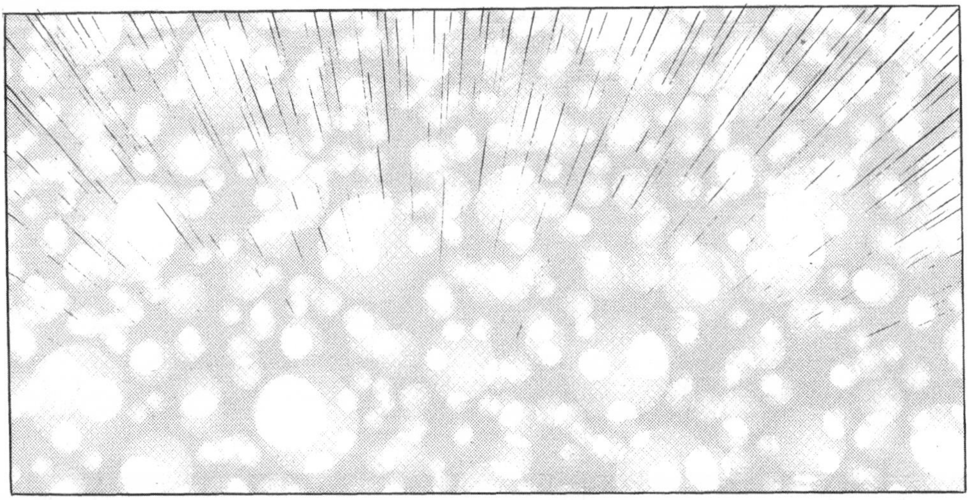

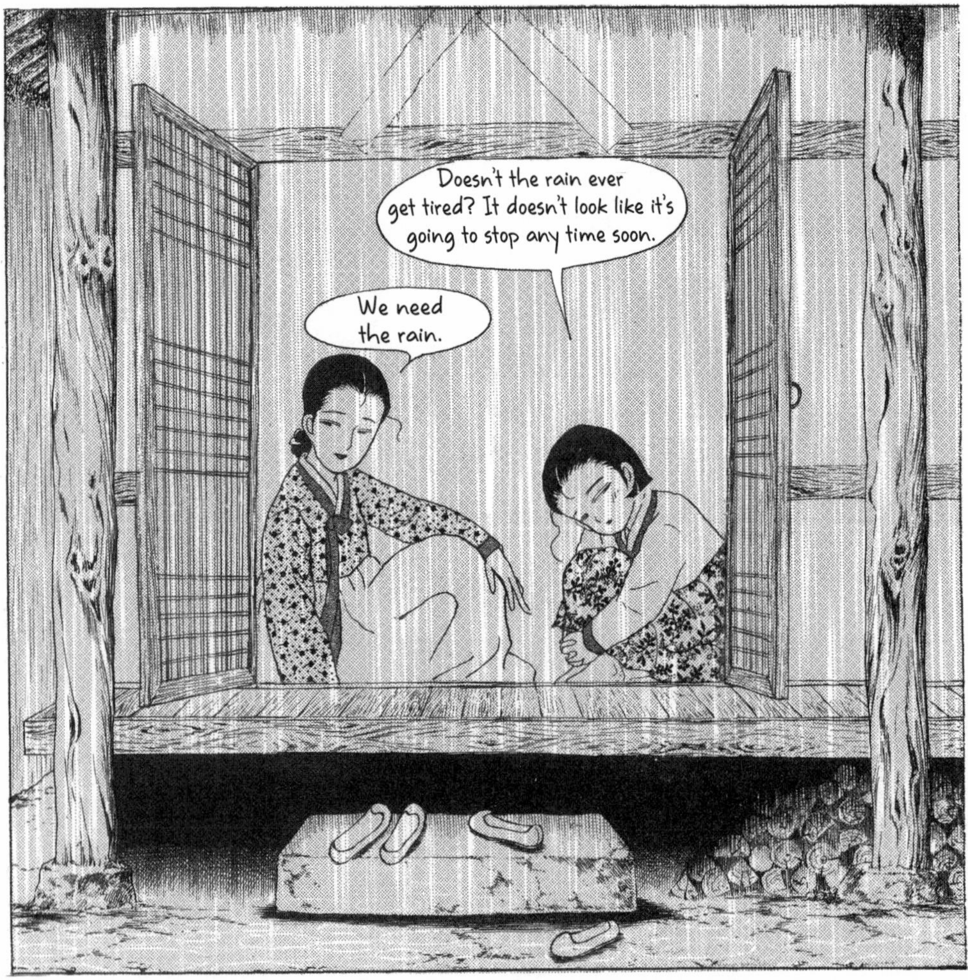
Doesn't the rain ever get tired? It doesn't look like it's going to stop any time soon.
We need the rain.

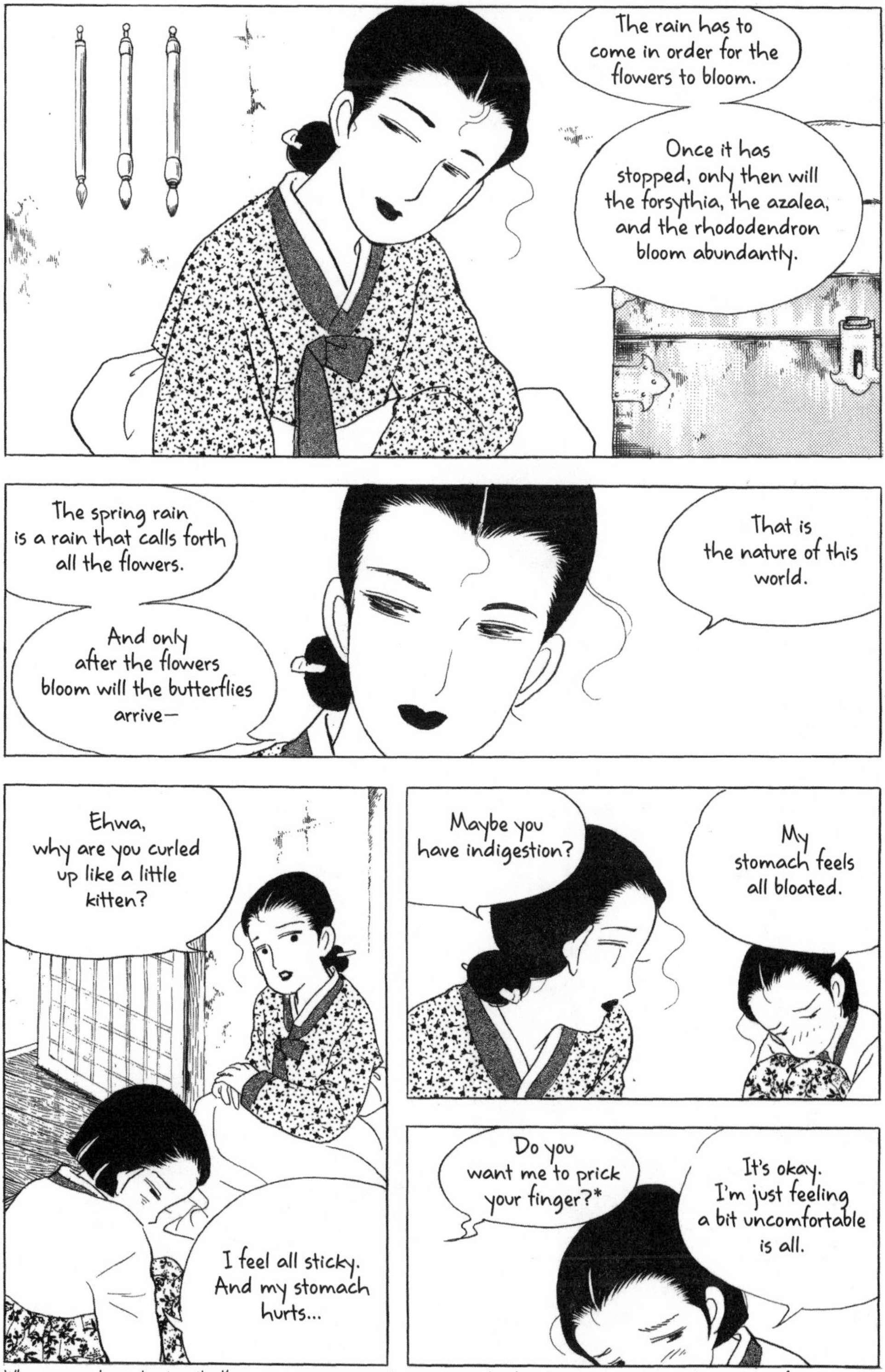
The rain has to come in order for the flowers to bloom.
Once it has stopped, only then will the forsythia, the azalea, and the rhododendron bloom abundantly.
The spring rain is a rain that calls forth all the flowers.
And only after the flowers bloom will the butterflies arrive—
That is the nature of this world.
Ehwa, why are you curled up like a little kitten?
I feel all sticky. And my stomach hurts...
Maybe you have indigestion?
My stomach feels all bloated.
Do you want me to prick your finger?*
It's okay. I'm just feeling a bit uncomfortable is all.

* When someone has indigestion, the Korean custom is to make a tourniquet on a thumb and prick its tip with a needle to release a few drops of blood. This method is thought to relieve indigestion.

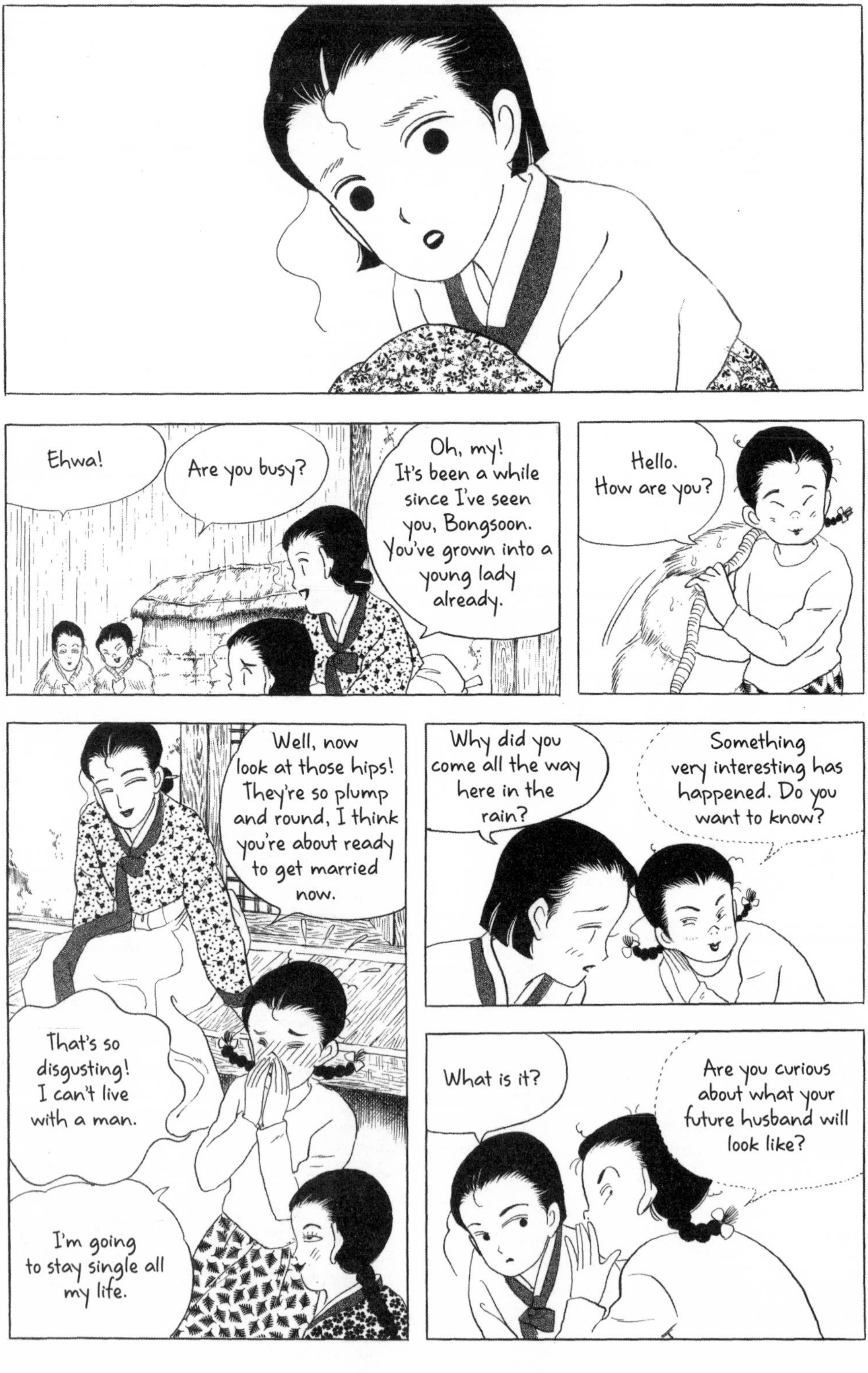
Ehwa!
Are you busy?
Oh, my! It's been a while since I've seen you, Bongsoon. You've grown into a young lady already.
Hello. How are you?
Well, now look at those hips! They're so plump and round, I think you're about ready to get married now.
That's so disgusting! I can't live with a man.
I'm going to stay single all my life.
Why did you come all the way here in the rain?
Something very interesting has happened. Do you want to know?
What is it?
Are you curious about what your future husband will look like?

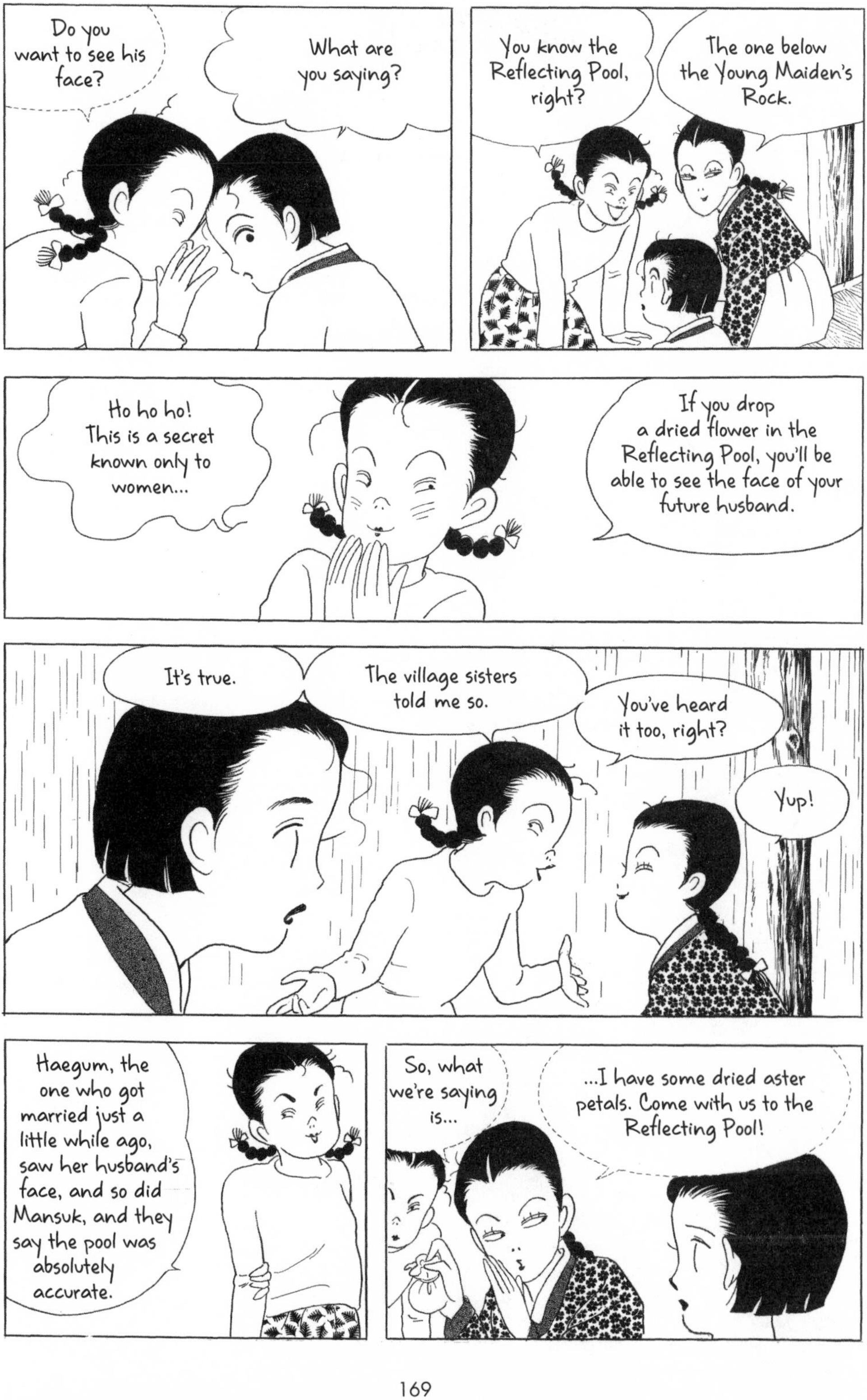
Do you want to see his face?
What are you saying?
You know the Reflecting Pool, right?
The one below the Young Maiden's Rock.
Ho ho ho! This is a secret known only to women...
If you drop a dried flower in the Reflecting Pool, you'll be able to see the face of your future husband.
It's true.
The village sisters told me so.
You've heard it too, right?
Yup!
Haegum, the one who got married just a little while ago, saw her husband's face, and so did Mansuk, and they say the pool was absolutely accurate.
So, what we're saying is...
...I have some dried aster petals. Come with us to the Reflecting Pool!

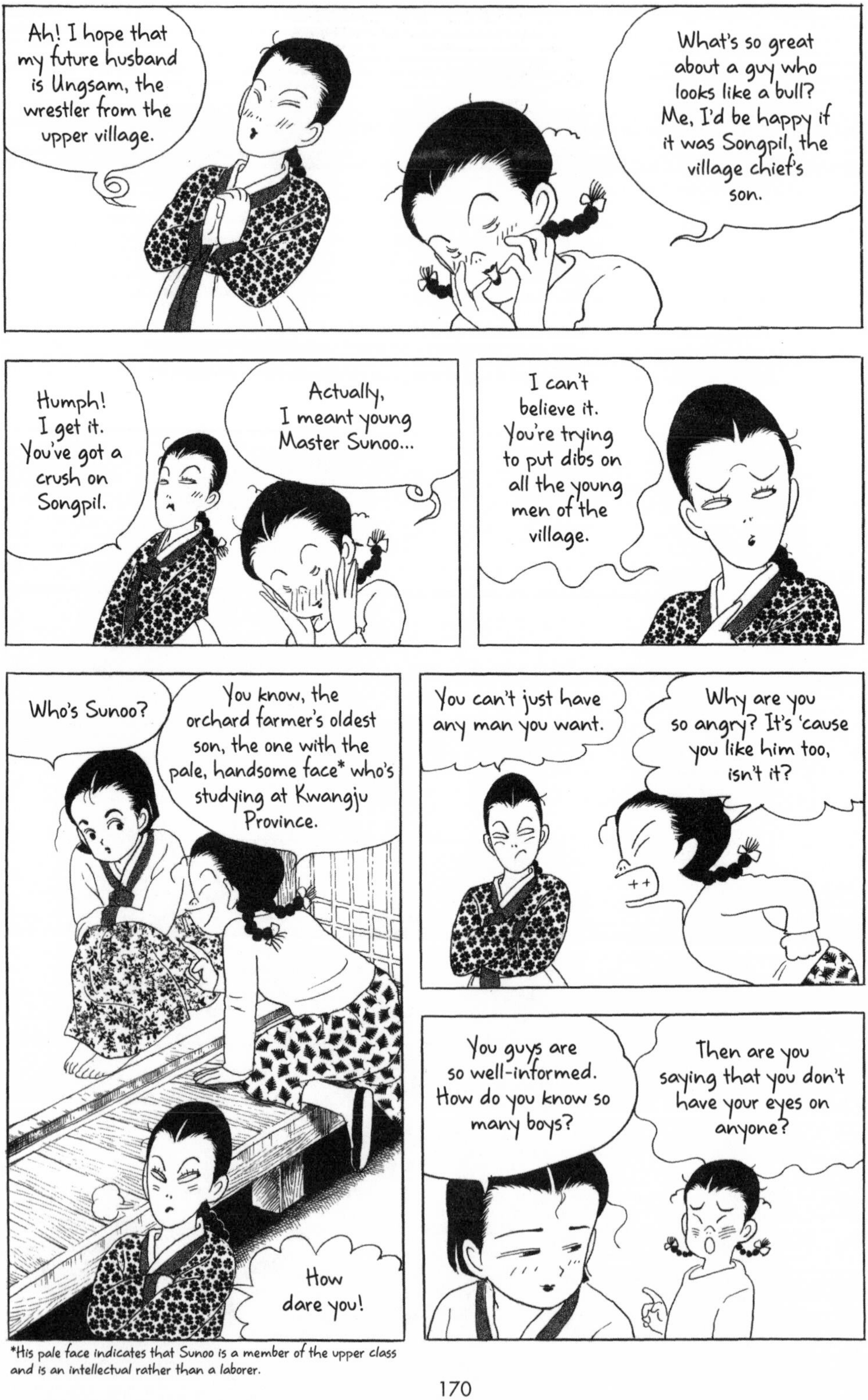
Ah! I hope that my future husband is Ungsam, the wrestler from the upper village.
What's so great about a guy who looks like a bull? Me, I'd be happy if it was Songpil, the village chief's son.
Humph! I get it. You've got a crush on Songpil.
Actually, I meant young Master Sunoo...
I can't believe it. You're trying to put dibs on all the young men of the village.
Who's Sunoo?
You know, the orchard farmer's oldest son, the one with the pale, handsome face* who's studying at Kwangju Province.
How dare you!
You can't just have any man you want.
Why are you so angry? It's 'cause you like him too, isn't it?
You guys are so well-informed. How do you know so many boys?
Then are you saying that you don't have your eyes on anyone?

*His pale face indicates that Sunoo is a member of the upper class and is an intellectual rather than a laborer.

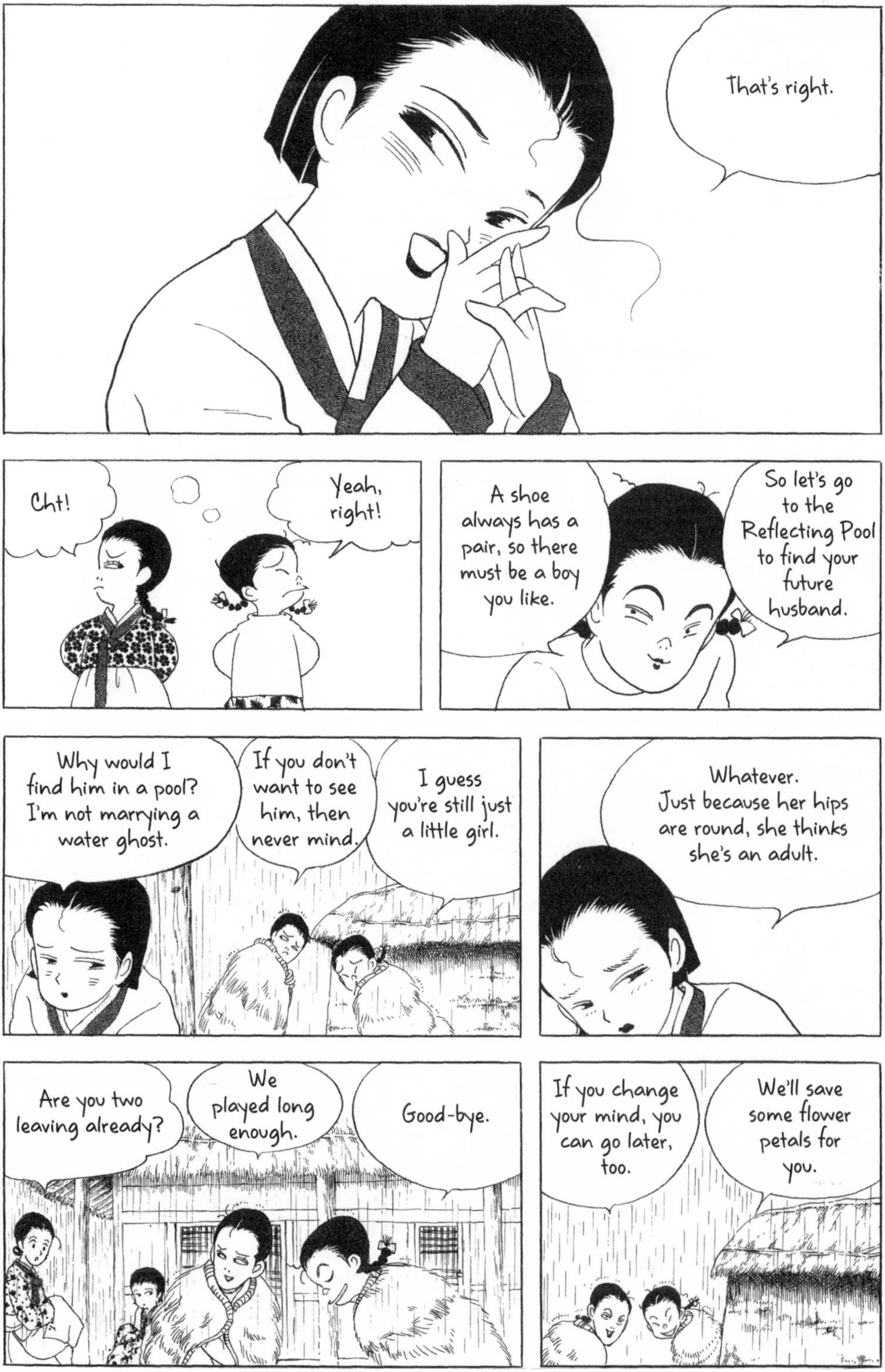
That's right.
Cht!
Yeah, right!
A shoe always has a pair, so there must be a boy you like.
So let's go to the Reflecting Pool to find your future husband.
Why would I find him in a pool? I'm not marrying a water ghost.
If you don't want to see him, then never mind.
I guess you're still just a little girl.
Whatever. Just because her hips are round, she thinks she's an adult.
Are you two leaving already?
We played long enough.
Good-bye.
If you change your mind, you can go later, too.
We'll save some flower petals for you.

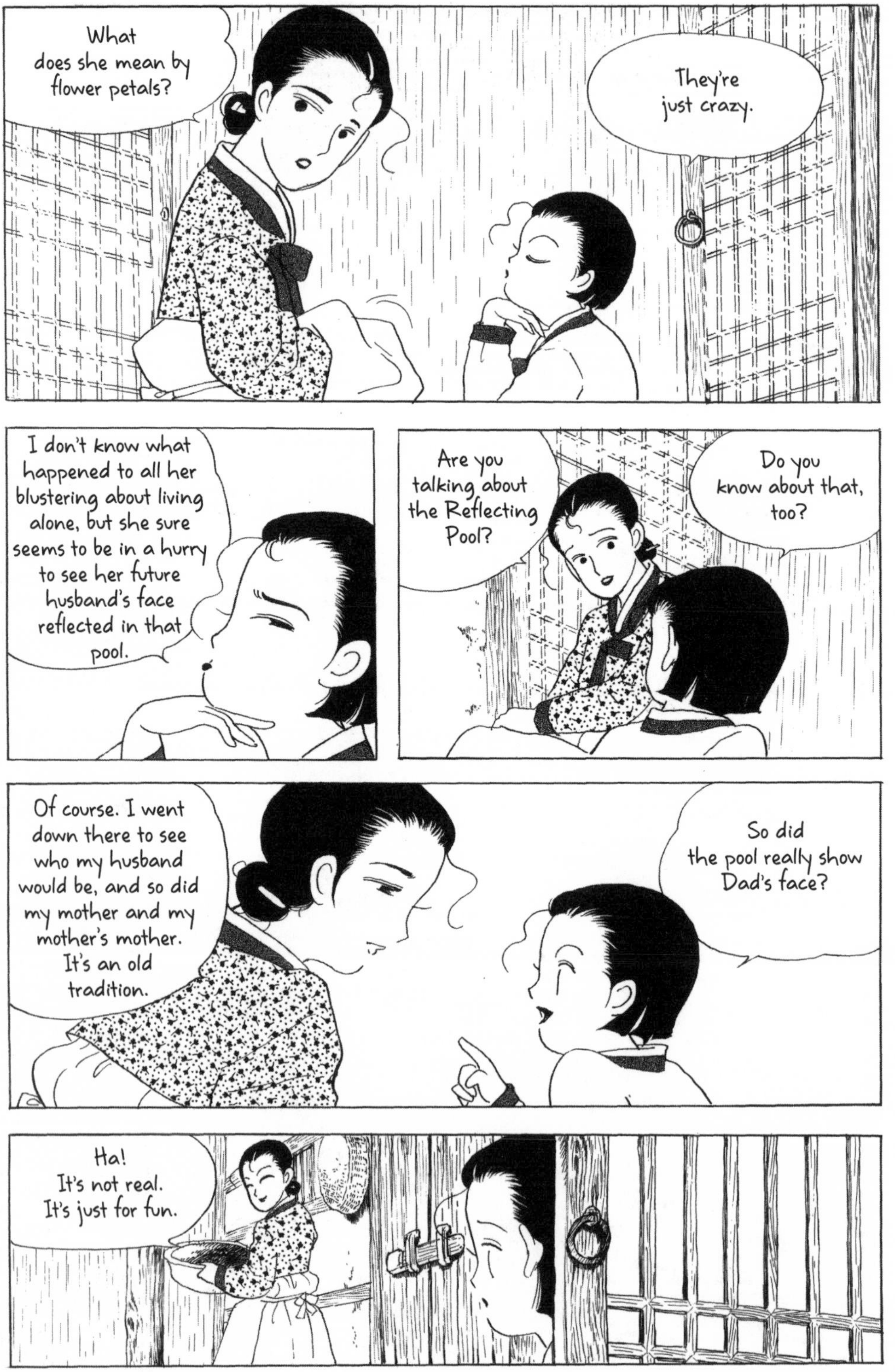
What does she mean by flower petals?
They're just crazy.
I don't know what happened to all her blustering about living alone, but she sure seems to be in a hurry to see her future husband's face reflected in that pool.
Are you talking about the Reflecting Pool?
Do you know about that, too?
Of course. I went down there to see who my husband would be, and so did my mother and my mother's mother. It's an old tradition.
So did the pool really show Dad's face?
Ha! It's not real. It's just for fun.

Huh?

What is this?

There's a bump on my chest.

What's going on? I don't remember bumping into anything...

First my stomach... And now my chest... I hope I'm not getting sick or anything.

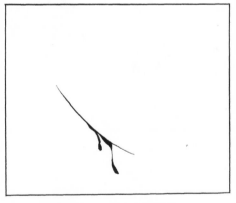

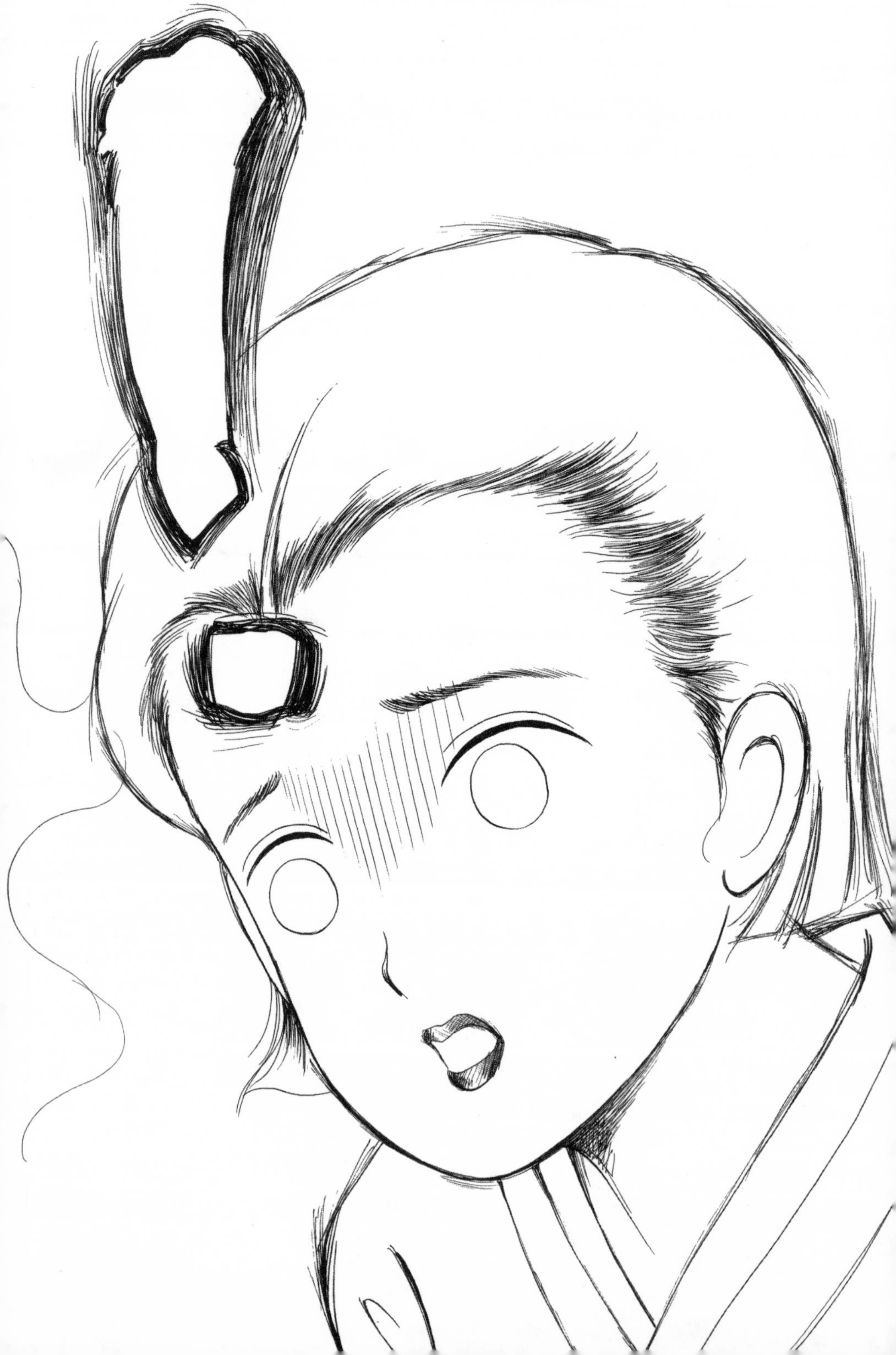

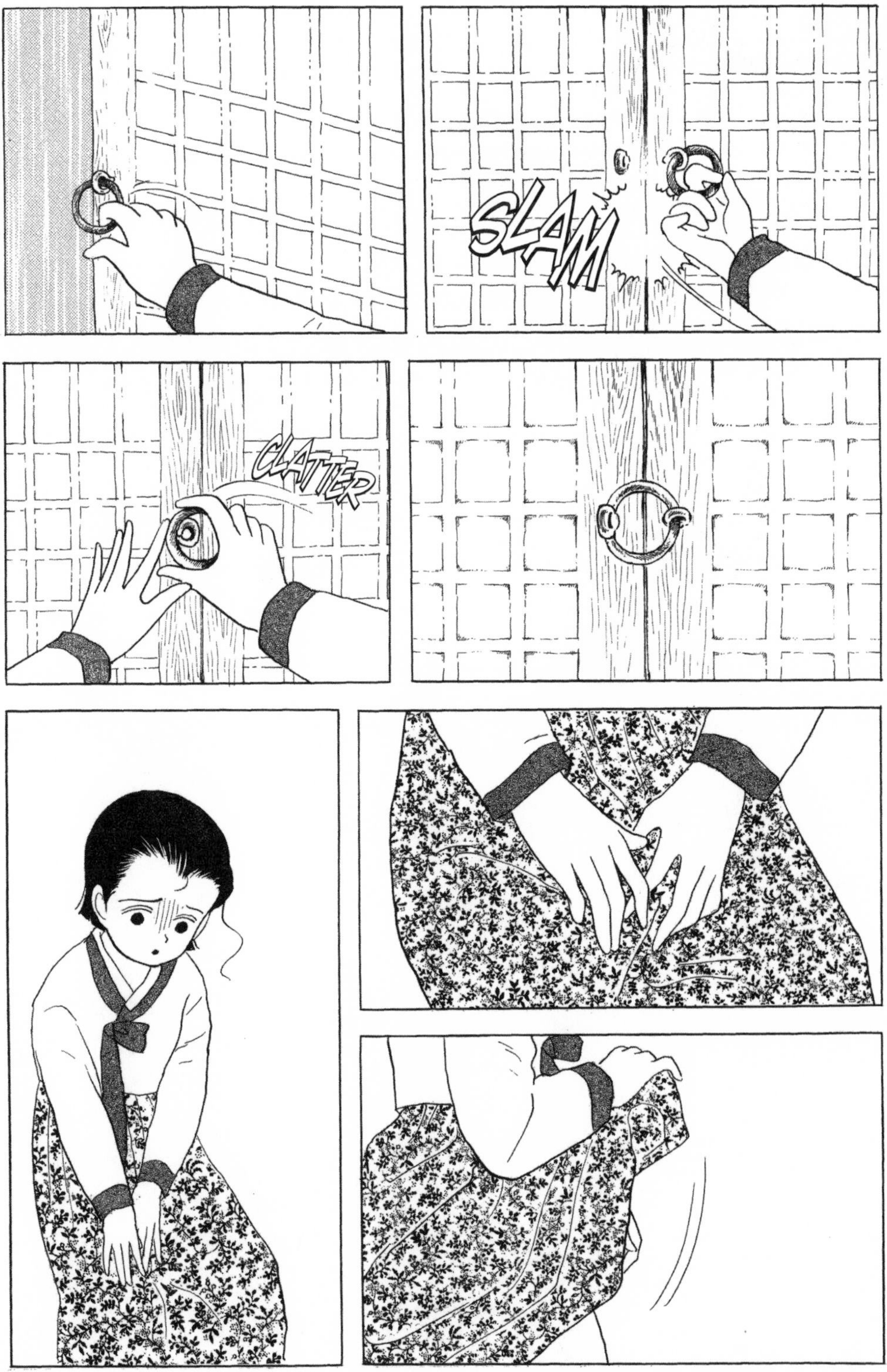
SLAM
CLATTER

Something is dripping down there!
It's wet.

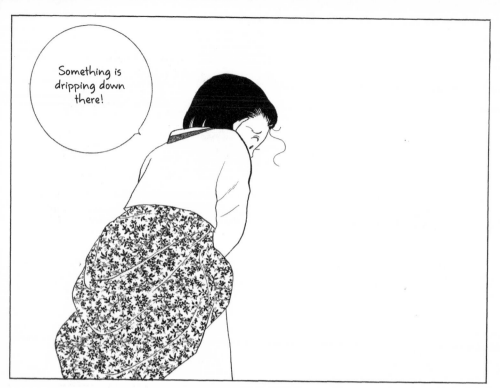

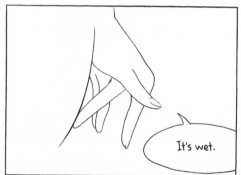

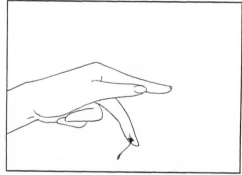

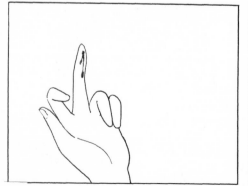

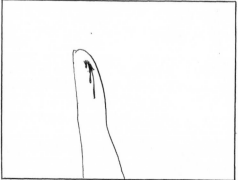

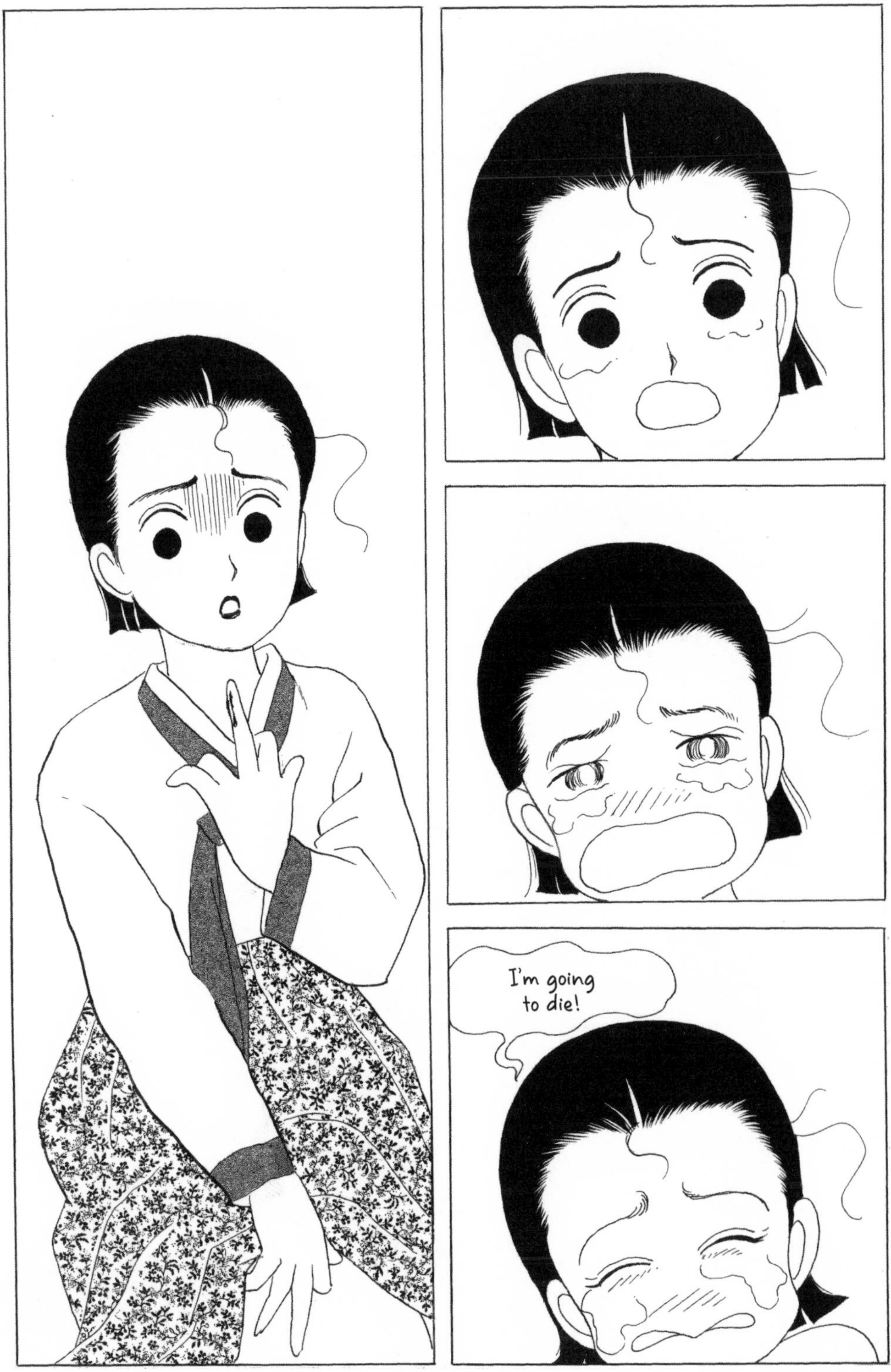
I'm going to die!

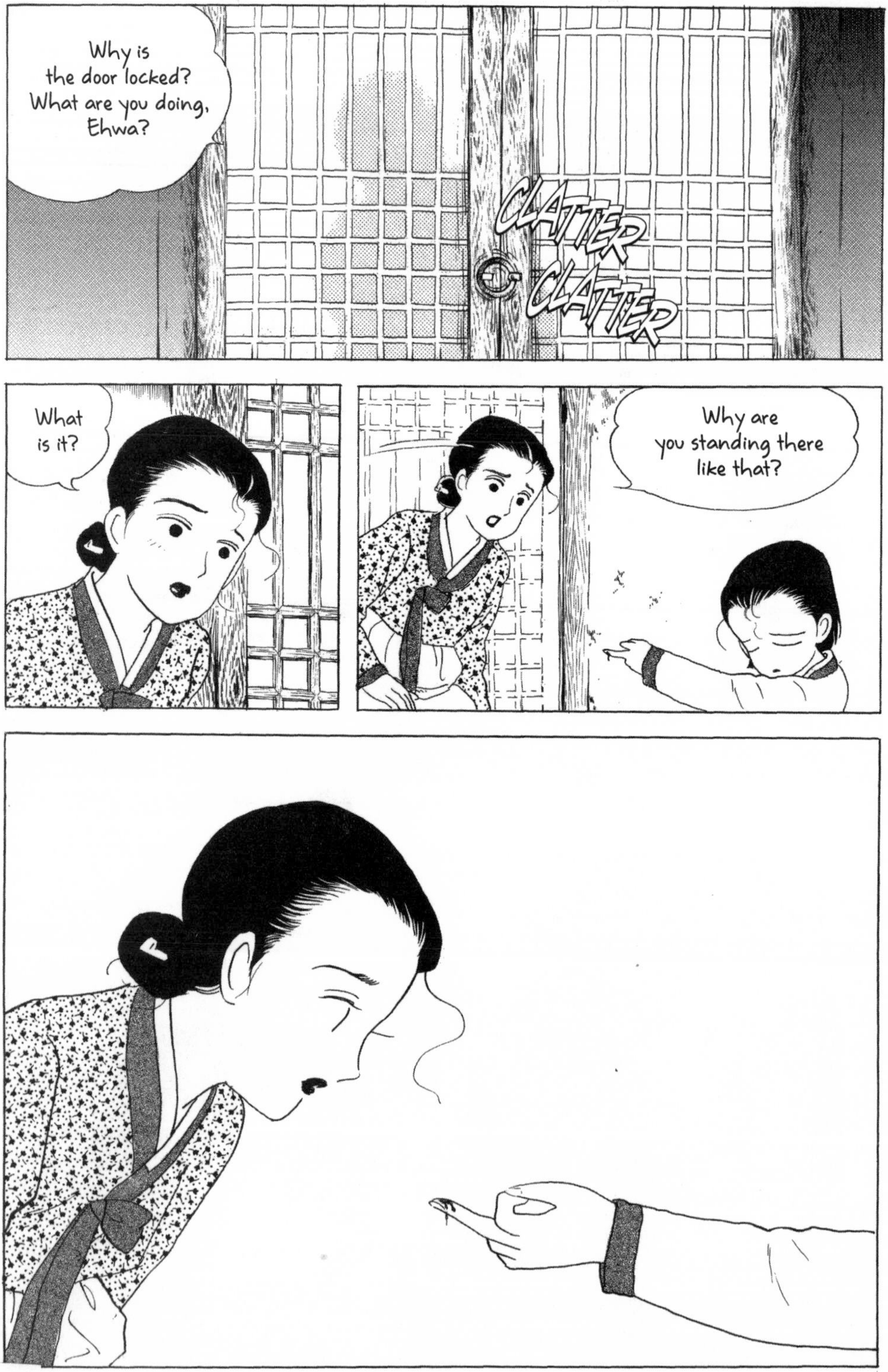
Why is the door locked? What are you doing, Ehwa?
CLATTER CLATTER
What is it?
Why are you standing there like that?

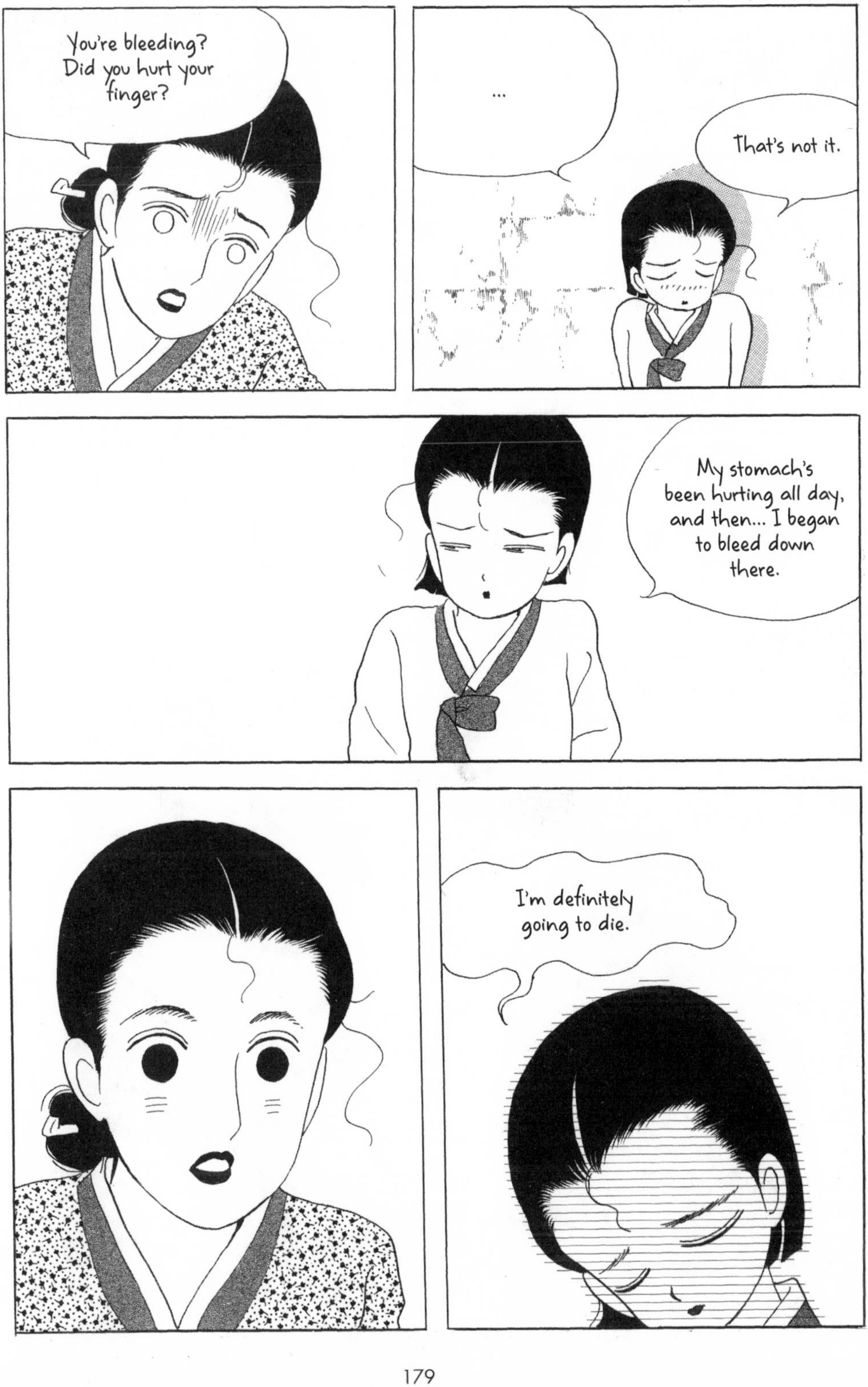
You're bleeding? Did you hurt your finger?
...
That's not it.
My stomach's been hurting all day, and then... I began to bleed down there.
I'm definitely going to die.

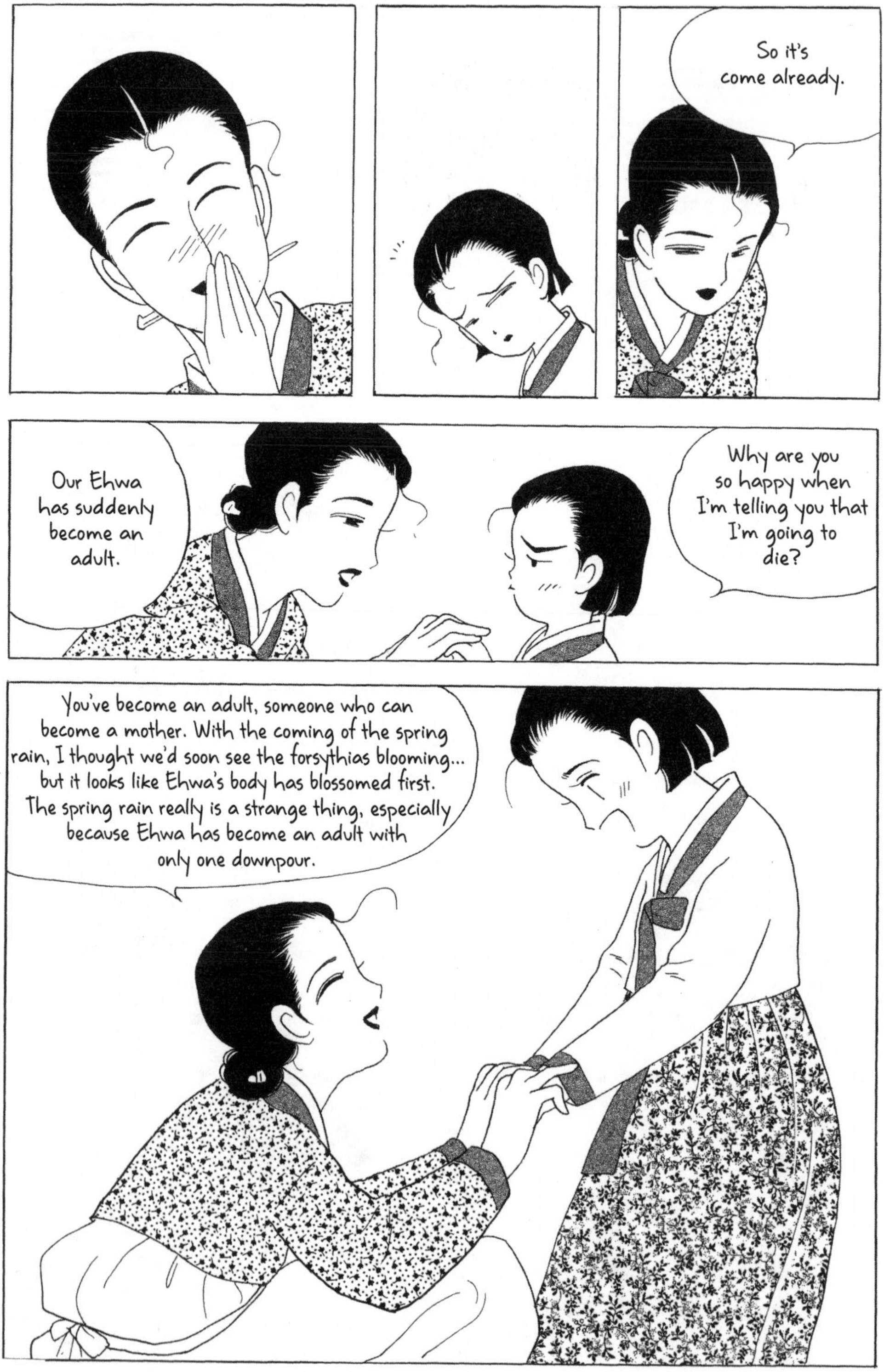
So it's come already.
Our Ehwa has suddenly become an adult.
Why are you so happy when I'm telling you that I'm going to die?
You've become an adult, someone who can become a mother. With the coming of the spring rain, I thought we'd soon see the forsythias blooming... but it looks like Ehwa's body has blossomed first. The spring rain really is a strange thing, especially because Ehwa has become an adult with only one downpour.

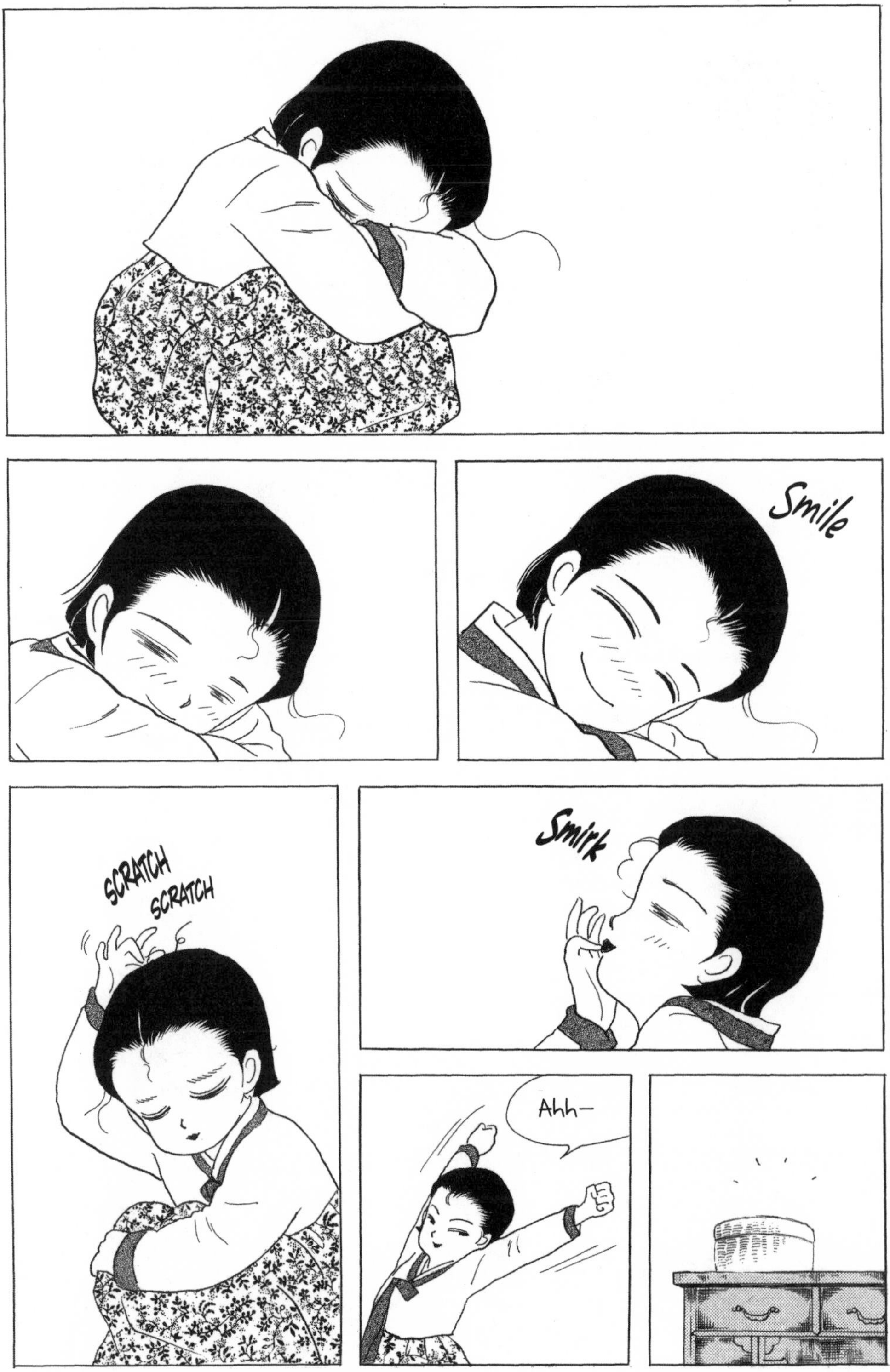
Smile
SCRATCH
SCRATCH
Smirk
Ahh-

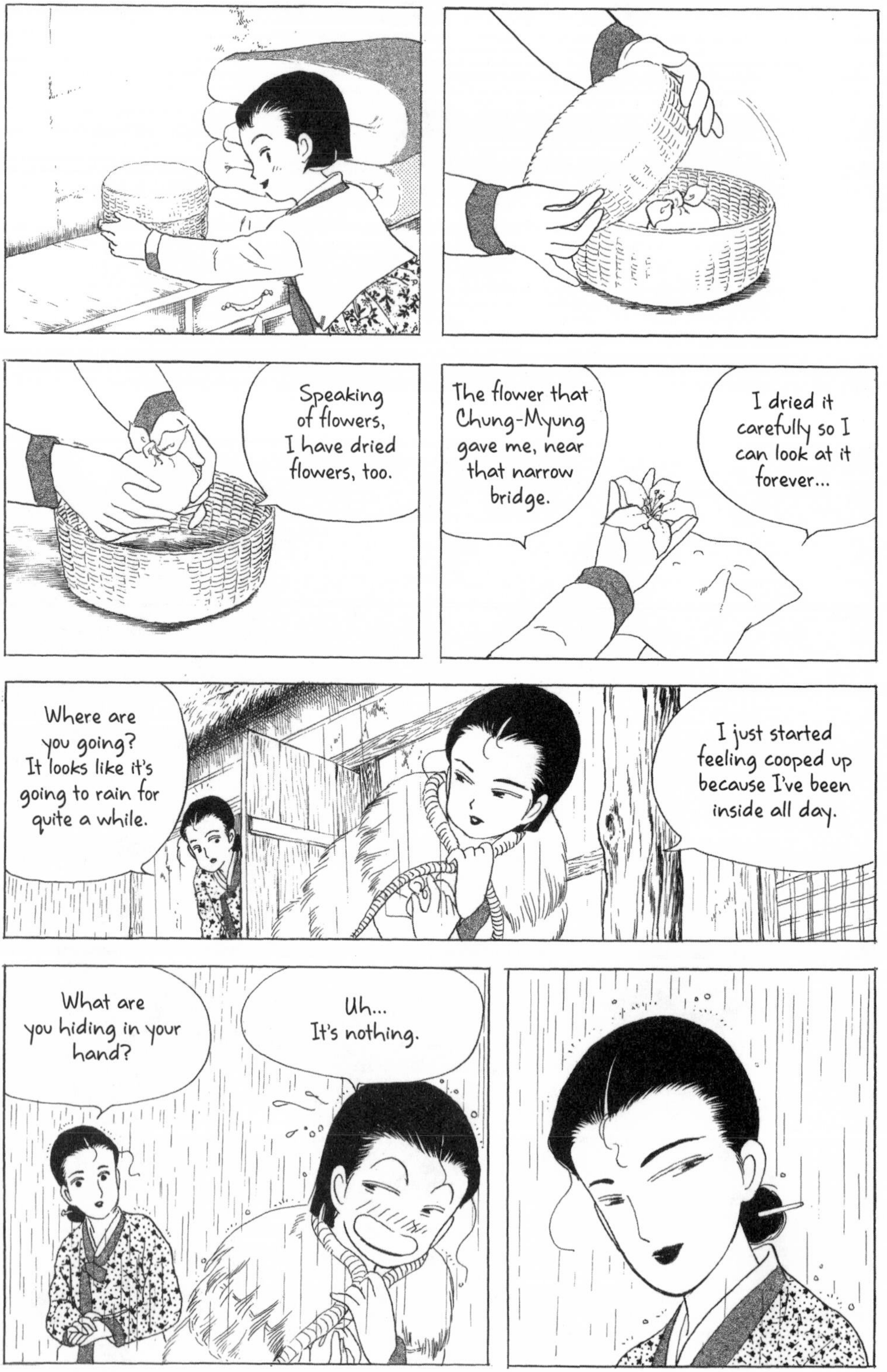
Speaking of flowers, I have dried flowers, too.
The flower that Chung-Myung gave me, near that narrow bridge.
I dried it carefully so I can look at it forever...
Where are you going? It looks like it's going to rain for quite a while.
I just started feeling cooped up because I've been inside all day.
What are you hiding in your hand?
Uh... It's nothing.

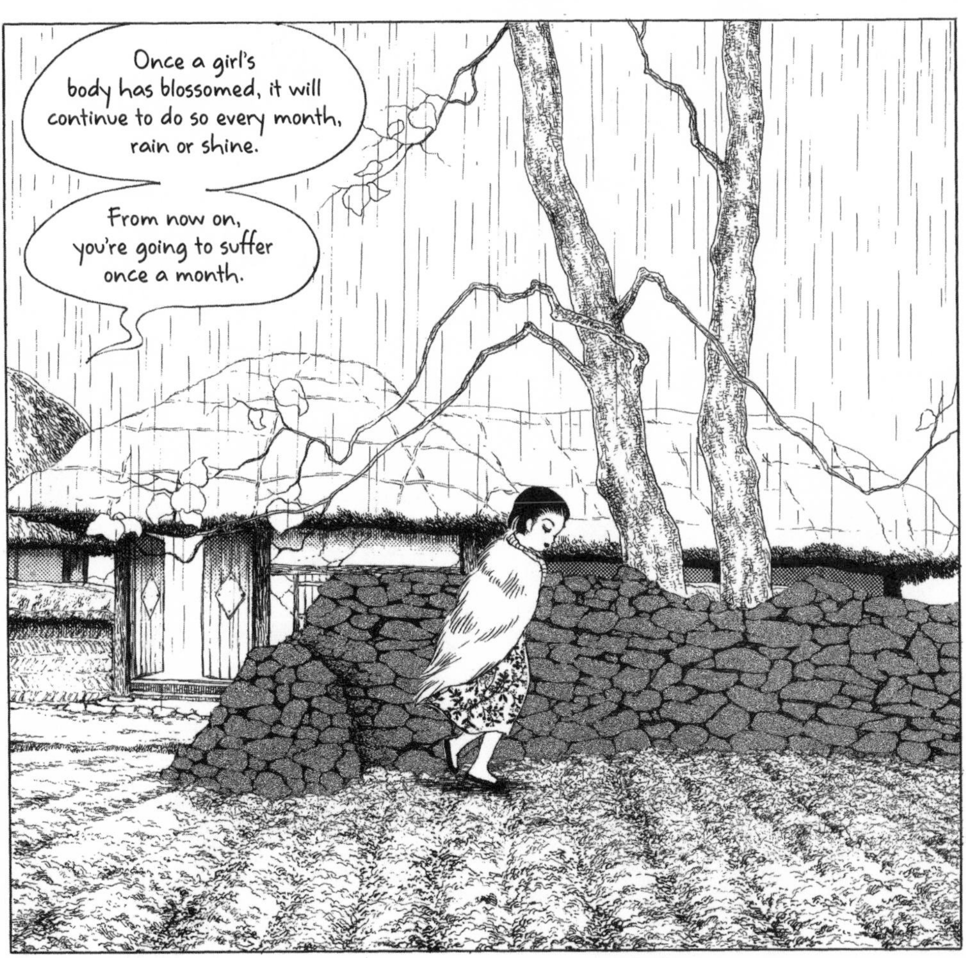
Once a girl's body has blossomed, it will continue to do so every month, rain or shine.
From now on, you're going to suffer once a month.

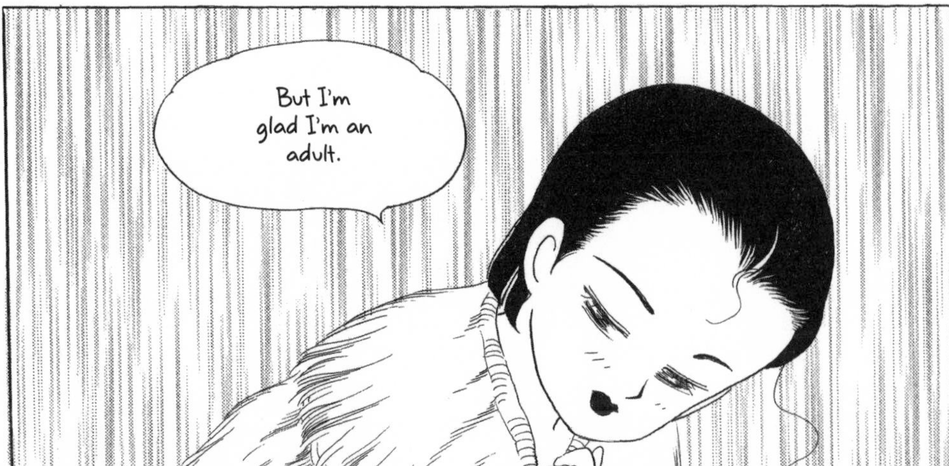
But I'm glad I'm an adult.

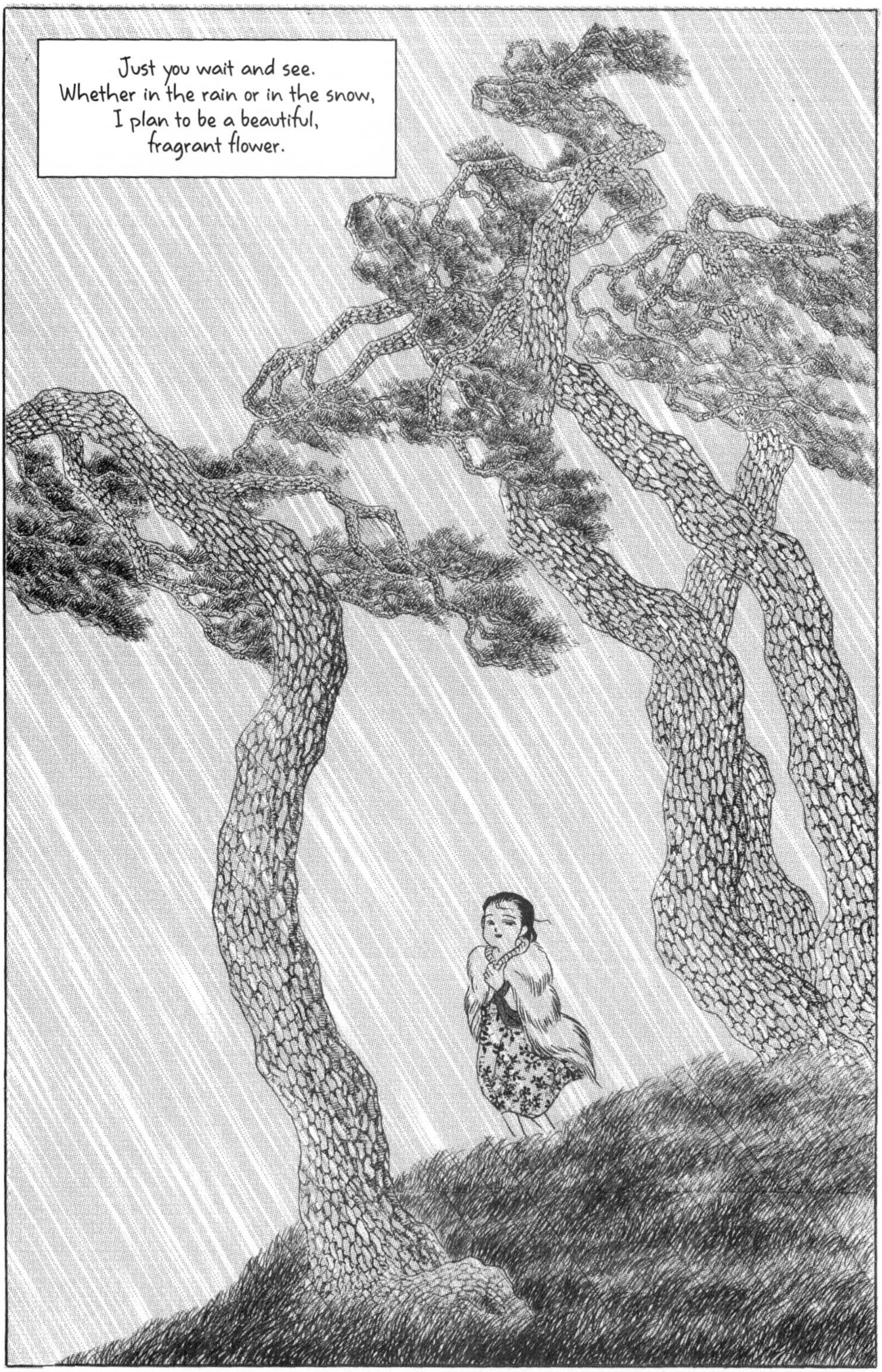
Just you wait and see.
Whether in the rain or in the snow,
I plan to be a beautiful,
fragrant flower.

It stopped raining. It looks like Mr. Rain is tired now.

I wonder who Bongsoon and Junghee saw in the Reflecting Pool?

I want to see, too.

Now that I've finally reached adulthood.

Who will come find me?

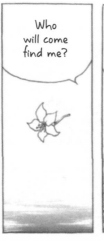

Who will wait for me?

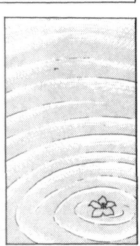

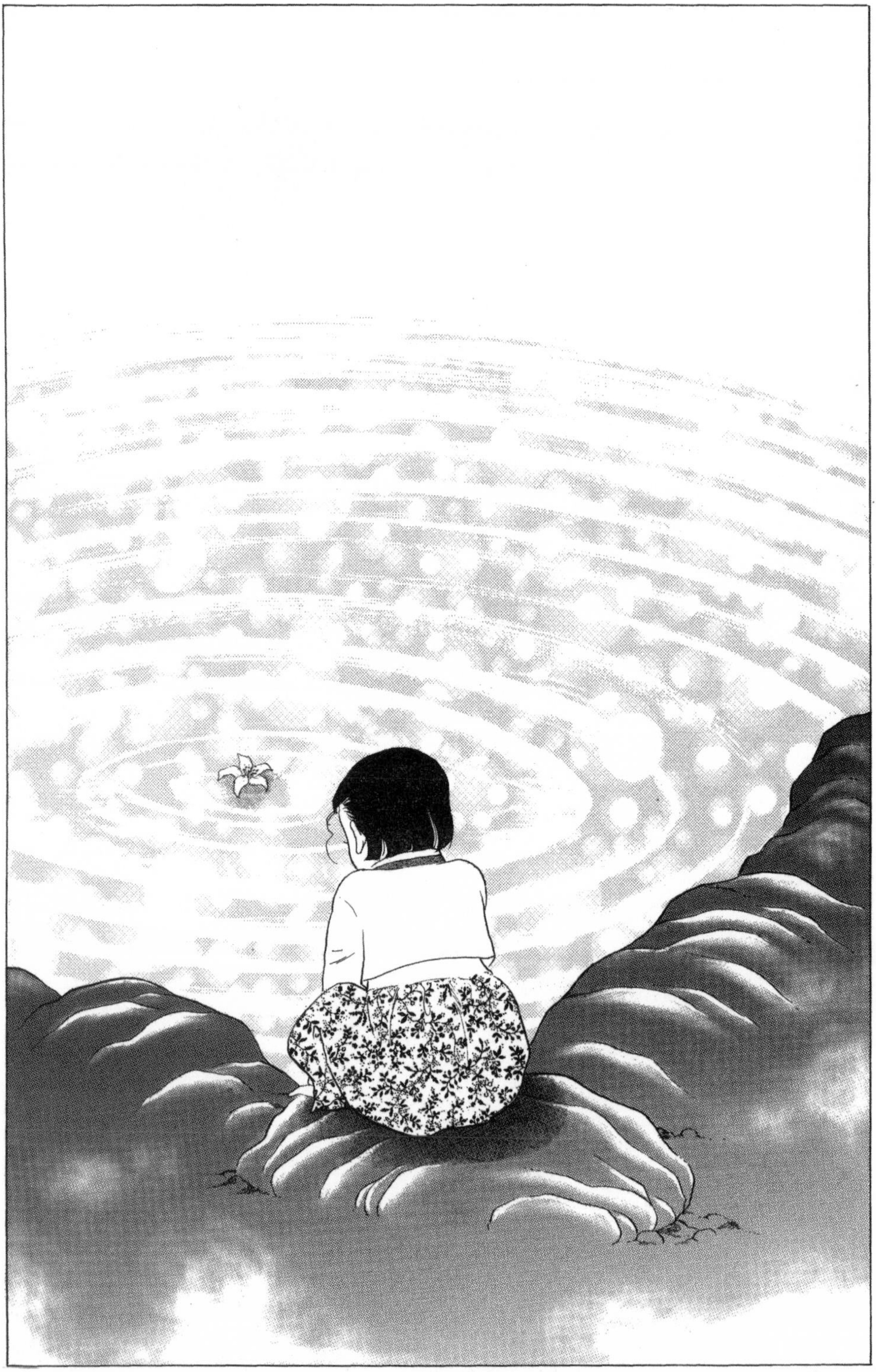

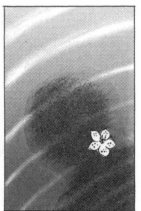

The pool really does work!

Gulp

Short hair, like Chung-Myung.

It doesn't look like a monk's garb...

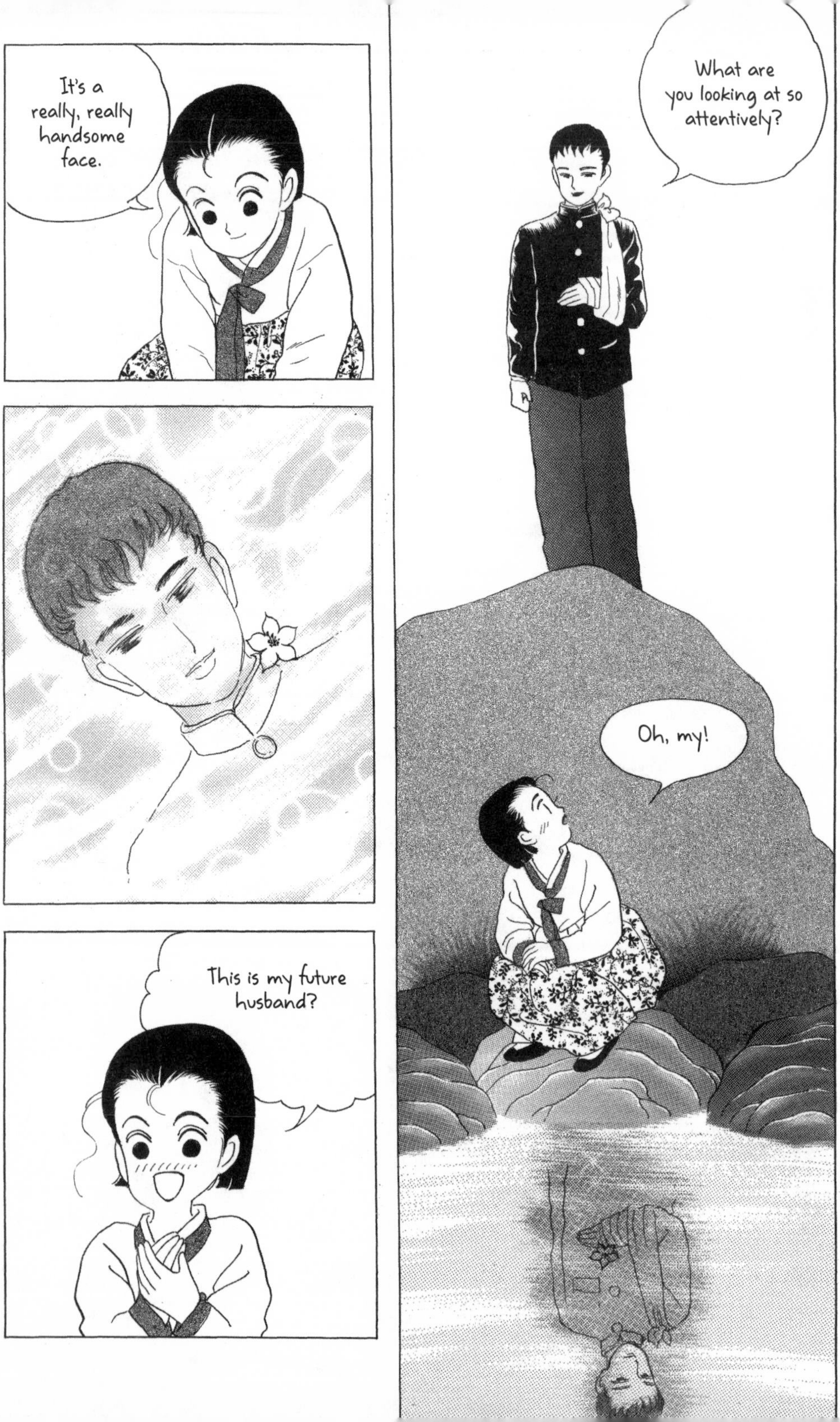
It's a really, really handsome face.
This is my future husband?
What are you looking at so attentively?
Oh, my!

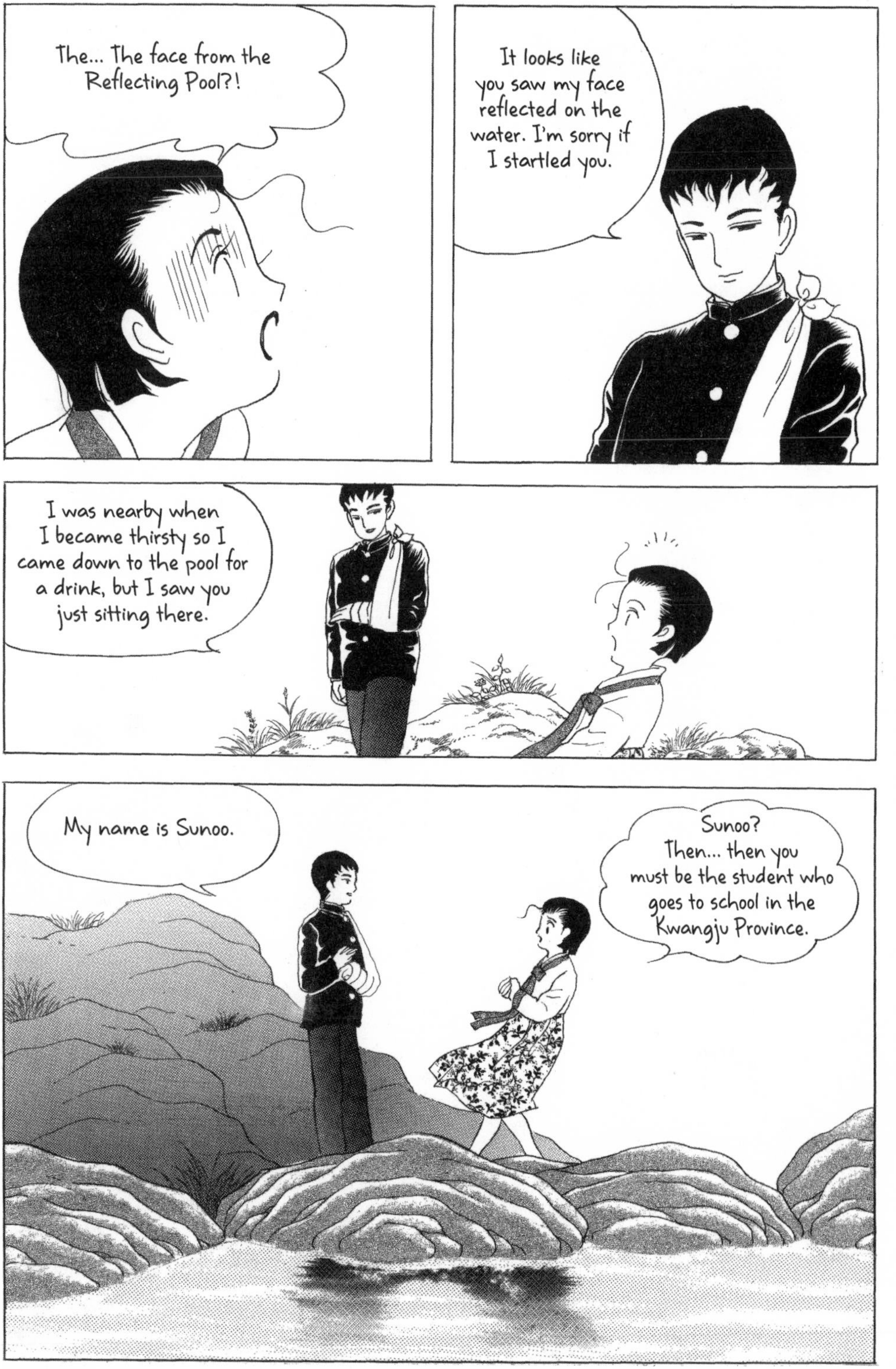
The... The face from the Reflecting Pool?!
It looks like you saw my face reflected on the water. I'm sorry if I startled you.
I was nearby when I became thirsty so I came down to the pool for a drink, but I saw you just sitting there.
My name is Sunoo.
Sunoo? Then... then you must be the student who goes to school in the Kwangju Province.

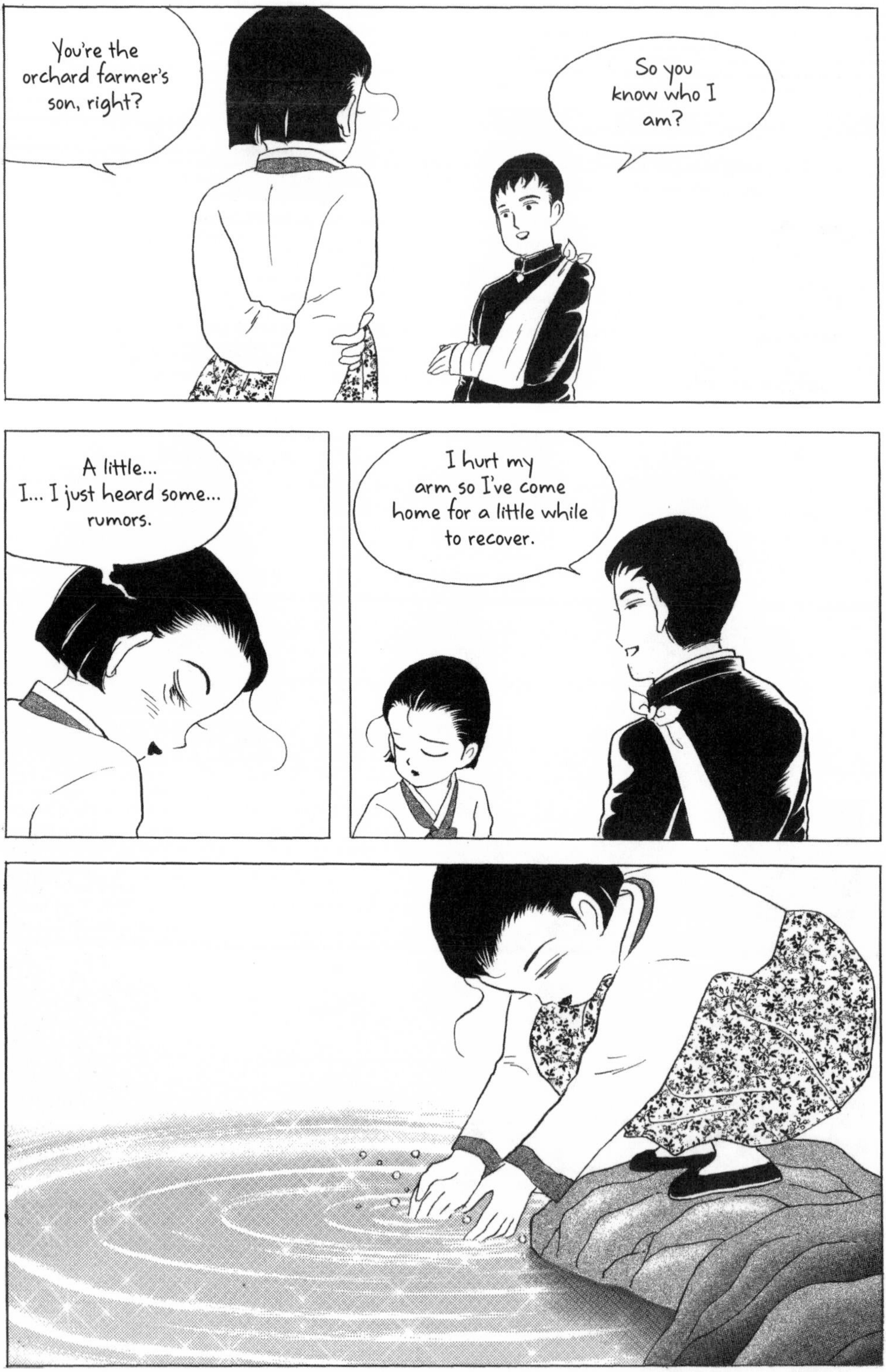
You're the orchard farmer's son, right?
So you know who I am?
A little... I... I just heard some... rumors.
I hurt my arm so I've come home for a little while to recover.

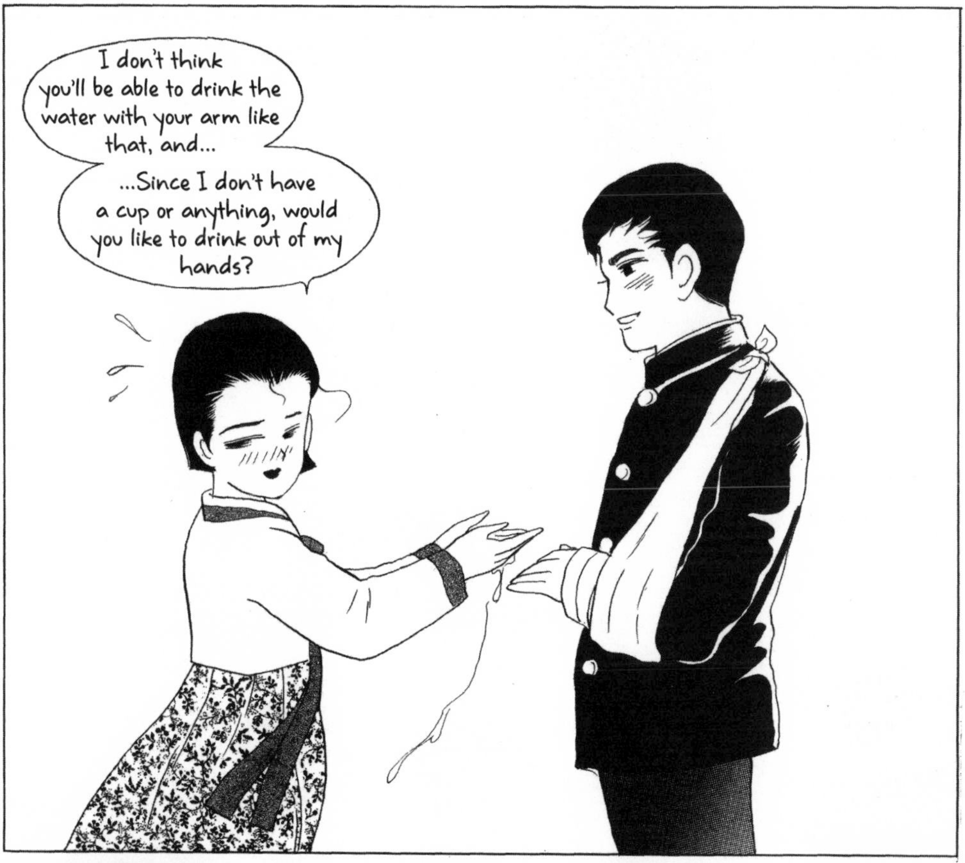
I don't think you'll be able to drink the water with your arm like that, and...
...Since I don't have a cup or anything, would you like to drink out of my hands?

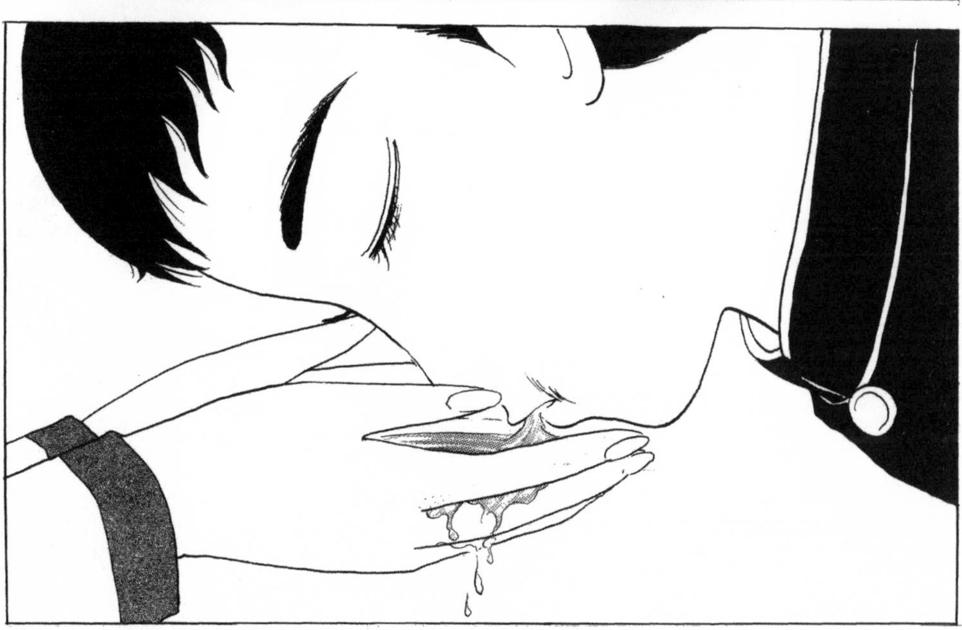

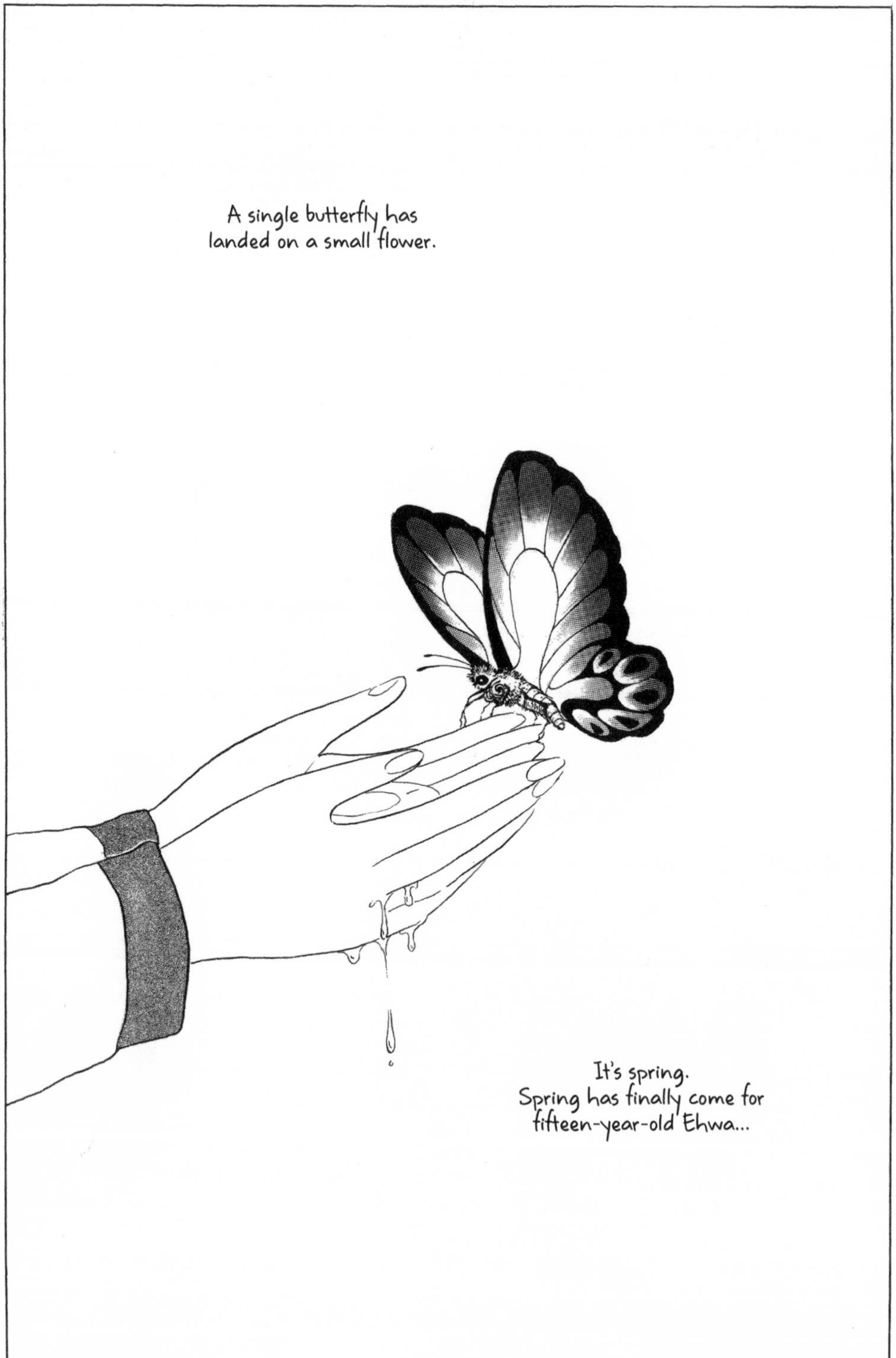
A single butterfly has landed on a small flower.
It's spring. Spring has finally come for fifteen-year-old Ehwa...

Chapter Seven

LOVE IS IN THE AIR

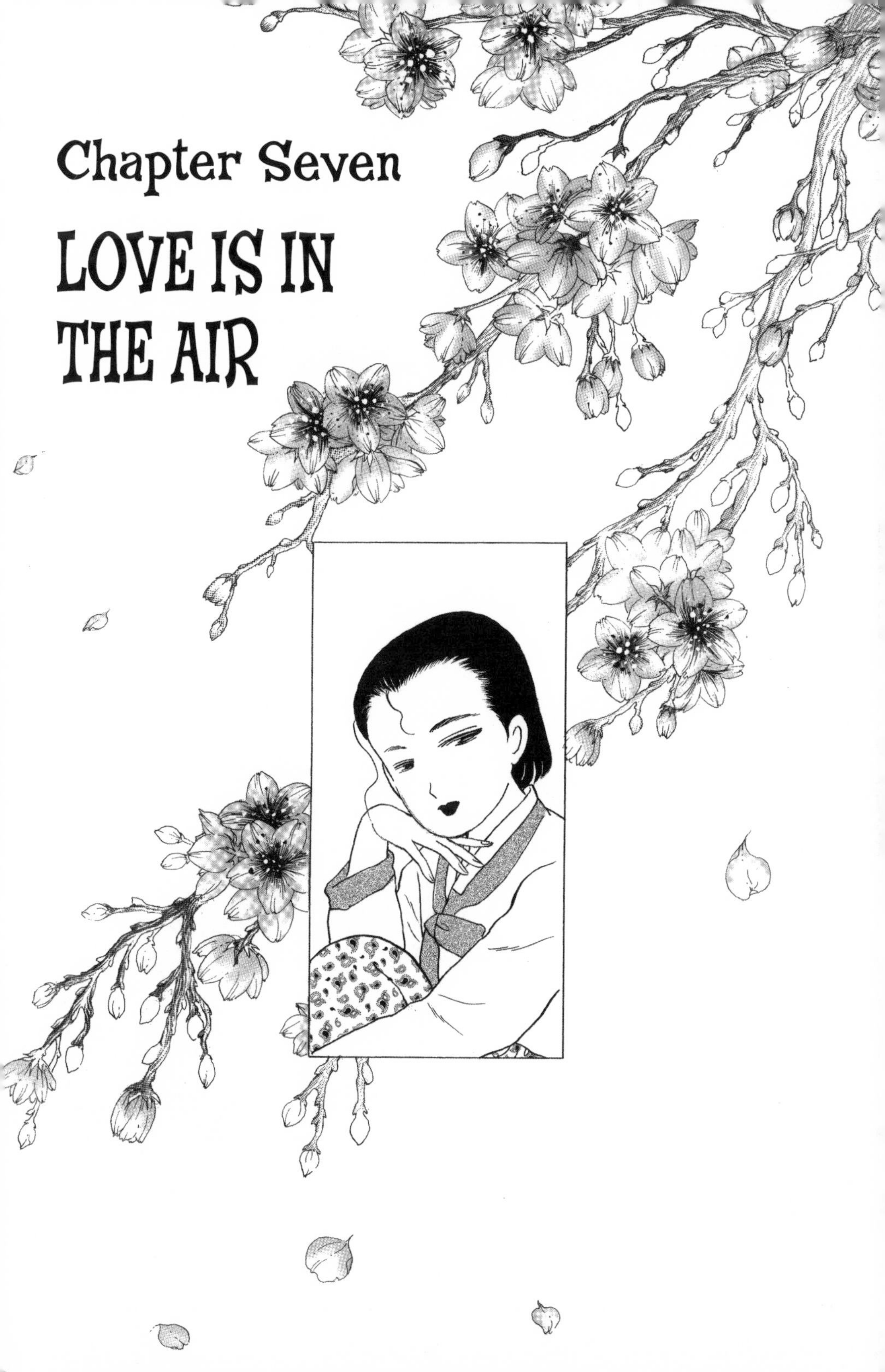

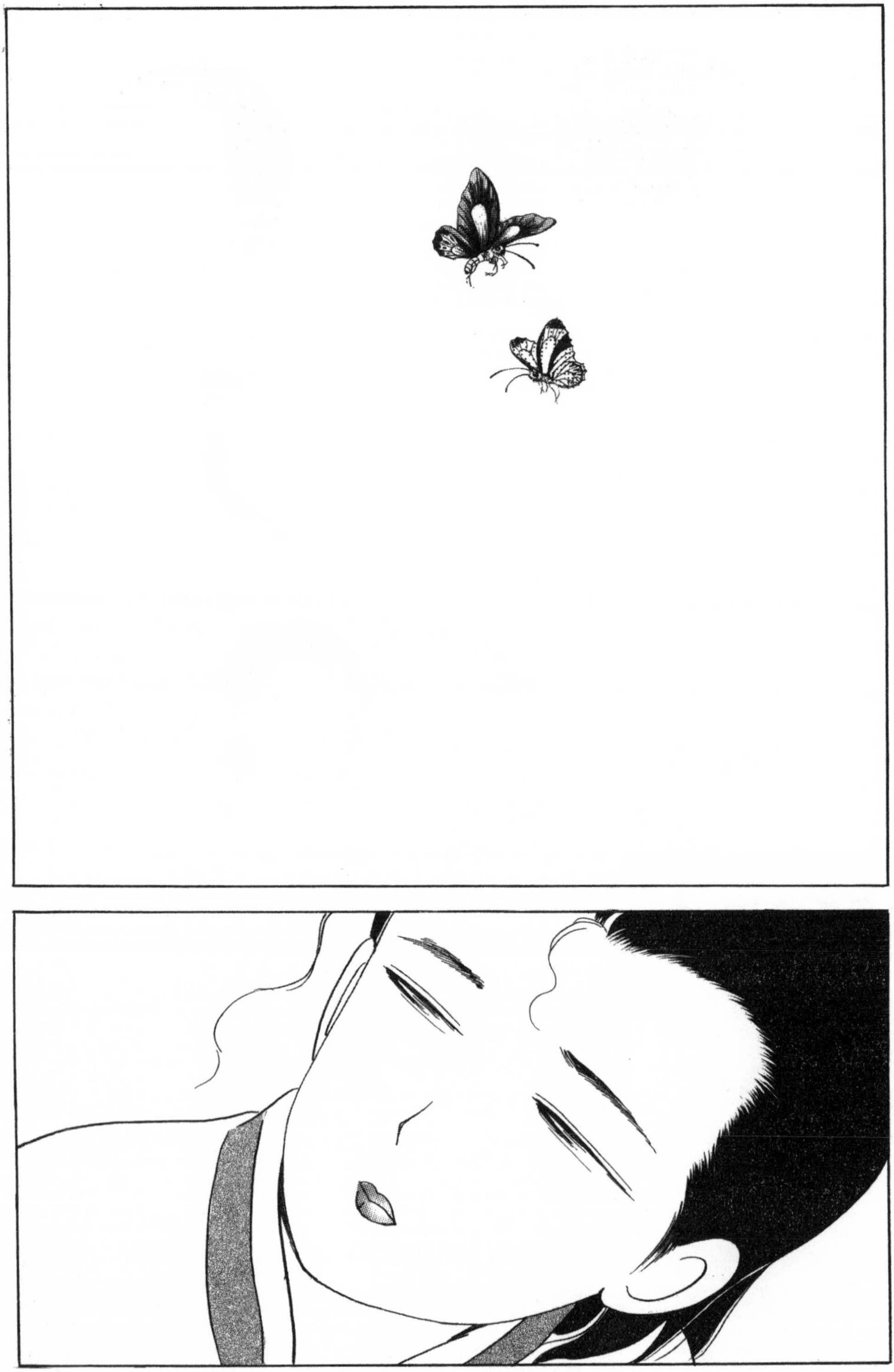

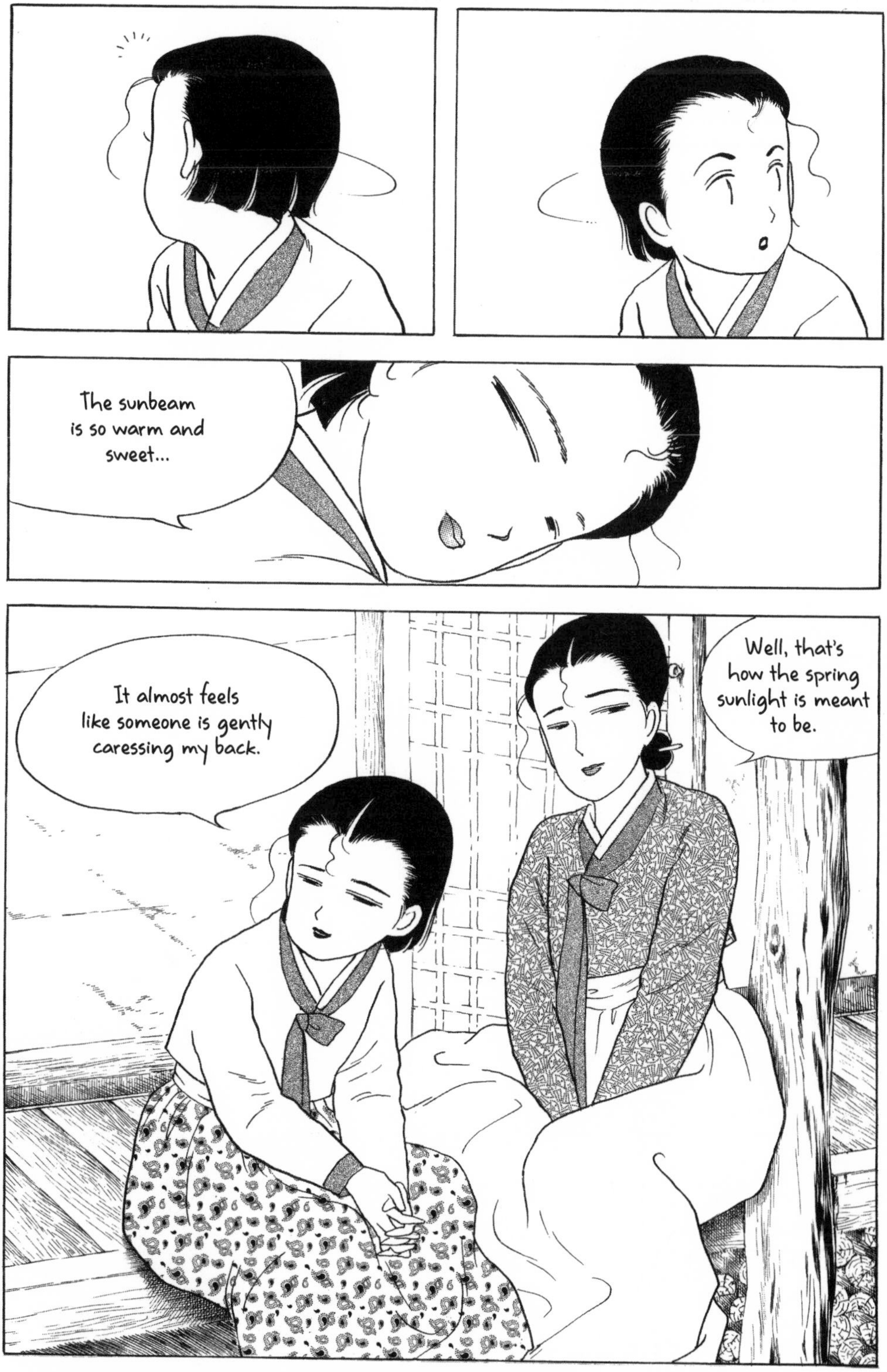
The sunbeam is so warm and sweet...
It almost feels like someone is gently caressing my back.
Well, that's how the spring sunlight is meant to be.

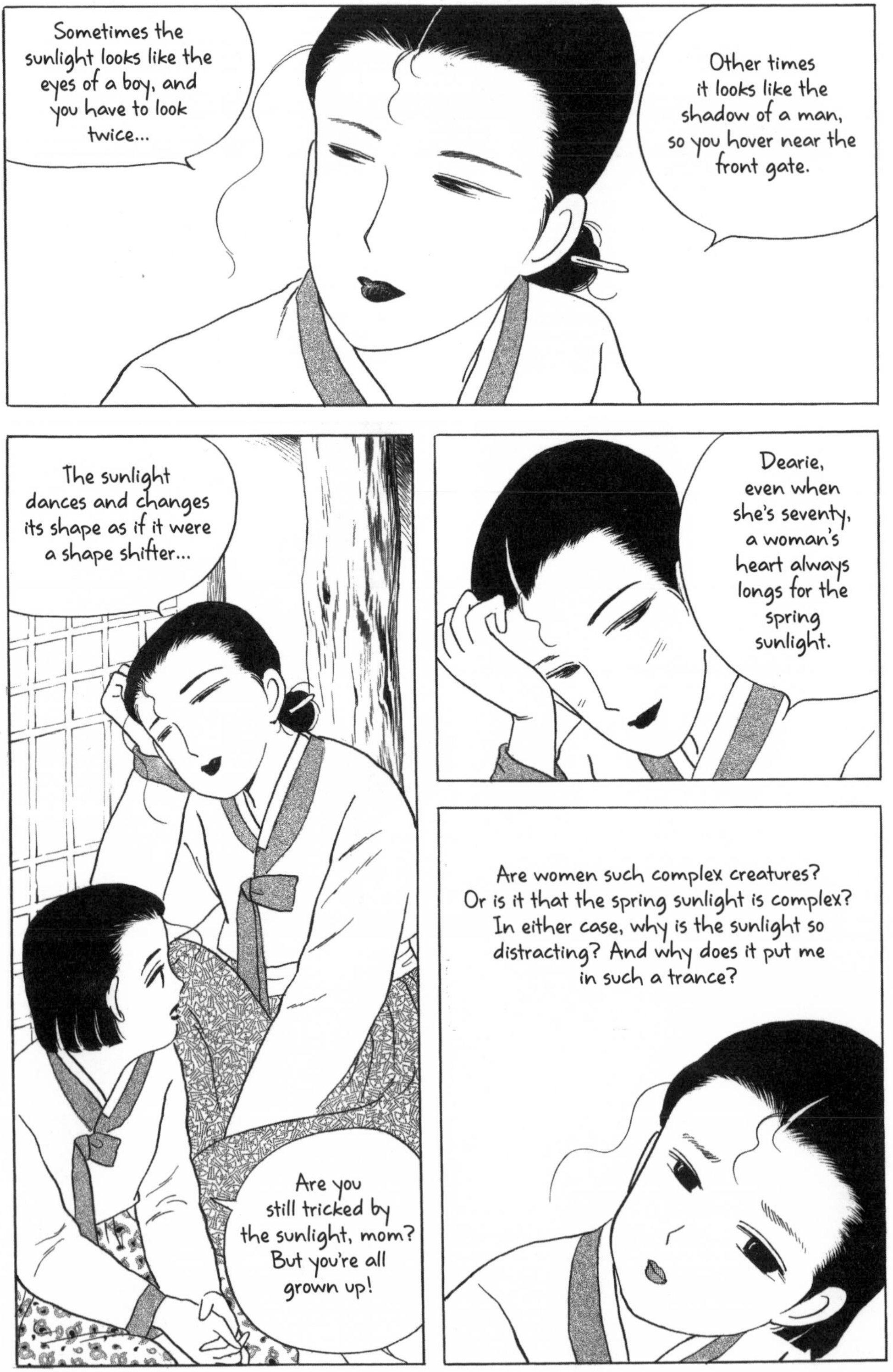
Sometimes the sunlight looks like the eyes of a boy, and you have to look twice...
Other times it looks like the shadow of a man, so you hover near the front gate.
The sunlight dances and changes its shape as if it were a shape shifter...
Dearie, even when she's seventy, a woman's heart always longs for the spring sunlight.
Are you still tricked by the sunlight, mom? But you're all grown up!
Are women such complex creatures? Or is it that the spring sunlight is complex? In either case, why is the sunlight so distracting? And why does it put me in such a trance?

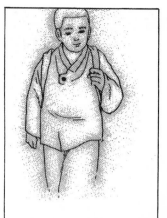

What am I doing?

Is it because of the sunlight that these two are always in my thoughts?

197

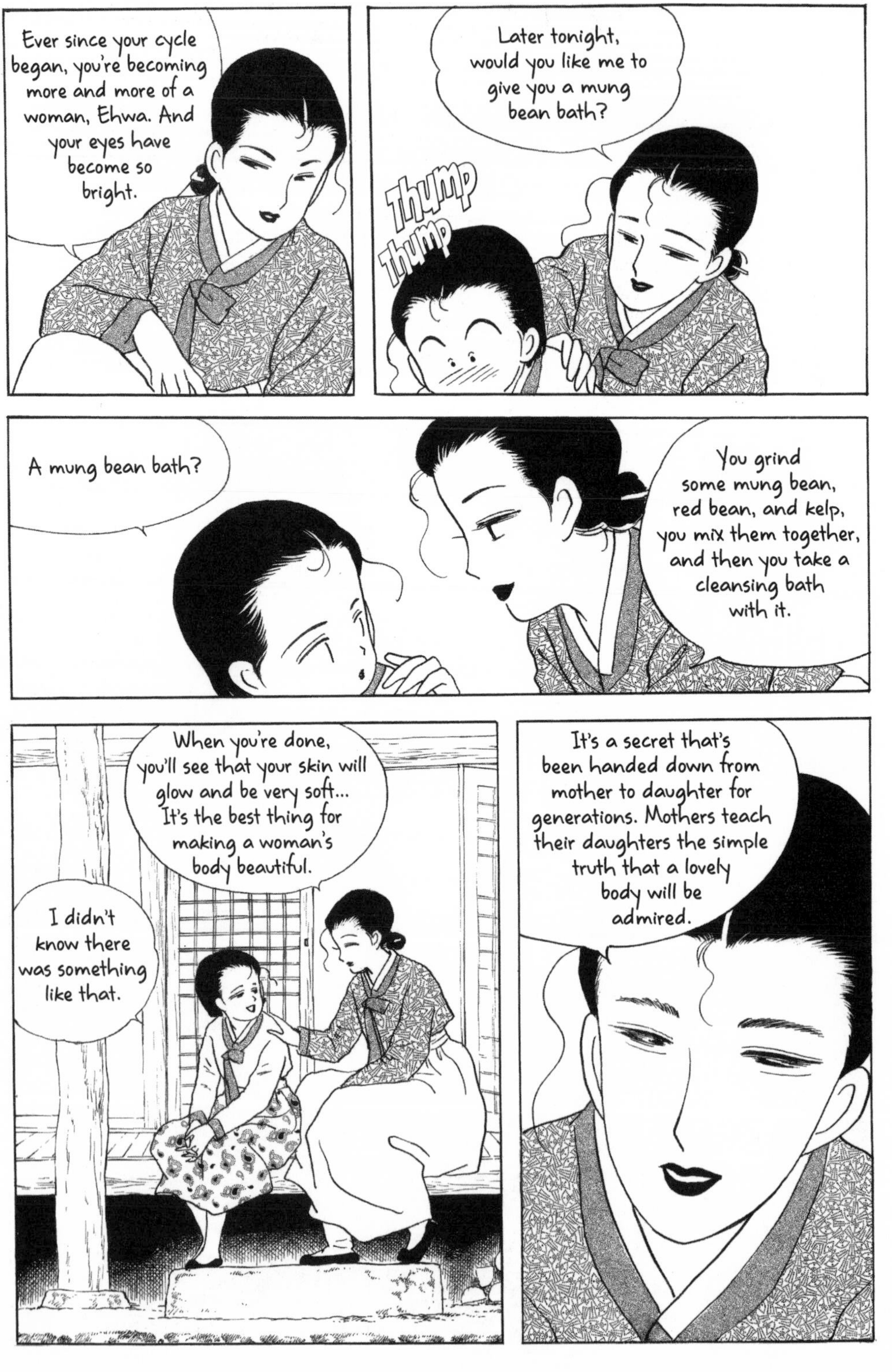

Ever since your cycle began, you're becoming more and more of a woman, Ehwa. And your eyes have become so bright.
Later tonight, would you like me to give you a mung bean bath?
Thump Thump
A mung bean bath?
You grind some mung bean, red bean, and kelp, you mix them together, and then you take a cleansing bath with it.
When you're done, you'll see that your skin will glow and be very soft... It's the best thing for making a woman's body beautiful.
I didn't know there was something like that.
It's a secret that's been handed down from mother to daughter for generations. Mothers teach their daughters the simple truth that a lovely body will be admired.

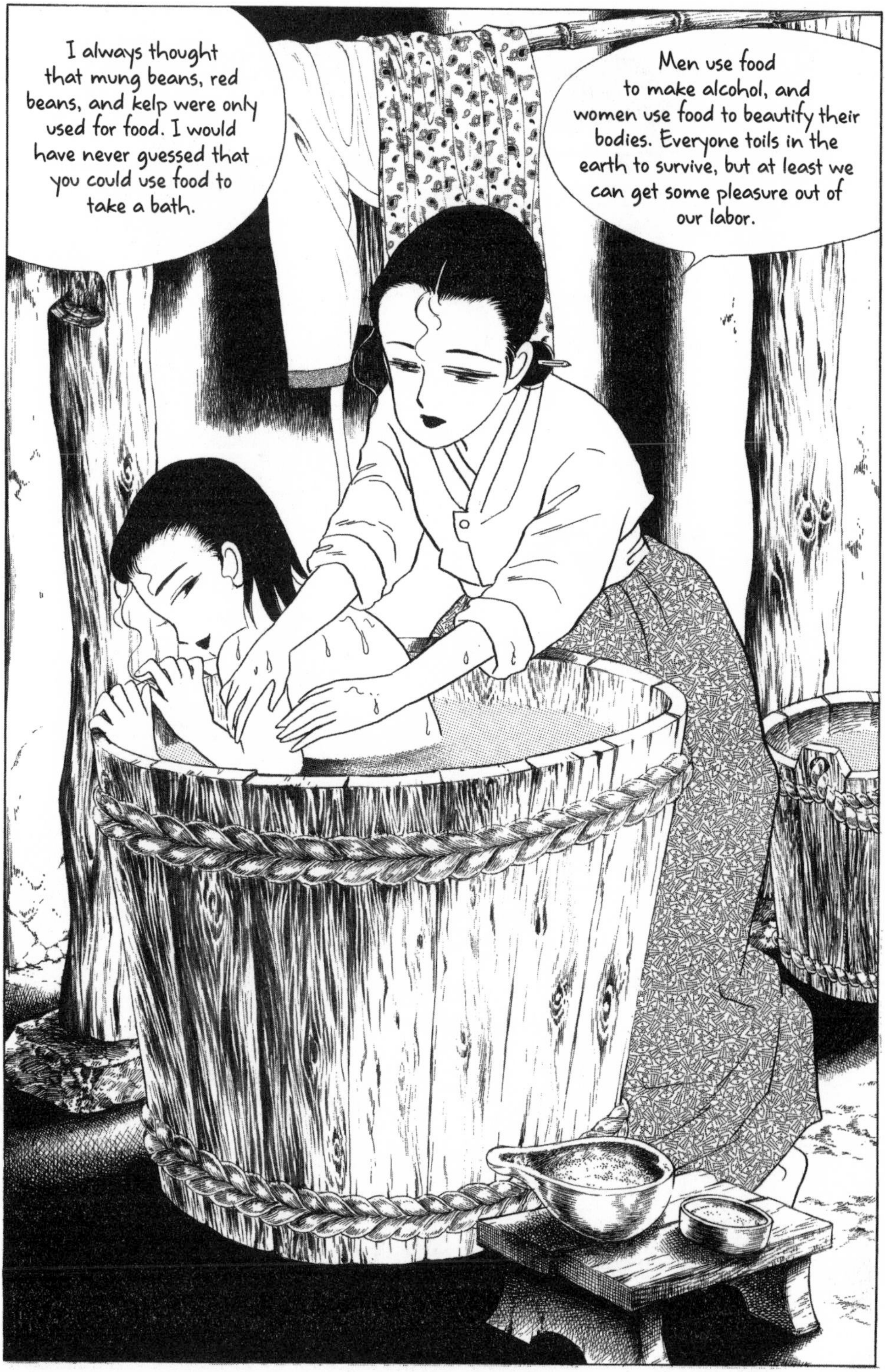
I always thought that mung beans, red beans, and kelp were only used for food. I would have never guessed that you could use food to take a bath.
Men use food to make alcohol, and women use food to beautify their bodies. Everyone toils in the earth to survive, but at least we can get some pleasure out of our labor.

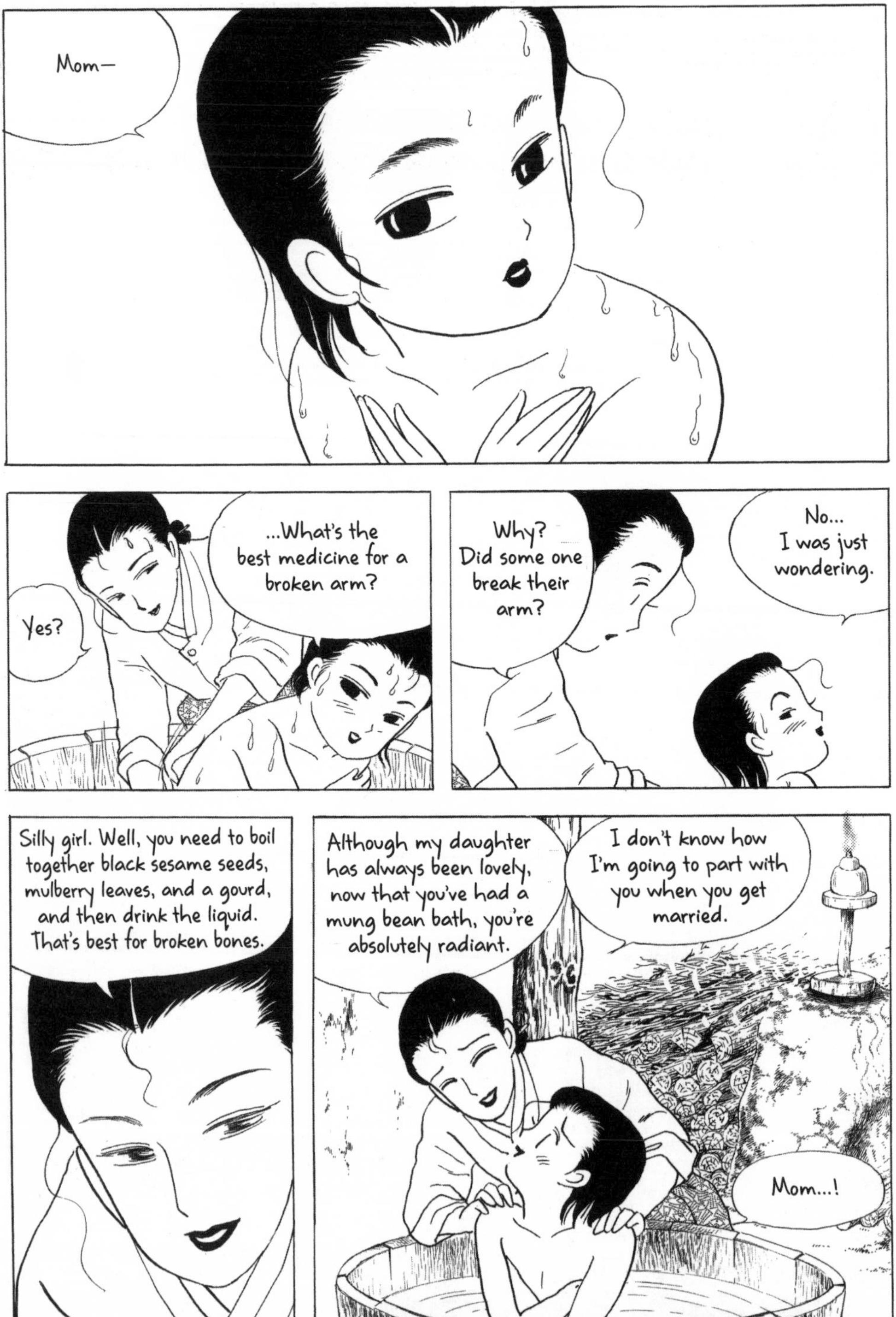
Mom—
Yes?
...What's the best medicine for a broken arm?
Why? Did some one break their arm?
No... I was just wondering.
Silly girl. Well, you need to boil together black sesame seeds, mulberry leaves, and a gourd, and then drink the liquid. That's best for broken bones.
Although my daughter has always been lovely, now that you've had a mung bean bath, you're absolutely radiant.
I don't know how I'm going to part with you when you get married.
Mom...!

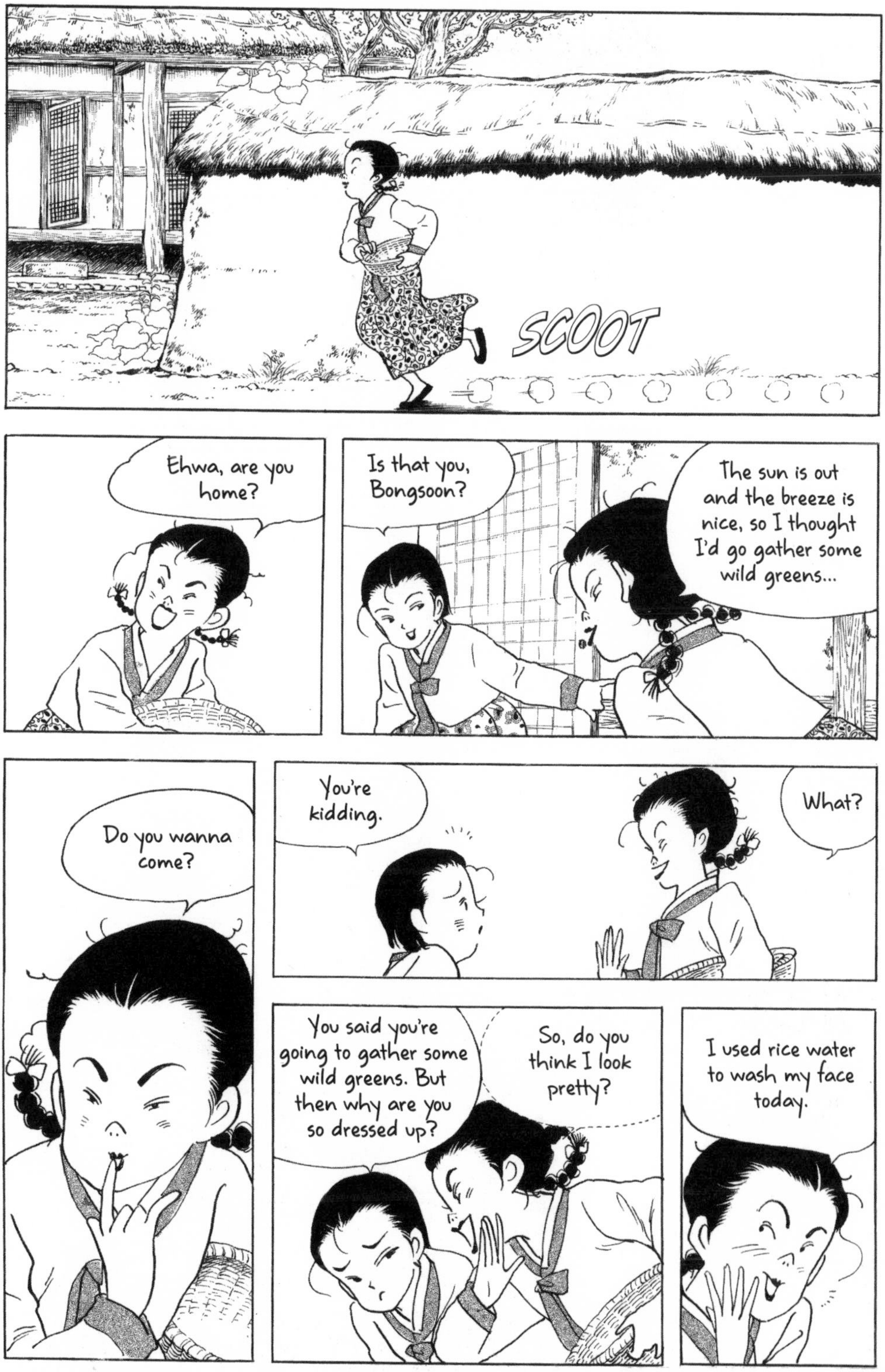
SCOOT
Ehwa, are you home?
Is that you, Bongsoon?
The sun is out and the breeze is nice, so I thought I'd go gather some wild greens...
Do you wanna come?
You're kidding.
What?
You said you're going to gather some wild greens. But then why are you so dressed up?
So, do you think I look pretty?
I used rice water to wash my face today.

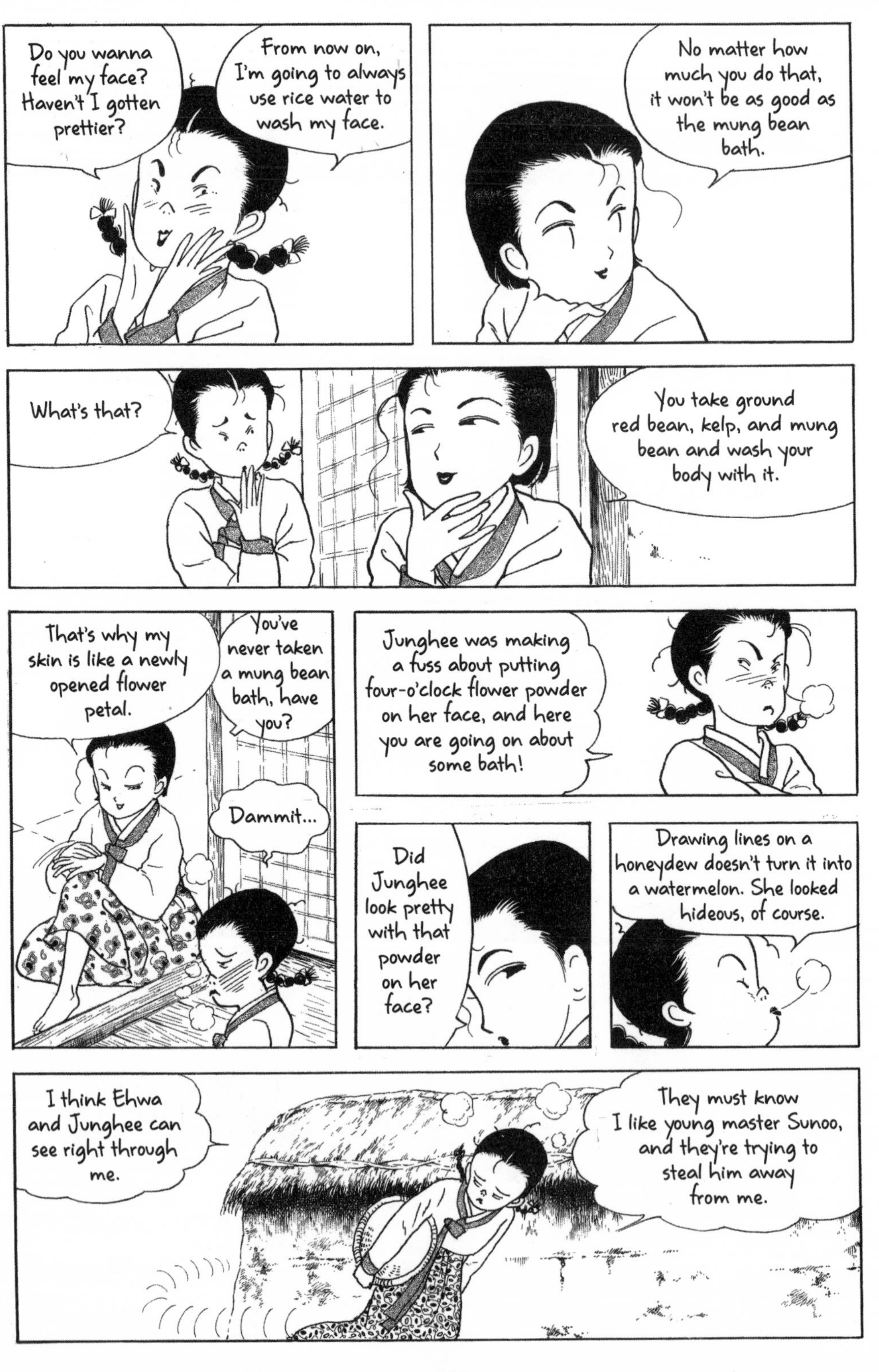

Do you wanna feel my face? Haven't I gotten prettier?
From now on, I'm going to always use rice water to wash my face.
No matter how much you do that, it won't be as good as the mung bean bath.
What's that?
You take ground red bean, kelp, and mung bean and wash your body with it.
That's why my skin is like a newly opened flower petal.
You've never taken a mung bean bath, have you?
Dammit...
Junghee was making a fuss about putting four-o'clock flower powder on her face, and here you are going on about some bath!
Did Junghee look pretty with that powder on her face?
Drawing lines on a honeydew doesn't turn it into a watermelon. She looked hideous, of course.
I think Ehwa and Junghee can see right through me.
They must know I like young master Sunoo, and they're trying to steal him away from me.

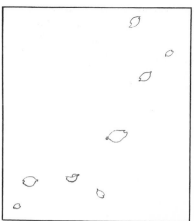

Look at the peach blossom petals flutter in the wind! It's the season for pretty girls to be fluttering about with love in their eyes.

Maybe that's why every nook and cranny of the village has the scent of a female animal in heat.

It's probably because the orchard owner's son is back home, and not because of the peach blossoms.

I heard he was studying in the Kwangju Province. Is he done with school already?

I heard he came home to recuperate, something about a broken arm.

What's the best medicine for a broken arm?

Perhaps that's why she asked that question.

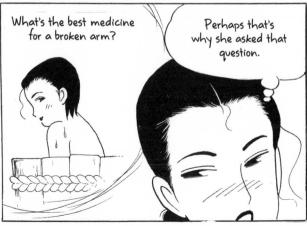

203

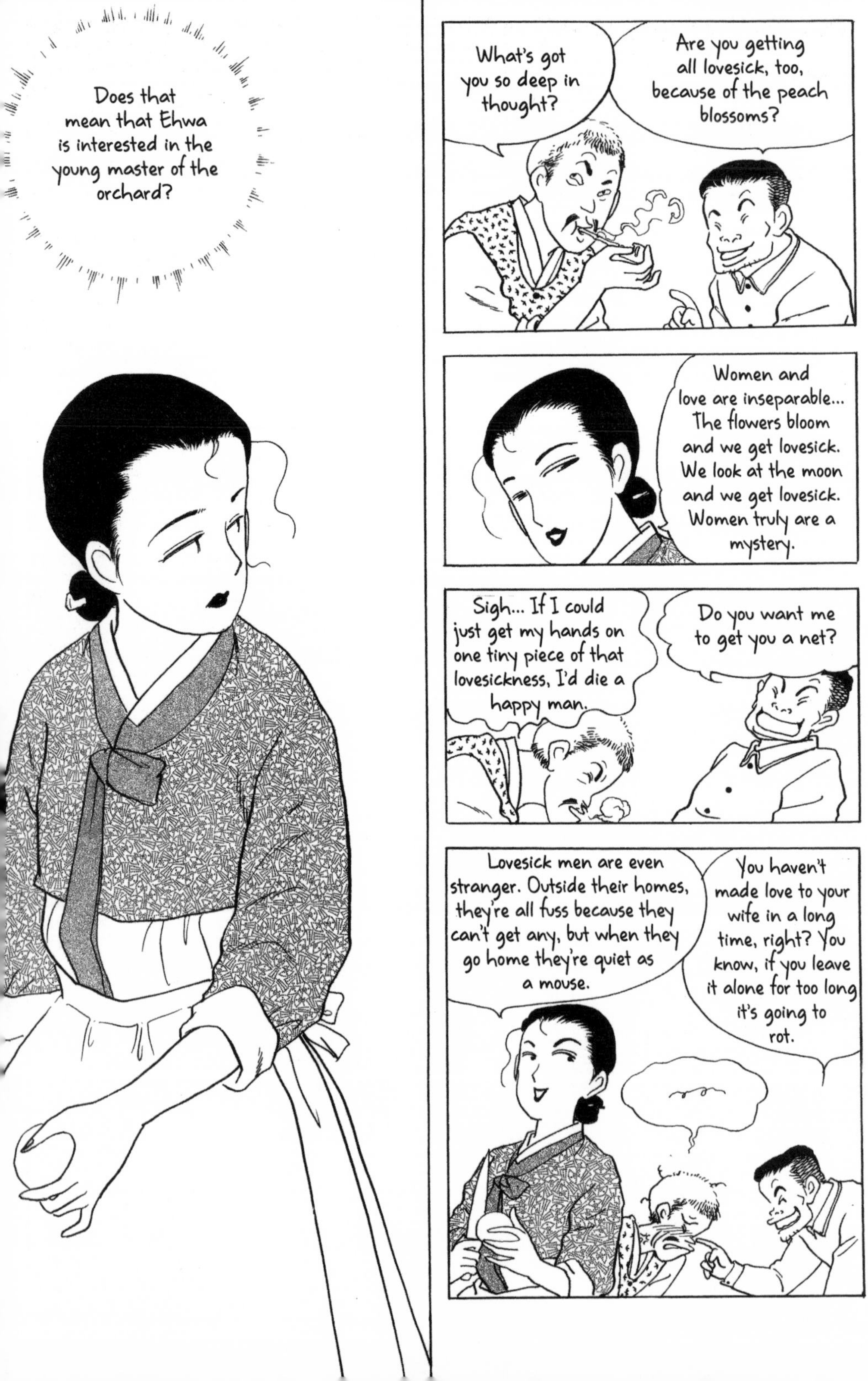

Does that mean that Ehwa is interested in the young master of the orchard?
What's got you so deep in thought?
Are you getting all lovesick, too, because of the peach blossoms?
Women and love are inseparable... The flowers bloom and we get lovesick. We look at the moon and we get lovesick. Women truly are a mystery.
Sigh... If I could just get my hands on one tiny piece of that lovesickness, I'd die a happy man.
Do you want me to get you a net?
Lovesick men are even stranger. Outside their homes, they're all fuss because they can't get any, but when they go home they're quiet as a mouse.
You haven't made love to your wife in a long time, right? You know, if you leave it alone for too long it's going to rot.

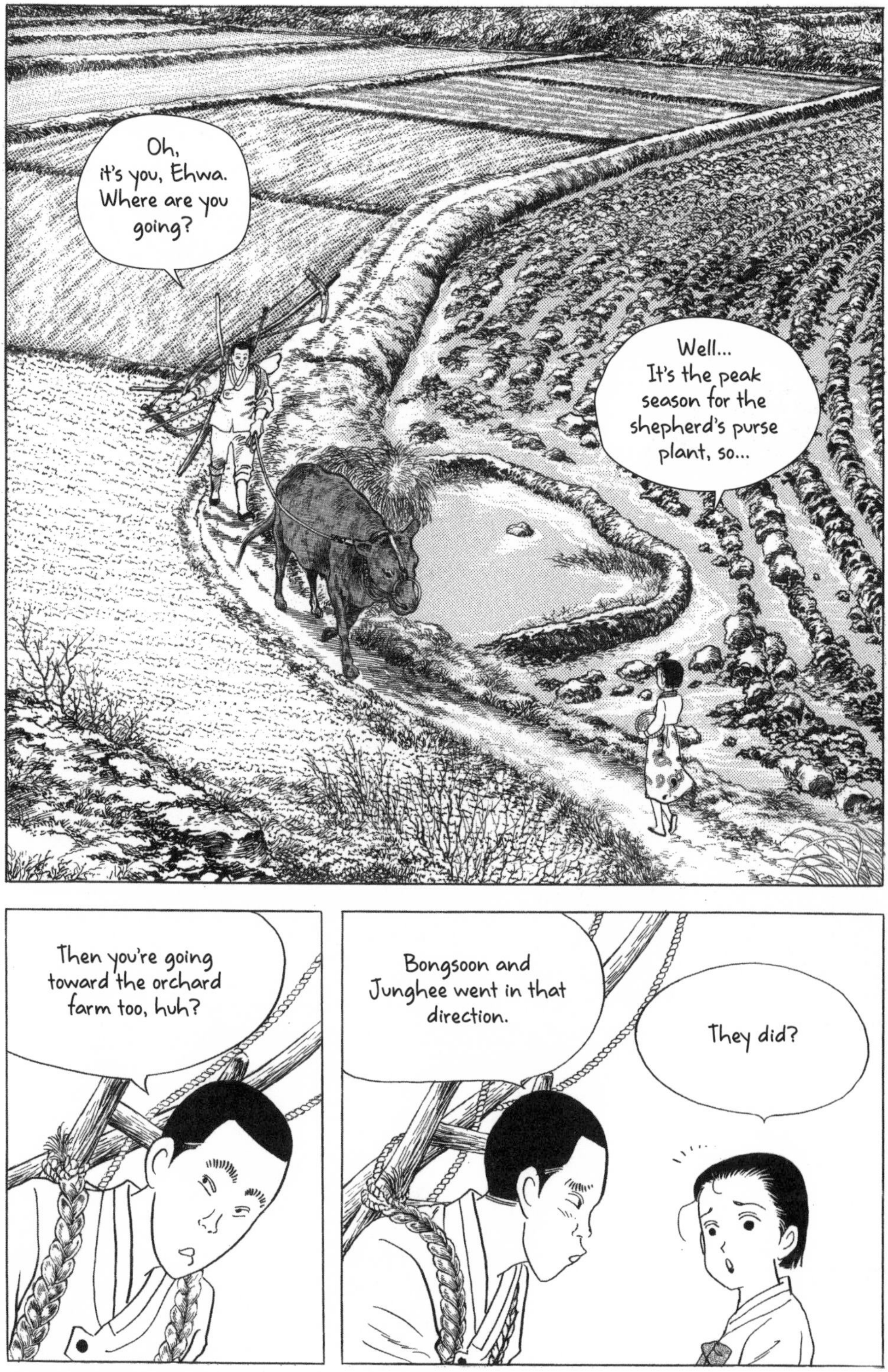
Oh, it's you, Ehwa. Where are you going?
Well... It's the peak season for the shepherd's purse plant, so...
Then you're going toward the orchard farm too, huh?
Bongsoon and Junghee went in that direction.
They did?

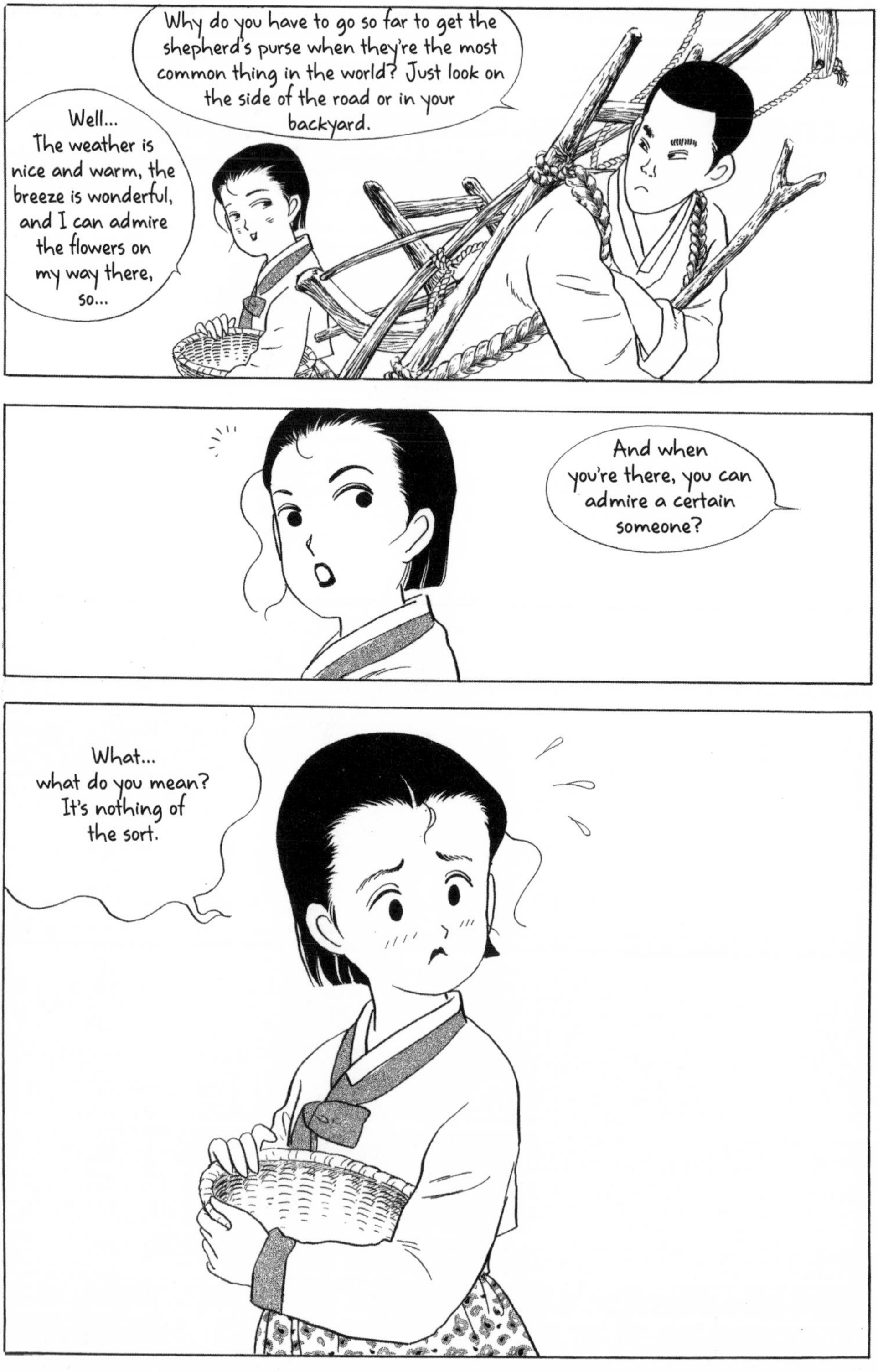
Why do you have to go so far to get the shepherd's purse when they're the most common thing in the world? Just look on the side of the road or in your backyard.
Well... The weather is nice and warm, the breeze is wonderful, and I can admire the flowers on my way there, so...
And when you're there, you can admire a certain someone?
What... what do you mean? It's nothing of the sort.

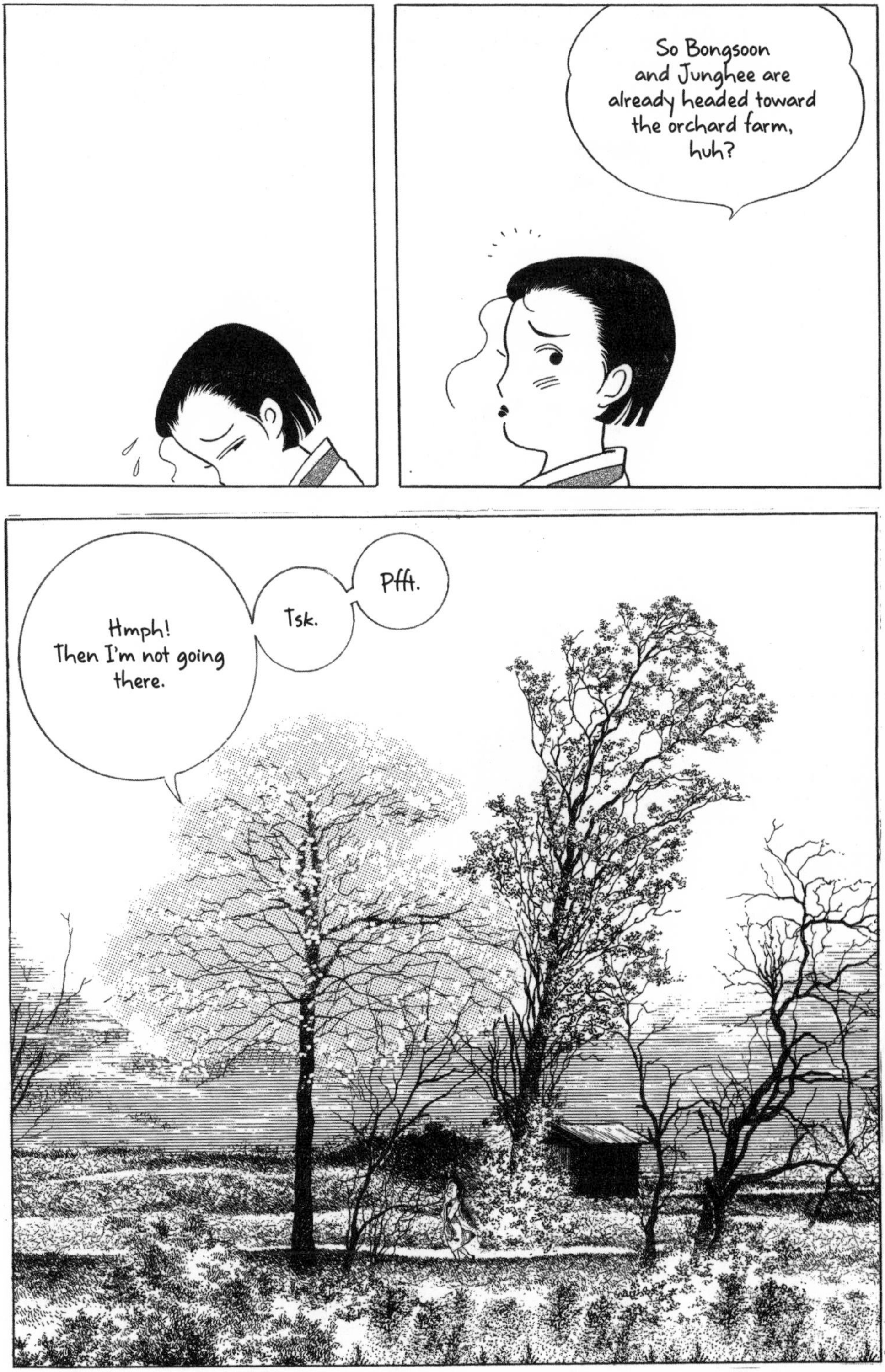
So Bongsoon and Junghee are already headed toward the orchard farm, huh?
Hmph! Then I'm not going there.
Tsk.
Pfft.

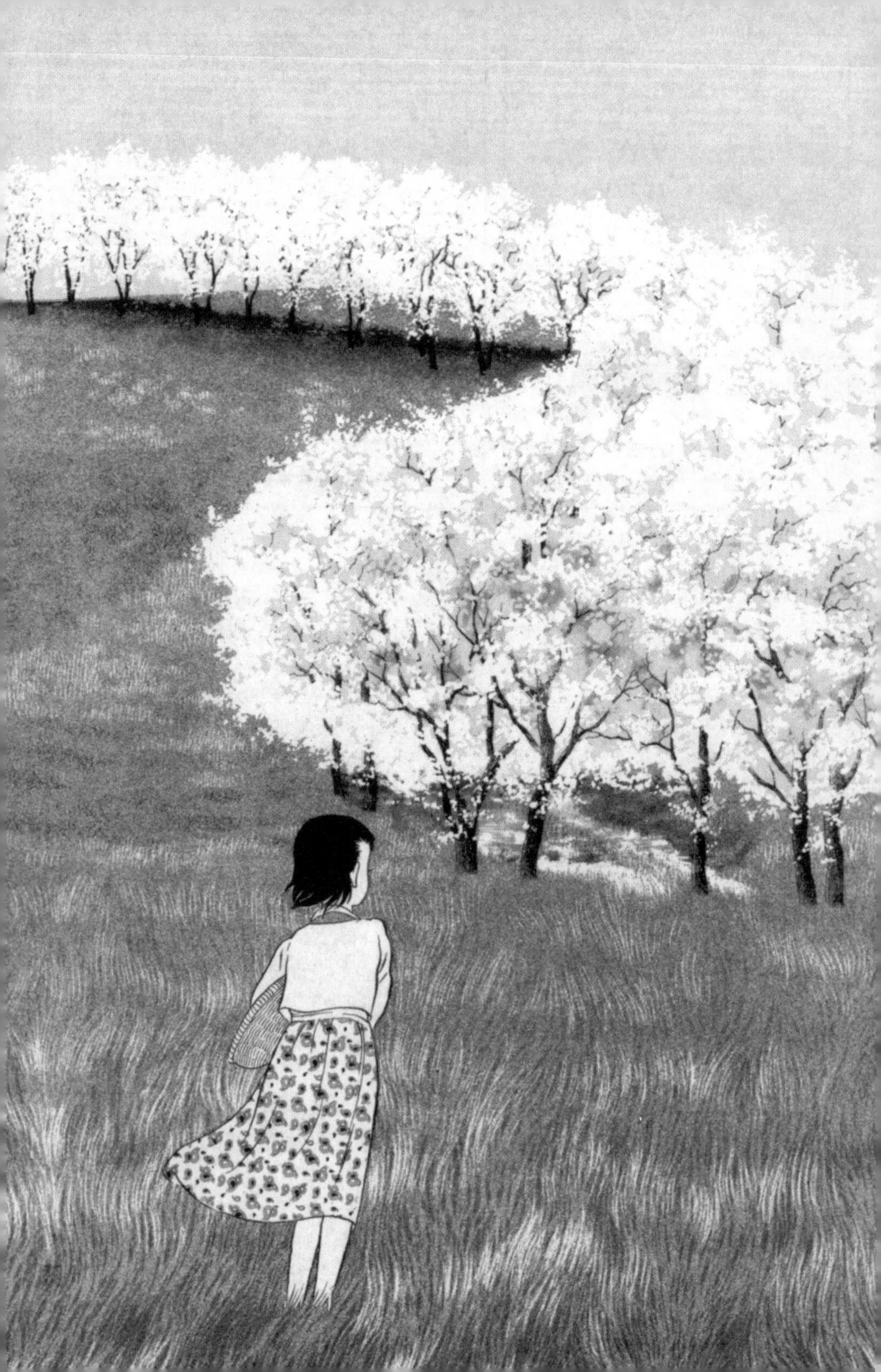

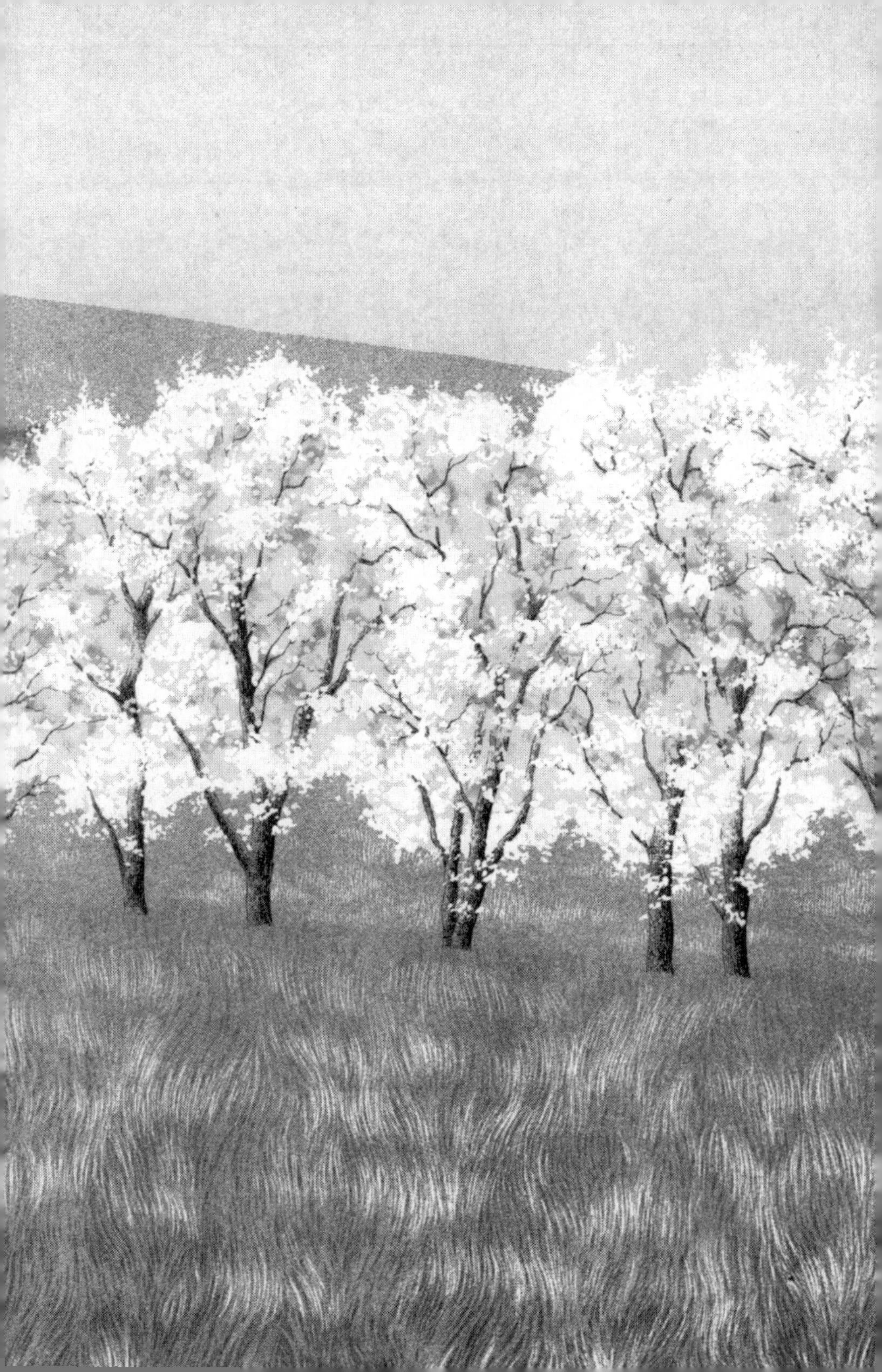

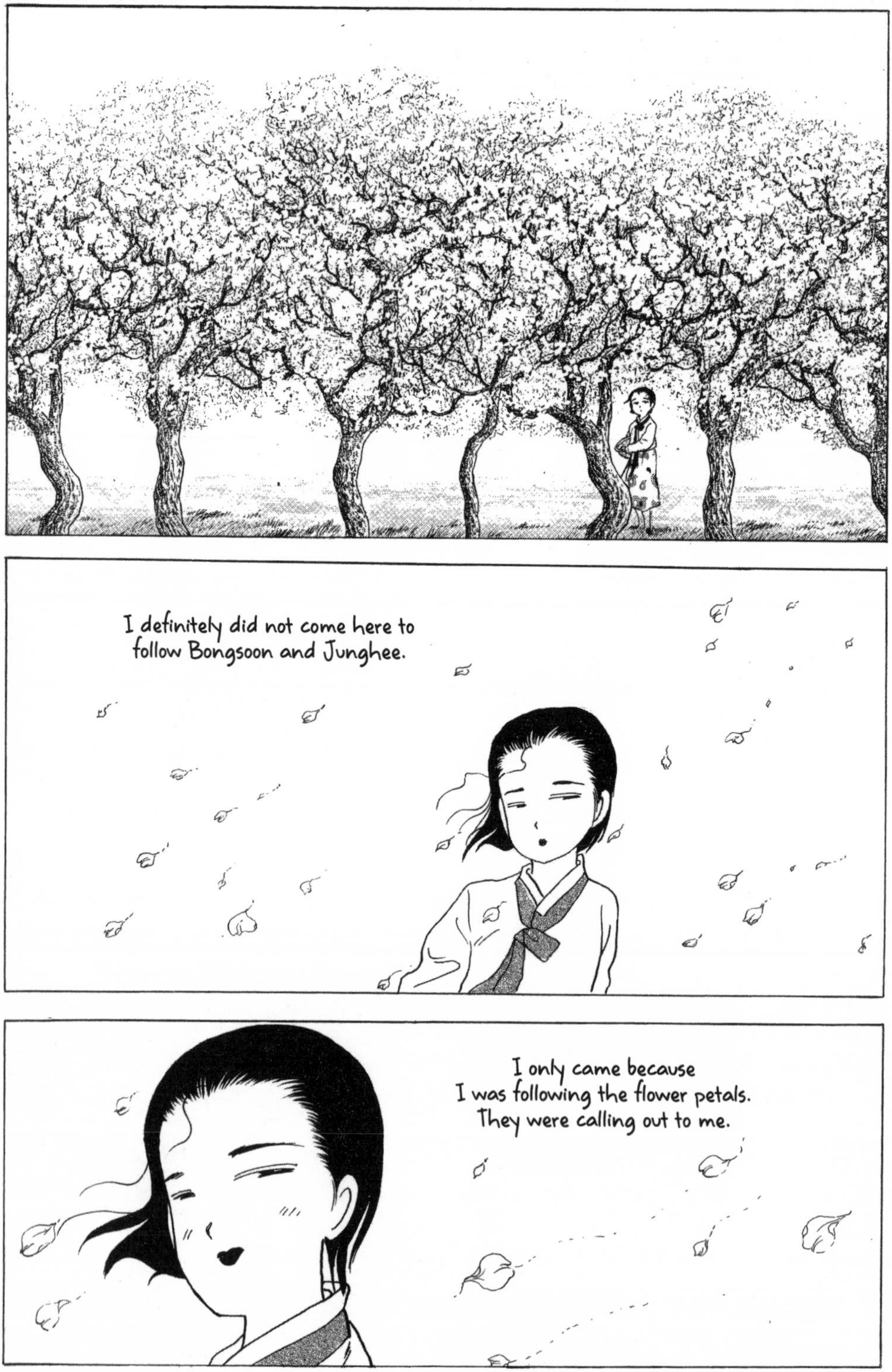
I definitely did not come here to follow Bongsoon and Junghee.
I only came because I was following the flower petals. They were calling out to me.

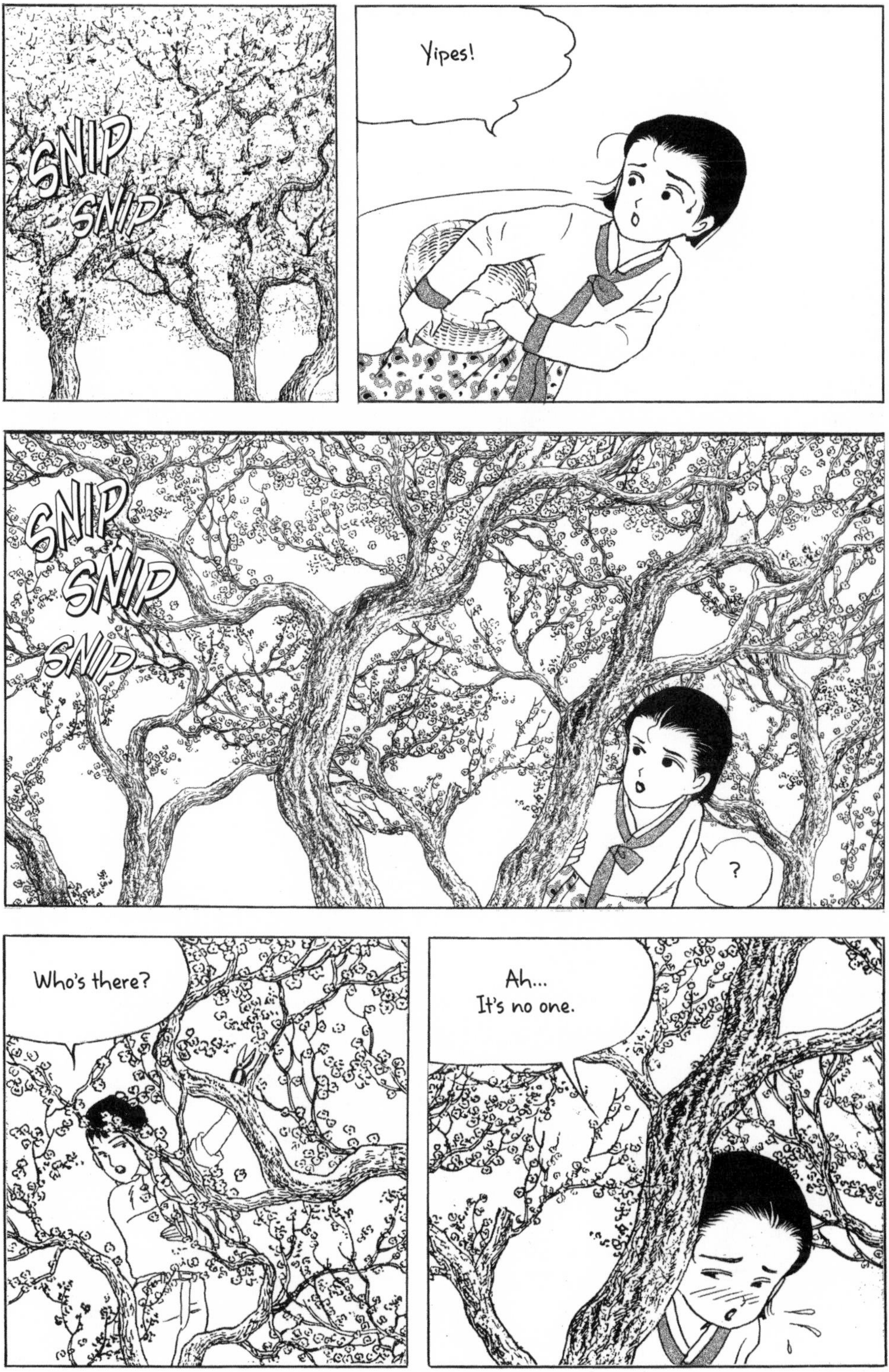
SNIP
SNIP
Yipes!
SNIP
SNIP
SNIP
?
Who's there?
Ah...
It's no one.

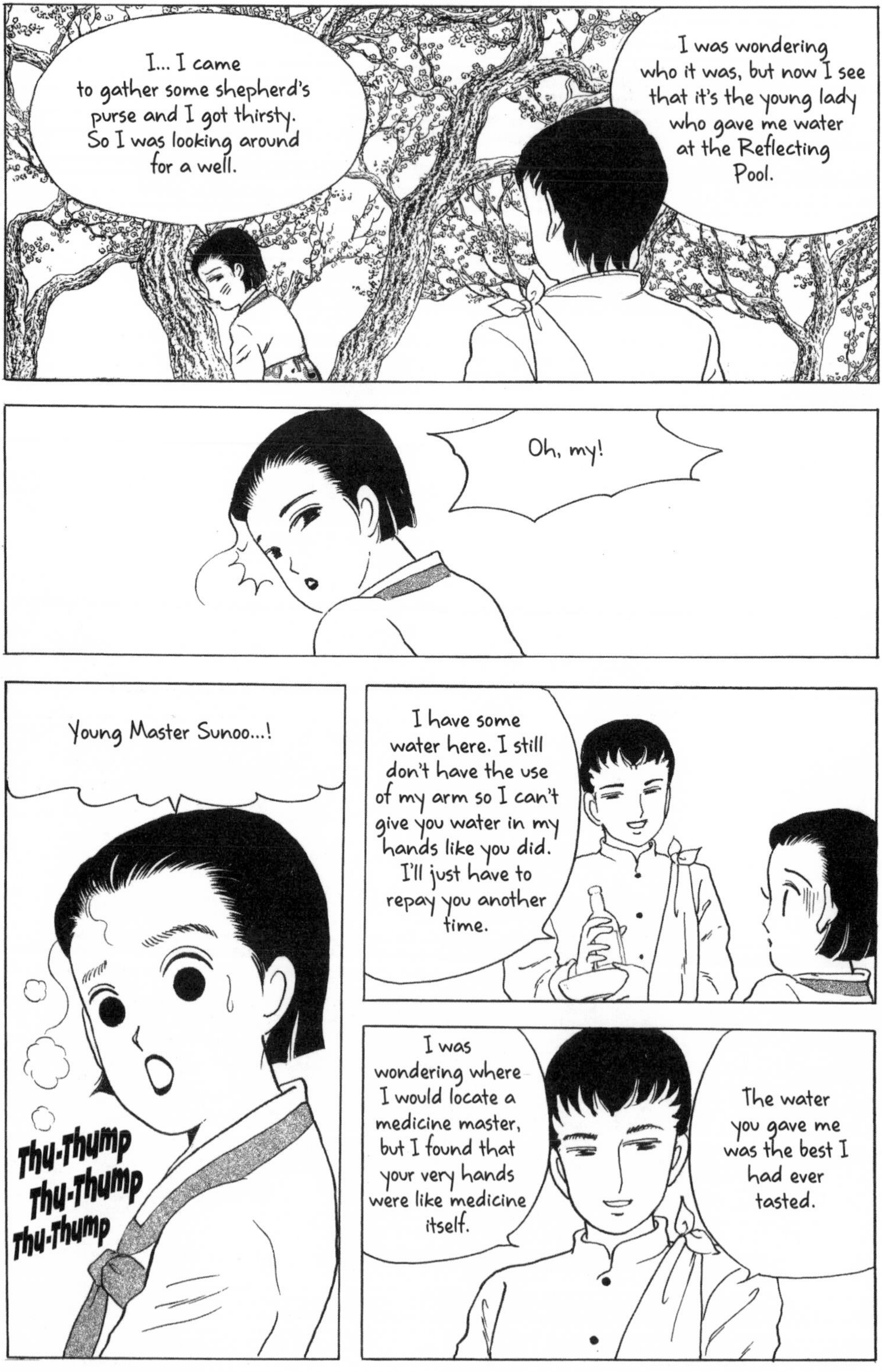
I... I came to gather some shepherd's purse and I got thirsty. So I was looking around for a well.
I was wondering who it was, but now I see that it's the young lady who gave me water at the Reflecting Pool.
Oh, my!
Young Master Sunoo...!
Thu-Thump Thu-Thump Thu-Thump
I have some water here. I still don't have the use of my arm so I can't give you water in my hands like you did. I'll just have to repay you another time.
I was wondering where I would locate a medicine master, but I found that your very hands were like medicine itself.
The water you gave me was the best I had ever tasted.

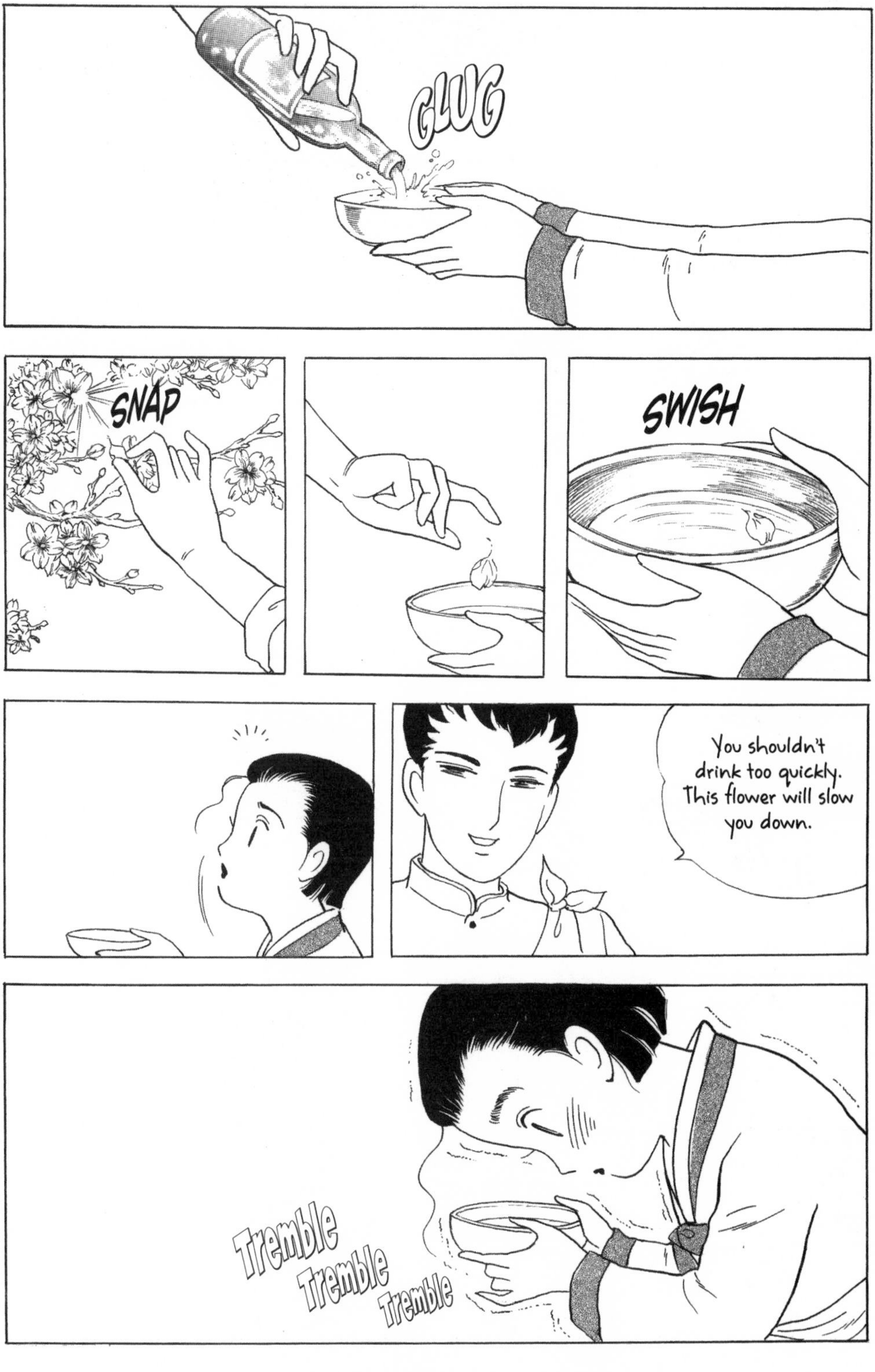
GLUG
SNAP
SWISH
You shouldn't drink too quickly. This flower will slow you down.
Tremble
Tremble
Tremble

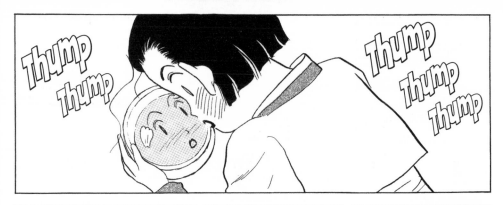

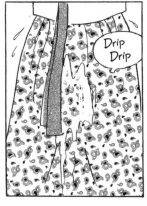

Thump
Thump
Thump
Thump
Thump
GLUG
GLUG
SPLOOSH
Drip
Drip
Oh, no!
You must have been distracted by the petal I placed in the bowl.
How embarrassing...
What am I going to do?

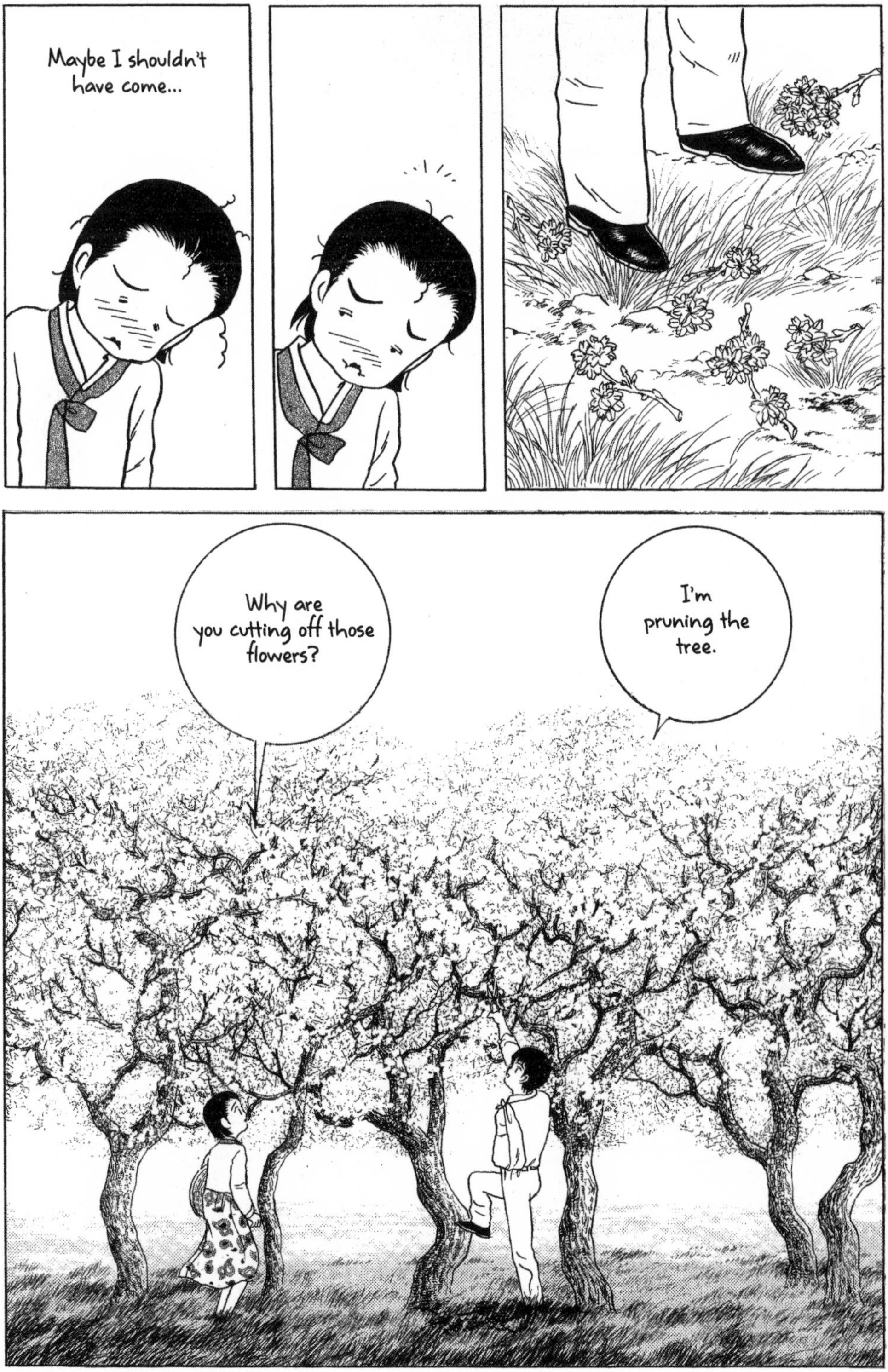
Maybe I shouldn't have come...
Why are you cutting off those flowers?
I'm pruning the tree.

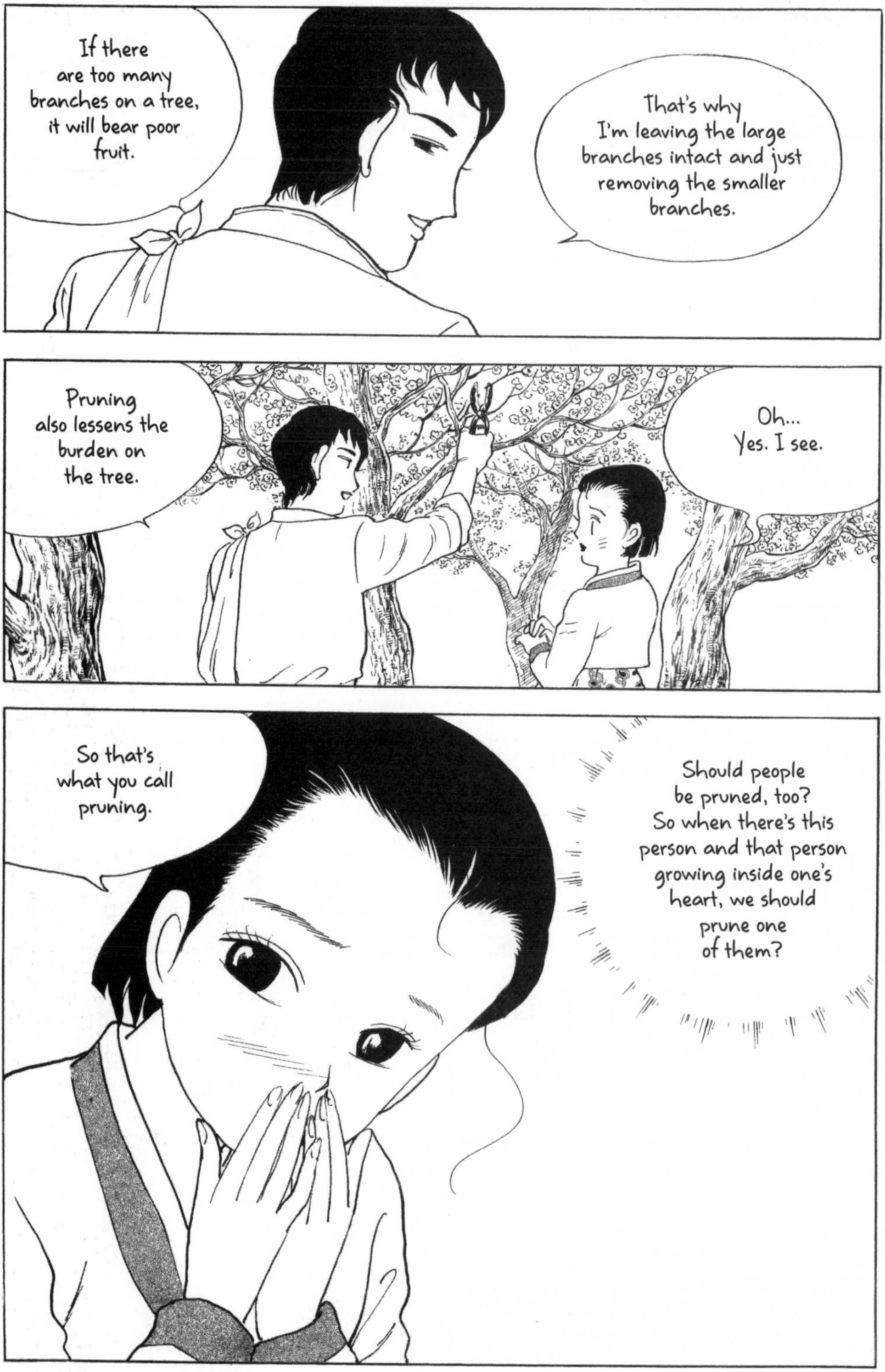
If there are too many branches on a tree, it will bear poor fruit.
That's why I'm leaving the large branches intact and just removing the smaller branches.
Pruning also lessens the burden on the tree.
Oh... Yes. I see.
So that's what you call pruning.
Should people be pruned, too? So when there's this person and that person growing inside one's heart, we should prune one of them?

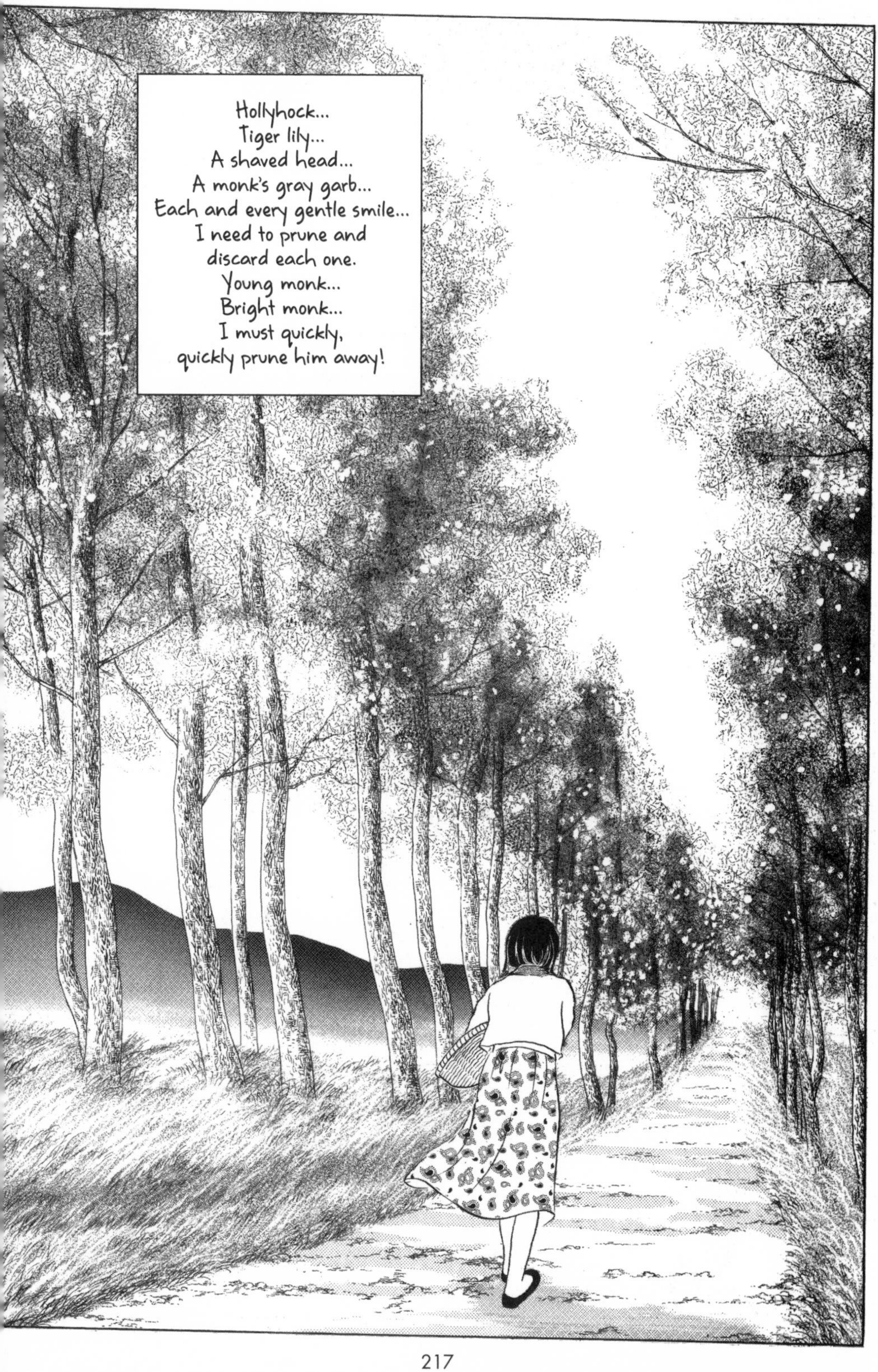
Hollyhock...
Tiger lily...
A shaved head...
A monk's gray garb...
Each and every gentle smile...
I need to prune and
discard each one.
Young monk...
Bright monk...
I must quickly,
quickly prune him away!

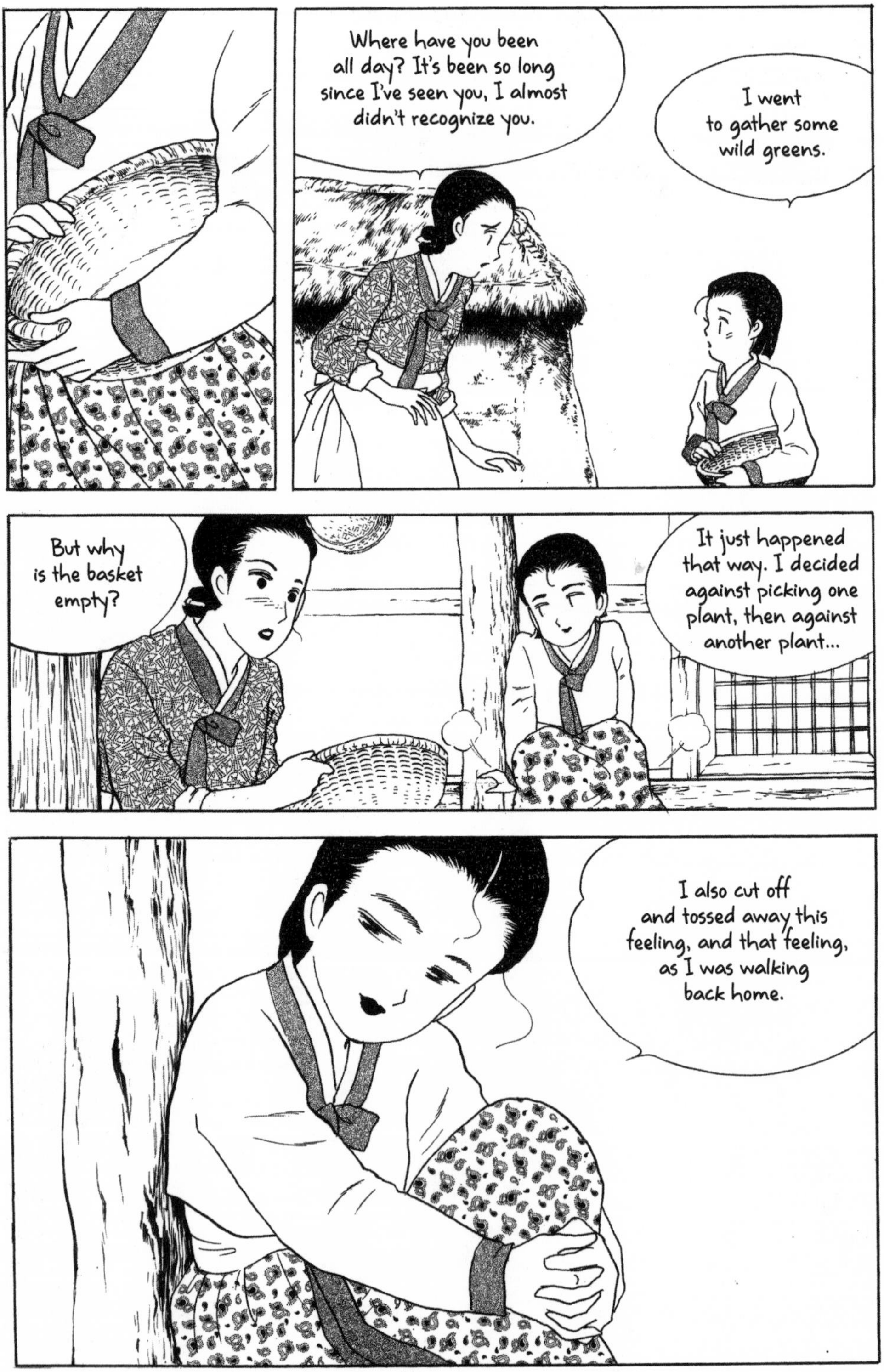
Where have you been all day? It's been so long since I've seen you, I almost didn't recognize you.
I went to gather some wild greens.
But why is the basket empty?
It just happened that way. I decided against picking one plant, then against another plant...
I also cut off and tossed away this feeling, and that feeling, as I was walking back home.

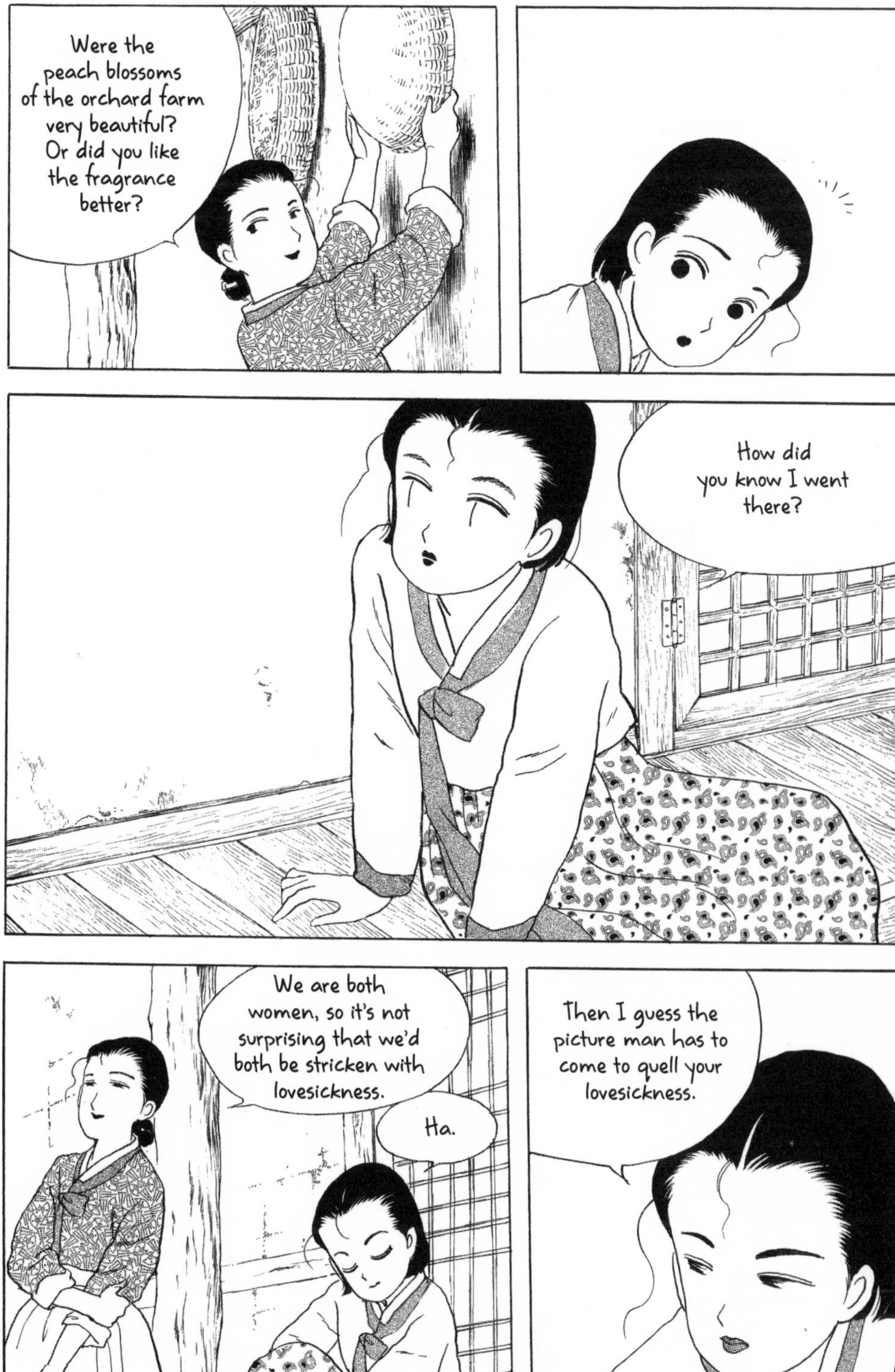
Were the peach blossoms of the orchard farm very beautiful? Or did you like the fragrance better?
How did you know I went there?
We are both women, so it's not surprising that we'd both be stricken with lovesickness.
Ha.
Then I guess the picture man has to come to quell your lovesickness.

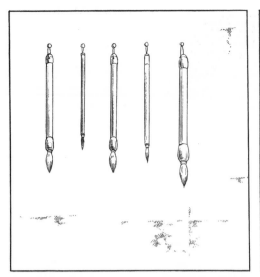

I can't believe he's already left five brushes with you. How long does he intend keep this up?

Who knows? Maybe he intends to leave his brushes one by one until he has no more to leave. And when that time comes, he'll just have to stay with us...

I think I'll plant the gourd seeds along the hedge tomorrow.

I guess you should.

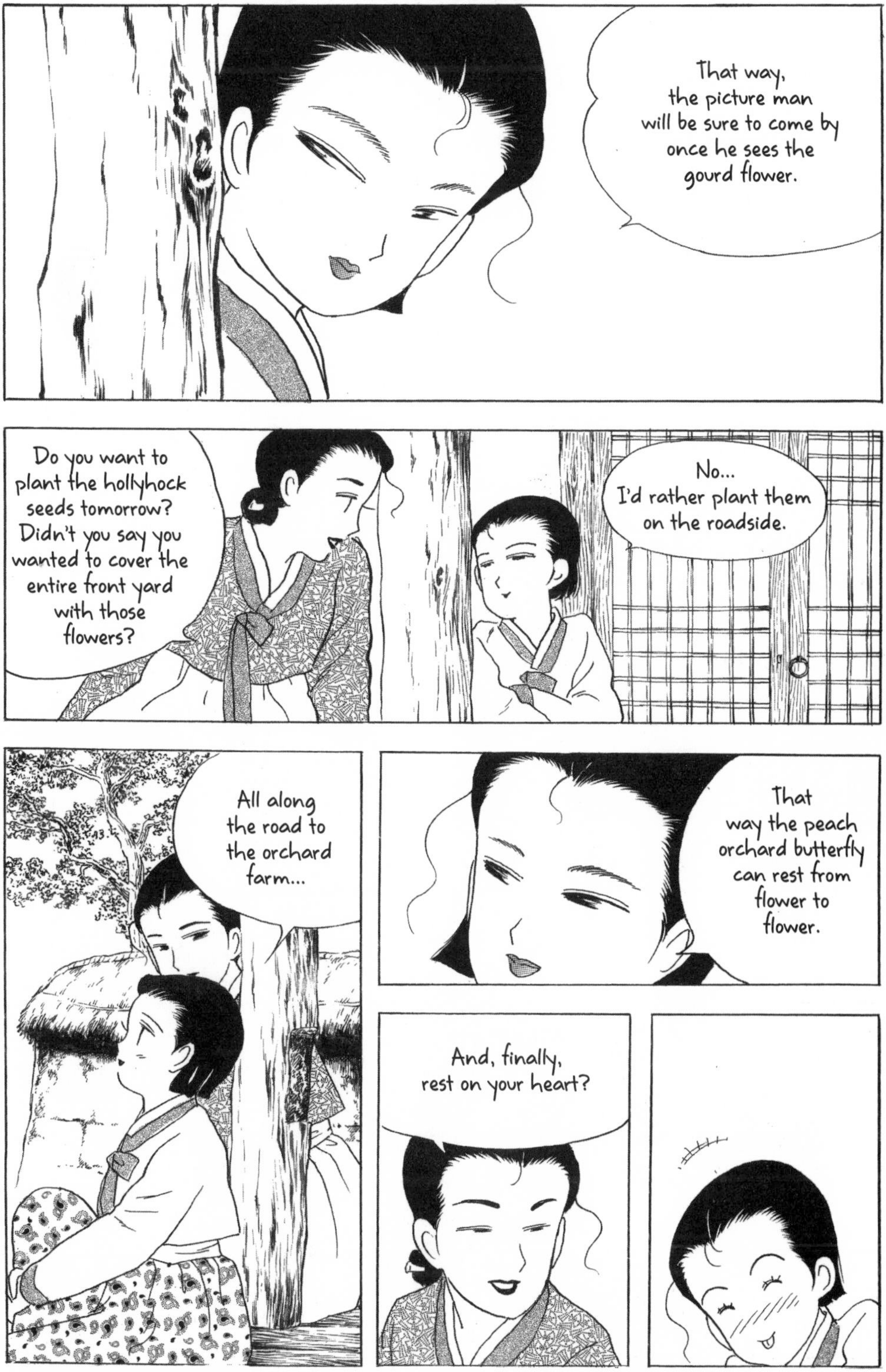
That way, the picture man will be sure to come by once he sees the gourd flower.
Do you want to plant the hollyhock seeds tomorrow? Didn't you say you wanted to cover the entire front yard with those flowers?
No... I'd rather plant them on the roadside.
All along the road to the orchard farm...
That way the peach orchard butterfly can rest from flower to flower.
And, finally, rest on your heart?

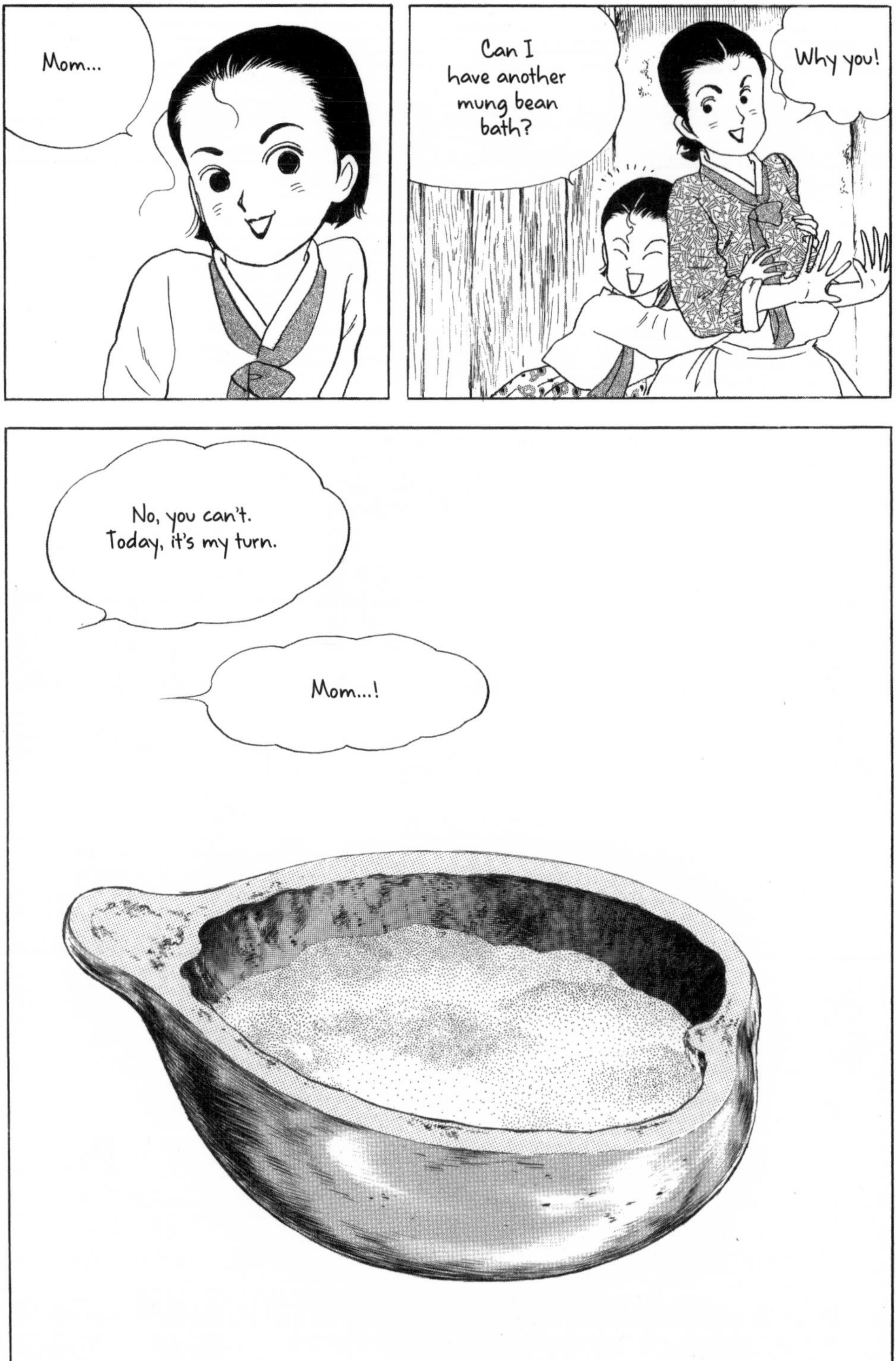
Mom...
Can I have another mung bean bath?
Why you!
No, you can't. Today, it's my turn.
Mom...!

Chapter Eight

THE SCENT OF FRESH YOUNG GREENS

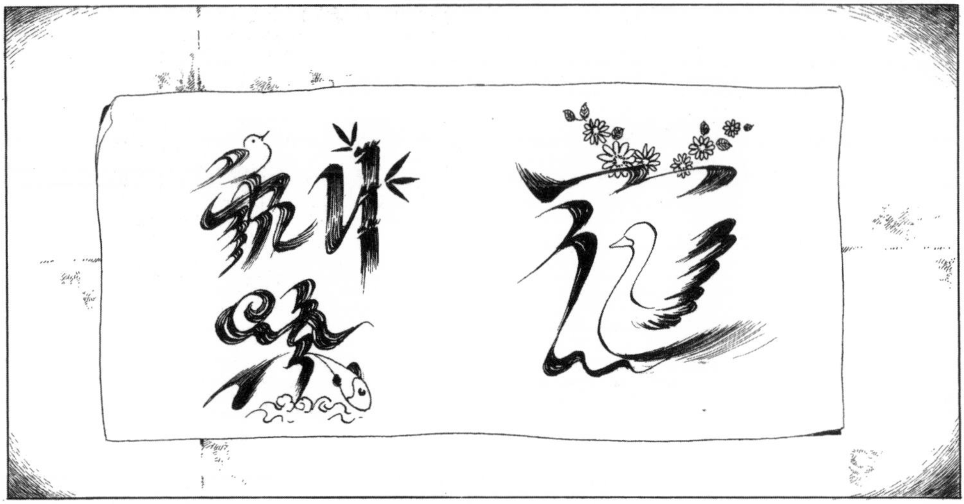

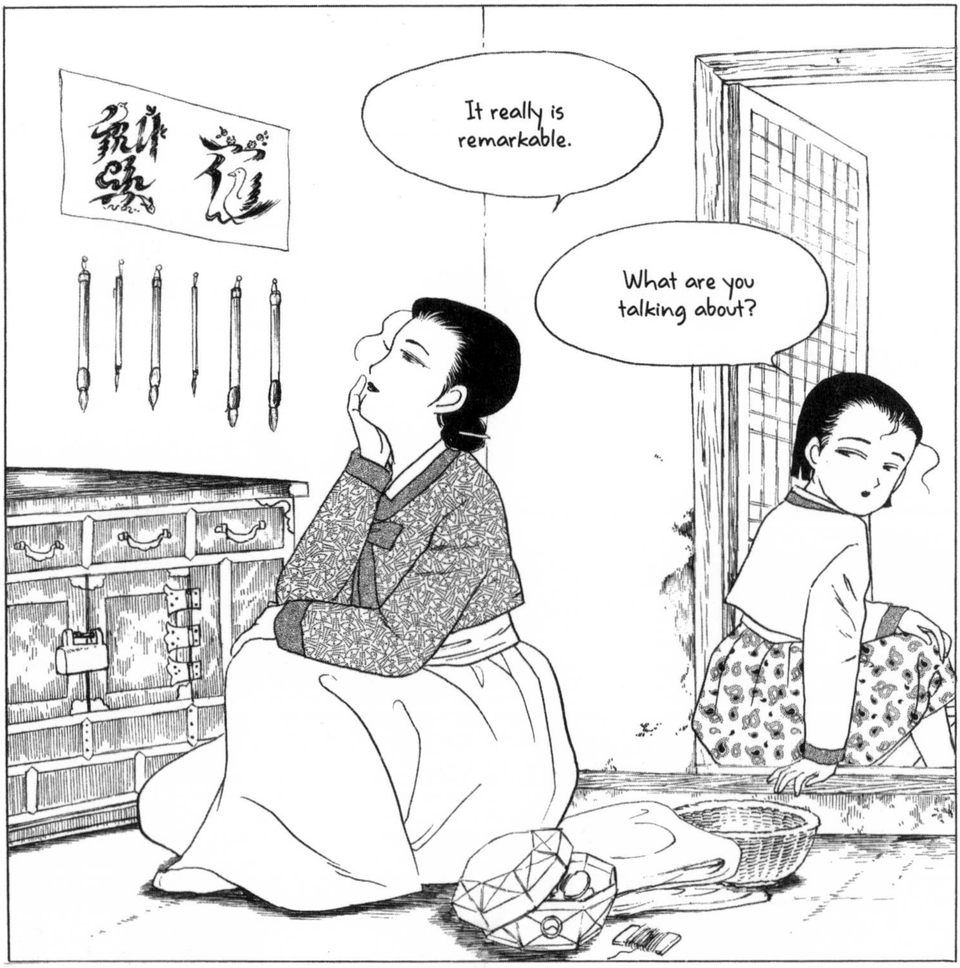
It really is remarkable.
What are you talking about?

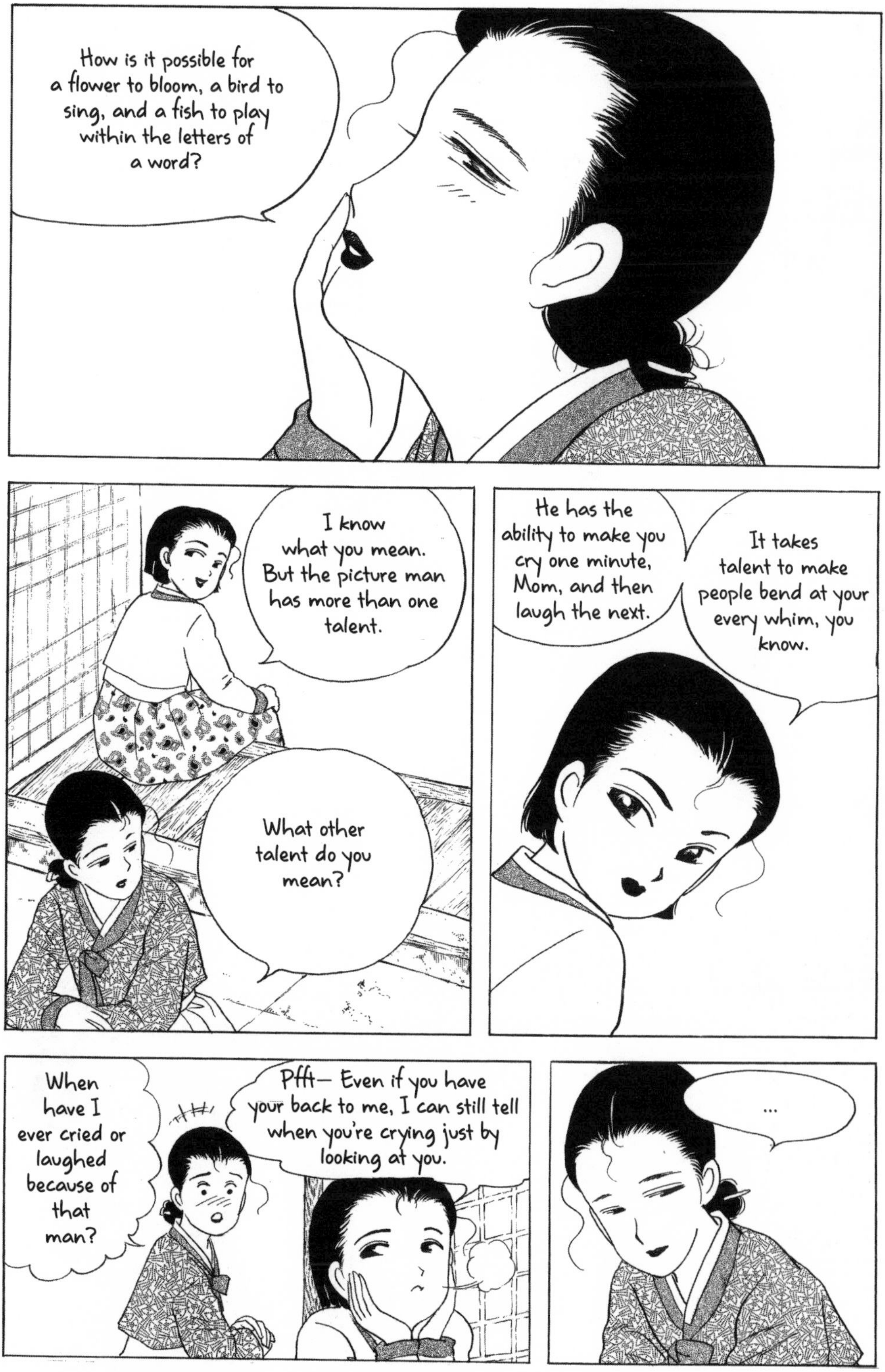
How is it possible for a flower to bloom, a bird to sing, and a fish to play within the letters of a word?
I know what you mean. But the picture man has more than one talent.
What other talent do you mean?
He has the ability to make you cry one minute, Mom, and then laugh the next.
It takes talent to make people bend at your every whim, you know.
When have I ever cried or laughed because of that man?
Pfft— Even if you have your back to me, I can still tell when you're crying just by looking at you.
...

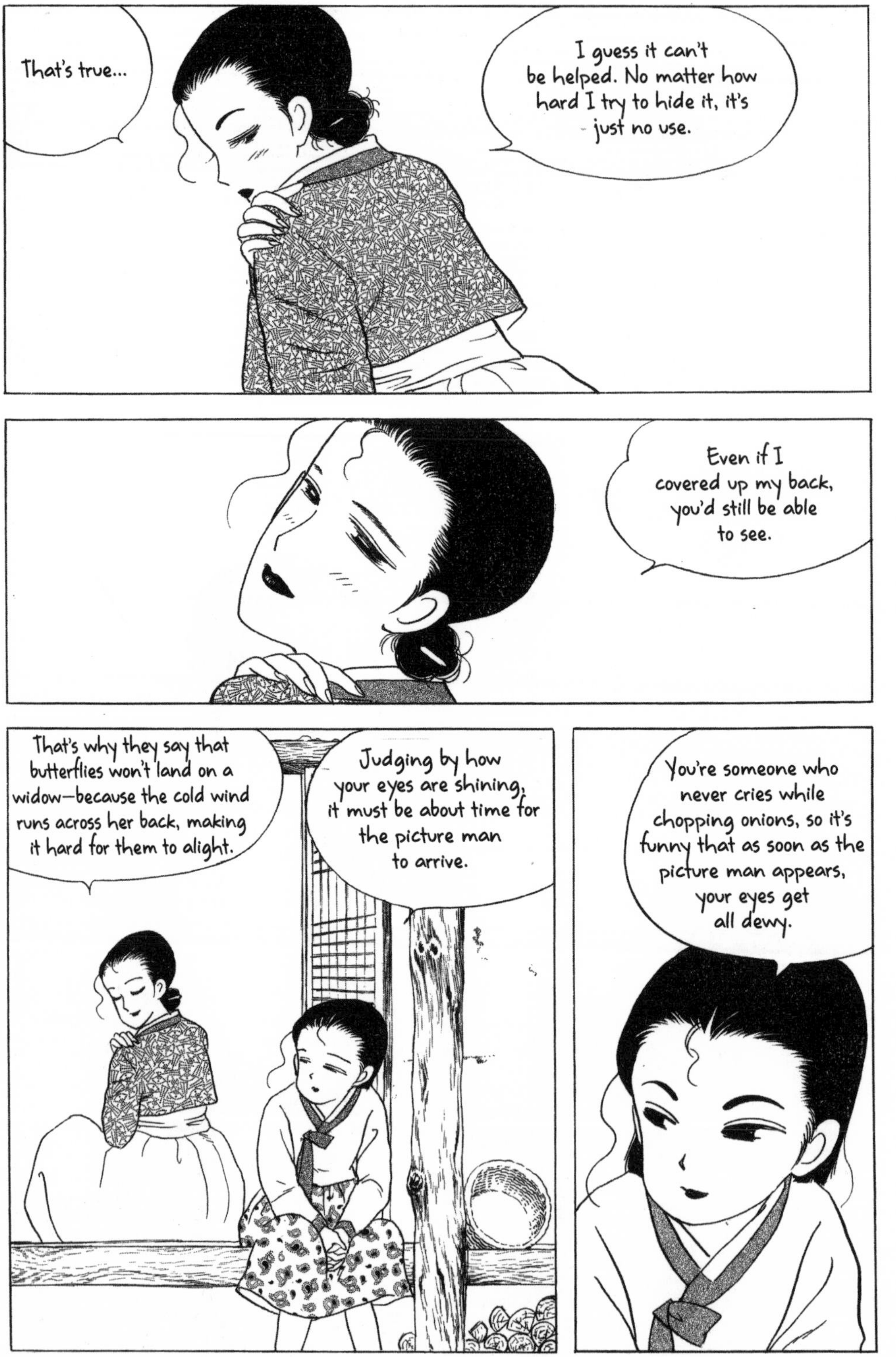
That's true...
I guess it can't be helped. No matter how hard I try to hide it, it's just no use.
Even if I covered up my back, you'd still be able to see.
That's why they say that butterflies won't land on a widow—because the cold wind runs across her back, making it hard for them to alight.
Judging by how your eyes are shining, it must be about time for the picture man to arrive.
You're someone who never cries while chopping onions, so it's funny that as soon as the picture man appears, your eyes get all dewy.

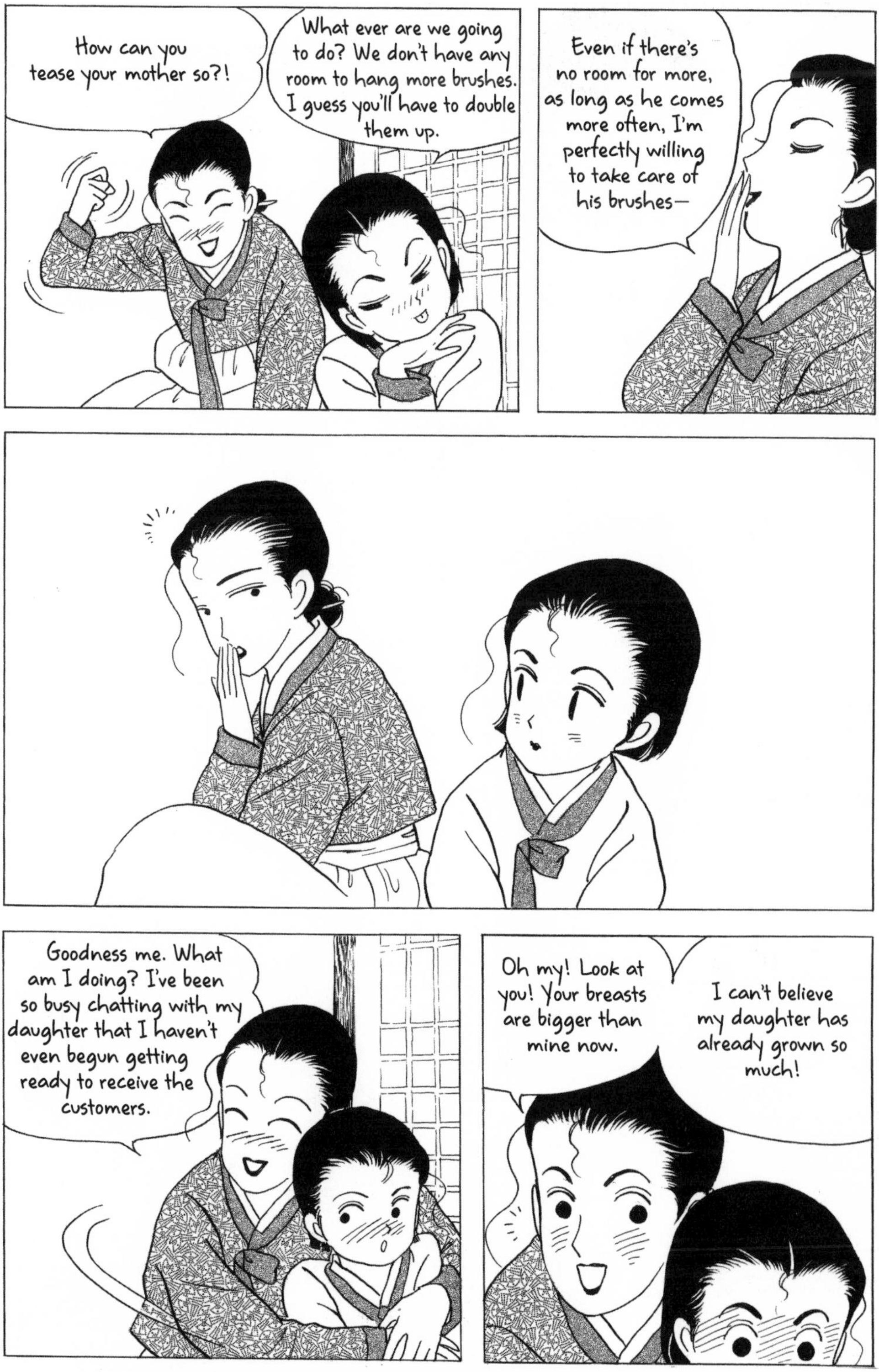
How can you tease your mother so?!
What ever are we going to do? We don't have any room to hang more brushes. I guess you'll have to double them up.
Even if there's no room for more, as long as he comes more often, I'm perfectly willing to take care of his brushes—
Goodness me. What am I doing? I've been so busy chatting with my daughter that I haven't even begun getting ready to receive the customers.
Oh my! Look at you! Your breasts are bigger than mine now.
I can't believe my daughter has already grown so much!

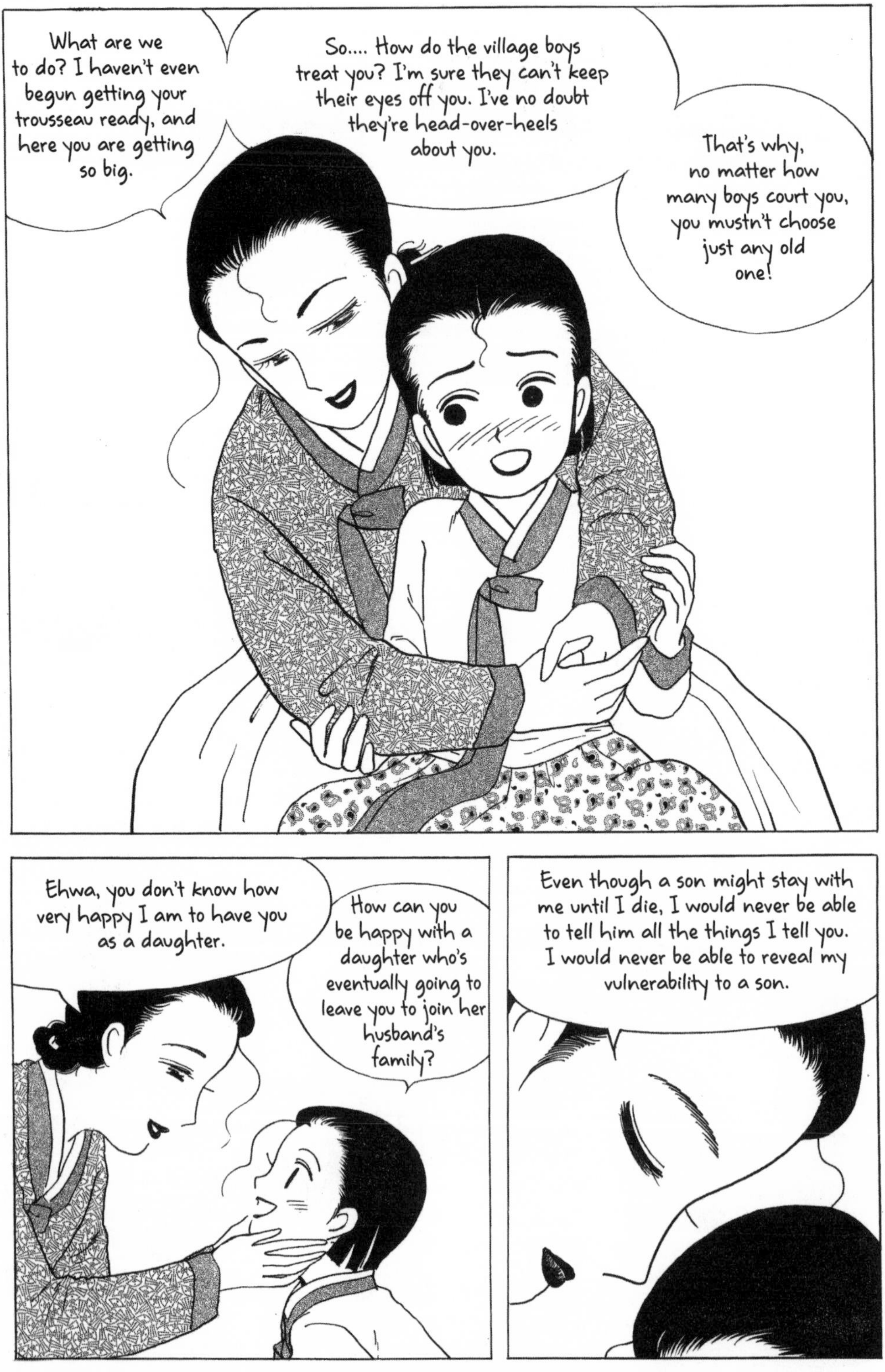
What are we to do? I haven't even begun getting your trousseau ready, and here you are getting so big.
So.... How do the village boys treat you? I'm sure they can't keep their eyes off you. I've no doubt they're head-over-heels about you.
That's why, no matter how many boys court you, you mustn't choose just any old one!
Ehwa, you don't know how very happy I am to have you as a daughter.
How can you be happy with a daughter who's eventually going to leave you to join her husband's family?
Even though a son might stay with me until I die, I would never be able to tell him all the things I tell you. I would never be able to reveal my vulnerability to a son.

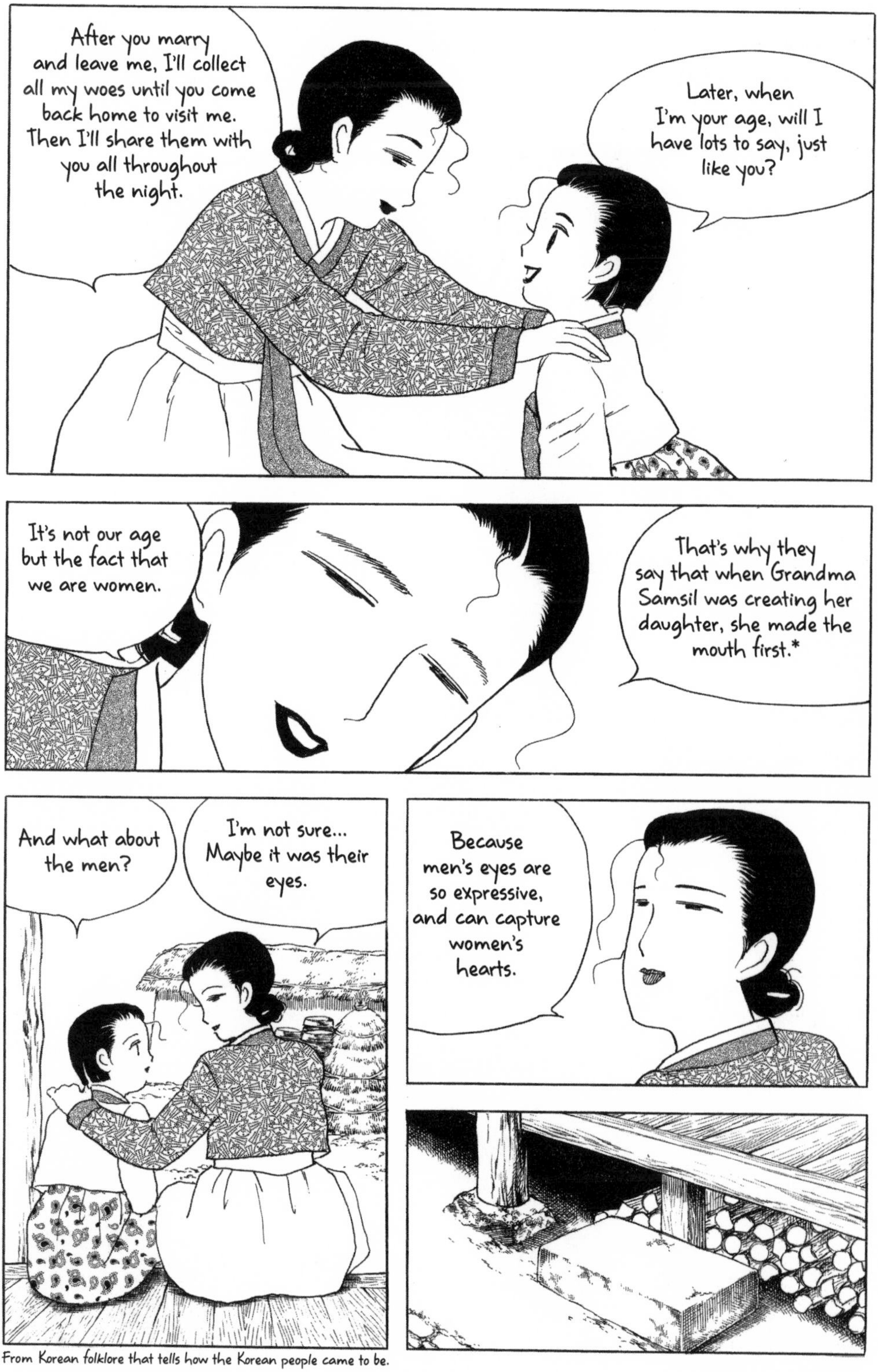
After you marry and leave me, I'll collect all my woes until you come back home to visit me. Then I'll share them with you all throughout the night.
Later, when I'm your age, will I have lots to say, just like you?
It's not our age but the fact that we are women.
That's why they say that when Grandma Samsil was creating her daughter, she made the mouth first.*
And what about the men?
I'm not sure... Maybe it was their eyes.
Because men's eyes are so expressive, and can capture women's hearts.

* From Korean folklore that tells how the Korean people came to be.

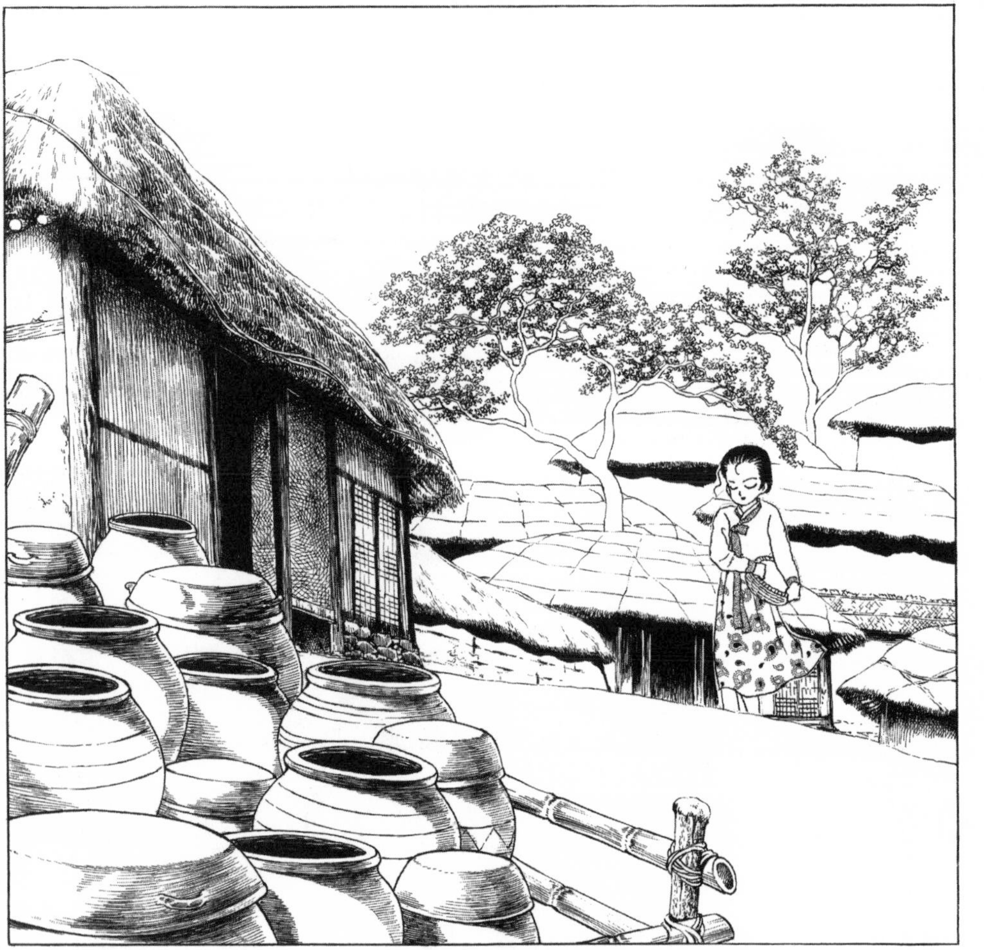

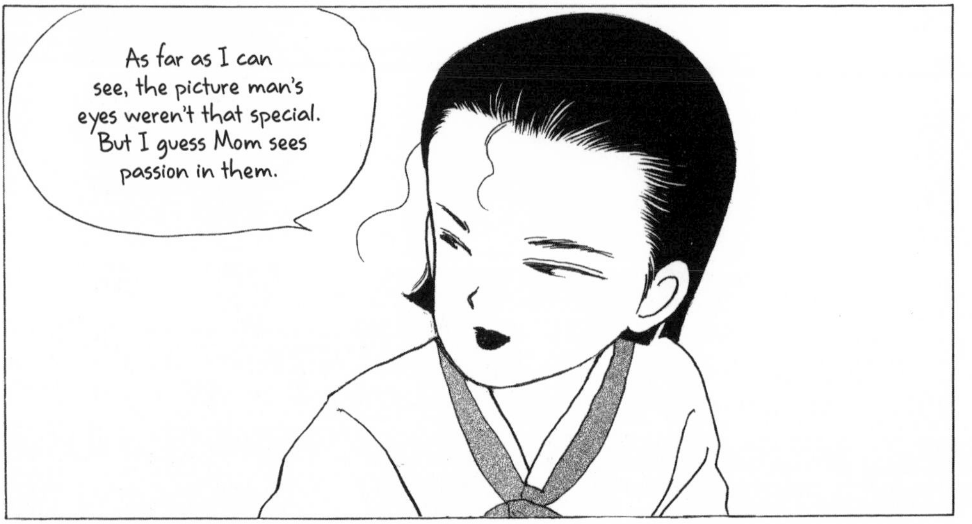
As far as I can see, the picture man's eyes weren't that special. But I guess Mom sees passion in them.

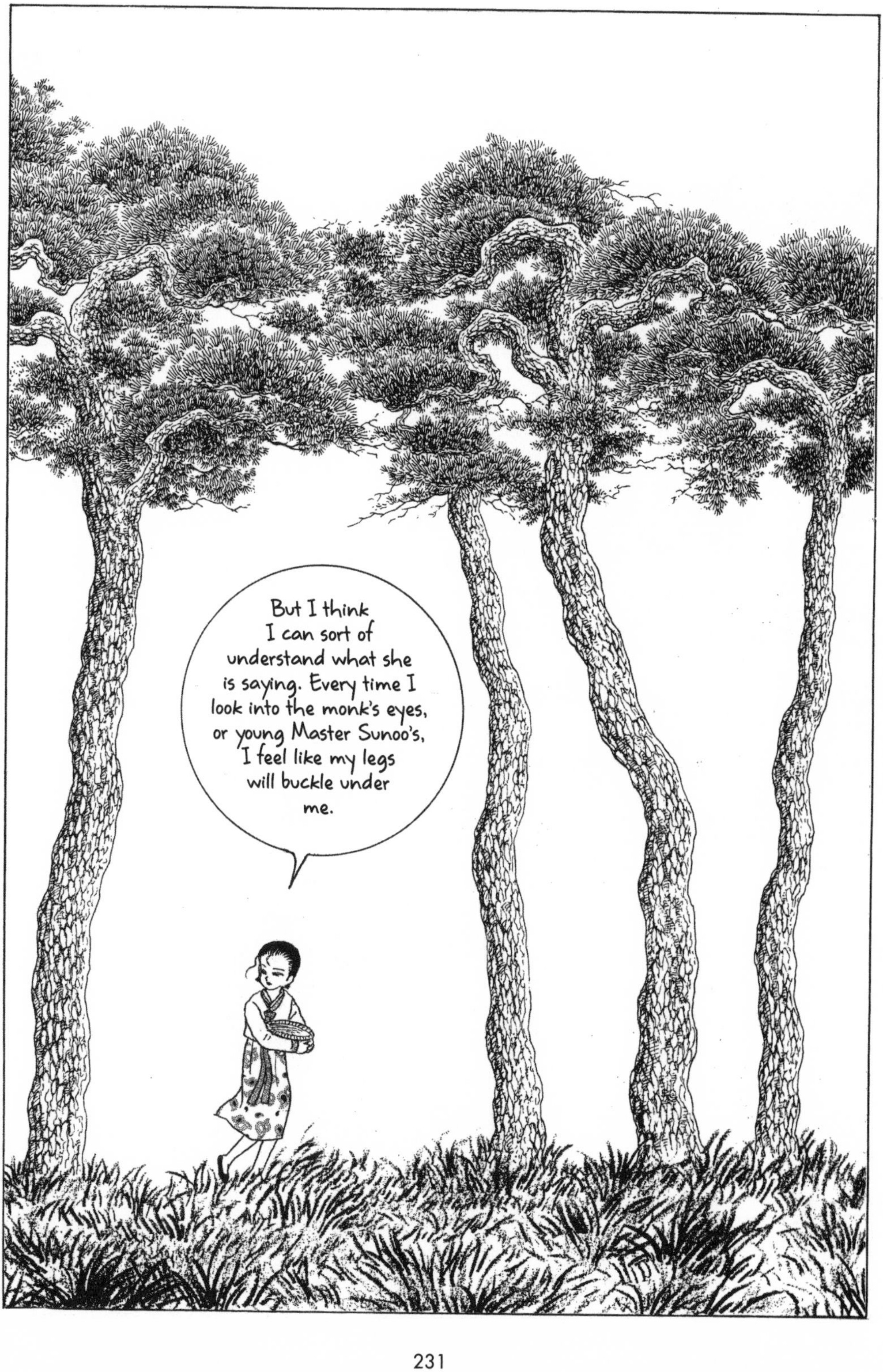
But I think I can sort of understand what she is saying. Every time I look into the monk's eyes, or young Master Sunoo's, I feel like my legs will buckle under me.

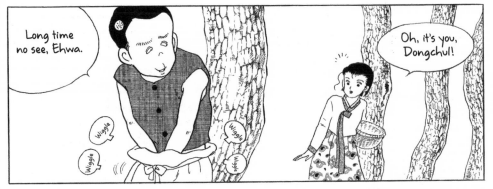

Long time no see, Ehwa.
Wiggle
Wiggle
Wiggle
Wiggle
Oh, it's you, Dongchul!
Are you still taking good care of your gochoo?
Wiggle
Wiggle
What's this about a gochoo all of a sudden?
You said your gochoo was the size of the kimjang gochoo, remember?
Do you wanna compare our gochoo size? My gochoo has grown really big now.
I... I said that back then as a joke because you guys were teasing me. A girl doesn't have a gochoo!
That's right. Later, I found out that a girl doesn't have a gochoo but has a persimmon seed instead.
Wiggle
Wiggle
Wiggle

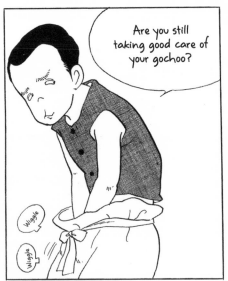

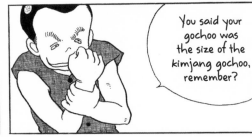

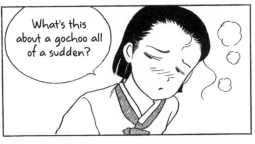

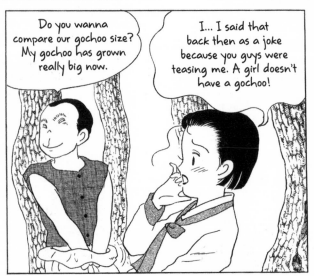

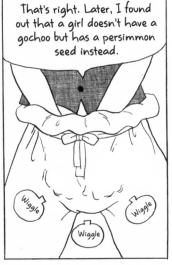

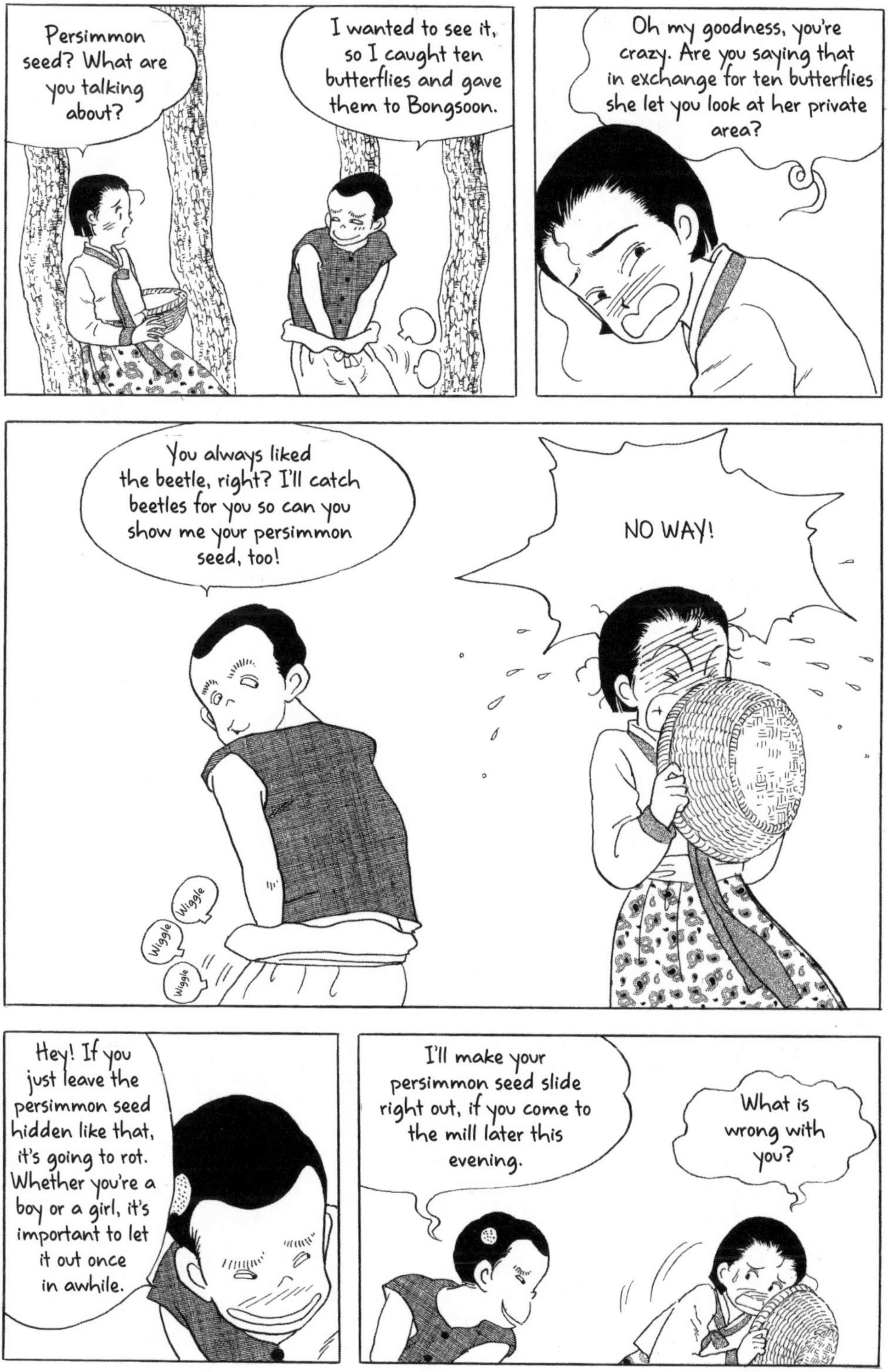
Persimmon seed? What are you talking about?
I wanted to see it, so I caught ten butterflies and gave them to Bongsoon.
Oh my goodness, you're crazy. Are you saying that in exchange for ten butterflies she let you look at her private area?
You always liked the beetle, right? I'll catch beetles for you so can you show me your persimmon seed, too!
NO WAY!
Wiggle
Wiggle
Wiggle
Hey! If you just leave the persimmon seed hidden like that, it's going to rot. Whether you're a boy or a girl, it's important to let it out once in awhile.
I'll make your persimmon seed slide right out, if you come to the mill later this evening.
What is wrong with you?

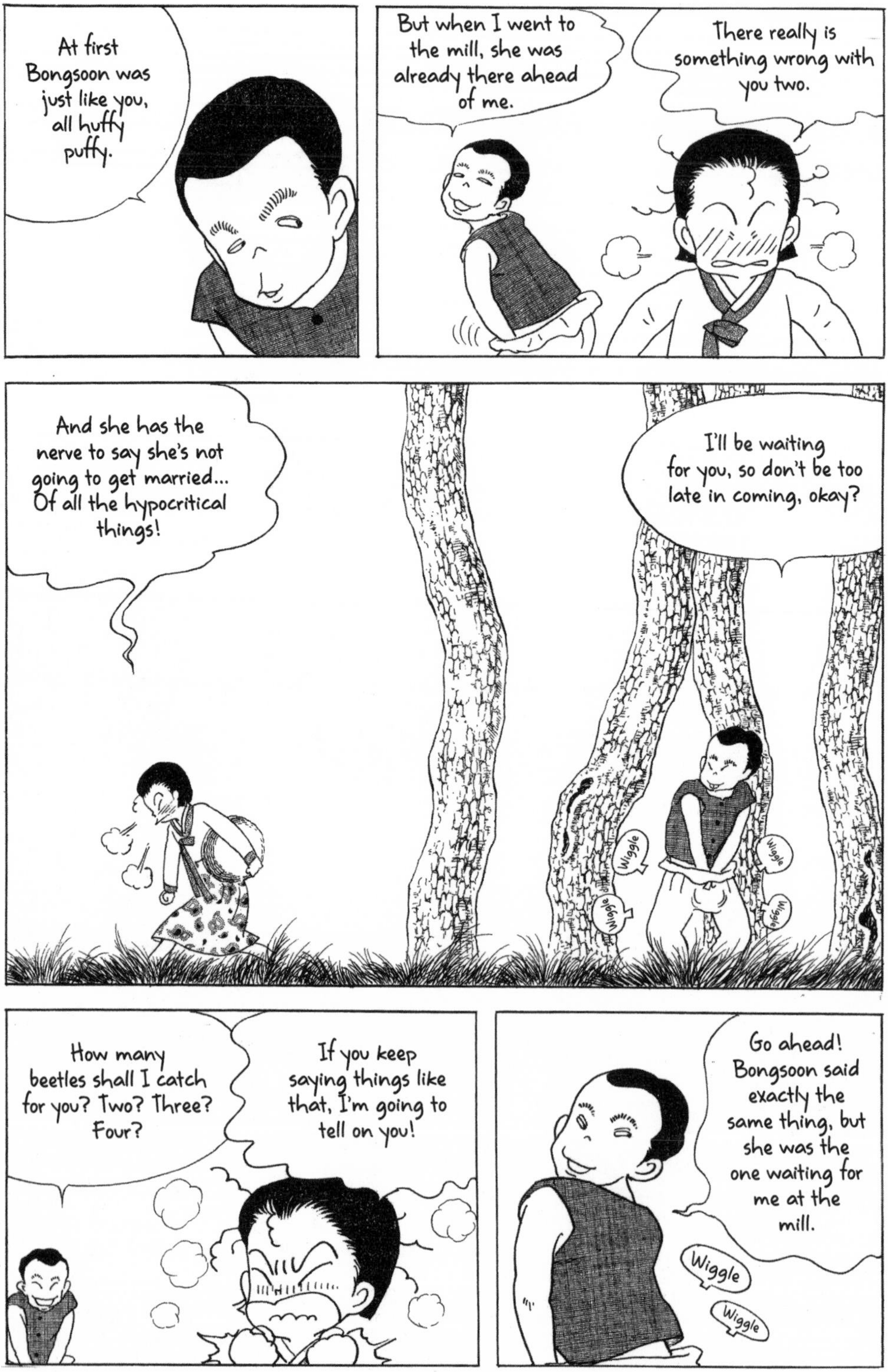
At first Bongsoon was just like you, all huffy puffy.
But when I went to the mill, she was already there ahead of me.
There really is something wrong with you two.
And she has the nerve to say she's not going to get married... Of all the hypocritical things!
I'll be waiting for you, so don't be too late in coming, okay?
Wiggle
Wiggle
Wiggle
Wiggle
How many beetles shall I catch for you? Two? Three? Four?
If you keep saying things like that, I'm going to tell on you!
Go ahead! Bongsoon said exactly the same thing, but she was the one waiting for me at the mill.
Wiggle
Wiggle

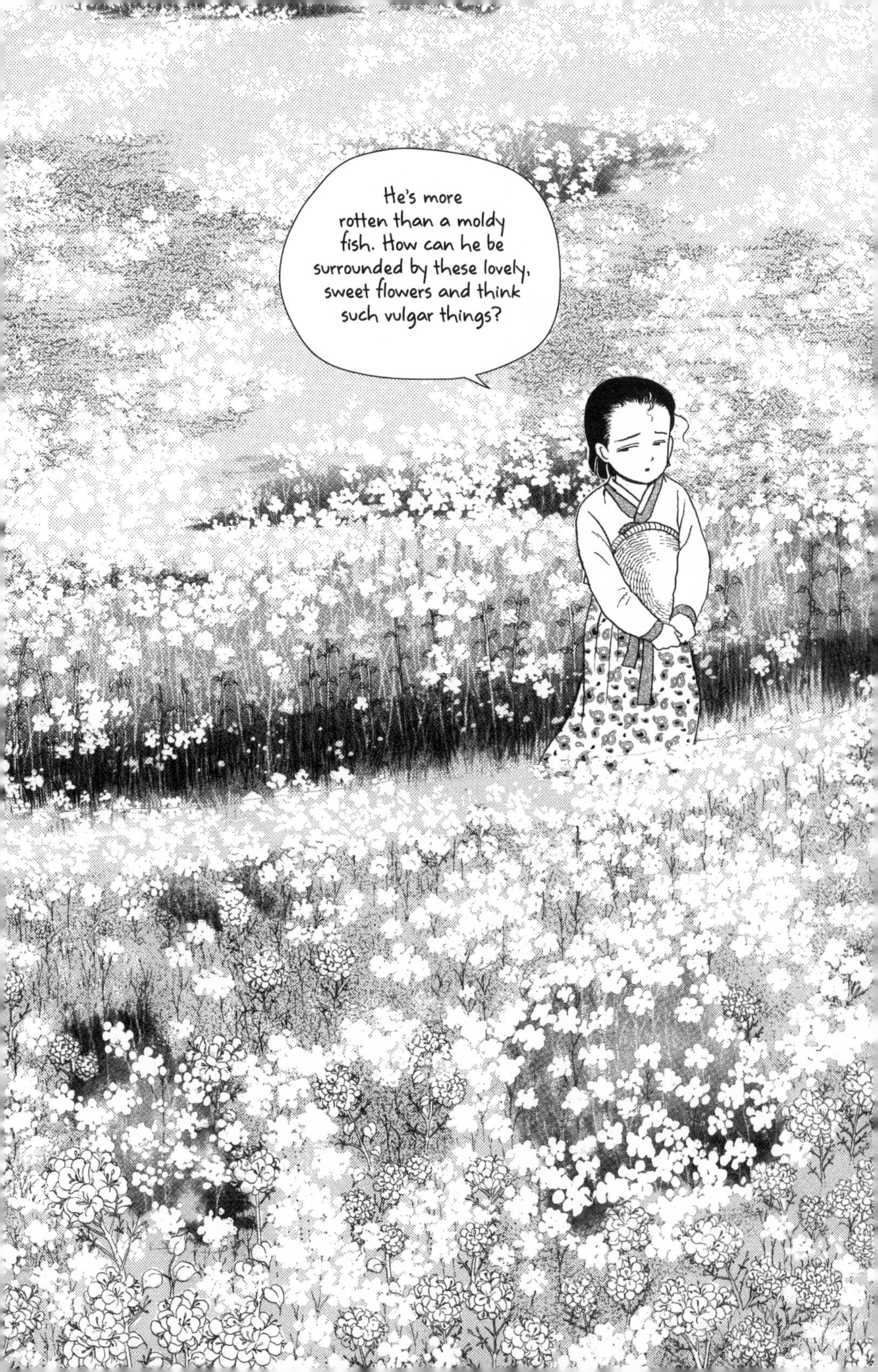
He's more rotten than a moldy fish. How can he be surrounded by these lovely, sweet flowers and think such vulgar things?

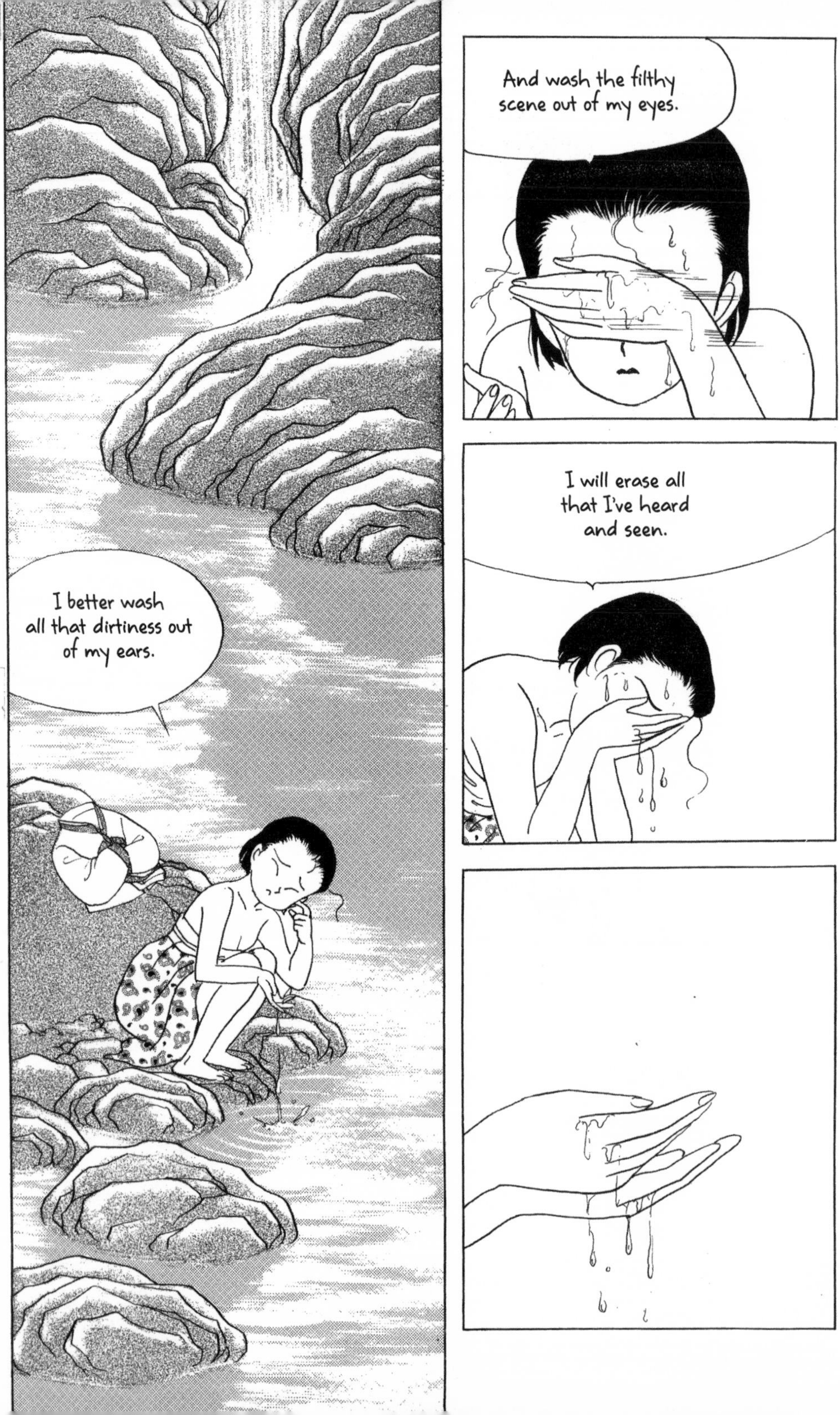
I better wash all that dirtiness out of my ears.
And wash the filthy scene out of my eyes.
I will erase all that I've heard and seen.

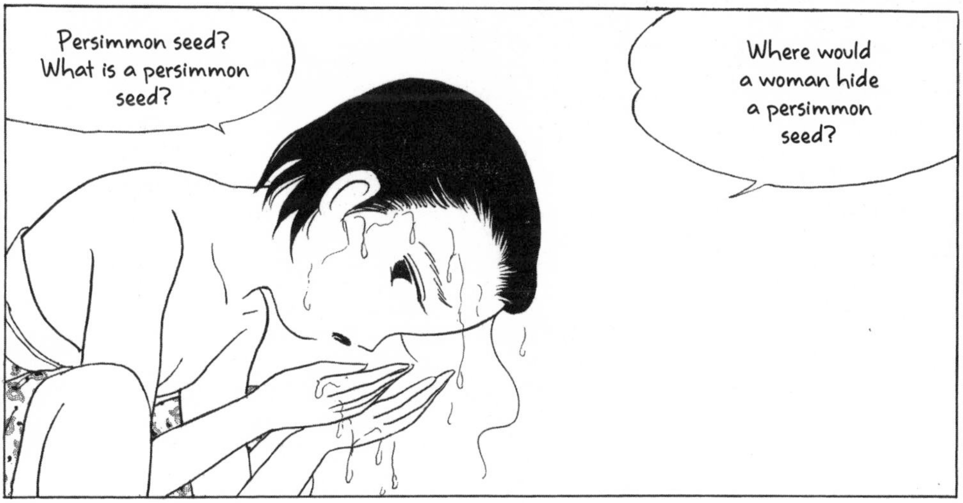
Persimmon seed? What is a persimmon seed?
Where would a woman hide a persimmon seed?

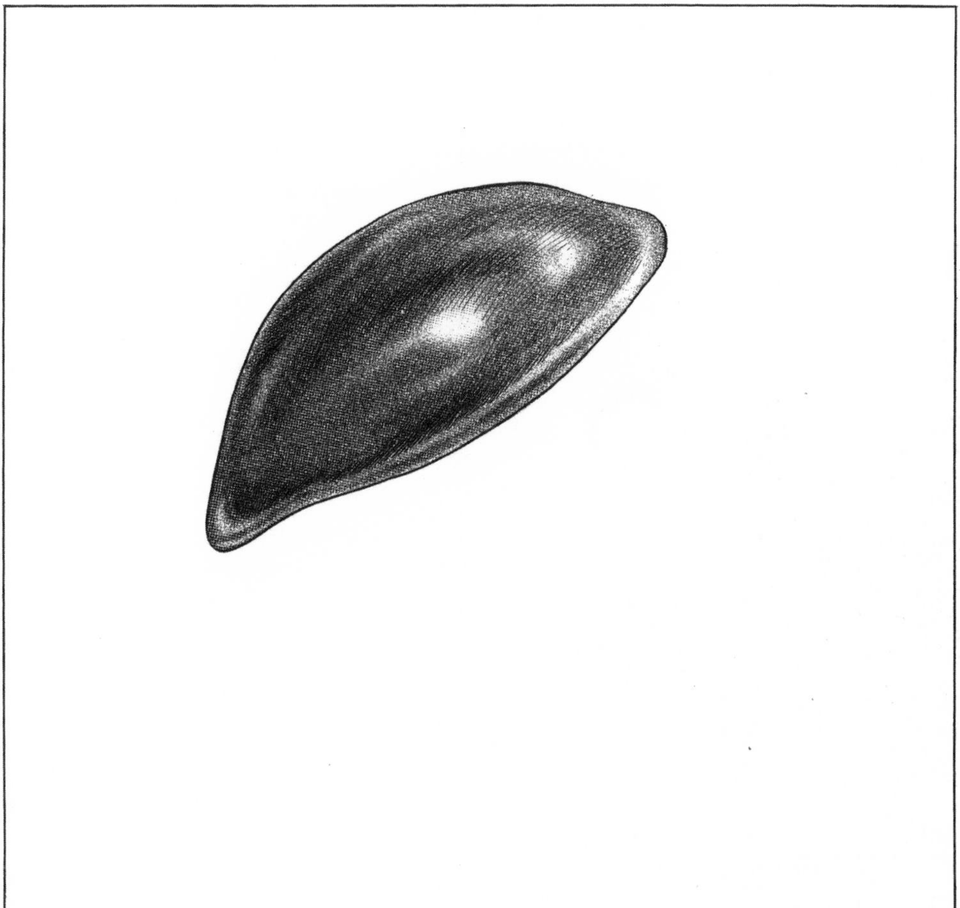

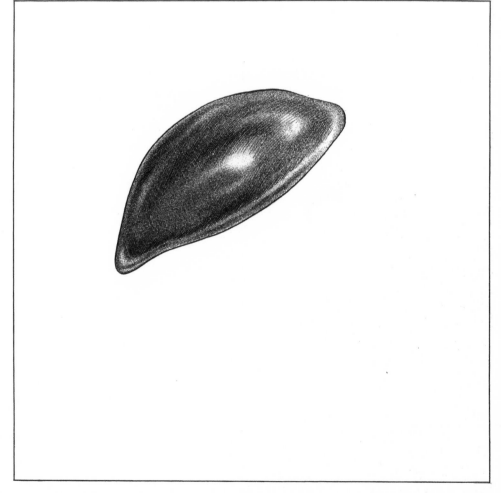

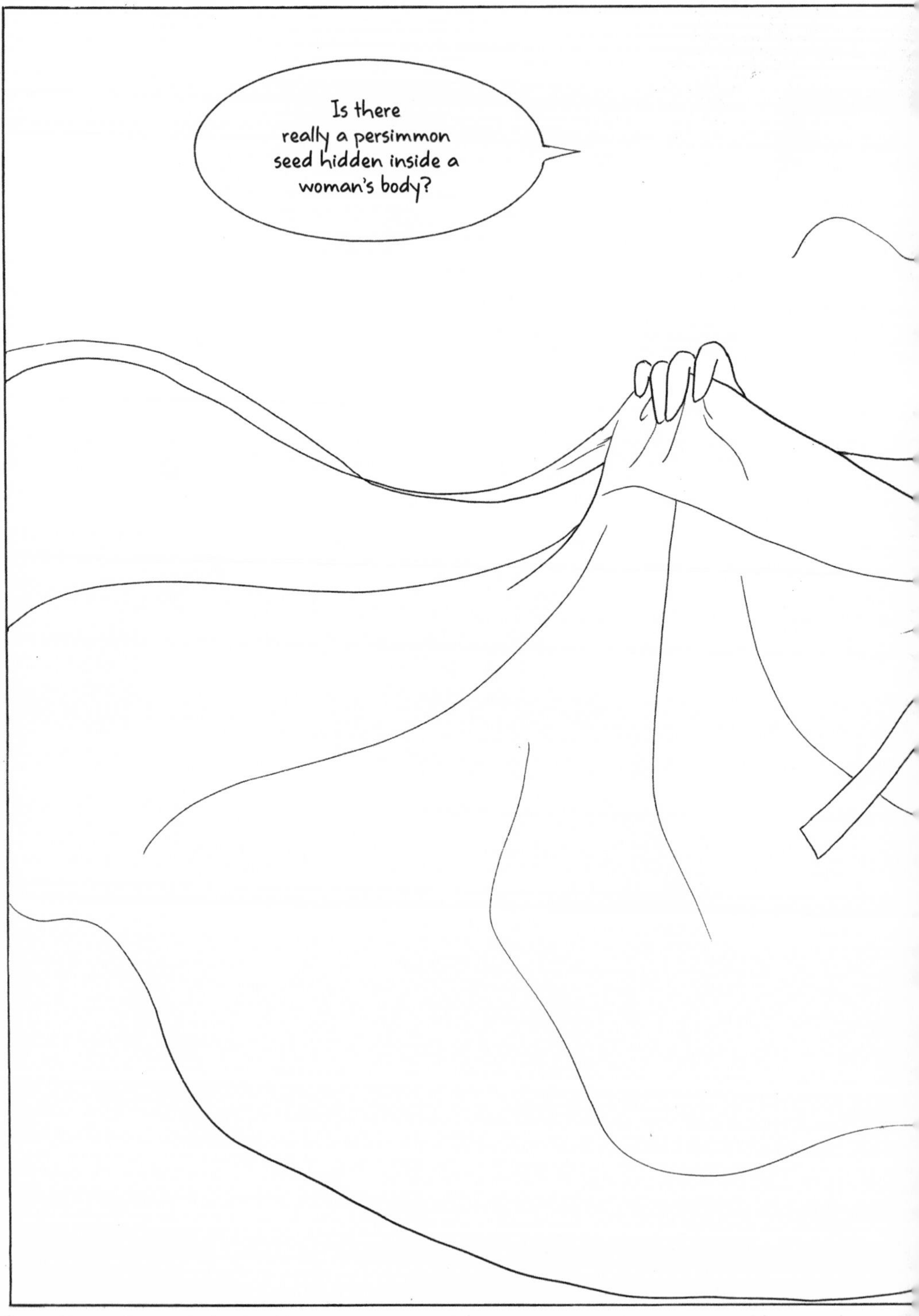
Is there really a persimmon seed hidden inside a woman's body?

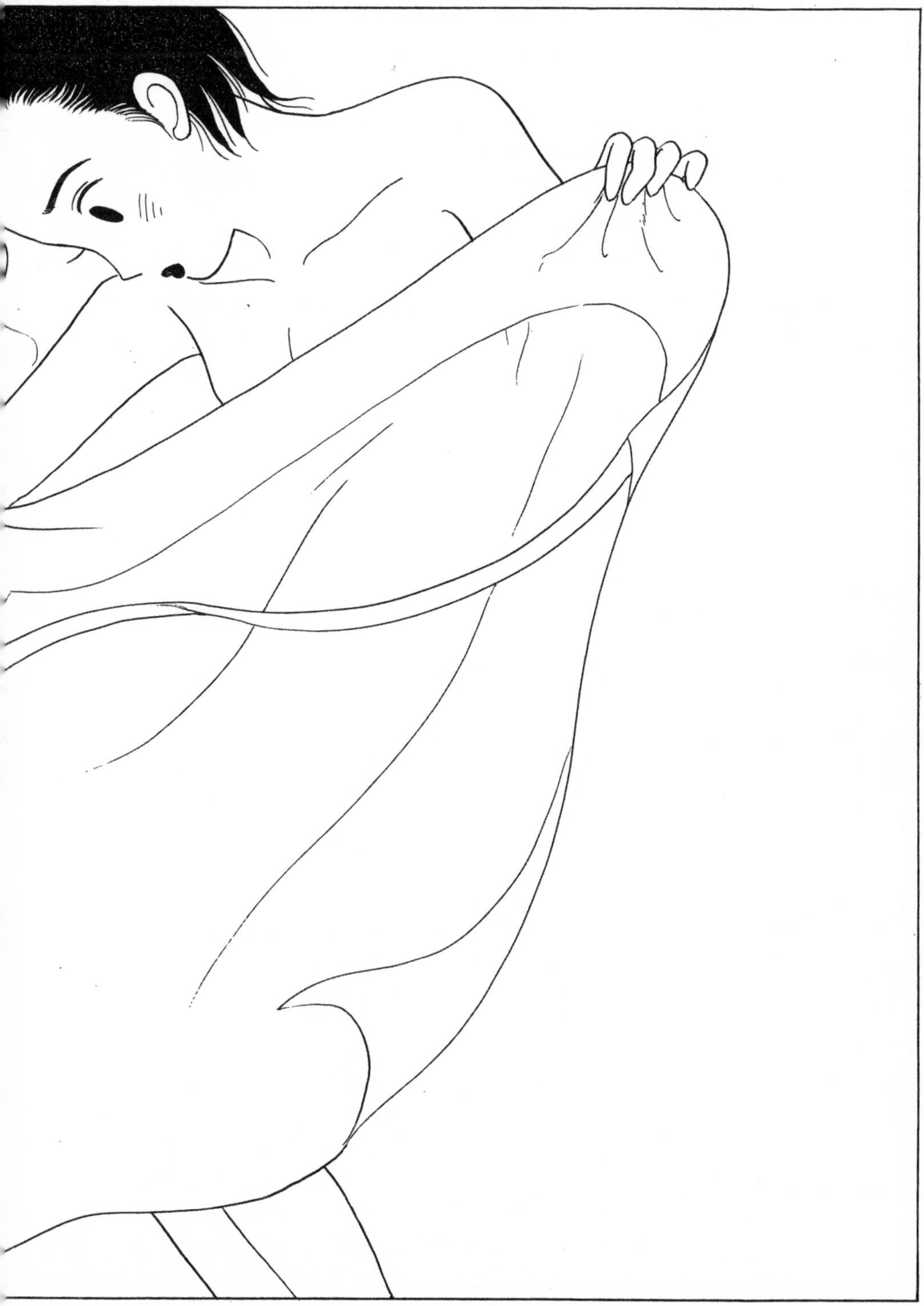

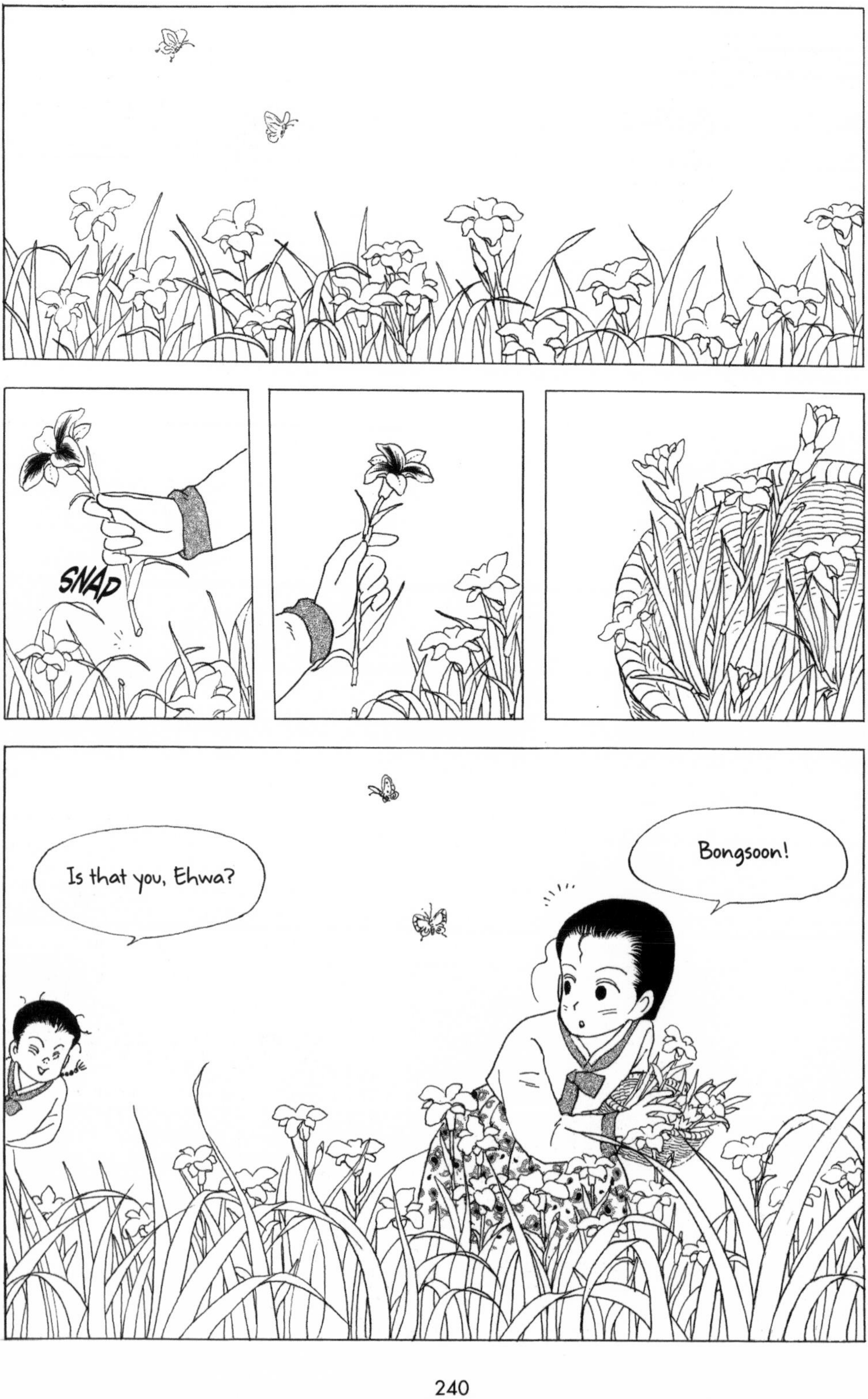
SNAP
Is that you, Ehwa?
Bongsoon!

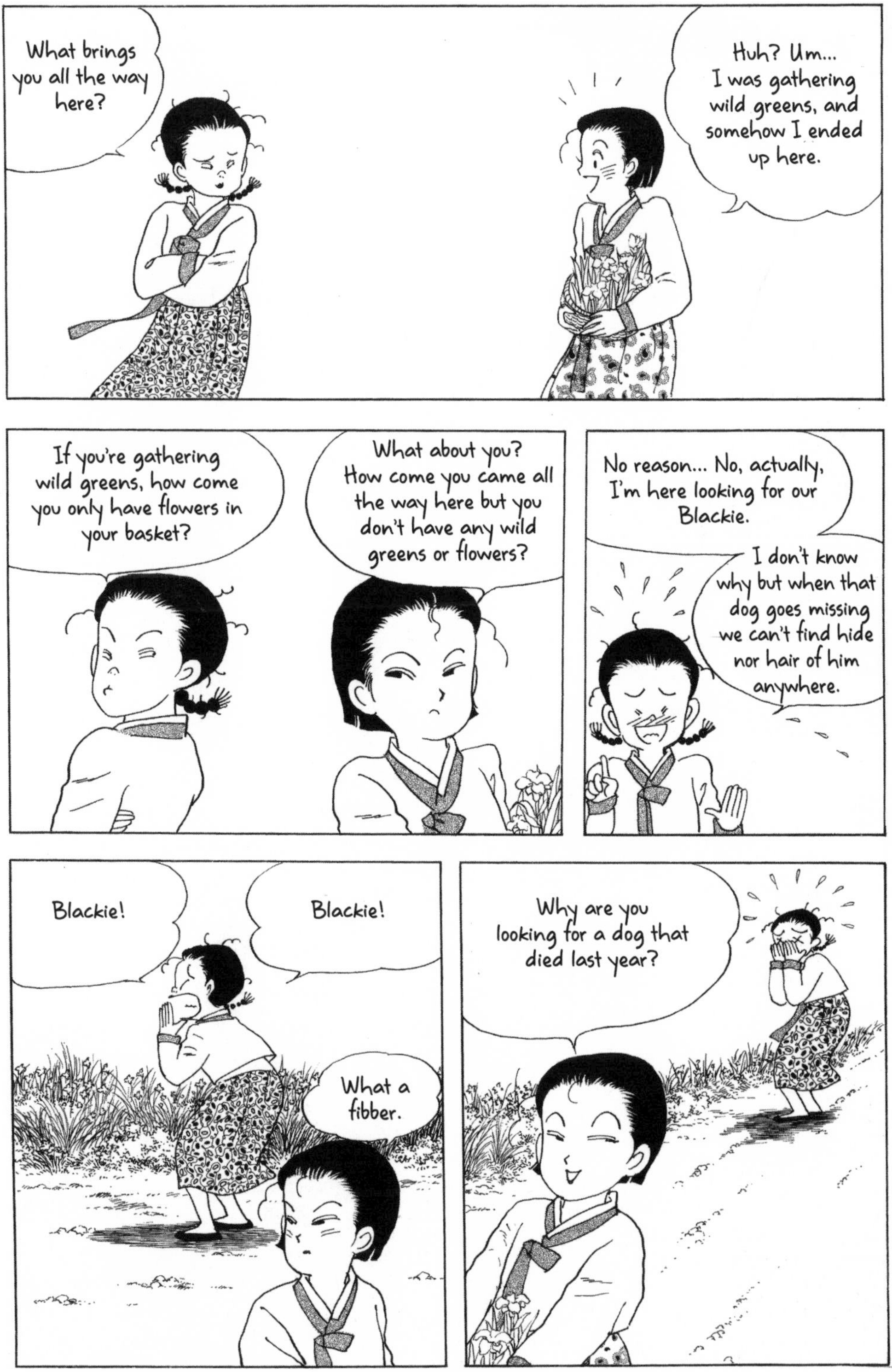
What brings you all the way here?
Huh? Um... I was gathering wild greens, and somehow I ended up here.
If you're gathering wild greens, how come you only have flowers in your basket?
What about you? How come you came all the way here but you don't have any wild greens or flowers?
No reason... No, actually, I'm here looking for our Blackie.
I don't know why but when that dog goes missing we can't find hide nor hair of him anywhere.
Blackie!
Blackie!
What a fibber.
Why are you looking for a dog that died last year?

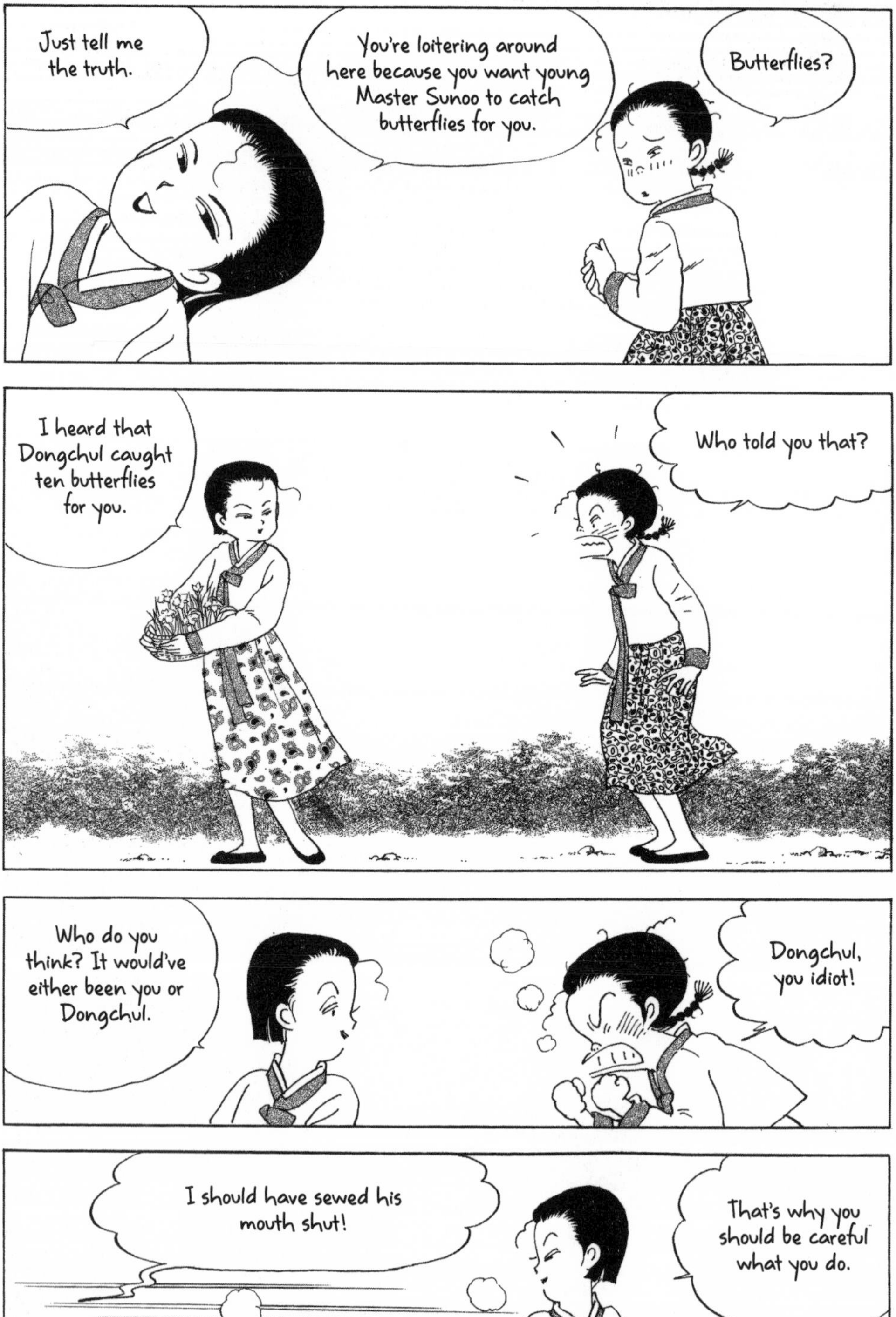
Just tell me the truth.
You're loitering around here because you want young Master Sunoo to catch butterflies for you.
Butterflies?
I heard that Dongchul caught ten butterflies for you.
Who told you that?
Who do you think? It would've either been you or Dongchul.
Dongchul, you idiot!
I should have sewed his mouth shut!
That's why you should be careful what you do.

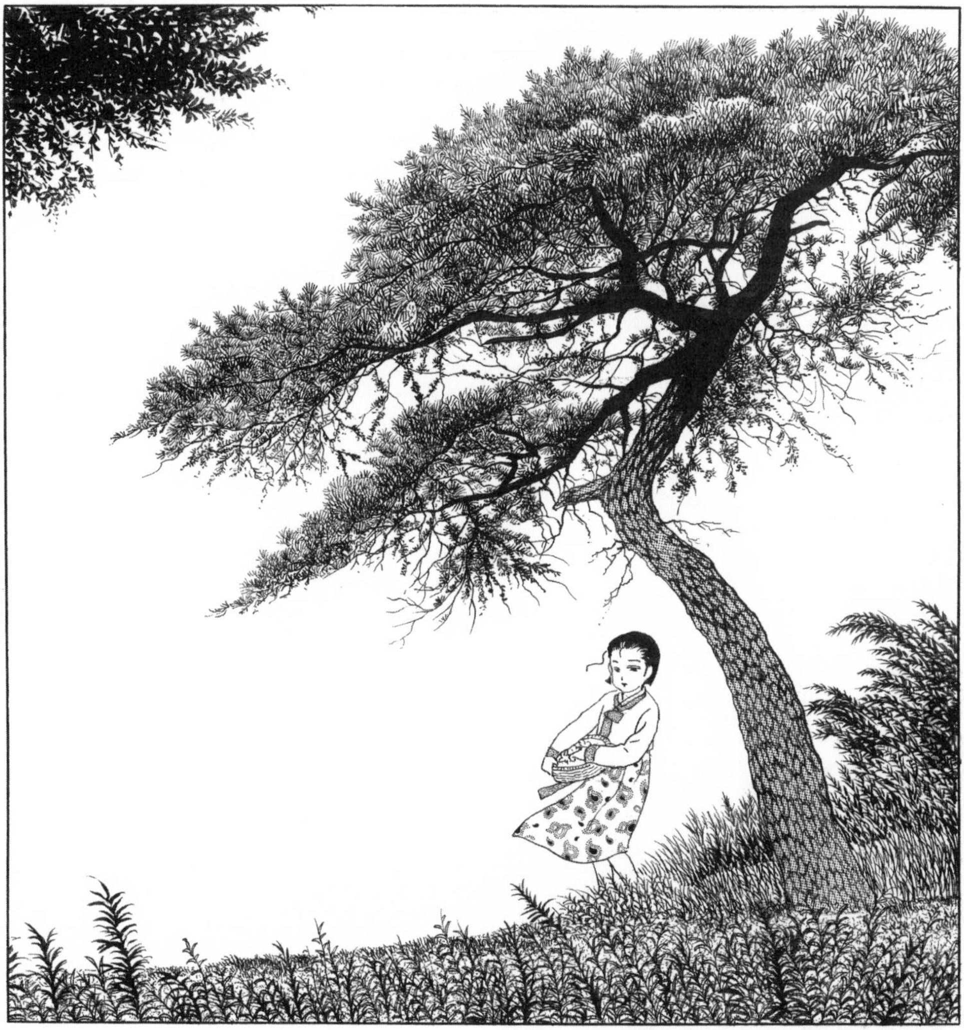

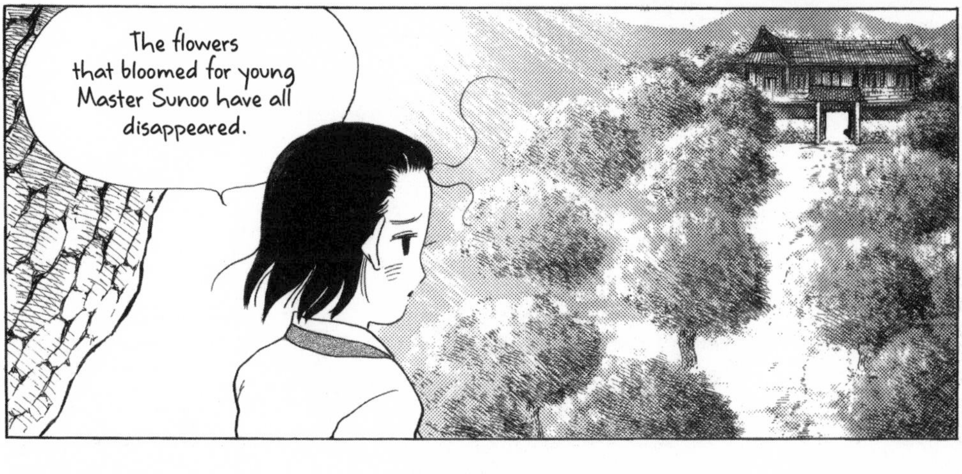
The flowers that bloomed for young Master Sunoo have all disappeared.

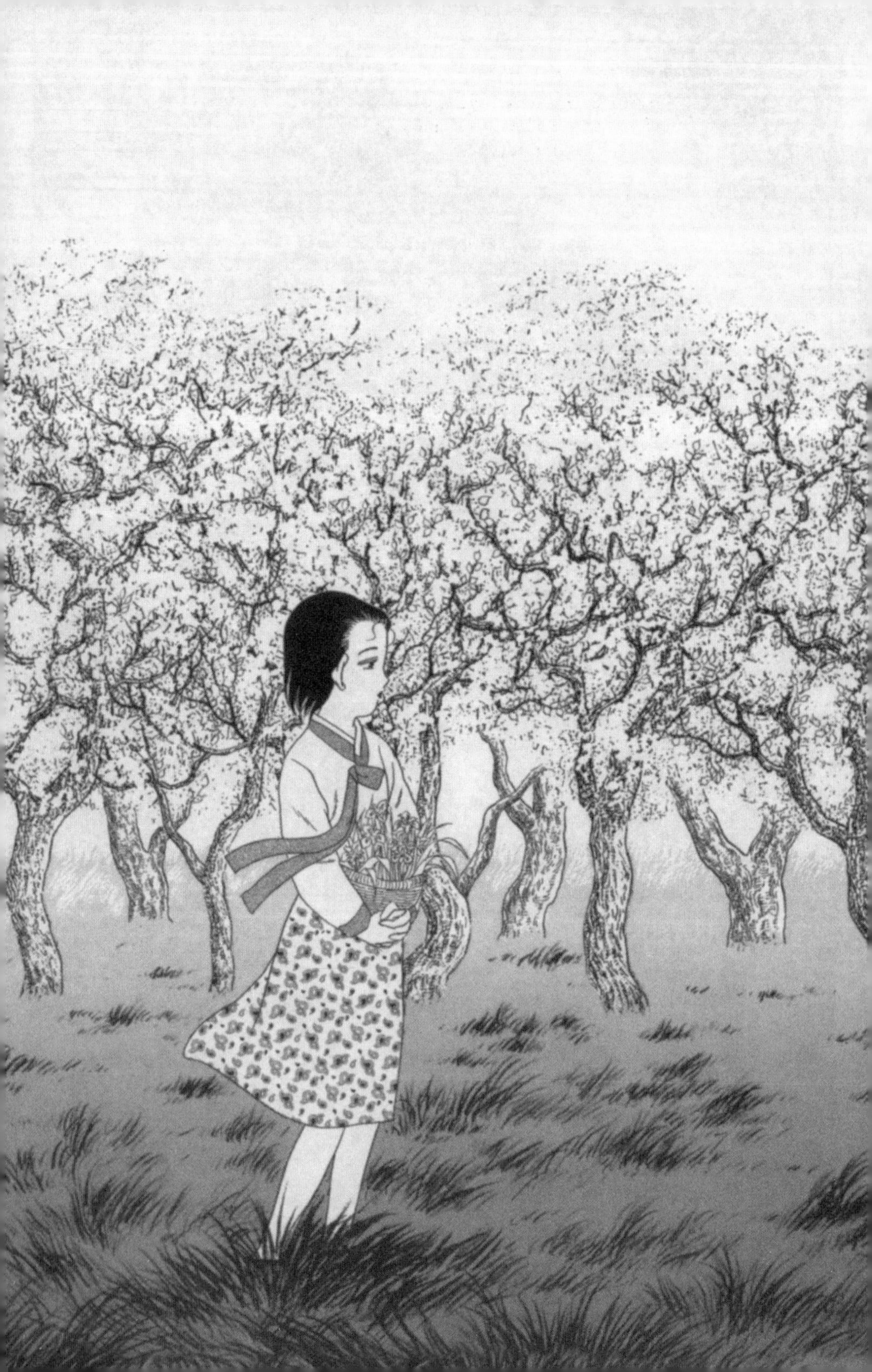

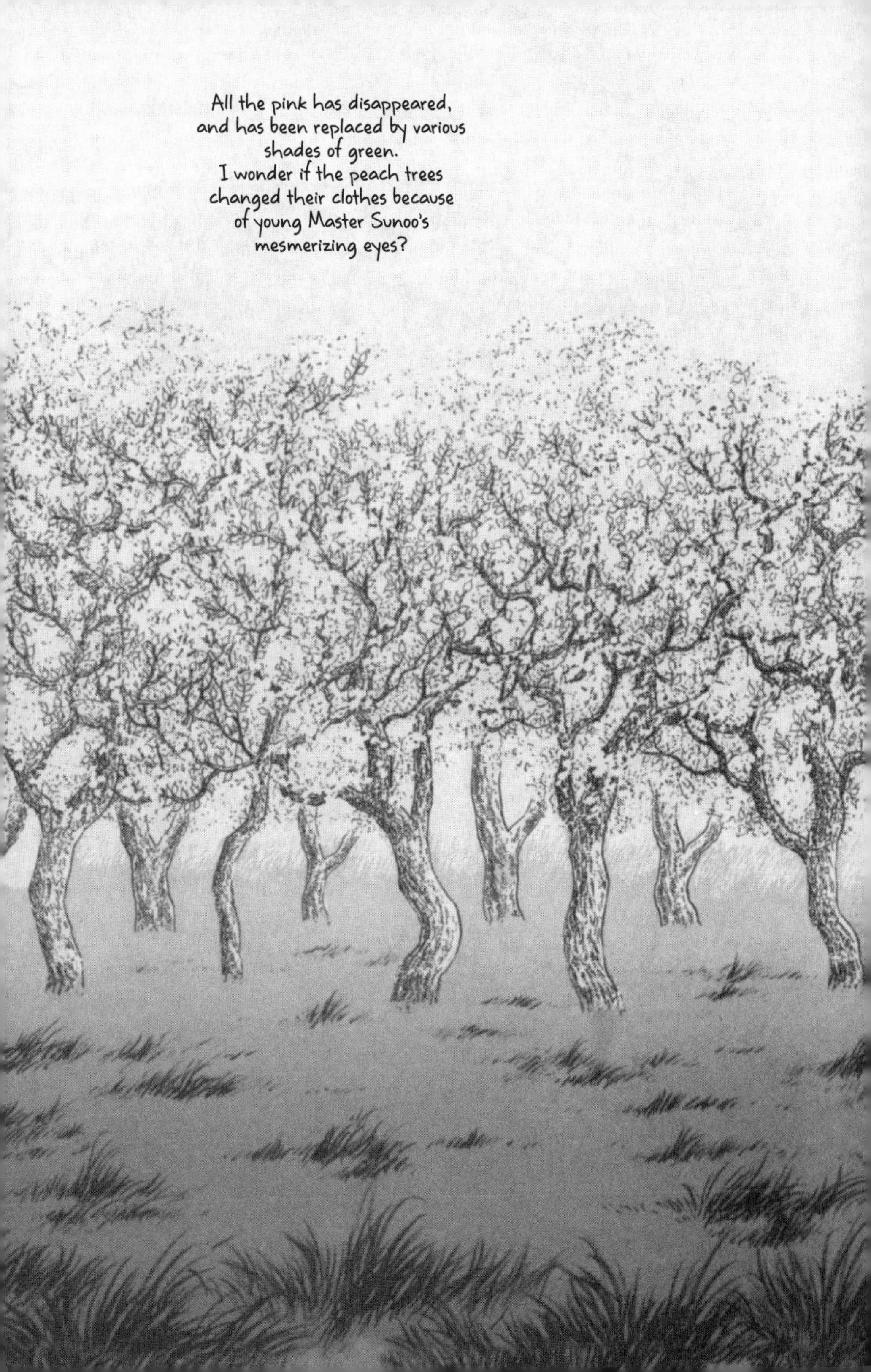
All the pink has disappeared, and has been replaced by various shades of green.
I wonder if the peach trees changed their clothes because of young Master Sunoo's mesmerizing eyes?

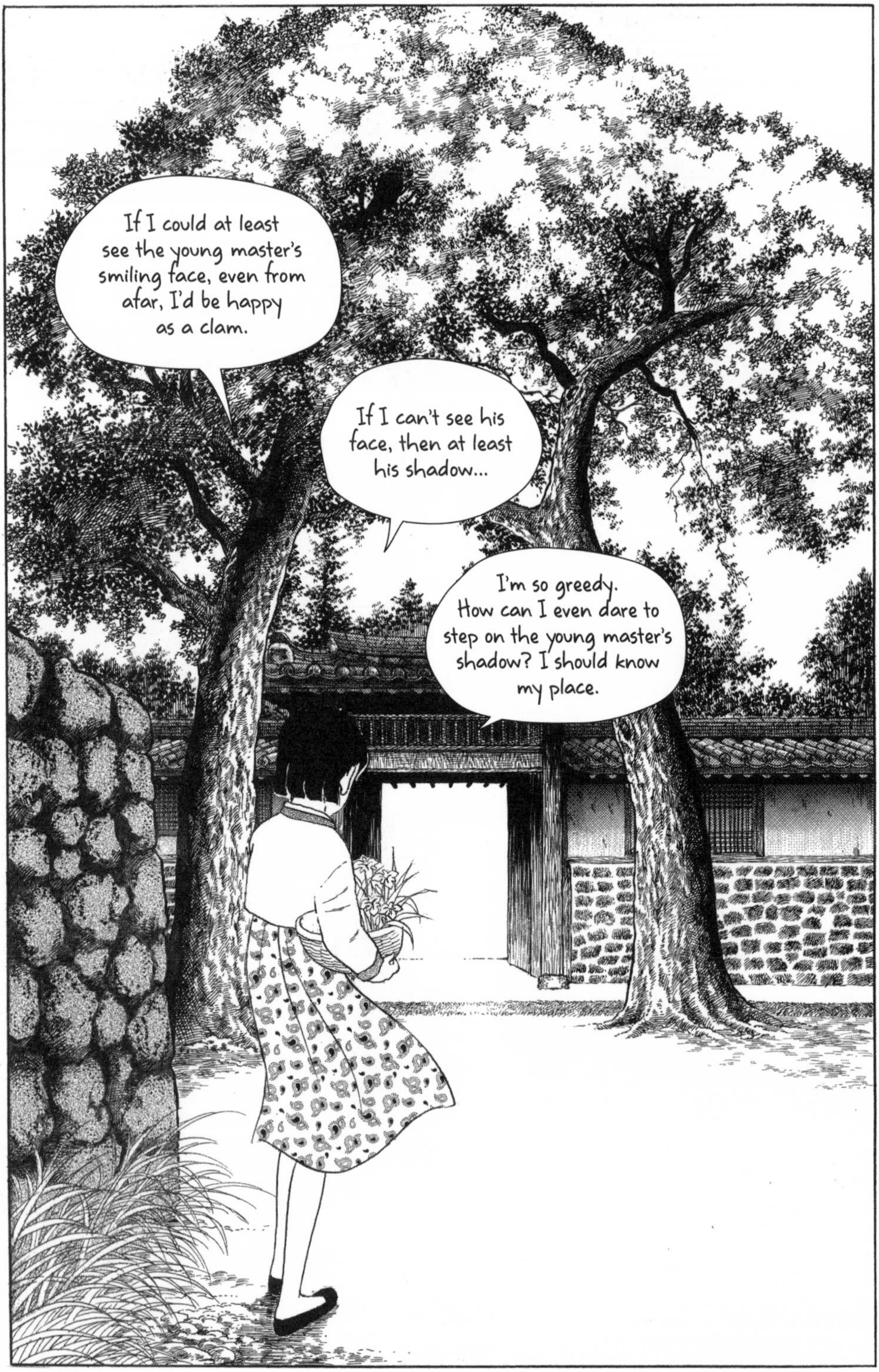
If I could at least see the young master's smiling face, even from afar, I'd be happy as a clam.
If I can't see his face, then at least his shadow...
I'm so greedy. How can I even dare to step on the young master's shadow? I should know my place.

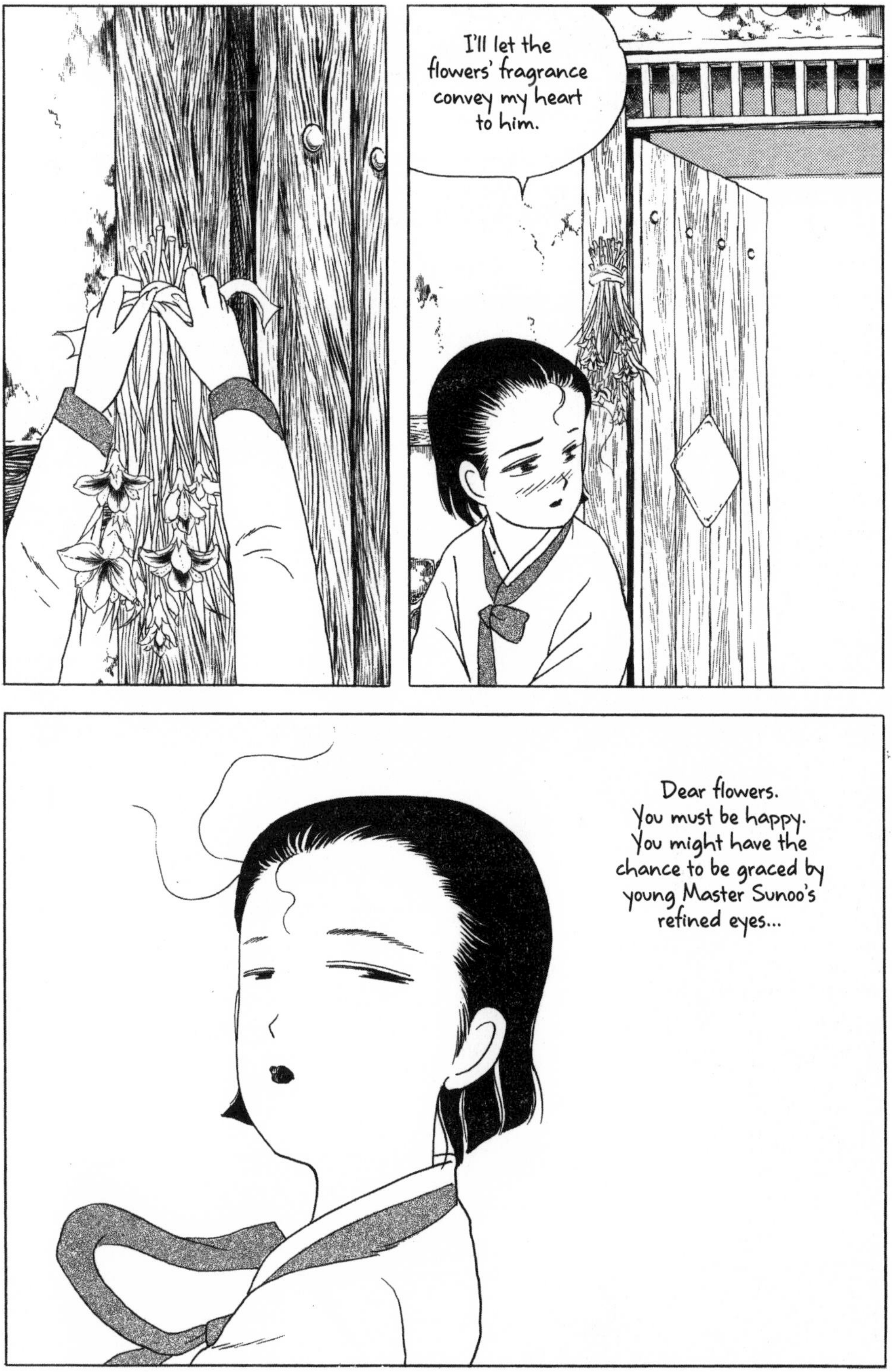
I'll let the flowers' fragrance convey my heart to him.
Dear flowers. You must be happy. You might have the chance to be graced by young Master Sunoo's refined eyes...

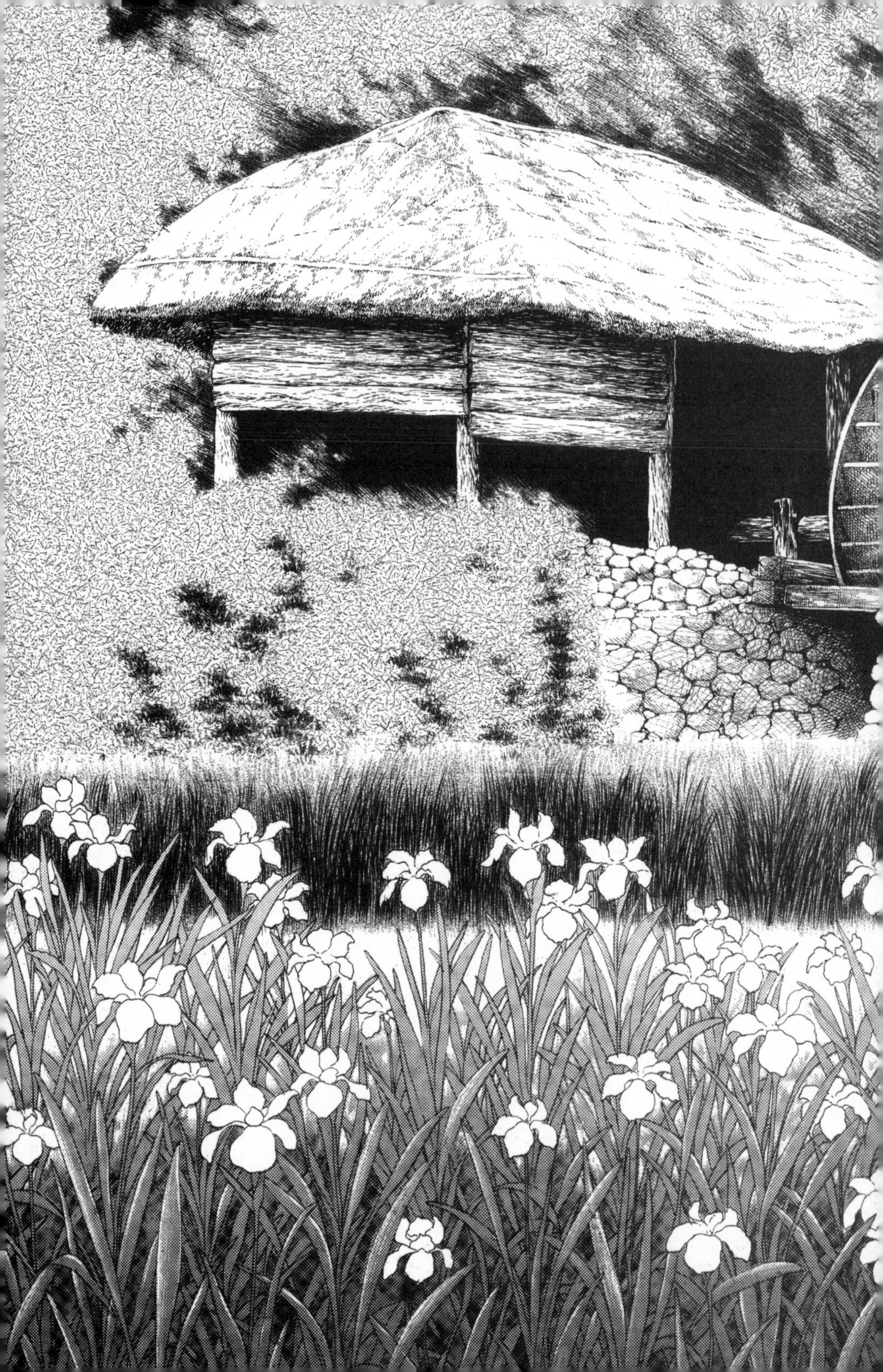

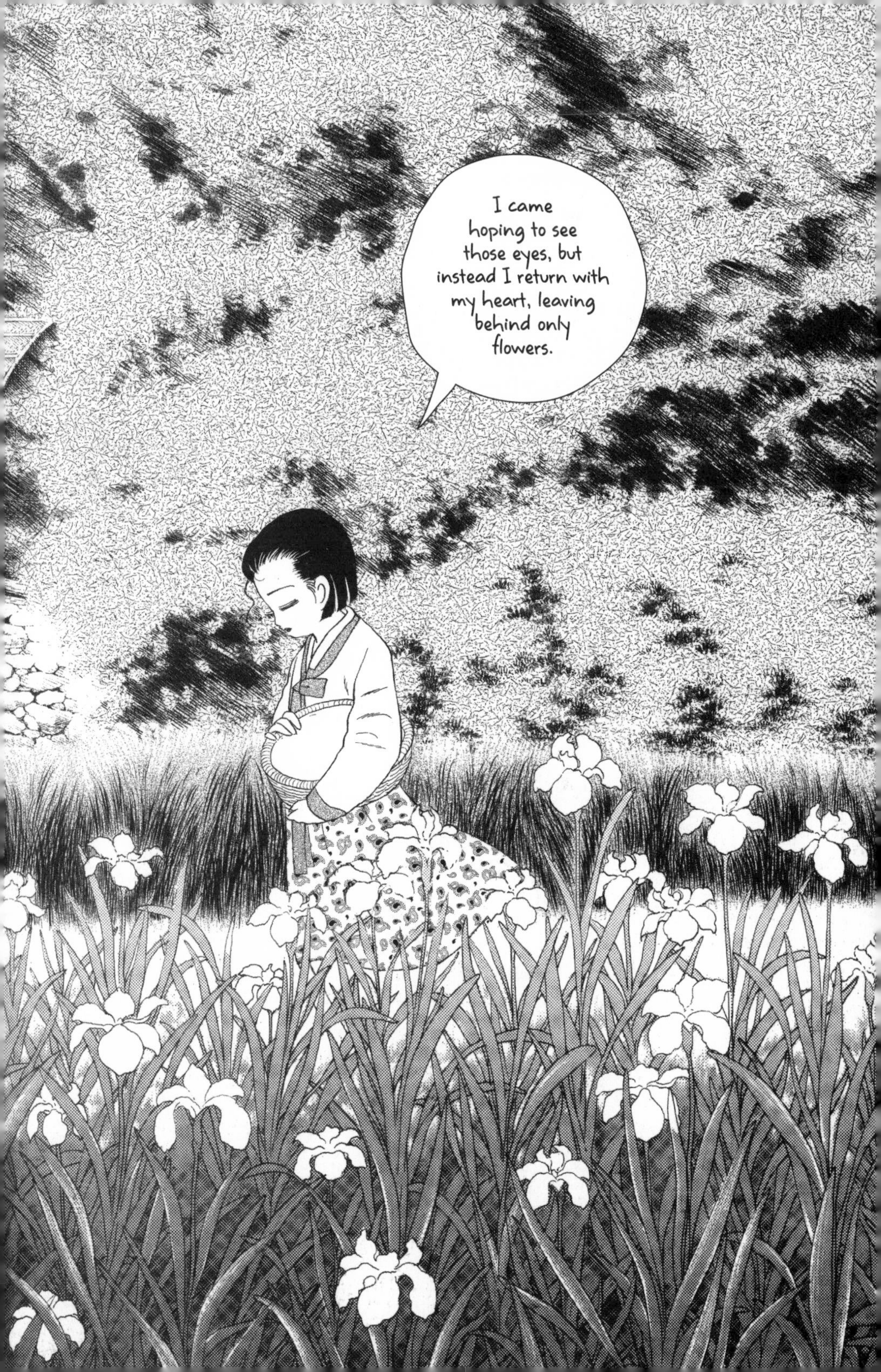
I came hoping to see those eyes, but instead I return with my heart, leaving behind only flowers.

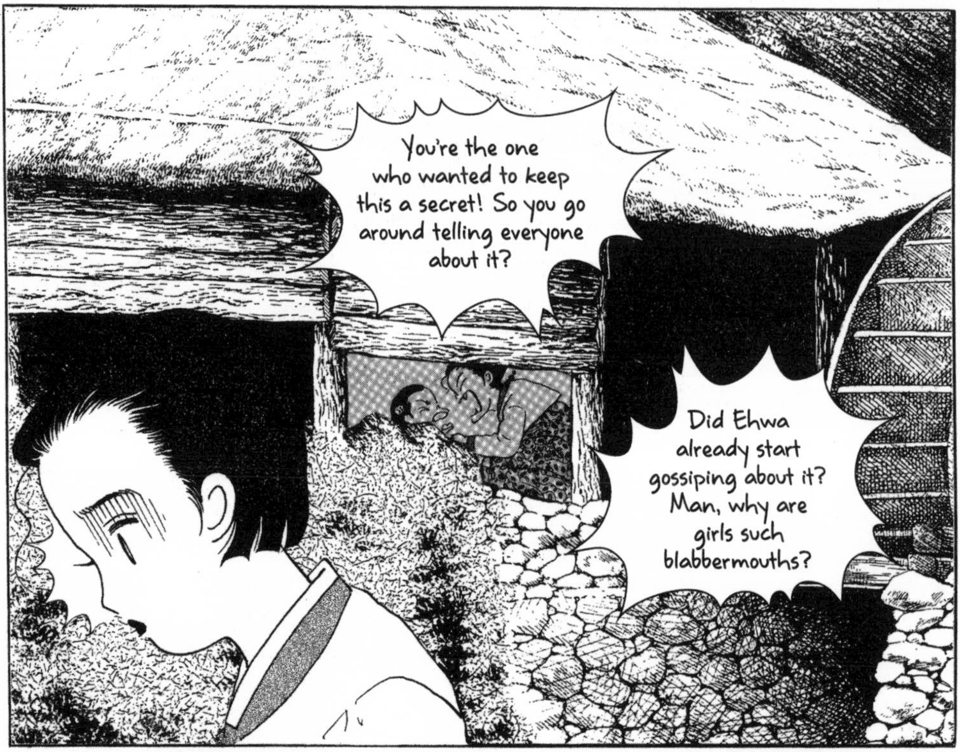
You're the one who wanted to keep this a secret! So you go around telling everyone about it?
Did Ehwa already start gossiping about it? Man, why are girls such blabbermouths?

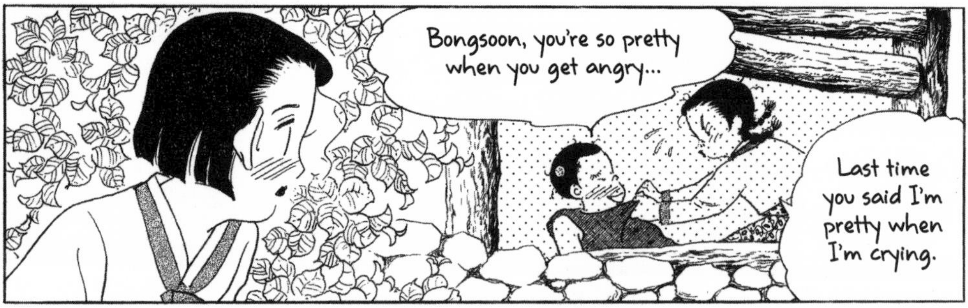
Bongsoon, you're so pretty when you get angry...
Last time you said I'm pretty when I'm crying.

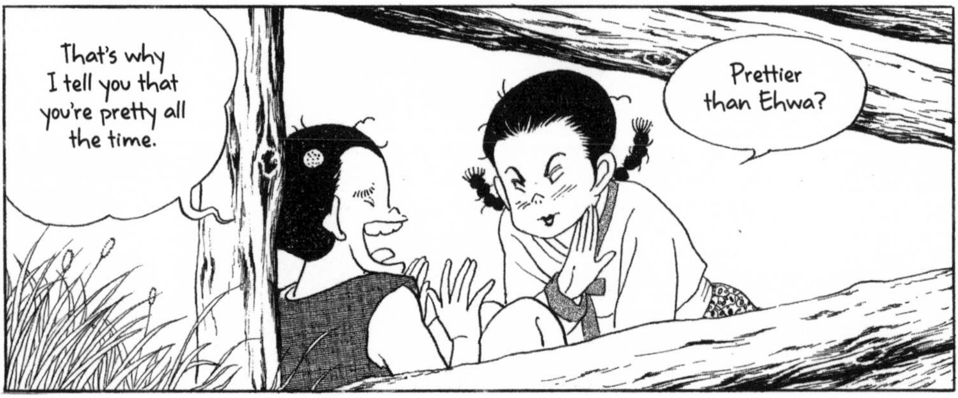
That's why I tell you that you're pretty all the time.
Prettier than Ehwa?

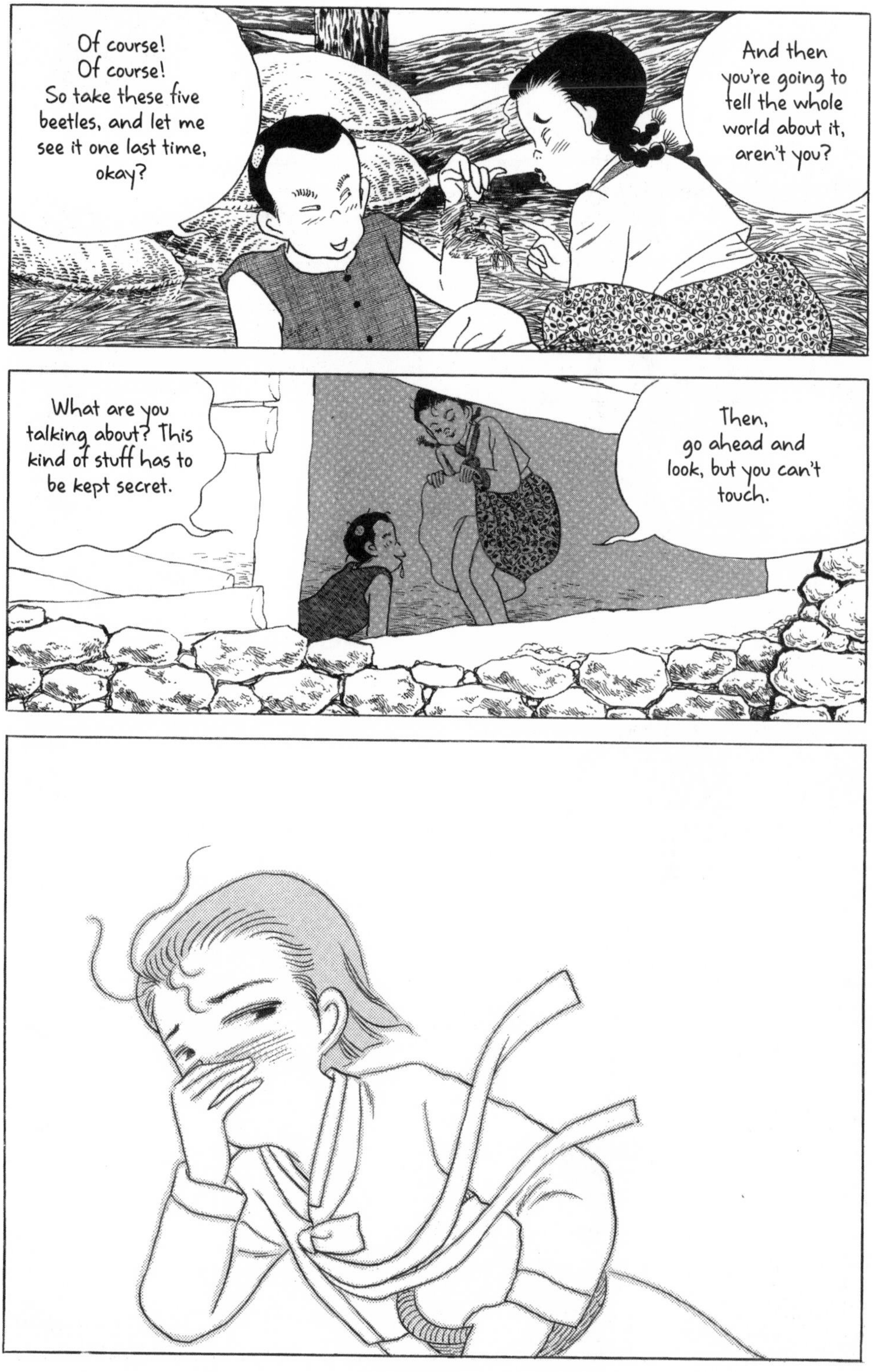
Of course! Of course! So take these five beetles, and let me see it one last time, okay?
And then you're going to tell the whole world about it, aren't you?
What are you talking about? This kind of stuff has to be kept secret.
Then, go ahead and look, but you can't touch.

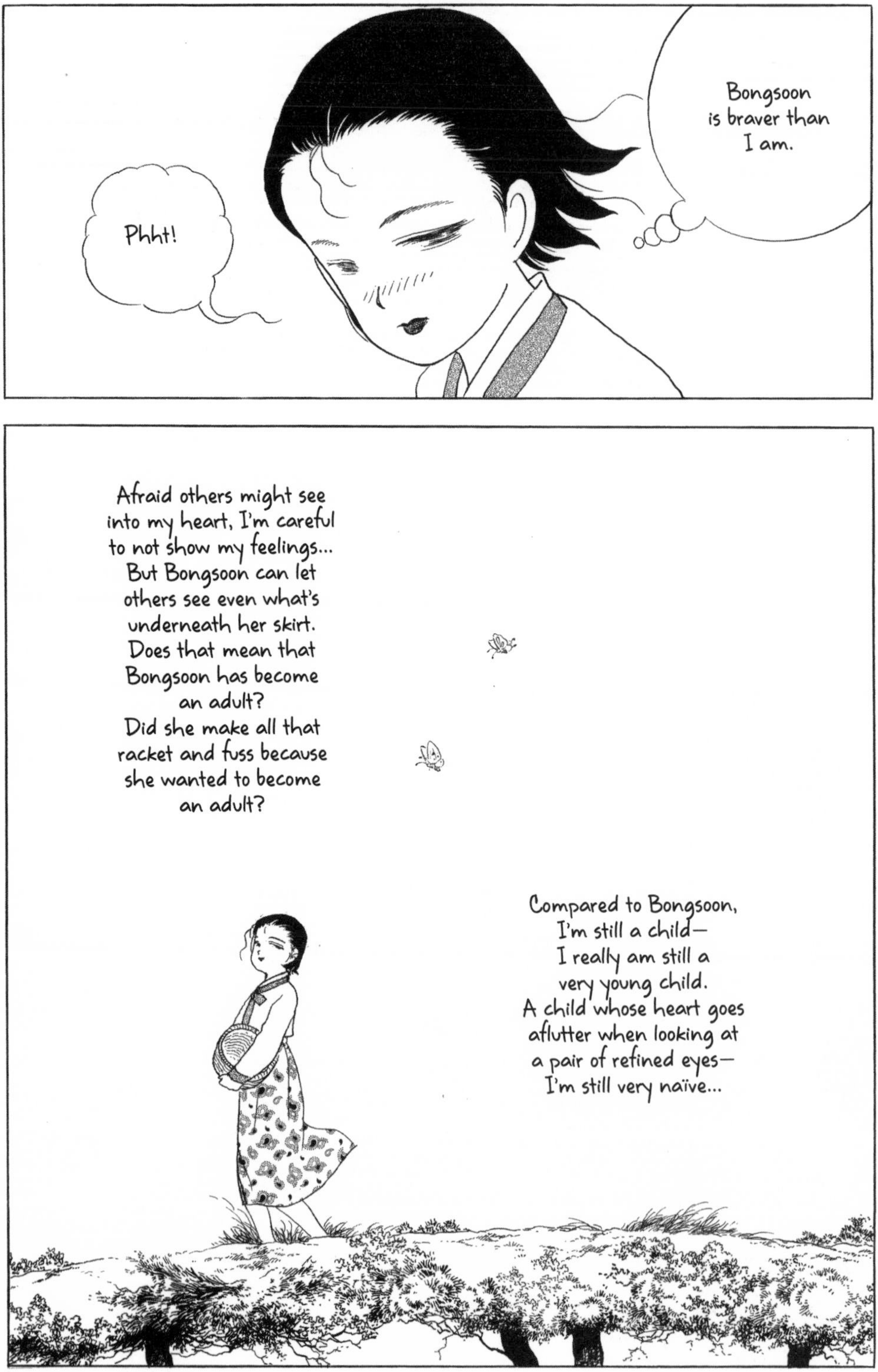
Bongsoon is braver than I am.
Phht!
Afraid others might see into my heart, I'm careful to not show my feelings... But Bongsoon can let others see even what's underneath her skirt. Does that mean that Bongsoon has become an adult? Did she make all that racket and fuss because she wanted to become an adult?
Compared to Bongsoon, I'm still a child— I really am still a very young child. A child whose heart goes aflutter when looking at a pair of refined eyes— I'm still very naïve...

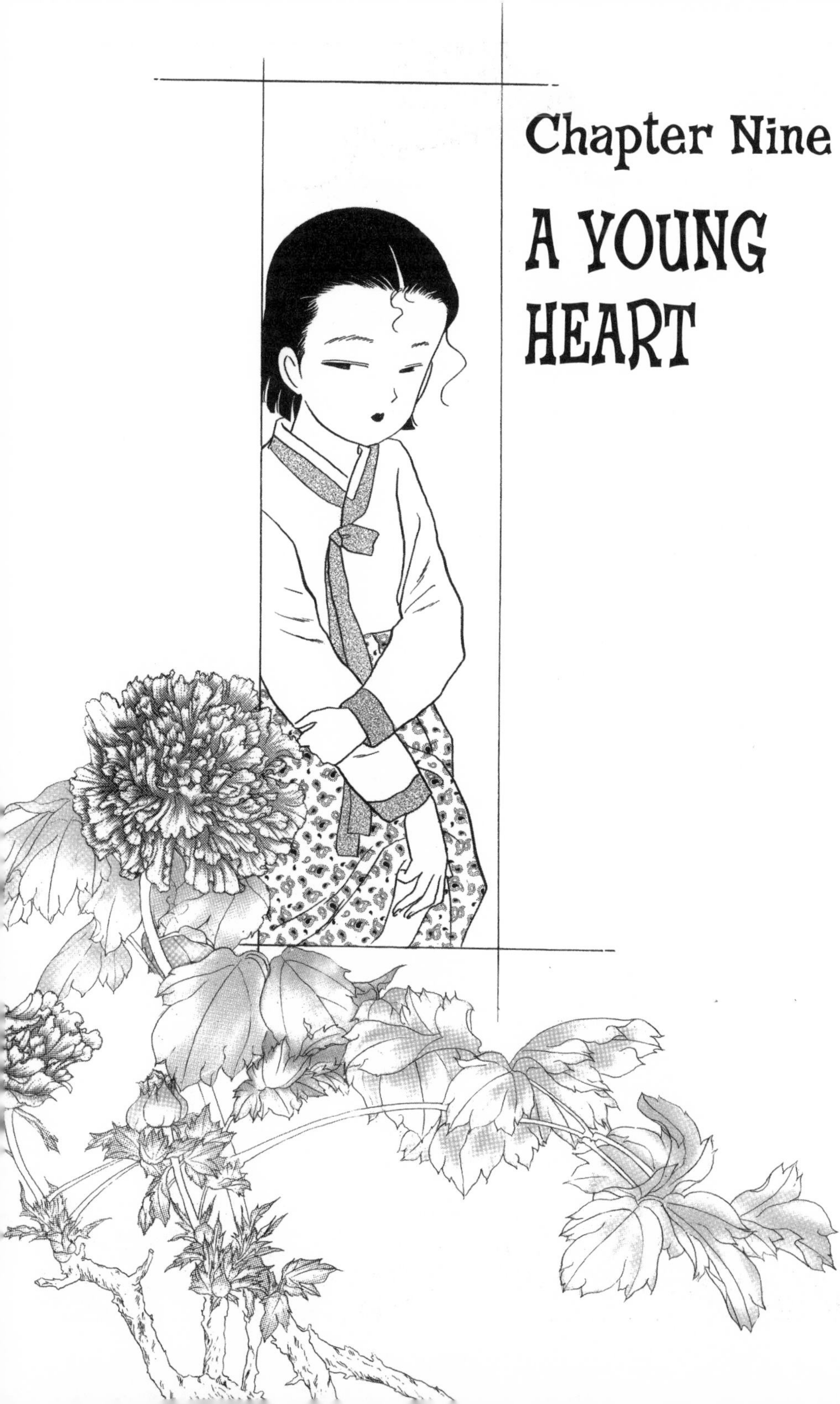

Chapter Nine

A YOUNG HEART

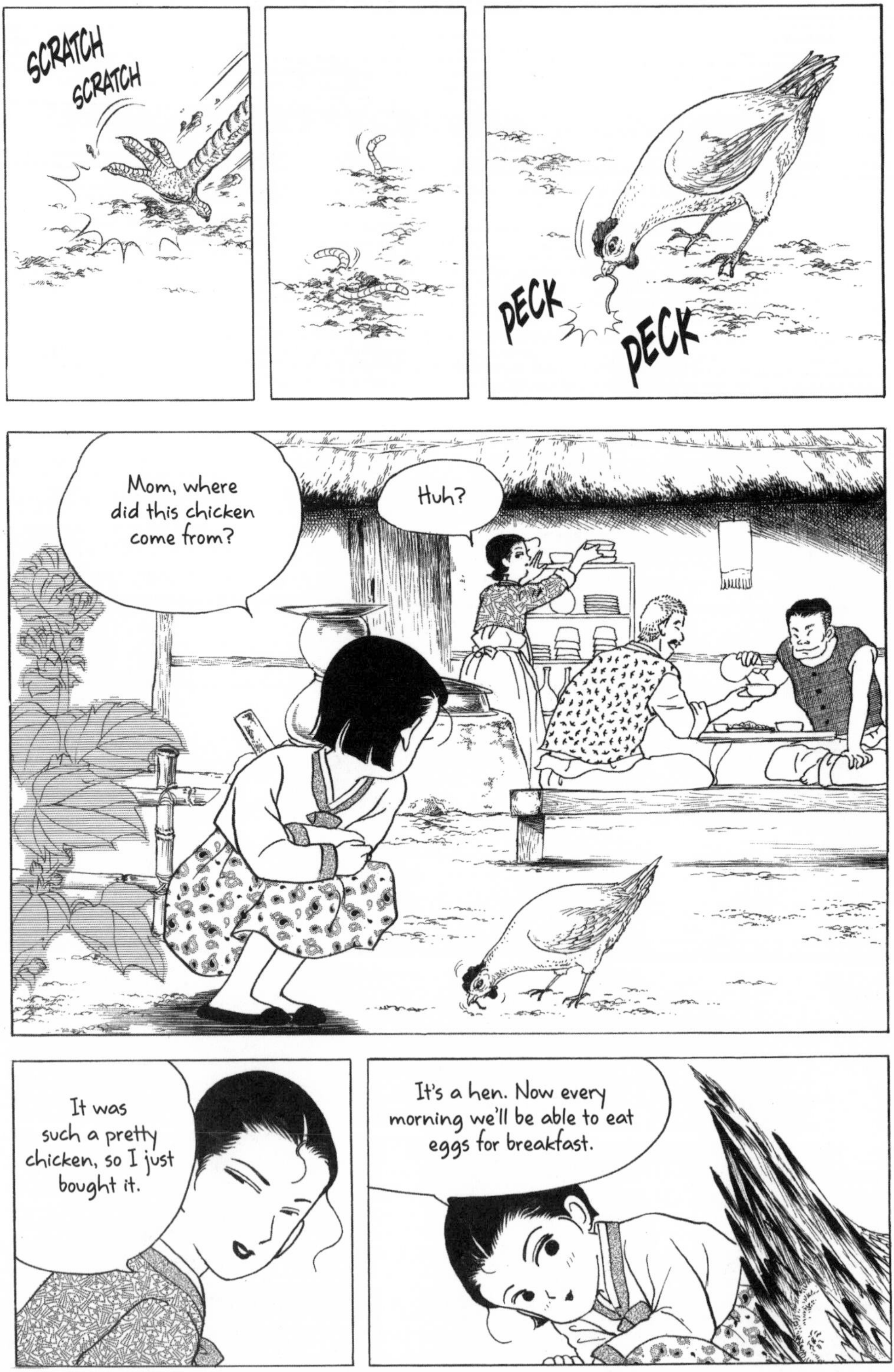
SCRATCH SCRATCH
PECK PECK
Mom, where did this chicken come from?
Huh?
It was such a pretty chicken, so I just bought it.
It's a hen. Now every morning we'll be able to eat eggs for breakfast.

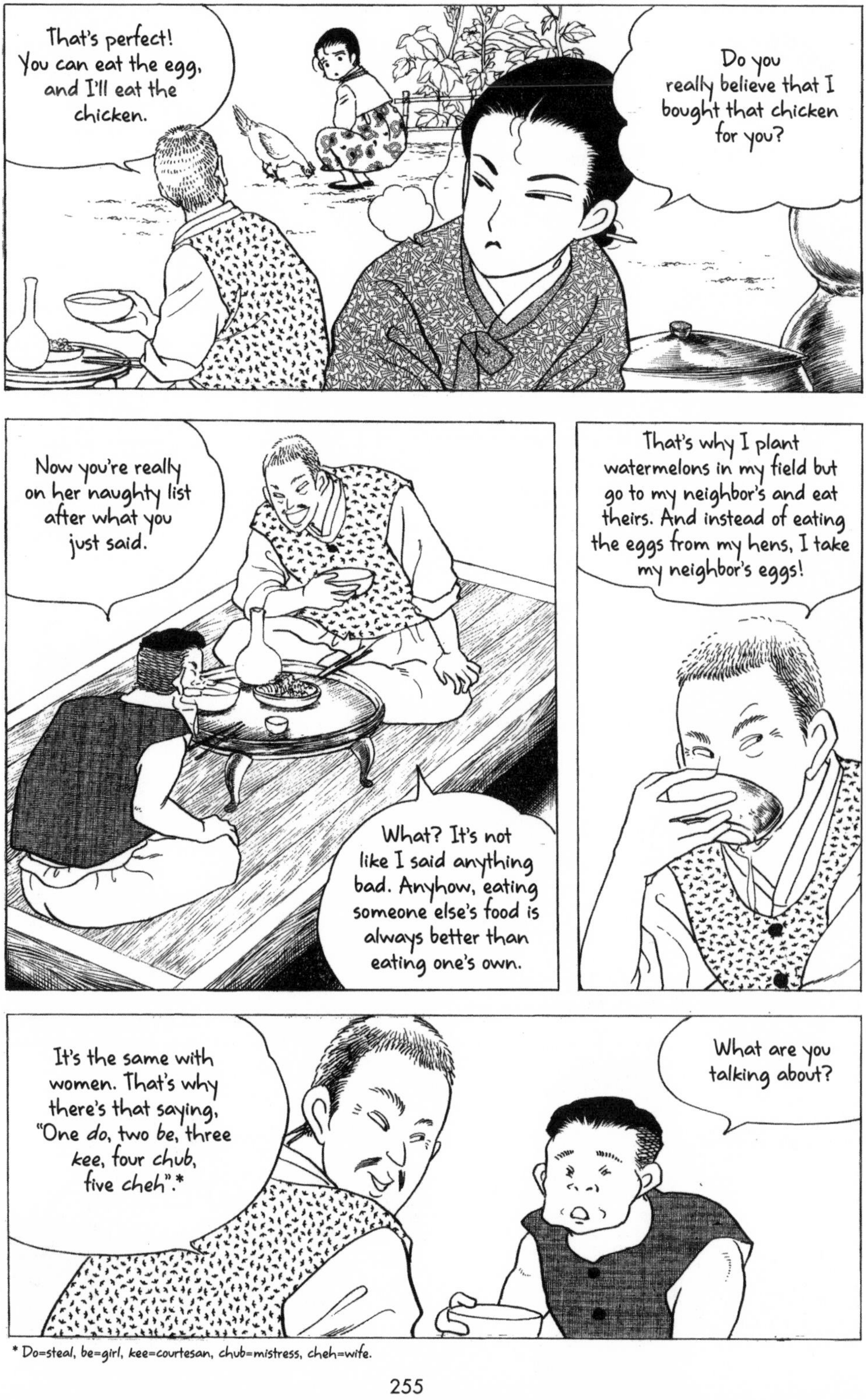
That's perfect! You can eat the egg, and I'll eat the chicken.
Do you really believe that I bought that chicken for you?
Now you're really on her naughty list after what you just said.
What? It's not like I said anything bad. Anyhow, eating someone else's food is always better than eating one's own.
That's why I plant watermelons in my field but go to my neighbor's and eat theirs. And instead of eating the eggs from my hens, I take my neighbor's eggs!
It's the same with women. That's why there's that saying, "One *do*, two *be*, three *kee*, four *chub*, five *cheh*".*
What are you talking about?

* *Do*=steal, *be*=girl, *kee*=courtesan, *chub*=mistress, *cheh*=wife.

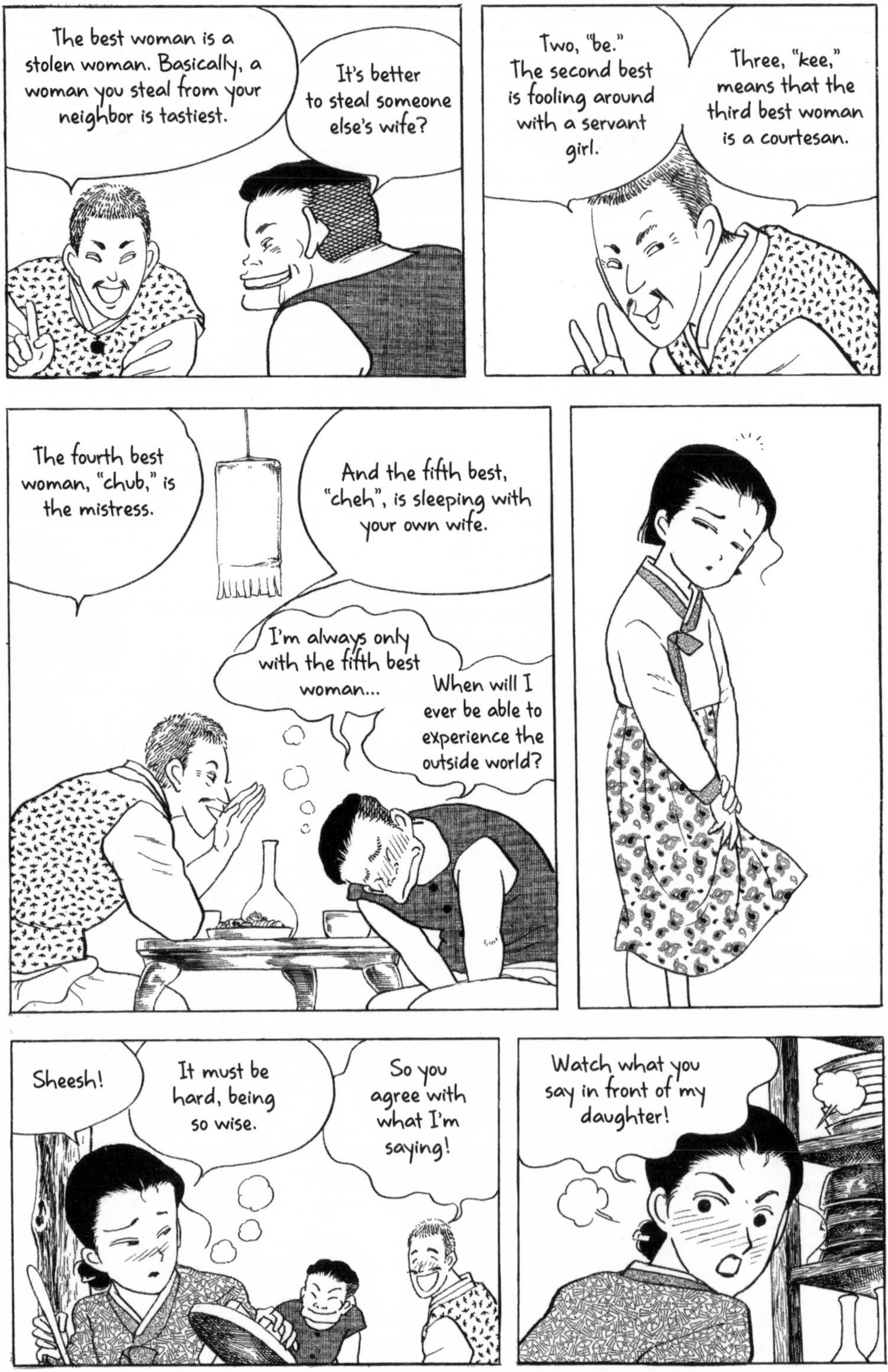
The best woman is a stolen woman. Basically, a woman you steal from your neighbor is tastiest.
It's better to steal someone else's wife?
Two, "be." The second best is fooling around with a servant girl.
Three, "kee," means that the third best woman is a courtesan.
The fourth best woman, "chub," is the mistress.
And the fifth best, "cheh", is sleeping with your own wife.
I'm always only with the fifth best woman...
When will I ever be able to experience the outside world?
Sheesh!
It must be hard, being so wise.
So you agree with what I'm saying!
Watch what you say in front of my daughter!

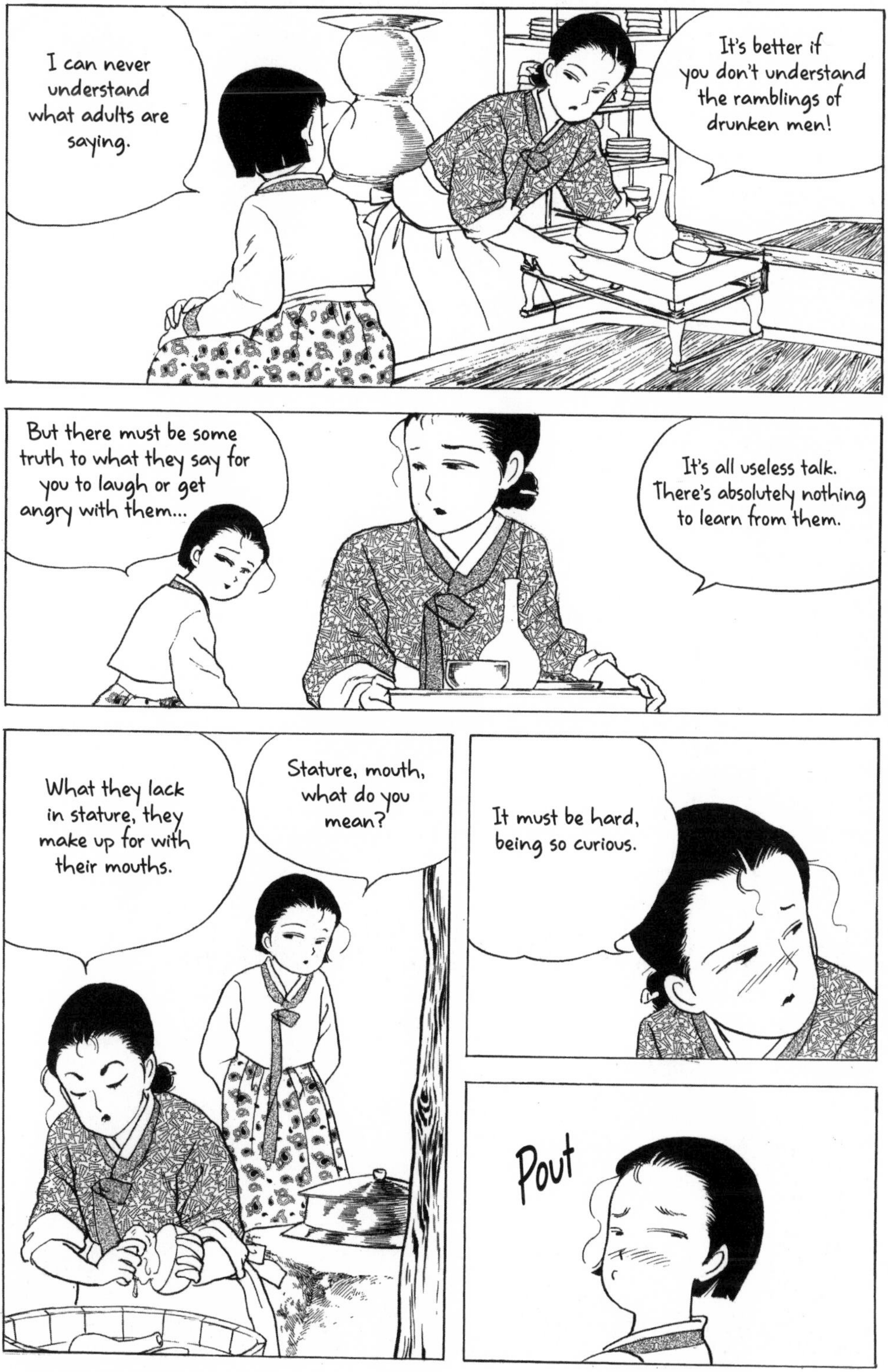
I can never understand what adults are saying.
It's better if you don't understand the ramblings of drunken men!
But there must be some truth to what they say for you to laugh or get angry with them...
It's all useless talk. There's absolutely nothing to learn from them.
What they lack in stature, they make up for with their mouths.
Stature, mouth, what do you mean?
It must be hard, being so curious.
Pout

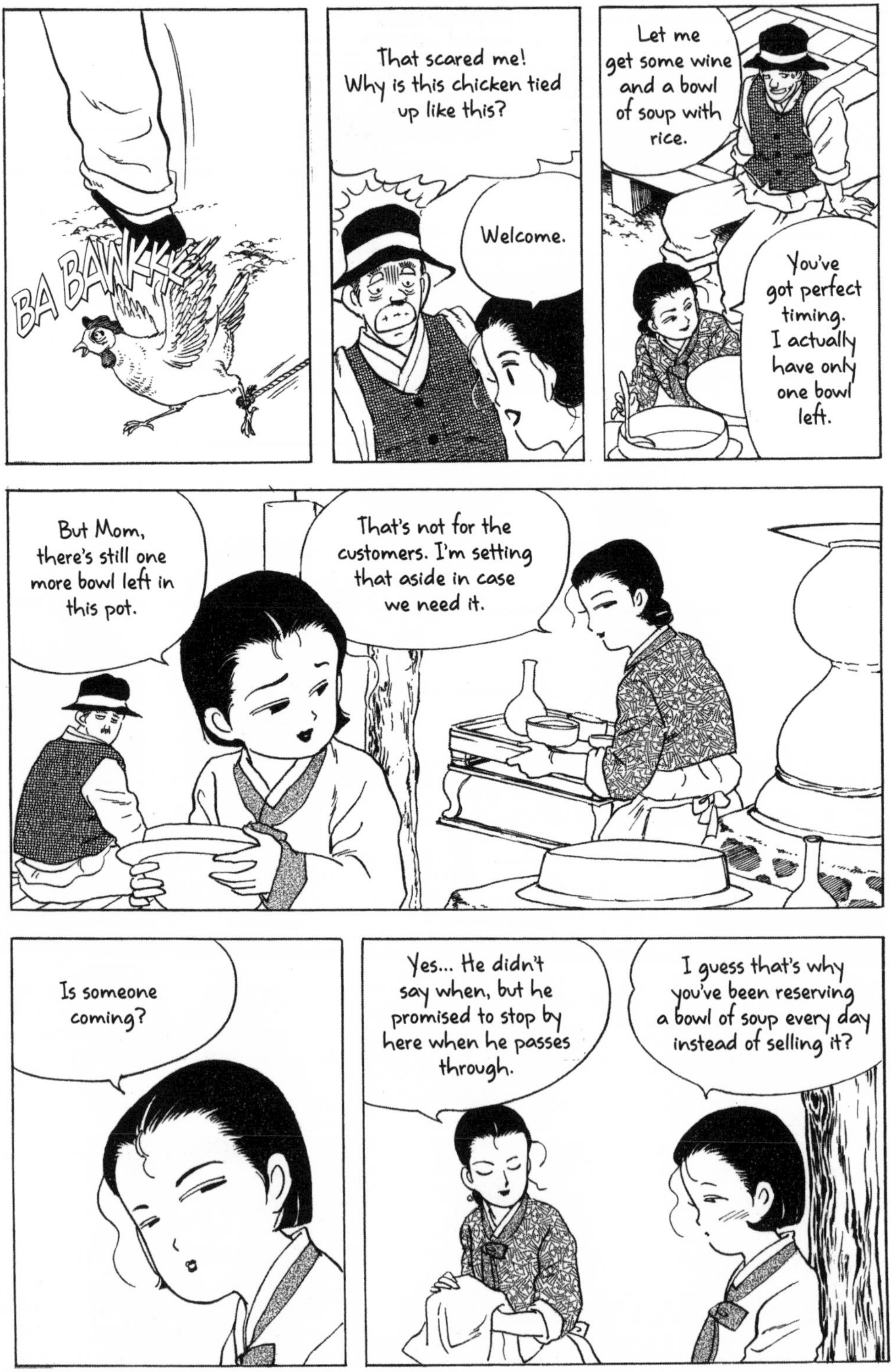
BA BAWKKK
That scared me! Why is this chicken tied up like this?
Welcome.
Let me get some wine and a bowl of soup with rice.
You've got perfect timing. I actually have only one bowl left.
But Mom, there's still one more bowl left in this pot.
That's not for the customers. I'm setting that aside in case we need it.
Is someone coming?
Yes... He didn't say when, but he promised to stop by here when he passes through.
I guess that's why you've been reserving a bowl of soup every day instead of selling it?

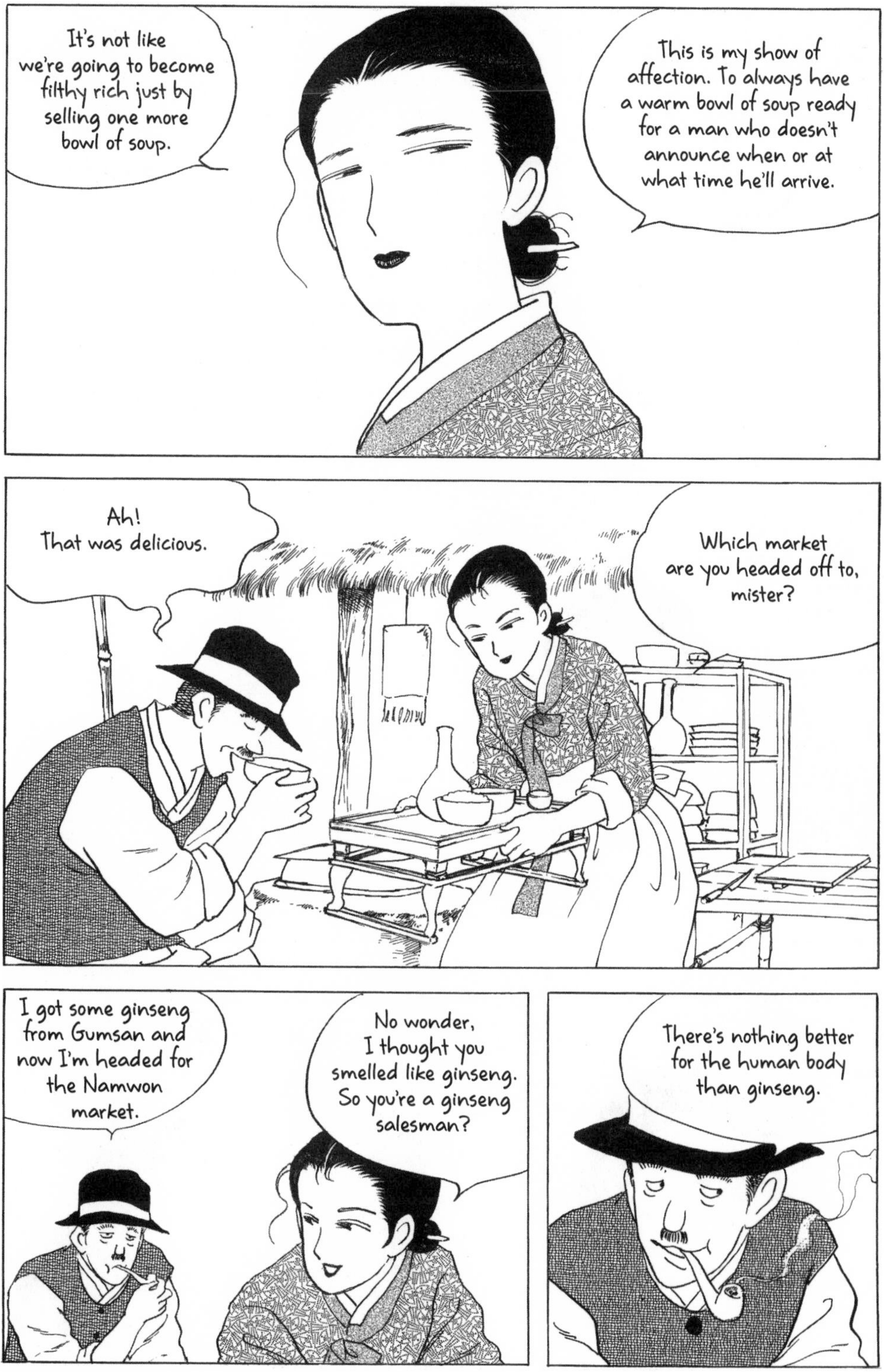
It's not like we're going to become filthy rich just by selling one more bowl of soup.
This is my show of affection. To always have a warm bowl of soup ready for a man who doesn't announce when or at what time he'll arrive.
Ah! That was delicious.
Which market are you headed off to, mister?
I got some ginseng from Gumsan and now I'm headed for the Namwon market.
No wonder, I thought you smelled like ginseng. So you're a ginseng salesman?
There's nothing better for the human body than ginseng.

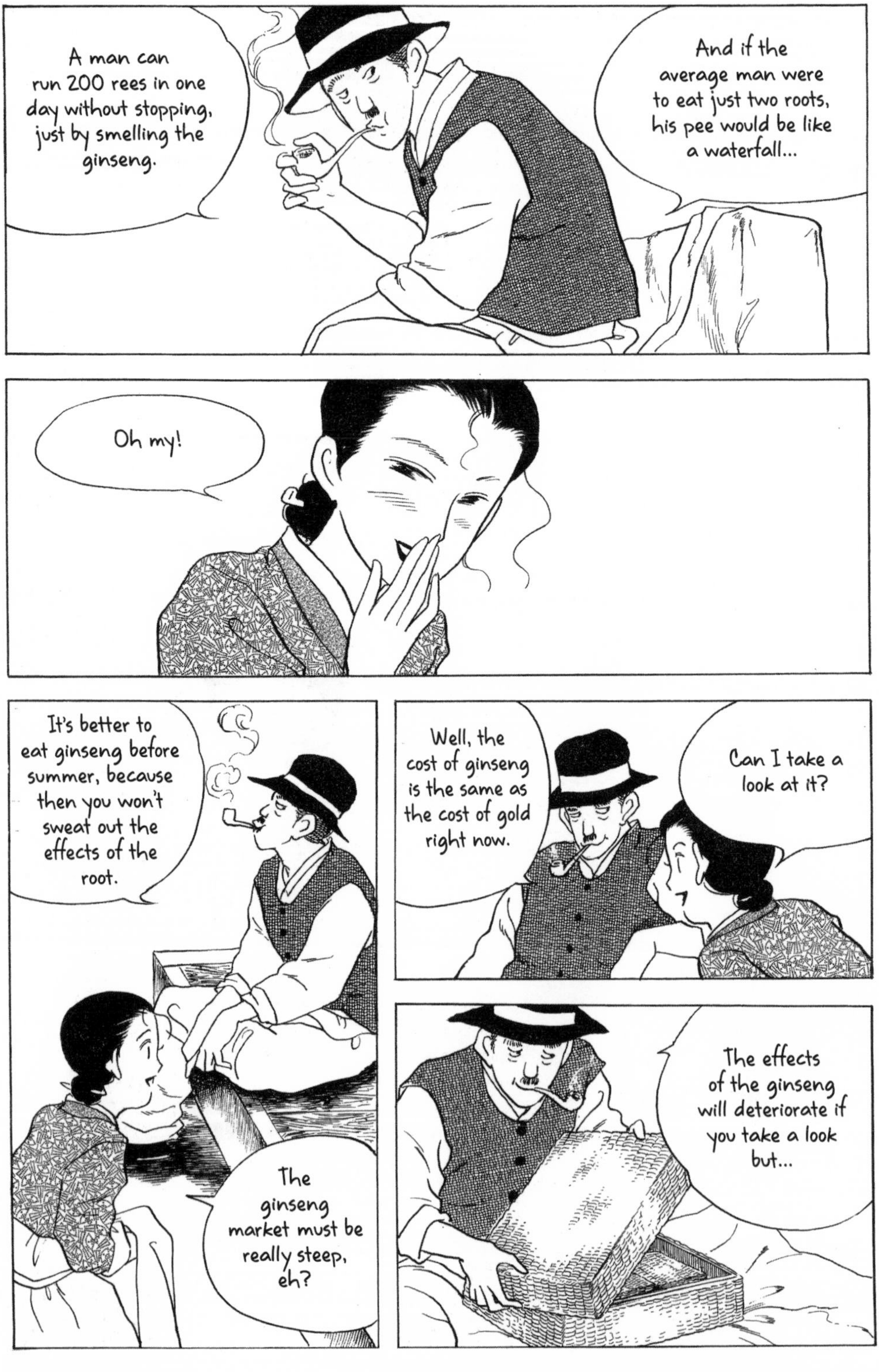
A man can run 200 rees in one day without stopping, just by smelling the ginseng.
And if the average man were to eat just two roots, his pee would be like a waterfall...
Oh my!
It's better to eat ginseng before summer, because then you won't sweat out the effects of the root.
The ginseng market must be really steep, eh?
Well, the cost of ginseng is the same as the cost of gold right now.
Can I take a look at it?
The effects of the ginseng will deteriorate if you take a look but...

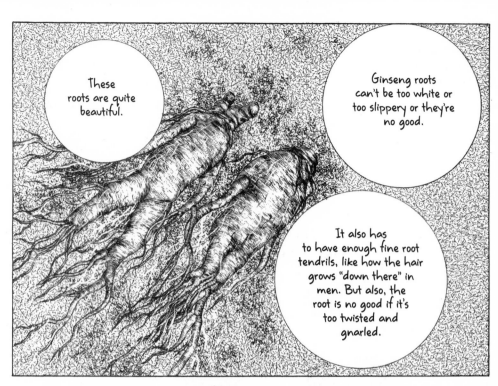

These roots are quite beautiful.

Ginseng roots can't be too white or too slippery or they're no good.

It also has to have enough fine root tendrils, like how the hair grows "down there" in men. But also, the root is no good if it's too twisted and gnarled.

The best ginseng is like this one with two main roots that look like a man lying with his legs stretched out.

I'll buy them both. Can you give me a good price?

You're a single woman. Why would you want to buy two?

Just because I'm single doesn't mean there's no one I might want to give ginseng to.

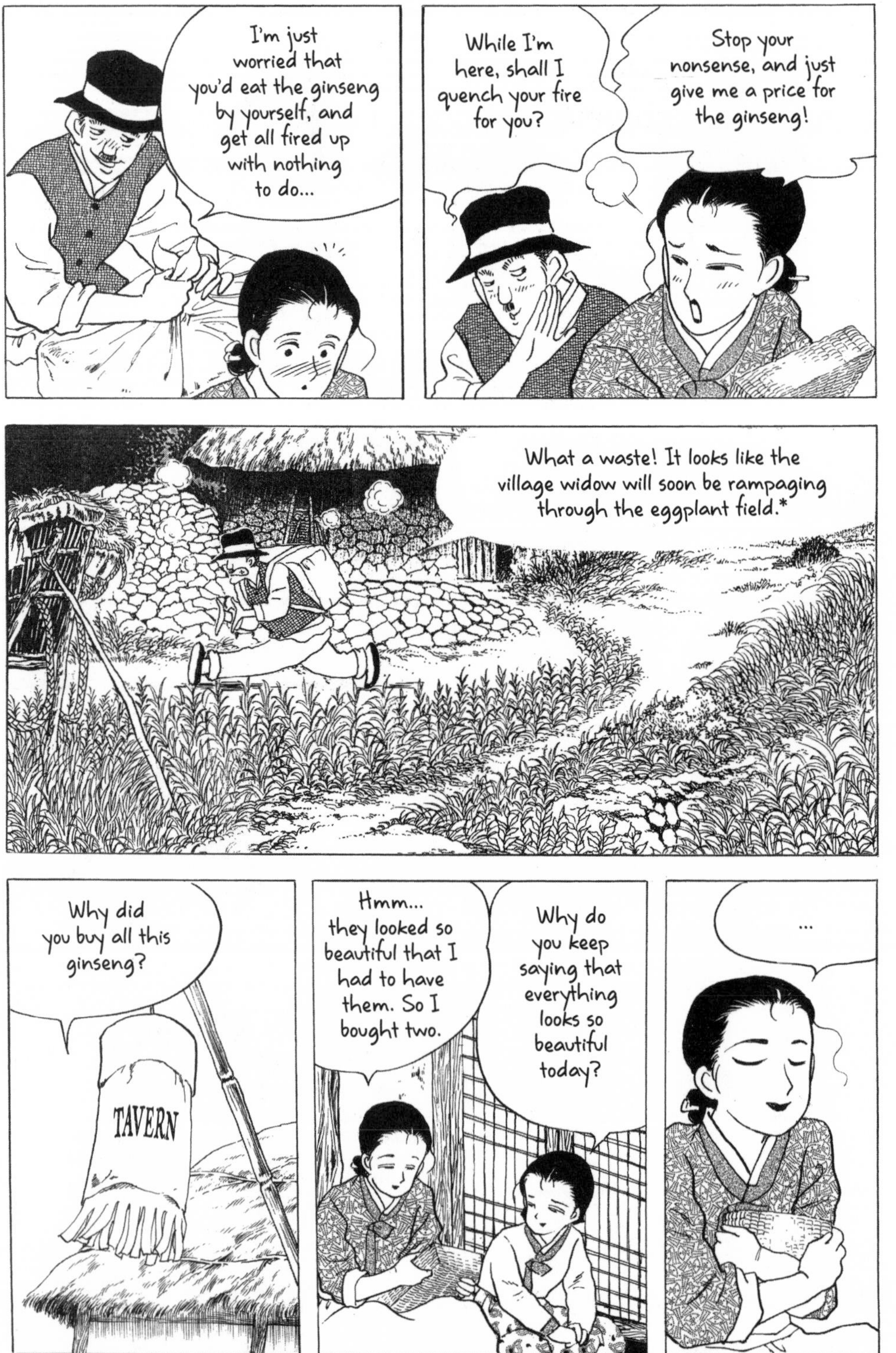
I'm just worried that you'd eat the ginseng by yourself, and get all fired up with nothing to do...
While I'm here, shall I quench your fire for you?
Stop your nonsense, and just give me a price for the ginseng!
What a waste! It looks like the village widow will soon be rampaging through the eggplant field.*
Why did you buy all this ginseng?
TAVERN
Hmm... they looked so beautiful that I had to have them. So I bought two.
Why do you keep saying that everything looks so beautiful today?
...

* "Eggplant field" is an expression for a field of men.

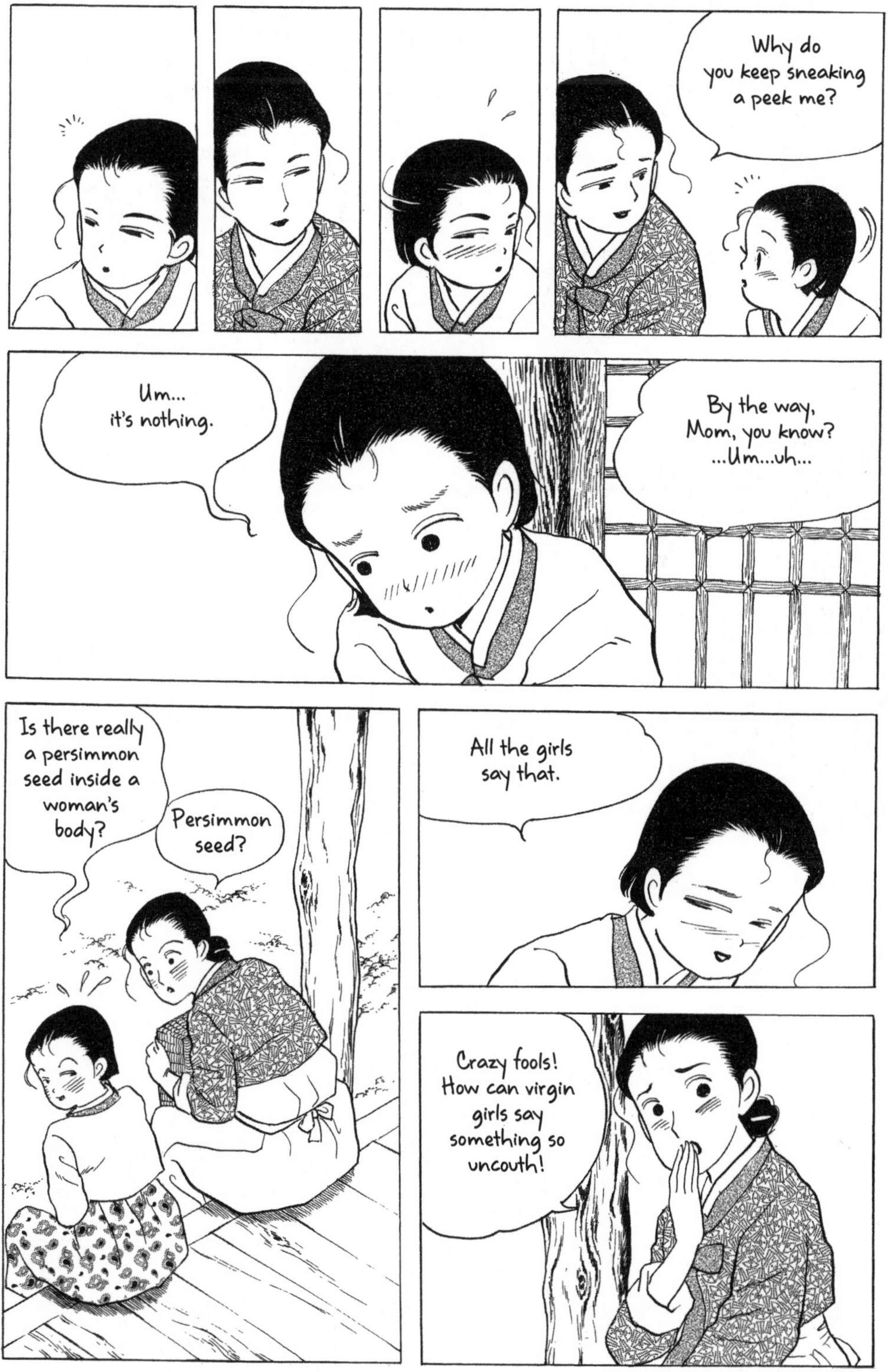
Why do you keep sneaking a peek me?
Um... it's nothing.
By the way, Mom, you know? ...Um...uh...
Is there really a persimmon seed inside a woman's body?
Persimmon seed?
All the girls say that.
Crazy fools! How can virgin girls say something so uncouth!

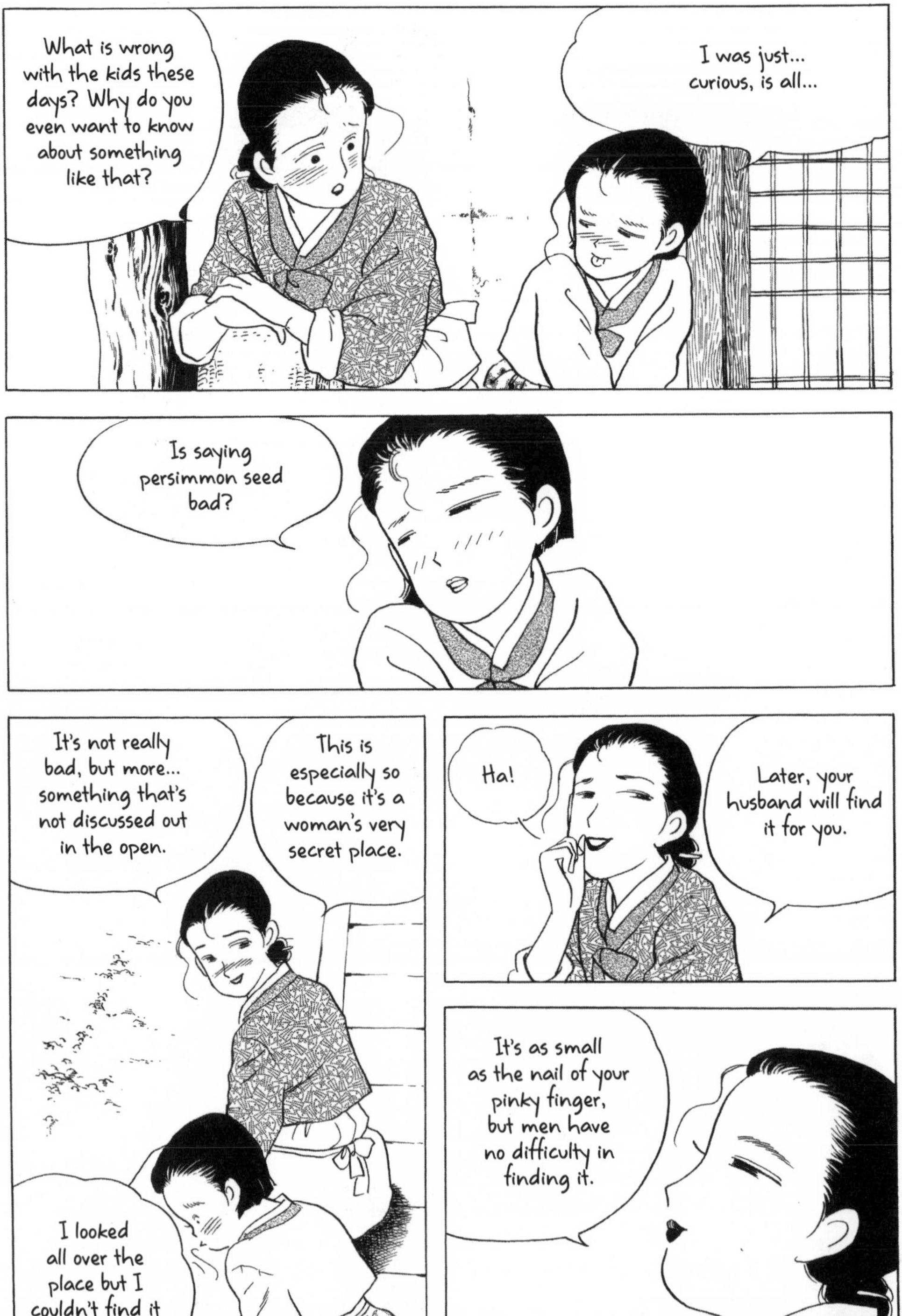
What is wrong with the kids these days? Why do you even want to know about something like that?
I was just... curious, is all...
Is saying persimmon seed bad?
It's not really bad, but more... something that's not discussed out in the open.
This is especially so because it's a woman's very secret place.
I looked all over the place but I couldn't find it on my body.
Ha!
Later, your husband will find it for you.
It's as small as the nail of your pinky finger, but men have no difficulty in finding it.

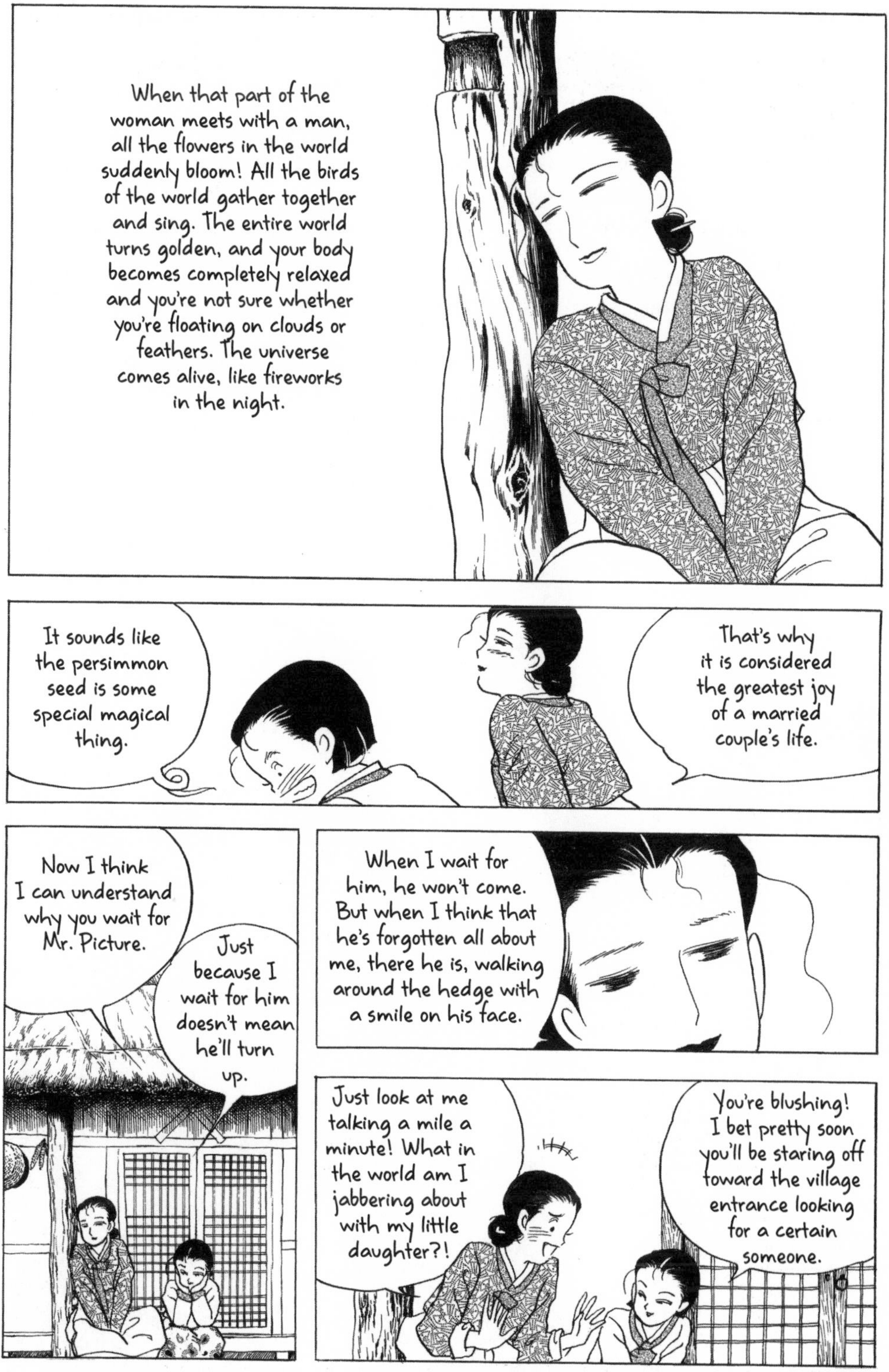
When that part of the woman meets with a man, all the flowers in the world suddenly bloom! All the birds of the world gather together and sing. The entire world turns golden, and your body becomes completely relaxed and you're not sure whether you're floating on clouds or feathers. The universe comes alive, like fireworks in the night.
It sounds like the persimmon seed is some special magical thing.
That's why it is considered the greatest joy of a married couple's life.
Now I think I can understand why you wait for Mr. Picture.
Just because I wait for him doesn't mean he'll turn up.
When I wait for him, he won't come. But when I think that he's forgotten all about me, there he is, walking around the hedge with a smile on his face.
Just look at me talking a mile a minute! What in the world am I jabbering about with my little daughter?!
You're blushing! I bet pretty soon you'll be staring off toward the village entrance looking for a certain someone.

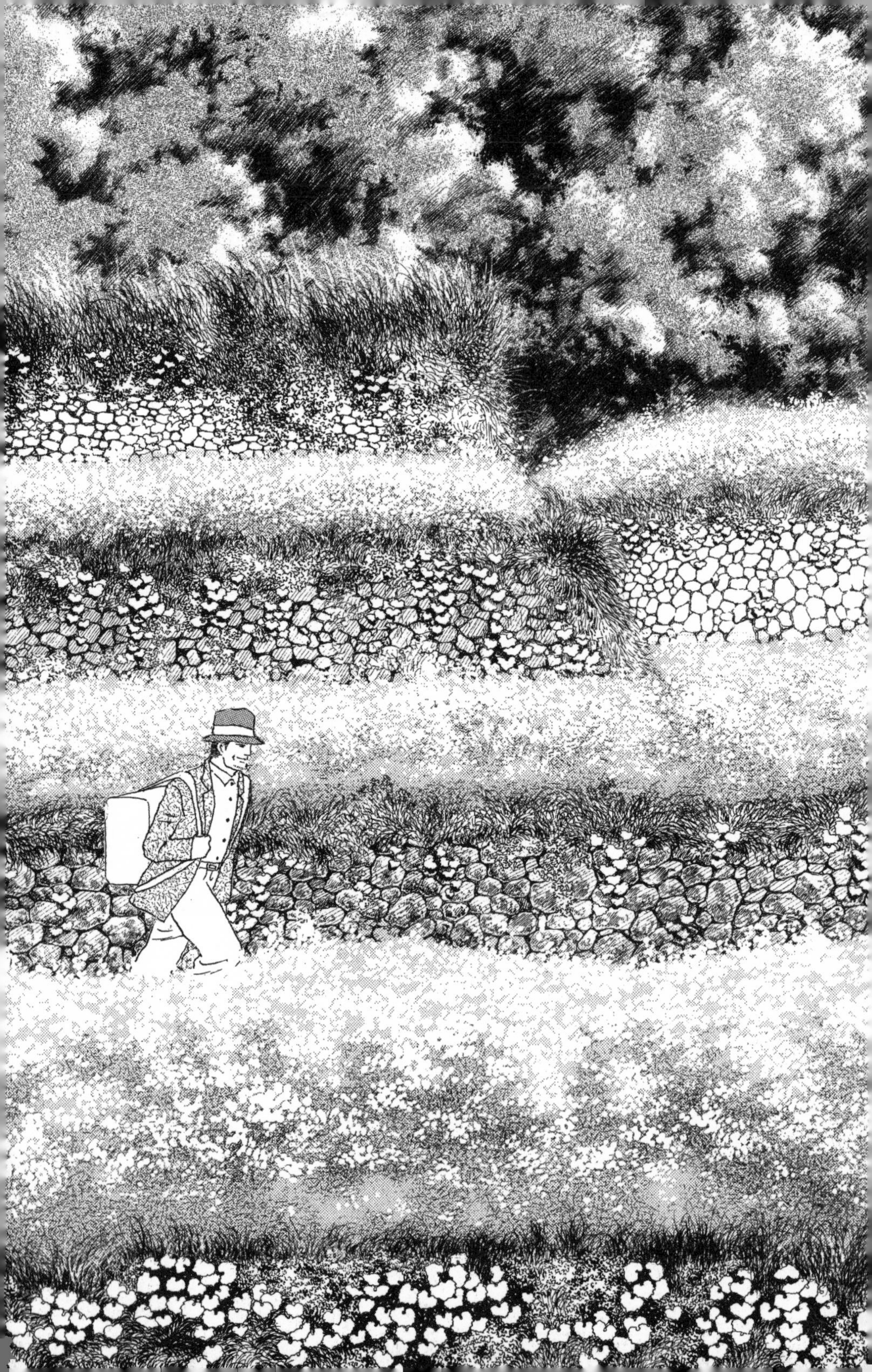

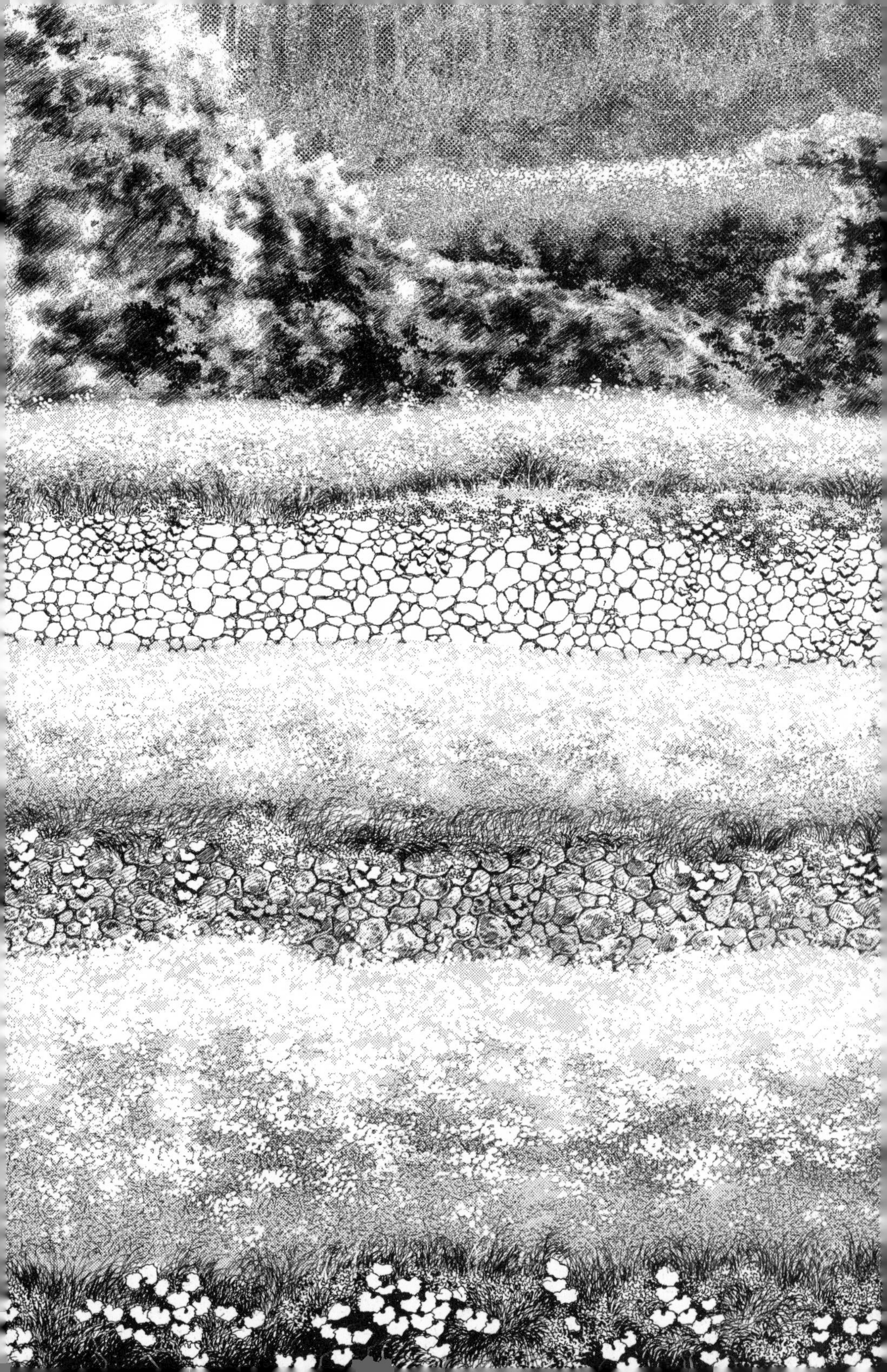

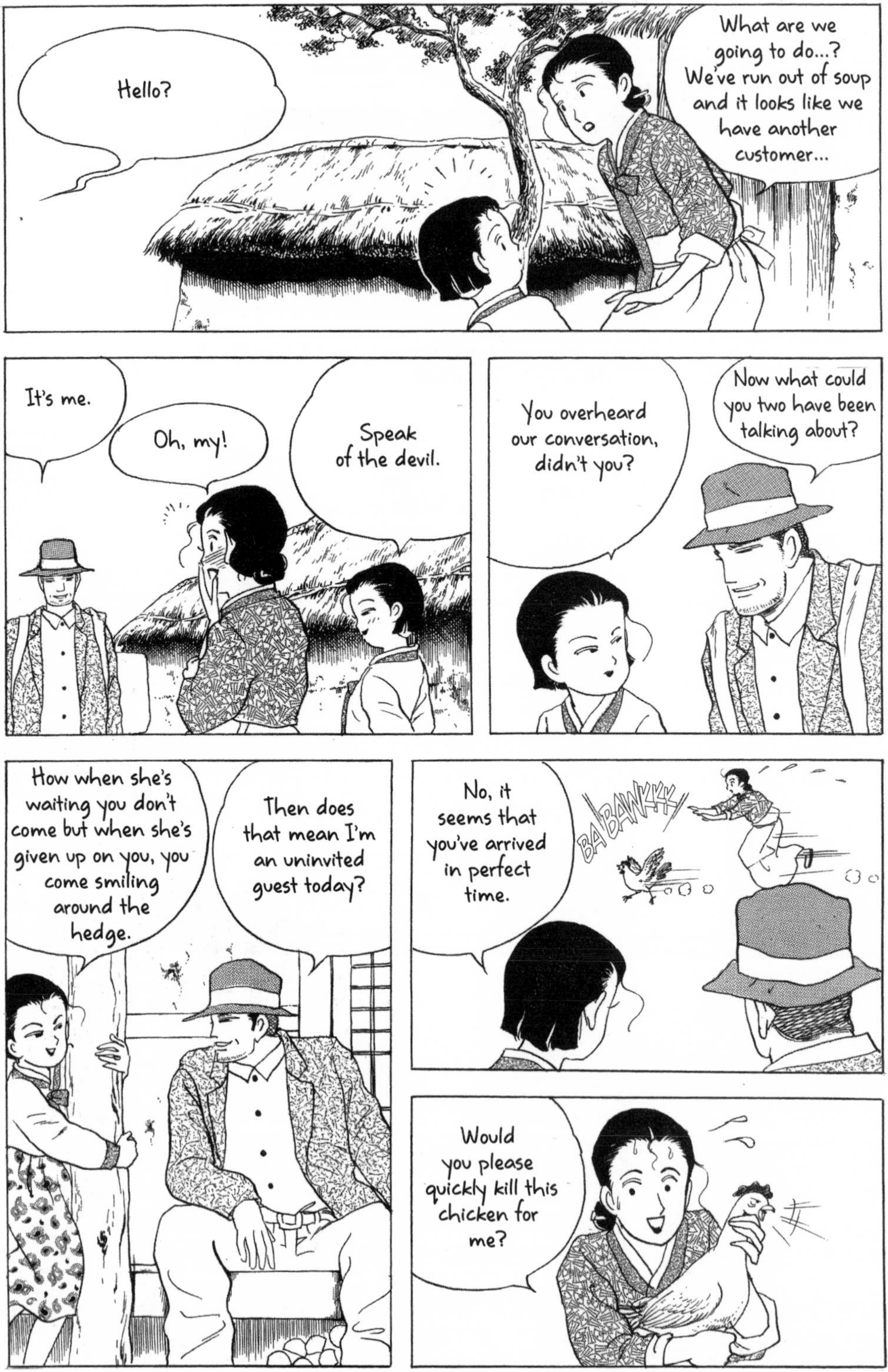
What are we going to do...? We've run out of soup and it looks like we have another customer...
Hello?
It's me.
Oh, my!
Speak of the devil.
You overheard our conversation, didn't you?
Now what could you two have been talking about?
How when she's waiting you don't come but when she's given up on you, you come smiling around the hedge.
Then does that mean I'm an uninvited guest today?
No, it seems that you've arrived in perfect time.
BABAWKKK
Would you please quickly kill this chicken for me?

Ehwa, would you please go buy me some dried chestnuts and jujubes?

What for?

Now that I have ginseng roots, I want to make samgaetang.*

He's always traveling, and I'm sure he never takes any herbal medicine so this will be a good opportunity for him to eat something healthy.

Haha! Just eating your soup and rice is enough to melt away all my fatigue...

When I saw that you bought a chicken and the ginseng, I already knew...

* Samgaetang is a soup made with game hen or chicken, ginseng, jujubes, chestnuts, and sweet rice. It's considered a health food that restores energy and stamina.

269

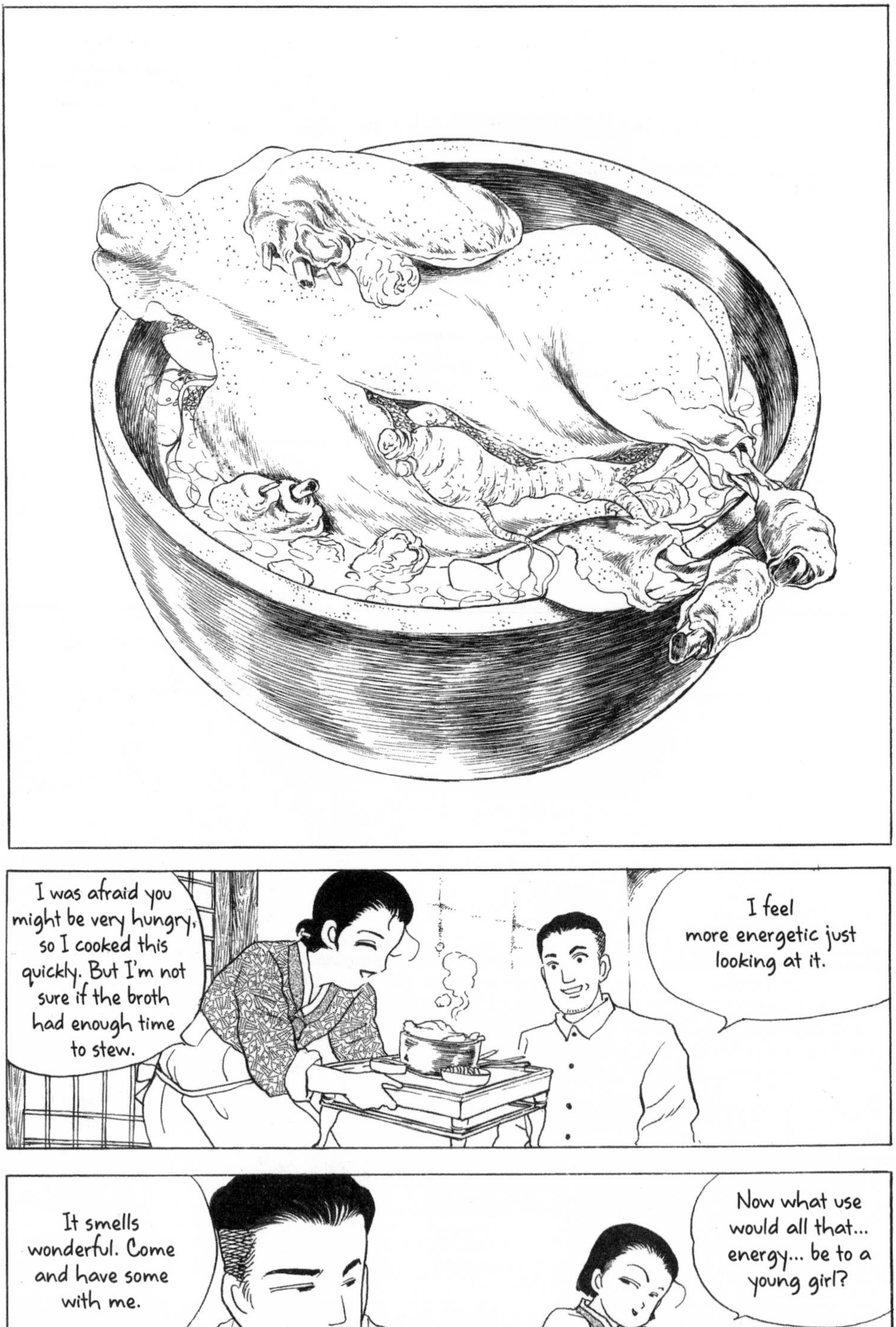
I was afraid you might be very hungry, so I cooked this quickly. But I'm not sure if the broth had enough time to stew.
I feel more energetic just looking at it.
It smells wonderful. Come and have some with me.
Now what use would all that... energy... be to a young girl?

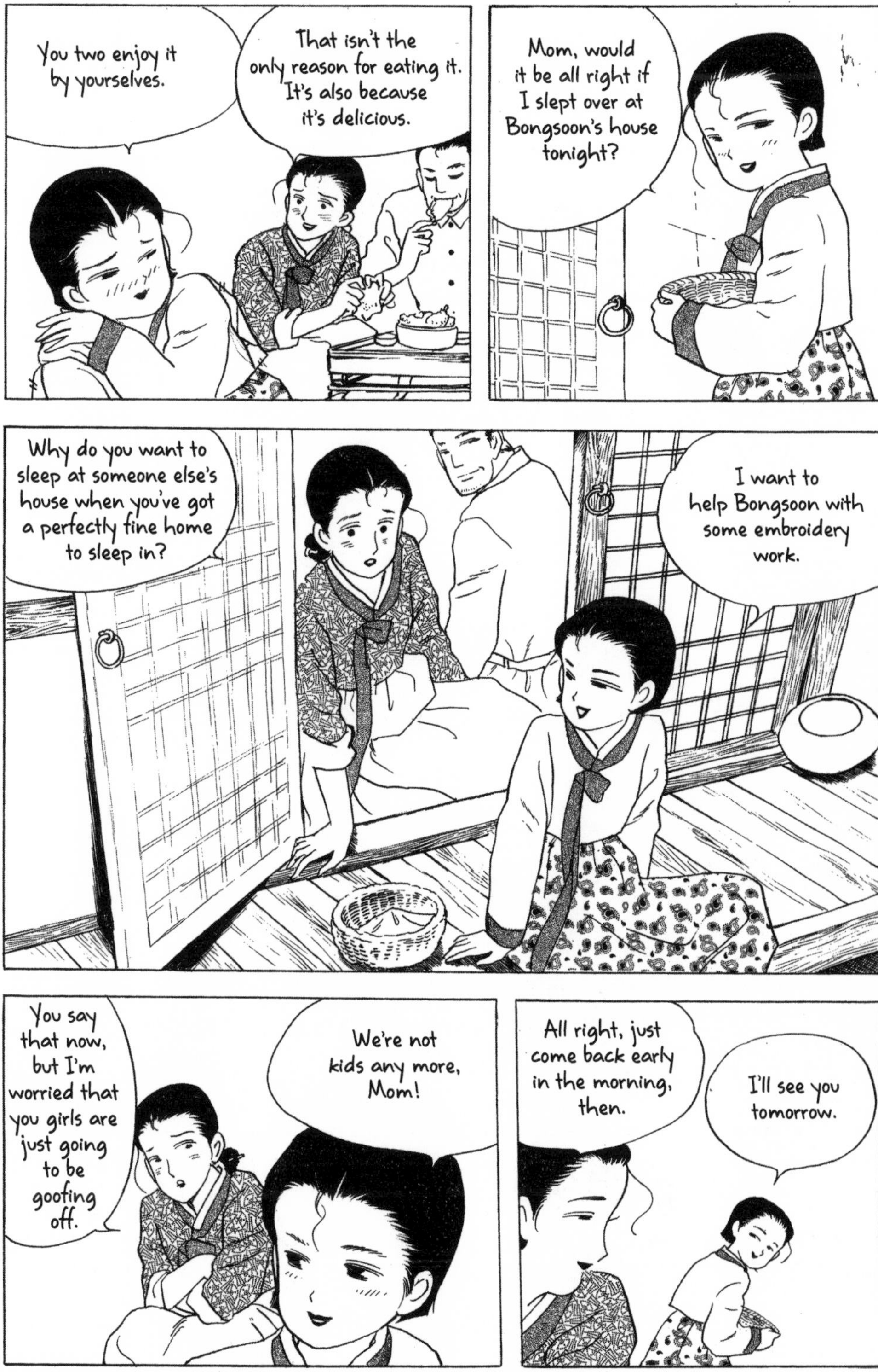
You two enjoy it by yourselves.
That isn't the only reason for eating it. It's also because it's delicious.
Mom, would it be all right if I slept over at Bongsoon's house tonight?
Why do you want to sleep at someone else's house when you've got a perfectly fine home to sleep in?
I want to help Bongsoon with some embroidery work.
You say that now, but I'm worried that you girls are just going to be goofing off.
We're not kids any more, Mom!
All right, just come back early in the morning, then.
I'll see you tomorrow.

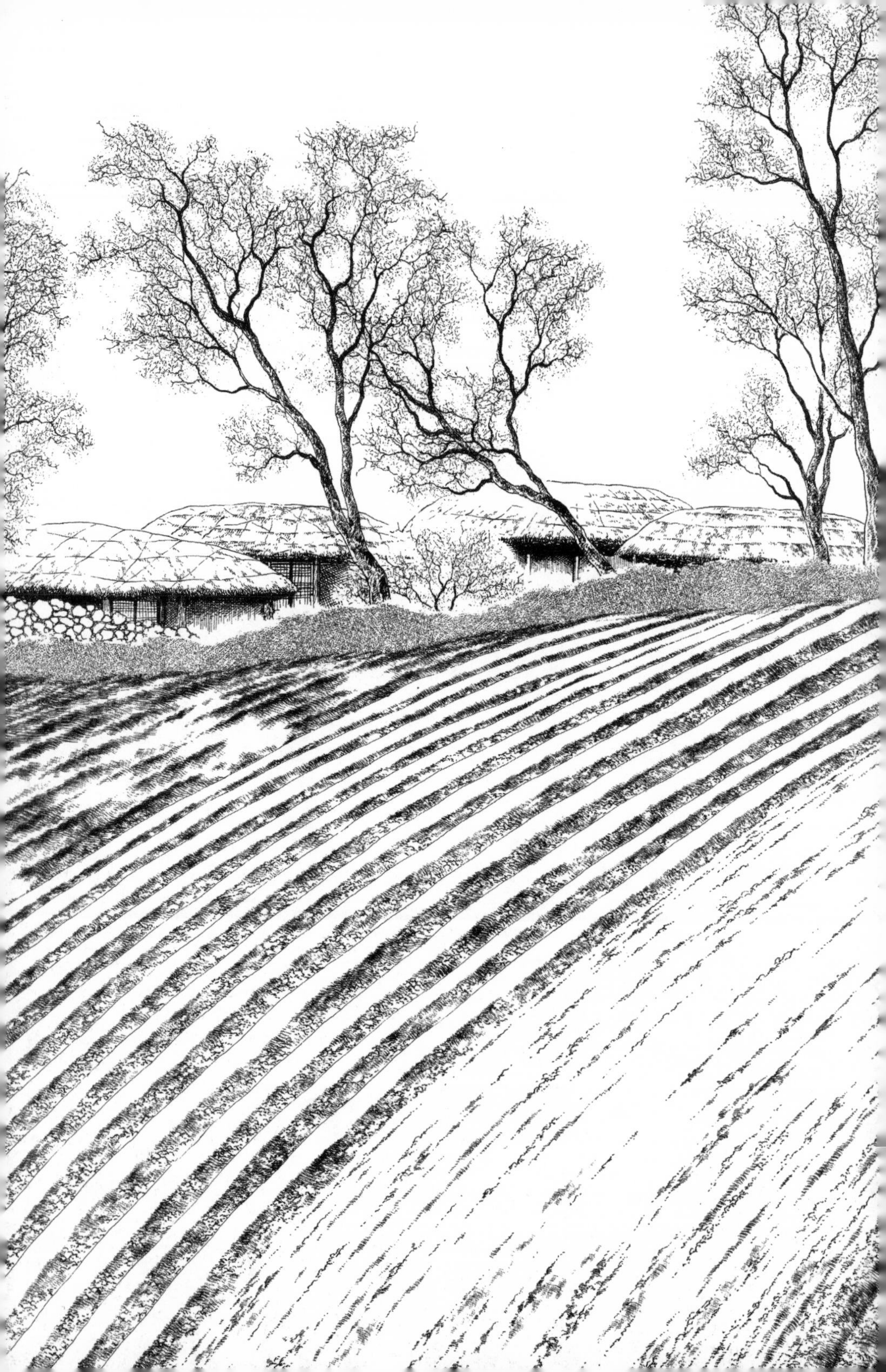

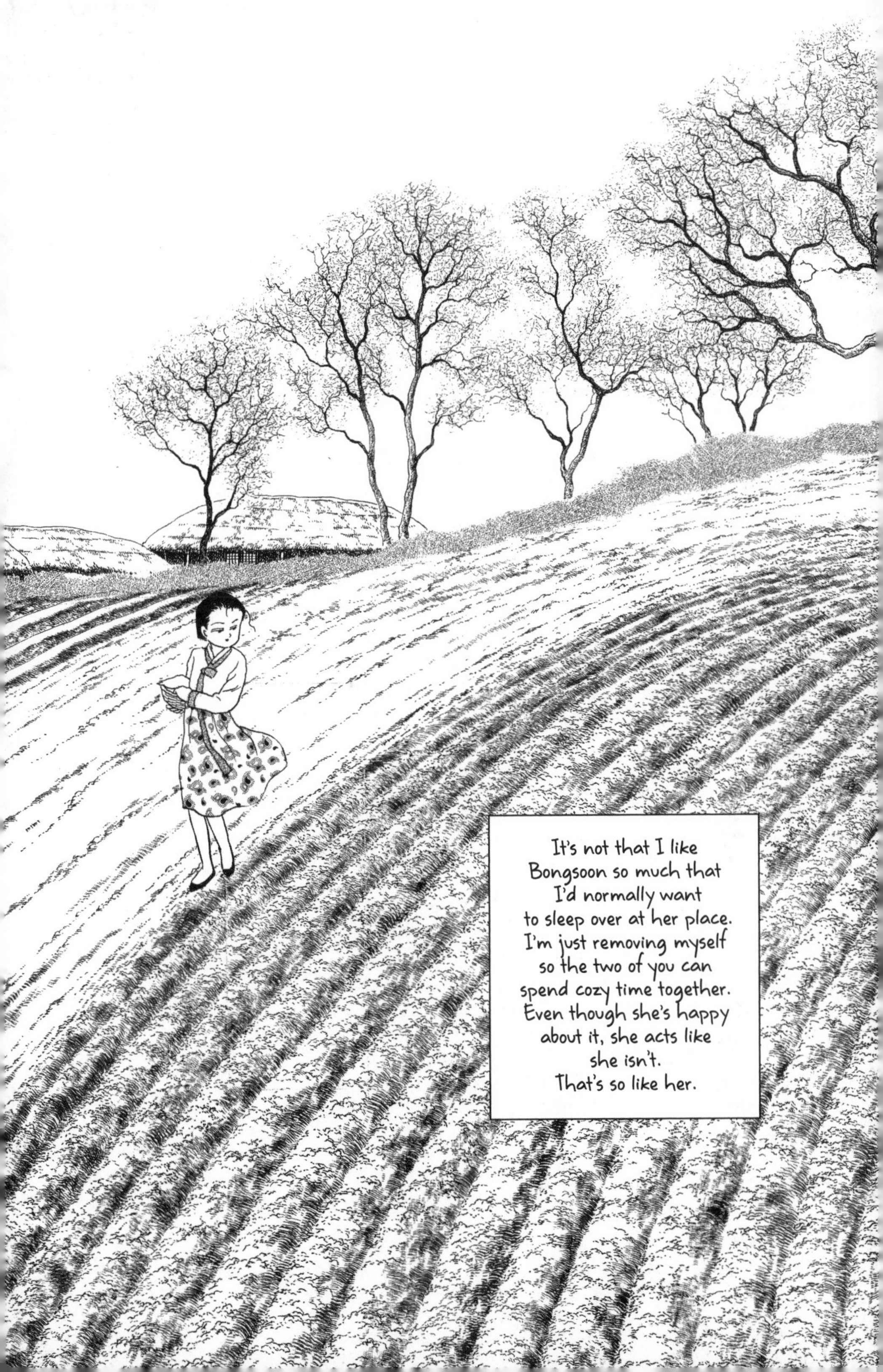
It's not that I like Bongsoon so much that I'd normally want to sleep over at her place. I'm just removing myself so the two of you can spend cozy time together. Even though she's happy about it, she acts like she isn't. That's so like her.

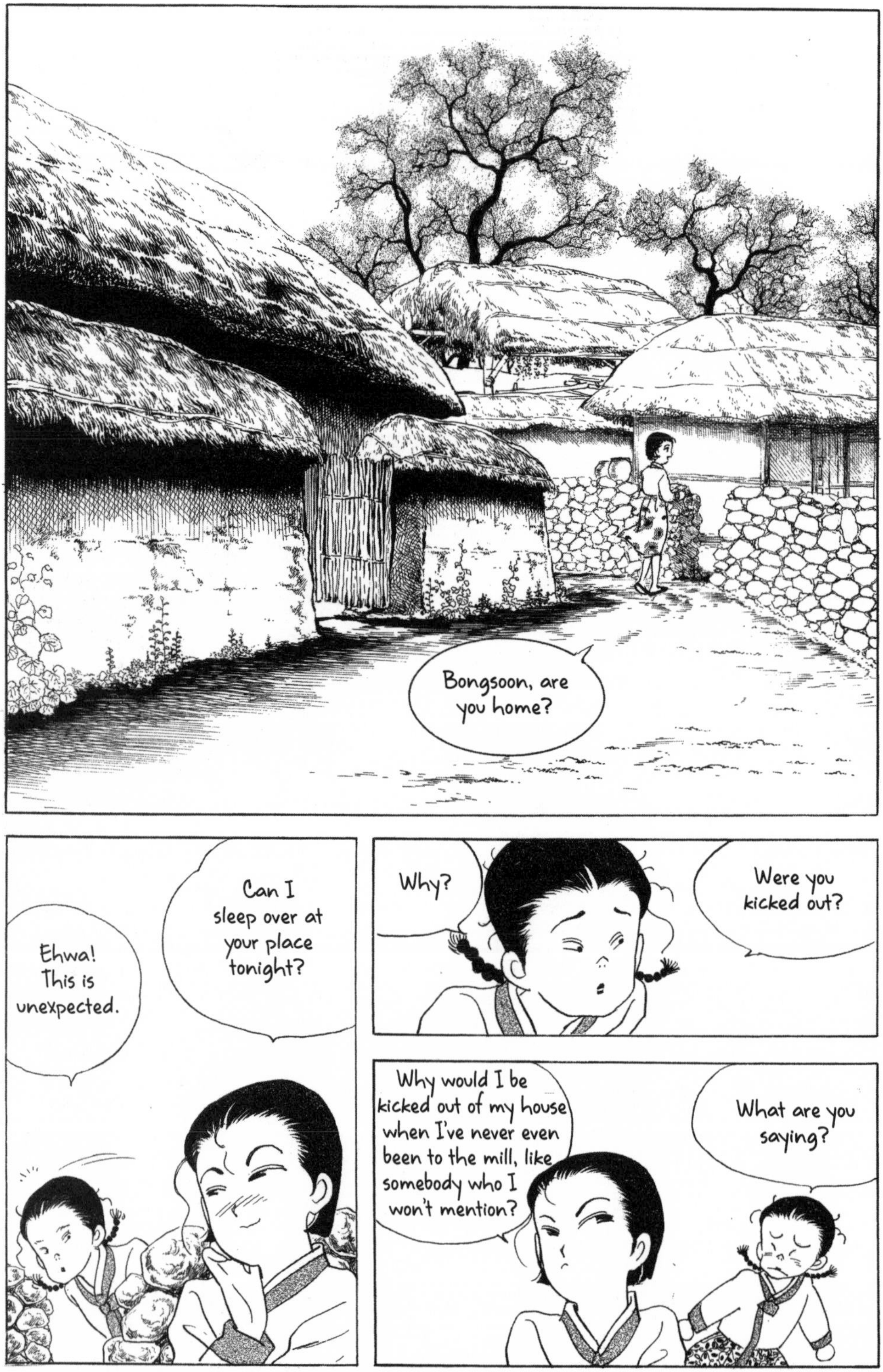
Bongsoon, are you home?
Can I sleep over at your place tonight?
Ehwa! This is unexpected.
Why?
Were you kicked out?
Why would I be kicked out of my house when I've never even been to the mill, like somebody who I won't mention?
What are you saying?

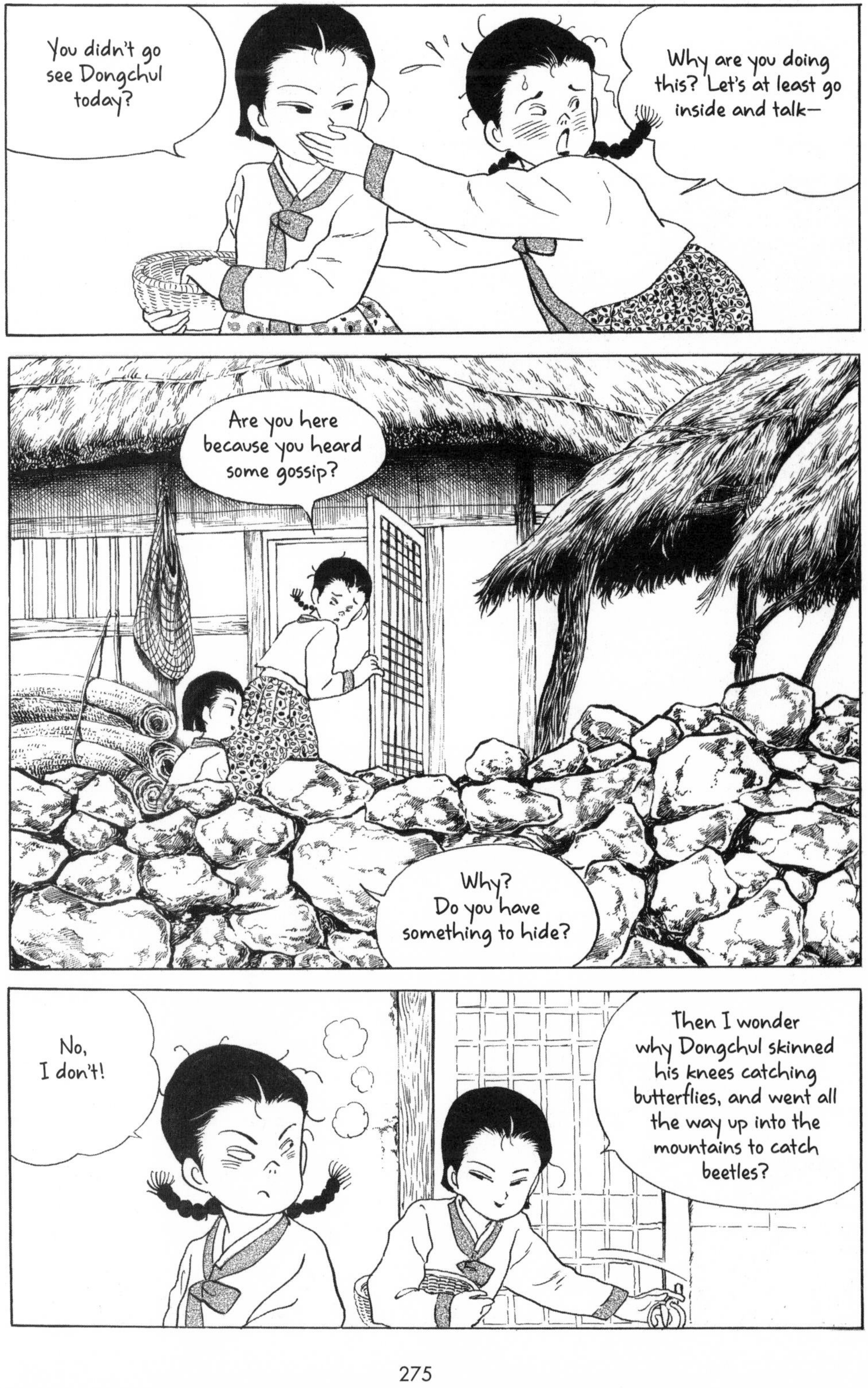
You didn't go see Dongchul today?
Why are you doing this? Let's at least go inside and talk—
Are you here because you heard some gossip?
Why? Do you have something to hide?
No, I don't!
Then I wonder why Dongchul skinned his knees catching butterflies, and went all the way up into the mountains to catch beetles?

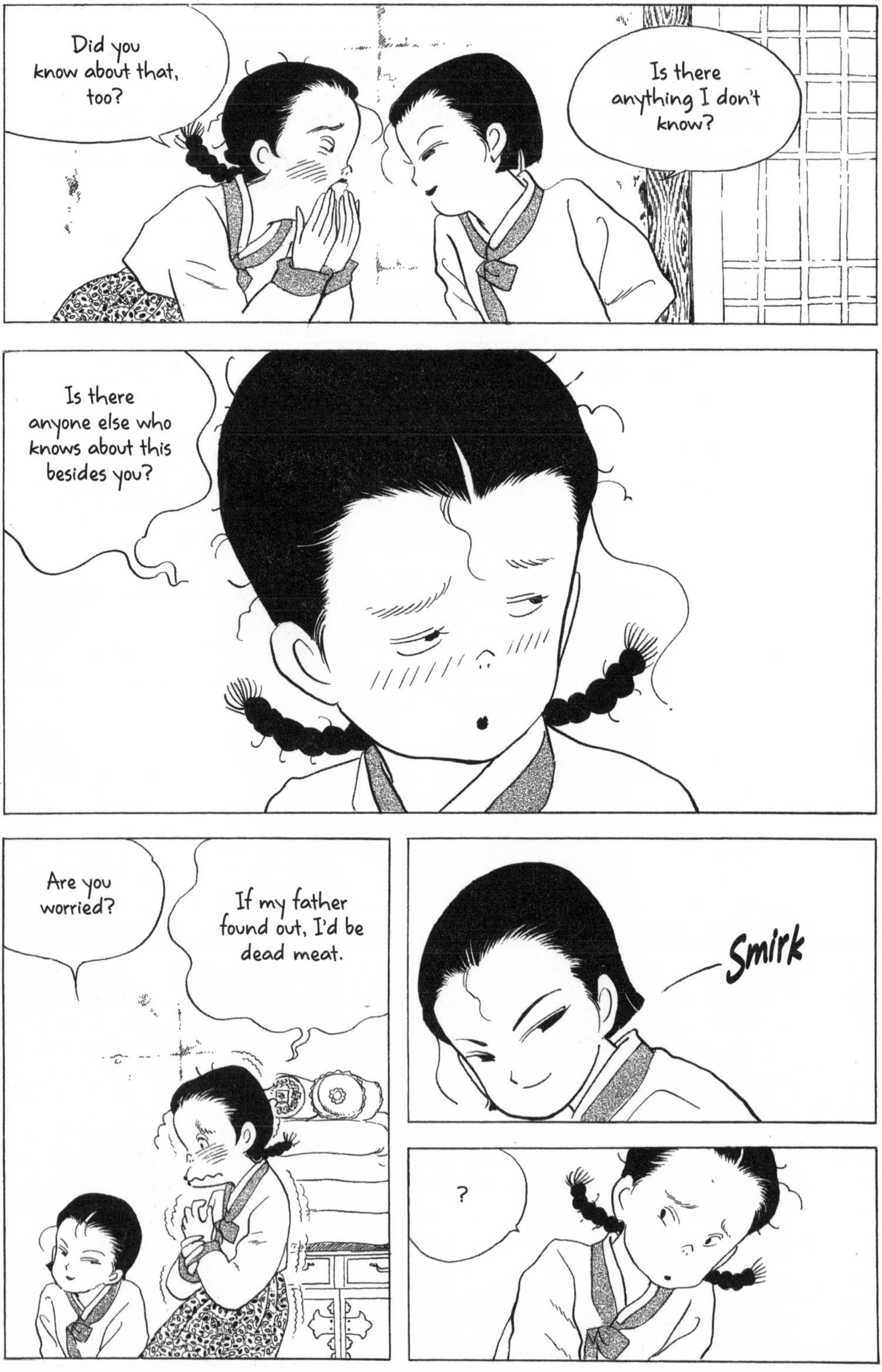
Did you know about that, too?
Is there anything I don't know?
Is there anyone else who knows about this besides you?
Are you worried?
If my father found out, I'd be dead meat.
Smirk
?

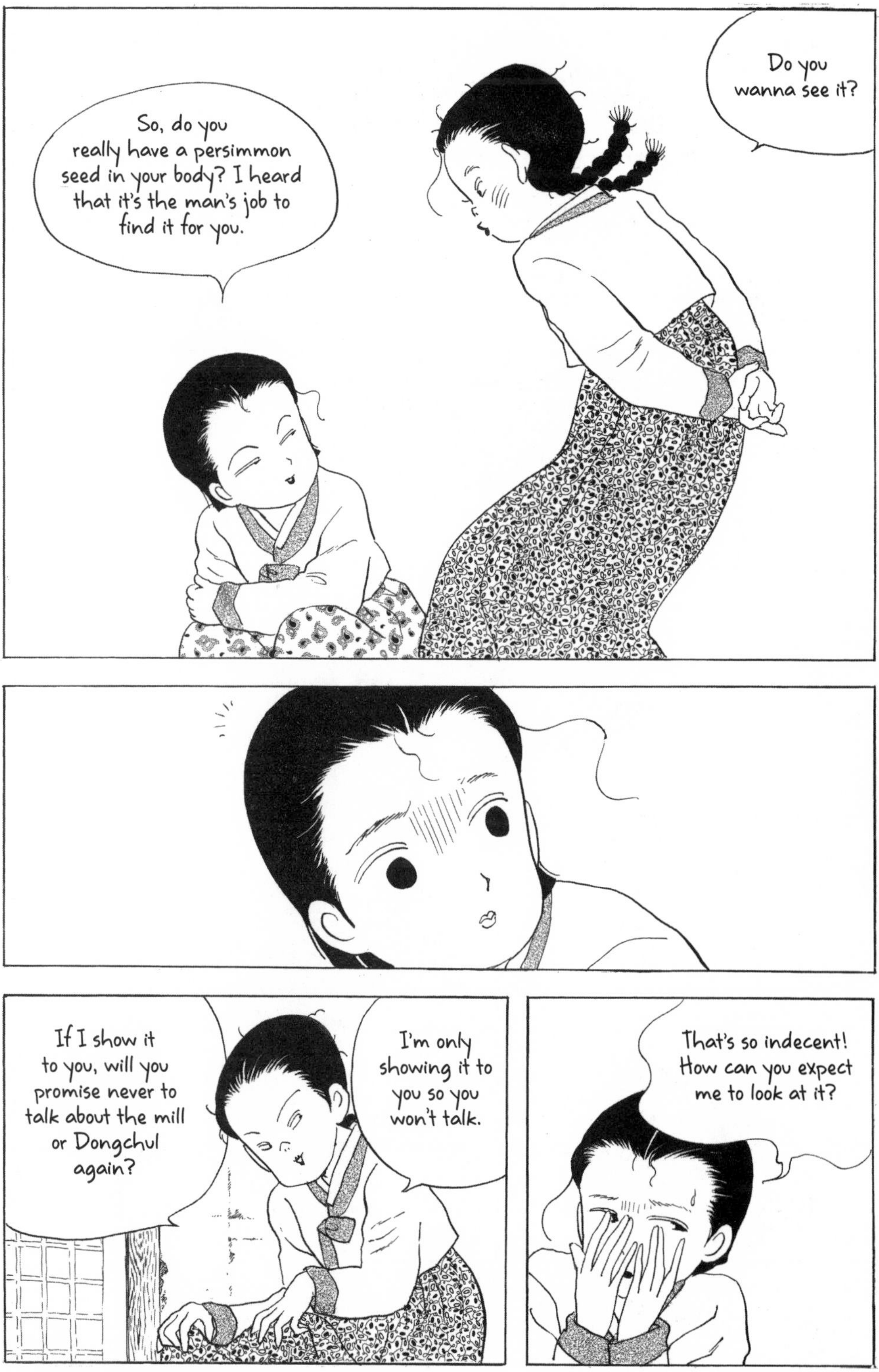

So, do you really have a persimmon seed in your body? I heard that it's the man's job to find it for you.
Do you wanna see it?
If I show it to you, will you promise never to talk about the mill or Dongchul again?
I'm only showing it to you so you won't talk.
That's so indecent! How can you expect me to look at it?

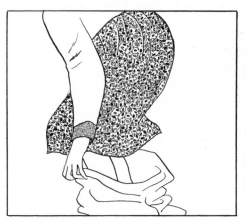

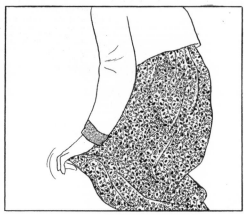

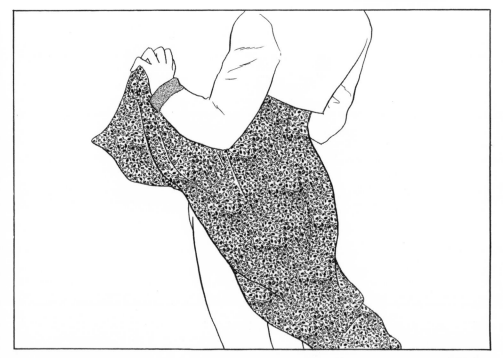

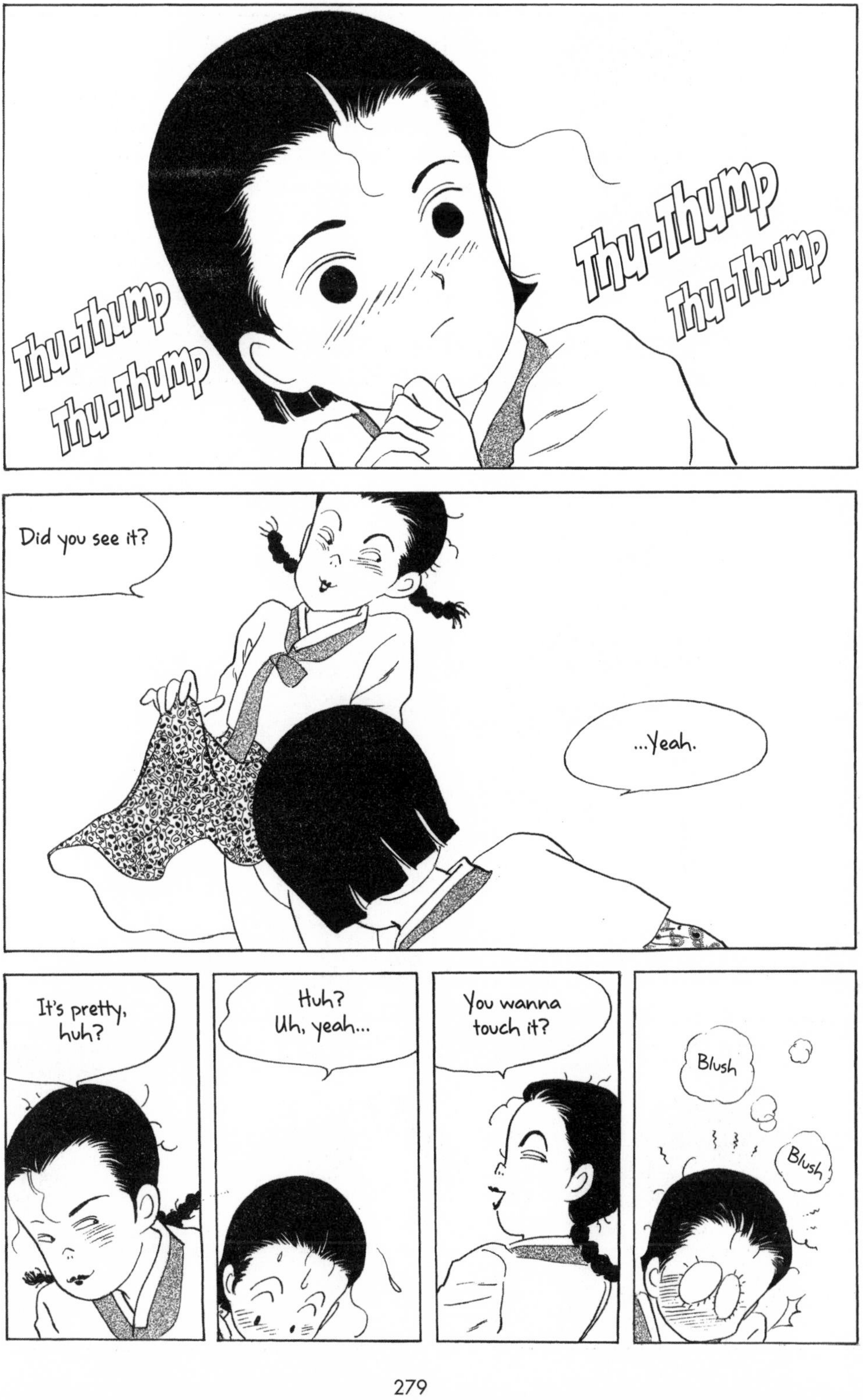
Thu-Thump
Thu-Thump
Thu-Thump
Thu-Thump
Did you see it?
...Yeah.
It's pretty, huh?
Huh? Uh, yeah...
You wanna touch it?
Blush
Blush

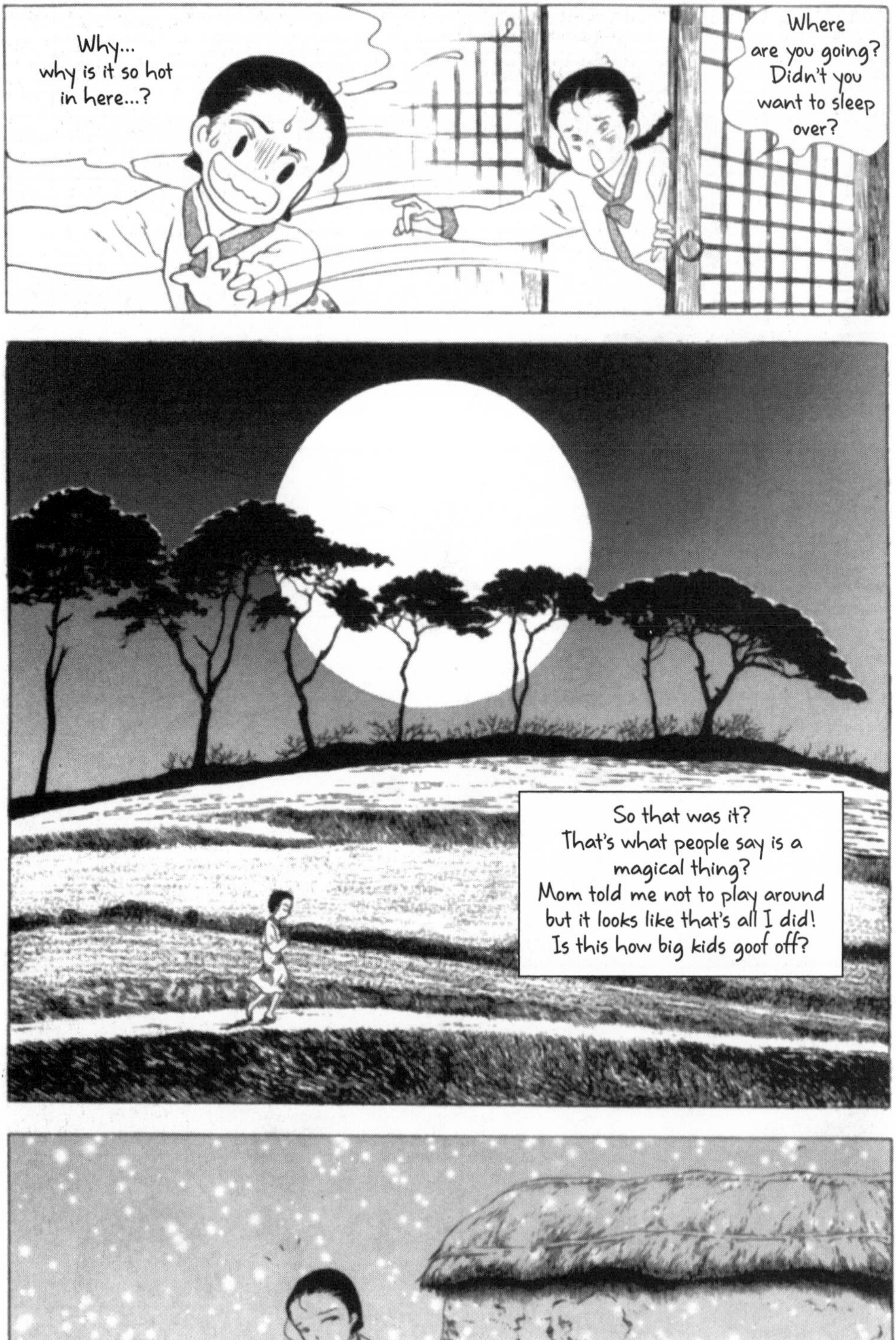
Why... why is it so hot in here...?
Where are you going? Didn't you want to sleep over?
So that was it? That's what people say is a magical thing? Mom told me not to play around but it looks like that's all I did! Is this how big kids goof off?

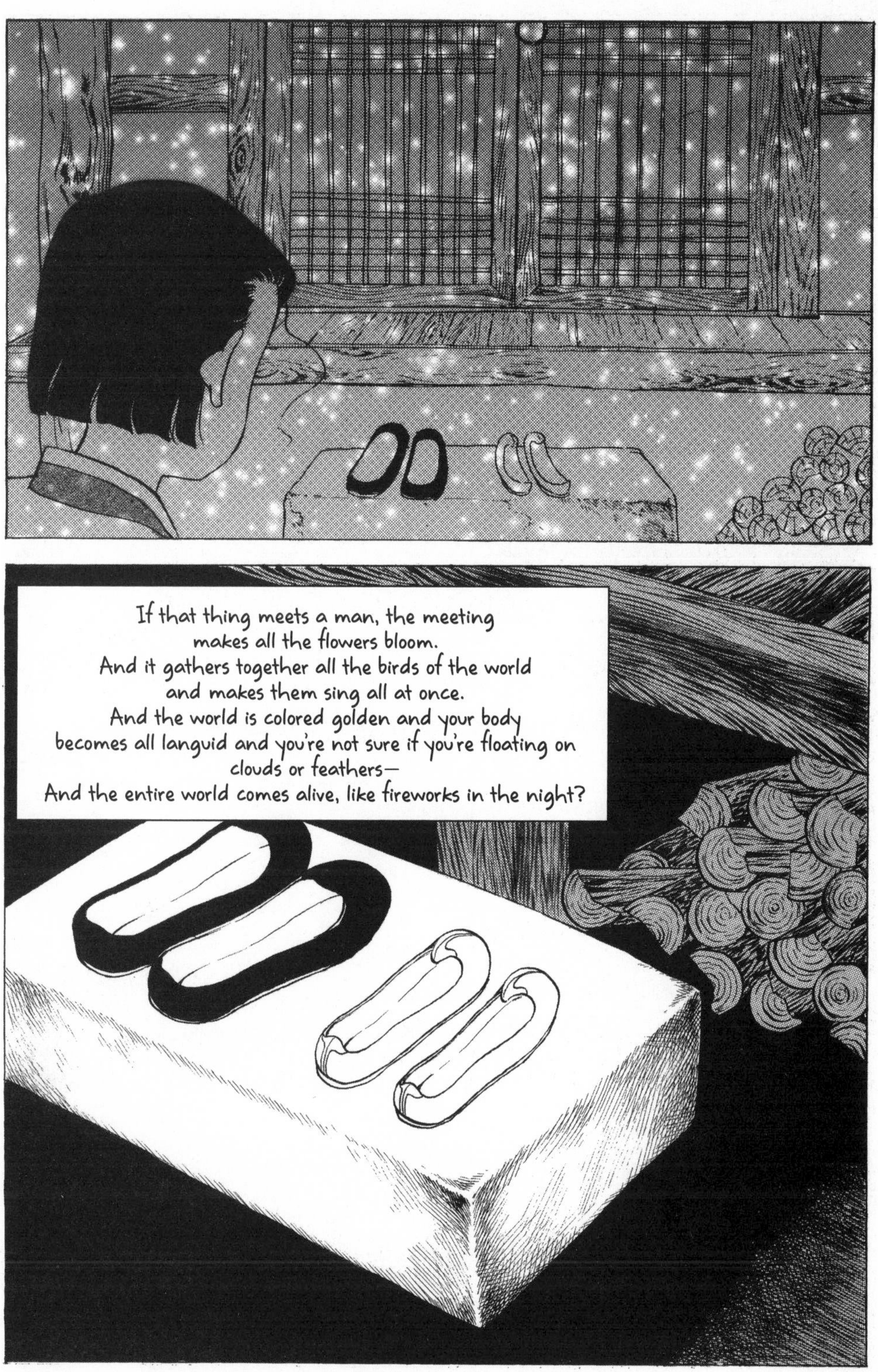
If that thing meets a man, the meeting makes all the flowers bloom.
And it gathers together all the birds of the world and makes them sing all at once.
And the world is colored golden and your body becomes all languid and you're not sure if you're floating on clouds or feathers—
And the entire world comes alive, like fireworks in the night?

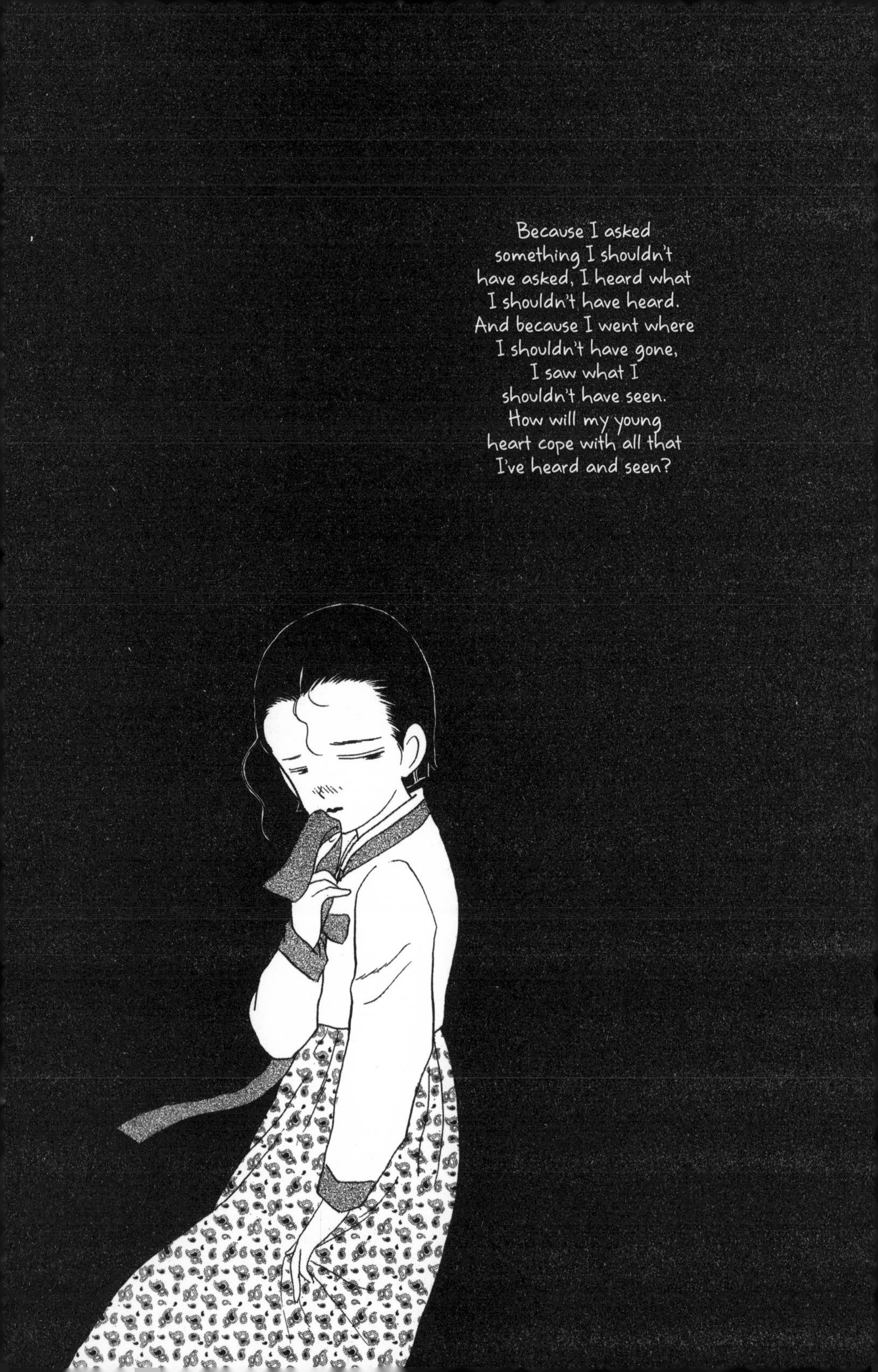
Because I asked something I shouldn't have asked, I heard what I shouldn't have heard. And because I went where I shouldn't have gone, I saw what I shouldn't have seen. How will my young heart cope with all that I've heard and seen?

Chapter Ten

UNREQUITED LOVE

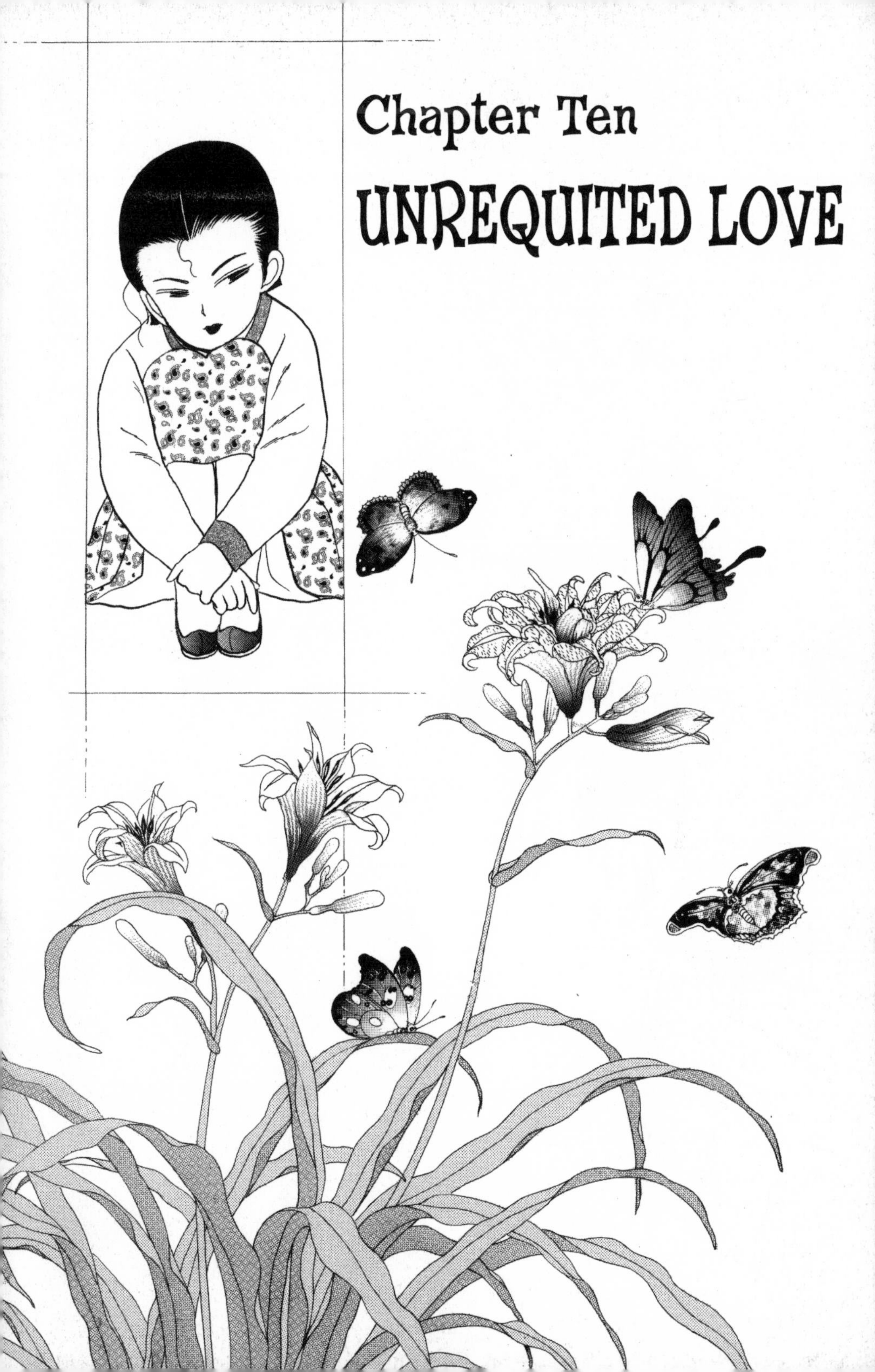

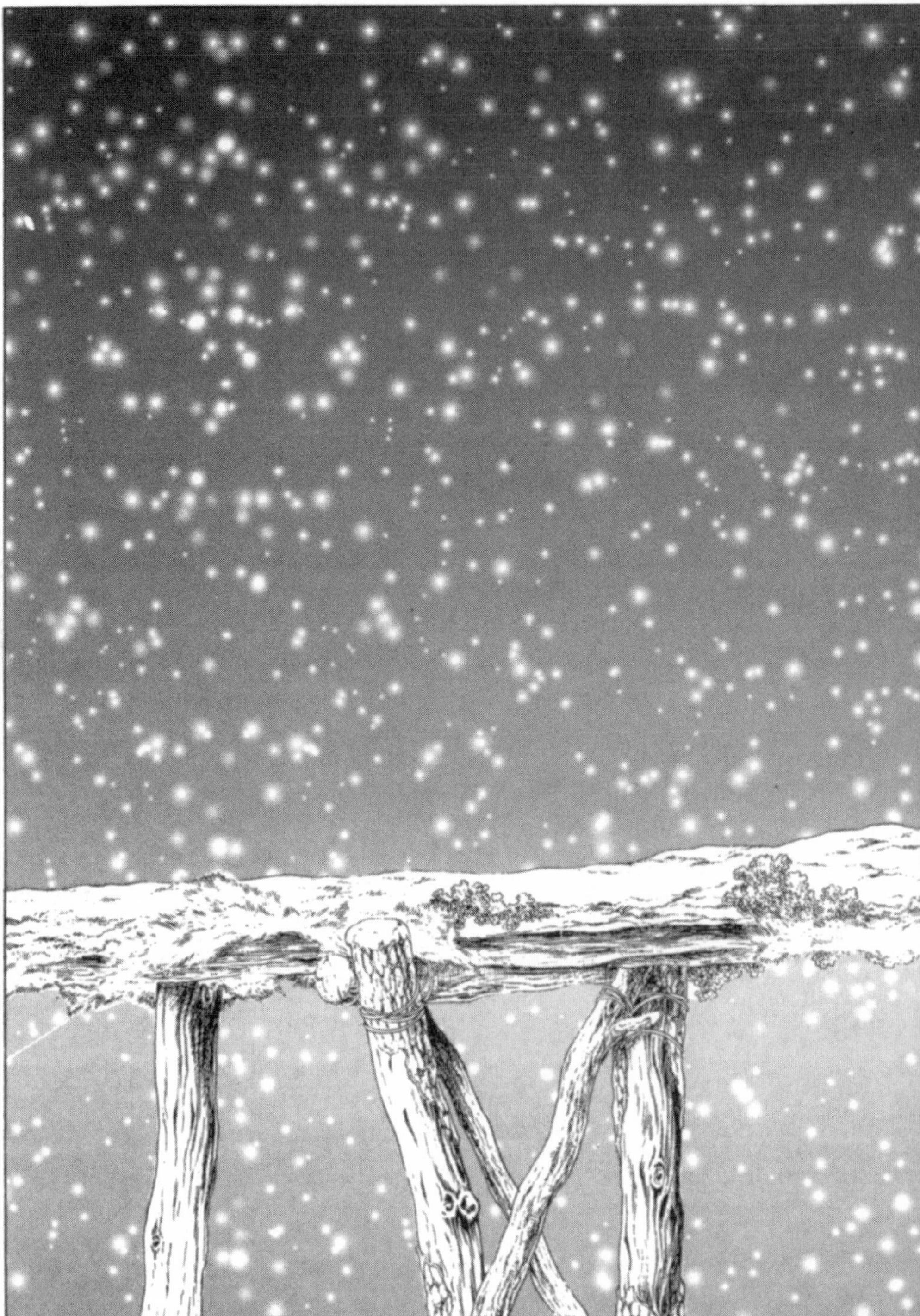

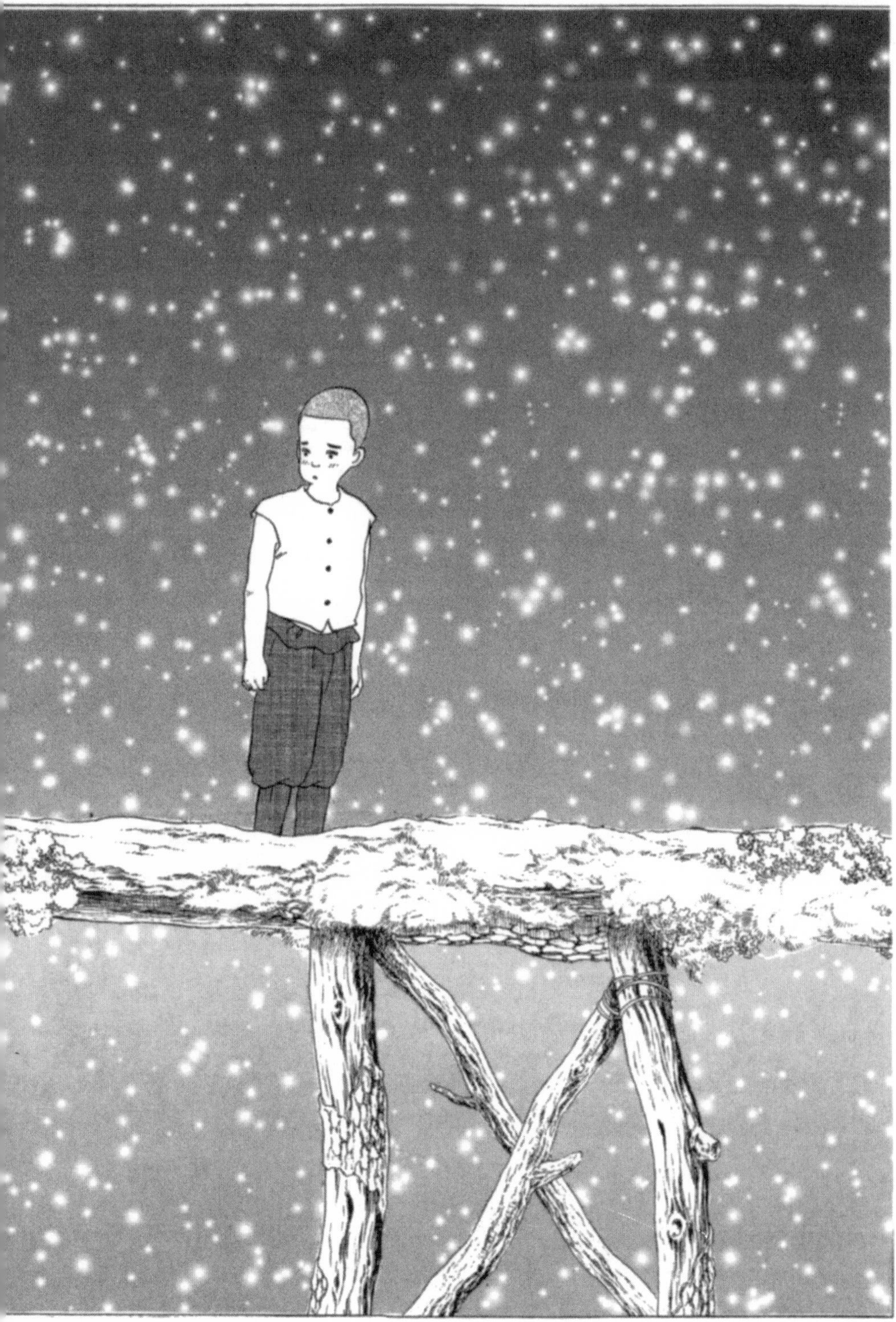

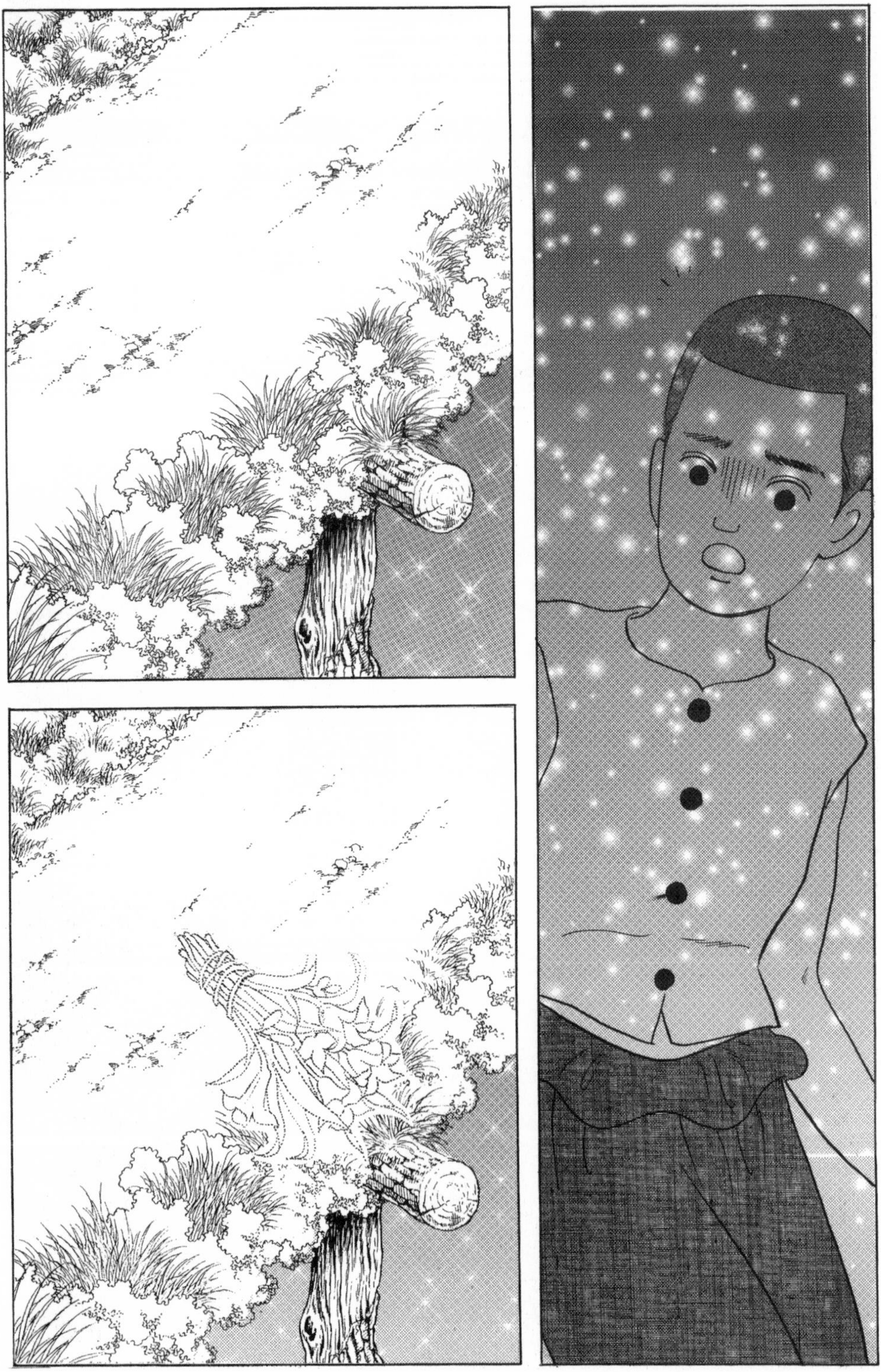

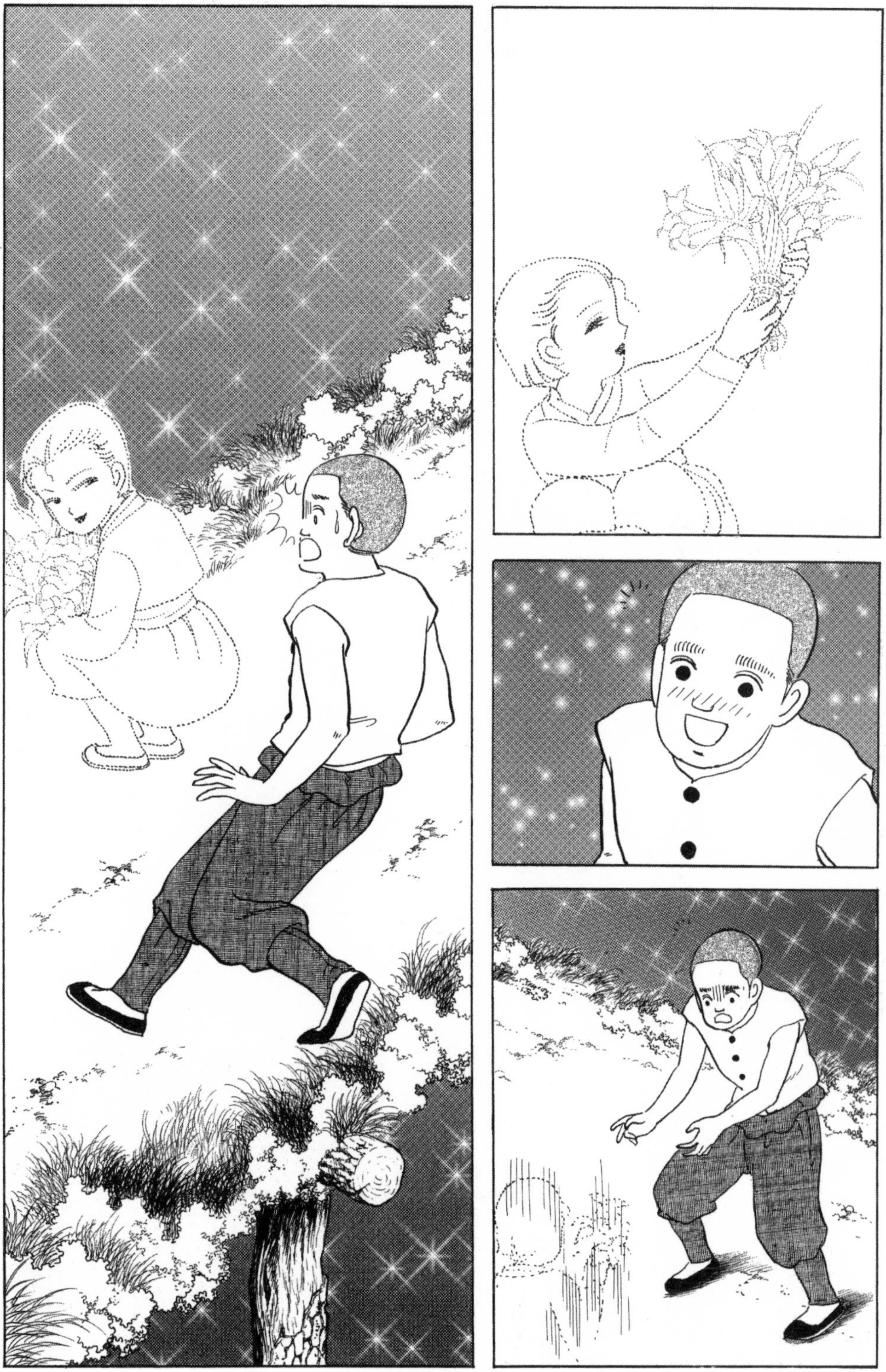

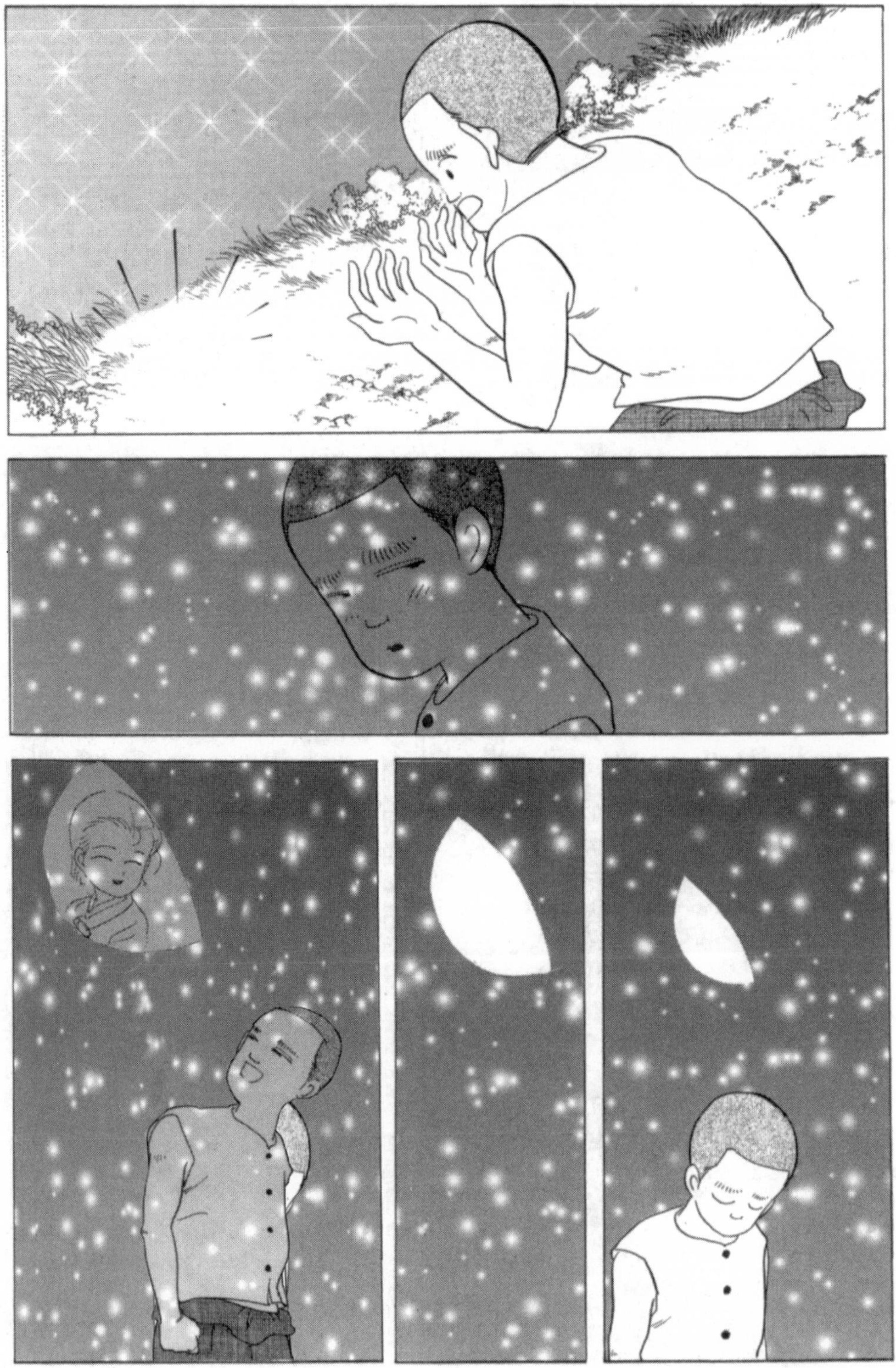

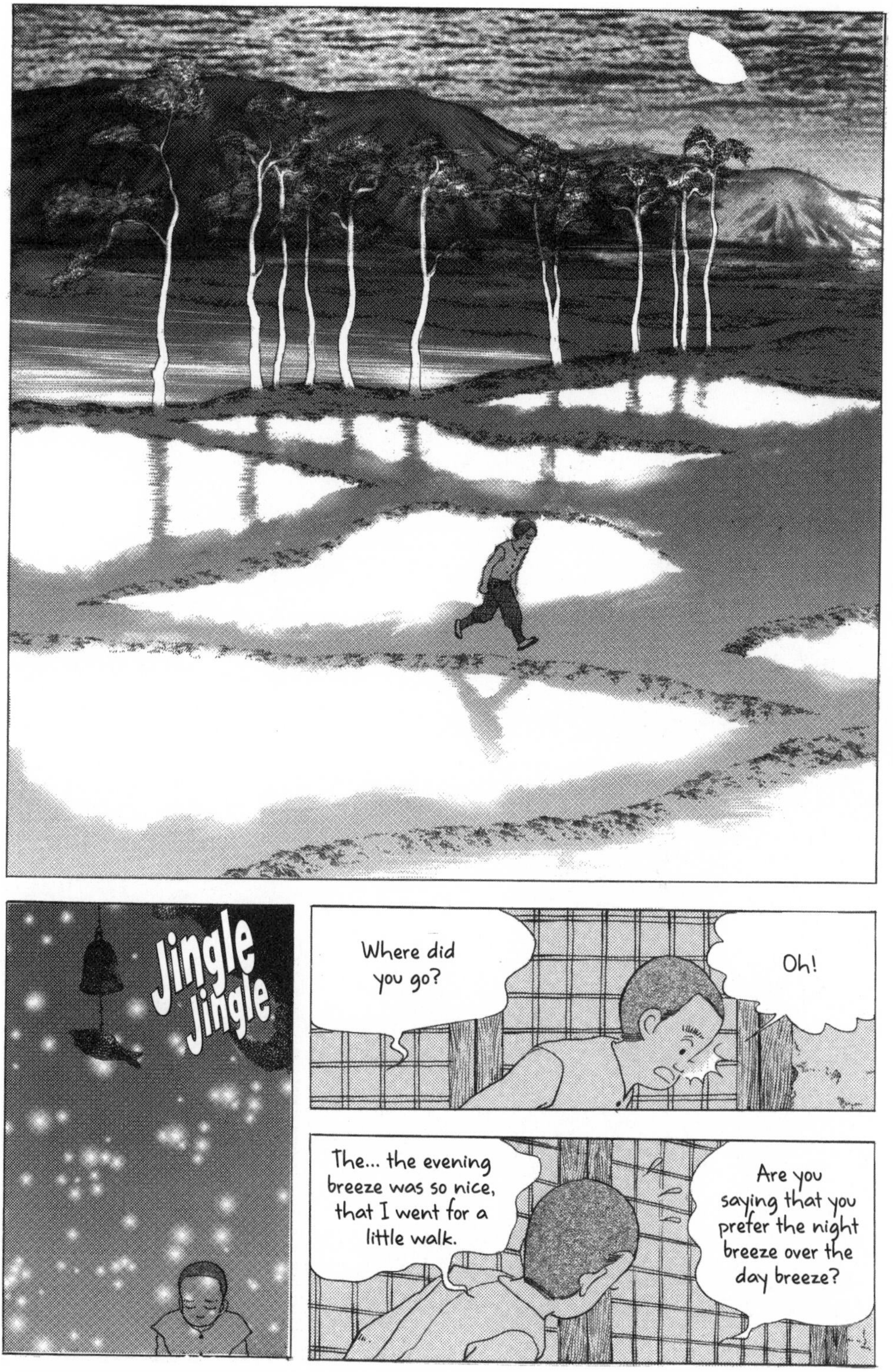
Jingle Jingle
Where did you go?
Oh!
The... the evening breeze was so nice, that I went for a little walk.
Are you saying that you prefer the night breeze over the day breeze?

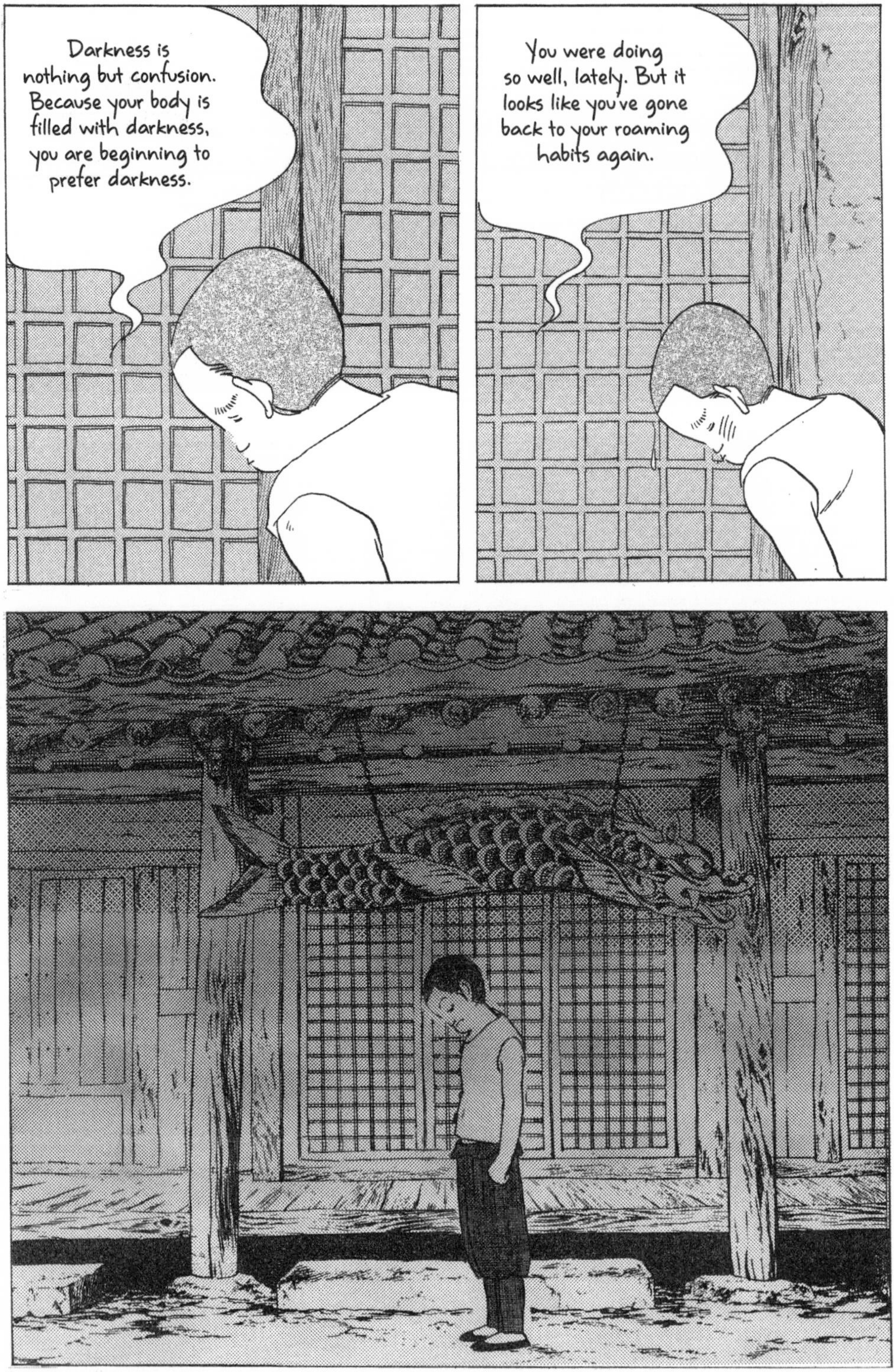
Darkness is nothing but confusion. Because your body is filled with darkness, you are beginning to prefer darkness.
You were doing so well, lately. But it looks like you've gone back to your roaming habits again.

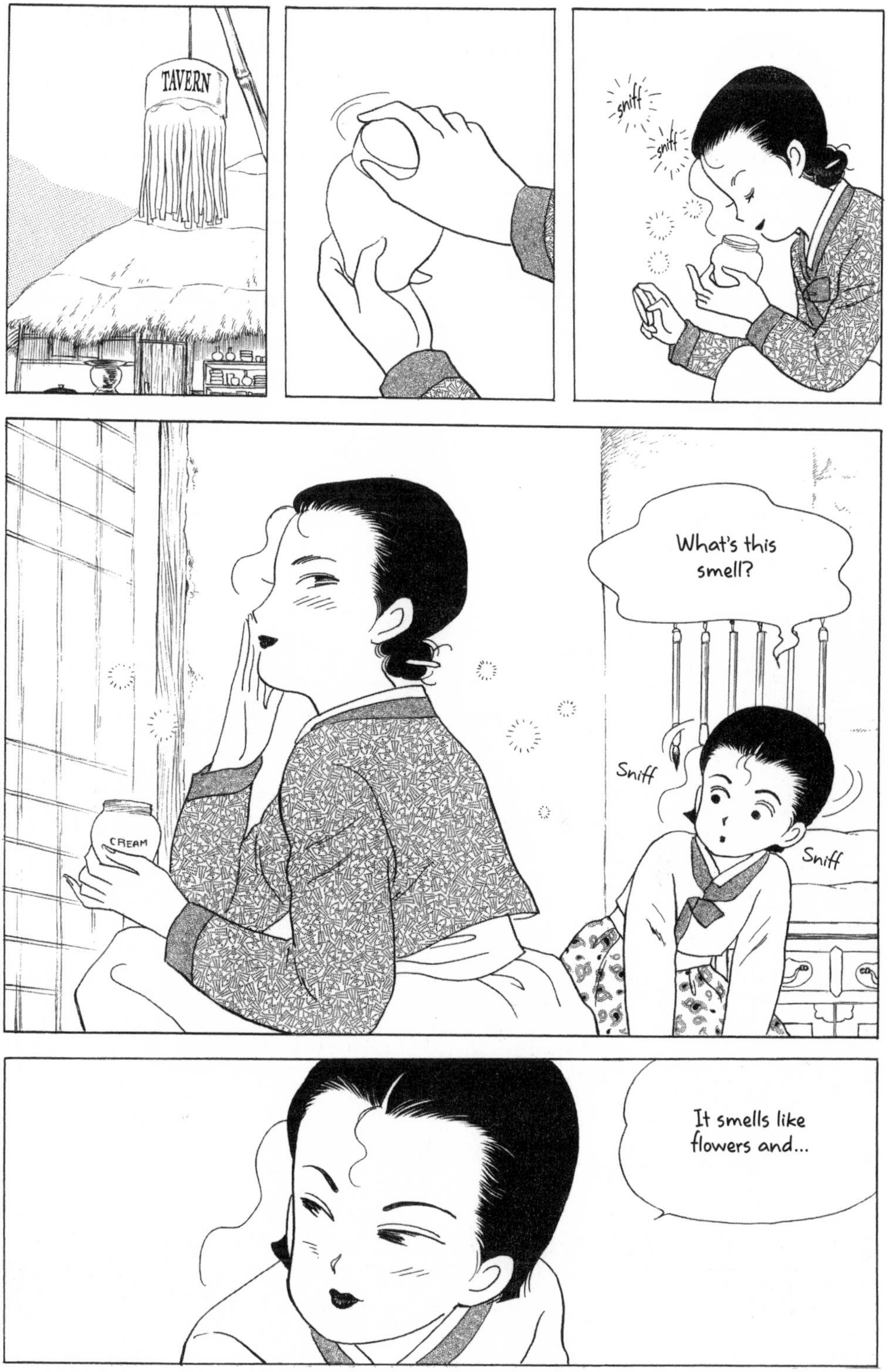
TAVERN
sniff
sniff
What's this smell?
Sniff
Sniff
CREAM
It smells like flowers and...

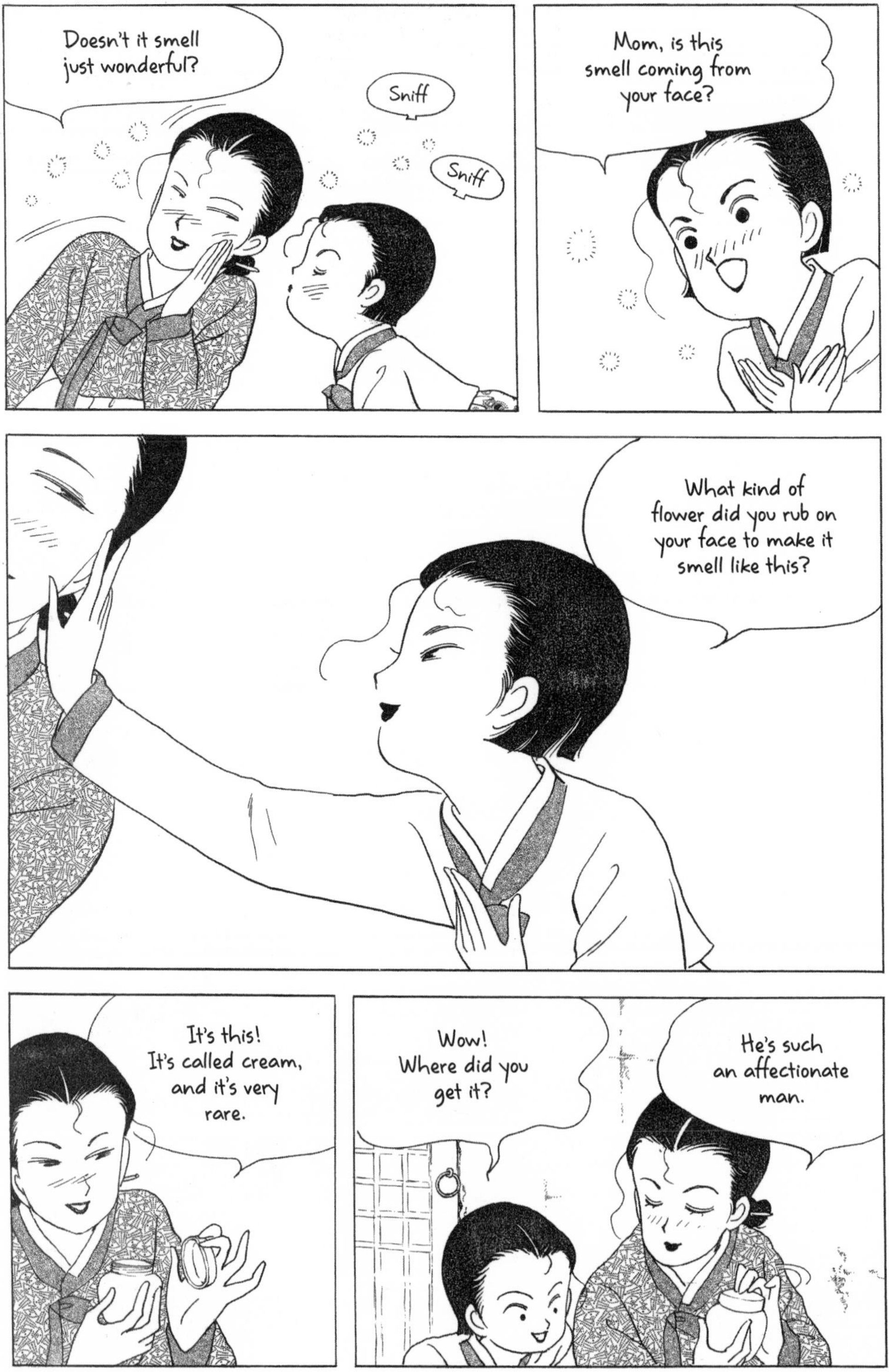
Doesn't it smell just wonderful?
Sniff
Sniff
Mom, is this smell coming from your face?
What kind of flower did you rub on your face to make it smell like this?
It's this! It's called cream, and it's very rare.
Wow! Where did you get it?
He's such an affectionate man.

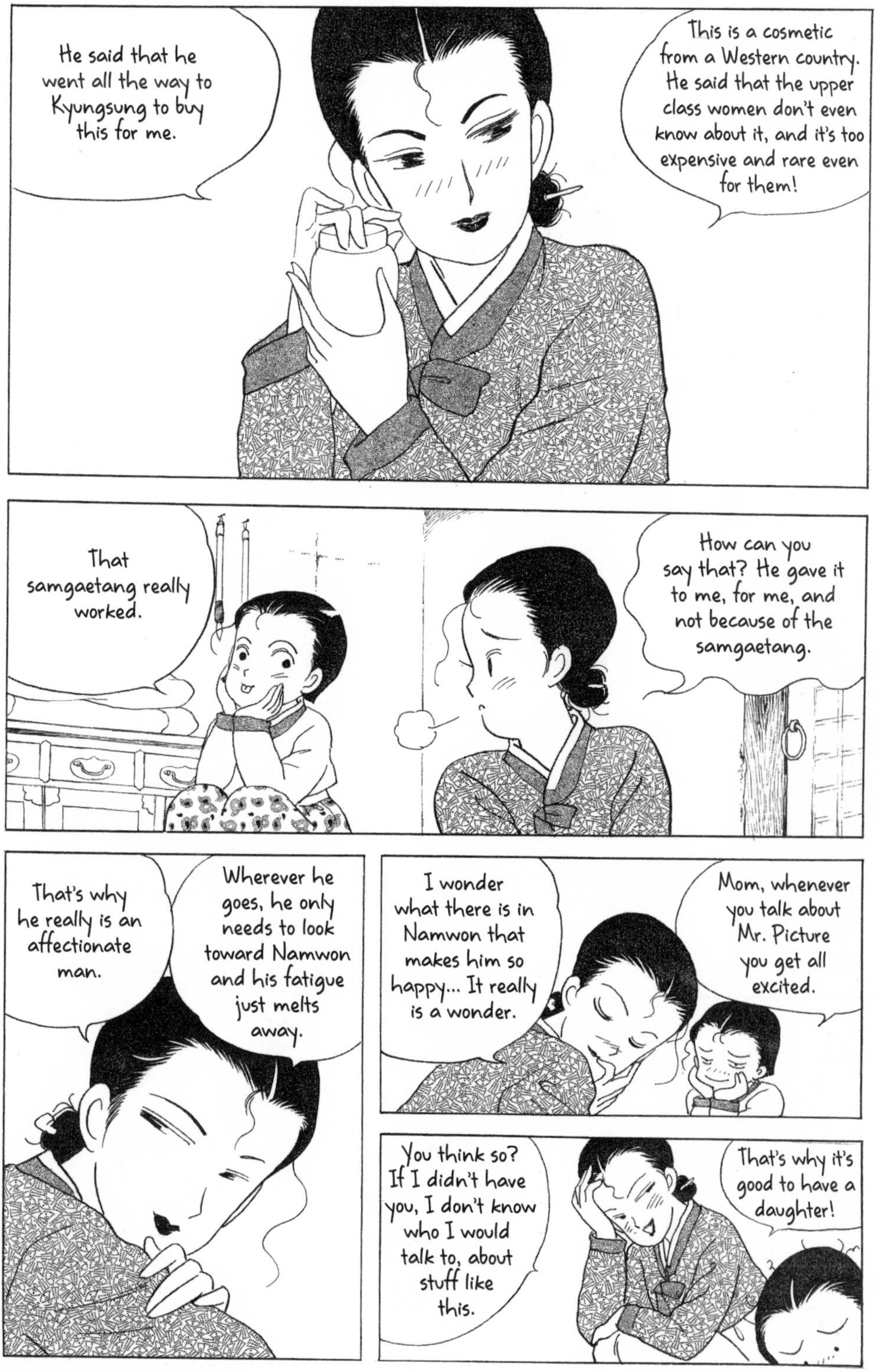
He said that he went all the way to Kyungsung to buy this for me.
This is a cosmetic from a Western country. He said that the upper class women don't even know about it, and it's too expensive and rare even for them!
That samgaetang really worked.
How can you say that? He gave it to me, for me, and not because of the samgaetang.
That's why he really is an affectionate man.
Wherever he goes, he only needs to look toward Namwon and his fatigue just melts away.
I wonder what there is in Namwon that makes him so happy... It really is a wonder.
Mom, whenever you talk about Mr. Picture you get all excited.
You think so? If I didn't have you, I don't know who I would talk to, about stuff like this.
That's why it's good to have a daughter!

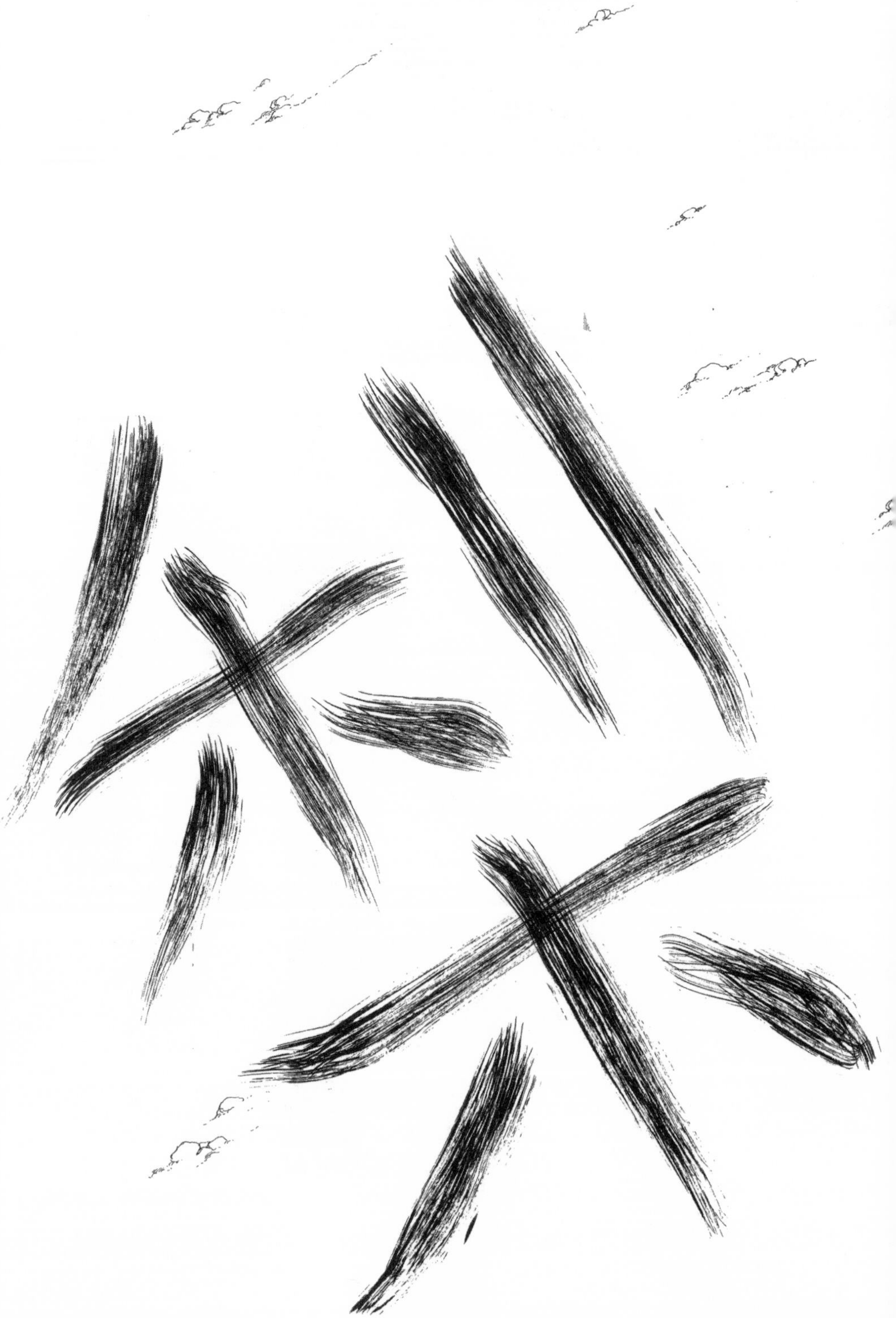

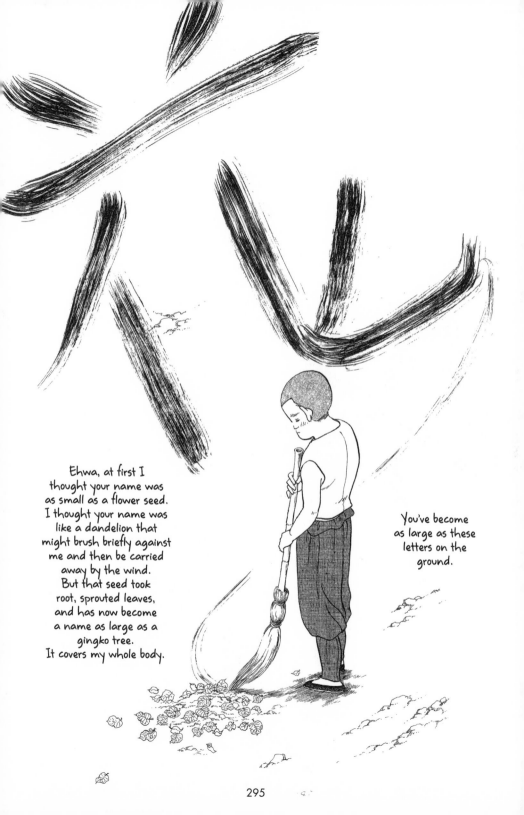

Ehwa, at first I
thought your name was
as small as a flower seed.
I thought your name was
like a dandelion that
might brush briefly against
me and then be carried
away by the wind.
But that seed took
root, sprouted leaves,
and has now become
a name as large as a
gingko tree.
It covers my whole body.

You've become
as large as these
letters on the
ground.

...

Chung-Myung.

Y—yes? Master?

Come inside for a moment.

SCRATCH

SCRATCH

SCRATCH

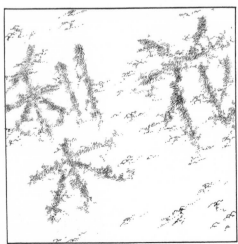

You called me?

Yes. As you know, to monks all things under the sun look like Buddha. But...

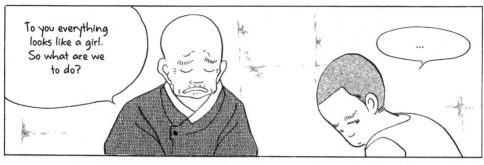

To you everything looks like a girl. So what are we to do?

...

If you behave this way, how will you ever attain enlightenment?

...

Chung-Myung, your entire body is restless, isn't it?

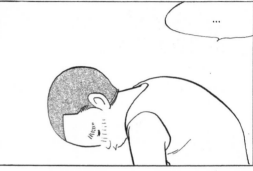

Why don't you go a bit farther to collect alms today? The tiger lilies in the Namwon area are quite spectacular this season. You can look at the flowers, and it'll be a nice change in scenery.

And when you look, be sure to look carefully with both your eyes. You're always looking at things with your eyes half closed and that's why, long after you've seen something, you continue to dwell on it. Put strength in your eyes and look, then you will see the world as it should be seen.

Then I'll be going.

But then again, even if you close your eyes to longing it won't disappear, and even if you turn your head away, longing will not cease.

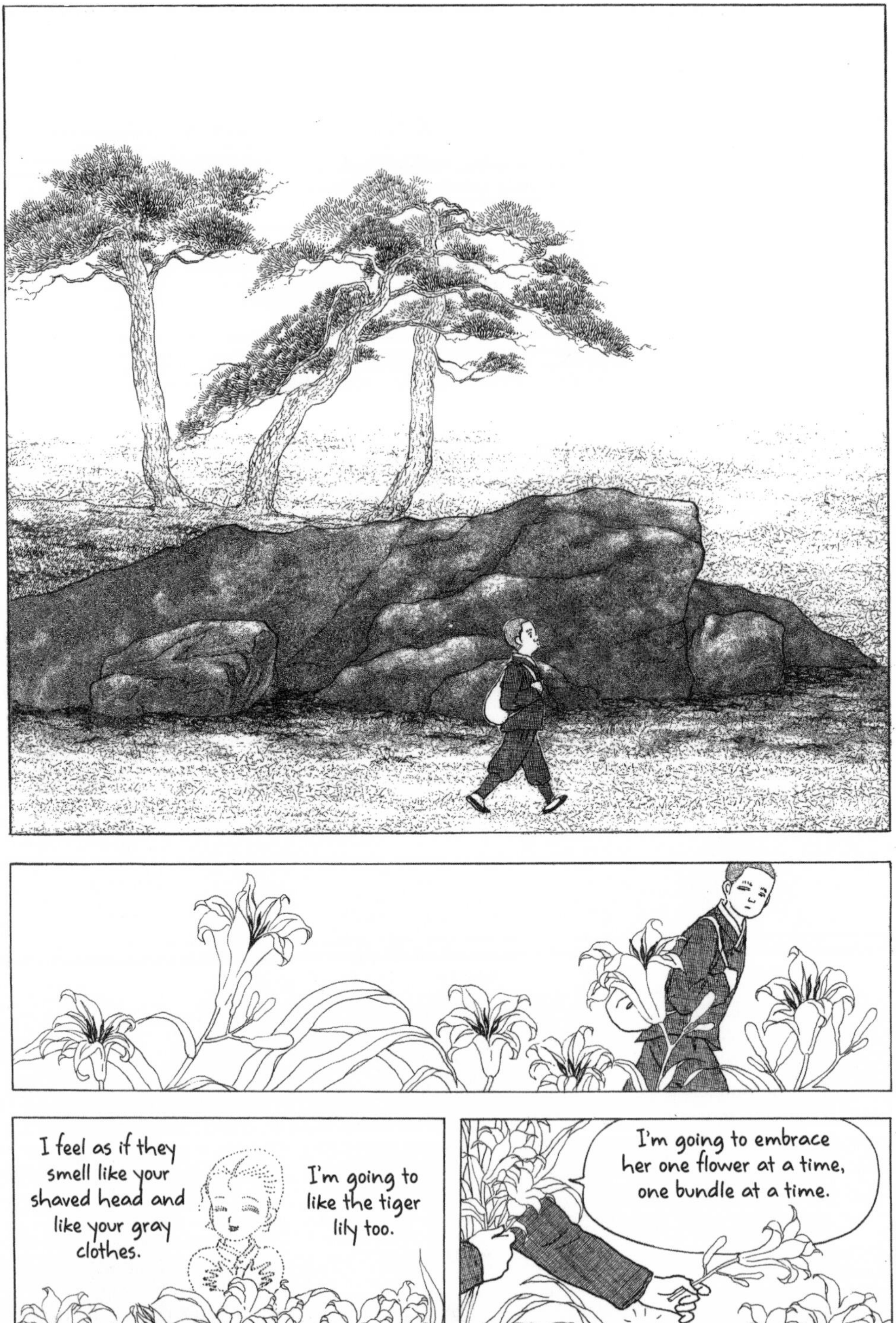
I feel as if they smell like your shaved head and like your gray clothes.
I'm going to like the tiger lily too.
I'm going to embrace her one flower at a time, one bundle at a time.

GRAB

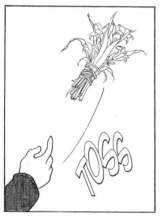

TOSS

GRAB

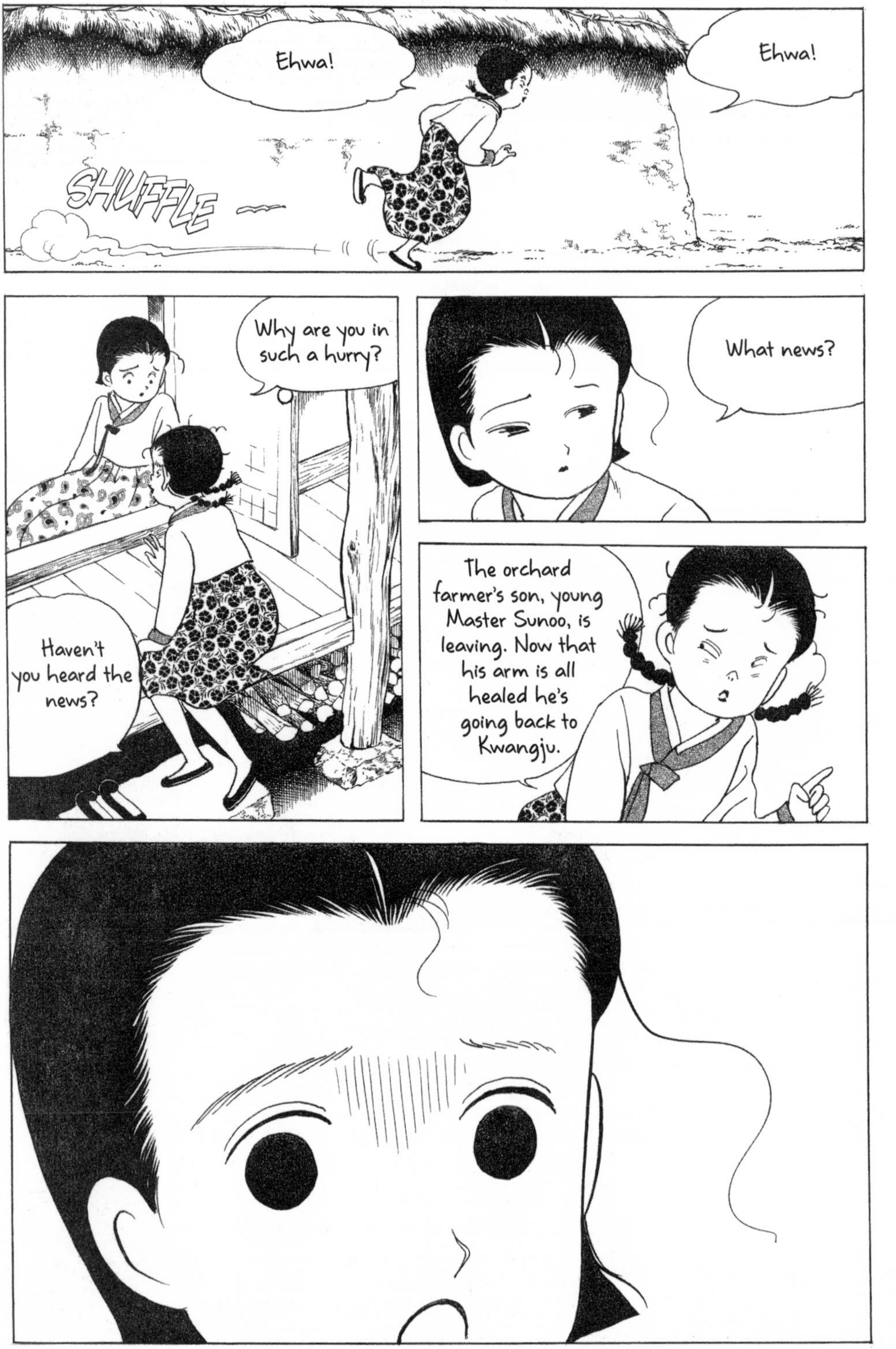
Ehwa!
Ehwa!
SHUFFLE
Why are you in such a hurry?
Haven't you heard the news?
What news?
The orchard farmer's son, young Master Sunoo, is leaving. Now that his arm is all healed he's going back to Kwangju.

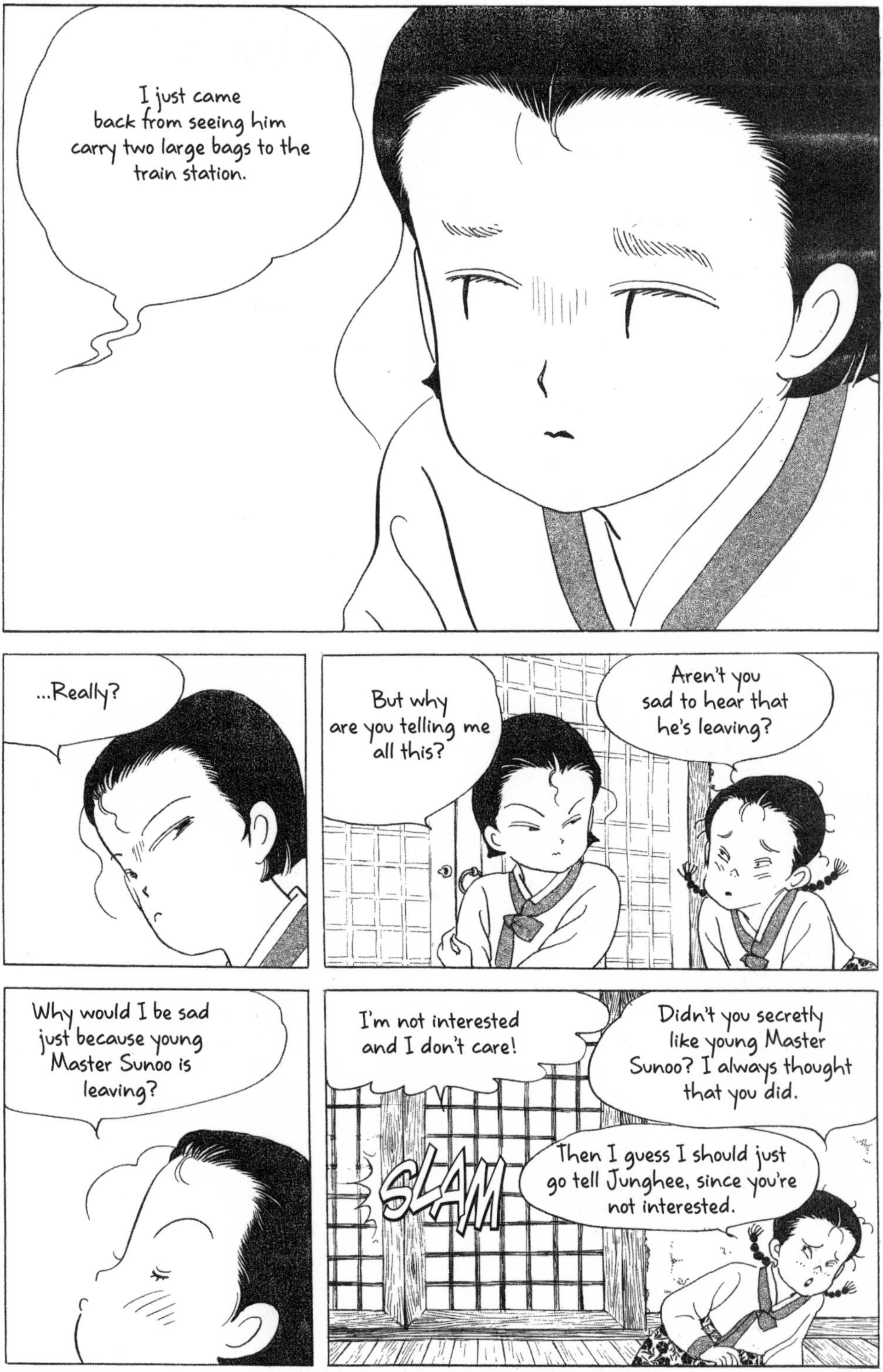

I just came back from seeing him carry two large bags to the train station.
...Really?
But why are you telling me all this?
Aren't you sad to hear that he's leaving?
Why would I be sad just because young Master Sunoo is leaving?
I'm not interested and I don't care!
Didn't you secretly like young Master Sunoo? I always thought that you did.
SLAM
Then I guess I should just go tell Junghee, since you're not interested.

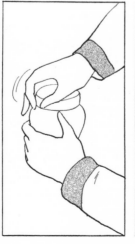

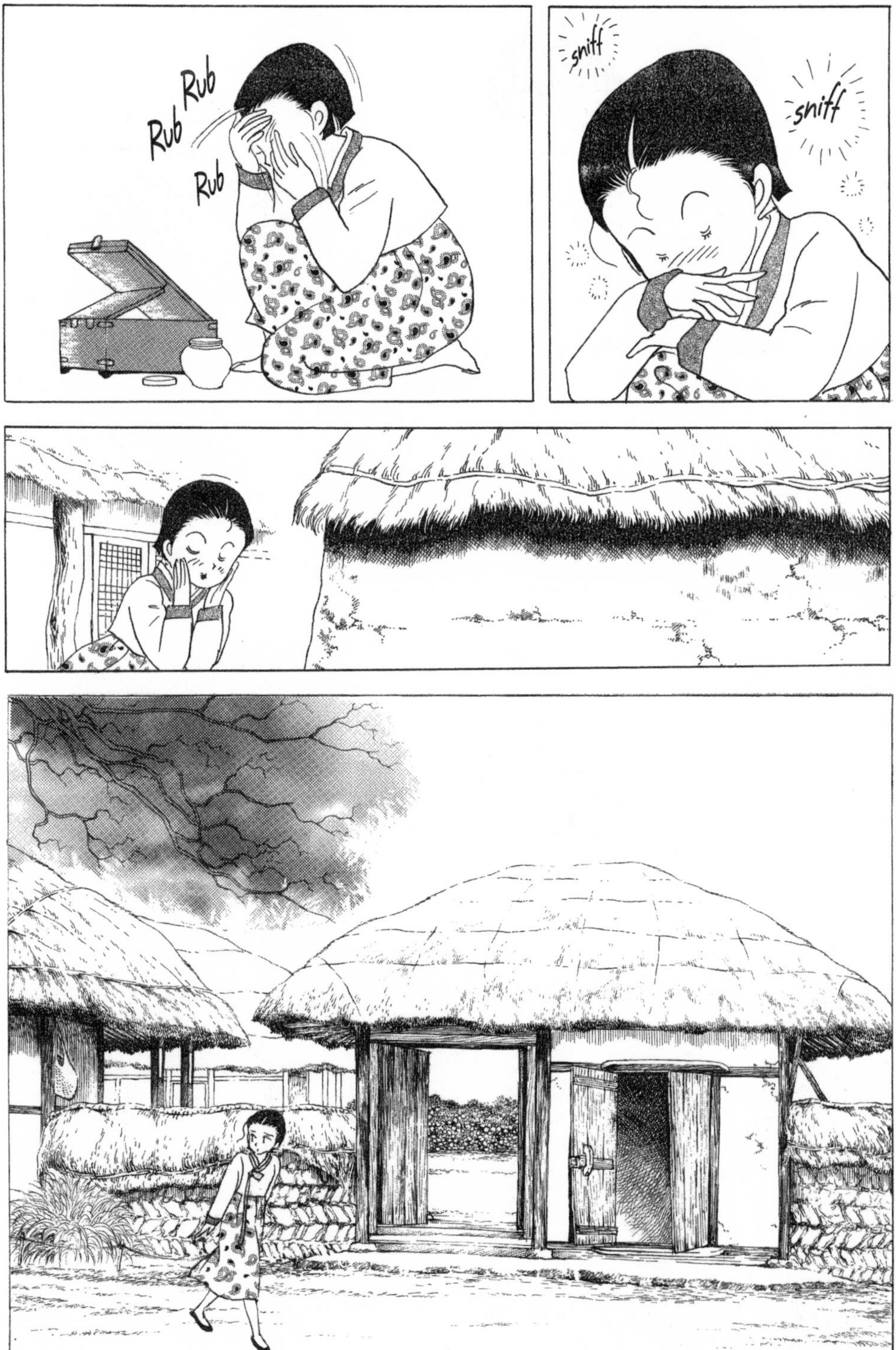
Rub
Rub
Rub
sniff
sniff

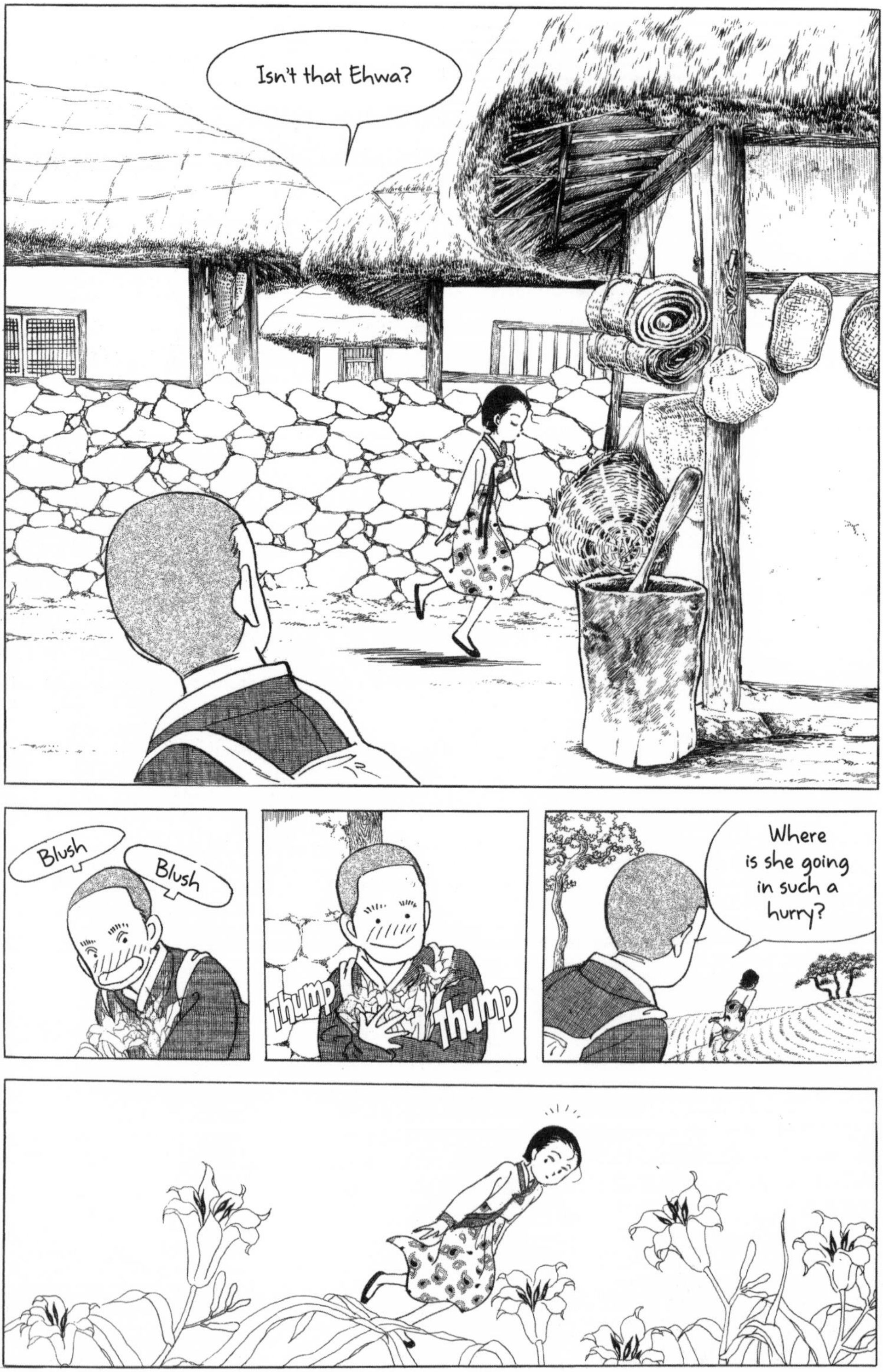
Isn't that Ehwa?
Blush
Blush
Thump
Thump
Where is she going in such a hurry?

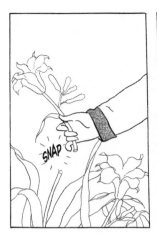

SNAP

SNAP

She's picking tiger lilies. Maybe she's headed for the bridge?

Just as we first exchanged flowers on that bridge, now maybe she's planning to give those flowers to me!

How silly... I have so many tiger lilies already!

I can just picture her face when she sees me. Should I call out to her or not?

Thu-Thump Thu-Thump

Call out to her? Or don't call out to her? Call out to her? Or don't call out to her?

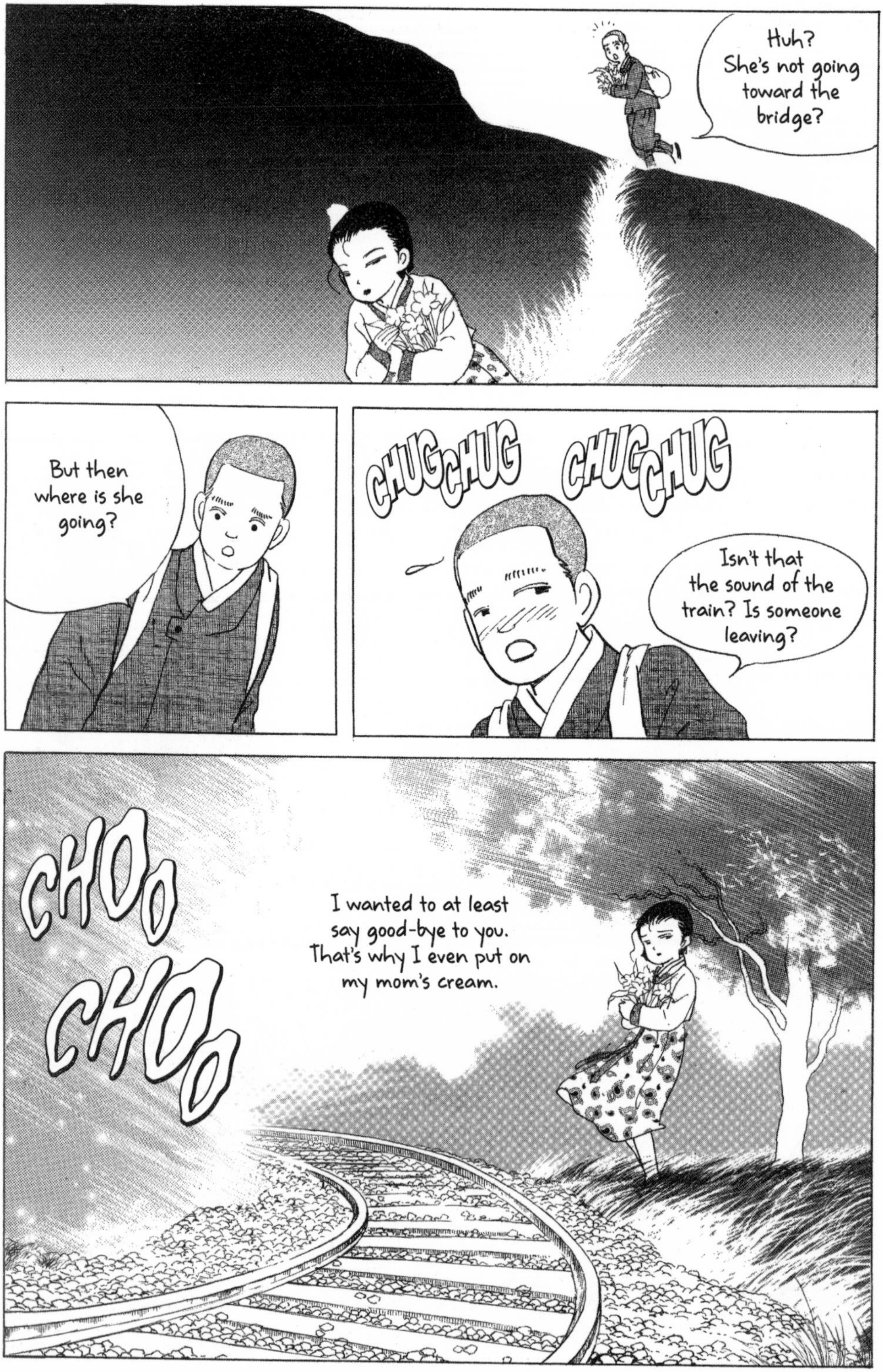
Huh? She's not going toward the bridge?
But then where is she going?
CHUGCHUG CHUGCHUG
Isn't that the sound of the train? Is someone leaving?
CHOO CHOO
I wanted to at least say good-bye to you. That's why I even put on my mom's cream.

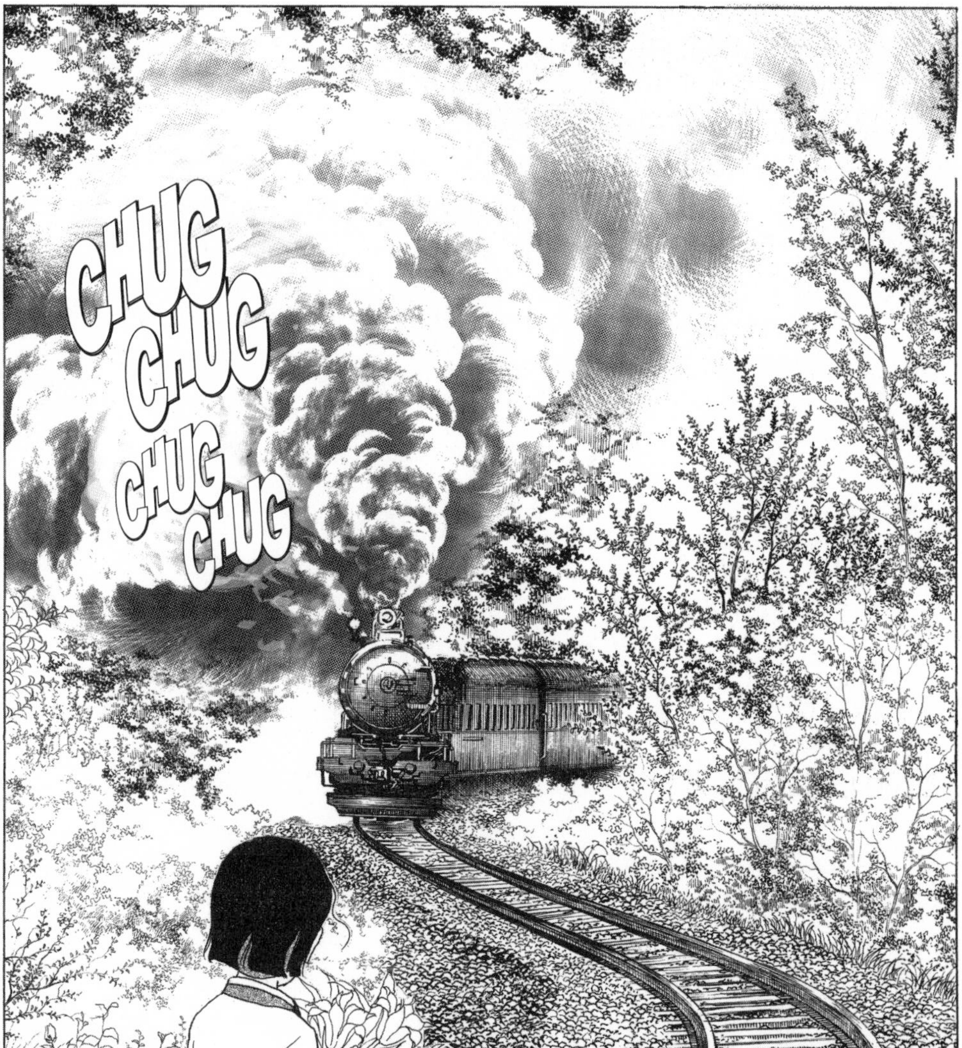
CHUG
CHUG
CHUG
CHUG

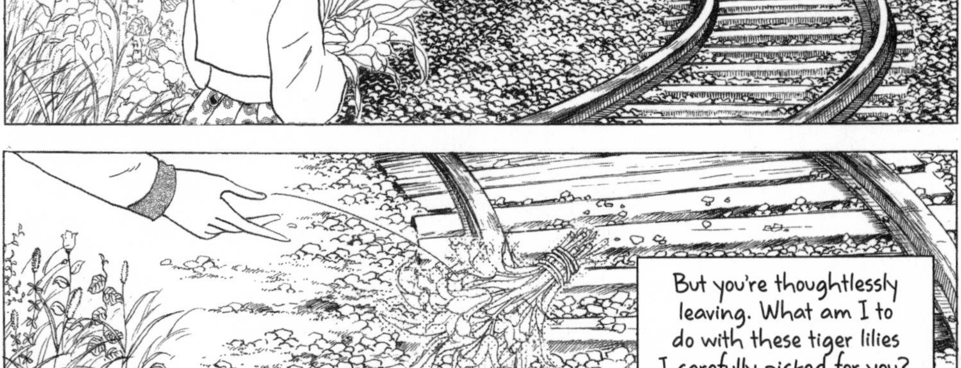
But you're thoughtlessly leaving. What am I to do with these tiger lilies I carefully picked for you?

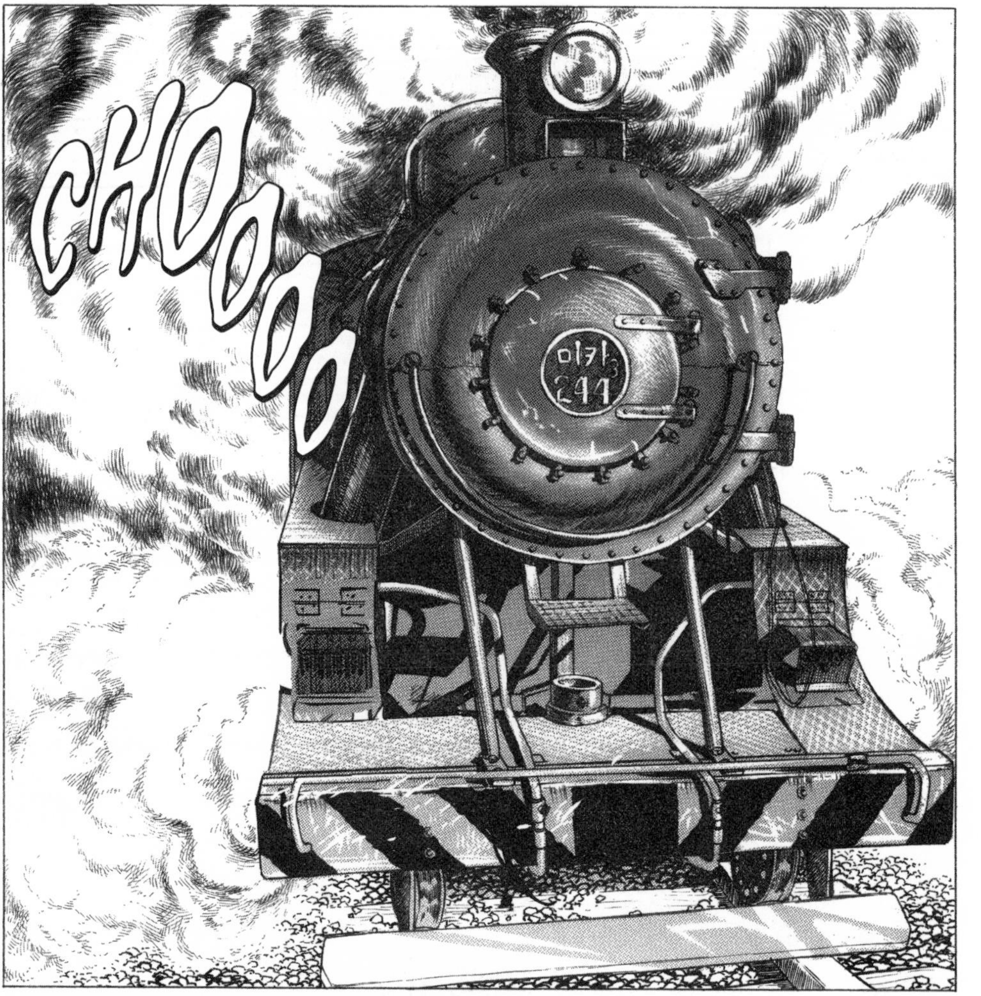
CHOOOOO

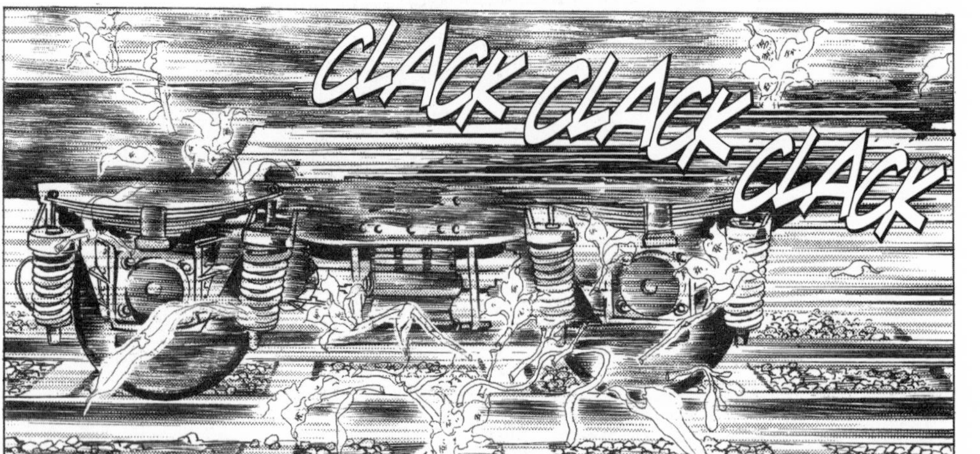
CLACK CLACK CLACK

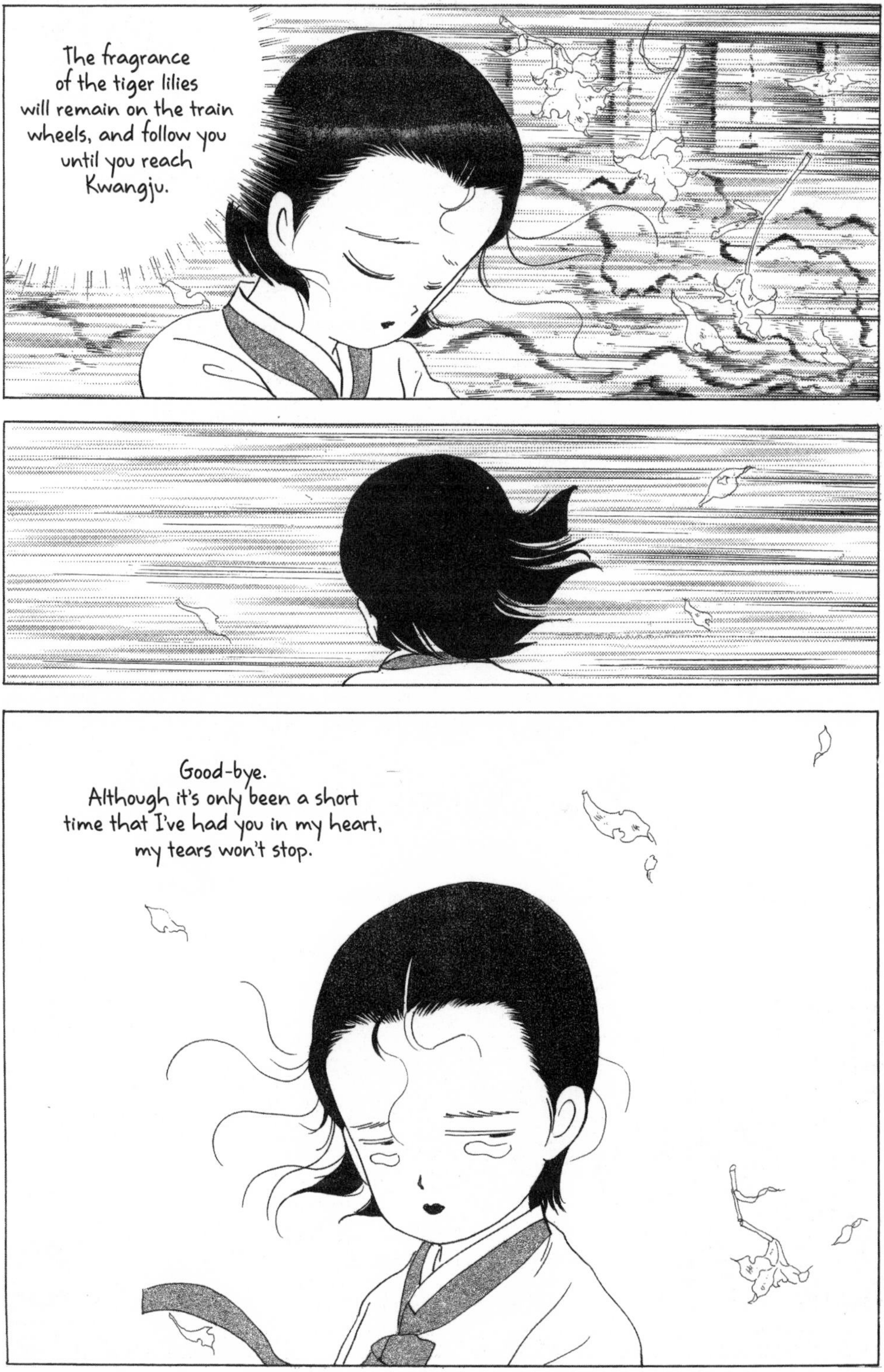
The fragrance of the tiger lilies will remain on the train wheels, and follow you until you reach Kwangju.
Good-bye. Although it's only been a short time that I've had you in my heart, my tears won't stop.

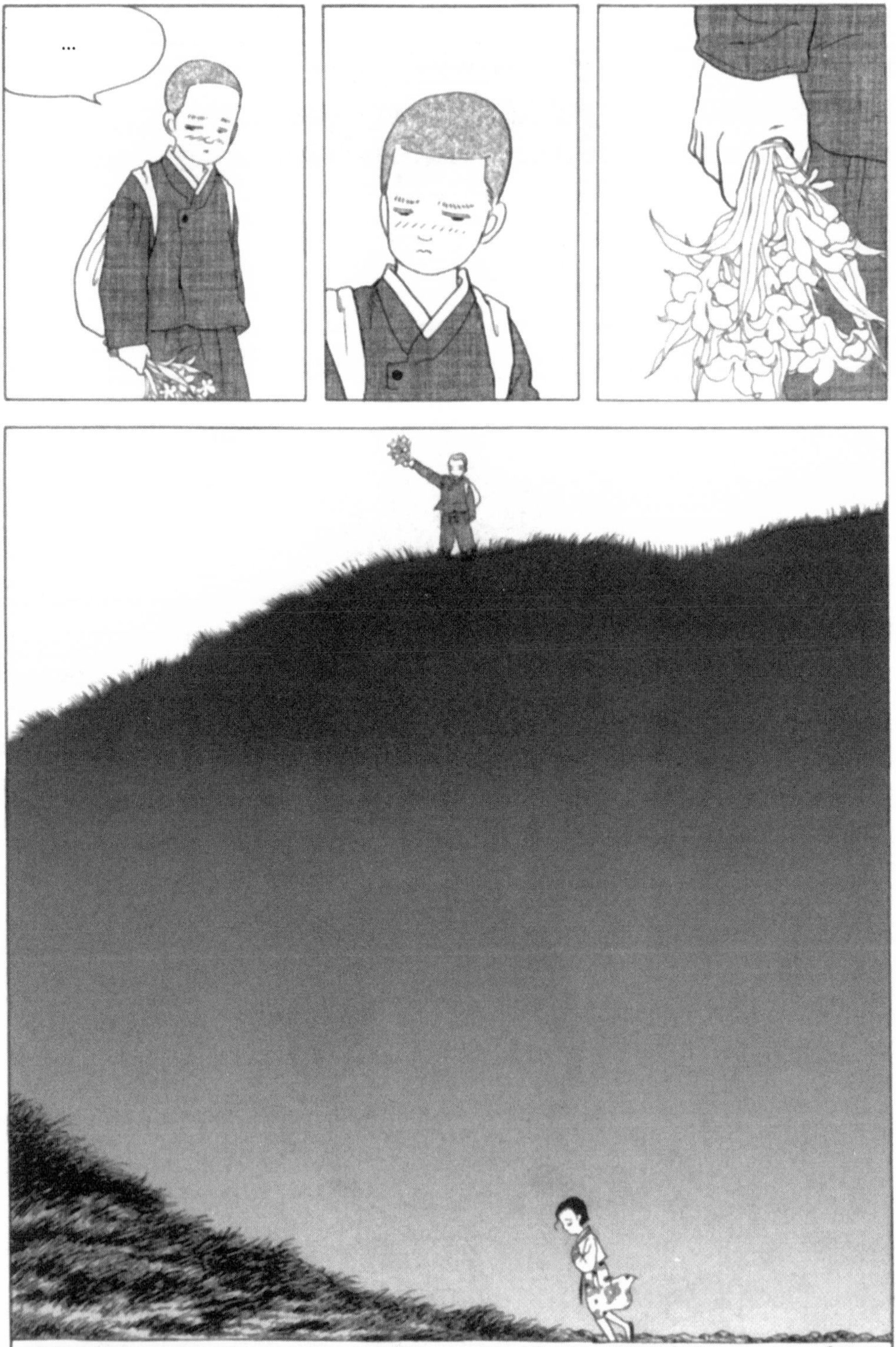
...

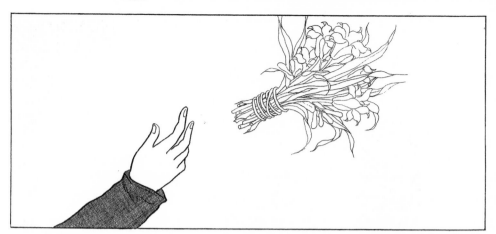

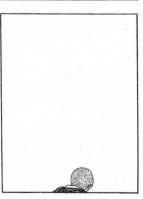

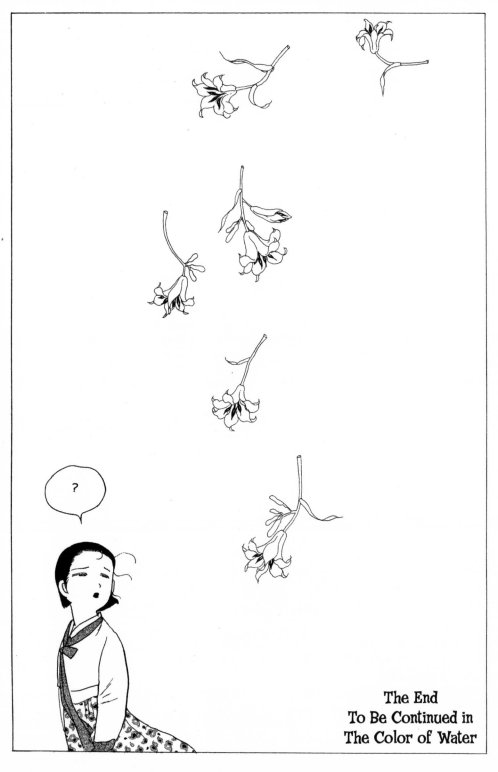

The End
To Be Continued in
The Color of Water

PAINTING THE LIVES
OF WOMEN WITH RAIN
AND FLOWERS

The Color of Earth is a lyrical poem laden with rain and flowers, a luminous *manhwa* (the equivalent of the Japanese *manga*) whose captivating presence and stunning beauty invite you to take plenty of time to appreciate it fully.

The author, Kim Dong Hwa, who was known previously as a master of the light, sweet *sunjung* genre of comics for girls (known as *shojo* in Japanese), took the risk of creating something completely new. His courage paid off, and The Color of Earth became a turning point in the history of *manhwa*. It was the first time that a book drawn in the *sunjung* style enjoyed such unparalleled success with an adult audience composed in equal measure of men and women.

The Color of Earth describes life and the world as seen through the eyes of two generations of women: a little girl named Ehwa and her mother, a widow of the town of Namwon. Ehwa is just setting out on the journey of becoming a woman, while her mother, widowed at a young age, finds herself missing the presence of a man at her side. As protagonists, they stand out in the Korean comics market, which is dominated by books whose stories are based on a male worldview. The author's markedly feminist approach is noteworthy not only because he is a man, but also because many of his readers are as well. In a previous work, *Spring Rain*, Kim Dong Hwa did not restrain his criticism of the vanity of men, old or young, who think themselves superior to women.

That chauvinism is evident among the villagers of *The Color of Earth*, who gossip about the young widow, comparing her to a beetle, and among the little boys, who tell Ehwa that anyone without male genitals is deformed. Fortunately, positive masculine characters like the pictograph artist and the young monk Chung-Myung help preserve a certain balance.

PAINTING LOVE WITH RAIN AND FLOWERS

Rain and flowers are symbols employed constantly throughout *The Color of Earth*. Many of the characters use bouquets of flowers to express their love for one another. Flowers even become a metaphor for a lover, or a beloved. The white gourd flower that blooms every evening at sunset symbolizes the waiting endured by the widow. The tiger lily comes to represent the young monk even as, in his heart, the hollyhock flower stands for Ehwa.

And the rain, the element of water, takes on the potency of a life force. With each rainy season, little Ehwa matures a bit more in mind and body. It is also on a rainy night that the young widow, who had been wasting away from loneliness, finally finds happiness in the arms of the pictograph artist. His warmth regenerates her, and the rain fully embodies its role as the bringer of growth. Young Ehwa, guessing at the scene unfolding behind the door, can only feel glad for her mother.

There's an interesting parallel between the mother-daughter relationship in *The Color of Earth* and that in Jane Campion's feminist-inclined film *The Piano*. Unlike the character of Flora, who disapproves of her mother's womanly desire and even betrays her to her stepfather, Ehwa never turns against her mother. Much to the contrary, the young girl becomes her mother's chief ally.

Why such a difference in behavior between the characters of two girls of about the same age, both raised by a lonely mother? Is it that Flora had a stepfather, unlike Ehwa? Or is it due to a difference in mentality between Eastern and Western cultures? No, the reason appears to lie elsewhere.

In *The Color of Earth*, a profound physical bond unites the mother and daughter. Scenes in which they bathe together or share the same bed at night give a sense of how close they are. The two identify with each other in a mirroring process that is even arguably tinged with a latent homoeroticism. It therefore follows naturally that Ehwa becomes her mother's main ally. Conversely, in *The Piano* there is no possibility of confusion between mother and daughter. Each remains solely committed to her own identity as well as to her own desires.

A SCRIPT THAT DOES JUSTICE TO OUTSTANDING ARTWORK

The Color of Earth offers a brilliant demonstration of the possibilities of manhwa. Landscapes are superbly rendered in exceptionally fine and delicate linework, and the artist's masterful use of space sometimes evokes India-ink paintings. The care invested in each drawing demonstrates the author's passion for his art, and the script is equally strong. The daily goings-on of characters and the psychological tensions at play are presented with realism and true empathy. There is unflinching verisimilitude in Chung-Myung's surprise as he discovers his stained pants in the early morning, as well as Ehwa's panic when she has her first period.

Several poignant scenes need no words, like the one in which the young monk daringly places his shoe on top of Ehwa's, or

Ehwa's half smile when she is both embarrassed and proud of having become a real woman. Throughout, the reader will find much to enjoy in Kim Dong Hwa's rich dialogue filled with cultural references and folk wisdom, and the high caliber of his writing in general.

A MOVING HOMAGE TO THE WOMEN
OF YESTERYEAR

The Color of Earth tells the story of two women at different stages of life, and we come to understand them through the mysteries of nature, rain, and flowers.

If one had to sum up the story in a few words, one could say that this book is about a young girl, who is seven years old at the outset, progressing from the curiosity of early childhood to the awakening of sexuality. Alongside the turbulence of her life, there is the gradual invasion of her mother's room by paintbrushes belonging to the pictograph artist. Here, it is the paintbrushes that reveal the changes taking place in the widow's life.

But above all, this work is a moving homage to Korean women of a generation or two ago, who bore up patiently under the weight of social codes and traditions. The author may have wanted to remind his male readers of this.

Kim Dong Hwa is famous for the ease with which he reinvents himself. At the time when he was working mainly on books of the *sunjung* genre, he would frequently alter his style, much to the delight of his young female readers. He even sometimes surprised everyone by publishing books intended for young boys. With *The Color of Earth*, he has produced a book that can warm even the toughened hearts of men.

In short, *The Color of Earth* is a rare gem, a book in which all the author's many talents find a unique and haunting expression.

Hwang Min-Ho

In addition to working for the Daiwon Ci publishing house, Hwang Min-Ho is a book critic and an emeritus professor at Myung Ji University. He is also a member of the Board of Seoul's Animation Film Center. He has published a book entitled From Ko Ba Woo to Duli.